Designing Network Security
Second Edition

Merike Kaeo

Copyright© 2004 Cisco Systems, Inc.

Published by:
Cisco Press
800 East 96th Street
Indianapolis, IN 46240 USA

Printed in the United States of America 2 3 4 5 6 7 8 9 0

Library of Congress Cataloging-in-Publication Number: 2002108489

ISBN: 1-58705-117-6

Second Printing March 2004

Warning and Disclaimer

This book is designed to provide information about designing network security. Every effort has been made to make this book as complete and as accurate as possible, but no warranty or fitness is implied.

The information is provided on an "as is" basis. The authors, Cisco Press, and Cisco Systems, Inc., shall have neither liability nor responsibility to any person or entity with respect to any loss or damages arising from the information contained in this book or from the use of the discs or programs that may accompany it.

The opinions expressed in this book belong to the author and are not necessarily those of Cisco Systems, Inc.

Feedback Information

At Cisco Press, our goal is to create in-depth technical books of the highest quality and value. Each book is crafted with care and precision, undergoing rigorous development that involves the unique expertise of members from the professional technical community.

Readers' feedback is a natural continuation of this process. If you have any comments regarding how we could improve the quality of this book, or otherwise alter it to better suit your needs, you can contact us through e-mail at feedback@ciscopress.com. Please make sure to include the book title and ISBN in your message.

We greatly appreciate your assistance.

Trademark Acknowledgments

All terms mentioned in this book that are known to be trademarks or service marks have been appropriately capitalized. Cisco Press or Cisco Systems, Inc. cannot attest to the accuracy of this information. Use of a term in this book should not be regarded as affecting the validity of any trademark or service mark.

Corporate and Government Sales

Cisco Press offers excellent discounts on this book when ordered in quantity for bulk purchases or special sales. For more information, please contact:

U.S. Corporate and Government Sales 1-800-382-3419 corpsales@pearsontechgroup.com

For sales outside of the U.S. please contact:

International Sales 1-317-581-3793 international@pearsoned.com

Designing Network Security
Second Edition

Merike Kaeo

Cisco Press

800 East 96th Street
Indianapolis, IN 46240 USA

Publisher	John Wait
Editor-in-Chief	John Kane
Cisco Representative	Anthony Wolfenden
Cisco Press Program Manager	Sonia Torres Chavez
Manager, Marketing Communications, Cisco Systems	Scott Miller
Cisco Marketing Program Manager	Edie Quiroz
Production Manager	Patrick Kanouse
Acquisitions Editor	Amy Moss
Development Editor	Andrew Cupp
Project Editor	Ginny Bess Munroe
Copy Editor	Keith Cline
Technical Editors	Ron da Silva
	Hank Mauldin
	Glen Zorn
Team Coordinator	Tammi Barnett
Cover Designer	Louisa Adair
Production Team	Mark Shirar
Indexer	Julie Bess

CISCO SYSTEMS

Corporate Headquarters
Cisco Systems, Inc.
170 West Tasman Drive
San Jose, CA 95134-1706
USA
www.cisco.com
Tel: 408 526-4000
 800 553-NETS (6387)
Fax: 408 526-4100

European Headquarters
Cisco Systems International BV
Haarlerbergpark
Haarlerbergweg 13-19
1101 CH Amsterdam
The Netherlands
www-europe.cisco.com
Tel: 31 0 20 357 1000
Fax: 31 0 20 357 1100

Americas Headquarters
Cisco Systems, Inc.
170 West Tasman Drive
San Jose, CA 95134-1706
USA
www.cisco.com
Tel: 408 526-7660
Fax: 408 527-0883

Asia Pacific Headquarters
Cisco Systems, Inc.
Capital Tower
168 Robinson Road
#22-01 to #29-01
Singapore 068912
www.cisco.com
Tel: +65 6317 7777
Fax: +65 6317 7799

Cisco Systems has more than 200 offices in the following countries and regions. Addresses, phone numbers, and fax numbers are listed on the **Cisco.com Web site at www.cisco.com/go/offices.**

Argentina • Australia • Austria • Belgium • Brazil • Bulgaria • Canada • Chile • China PRC • Colombia • Costa Rica • Croatia • Czech Republic Denmark • Dubai, UAE • Finland • France • Germany • Greece • Hong Kong SAR • Hungary • India • Indonesia • Ireland • Israel • Italy Japan • Korea • Luxembourg • Malaysia • Mexico • The Netherlands • New Zealand • Norway • Peru • Philippines • Poland • Portugal Puerto Rico • Romania • Russia • Saudi Arabia • Scotland • Singapore • Slovakia • Slovenia • South Africa • Spain • Sweden Switzerland • Taiwan • Thailand • Turkey • Ukraine • United Kingdom • United States • Venezuela • Vietnam • Zimbabwe

About the Author

Merike Kaeo, CCIE No. 1287, is currently a consultant focusing primarily on security-related products and network design solutions. She has been in the networking industry more than 15 years, starting out at the National Institutes of Health in Bethesda, MD, from 1988 to 1993, designing and implementing the original FDDI backbone for the NIH campus using Cisco routers. From 1993 to 2000, Merike was employed by Cisco Systems, Inc., where she worked primarily on technical issues relating to router performance, network routing protocols, network design, and network security. She was a lead member of the Cisco security initiative, has acted as a technical advisor for security startup companies, and has been an instructor and speaker in a variety of security-related conferences. Merike received her BSEE from Rutgers University in 1987 and completed her MSEE degree from George Washington University in 1998.

About the Technical Reviewers

Ron da Silva is the principal network architect at America Online, Inc., an AOL Time Warner company. He is responsible for designing and scaling the company's data networks. He is involved in developing future cable architectures, researching access technologies, business development, broadband strategy, and most every other initiative within AOL. Ron serves as strategic advisor for product development, research, and new technology evaluation. Ron has extensive experience in managing large IP networks. In particular, during his time with AOL, Ron was responsible for building AOLTW Transit Data Network (ATDN), an international tier-1 oc192 backbone ISP that spans five continents, serving AOLTW and its subsidiaries. In addition, Ron oversaw the development of the data-center hosting networks as the business experienced some of its greatest success. Prior to joining AOL in 1998, Ron served as a principal engineer for Sprint's Internet backbone after ranking first in the competitive Associate Engineering Program. Ron began his career in 1992, when he started systems and LAN administration while completing his Bachelor of Science degree in applied mathematics and English at Old Dominion University (1994). Ron is well known in the service provider community and is very active in various industry organizations. He serves on the technical advisory council for ARIN.

Hank Mauldin is a corporate consulting engineer for Cisco Systems specializing in network design and security. He has worked for Cisco Systems for more than nine years evaluating and designing data networks. He has been involved with IPsec and done extensive testing of interoperability among IPsec products. He is working on evaluating, testing, and mitigation of network threats. Prior to working at Cisco, he worked for several network integrators and has more than 20 years of data networking experience. Hank holds a master's degree in information system technology from George Washington University. He lives with his wife in San Diego, and has one son away at college. His other interests are travel and digital video production.

Glen Zorn has worked with computer networks since 1982, with the past 10 years devoted to the design and implementation of distributed authentication and authorization protocols. He is the author of more than 20 IETF RFCs and has been an active participant in the development of security protocols for wireless LANs and 3G cellular networks. Zorn is currently employed by Cisco Systems as a corporate development consulting engineer in the Security and Integrity group.

Dedication

Dedicated to Cathy...

For your friendship throughout this past tumultuous decade and for keeping FMS a shared secret.

Acknowledgments

It happened—I wrote a second edition despite declarations of insanity and ravings of "I will never do this again" upon completion of the first edition of this book. Funny how things change after a few years.

There were, of course, many people who helped with this process, and I would like to thank the following folks for providing insightful discussions to help me understand the myriad security technologies and subtle nuances of many protocols. The list includes (in no particular order) Rohan Mahy, Elizabeth McGee, Ian Cox, Bill Woodcock, Cheryl Madson, Jan Vilhuber, Derrell Piper, and Dan Harkins. I would also like to thank my reviewers for this second edition: Ron da Silva, Hank Mauldin, and Glen Zorn. They provided many useful corrections and comments. The patient proddings from the staff at Cisco Press, primarily Amy Moss and Andrew Cupp, is also appreciated. And thanks to John Kane who apparently told his staff not to prod too much to avoid further stressing this particular author.

I would never have had the courage to begin this endeavor in the first place had it not been for the mentoring I received from Harold Ostrow and Bill Kelly. My bosses at NIH and Cisco, respectively, each for approximately five years, both gave me incredible freedom to explore the world of networking and security. I want to thank you both for simply trusting me.

Finally, I would like to thank my family and friends who patiently understood my last-minute cancellations and panic-stricken phone calls because I had to meet yet another deadline (which were invariably missed anyhow). I now have to come up with new excuses.

—Merike Kaeo

Contents at a Glance

Contents

Introduction

Security is hard. Security is expensive. Both statements seem to reflect the sentiment of the general population who is in dire need of securing the electronic communications that have become the ubiquitous means of business communication today. The term *enterprise network security* is becoming more and more prevalent as corporations try to understand and manage the risks associated with the rapidly developing business applications and practices deployed over corporate network infrastructures. Although this statement may at first seem rather dismal, it is just stating reality: Absolute security does *not* exist. Facts of life: Devices will be misconfigured, new attacks will be created, and software has bugs. The best any corporation can do is assess its risks and vulnerabilities, make decisions on what is critical, and then go on to implement its defined security policy as efficiently as possible. It is also important to verify that the implementation of the defined security policy is adhered to, which entails actively monitoring traffic on your networks and performing regularly scheduled security audits. Network security is a complex subject. This is partly because of the abundance of security technologies available today, some of which solve similar security issues and exist as an evolutionary cycle to a more comprehensive security strategy. Recently, the mechanisms to implement security into your corporate networks have become easier even though the underlying technologies remain complex.

Many outstanding books have been written on the subject of computer security, ranging from simplistic introductory books for the layperson to understand a specific concentrated area to more intricate technical details of security that are necessary for implementers of security products. When starting to teach network security fundamentals to people responsible for designing and operating corporate network infrastructures, I found that there was an overwhelming abundance of information to digest—all are available from many different books for the layperson. Often, these books either concentrated on host security issues, or concentrated specifically on security when connecting to the Internet. There was no single source that provided the fundamentals of cryptography, gave a good overview of some currently used and newly developing security technologies, and showed how these technologies could be used to provide a secure network infrastructure given a specified corporate security policy.

The first edition of this book was an attempt to provide a single starting point for understanding network security and to give enough technical details on cryptography fundamentals and security technologies for those who are new to security. In this revised edition, more recent technical developments have been added as well as chapters that
discuss practical deployment issues for virtual private networks, wireless networks, and Voice over IP networks. In addition, a chapter has been added that focuses solely on routing protocol security. By reading this book, you will obtain a good basic understanding of security technologies and issues, recognize the fundamental need to create a corporate security policy, and use the policy as a guide to implement a secure corporate network infrastructure. Topics that have been covered by other books in extensive expert detail are addressed (such as firewalls or intrusion detection systems), but the references in Appendix A, "Sources of Technical Information," should be also read to get the detailed knowledge.

This book focuses on securing the corporate infrastructure. In the ideal secure networking environment, security would be host-based and all security services would be implemented between the originator and the recipient of the information. In practicality, however, there is no complete control of desktop systems in many corporations, and a corporate security policy must be enforced by all departments at the level of control of the given department.

Most corporations have in place departments that handle any one or a combination of the following functions:

- Networking infrastructure
- Desktop requirements
- Security requirements

The network infrastructure group designs and enforces the overall corporate network design. The desktop requirements group defines specifications for all desktop computers (PCs and workstations) and their supported applications. The security requirements group evaluates security risks and creates appropriate security policies to be enforced by all other corporate departments. All departments need to look at what security measures need to be implemented under their realm of control. This book focuses on the security services that can be used to protect the network infrastructure and the data traversing it.

I would like to emphasize that there is no such thing as absolute security. As stated in the movie *The Avengers*, "Nothing is impossible, only mathematically improbable." When a network is called a secure network, it is often misunderstood to mean that there is no possibility of an intrusion or security breach. On the contrary, a secure network means that there are mechanisms in place that will mitigate most of the risks to corporate assets. However slight, some vulnerability will always be there, but as long as it is recognized and understood, it can be dealt with appropriately.

A book that was an inspiration in many ways and that has a great anecdotal chapter on the misconceptions of security is *Surely You're Joking, Mr. Feynman*, an autobiography of the Nobel Prize-winning physicist, Richard P. Feynman. There is a chapter in which Mr. Feynman recounts how easy he found it to crack safes and file cabinets that were thought to be secure—those containing the secrets of the atomic bomb. Most of his success at breaking in was due to people not locking their file cabinets, not changing default combinations, writing down combinations in obvious places, and keeping the combinations the same for multiple safes. He figured out the obvious method to break in, which nobody had considered because they had concentrated on figuring out only part of the problem. All threats and vulnerabilities must be considered when you create an effective corporate security policy.

Objectives

The purpose of this book is to help you understand the fundamentals of securing a network infrastructure. Whether you already have a fundamental knowledge of security or are completely new to the topic, this book offers a detailed look at designing and implementing a secure corporate infrastructure. After completing this book, you will have a thorough understanding of basic cryptography, the most widely deployed security technologies, newly emerging security technologies, and how the technologies relate in the context of virtual private networks, wireless networks, and Voice over IP networks. You will be able to guide the architecture and implementation of a security policy for any corporate environment by understanding the steps required for risk management and the specific details needed. You will also be able to specify the features required in network infrastructure equipment to implement the given security policy.

Audience

This book is written for internetworking professionals who are responsible for designing and maintaining security services for enterprise network infrastructures. If you are a network engineer, architect, or technician who has a rudimentary knowledge of security protocols and technologies, this book will provide you with practical insights on what you need to consider to design and implement varying degrees of a security policy.

This book also includes useful information for consultants, systems engineers, and sales engineers who design corporate networks for clients. The information in this book covers a wide audience because incorporating some measure of security services is an integral part of any network design process.

Organization

This book is organized into four parts. Part I establishes the technical background. Part II focuses on your corporate environment, such as how to determine possible vulnerabilities and create an appropriate security policy. Part III demonstrates the practical implementations with sample configurations using Cisco equipment. Finally, Part IV is a set of appendixes that lists references for further information on network security and gives additional examples for security contingency plans and steps to mitigate distributed denial-of-service attacks.

Part I, "Security Fundamentals"

The first part of the book is dedicated to explaining the fundamentals of cryptography, some of the more widely deployed security technologies, and how these technologies apply to specific networking scenarios including virtual private networks, wireless networks, and Voice over IP networks.

Chapter 1, "Basic Cryptography," focuses on cryptography basics; the emphasis is placed on explaining what the differences are between different cryptographic functions and how they are used in practical implementations. The intent is to give enough detail to understand some relative strengths and weaknesses and get the technical realities to combat marketing hype. Many of the mathematical complexities are avoided because they are mainly required for implementers of security products. Interested parties can get the details from the books referenced in Appendix A, which were written by the ultimate crypto experts.

Chapter 2, "Security Technologies," details emerging security technologies that are widely deployed. This chapter is quite expansive and was the most difficult to represent because it could easily be a book of its own. It is organized in a way that helps you make comparative decisions about which technology is best suited for you when you decide how to implement a given security policy. Many of the technologies overlap because they provide similar solutions to similar problems, and many are stepping stones to the more secure solutions that, in the past, were too complex to implement.

Chapter 3, "Applying Security Technologies to Real Networks," shows how the technologies discussed in Chapter 3 can be used and applied to secure specific scenarios: virtual private networks, wireless networks, and Voice over IP networks.

Chapter 4, "Routing Protocol Security," details some commonly used routing protocols and what built-in functionality exists to effectively secure them (at least to the extent possible today). Most of the mechanisms to provide security have been available for years but have not been widely deployed or are not clearly understood (probably leading to the nondeployment issue). The discussion focuses on most of the routing protocols used in deploying IP routing architectures: RIP, EIGRP, OSPF, IS-IS, and BGP.

Part II, "The Corporate Security Policy"

Understanding the vulnerabilities and risks is the most important step in defining a security policy. The second part of the book focuses on how to go about creating a security policy—the practicalities of what you should think about when designing a policy to fit into your particular environment.

Chapter 5, "Threats in an Enterprise Network," introduces you to the possible threats and common attacks to a
network infrastructure.

Chapter 6, "Considerations for a Site Security Policy," details the considerations for a security policy and describes how to carry out a risk management analysis.

Chapter 7, "Design and Implementation of the Corporate Security Policy," is dedicated to the design of the security policy after a risk analysis has been completed; it presents guidelines and procedures that a corporation should follow.

Chapter 8, "Incident Handling," is dedicated to describing how to handle and recover from a security breach.

Part III, "Practical Implementation"

The third part of the book is dedicated to explaining implementation scenarios. Many specific configuration examples are given for Cisco-specific devices. The implementations will vary greatly depending on your established security policy but should be used as guidelines for what features to think about when implementing a given corporate security policy.

Chapter 9, "Securing the Corporate Network Infrastructure," focuses on security requirements for the internal corporate infrastructure to ensure restricted, confidential access to network infrastructure equipment and network areas.

Chapter 10, "Securing Internet Access," concentrates on securing Internet access as well as any defined network perimeters.

Chapter 11, "Securing Remote Dial-In Access," is dedicated to securing the remote access environment where emphasis is placed on dial-in environments.

Chapter 12, "Securing VPN, Wireless, and VoIP Networks," provides comprehensive design considerations and examples for securing virtual private networks, wireless networks, and Voice over IP networks.

Part IV, "Appendixes"

Appendix A, "Sources of Technical Information," lists sources of more information. It includes books specifically tailored to cryptography and firewalls, points you to IETF working groups for more detailed information about current work on security technologies, and directs you to information that provides guidance for creating network security policies and incident response teams.

Appendix B, "Reporting and Prevention Guidelines: Industrial Espionage and Network Intrusions," shows an example of a contingency planning guide for reporting and preventing industrial espionage and network intrusions. It was created by John C. Smith to help organizations develop the ability to prevent proprietary theft and network intrusion and to know how to respond to recover their property and stop further intrusions when they do occur.

Appendix C, "Port Numbers," is a list of assigned port numbers from the Internet Assigned Numbers Authority (IANA) that specifically relate to the security technologies discussed in Chapter 2.

Appendix D, "Mitigating Distributed Denial-of-Service Attacks," details the steps that should be taken on network infrastructure routers to cause the least amount of harm in any network due to distributed denial-of-service attacks.

Appendix E, "Answers to Review Questions," provides answers and explanations to the questions found at the end of each chapter.

Finally, there is a glossary of the most important terms used in this book.

Cisco Systems Networking Icon Legend

Cisco Systems, Inc. uses a standardized set of icons to represent devices in network topology illustrations. The icon legend that follows shows the most commonly used icons that you might encounter throughout this book.

Router

Bridge

Hub

DSU/CSU

Catalyst
Switch

Multilayer
Switch

ATM
Switch

ISDN/Frame Relay
Switch

Communication
Server

Gateway

Access
Server

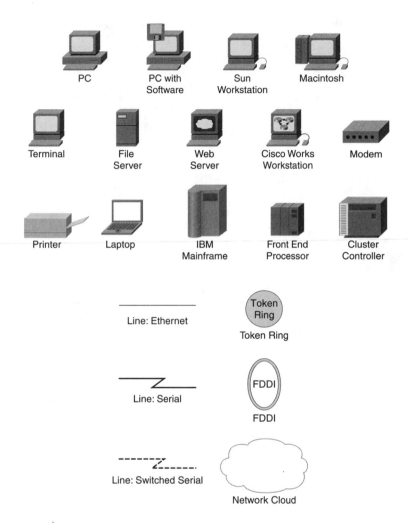

Command Syntax Conventions

The conventions used to present command syntax in this book are the same conventions used in the Cisco IOS Software Command Reference. The Command Reference describes these conventions as follows:

- Vertical bars (l) separate alternative, mutually exclusive elements.

- Square brackets ([ ]) indicate optional elements.

- Braces ({ }) indicate a required choice.

- Braces within brackets ([{ }]) indicate a required choice within an optional element.

- **Boldface** indicates commands and keywords that are entered exactly as shown.

- *Italic* indicates arguments for which you supply values.

Security Fundamentals

## CHAPTER 1

Basic Cryptography

This chapter details the basic building blocks and fundamental issues you need to understand before moving on to more complex security technologies. *Cryptography* is a basis for secure communications; it is, therefore, important that you understand three basic cryptographic functions: symmetric encryption, asymmetric encryption, and one-way hash functions. Most current authentication, integrity, and confidentiality technologies derive from these three cryptographic functions. This chapter also introduces digital signatures as a practical example of how you can combine asymmetric encryption with one-way hash algorithms to provide data authentication and integrity.

Authentication, authorization, and key management issues are critical for you to understand because the compromise of either identity or secret keys is the most common form of security compromise. Authentication technologies are introduced in Chapter 2, "Security Technologies," but this chapter explores the methods of authentication, the establishment of trust domains for defining authorization boundaries, and the importance of the uniqueness of namespace.

A cryptographic *key* is a digital object that you can use to encrypt, decrypt, and sign information. Some keys are kept private, whereas others are shared and must be distributed in a secure manner. The area of key management has seen much progress in the past years; this is mainly because it makes key distribution secure and scalable in an automated fashion. Important issues with key management are creating and distributing the keys securely. This chapter introduces some common mechanisms used to securely create and distribute secret and public keys. The controversial area of *key escrow*, where a third party has access to a confidential cryptographic key, is explored to raise your awareness of what the controversy is all about and what role key escrow may play in a secure enterprise infrastructure.

Cryptography

Cryptography is the science of writing or reading coded messages; it is the basic building block that enables the mechanisms of authentication, integrity, and confidentiality. *Authentication* establishes the identity of either the sender or the receiver of information, or both. In some communication instances, it is not always a requirement to have mutual authentication of both parties. *Integrity* ensures that the data has not been altered in transit, and *confidentiality* ensures that no one except the sender and receiver of the data can actually understand the data.

Usually, cryptographic mechanisms use both an *algorithm* (a mathematical function) and a secret value known as a *key*. Most algorithms undergo years of scrutiny by the world's best cryptographers, who validate the strength of the algorithm. The algorithms are widely known and available; it is the key that is kept secret and provides the required security. The key is analogous to the combination to a lock. Although the concept of a combination lock is well known, you can't open a combination lock easily without knowing the combination. In addition, the more numbers a given combination has, the more work must be done to guess the combination—the same is true for cryptographic keys. The more bits that are in a key, the less susceptible a key is to being compromised by a third party.

The number of bits required in a key to ensure secure encryption in a given environment can be controversial. The longer the *keyspace*—the range of possible values of the key— the more difficult it is to learn (often referred to as *breaking*) the key in a brute-force attack. In a *brute-force attack*, you apply all combinations of a key to the algorithm until you succeed in deciphering the message. Table 1-1 shows the number of keys that must be tried to exhaust all possibilities, given a specified key length.

Table 1-1 *Brute-Force Attack Combinations*

Key Length (in bits)	Number of Combinations
40	$2^{40} = 1,099,511,627,776$
56	$2^{56} = 7.205759403793 \times 10^{16}$
64	$2^{64} = 1.844674407371 \times 10^{19}$
112	$2^{112} = 5.192296858535 \times 10^{33}$
128	$2^{128} = 3.402823669209 \times 10^{38}$

A natural inclination is to use the longest key available, which makes the key more difficult to discover. However, the longer the key, the more computationally expensive the encryption and decryption process can be. The goal is to make breaking a key "cost" more than the worth of the information the key is protecting.

Three types of cryptographic functions enable authentication, integrity, and confidentiality: symmetric key encryption, asymmetric key encryption, and one-way hash functions.

Symmetric Key Encryption

Symmetric encryption, often referred to as *secret key encryption*, uses a common key and the same cryptographic algorithm to scramble and unscramble a message. Figure 1-1 shows two users, Alice and Bob, who want to communicate securely with each other. Both Alice and Bob have to agree on the same cryptographic algorithm to use for encrypting and decrypting data. They also have to agree on a common key—the secret key—to use with their chosen encryption/decryption algorithm.

Figure 1-1   *Secret Key Encryption*

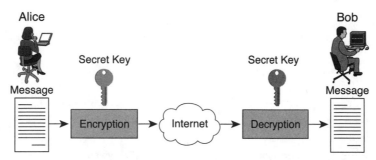

A simplistic secret key algorithm is the Caesar Cipher. The *Caesar Cipher* replaces each letter in the original message with the letter of the alphabet *n* places further down the alphabet. The algorithm shifts the letters to the right or left (depending on whether you are encrypting or decrypting). Figure 1-2 shows Alice and Bob communicating with a Caesar Cipher where the key, *n*, is three letters. For example, the letter A is replaced with the letter D (the letter of the alphabet three places away). The steps of the Caesar Cipher are as follows:

1   Alice and Bob agree to use the Caesar Cipher to communicate and pick *n* = 3 as the secret key.

2   Alice uses the Caesar Cipher to *encrypt* a confidential message to Bob and mails the message.

3   When he receives Alice's mail, Bob *decrypts* the message and reads the confidential message.

Anyone intercepting the message without knowing the secret key is unable to read it. However, you can see that if anyone intercepts the encrypted message and knows the algorithm (for example, shift letters to the right or left), it is fairly easy to succeed in a brute-force attack. Assuming the use of a 26-letter alphabet, the interceptor has to try at most 25 keys to determine the correct key.

Some secret key algorithms operate on fixed-length message blocks. Therefore, it is necessary to break up larger messages into *n*-bit blocks and somehow chain them together. The chaining mechanisms can also offer additional protection from tampering with the transmitted data.

Four common modes exist in which each mode defines a method of combining the plaintext (the message that is not encrypted), the secret key, and the ciphertext (the encrypted text) to generate the stream of ciphertext that is actually transmitted to the recipient, as follows:

- Electronic CodeBook (ECB)
- Cipher Block Chaining (CBC)
- Cipher FeedBack (CFB)
- Output FeedBack (OFB)

Figure 1-2   *Encryption and Decryption Using the Caesar Cipher Algorithm*

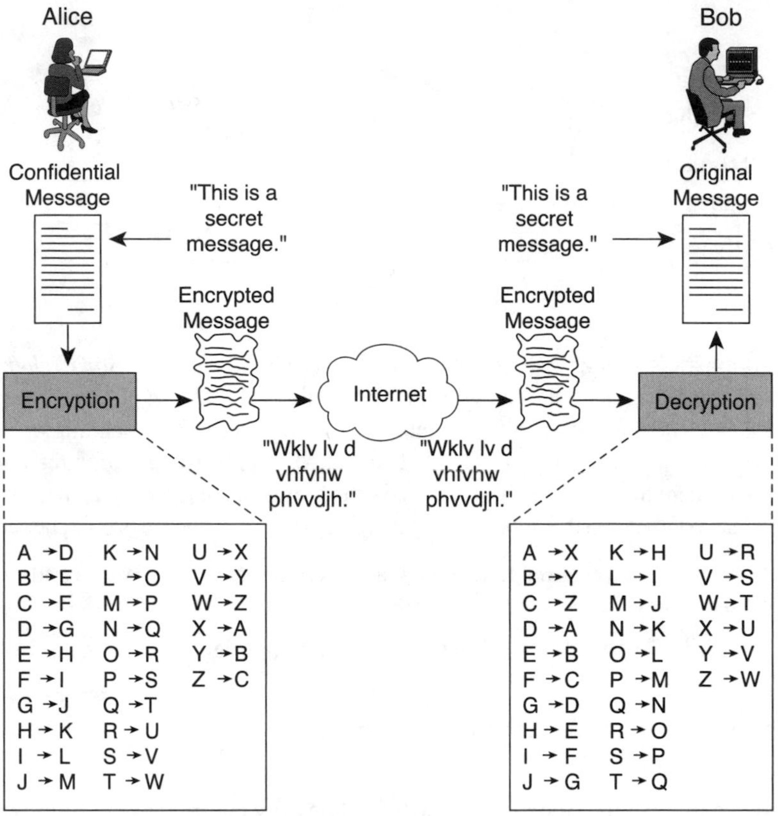

The ECB chaining mechanism encodes each *n*-bit block independently—but uses the same key. An avid snooper interested only in changes in information and not the exact content can easily exploit this weakness. For example, consider someone snooping a certain employee's automatic payroll transactions to a bank. Assuming that the amount is the same for each paycheck, each ECB-encoded ciphertext message appears the same. If the ciphertext changes, the snooper could conclude that the payroll recipient received a raise and perhaps was promoted.

The remaining three algorithms (CBC, CFB, and OFB) have inherent properties that add an element of randomness to the encrypted messages. If you send the same plaintext block through one of these three algorithms, you get back different ciphertext blocks each time. This is accomplished by using different encryption keys or an *initialization vector* (IV). An IV is an encrypted block of random data used as the first *n*-bit block to begin the chaining process. The IV is implementation specific but can be taken from a time stamp or some other random bit of data. If a snooper is listening to the encrypted traffic on the wire, and you are to send the same message 10 times using a different key or IV to encrypt the data, it would look like a different message each time. The snooper would gain virtually no information.

Most secret key algorithms use one of these four modes to provide additional security for the transmitted data. Some of the more common secret key algorithms used today include the following:

- Data Encryption Standard (DES)
- 3DES (read "triple DES")
- Rivest Cipher 4 (RC-4)
- International Data Encryption Algorithm (IDEA)
- Advanced Encryption Standard (AES)

DES

DES is the most widely used encryption scheme today. In 1972, the National Institute of Standards and Technology (NIST, called the National Bureau of Standards at the time) asked for public proposals for an algorithm that would provide strong cryptographic means to protect nonclassified information. In 1974, IBM submitted the Lucifer algorithm, which appeared to meet most of NIST's design requirements. NIST evaluated this program with help from the National Security Agency (NSA). Due to the general distrust of NSA activities, there was quite a bit of skepticism regarding the analysis of Lucifer, especially when it came to the key length, which was reduced from the originally proposed 128 bits down to 56 bits, weakening it significantly.

The NSA was also accused of changing the algorithm to provide a "backdoor" in it that would allow agents to decrypt any information without having to know the encryption key. This fear proved unjustified, however, and no such backdoor has ever been found.

The modified Lucifer algorithm was adopted by NIST as a federal standard in November 1976 and became known as the Data Encryption Standard (DES).

DES operates on 64-bit message blocks. The algorithm uses a series of steps to transform 64 input bits into 64-output bits. In its standard form, the algorithm uses 64-bit keys—of which 56 bits are chosen randomly. The remaining 8 bits are parity bits (one for each 7-bit block of the 56-bit random value). DES is widely used in many commercial applications today, and can be used in all four modes: ECB, CBC, CFB, and OFB. Generally, however, DES operates in either the CBC mode or the CFB mode.

In 1998, the Electronic Frontier Foundation, using a specially developed computer called the DES Cracker, managed to break DES in fewer than 3 days. The cost was less than $250,000, and the encryption chip that powered the DES Cracker was capable of processing 88 billion keys per second. It has also been shown that for a cost of a million dollars a dedicated hardware device can be built that can search all possible DES keys in about 3.5 hours. Because of the relative ease of breaking DES encryption, it is being phased out of use. NIST has depracated DES in favor of AES.

3DES

Triple DES (3DES) is an alternative to DES that preserves the existing investment in software but makes a brute-force attack more difficult. It has the advantage of proven reliability and a longer key length that eliminates many of the shortcut attacks that can be used to reduce the amount of time it takes to break DES. 3DES takes a 64-bit block of data and performs the operations of encrypt, decrypt, and encrypt. 3DES can use one, two, or three different keys. The advantage of using one key is that, with the exception of the additional processing time required, 3DES with one key is the same as standard DES (for backward compatibility). 3DES in ECB mode is the most commonly used mode of operation. At least two keys must be used if 3DES is to be more secure than DES. Triple DES was endorsed by NIST as a temporary standard to be used until the AES specifications was finalized (described later).

RC-4

RC-4 is a proprietary algorithm invented by Ron Rivest and marketed by RSA Data Security. It is used often with a 128-bit key, although its key size can vary. It is unpatented, but is protected as a trade secret—although it was leaked to the Internet in September 1994. Historically, because the U.S. government at one time only allowed encryption algorithms to be exported when using secret key lengths of 40 bits or less, some implementations use a very short key length for compatibility purposes with other 40-bit systems.

IDEA

IDEA was developed to replace DES. It also operates on 64-bit message blocks but uses a 128-bit key. As with DES, IDEA can operate in all four modes: ECB, CBC, CFB, and OFB. IDEA was designed to be efficient in both hardware and software implementations. However, IDEA has a major shortcoming in that it is not available in the public domain. It is a patented algorithm and requires a license for commercial use.

AES

In 1997, NIST abandoned their official endorsement of DES and began work on a replacement, to be called the Advanced Encryption Standard (AES). In November 2001, the AES standard was published as the Federal Information Processing Standards Publication 197 (FIPS 197). It specifies the Rijndael algorithm, which was developed and by two cryptographers from Belgium: Dr. Joan Daemen and Dr. Vincent Rijmen. The Rijndael algorithm is a symmetric block cipher that can process data blocks of 128 bits, using 3 different key lengths: 128, 192, and 256 bits. In decimal terms, this means that there are approximately the following:

- 3.4×10^{38} possible 128-bit keys
- 6.2×10^{57} possible 192-bit keys
- 1.1×10^{77} possible 256-bit keys

Rijndael was designed to handle additional block sizes and key lengths, but these are not adopted in the AES standard. Rijndael's symmetric and parallel structure gives implementors a lot of flexibility and can be efficiently implemented in both hardware and software across a wide range of computing environments. Rijndael's very low memory requirements make it very well suited for mobile and wireless environments, in which it also demonstrates excellent performance. Rijndael's operations are among the easiest to defend against power and timing attacks. These are attacks where the power consumption or radiation emission is measured to aid in breaking the cryptosystem or where private keys can be recovered by measuring how long a particular encryption operation takes. The AES algorithm is gaining wide adoption across many security implementations.

NOTE   References to specific algorithms are given to get you familiar with which algorithms pertain to which basic encryption concepts. Because most of the crypto analytical and performance comparisons are useful more for implementers of the technology, they are not deeply explored here. Appendix A, "Sources of Technical Information," provides references for more in-depth studies.

Secret key encryption is most often used for data confidentiality because most symmetric key algorithms have been designed to be implemented in hardware and have been optimized for encrypting large amounts of data at one time. Challenges with secret key encryption include the following:

- Changing the secret keys frequently to avoid the risk of compromising the keys
- Securely generating the secret keys
- Securely distributing the secret keys

A commonly used mechanism to derive and exchange secret keys securely is the Diffie-Hellman algorithm. This algorithm is explained later in this chapter in the "Key Management" section.

Asymmetric Encryption

Asymmetric encryption is often referred to as *public key encryption*. It can use either the same algorithm, or different but complementary algorithms, to scramble and unscramble data. Two different, but related, key values are required: a public key and a private key. If Alice and Bob want to communicate using public key encryption, both need a public key and private key pair. (See Figure 1-3.) Alice has to create her public key/private key pair, and Bob has to create his own public key/private key pair. When communicating with each other securely, Alice and Bob use different keys to encrypt and decrypt data.

Figure 1-3   *Public Key Encryption*

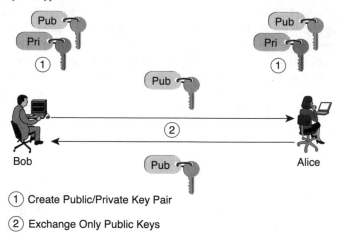

① Create Public/Private Key Pair

② Exchange Only Public Keys

Some of the more common uses of public key algorithms include the following:

- Data integrity
- Data confidentiality
- Sender nonrepudiation
- Sender authentication

Data confidentiality and sender authentication can be achieved using the public key algorithm. Figure 1-4 shows how data integrity and confidentiality is provided using public key encryption.

The following steps have to take place if Alice and Bob are to have *confidential data exchange*:

Step 1   Both Alice and Bob create their individual public/private key pairs.

Step 2   Alice and Bob exchange their public keys.

Step 3   Alice writes a message to Bob and uses *Bob's public key* to encrypt her message. Then, she sends the encrypted data to Bob over the Internet.

Step 4   Bob uses *his private key* to decrypt the message.

Step 5   Bob writes a reply, encrypts the reply with *Alice's public key*, and sends the encrypted reply over the Internet to Alice.

Step 6   Alice uses *her private key* to decrypt the reply.

Figure 1-4   *Ensuring Data Integrity and Confidentiality with Public Key Encryption*

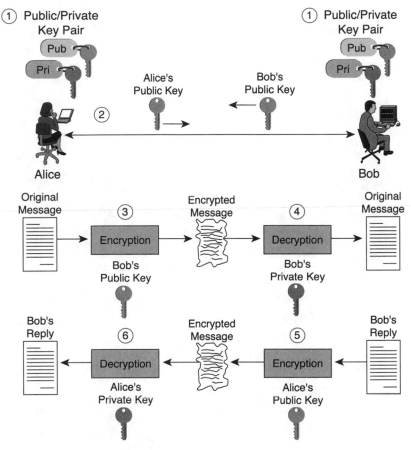

Data confidentiality is ensured when Alice sends the initial message because only Bob can decrypt the message with his private key. Data integrity is also preserved because, to modify the message, a malicious attacker would need Bob's private key again. Data integrity and confidentiality are also ensured for the reply because only Alice has access to her private key and is the only one who can modify or decrypt the reply with her private key.

However, this exchange is not very reassuring because it is easy for a third party to pretend to be Alice and send a message to Bob encrypted with Bob's public key. The public key is, after all, widely available. Verification that it was Alice who sent the initial message is important. Figure 1-5 shows how public key cryptography resolves this problem and provides for sender authentication and nonrepudiation.

Figure 1-5   *Sender Authentication and Nonrepudiation Using Public Key Encryption*

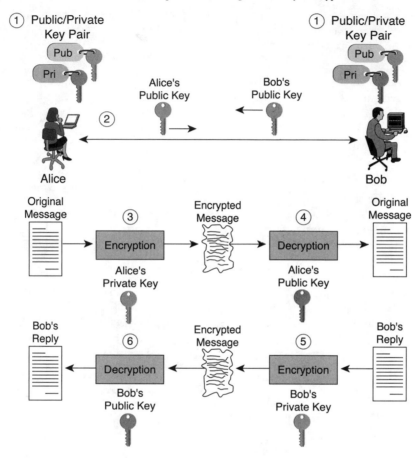

The following steps have to take place if Alice and Bob are to have an *authenticated data exchange*:

Step 1   Both Alice and Bob create their public/private key pairs.

Step 2   Alice and Bob exchange their public keys.

Step 3   Alice writes a message for Bob, uses *her private key* to encrypt the message, and then sends the encrypted data over the Internet to Bob.

Step 4   Bob uses *Alice's public key* to decrypt the message.

Step 5   Bob writes a reply, encrypts the reply with *his private key*, and sends the encrypted reply over the Internet to Alice.

Step 6   Alice uses *Bob's public key* to decrypt the reply.

An authenticated exchange is ensured because only Bob and Alice have access to their respective private keys. Bob and Alice meet the requirement of nonrepudiation—they cannot later deny sending the given message if their keys have not been compromised. This, of course, lends itself to a hot debate on how honest Bob and Alice are; they can deny sending messages by just stating that their private keys have been compromised.

To use public key cryptography to perform an authenticated exchange as well as ensure data integrity and confidentiality, double encryption needs to occur. Alice first encrypts her confidential message to Bob with Bob's public key and then encrypts again with her private key. Anyone can decrypt the first message to get the embedded ciphertext, but only Bob can decrypt the ciphertext with his private key.

NOTE   A crucial aspect of asymmetric encryption is that the private key *must* be kept private. If the private key is compromised, an evil attacker can impersonate you and send and receive messages as you.

The mechanisms used to generate these public/private key pairs are complex, but they result in the generation of two very large random numbers, one of which becomes the public key and the other becomes the private key. Because these numbers *as well as their product* must adhere to stringent mathematical criteria to preserve the uniqueness of each public/private key pair, generating these numbers is fairly processor intensive.

NOTE   Key pairs are not guaranteed to be unique by any mathematical criteria. However, the math ensures that no *weak keys* are generated.

Public key encryption algorithms are rarely used for data confidentiality because of their performance constraints. Instead, public key encryption algorithms are typically used in applications involving authentication using digital signatures and key management.

Some of the more common public key algorithms are the Ron Rivest, Adi Shamir, and Leonard Adleman (RSA) algorithm and the El Gamal algorithm.

Hash Functions

A *hash function* takes an input message of arbitrary length and outputs fixed-length code. The fixed-length output is called the *hash*, or the *message digest*, of the original input message. If an algorithm is to be considered cryptographically suitable (that is, secure) for a hash function, it must exhibit the following properties:

- The function must be consistent; that is, the same input must always create the same output.

- The function must be one way (that is, irreversible); if you are given the output, it must be extremely difficult, if not impossible, to ascertain the input message.

- The output of the function must be random—or give the appearance of randomness—to prevent guessing of the original message.

- The output of the function must be unique; that is, it should be nearly impossible to find two messages that produce the same message digest.

One-way hash functions are typically used to provide a *fingerprint* of a message or file. Much like a human fingerprint, a hash fingerprint is unique and thereby proves the integrity and authenticity of the message.

Consider the example shown in Figure 1-6; Alice and Bob are using a one-way hash function to verify that no one has tampered with the contents of the message during transit.

Figure 1-6   *Using a One-Way Hash Function for Data Integrity*

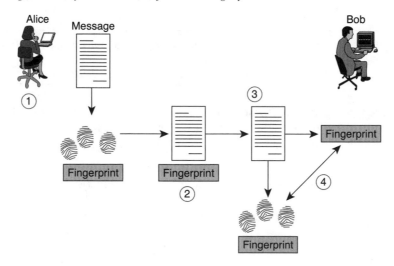

The following steps have to take place if Alice and Bob are to keep the integrity of their data:

Step 1   Alice writes a message and uses the message as input to a one-way hash function.

Step 2   The result of the hash function is appended as the fingerprint to the message sent to Bob.

Step 3   Bob separates the message and the appended fingerprint and uses the message as input to the same one-way hash function that Alice used.

Step 4   If the hashes match, Bob can be assured that the message was not tampered with.

The problem with this simplistic approach is that the fingerprint itself could be tampered with and is subject to the man-in-the-middle attack. The *man-in-the-middle attack* refers to an entity listening to a believed secure communication and impersonating either the sender or receiver. A variant to make hash functions more secure is to use a keyed hash function, where the input to the algorithm is a shared secret key as well as the original message. To more effectively use hash functions as fingerprints, however, you can combine them with public key technology to provide digital signatures, which are discussed in the next section, "Digital Signatures."

Common hash functions include the following:

- Message Digest 4 (MD4) algorithm
- Message Digest 5 (MD5) algorithm
- Secure Hash Algorithm (SHA)

MD4 and MD5 were designed by Ron Rivest of MIT. SHA was developed by the National Institute of Standards and Technology (NIST). MD5 and SHA are the hash functions used most often in current security product implementations—both are based on MD4. MD5 processes its input in 512-bit blocks and produces a 128-bit message digest. SHA also processes its input in 512-bit blocks but produces a 160-bit message digest. SHA is more processor intensive and may run a little more slowly than MD5.

Digital Signatures

A *digital signature* is an encrypted message digest appended to a document. It is sometimes also referred to as a digital fingerprint. Digital signatures enable you to confirm the identity of the sender and the integrity of the document. Digital signatures are based on a combination of public key encryption and one-way secure hash function algorithms. Figure 1-7 shows an example of how to create a digital signature.

Figure 1-7   *Creating a Digital Signature*

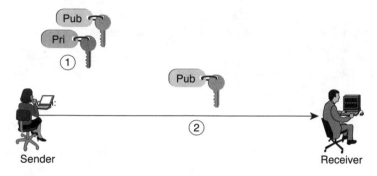

① Sender Creates Public/Private Key Pair

② Sender Sends its Public Key to Receiver

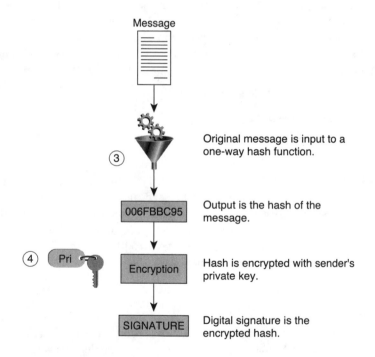

The following steps must be followed for Bob to create a digital signature:

Step 1   Bob creates a public/private key pair.

Step 2   Bob gives his public key to Alice.

Step 3   Bob writes a message for Alice and uses the document as input to a one-way hash function.

Step 4   Bob encrypts the output of the hash algorithm, the message digest, with his private key, resulting in the digital signature.

The combination of the document and the digital signature is the message that Bob sends to Alice. Figure 1-8 shows the verification of the digital signature.

Figure 1-8   *Verifying a Digital Signature*

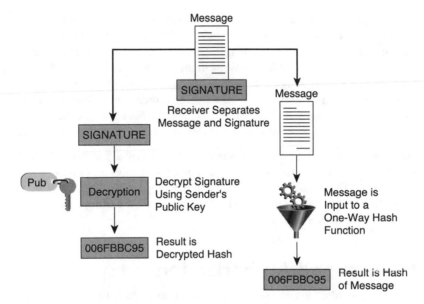

On the receiving side, Alice follows these steps to verify that the message is indeed from Bob—that is, to verify the digital signature:

Step 1   Alice separates the received message into the original document and the digital signature.

Step 2   Alice uses Bob's public key to decrypt the digital signature, which results in the original message digest.

Step 3   Alice takes the original document and uses it as input to the same hash function Bob used, which results in a message digest.

Step 4   Alice compares both of the message digests to see whether they match.

If Alice's calculation of the message digest matches Bob's decrypted message digest, the integrity of the document as well as the authentication of the sender are proven.

NOTE   The initial public key exchange must be performed in a trusted manner to preserve security. This is critical and is the fundamental reason for the need for digital certificates. A digital certificate is a message that is digitally signed with the private key of a trusted third party stating that a specific public key belongs to someone or something with a specified name and set of attributes. If the initial public key exchange wasn't performed in a trusted manner, someone could easily impersonate a given entity.

Digital signatures do not provide confidentiality of the message contents. However, it is frequently more imperative to produce proof of the originator of a message than to conceal the contents of a message. It is plausible that you could want authentication and integrity of messages without confidentiality, as in the case where routing updates are passed in a core network. The routing contents may not be confidential, but it's important to verify that the originator of the routing update is a trusted source. An additional example of the importance of authenticating the originator of a message is in online commerce and banking transactions, where proof of origin is imperative before acting on any transactions.

Some of the more common public key digital signature algorithms are the RSA algorithm and the Digital Signature Standard (DSS) algorithm. DSS was proposed by NIST and is based on the El Gamal public key algorithm. Compared to RSA, DSS is faster for key generation and has about the same performance for generating signatures but is much slower for signature verification.

Authentication and Authorization

Because authentication and authorization are critical parts of secure communications, they must be emphasized. *Authentication* establishes the identity of the sender and/or the receiver of information. Any integrity check or confidential information is often meaningless if the identity of the sending or receiving party is not properly established.

Authorization is usually tightly coupled to authentication in most network resource access requirements. Authorization establishes what you are allowed to do after you've identified yourself. (It is also called *access control*, *capabilities*, and *permissions*.) It can be argued that authorization does not always require *a priori* authentication, but in this book, authentication and authorization are tightly coupled; authorization usually follows any authentication procedure.

Issues related to authentication and authorization include the robustness of the methods used in verifying an entity's identity, the establishment of trusted domains to define authorization boundaries, and the requirement of uniqueness in namespace.

Methods of Authentication

All methods of authentication require you to specify who or what you are and to relay appropriate credentials to *prove* that you are who you say you are. These credentials generally take the form of something you know, something you have, or something you are. *What you know* may be a password. *What you have* could be a smart card. *What you are* pertains to the field of biometrics, in which sophisticated equipment is used to scan a person's fingerprint or eye or to recognize a person's voice to provide authentication.

Authentication technologies are discussed in detail in Chapter 2. Here, the important element is to recognize that different mechanisms provide authentication services with varying degrees of certainty. Choosing the proper authentication technology largely depends on the location of the entities being authenticated and the degree of trust placed in the particular facets of the network.

Trust Models

Trust is the firm belief or confidence in the honesty, integrity, reliability, justice, and so on of another person or thing. *Authorization* is what you are allowed to do once your identity is established. All secure systems must have a framework for an organizational policy for authorization—this framework is called a *trust model*.

If something is difficult to obtain in a dishonest manner or is difficult to forge, we have inherent trust in that system. An example is the title to a car: This document is used as proof of ownership of a car because it is difficult to forge. It is this proof that authorizes a person to resell his or her car with the relative certainty that the car is actually his or hers to sell.

In the network world, trust models can be very complex. Suppose that we have a large corporation with a number of different affiliated departments—the research department, the marketing department, and the payroll department. These individual departments could structure their networks autonomously but with a spirit of cooperation. Each department sets up a trusted intermediary, which is the entity that keeps all the authentication and authorization information for the employees in that department. (See Figure 1-9.)

When an executive member of the research department wants to access a document off one of the research servers, the research department's authentication/authorization server authenticates the executive member. Now if that same executive wants to access salary information for his employees, there must be a mechanism for authenticated and authorized access to the payroll department. Instead of each department server having separate account information for every user (this arrangement could become an administrative nightmare with large numbers of users), it may be necessary to create *groups* with *inherited trust*. For example, you can create an executive group on the payroll server that permits any executive member of the company to access payroll information.

Figure 1-9 *Trusted Intermediaries for Individual Corporate Departments*

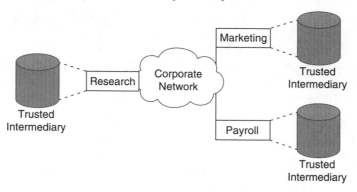

Delegation of trust refers to giving someone or something permission to act on your behalf. If the executive from the research department went on vacation and left someone else in charge, this individual could have permission to act on the executive's behalf to carry out a salary modification. When the executive returns, the authorization must be revoked because it was granted only on a temporary basis.

The difficulty in many trust models is deciding whom to trust. Weighting risk factors (the amount of damage that can be done if trust is inappropriately placed) and having adequate mechanisms to deal with misplaced trust should be a part of every corporate security policy. Creating a security policy is discussed in more detail in Chapter 7, "Design and Implementation of the Corporation Security Policy."

NOTE   It is important to recognize that *trust* does not mean *implicit* trust. You should have a trust model that works in high probability, but you must verify the trust relationships and put in place checks to verify that information has not been compromised. As Ronald Reagan once said, "Trust, but verify."

Namespace

Trust domains define authorization boundaries. For each trust domain, it is important that a unique identifier exists to identify what is being acted on. At first, creating unique identifiers may seem trivial, but as the size and numbers of trust domains grow, the problem can get very complex.

Take the simple scenario of a typical enterprise network. Company A is a small startup enterprise, and employees use their first names as login IDs. Company B decides to acquire Company A. Now there are a number of employees who have the same login ID. As you know, the IDs must be unique to preserve authentication and authorization rights. Typically, companies have a naming convention for this situation: Login IDs consist of the user's first initial and last name; any duplicates use the first two initials and last name, or the first three initials and last name, and so on.

Many large corporations create standard naming conventions for all entities that may require authentication (for example, employees and any and all network infrastructure devices). The concept of an object identifier has been used in the industry to veer away from the common notion that an entity has to have a specific name. The object identifier also can be an employee badge number, an employee social security number, a device IP address, a MAC address, or a telephone number. These object identifiers must be unique within given trust domains.

Key Management

Key management is a difficult problem in secure communications, mainly because of social rather than technical factors. Cryptographically secure ways of creating and distributing keys have been developed and are fairly robust. However, the weakest link in any secure system is that humans are responsible for keeping secret and private keys confidential. Keeping these keys in a secure place and not writing them down or telling other people what they are is a socially difficult task — especially in the face of greed and anger. Some people find it quite difficult not to divulge a secret in exchange for a million dollars or to get back at a seemingly unfair employer. Other people do not take secure procedures seriously — sometimes considering them just a nuisance — and are careless in keeping keys private. The human factor will always be an issue that necessitates sufficient checks to ensure that keys have not been compromised.

Creating and Distributing Secret Keys

For a small number of communicating entities, it is not unreasonable to create a key and manually deliver it. In most wide-scale corporations, however, this mechanism is awkward and outdated. Because secret key encryption is often used in applications requiring confidentiality, it is reasonable to assume that there may exist a secret key per session, a *session* being any single communication data transfer between two entities. For a large network with hundreds of communication hosts, each holding numerous sessions per hour, assigning and transferring secret keys is a large problem. Key distribution is often performed through centralized key distribution centers (KDCs) or through public key algorithms that establish secret keys in a secure, distributed fashion.

The centralized key distribution model relies on a trusted third party, the KDC, which issues the session keys to the communicating entities. (See Figure 1-10.)

Figure 1-10   *Distributing Keys through a Key Distribution Center*

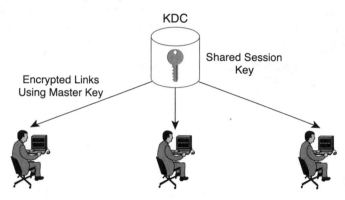

The centralized distribution model requires that all communicating entities have a shared secret key with which they can communicate with the KDC confidentially. The problem of how to distribute this shared secret key to each of the communicating nodes still exists, but it is much more scalable. The KDC is manually configured with every shared key, and each communicating node has its corresponding shared key configured. Keys can be distributed physically to employees when they get an employee badge or to devices from the IS department as part of the initial system setup.

NOTE   If a device is given the key, anyone using that device may be authorized for accessing certain network resources. In this age of mobile hosts, it is good practice to authenticate a device as well as the user using the device to access network resources.

A common method used to create secret session keys in a distributed manner is the *Diffie-Hellman algorithm*. The Diffie-Hellman algorithm provides a way for two parties to establish a shared secret key that only those two parties know—even though they are communicating over an insecure channel. This secret key is then used to encrypt data using their favorite secret key encryption algorithm. Figure 1-11 shows how the Diffie-Hellman algorithm works.

Figure 1-11   *Establishing Secret Keys Using the Diffie-Hellman Algorithm*

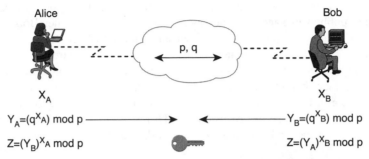

By exchanging numbers (p,q) in the clear, two entities can determine
a new unique number (z) known only to them.

The following steps are used in the Diffie-Hellman algorithm:

1   Alice initiates the exchange and transmits two large numbers (p and q) to Bob.

2   Alice chooses a random large integer X_A and computes the following equation:

$$Y_A = (q^{XA}) \bmod p$$

3   Bob chooses a random large integer X_B and computes this equation:

$$Y_B = (q^{XB}) \bmod p$$

4   Alice sends Y_A to Bob. Bob sends Y_B to Alice.

5   Alice computes the following equation:

$$Z = (Y_B)^{XA} \bmod p$$

6   Bob computes this equation:

$$Z' = (Y_A)^{XB} \bmod p$$

The resulting shared secret key is as follows:

$$Z = Z' = q^{(XAXB)} \bmod p$$

The security of Diffie-Hellman relies on two very difficult mathematical problems:

- Any eavesdropper has to compute a discrete logarithm to recover X_A and X_B. (That is, the eavesdropper has to figure out X_A from seeing q^{XA} or figure out X_B from seeing q^{XB}.)

- Any eavesdropper has to factor large prime numbers—numbers on the order of 100 to 200 digits can be considered *large*. Both p and q should be large prime numbers and $(p - 1)/2$ should be a prime number.

For the reader interested in a more detailed mathematical explanation, see the following sidebar.

The Diffie-Hellman exchange is subject to a man-in-the-middle attack because the exchanges themselves are not authenticated. In this attack, an opponent, Cruella, intercepts Alice's public value and sends her own public value to Bob. When Bob transmits his public value, Cruella substitutes it with her own and sends it to Alice. Cruella and Alice thus agree on one shared key, and Cruella and Bob agree on another shared key. After this exchange, Cruella just decrypts any messages sent out by Alice or Bob, and then reads and possibly modifies them before re-encrypting with the appropriate key and transmitting them to the correct party. To circumvent this problem and ensure authentication and integrity in the exchange, the two parties involved in the Diffie-Hellman exchange can authenticate themselves to each other through the use of digital signatures and public key certificates.

More About the Diffie-Hellman Algorithm

Two basic mathematical transforms are necessary to understand the Diffie-Hellman exchange. The first transform to understand is a property of exponents:

$$(n^x)^y = n^{xy} = n^{yx} = (n^y)^x$$

If you substitute $n = 2$, $x = 2$, and $y = 3$ to get the following for $(n^x)^y$:

$$(2^2)^3 = 4^3 = 4 \times 4 \times 4 = 64$$

You can swap the exponents x and y to get the same results:

$$(2^2)^3 = (2^3)^2 = 2^6 = 2 \times 2 \times 2 \times 2 \times 2 \times 2 = 64$$

Finally, you can swap the exponents x and y in the original expression $(n^y)^x$ and get the same results:

$$(2^3)^2 = 8^2 = 8 \times 8 = 64$$

This transform is important to the Diffie-Hellman algorithm because the two endpoints of the encrypted transmission exchange use this concept to scramble their private keys and exchange the keys as exponents. If Alice and Bob are the two endpoints, and Alice chooses the private key A while Bob chooses the private key B, and they both know a number q, they can do the following:

- Alice sends her public key q^A to Bob.
- Bob sends his public key q^B to Alice.
- Alice computes $(q^B)^A$.
- Bob computes $(q^A)^B$.

Now Bob and Alice both know the secret number q^{AB} and can use it as a session key.

The trouble is that anyone else who knows q can calculate A and B, and will know q^{AB} as well, and can decode the ciphertext encrypted with the key. That's where the next mathematical operation comes in.

The operator *modulus*, or *mod*, is used quite regularly in number theory and some other branches of mathematics. Remember from your arithmetic classes that any integer can be divided by any other integer, to produce a quotient and a remainder. This is usually expressed as follows:

$$x \div y = (\text{quotient}, \text{remainder})$$

Here's an example:

$$5 \div 3 = (1, 2)$$

Usually, we are more interested in the quotient than in the remainder when we perform a division operation. In modular arithmetic, however, the remainder is the important part:

$$x \bmod y = r$$

Here's an example:

$$5 \bmod 3 = 2$$

One of the interesting things to notice is that there are an infinite number of numbers x such that x mod 3 equals 2. Substitute these values for x to prove that there are many x's to solve the equation x mod 3 = 2: 2, 5, 8, 11, 14, 17, 20, and so on.

How does modular arithmetic help Bob and Alice? If they share another number, p, then instead of using q^A and q^B as their public keys, they can exchange ($q^A \bmod p$) and ($q^B \bmod p$) as public keys without risk of exposing their private keys, even if q and p are well-known numbers, because this statement is true:

$$(q^A \bmod p)^B = (q^B \bmod p)^A$$

Because many numbers equal $q^X \bmod p$, many computations must be performed to find x. To complicate the process of finding x even further, q and p should be large *prime* numbers and (p − 1)/2 should be prime.

A *prime number* is a number that has only 1 and itself as factors. The number of integers over 100 digits long and known with absolute certainty to be prime is small and, among the mathematical community, very well known. With the choice between using well-known, proven, large prime numbers and the immense task of proving for yourself that the numbers p and q you are choosing are, in fact, primes, you have to compromise: You choose numbers that are relatively prime. A *relatively prime* number is one that is *fairly likely* to be prime. This modification of the rule enables you to choose numbers that are still computationally difficult but that can be generated in much less time than what is needed to prove that the numbers are absolute primes.

Creating and Distributing Public Keys

For public key algorithms, creating the public/private key pairs is complex. The pairs adhere to stringent rules as defined by varying public key algorithms to ensure the uniqueness of each public/private key pair. Uniqueness is "statistically" guaranteed; that is, the odds of two identical keys being generated independently are astronomical. The complexity associated with generating public/private key pairs is the creation of sets of parameters that meet the needs of the algorithm (for example, primarily for RSA and many other algorithms).

NOTE   It is ideal for the end user (the person or thing being identified by the key) to generate the key pair themselves. The private key should *never* leave the end user's possession. In corporate environments where this may not be practical or where key escrow is required, different rules apply. However, all technical solutions should attempt self-generation as the first goal of a design architecture so that the private key is known only to the entity creating the key pair.

The problem is how you can distribute the public keys in a secure manner and how you can trust the entity that gives you the key. For a small number of communicating parties, it may be manageable to call each other or to meet face to face and give out your public key.

It should *never* be taken on faith that a public key belongs to someone. Many organizations today have so-called *key-signing parties*, a time in which people get together in the same room and exchange respective public keys. Someone in the room may know for sure that a person is who he says he is; however, it may be necessary to provide proof of identity with a drivers license or passport.

The key-signing parties are necessary when there is a lack of a trusted third party. A more scalable approach is to use digital certificates to distribute public keys. Digital certificates require the use of a trusted third party—the *certificate authority*.

NOTE   There is no need for complex key distribution methods of a public key cryptosystem to ensure data confidentiality. The security of the data encrypted with the public key doesn't depend on the authenticity of the person advertising the public key. A public key cryptosystem encrypts a message just as strongly with a public key that is widely known by broadcasting it as it does with a public key obtained from a trusted certificate authority. Key distribution in public key systems is a problem only if you want true authentication of the person claiming to be associated with the public key.

Digital Certificates

A *digital certificate* is a digitally signed message that is typically used to attest to the validity of a public key of an entity. Certificates require a common format and are largely based on the ITU-T X.509 standard today. Figure 1-12 shows an example of a digital certificate format using the X.509 standard.

Figure 1-12 *The X.509 Certificate Format*

```
Version number: 3
Serial number: 0000123
Issuing algorithms: SHA, DH, 3837829...
Issued by: Me
Valid from/to: 1/1/93 to 12/31/98
Subject name: Alice Smith
Subject public key information: DH, 3813710...
Signature: 2393702347...
```

The general format of an X.509 certificate includes the following elements:

- Version number
- Serial number of certificate
- Issuer algorithm information
- Issuer of certificate
- Valid to/from date
- Public key algorithm information of the subject of the certificate
- Digital signature of the issuing authority

Digital certificates are a way to prove the validity of an entity's public key and may well be the future mechanism to provide single login capabilities in today's corporate networks. However, this technology is still in its infancy as far as deployment is concerned. Much of the format of certificates has been defined, but there is still the need to ensure that certificates are valid, manageable, and have consistent semantic interpretation.

Certificate Authorities

The *certificate authority* (CA) is the trusted third party that vouches for the validity of the certificate. It is up to the CA to enroll certificates, distribute certificates, and finally to remove (revoke) certificates when the information they contain becomes invalid. Figure 1-13 shows how Bob can obtain Alice's public key in a trusted manner using a CA.

Figure 1-13 *Obtaining a Digital Certificate Through a Certificate Authority*

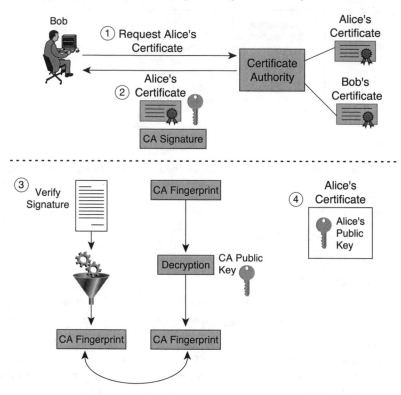

Assume that Alice has a valid certificate stored in the CA and that Bob has securely obtained the CA's public key. The steps that Bob follows to obtain Alice's public key in a reliable manner are as follows:

Step 1 Bob requests Alice's digital certificate from the CA.

Step 2 The CA sends Alice's certificate, which is signed by the CA's private key.

Step 3 Bob receives the certificate and verifies the CA's signature.

Step 4 Because Alice's certificate contains her public key, Bob now has a "notarized" version of Alice's public key.

This scheme relies on the CA's public key to be distributed to users in a secure way. Most likely, this occurs using an out-of-band mechanism. There is still much debate over who should maintain CAs on the Internet. Many organizations (including financial institutions, government agencies, and application vendors) have expressed interest in offering certificate services. In all cases, it's a decision based on trust. Some corporations may want to control their own certificate infrastructure, and others may choose to outsource the control to a trusted third party.

The issues still being finalized in the industry include how to perform efficient certificate enrollment, how to revoke certificates, and how to handle cross-certifications in CA hierarchies. These issues are discussed in more detail in Chapter 2 in the section "Public Key Infrastructure and Distribution Models."

Key Escrow

Key escrow is the notion of putting a confidential secret key or private key in the care of a third party until certain conditions are fulfilled. This, in itself, is not a bad idea because it is easy to forget a private key, or the key may become garbled if the system it is stored on goes berserk. The controversy revolves around which keys should be in escrow and who becomes the trusted third party who has access to confidential keys while still protecting the privacy of the owners of the keys.

By far the most controversial key escrow issue surrounds whether cryptosystems should be developed to have a backdoor for wire-tapping purposes. The U.S. government for one would like secret keys and private keys to be made available to law and government officials for wire-tapping purposes. Many leading security and cryptography experts have found flaws in cryptographic systems that support key recovery. All the current algorithms operate on the premise that the private and secret keys cannot be compromised (unless they are written down or conveyed). Key recovery goes against all these assumptions.

The Business Case

In a corporate environment, many business needs for key escrow exist. It would not seem unreasonable for a corporation to keep in escrow keys used to encrypt and decrypt corporate secrets. The corporation must make a business decision about which kinds of traffic require encryption and which information is critical to be able to retrieve. Typically, the encryption/decryption is performed at the application level; the keys used can be offered to trusted key escrow personnel. In all cases, the business keeps all parts of a key and the cryptosystem private within the business. No external escrow agent is needed.

The Political Angle

Government policy is still being defined for key escrow. A technical solution initially proposed by NIST and the NSA during the Bush Sr. administration was a new tamper-proof encryption chip called the *Clipper chip*. The algorithm it used contained a superkey—essentially a law enforcement agency field in the key. Each Clipper chip is unique and has a key field tied to the chip's serial number. The FBI, supposedly only with a court-ordered warrant, could use the superkey to open up your message. Matt Blaze, principal research scientist at AT&T Laboratories, and others showed that the Clipper chip is not secure; the Clipper proposals have mostly been cast aside.

Now the government is back to brute-force escrow: You give your private key or keys to the escrow agency. The government has "compromised" by allowing in its proposal that the escrow agency can be a private business that has been "certified" by the U.S. government.

The Clinton administration continued to pursue a policy of key recovery both inside the United States and abroad. An extensive study on the risks of key recovery mechanisms was conducted by a group of leading computer scientists and cryptographers. This report attempted to outline the technical risks, costs, and implications of deploying systems that provide government access to encryption keys. You can find this report at http://www.cdt.org/crypto/risks98/.

You can find updates on the U.S. government's position on key escrow at http://www.cdt.org/crypto/ and http://www.epic.org.

The Human Element

Aside from the political and business problems with government key escrow (who wants to buy a cryptosystem for which you know someone else has the keys?), there is the critical human element to key escrow. Assume that there is a government key escrow system in which all keys are escrowed with a very few "trusted" agents. Further, assume that a large amount of commerce, trade, banking, currency transfer, and so on is performed on these escrowed cryptosystems.

The equivalent of a huge pot of gold is now concentrated in a few, well-known places: the escrow agencies. All you have to do is get a few escrowed keys, tap in to some secure banking or currency transfer sessions, and you can quickly become a very wealthy thief. There is no need to spoof an encrypted session or spoof a wire transaction to put a lot of money in an offshore bank account. In the world of finance and banking, having prior knowledge of significant events coupled with fully legitimate investments or trading moves in the open market can make you extremely wealthy without having to resort to anything more than mere eavesdropping on what are thought to be "secure" channels.

Greed and anger are the issues that most severely weaken a cryptosystem. If a large amount of wealth is tied up in one place (the key escrow system), a foreign government or economic terrorist would conceivably offer a large amount of money to escrow agency employees. In the example of a compromised escrowed key being used to get rich in open markets with insider knowledge, an unscrupulous person could offer an escrow agent a million dollars as well as a percentage of the gains. In this way, the more keys the employee reveals, the more money he makes. Greed can be a major factor in causing the entire escrowed key system to crumble. It is more because of human reasons than technical or legal ones that escrowed encryption is largely not workable.

Summary

This chapter has explored many fundamental security concepts. The intent was to provide you with a precursory understanding of three basic cryptographic functions: symmetric encryption, asymmetric encryption, and one-way hash functions. You also learned how these cryptographic functions can be used to enable security services such as authentication, integrity, and confidentiality.

In many systems today, end-user or device authentication can be established using public key technology, where the public keys are distributed in some secure manner, possibly through the use of digital certificates. Digital signatures are created through the use of hash functions and ensure the integrity of the data within the certificate. Data confidentiality is typically achieved through the use of some secret key algorithm where the Diffie-Hellman exchange is used to derive the shared secret key used between the two communicating parties.

Authentication and authorization issues were discussed. It is important to recognize that different mechanisms provide authentication services with varying degrees of certainty. Choosing the proper authentication technology largely depends on the location of the entities being authenticated and the degree of trust placed in the particular facets of the network.

Also, the issues of key management systems were explored. How to effectively generate and distribute cryptographic keys will probably change over time and will require a periodic assessment. The human factor will always be an issue that necessitates sufficient checks to ensure that keys have not been compromised.

Review Questions

The following questions provide you with an opportunity to test your knowledge of the topics covered in this chapter. You can find the answers to these questions in Appendix E, "Answers to Review Questions."

1 Cryptography is the basic building block that enables which of the following?

   A   Authentication

   B   Integrity

   C   Confidentiality

   D   All of the above

2 True or false: The best security algorithms are designed in secret.

3 What is a brute-force attack?

4 Name three fundamental cryptographic functions.

5 What is the inherent weakness in the ECB chaining mechanism?

6 Which of the following algorithms is specified as the symmetric key encryption AES standard?

   A 3DES

   B RC4

   C Rijndael

   D IDEA

7 What are three challenges with secret key encryption?

8 What is another term for asymmetric encryption?

9 Name three common uses of asymmetric encryption algorithms.

10 True or false: The crucial aspect of asymmetric encryption is that the public key needs to be kept confidential.

11 Which of the following properties is *not* suitable for a hash function?

   A It must be random—or give the appearance of randomness.

   B It must be unique.

   C It must be reversible.

   D It must be consistent.

12 What is a digital signature?

13 How do keyed hash functions and digital signatures differ?

14 A centralized key distribution model relies on what entity to issue keys?

15 Which algorithm is commonly used to create secret session keys in a distributed manner?

16 Name five elements commonly found in an X.509 certificate.

CHAPTER 2

Security Technologies

A wide range of security technologies exists that provides solutions for securing network access and data transport mechanisms within the corporate network infrastructure. Many of the technologies overlap in solving problems that relate to ensuring user or device identity, data integrity, and data confidentiality.

NOTE Throughout this book, *authentication*, *authorization*, and *access control* are incorporated into the concept of *identity*. Although these concepts are distinct, they all pertain to each individual user of the network—be it a person or device. Each person or device is a distinct entity that has separate abilities within the network and is allowed access to resources based on who they are. Although in the purest sense, identity really pertains only to authentication, in many cases, it makes sense to discuss the entities' authorization and access control at the same time.

Authentication refers to the process of validating the claimed identity of an end user or a device (such as clients, servers, switches, routers, firewalls, and so on). *Authorization* refers to the process of granting access rights to a user, groups of users, or specified system; *access control* refers to limiting the flow of information from the resources of a system to only the authorized persons or systems in the network. In most of the cases studied here, authorization and access control are subsequent to successful authentication.

This chapter describes security technologies commonly used to establish identity (authentication, authorization, and access control) and to ensure some degree of data integrity and confidentiality in a network. Data *integrity* ensures that any alteration or destruction of data by people who are not explicitly intended to modify it is detected; data *confidentiality* ensures that only the entities allowed to see the data see it in a usable format.

The intent is to develop a basic understanding of how these technologies can be implemented in corporate networks and to identify their strengths and weaknesses. The following categories have been selected in an attempt to group the protocols according to shared attributes:

- Identity technologies
- Application layer security protocols
- Transport layer security protocols

- Network layer security
- Link layer security protocols
- Public key infrastructure and distribution models

NOTE Many of the technologies discussed here either have been or are in the process of being standardized by the IETF. For information on more technical details and the latest developments, refer to Appendix A, "Sources of Technical Information." Appendix A contains pointers to the IETF working groups that produce the RFCs and drafts relating to the technologies discussed here.

Identity Technologies

This section describes the primary technologies used to establish identity for a host, an end-user, or both. Authentication is an extremely critical element because everything is based on who you are. In many corporate networks, you would not grant authorized access to specific parts of the network before establishing who is trying to gain access to restricted resources. Who needs to identify who is a consideration. In some instances, the initiator of a communication is the required entity to authenticate, in others it is the responder. Sometimes mutual authentication is required. To complicate things even further, there is the additional consideration of whether to authenticate only the end device or also the actual user and possibly to associate them together. In many instances, multiple end users use the same device and may need different privileges across the network. Also, the proliferation of laptops make it easier for people to travel and get connected back to corporate offices anywhere on the globe. If a laptop gets stolen and if an automated authentication scheme is used to authenticate and allow access privileges based only on the device identity, however, large security implications apply.

How foolproof the authentication method is depends on the technology used and how foolproof the procedures are.

Authentication methods can loosely be categorized as those where there is *local control* and those where you provide authentication verification through a *trusted third party*.

One of the potential weaknesses in some authentication methods is who you trust. Many authentication methods rely on a third party to verify someone's identity. The strength of this verification is the limiting factor in the strength of the authentication. When using a third party to authenticate an end user or device, ask yourself, "What is the likelihood that the third party I'm counting on to provide the authentication verification has been compromised?"

The technologies discussed in this section include variants of secure passwords, which provide varying degrees of security and are offered by most vendors today. Many protocols authorize some form of connection setup after authentication has been successfully verified. In dialup environments, a peer-to-peer, link-level connection is established; sometimes, additional access control mechanisms can be used at higher levels of the protocol stack, such as permitting access to hosts with certain IP addresses accessing specific applications. This discussion covers different protocols that often use an initial authentication process to then grant authorization and access control.

NOTE You can use digital certificates as an authentication method, as discussed in detail in the "Public Key Infrastructure and Distribution Models" section later in this chapter.

Secure Passwords

Although passwords are often used as proof for authenticating a user or device, passwords can easily be compromised if they are easy to guess, if they are not changed often enough, and if they are transmitted in cleartext across a network. To make passwords more secure, more robust methods are offered by encrypting the password or by modifying the encryption so that the encrypted value changes each time. This is the case with most one-time password schemes; the most common being the S/Key protocol and the token password authentication schemes.

S/Key Password Protocol

The *S/Key One-Time Password System*, released by Bellcore and defined in RFC 1760, is a one-time, password-generation scheme based on MD4 and MD5. The S/Key protocol is designed to counter a replay attack when a user is attempting to log in to a system. A replay attack in the context of login is when someone eavesdrops on a network connection to get the login ID and password of a legitimate user and later uses it to gain access to the network.

The operation of the S/Key protocol is client/server-based; the client is typically a PC, and the server is some flavor of UNIX. Initially, both the client and the server must be configured with the same pass phrase and an iteration count. The *iteration count* specifies how many times a given input will be applied to the hash function. The client initiates the S/Key exchange by sending an initialization packet; the server responds with a sequence number and seed, as shown in Figure 2-1.

Figure 2-1   *The Initial S/Key Exchange*

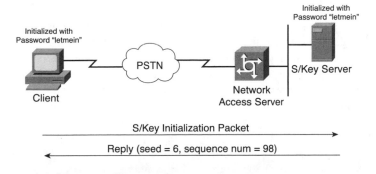

The client then computes the one-time password, a process that involves three distinct steps: a preparatory step, a generation step, and an output function. (See Figure 2-2.)

Step 1   In the preparatory step, the client enters a secret pass phrase. This pass phrase is concatenated with the seed that was transmitted from the server in cleartext.

Step 2   The generation step applies the secure hash function multiple times, producing a 64-bit final output.

Step 3   The output function takes the 64-bit one-time password and displays it in readable form.

Figure 2-2   *Computing the S/Key One-Time Password*

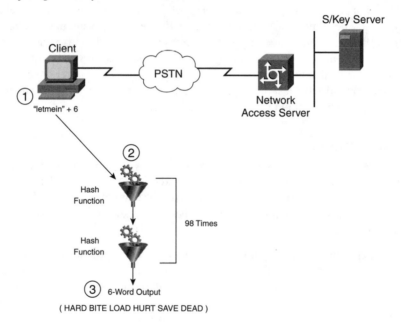

The last phase is for the client to pass the one-time password to the server, where it can be verified. (See Figure 2-3.)

The server has a file (on the UNIX reference implementation, it is /etc/skeykeys) containing, for each user, the one-time password from the last successful login. To verify an authentication attempt, the authentication server passes the received one-time password through the secure hash function once. If the result of this operation matches the stored previous one-time password, the authentication is successful and the accepted one-time password is stored for future use.

Figure 2-3   *Verifying the S/Key Password*

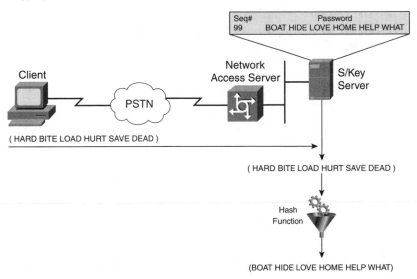

Because the number of hash function applications executed by the client decreases by one each time, this ensures a unique sequence of generated passwords. However, at some point, the user must re-initialize the system to avoid being unable to log in again. The system is re-initialized using the **keyinit** command, which allows the changing of the secret pass phrase, the iteration count, and the seed.

When computing the S/Key password on the client side, the client pass phrase can be of any length—more than eight characters is recommended. The use of the nonsecret seed allows a client to use the same secret pass phrase on multiple machines (using different seeds) and to safely recycle secret pass phrases by changing the seed.

NOTE	Many implementations require the generated one-time password to be entered either using a cut-and-paste approach, or manually. In manual entry scenarios, the one-time password is converted to, and accepted, as a sequence of six short (one- to four-letter) English words. Each word is chosen from a dictionary of 2048 words; at 11 bits per word, all one-time passwords may be encoded. Interoperability requires that all S/Key system hosts and calculators use the same dictionary.

S/Key is an alternative to simple passwords. Free as well as commercial implementations are widely available.

Token Password Authentication Schemes

Token authentication systems generally require the use of a special card (called a *token card*), although some implementations are done using software to alleviate the problem of losing the token card. These types of authentication mechanisms are based on one of two alternative schemes: challenge-response and time-synchronous authentication.

The challenge-response approach is shown in Figure 2-4. The following steps carry out the authentication exchange:

Step 1   The user dials in to an authentication server, which then issues a prompt for a user ID.

Step 2   The user provides the ID to the server, which then issues a *challenge*—a random number that appears on the user's screen.

Step 3   The user enters that challenge number into the token card, a credit card type of device, which then encrypts the challenge with the user's encryption key and displays a response.

Step 4   The user types this response and sends it to the authentication server. While the user is obtaining a response from the token, the authentication server calculates what the appropriate response should be based on its database of user keys.

Step 5   When the server receives the user's response, it compares that response with the one it has calculated.

If the two responses match, the user is granted access to the network. If they don't match, access is denied.

Figure 2-5 shows the time-synchronous authentication scheme. In this scheme, a proprietary algorithm executes in the token and on the server to generate identical numbers that change over time. The user dials in to the authentication server, which issues a prompt for an access code. The user enters a personal identification number (PIN) on the token card, resulting in digits displayed at that moment on the token. These digits represent the one-time password and are sent to the server. The server compares this entry with the sequence it generated; if they match, it grants the user access to the network.

A popular variant is to require a password prompt in addition to the PIN to increase the amount of information required to compromise the identity. In some cases, the time-synchronous token systems can be set up without the user being required to enter a PIN on the token card to obtain the present access code. The motivation in these cases is that administrators have found that employees would etch or write the PIN onto the token card directly; however, should the card be misplaced or stolen, the card would be easily abused. This latter scenario, where the user is not required to enter any information on the token card, is strongly discouraged.

Figure 2-4   *Challenge-Response Token Authentication*

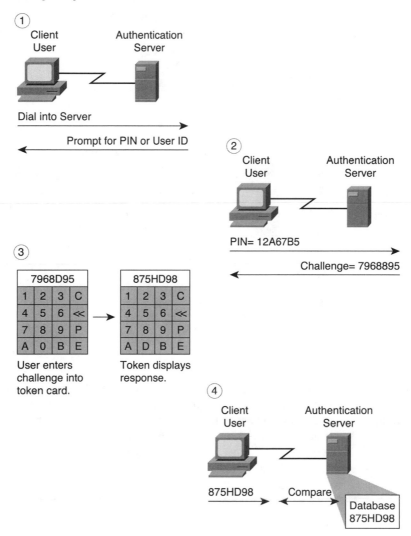

Figure 2-5   *Time-Synchronous Token Authentication*

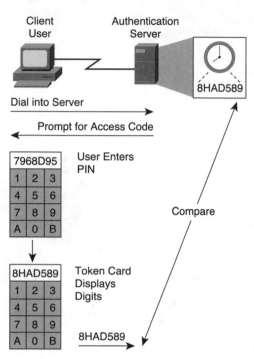

Use of either the challenge-response or time-synchronous token password authentication scheme generally requires the user to carry a credit card type of device to provide authentication credentials. This can be a burden to some users because they have to remember to carry the device, but it has the flexibility to allow fairly secure authenticated access from anywhere in the world. It is extremely useful for mobile users who frequently log in from remote sites. If the mobile users have their own laptop, the token can be installed as software, which relieves the burden of remembering to carry an additional device. These schemes are very robust and scalable from a centralized database point of view.

NOTE   Using the one-time password scheme only protects you from replay attacks when initially logging in to the site. If you then continue to log in to other machines at the campus site, the password will be sent in the clear. It is best to combine one-time password use with some form of confidentiality (encryption) technique if protection is required for more than just the initial login sequence.

PPP Authentication Protocols

Passwords are incorporated into many protocols that provide authentication services. For dial-in connections, the Point-to-Point Protocol (PPP) is most often used to establish a dial-in connection over serial lines or ISDN. PPP authentication mechanisms include the Password Authentication Protocol (PAP), the Challenge Handshake Protocol (CHAP), and the Extensible Authentication Protocol (EAP). In some of these cases, the peer device is being authenticated rather than the user of the device.

NOTE	In the section "Link Layer Security Technologies" later in this chapter, other protocols such as L2TP and PPPoE are discussed; these other protocols rely on the PPP authentication mechanisms. These technologies extend the point-to-point link across non-point-to-point networks and because the PPP frames may be forwarded beyond the local loop of a dialup connection, additional considerations need to be taken into account for the path over which those frames traverse.

The PPP Protocol

PPP is a standardized Internet encapsulation of IP over point-to-point links. PPP addresses issues such as assignment and management of IP addresses, asynchronous (start/stop) and bit-oriented synchronous encapsulation, network protocol multiplexing, link configuration, link quality testing, error detection, and option negotiation for such capabilities as network layer address negotiation and data compression negotiation. PPP addresses these issues by providing an extensible Link Control Protocol (LCP) and a family of Network Control Protocols (NCPs) to negotiate optional configuration parameters and facilities. After the link has been established, PPP provides for an optional authentication phase before proceeding to the network layer protocol phase.

PPP Link Layer

The PPP protocol data unit (PDU) uses the High-Level Data Link Control (HDLC) frame as stipulated in ISO 3309-1979 (and amended by ISO 3309-1984/PDAD1).

Figure 2-6 shows the PPP frame format.

Figure 2-6   *The PPP Frame Format*

Flag	Address	Control	Protocol	Data	FCS
1	1	1	1	Variable	2 or 4

Bytes:

The fields of a PPP frame are as follows:

- **Flag**—A single byte that indicates the beginning or end of a frame. The Flag field consists of the binary sequence 01111110.

- **Address**—A single byte that contains the binary sequence 11111111, the standard broadcast address. PPP does not assign individual station addresses.

- **Control**—A single byte that contains the binary sequence 00000011, which calls for transmission of user data in an unsequenced frame.

- **Protocol**—Two bytes that identify the protocol encapsulated in the Information field of the frame. The most current values of the Protocol field are specified in the most recent Assigned Numbers Request for Comments (RFCs).

- **Data**—Zero or more bytes that contain the datagram for the protocol specified in the Protocol field. The end of the Information field is found by locating the closing flag sequence and allowing two bytes for the FCS field. The default maximum length of the Information field is 1500 bytes. By prior agreement, consenting PPP implementations can use other values for the maximum Information field length.

- **Frame Check Sequence (FCS)**—Normally two bytes. By prior agreement, consenting PPP implementations can use a four-byte FCS for improved error detection.

The LCP can negotiate modifications to the standard PPP frame structure. However, modified frames will always be clearly distinguishable from standard frames.

PPP Negotiations

PPP negotiation consists of LCP and NCP negotiation. LCP is responsible for establishing the connection with certain negotiated options, maintaining the connection, and providing procedures to terminate the connection. To perform these functions, LCP is organized into the following four phases:

1 Link establishment and configuration negotiation

2 Link quality determination

3 Network layer protocol configuration negotiation

4 Link termination

To establish communications over a point-to-point link, each end of the PPP link must first send LCP packets to configure the data link during the link establishment phase. After the link has been established, PPP provides for an optional authentication phase before proceeding to the network layer protocol phase. The NCP phase then establishes and configures different network layer protocols such as IP.

By default, authentication before the NCP phase is not mandatory. If authentication of the link is desired, an implementation will specify the authentication protocol configuration option during the link establishment phase. These authentication protocols are intended for use primarily by hosts and routers that connect to a PPP network server through switched circuits or dialup lines, but can be applied to dedicated links too. The server can use the identification of the connecting host or router in the selection of options for network layer negotiations.

PPP Password Authentication Protocol

The *Password Authentication Protocol* (PAP) provides a simple way for a peer to establish its identity to the authenticator using a two-way handshake. This is done only at initial link establishment. There exist three PAP frame types, as shown in Figure 2-7.

Figure 2-7   *The Three PPP PAP Frame Types*

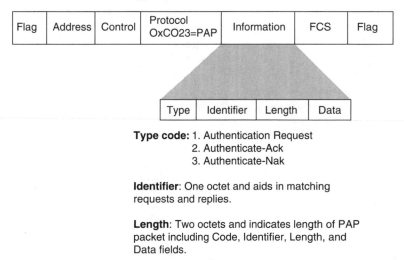

Type code: 1. Authentication Request
2. Authenticate-Ack
3. Authenticate-Nak

Identifier: One octet and aids in matching requests and replies.

Length: Two octets and indicates length of PAP packet including Code, Identifier, Length, and Data fields.

Data: 0 or more octets.

After the link establishment phase is completed, the authenticate-request packet is used to initiate the PAP authentication. This packet contains the peer name and password, as shown in Figure 2-8.

Figure 2-8   *PPP PAP Authentication Request*

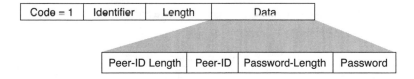

This request packet is sent repeatedly until a valid reply packet is received or an optional retry counter expires. If the authenticator receives a Peer-ID/Password pair that is both recognizable and acceptable, it should reply with an Authenticate-Ack (where Ack is short for *acknowledge*). If the Peer-ID/Password pair is not recognizable or acceptable, the authenticator should reply with an Authenticate-Nak (where Nak is short for *negative acknowledge*).

Figure 2-9 shows the sequence of PPP negotiations between a branch router (the peer) trying to authenticate to the network access server (NAS, the authenticator).

Figure 2-9   *PPP PAP Authentication*

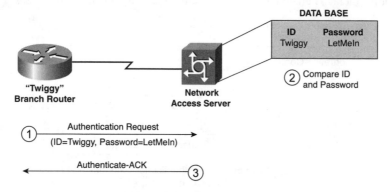

PAP is not a strong authentication method. PAP authenticates only the peer, and passwords are sent over the circuit "in the clear." PAP authentication is only performed once during a session. There is no protection from replay attacks or repeated trial-and-error attacks. The peer is in control of the frequency and timing of the attempts.

PPP Challenge Handshake Authentication Protocol

The *Challenge Handshake Authentication Protocol* (CHAP), defined in RFC 1994, is used to periodically verify the identity of a host or end user using a three-way handshake. CHAP is performed at initial link establishment and can be repeated any time after the link has been established. Four CHAP frame types exist, as shown in Figure 2-10.

Figure 2-10   *PPP CHAP Frame Types*

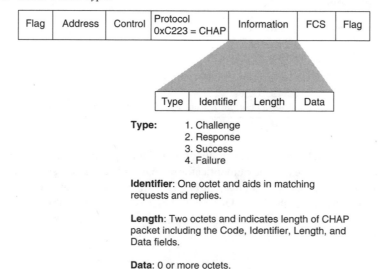

Figure 2-11 shows a scenario in which a branch router (the peer) is trying to authenticate to the NAS (the authenticator).

Figure 2-11 *PPP CHAP Authentication*

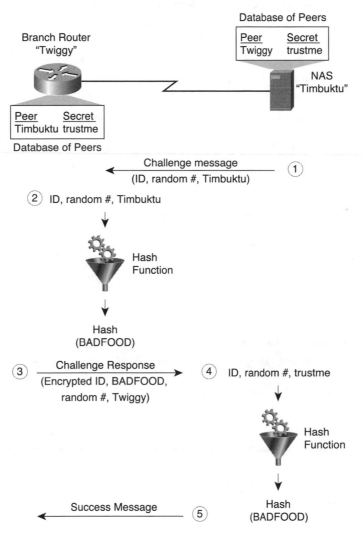

CHAP imposes network security by requiring that the peers share a plaintext secret. This secret is never sent over the link. The following sequence of steps is carried out:

Step 1 After the link establishment phase is complete, the authenticator sends a challenge message to the peer. The challenge consists of an identifier (ID), a random number (the challenge value), and either the host name of the local device or the name of the user on the remote device.

Step 2 The receiving peer calculates a response value using a one-way hash function; the input to the one-way hash function is the ID, the secret, and the challenge value, concatenated in that order.

Step 3 The peer sends the challenge response, which consists of the following:

— The ID

— A response value (the calculated hash value from Step 2)

— Either the host name of the remote device, or the name of the user on the remote device

Step 4 When the authenticator receives the challenge response, it verifies the secret by looking up the name given in the response and performing the same encryption operation. The authenticator checks the response against its own calculation of the expected hash value.

Step 5 If the values match, the authenticator acknowledges the authentication and sends a success message, and the LCP establishes the link.

The secret passwords must be identical on the remote and local devices. These secrets should be agreed on, generated, and exchanged out of band in a secure manner. Because the secret is never transmitted, other devices are prevented from stealing it and gaining illegal access to the system. Without the proper response, the remote device cannot connect to the local device.

CHAP provides protection against playback attack through the use of an incrementally changing identifier and a variable challenge value. The use of repeated challenges is intended to limit the time of exposure to any single attack. The authenticator is in control of the frequency and timing of the challenges.

Either CHAP peer can act as the authenticator; there is no requirement in the specification that authentication must be full duplex or that the same protocol must be used in both directions.

NOTE	Typically, MD5 is used as the CHAP one-way hash function; the shared secrets are required to be stored in plaintext form. Despite the claim in RFC 1994 to the contrary, however, irreversably encrypted passwords can be used as long as the password is correctly preprocessed (that is, encrypted) by the peer before being processed by the CHAP algorithm. Microsoft has a variation of CHAP (MS-CHAP and MS-CHAPv2), in which the password is stored encrypted in both the peer and the authenticator. Therefore, MS-CHAP can take advantage of irreversibly encrypted password databases commonly available, whereas the standards-based CHAP cannot.

PPP Extensible Authentication Protocol

The PPP *Extensible Authentication Protocol* (EAP) is defined in RFC 2284, although there is a newer draft version numbered RFC 2284bis. EAP is a general protocol for PPP authentication that supports multiple authentication mechanisms. It provides its own support for duplicate elimination and retransmission. Fragmentation is not supported within EAP itself; however, individual EAP methods may support this.

EAP does not select a specific authentication mechanism at the link control phase; rather, it postpones this until the authentication phase so that the authenticator can request more information before determining the specific authentication mechanism. This arrangement also permits the use of a "back-end" server, which actually implements the various authentication mechanisms, whereas the PPP authenticator merely passes through the authentication exchange. This has the added benefit of not requiring the authenticator to be updated to support each new authentication method.

Figure 2-12 shows the EAP packet format.

Figure 2-12 *EAP Packet Format*

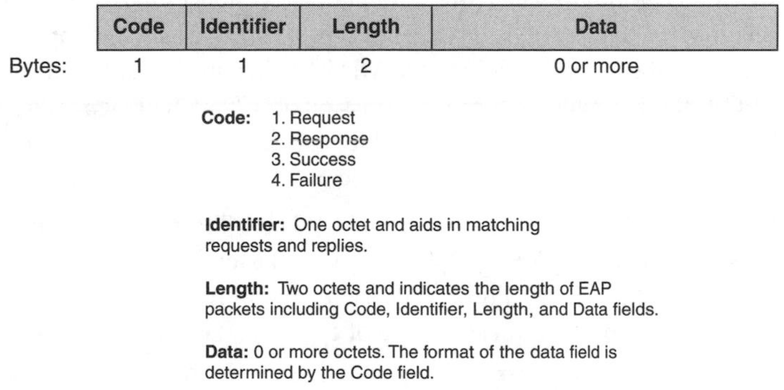

Code	Identifier	Length	Data
1	1	2	0 or more

Bytes:

Code: 1. Request
2. Response
3. Success
4. Failure

Identifier: One octet and aids in matching requests and replies.

Length: Two octets and indicates the length of EAP packets including Code, Identifier, Length, and Data fields.

Data: 0 or more octets. The format of the data field is determined by the Code field.

Additional code types are specified in the data portion of the EAP request/response packets, as shown in Figure 2-13.

Figure 2-13 *EAP Request/Response Packet Format*

Code	Identifier	Length	Type	Type Data
Bytes: 1	1	2	1	0 or more

Code: 1) Request
2) Response

Identifier: One octet and aids in matching requests and replies.

Length: Two octets and indicates the length of EAP packets including Code, Identifier, Length Type, and Type Data fields.

Type: 1 octet and identifies the type of request of response.

Type-Data: Varies with the type of request and the associated response.

New code types are continually being defined to allow for various authentication mechanisms. The following are some commonly used ones:

- **Identity type (1)**—Used to query the identity of the peer. Generally, the authenticator issues this as the initial request. An optional displayable message could be included to prompt the peer in the case where there is the expectation of interaction with a user. A response message is typically sent of the same type containing the requested information.

- **Notification type (2)**—Optionally used to display a message from the authenticator to the peer. For example, it could be a notification that a password is about to expire.

- **Nak type (response only) (3)**—Valid only in a response message. It is sent in reply to a request where the desired authentication type is unacceptable.

- **MD5-Challenge type (4)**—Analogous to the PPP CHAP protocol(with MD5 as the specified algorithm). The request contains a "challenge" message to the peer. The response sent in reply to the request is either of type 4 (MD5-Challenge) or type 3 (Nak). Note that the use of the Identifier field in the MD5-Challenge type differs from that described in RFC 1994. EAP allows for retransmission of MD5-Challenge request packets, whereas RFC 1994 states that both the Identifier and Challenge fields must change each time a Challenge (the CHAP equivalent of the MD5-Challenge request packet) is sent.

- **One-Time Password (OTP) type (5)**—The OTP system is defined in "A One-Time Password System" (RFC 2289) and "OTP Extended Responses" (RFC 2243). The request contains a displayable message containing an OTP challenge. The response sent in reply to the request will be of type 5 (OTP) or type 3 (Nak).

- **Generic Token Card (GTC) type (6)**—Defined for use with various token card implementations that require user input. The request contains a displayable message, and the response contains the token card information necessary for authentication. Typically, this is information read by a user from the token card device and entered as ASCII text. The response sent in reply to the request will be of type 6 (GTC) or type 3 (Nak).

Figure 2-14 shows how PPP EAP works between two network infrastructure devices.

Figure 2-14   *PPP EAP Authentication*

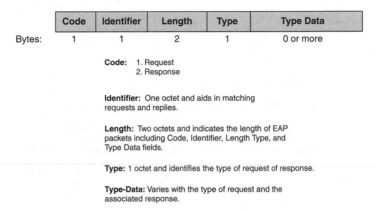

In Figure 2-14, the branch router (the peer) is trying to authenticate to the NAS (the authenticator). The sequence of steps is as follows:

Step 1   When the link establishment phase is complete, the authenticator sends one or more requests to authenticate the peer. The request has a Type field to indicate what is being requested.

NOTE   Typically, the authenticator sends an initial identity request followed by one or more requests for authentication information. However, an initial identity request is not required and may be bypassed in cases where the identity is presumed (for example, with leased lines, dedicated dialups, and so on).

Step 2   The peer sends a response packet in reply to each request. As with the request packet, the response packet contains a Type field that corresponds to the Type field of the request.

Step 3   The authenticator ends the authentication phase with a success or failure packet.

Figure 2-15 shows an example where a RADIUS server is used as a back-end server to actually implement the authentication mechanism. In this case, the client is a telecommuter dialing in to a NAS to access the corporate network. The NAS (PPP authenticator) merely passes through the authentication exchange.

Figure 2-15   *PPP EAP Using RADIUS*

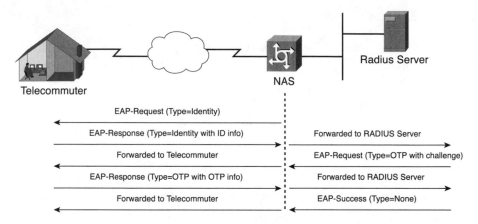

EAP adds more flexibility to PPP authentication and provides the capability to use new technologies—such as digital certificates—when they become widely available. The EAP protocol can support multiple authentication mechanisms without having to prenegotiate a particular one. Devices (for instance, a NAS, switch, or access point) do not have to understand each authentication method and can act as a passthrough agent for a backend authentication server. Although the support for passthrough is optional in the specification, many vendors are implementing it. An authenticator can authenticate local users while at the same time acting as a passthrough for nonlocal users and authentication methods it does not implement locally.

PPP Authentication Summary

PPP authentication is required for dial-in connectivity. Any of the three standard mechanisms—PAP, CHAP, and EAP—can be used. Most current implementations are taking advantage of the flexibility of EAP, and it is widely available. Table 2-1 gives a summary of the strengths and weaknesses of these mechanisms.

Table 2-1   *PPP Authentication Summary*

Protocol	Strength	Weakness
PAP	Easy to implement	Does not have strong authentication; password is sent in the clear between client and server; no playback protection.
CHAP	Password encrypted	Password must be stored in cleartext on server.
EAP	Flexible, more robust authentication support	Physically insecure networks will not provide protection of authentication mechanism used.

Protocols Using Authentication Mechanisms

Many protocols require authentication verification before providing authorization and access rights to the user or device. The previous sections of this chapter discussed a variety of authentication methods. This section details the protocols that make use of these authentication mechanisms. TACACS+, RADIUS, Kerberos, DCE, and FORTEZZA are examples of such protocols. TACACS+ and RADIUS are often used in dial-in environments to provide a scalable authentication database and can incorporate a variety of authentication methods. Kerberos is a protocol used in some campus environments to first verify that users and the network services they use are really who and what they claim to be before granting access privileges. For completeness, the Distributed Computing Environment (DCE) and FORTEZZA authentication mechanisms are included in this section, although their use is not widespread.

802.1x is an IEEE specification that enables authentication and key management for IEEE 802 local-area networks. IEEE 802.1x is not a single authentication method; rather it uses the Extensible Authentication Protocol (EAP) as its authentication framework. This technology is also included because its application is widely deployable in many networking scenarios.

The TACACS+ Protocol

The *TACACS+* protocol is the latest generation of TACACS. TACACS is a simple UDP-based access control protocol originally developed by BBN for the MILNET. Cisco has enhanced (extended) TACACS several times, and Cisco's implementation, based on the original TACACS, is referred to as *XTACACS*. The fundamental differences between TACACS, XTACACS, and TACACS+ are given here:

- **TACACS**—Combined authentication and authorization process
- **XTACACS**—Separated authentication, authorization, and accounting
- **TACACS+**—XTACACS with extended attribute control and accounting

TACACS+ uses TCP for its transport. The server daemon usually listens at port 49, the login port assigned for the TACACS protocol. This port is reserved in the assigned number's RFC for both UDP and TCP. Current TACACS and extended TACACS implementations also use port 49.

TACACS+ is a client/server protocol; the TACACS+ client is typically a NAS, and the TACACS+ server is usually a daemon process running on a UNIX or Windows NT machine. A fundamental design component of TACACS+ is the separation of authentication, authorization, and accounting. Figure 2-16 shows the TACACS+ header format.

Figure 2-16 *TACACS+ Header*

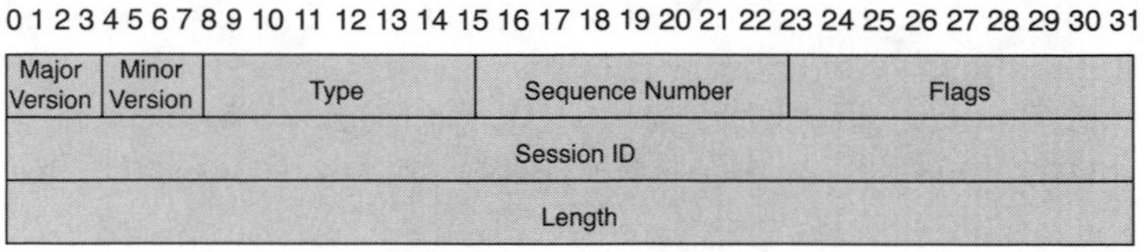

0 1 2 3 4 5 6 7 8 9 10 11 12 13 14 15 16 17 18 19 20 21 22 23 24 25 26 27 28 29 30 31

Major Version	Minor Version	Type	Sequence Number	Flags
Session ID				
Length				

Major Version: Major TACAS+ version number.

Minor Version: Minor TACACS+ version number, which allows revisions to the TACACS+ protocol while maintaining backwards compatibility.

Type: 0x01=authentication
0x02=authorization
0x03=accounting

Seq_num: The first TACACS+ packet in a session must start with 1 and each subsequent packet increments the sequence number by 1.

Flags: Specifies whether encryption or multiplexing is used.

Session ID: Randomly chosen and does not change for the duration of the TACACS+ session.

Length: Total length of the TACACS+ packet excluding the header.

TACACS+ Authentication

TACACS+ allows for arbitrary length and content authentication exchanges, which allows any authentication mechanism to be used with TACACS+ clients (including PPP PAP, PPP CHAP, PPP EAP, token cards, and Kerberos). Authentication is not mandatory; it is a site-configured option. Some sites do not require it at all; others require it only for certain services.

TACACS+ authentication has three packet types:

- START, which is always sent by the client
- CONTINUE, which is always sent by the client
- REPLY, which is always sent by the server

Authentication begins when the NAS (TACACS+ client) receives a connection request that needs to be authenticated. The client then sends a START message to the server. The START message describes the type of authentication to be performed (for example, simple cleartext password, PAP, or CHAP), and may contain the username and some authentication data. The START packet is sent only as the first message in a TACACS+ authentication session, or as the packet immediately following a restart. (A restart may be requested by the server in a REPLY packet.) A START packet always has a sequence number equal to 1.

In response to a START packet, the server sends a REPLY, which includes the authentication result. The REPLY message indicates whether the authentication is finished, or whether it should continue. If the REPLY indicates that authentication should continue, the message also indicates what new information is requested. The client gets that information and returns it in a CONTINUE message. This process repeats until all authentication information is gathered, and the authentication process concludes. The server responds to the last CONTINUE message with a REPLY.

The authentication result contained in a TACACS+ server REPLY can be one of the following three messages:

- **ACCEPT**—The user is authenticated and if authorization is configured on the NAS, the authorization process can start.
- **REJECT**—The user failed to authenticate, in which case the user might be denied further access or is prompted to retry the login sequence.
- **ERROR**—Indicates that an error occurred sometime during the authentication process; in which case, the NAS may try to use an alternative method to authenticate the user.

TACACS+ Authorization

Authorization is the action of determining what a user is allowed to do. Generally, authentication precedes authorization, but, this is not required. An authorization request may indicate that the user is not authenticated. (That is, we don't know who they are.) In this case, it is up to the authorization agent to determine whether an unauthenticated user is allowed the services in question.

When authentication is completed (if authentication is used), the client can start the authorization process, if authorization is required. An *authorization session* is defined as a single pair of messages: a request followed by a response. The authorization Request message contains a fixed set of fields that describe the authenticity of the user or process, and a variable set of arguments that describes the services and options for which authorization is requested.

NOTE   In TACACS+, authorization does not merely provide yes or no answers—it may also customize the service for the particular user. Here are some examples of when authorization would be performed: when a user first logs in and wants to start a shell, and when a user starts PPP and wants to use IP over PPP with a particular IP address. The TACACS+ server daemon might respond to these requests by allowing the service, by placing a time restriction on the login shell, or by requiring IP access lists on the PPP connection.

TACACS+ Accounting

Accounting is typically the third action after authentication and authorization. Accounting is the action of recording what a user is doing or has done. Accounting in TACACS+ can serve two purposes:

- It may be used to account for services used, such as in a billing environment.
- It may be used as an auditing tool for security services.

To this end, TACACS+ supports three types of accounting records:

- **Start records** indicate that a service is about to begin.
- **Stop records** indicate that a service has just terminated.
- **Update records** are intermediate notices that indicate that a service is still being performed.

TACACS+ accounting records contain all the information used in the authorization records and also contain accounting-specific information such as start and stop times (when appropriate) and resource usage information.

TACACS+ Transactions

Transactions between the TACACS+ client and TACACS+ server are authenticated through the use of a shared secret, which is never sent over the network. Typically, the secret is manually configured in both entities. TACACS+ encrypts all traffic between the TACACS+ client and the TACACS+ server daemon. The encryption is done through the use of MD5 and the XOR functionality. (See the following sidebar on XOR.) The following steps are used to create the ciphertext:

Step 1 A hash (message digest) is calculated by using a concatenation of the session ID, shared secret key, version number, and sequence number as input to the MD5 algorithm. From this first hash, a second one is calculated by concatenating the first hash, session ID, version number, and sequence number as input to the MD5 algorithm. This process is repeated an implementation specific number of times.

Step 2 All the calculated hashes are concatenated and then truncated to the length of the data that is to be encrypted, which results in what is termed the *pseudo_pad*.

Step 3 A bytewise XOR is done on the pseudo_pad with the data that is to be encrypted, and this produces the resulting ciphertext.

The recipient of the ciphertext can calculate the pseudo_pad on its own because it is already preconfigured with a shared secret. An XOR of this pseudo_pad with the ciphertext results in the cleartext data.

Figure 2-17 shows the interaction between a dial-in user and the TACACS+ client and server.

Figure 2-17 *A TACACS+ Exchange*

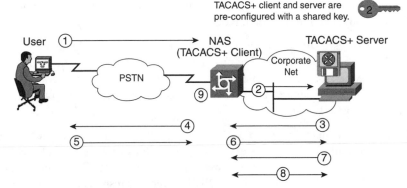

1. User initiates PPP authentication to NAS.
2. NAS sends START packet to TACACS+ server.
3. TACACS+ server responds with GETUSER packets that
   contain the prompts for username/password (PAP) or challenge (CHAP).
4. NAS sends the display to the user.
5. User responds to NAS.
6. NAS sends encrypted packet to TACACS+ server.
7. TACACS+ server responds to NAS with authentication result.
8. NAS and TACACS+ server exchange authorization requests and replies.
9. NAS acts upon authorization exchange.

The Exclusice OR (XOR) Function

This function is used rather extensively in many cryptographic operations. It essentially takes an input string of binary digits and a second string of binary digits (where both strings are the same length) and produces a third string of binary digits as output by following a specified set of rules. You can then take the resulting string and apply the same operation with the same second bit string and get back the original input. Therefore, the operation is symmetric. The rules for XOR are as follows:

- 1 XOR 1 = 0
- 0 XOR 0 = 0
- 1 XOR 0 = 1
- 0 XOR 1 = 1

If you XOR the input string 01100101 with a second string 11010011, for example, the result is 10110110.

Now you XOR the output string 10110110 with the second string 11010011 and obtain the result 01100101. And you see that this is the input string you started with.

The RADIUS Protocol

The *Remote Address Dial-In User Service* (RADIUS) protocol was developed by Livingston Enterprises, Inc., as an access server authentication and accounting protocol. In June 1996, the RADIUS protocol specification was submitted to the IETF. The RADIUS specification (RFC 2865) is a proposed standard, and the RADIUS accounting specification (RFC 2866) is an informational RFC.

RADIUS uses UDP as its transport. Although some early implementations of RADIUS used port 1645, the official UDP port to use is 1812. Generally, the RADIUS protocol is considered to be a connectionless service. Issues related to server availability, retransmission, and timeouts are handled by the RADIUS-enabled devices rather than by the transmission protocol.

RADIUS is a client/server protocol. The RADIUS client is typically a NAS; the RADIUS server is usually a daemon process running on a UNIX or Windows NT machine. The client is responsible for passing user information to designated RADIUS servers and then acting on the response that is returned. RADIUS servers are responsible for receiving user connection requests, authenticating the user, and then returning all configuration information necessary for the client to deliver the service to the user. A RADIUS server can act as a proxy client to other RADIUS servers or to other kinds of authentication servers. Figure 2-18 shows the RADIUS packet format.

Figure 2-18 *RADIUS Packet Format*

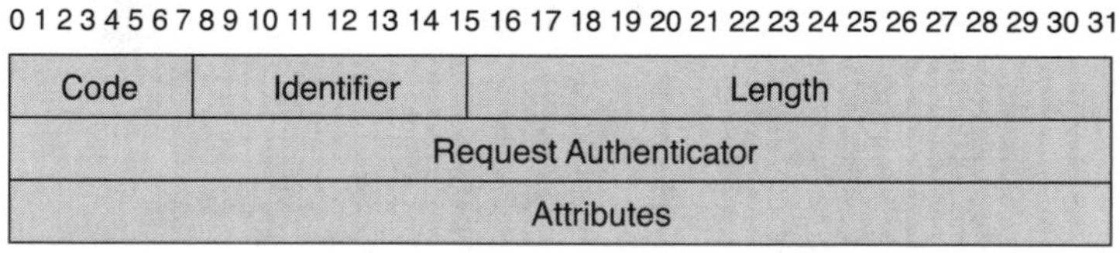

0 1 2 3 4 5 6 7 8 9 10 11 12 13 14 15 16 17 18 19 20 21 22 23 24 25 26 27 28 29 30 31

Code	Identifier	Length
Request Authenticator		
Attributes		

Code: One octet and identifies the type of RADIUS packet.

Identifier: One octet and aids in identifying requests and replies.

Length: Two octets and indicates the length of the packet including the Code, Identifier, Length, Authenticator, and Attribute fields. The minimum length is 20 and the maximum is 4096 octets.

Authenticator: 16 octets whose value is used to authenticate the reply from a RADIUS server (it may contain a 16-octet CHAP challenge if the CHAP-Challenge attribute isn't included in the Access-Request message).

Attributes: Specifies what network services are used.

RADIUS Authentication

The RADIUS server can support a variety of methods to authenticate a user. When the server is provided with the username and original password given by the user, the server can support PPP PAP or CHAP, UNIX login, and other authentication mechanisms. What is supported depends on what a vendor has implemented.

Typically, a user login consists of a query (access-request) from the NAS to the RADIUS server and a corresponding response (access-accept or access-reject) from the server. The access-request packet contains the username, encrypted password, NAS IP address, and port. The format of the request also provides information about the type of session the user wants to initiate.

When the RADIUS server receives the access-request packet from the NAS, it searches a database for the username listed. If the username does not exist in the database, either a default profile is loaded or the RADIUS server immediately sends an access-reject message. This access-reject message can be accompanied by an optional text message, which may indicate the reason for the refusal.

RADIUS Authorization

In RADIUS, the authentication and authorization functionalities are coupled together. If the username is found and the password is correct, the RADIUS server returns an access-accept response, including a list of attribute-value pairs that describe the parameters to be used for this session. Typical parameters include service type (shell or framed), protocol type, IP address to assign the user (static or dynamic), access list to apply, or a static route to install in the NAS routing table. The configuration information in the RADIUS server defines what will be installed on the NAS.

RADIUS Accounting

The accounting features of the RADIUS protocol can be used independently of RADIUS authentication or authorization. The RADIUS accounting functions allow data to be sent at the start and end of sessions, indicating the amount of resources (such as time, packets, bytes, and so on) used during the session. An Internet service provider (ISP) might use RADIUS access control and accounting software to meet special security and billing needs.

RADIUS Transactions

Transactions between the RADIUS client and RADIUS server are authenticated through the use of a shared secret, which is never sent over the network. However, communication between the client and server is in the clear except for the user passwords, which are encrypted. The following steps are used to encrypt the user-supplied password:

Step 1   The 16-byte random number from the Request Authenticator field and the preconfigured shared secret are input to an MD5 hash function, which results in a 16-byte hash.

Step 2   The user-provided password is padded at the end with nulls until it is 16 bytes in length.

Step 3   The hash from Step 1 is XOR'd with the padded password to create the encrypted password.

The recipient of the encrypted password calculates its own hash because it also has knowledge of the preconfigured shared secret. When this hash is XOR'd with the encrypted password, the result is the password in cleartext.

Figure 2-19 shows the RADIUS login and authentication process.

Figure 2-19   *RADIUS Login and Authentication*

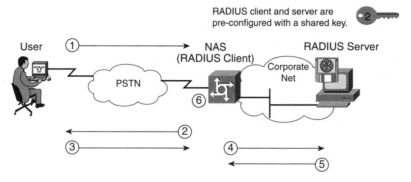

1. User initiates PPP authentication to NAS.
2. NAS prompts user for username/password (PAP) or challenge (CHAP).
3. User replies.
4. NAS sends username and encrypted password to RADIUS server.
5. RADIUS server responds with Accept, Reject or Challenge.
6. NAS acts upon services and service parameters bundled with Accept or Reject.

NOTE   With both TACACS+ and RADIUS, it is important to remember that encryption is performed between the TACACS+/RADIUS client and the TACACS+/RADIUS server. If the TACACS+/RADIUS client is a NAS and not the client PC, any communication between the PC and the NAS is not encrypted. (See Figure 2-20.) In addition, the communication between the NAS and the TACACS+/RADIUS server may traverse networks, which can easily be tapped into and snooped. Therefore, any authentication mechanism using cleartext passwords, such as PPP PAP, should not be used.

Figure 2-20   *TACACS+/RADIUS Encryption*

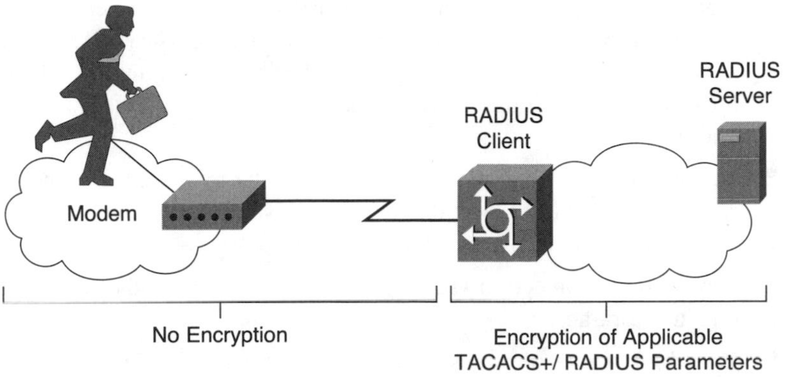

The Kerberos Protocol

Kerberos is a secret-key network authentication protocol, developed at Massachusetts Institute of Technology (MIT), that uses the Data Encryption Standard (DES) cryptographic algorithm for encryption and authentication. The Kerberos version 5 protocol is an Internet standard specified by RFC 1510.

Kerberos was designed to authenticate user requests for network resources. Kerberos is based on the concept of a trusted third party that performs secure verification of users and services. In the Kerberos protocol, this trusted third party is called the *key distribution center* (KDC), sometimes also called the *authentication server*. The primary use of Kerberos is to verify that users and the network services they use are really who and what they claim to be. To accomplish this, a trusted Kerberos server issues "tickets" to users. These tickets have a limited life span and are stored in the user's credential cache. They can later be used in place of the standard username-and-password authentication mechanism.

Kerberos Terminology

A number of Kerberos-related terms are defined here. The following definitions will make the subsequent text easier to understand:

- **Credential**—A general term that refers to authentication tickets, such as ticket-granting tickets (TGTs) and service credentials. Kerberos credentials verify the identity of a user or service. If a network service decides to trust the Kerberos server that issued a ticket, it can be used in place of retyping in a username and password. Credentials have the default life span of 8 hours.

- **Instance**—An authorization-level label for Kerberos principals.

- **Kerberized**—Applications and services that have been modified to support the Kerberos credential infrastructure.

- **Kerberos realm**—A domain consisting of users, hosts, and network services that are registered to a Kerberos server. The Kerberos server is trusted to verify a user's or network service's identity to another user or network service. Kerberos realms must always be in uppercase characters. TCP fragmentation must also be defined on the KDC server. The Kerberos realm is also used to map a DNS domain to a Kerberos realm.

- **Kerberos sever**—A daemon running on a network host. Users and network services register their identities with the Kerberos server. Network services query the Kerberos server to authenticate to other network services.

- **Key distribution center (KDC)**—A Kerberos server and database program running on a network host.

- **Principal**—Also known as a *Kerberos identity*, this is who you are or what a service is according to a Kerberos server.

- **Service credential**—A credential for a network service. When issued from the KDC, this credential is encrypted with the password shared by the network service and the KDC, and with the user's TGT.

- **SRVTAB**—A password that a network service shares with the KDC. The network service authenticates an encrypted service credential using the SRVTAB (also known s *KEYTAB*) to decrypt it.

- **Ticket-granting ticket (TGT)**—A credential that the KDC issues to authenticate users. When users receive a TGT, they can authenticate to network services within the Kerberos realm represented by the KDC.

Kerberos Authentication Request and Reply

Initially, the Kerberos client has knowledge of an encryption key known only to the user and the KDC, K_{client}. Similarly, each application server shares an encryption key with the KDC, K_{server}. (See Figure 2-21.)

Figure 2-21   *Kerberos Keys*

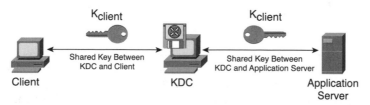

When the client wants to create an association with a particular application server, the client uses the authentication request and response to first obtain a ticket and a session key from the KDC. (See Figure 2-22.)

Figure 2-22   *Kerberos Authentication Request and Reply*

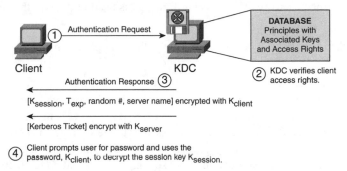

The steps are as follows:

Step 1   The client sends an authentication request to the KDC. This request contains the following information:

— Its claimed identity

— The name of the application server

— A requested expiration time for the ticket

— A random number that will be used to match the authentication response with the request

Step 2   The KDC verifies that the claimed identity exists in the Kerberos database and creates an authentication response. If pre-authentication is used, the client access rights are also verified.

Step 3   The KDC returns the response to the client. The authentication response contains the following information:

— The session key, $K_{session}$

— The assigned expiration time

— The random number from the request

— The name of the application server

— Other information from the ticket

This information is all encrypted with the user's password, which was registered with the authentication server, K_{client}. The KDC also returns a Kerberos ticket containing the random session key, $K_{session}$, which will be used for authentication of the client to the application server; the name of the client to whom the session key was issued; and an expiration time after which the session key is no longer valid. The Kerberos ticket is encrypted using K_{server}.

Step 4   When the client receives the authentication reply, it prompts the user for the password. This password, K_{client}, is used to decrypt the session key, $K_{session}$.

Now the client is ready to communicate with the application server.

NOTE K_{client} is used as the bootstrap mechanism, but in subsequent communication between the KDC and the client, a short-term client key, $K_{client-session}$, is used. $K_{client-session}$ is created by having the KDC convert the user's password to the short-term client key. The KDC sends the short-term client key, $K_{client-session}$, encrypted with the user's password, to the client. The user decrypts the short-term client key and subsequent KDC to client communication use $K_{client-session}$.

Kerberos Application Request and Response

The application request and response is the exchange in which a client proves to an application server that it knows the session key embedded in a Kerberos ticket. Figure 2-23 shows the exchange.

Figure 2-23   *Kerberos Application Request and Reply*

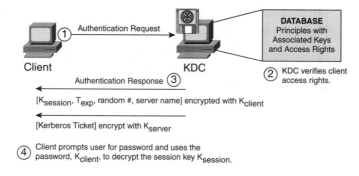

The steps in the application request and response are as follows:

Step 1   The client sends two things to the application server as part of the application request:

— The Kerberos ticket (described earlier)

— An authenticator, which includes the following (among other fields):

— The current time

— A checksum

— An optional encryption key

These elements are all encrypted with the session key, $K_{session}$, from the accompanying ticket.

Step 2   After receiving the application request, the application server decrypts the ticket with K_{server}, extracts the session key, $K_{session}$, and uses the session key to decrypt the authenticator.

If the same key was used to encrypt the authenticator as was used to decrypt it, the checksum will match, and the verifier can assume that the authenticator was generated by the client named in the ticket and to whom the session key was issued. By itself, this check is not sufficient for authentication because an attacker can intercept an authenticator and replay it later to impersonate the user. For this reason, the verifier also checks the time stamp. If the time stamp is within a specified window (typically 5 minutes), centered around the current time on the verifier, and if the time stamp has not been seen on other requests within that window, the verifier accepts the request as authentic.

At this point, the identity of the client has been verified by the server. For some applications, the client also wants to be sure of the server's identity. If such mutual authentication is required, a third step is required.

Step 3   The application server generates an application response by extracting the client's time from the authenticator and returns it to the client together with other information, all encrypted using the session key, $K_{session}$.

Reuse of Credentials

The basic Kerberos authentication protocol allows a client with knowledge of the user's password to obtain a ticket and session key and to prove its identity to any verifier (usually an application server) registered with the KDC. The user's password must be presented each time the user performs authentication with a new verifier. A system should support *single sign-on*, where the user logs in to the system once and provides the password at that time; subsequent authentication occurs automatically.

The obvious way to cache the user's password on the workstation is dangerous. Although a Kerberos ticket and the key associated with it are valid for only a short time, an intruder knowing the user's password can obtain valid tickets and impersonate the user until the password is changed. This is why the short-term client key, $K_{client-session}$, is used in place of the user's actual password in all but the initial bootstrap communication. The Kerberos approach is to cache only tickets and encryption keys (collectively called *credentials*) that will work for a limited time period.

The ticket-granting exchange of the Kerberos protocol allows a user to obtain tickets and encryption keys using such short-lived credentials, without re-entering the user's password. When the user first logs in, an authentication request is issued, and a ticket and the client session key for the ticket-granting service is returned by the KDC. This ticket, called a *ticket-granting ticket* (TGT), has a relatively short life (typically on the order of 8 hours). The response is decrypted, the ticket and session key are saved, and the user's password is forgotten. Subsequently, when the user wants to prove its identity to a new verifier, a new ticket is requested from the KDC using the ticket-granting exchange.

NOTE   The ticket-granting exchange is identical to the authentication exchange except that the ticket-granting request has embedded within it an application request (authenticating the client to the authentication server), and the ticket-granting response is encrypted using the client session key from the ticket-granting ticket rather than from the user's password.

Practical Considerations

Multiple realms, or domains, are supported in Kerberos to allow for scalable implementations. Assume that a corporation has implemented a Kerberos system with two separate realms, Italy and Hungary. When a client in Italy's realm connects to a server in Hungary's realm, Italy's KDC authenticates the client to Hungary's KDC. Hungary's KDC authenticates the client to Hungary's server. Multi-KDC chaining is not allowed, and trust for KDC chaining should go back only one level.

Several utility programs must be installed on the workstation to allow users to obtain Kerberos credentials (kinit), destroy credentials (kdestroy), list credentials (klist), and change their Kerberos passwords (kpasswd). Some sites choose to integrate the Kerberos login tool, kinit, with the workstation login program so that users do not have to type their password twice. This makes the use of Kerberos nearly transparent; users may not even be aware they are using Kerberos.

NOTE   Client/server applications must be modified to use Kerberos for authentication; such Kerberos-aware applications are said to be *Kerberized*.

You should also consider using a method of accurate time in all systems because Kerberos has a time-dependency issue through the use of time stamps. A synchronized, dependable mechanism of obtaining time is needed; most likely, the use of NTP is warranted.

The Distributed Computing Environment

The *Distributed Computing Environment* (DCE) is a set of functional specifications from the Open Software Foundation (OSF), found at http://www.opengroup.org/. DCE is a set of distributed computing technologies that provides security services to protect and control access to data; name services that make it easy to find distributed resources; and a highly scalable model for organizing widely scattered users, services, and data.

DCE has a modular design and supports authentication and authorization. The implemented authentication part is Kerberos version 5 (although, in theory, another mechanism can be substituted). The authorization part works in a manner similar to Kerberos but is implemented by privilege servers and registration servers. In practice, these are usually delivered with the KDC. The registration server ties the KDC with the user's privileges, which are found in the privilege server. The privilege server combines the universal unique ID (UUID) and the groups into a Kerberos ticket for secure transmission. Kerberos uses usernames (which may not always be consistent or unique across the enterprise). DCE uses the UUIDs, which are 128 bits long. On most systems, the user ID (UID) and group ID (GID) fields are 32 bits each.

In practice, a user can authenticate from any workstation with a username and password. The TGT is issued by the KDC. The workstation then uses that session key to form a session to the privilege server. The UUID and access control list (ACL) information is then passed to the workstation through a privilege ticket-granting ticket (PTGT) from the privilege server. The session key encrypted in the PTGT is used. The UUID and the group information are then used as the authorization information to allow or disallow access to services and resources.

NOTE   The DCE effort has not produced the groundswell effect its supporters hoped for. Today, some organizations have embraced it, but it is manpower-intensive to support (as is Kerberos) because it is fairly complex and relies on several other DCE services being implemented. Therefore, it is not found in use very often.

FORTEZZA

Multilevel Information Systems Security Initiative (MISSI) is a network security initiative, under the leadership of the National Security Agency (NSA). MISSI provides a framework for the development and evolution of interoperable, complementary security products to provide flexible, modular security for networked information systems across the Defense Information Infrastructure (DII) and the National Information Infrastructure (NII). These MISSI building blocks share a common network security infrastructure and are based on common security protocols and standards. Flexible solutions are tailored from these building blocks to meet a system's security requirements and may easily evolve, as future

MISSI components provide additional backward-compatible security services and assurance.

Although some MISSI components result from government-contracted developments, most components are offered by commercial vendors as off-the-shelf products. The MISSI building blocks include the following:

- FORTEZZA and FORTEZZA Plus
- Firewalls
- Guards
- Inline encryptors
- Trusted computing

FORTEZZA, combined with FORTEZZA-enabled applications, provides security services appropriate for protecting sensitive-but-unclassified (SBU) data. FORTEZZA provides the following features:

- Protection for SBU data when used on a commercial off-the-shelf (COTS) workstation in LAN or WAN environments
- Identification and authentication, confidentiality, data integrity, and nonrepudiation services
- Support for various workstation operating systems (DOS/Windows and UNIX at a minimum)

FORTEZZA Plus supports users of classified information with strong encryption methods. FORTEZZA Plus is an upgraded version of FORTEZZA that can be used to encrypt classified information up through Top Secret information. FORTEZZA Plus must be used in conjunction with a high assurance guard such as the secure network server (SNS), which ensures that the encryption of information is invoked. The use of FORTEZZA Plus to process classified information at different levels can be affected by the security limitations of other components in the system.

The FORTEZZA card is a cryptographic token in a PCMCIA form factor that provides encryption/ decryption and digital signature functions. It uses DSA and SHA for signature and message digests but NSA-designed key agreement and encryption algorithms. The key agreement algorithm is a variant of Diffie-Hellman called *Key Exchange Algorithm* (KEA) and the encryption algorithm is a block cipher called *SKIPJACK*. The card also stores certificates that include individualized key material used by the cryptographic and signature functions. The software on the workstation (PC, UNIX, and so on) exchanges commands and data with the FORTEZZA card to encrypt and sign messages before it sends them. It likewise uses the card to decrypt and verify the signatures of received messages. Each time the card is inserted into a workstation, the owner must unlock the card by entering a PIN. FORTEZZA card PINs can range from 4 to 12 characters. PINs may be a combination of alpha and numeric characters.

To perform application functions for the user, FORTEZZA must interoperate with FORTEZZA-enabled applications. These applications are either government developed or COTS applications (such as e-mail) that have been modified to interface with and use FORTEZZA security features. A large variety of such applications exist; more are being added as they are developed and tested.

Major types of FORTEZZA-enabled applications include these:

- **Electronic messaging**—FORTEZZA can secure e-mail, electronic data interchange (EDI), electronic commerce, and facsimile to provide message encryption, authentication, and data integrity.

- **World Wide Web (WWW)**—FORTEZZA can protect secure web transactions using strong identification and authentication and Secure Sockets Layer (SSL) interactions. Netscape has built a FORTEZZA-enabled version of its browser that links SSL with FORTEZZA.

- **File and media encryptors**—These encryptors are applications written to enable FORTEZZA to secure user files on storage media.

- **Identification and authentication**—After the FORTEZZA card has been installed in the workstation and the PIN has been correctly entered, the identity of the user is known and trusted. Access to other devices across a network can be authorized by exchanging this identification and authentication information in a trusted manner.

NOTE   FORTEZZA was originally designed by the NSA to provide strong cryptography while allowing the NSA to incorporate key escrow into the device. This was done using the Law Enforcement Access Field (LEAF), which contained the session key used to encrypt the transmitted traffic. The NSA could decrypt a communication by recovering the session key from the LEAF. The LEAF was embedded in the IV (initialization vector), which is a random block of data used to add randomness for key-generation material. However, due to the large key escrow controversy, in 1997 the NSA removed the LEAF. A dummy LEAF is now used for the IV for backward compatibility.

IEEE 802.1x

802.1x is the standard developed by the IEEE that enables authentication and key management for IEEE 802 local area networks. It allows for devices to be authenticated and authorized before they can logically connect to a port on a switch. In the case of Ethernet or Token Ring, these ports are physical entities that the device plugs into. In the case of wireless networks, however, these ports are logical entities known as *associations*.

The 802.1x standard defines three main logical entities (which may or may not reside on separate devices) as illustrated in Figure 2-24:

- **Supplicant**—A device that needs access to a LAN (for example, a laptop or workstation).
- **Authenticator**—A device that is responsible for initiating the authentication process and subsequently acts as a relay between the actual authentication server and the supplicant.
- **Authentication server**—A device that is responsible for performing the actual authentication and authorization on behalf of the authenticator. It contains profile information for all the users on the network and can use that information to authenticate and authorize users to connect to the ports on the authenticator.

Figure 2-24   *IEEE 802.1x Entities*

The authentication data between the three entities is exchanged using EAP packets, which are carried in varying protocol packets. An encapsulation mechanism known as EAP over LANs (EAPOL) is defined in 802.1x to allow communication between the supplicant and the authenticator. EAPOL is defined separately for both Ethernet and Token Ring. The EAP messages are thus encapsulated using the EAPOL frames for transport between the supplicant and the authenticator. Upon receiving the EAPOL frame, the authenticator strips off the headers and, if the authenticator and authentication server reside on different devices, forwards the EAP message using another protocol. Communication between the authenticator and the authentication server is typically done via TACACS+ or RADIUS. RADIUS is generally preferred because it has EAP encapsulation extensions built into it. An example of the 802.1x transaction for authenticating a workstation to a LAN switch is shown in Figure 2-25. A RADIUS server is used as the authentication server.

Figure 2-25   *802.1x Transaction Example*

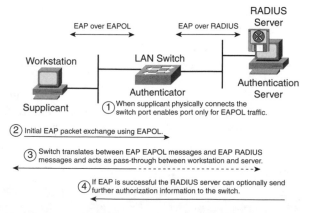

Application Layer Security Protocols

This section focuses on technologies designed to address security needs for specific application protocols. The intent of this chapter is to familiarize the reader with most of the underlying security technologies available today, which form the basis for securing the network infrastructure. Some of the application layer security protocols are used as security solutions for specific environments, such as securing Voice over IP networks, as discussed in the next chapter.

The application layer pertains to the details of a particular application such as Telnet, FTP, or HTTP, and doesn't concern itself with the details of the movement of data across a network. This layer uses end-to-end protocols, in which end systems are responsible for providing security for the application protocol. Not many security protocols are specifically designed for individual applications. There are too many applications to make such an approach scalable. However, a few merit mentioning. Because the World Wide Web has become one of the fastest growing applications in the Internet, a specific security protocol was designed to be used for secure web transactions: Secure HyperText Transport Protocol (SHTTP). The Secure Multipurpose Internet Mail Extensions (S/MIME) protocol was designed to build security functionality on top of the MIME protocol to be easily integrated into e-mail and messaging products. Both are detailed here.

SHTTP

SHTTP is a secure message-oriented communications protocol designed to be used for securing messages using the HTTP protocol. The protocol preserves the characteristics of HTTP while allowing request and reply messages to be signed, authenticated, encrypted, or any combination of these (including no protection). SHTTP clients can communicate with non-HTTP-supported servers (although in these cases, the security features of SHTTP would not be applied).

Multiple key-management mechanisms are supported, including password-style manually shared secrets, and public key exchange. If some hosts do not have a public key pair, it is possible to use pre-arranged symmetric session keys to send confidential messages. These would usually be provided out of band.

Secure HTTP can verify message integrity and sender authenticity for a message using the computation of a message authentication code (MAC). The MAC is computed as a keyed hash over the document using a shared secret.

SHTTP uses *option negotiation* to allow clients and servers to agree on the following:

- **Transaction modes**—What should be signed or encrypted or both?
- **Cryptographic algorithms**—Which algorithm should be used for signing and encrypting?
- **Certificate selection**—Which certificate should be used (Verisign, Entrust, other)?

The main benefit of using an application-specific protocol such as SHTTP is that very specific security needs can be met. Consider these examples:

- The application could deal with a message containing digital signatures by several different agents and make decisions based on who signed what.

- Cryptographic security measures could be defined for individual web pages such that individually encrypted web pages could be published on any web server but could only be read by those with authorized keys.

In practice, SHTTP has achieved limited use. Transport layer security implementations are more easily available and more often used for web security.

S/MIME

S/MIME is short for Secure Multipurpose Internet Mail Extensions. The specification was designed to be easily integrated into e-mail and messaging products. S/MIME builds security on top of the industry-standard MIME protocol according to an equally important set of cryptographic standards, the Public Key Cryptography Standards (PKCS). Public key technologies are discussed later in this chapter. MIME was an enhancement to the original messaging specification defined in RFC 822, which restricted the message body to ASCII text. MIME added other forms of content by providing specifications for binary data.

S/MIME was originally developed by RSA Data Security, Inc., and was based on the PKCS #7 data format for the messages, and the X.509v3 format for certificates. PKCS#7 only supported RSA for key exchange, which meant that S/MIMEv2 only had support for RSA. The S/MIME working group was created in the IETF to add support for other key exchange and signature algorithms.

The S/MIMEv3 standard consists of five parts:

- Cryptographic message syntax (RFC 3369)
- Cryptographic message syntax (CMS) algorithms (RFC 3370)
- S/MIME version 3 message specification (RFC 2633)
- S/MIME version 3 certificate handling (RFC 2632)
- Diffie-Hellman key agreement method (RFC 2631)

An additional protocol, Enhanced Security Services for S/MIME (RFC 2634), is a set of extensions to S/MIME to allow signed receipts, security labels, and secure mailing lists. The first two of these extensions work with either S/MIMEv2 or S/MIMEv3; secure mailing lists only work with S/MIMEv3.

NOTE   S/MIMEv2 is not an IETF standard. S/MIMEv2 requires the use of RSA key exchange, which is encumbered by U.S. patents held by RSA Data Security, Inc.; further, S/MIMEv2 requires the use of weak cryptography (40-bit keys). Both of these issues have prevented the protocol from being accepted as an IETF standard.

The Cryptographic Message Syntax (CMS)

CMS is a protocol for cryptographically securing messages. It provides encryption and signatures for arbitrary content. The CMS can support a variety of architectures for certificate-based key management. The CMS is derived from PKCS #7 version 1.5 as specified in RFC 2315. Password-based key management is included in the CMS specification, and an extension mechanism to support new key management schemes without further changes to the CMS is specified. Protocols that rely on the CMS are expected to choose appropriate algorithms for their environment.

Every CMS message has a type that describes which form of cryptographic service has been applied. These messages may be recursively encapsulated to offer multiple cryptographic services. CMS defines six basic content types:

- **Data**—The data content type is intended to refer to arbitrary octet strings, such as ASCII text files or MIME content.

- **Signed data**—The signed data content type consists of some content and one or more signatures over that content. The signature is derived by using a hash function over the content and encrypting the resulting hash with the sender's private key. A recipient independently computes the message digest. This message digest and the signer's public key are used to verify the signature value. The message usually contains the appropriate certificates needed to certify the key(s) used to sign the message. The message can also contain CRLs needed to check the validity of the certificate. If the message has no content, it is called a *detached signature* and represents a signature over some data that must be externally specified.

- **Enveloped data**—The enveloped data content type contains encrypted data using a randomly generated symmetric content encryption key (CEK). The encrypted content is encapsulated in a wrapper that contains the encrypted CEK for a given recipient. The CEK can be encrypted in four ways:

    - Key transport—The CEK is encrypted in the recipient's public key (typical algorithm is RSA).

    - Key agreement—The recipient's public key and the sender's private key are used to generate a pairwise symmetric key, and then the CEK is encrypted in the pairwise symmetric key (typically using Diffie-Hellman).

    - Symmetric key encryption keys—The CEK is encrypted in a previously distributed symmetric key-encryption key.

    - Passwords—The CEK is encrypted in a key-encryption key that is derived from a password or other shared secret value.

- **Digest data**—The digested data content type consists of content of any type and a message digest of the content. Typically, the digested data content type is used to provide content integrity, and the result generally becomes an input to the enveloped data content type.

- **Encrypted data**—The encrypted data content type consists of encrypted content of any type. Unlike the enveloped data content type, the encrypted data content type has neither recipients nor encrypted CEKs. Keys need to be managed by other means. The typical application of this content type will be to encrypt the content of the data content type for local storage, perhaps where the encryption key is derived from a password.

- **Authenticated data**—The authenticated data content type consists of content of any type, a message authentication code (MAC), and encrypted authentication keys for one or more recipients. The combination of the MAC and one encrypted authentication key for a recipient is necessary for that recipient to verify the integrity of the content. Any type of content can be integrity protected for an arbitrary number of recipients.

To apply both a signature and encryption to some content, CMS requires the service to be recursively applied. Typically, the data is first signed, and then the signed data is encrypted.

S/MIME provides a consistent way to send and receive secure MIME data by adding cryptographic signature and encryption services. It provides the following cryptographic security services for electronic messaging applications: authentication, message integrity and nonrepudiation of origin (using digital signatures), and privacy and data security (using encryption).

Separate requirements and recommendations are made for how receiving agents handle incoming messages and for how sending agents create outgoing messages. In general, they are based on the following strategy: Be liberal in what you receive and conservative in what you send. The separation for requirements on receiving agents and sending agents derives from the likelihood that there will be S/MIME systems that involve software other than traditional Internet mail clients. S/MIME is not restricted to mail; it can be used with any transport mechanism that transports MIME data, such as HTTP. Further, S/MIME can be used in automated message transfer agents that use cryptographic security services that do not require any human intervention, such as the signing of software-generated documents and the encryption of fax messages sent over the Internet.

The mandatory features required for S/MIME communication are as follows:

- **Message format**—Binary, based on CMS
- **Certificate format**—Binary, based on x.509v3
- **Symmetric encryption algorithm**—3DES
- **Signature algorithm**—Diffie-Hellman with DSS
- **Hash algorithm**—SHA-1

A sender may, of course, support other encryption algorithms. The sender is able to advertise the user's capabilities and preference for a choice of encryption algorithms.

The specification leaves it up to the implementers and users whether to either sign a message first or to provide confidentiality by encrypting the message first. When signing first, the signatories are then securely obscured by the encryption. When encrypting first, the signatories are exposed, but it is possible to verify signatures without removing the privacy protection. This may be useful in an environment were automatic signature verification is desired, because no private key material is required to verify a signature.

There are security ramifications to choosing whether to sign first or encrypt first. A recipient of a message that is encrypted and then signed can validate that the encrypted block was unaltered, but cannot determine any relationship between the signer and the unencrypted contents of the message. A recipient of a message that is signed and then encrypted can assume that the signed message itself has not been altered, but that a careful attacker may have changed the unauthenticated portions of the encrypted message.

Several characteristics of S/MIME make it a very flexible security solution for a variety of messaging applications:

- **Multiple signers**—Because CMS supports multiple signatures on a single message, S/MIME supports having a message signed by multiple senders.

- **Multiple recipients**—It is possible to send the same message securely to multiple recipients by encrypting the message with a single CEK and then encrypting the CEK individually for each recipient.

- **Receipt**—The ability to provide a receipt allows a sender to be sure that the recipient received a message and that it wasn't altered in transit. However, the recipient is not required to generate a receipt, and therefore lack of a receipt does not indicate that the recipient did not receive the message.

- **Forwarding**—Messages can be forwarded from one recipient to another while leaving the message signature intact and verifiable. This is possible because S/MIME uses a digital signature that signs the whole message.

- **Transport independence**—S/MIME provides end-to-end security at the application layer and is independent of any underlying transport. Therefore, in IP networks it can run over either TCP or UDP.

S/MIMEv3 is becoming widely deployed and is an underlying requirement for providing security services in Session Initiation Protocol (SIP)-based telephony networks, discussed in the next chapter.

Transport Layer Security Protocols

The transport layer provides the details of moving the flow of data between two hosts. The following sections describe the security protocols that operate over TCP/IP or some other reliable but insecure transport. They are categorized as *transport layer security protocols* because their intent is to secure the transport layer and to provide methods for implementing privacy, authentication, and integrity above the transport layer. This layer uses end-to-end protocols, in which end systems are responsible for providing security for the transport protocol.

The Secure Socket Layer/Transport Layer Security Protocol

The Secure Socket Layer (SSL)/Transport Layer Security (TLS) protocol specifies a mechanism for providing data security layered between application protocols (such as HTTP, Telnet, NNTP, or FTP) and TCP/IP. It provides data encryption, server authentication, message integrity, and optional client authentication for a TCP/IP connection.

The original proprietary SSLv1 specification was designed by Netscape, and was subsequently modified into SSLv2 and publicly released in 1994. While SSLv2 was being deployed, Microsoft was coming up with its own incompatible variant, PCT. SSLv2 contained a number of security flaws, some of which PCT corrected, that ultimately led to the design of SSLv3. SSLv2 used RC4 for encryption and the MD5 algorithm for authentication. RSA keys were used for both authentication and key exchange; and at the time the SSLv2 specification came out, the U.S. government export laws limited the key length of a cryptographic algorithm to 40-bits, which many implementations supported. SSLv3 added support for DSS for authentication and DH for key agreement. The Transport Layer Security (TLS) working group was formed in 1996 to try and standardize an SSL-like protocol. TLS is based on SSLv3 and requires the use of DSS for authentication, DH for key agreement, and 3DES for encryption. In the following text, any reference to SSL is meant to imply SSLv3. Only the SSL operation is described because TLS is essentially the same.

NOTE	Although the TLS protocol operation is very similar to that of SSLv3, the key expansion and message authentication computations are incompatibe and therefore TLS and SSLv3 will not necessarily interoperate.

SSL assumes that the underlying packet delivery mechanism is reliable, and although in theory there are a number of transport protocols that could provide this service, SSL nearly always uses TCP as its transport.

The primary goal of SSL is to provide privacy and reliability between two communicating applications. SSL is a layered protocol consisting of the record protocol, which provides the envelope and security services for the four content layer protocols (handshake, alert, change cipher spec, and application). These are described as follows:

- **The record protocol**—This protocol is used to exchange application layer data. Application messages are fragmented into manageable blocks, optionally compressed, and a MAC (message authentication code) is applied. (SSL uses the term MAC, which is really a hash or message digest.) The result is encrypted and transmitted. The recipient takes the received data and decrypts it, verifies the MAC, decompresses and reassembles it, and delivers the result to the application protocol.

- **The handshake protocol**—This protocol negotiates the cryptographic parameters to be used between the client and the server session. When an SSL client and server first start communicating, they agree on a protocol version, select cryptographic algorithms, optionally authenticate each other, and use public key encryption techniques to generate shared secrets.

- **The alert protocol**—This protocol is used to indicate when errors have occurred or when a session between two hosts is being terminated. It is a one-way information-error message.

- **The change cipher spec protocol**—This protocol indicates a change in the encryption and authentication of records. It is a one-way messge and instigates a new handshake.

- **The application protocols**—These define any client/server protocols that use SSL and have specified ports defined. For example POP3S (995), NNTPS 563), HTTPS (443), LDAPS (636), and IRCS (994).

NOTE   Although the SSLv3 and TLS specifications allow for compression, the only compression currently stipulated is NULL. Therefore, compression is not commonly used.

Figure 2-26 shows a diagram of a SSL/TLS record. The content type specifies the content protocol used to process the plaintext fragment. A *fragment* is the portion of the data stream that is being transmitted. The protocol version is 3.0 for SSL and 3.1 for TLS. The record length is the length of the fragments, in bytes. These three fields comprise the header and are sent in the clear. The rest of the fragment is encrypted. It consists of the data that is sent, the computed MAC, and possibly some padding. The padding is required when using block ciphers such as DES because a block cipher requires the data to be encrypted to be a multiple of the block length.

Figure 2-26 *SSL/TLS Record Format*

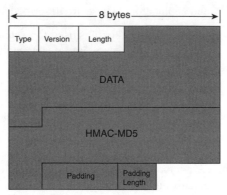

The SSL handshake protocol provides connection security that has three basic properties:

- The peer's identity can be authenticated using asymmetric, or public key, cryptography (for instance, RSA, DSS, and so on). This authentication can be made optional, but is generally required for at least one of the peers.

- The negotiation of a shared secret is secure—the negotiated secret is unavailable to eavesdroppers, and for any authenticated connection the secret cannot be obtained, even by an attacker who can place himself in the middle of the connection.

- The negotiation is reliable—no attacker can modify the negotiation communication without being detected by the parties to the communication.

Consider an example using a web client and server. The web client initiates an SSL session by connecting to an SSL-capable server. A typical SSL-capable web server accepts SSL connection requests on a different port (port 443 by default) than standard HTTP requests (port 80 by default). When the client connects to this port, it initiates a handshake that establishes the SSL session. After the handshake finishes, communication is encrypted using the negotiated shared session key and message integrity checks are performed until the SSL session expires. SSL creates a session during which the handshake must happen only once.

Figure 2-27 shows the SSL handshake process. (See the section "Public Key Infrastructure and Distribution Models" later in this chapter for more information about digital certificates.) The steps in the process are as follows:

Step 1 The SSL client connects to the SSL server and requests the server to authenticate itself. It also includes the cipher suites it supports.

Step 2 The server proves its identity by sending its digital certificate, which has its public key attached to it. This exchange may optionally include an entire certificate chain, up to some root certificate authority (CA).

Certificates are verified by checking validity dates and verifying that the certificate bears the signature of a trusted CA. The certificate is signed but not encrypted.

The server also returns a selected ciphersuite to use for the initial secure tunnel.

Step 3   The client generates a random secret key, encrypts it with the server's public key, and sends it to the SSL server. Communication from now on is encrypted using the shared secret and specified cipher suite.

Step 4   The message encryption algorithm and the hash function for integrity are negotiated for the session. Usually the client presents a list of all the algorithms it supports, and the server selects the strongest cipher available.

Step 5   The client and server generate the session keys by following these steps:

(a)   The client generates a random number that it sends to the server, encrypted with the server's public key (obtained from the server's certificate).

(a)   The server responds with more random data (encrypted with the client's public key, if available; otherwise, it sends the data in cleartext).

(a)   The encryption keys are generated from this random data using hash functions.

Step 6   The handshake process is complete and a secure session tunnel is created.

Figure 2-27   *The SSL Handshake Process*

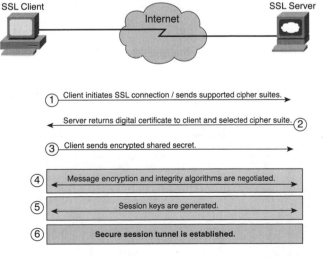

NOTE   Mutual authentication can be carried out by using the optional client-based authentication mechanism. This would occur after Step 3 in the preceding example. However, SSL only supports certificate-based client authentication, which is not often used due to the lack of a public key infrastructure. Instead, many application protocols incorporate their own client authentication mechanism, such as username/password or a one-time password technology such as S/Key. These authentication mechanisms are more secure when run over SSL.

The advantage of the SSL protocol is that it provides connection security that has three basic properties:

- The connection is private. Encryption is used after an initial handshake to define a secret key. Symmetric cryptography is used for data encryption (for example, DES and RC4).

- The peer's identity can be authenticated using asymmetric, or public key, cryptography (for example, RSA, and DSS).

- The connection is reliable. Message transport includes a message integrity check using a keyed MAC. Secure hash functions (such as SHA and MD5) are used for MAC computations.

SSL/TLS is widely used with HTTP traffic. Other protocols are also starting to use SSL/TLS and have specific port numbers defined. Refer to http://www.iana.org/assignments/port-numbers for a list of officially assigned application port numbers. Table 2-2 lists some applications that are starting to use TLS to provide application-specific security. Note that most of these port numbers are specified for TCP and UDP.

Table 2-2   *IANA-Assigned Port Numbers for Applications Using SSL/TLS*

Protocol	Defined Port Number	SSL/TLS Port Number
HTTP	80	443
NNTP	119	563
LDAP	389	636
FTP-data	20	989
FTP-control	21	990
Telnet	23	992
IMAP	143	993
POP3	194	994
SMTP	110	995

The Secure Shell Protocol

The *Secure Shell* (SSH) is a protocol for secure remote login and other secure network services over an insecure network. It provides support for secure remote login, secure file transfer, and the secure forwarding of TCP/IP and X Window System traffic. It can automatically encrypt, authenticate, and compress transmitted data. The work in progress to define the SSH protocol ensures that the SSH protocol can provide strong security against cryptanalysis and protocol attacks, can work reasonably well without a global key management or certificate infrastructure, and can use existing certificate infrastructures (such as DNSSEC and X.509) when available.

The SSH protocol consists of three major components:

- The transport layer protocol, which provides server authentication, confidentiality, and integrity with perfect forward secrecy. Optionally, it may also provide compression.
- The user authentication protocol, which authenticates the client to the server.
- The connection protocol, which multiplexes the encrypted tunnel into several logical channels.

The SSH transport layer is a secure low-level transport protocol. It provides strong encryption, cryptographic host authentication, and integrity protection. Authentication in SSH is host based; this protocol does not perform user authentication. A higher-level protocol for user authentication can be designed on top of SSH.

The protocol has been designed to be simple and flexible enough to allow parameter negotiation and to minimize the number of round trips. The key exchange method, the public key algorithm, the symmetric encryption algorithm, the message authentication algorithm, and the hash algorithm are all negotiated.

Data integrity is protected by including with each packet a MAC computed from a shared secret, a packet sequence number, and the contents of the packet.

SSH implementations can be found for UNIX, Windows, and Macintosh systems. It is a widely accepted protocol that uses well-known and well-established encryption, integrity, and public key algorithms.

The SOCKS Protocol

Socket Security (SOCKS) is a transport layer-based secure networking proxy protocol. It is designed to provide a framework for client/server applications in both the TCP and UDP domains to conveniently and securely use the services of a network firewall.

SOCKS was originally developed by David and Michelle Koblas; the code was made freely available on the Internet. Several major revisions have occurred since then, but the software has remained freely available. SOCKS version 4 provides for unsecured firewall traversal for TCP-based client/server applications (including Telnet, FTP, and the popular information discovery protocols such as HTTP, WAIS, and Gopher). SOCKS version 5, defined in RFC 1928, extends the SOCKS version 4 model to include UDP, extends the framework to include provisions for generalized strong authentication schemes, and extends the addressing scheme to encompass domain name and IPv6 addresses.

A proposal currently exists to create a mechanism for managing the entrance or exit of IP multicast through a firewall. It does this by defining extensions to the existing SOCKS version 5 protocol, which provides a framework for user-level, authenticated firewall traversal of unicast TCP and UDP traffic. Because the current UDP support in SOCKS version 5 has scalability problems and other deficiencies (which must be addressed before multicast support can be achieved), however, the extensions are defined in two parts:

- Base-level UDP extensions
- Multicast UDP extensions

SOCKS works by replacing the standard network system calls in an application with special versions. (This is why SOCKS is sometimes referred to as an *application-level proxy*.) These new system calls open connections to a SOCKS proxy server (configured in the application by the user, or by a system configuration file) on a well-known port (usually 1080/TCP). If the connection request succeeds, the client enters a negotiation for the authentication method to be used, authenticates with the chosen method, and then sends a relay request. The SOCKS server evaluates the request and either establishes the appropriate connection or denies it. After the connection is established with the SOCKS server, the client application sends the server the name of the machine and the port number to which the user wants to connect. The SOCKS server actually makes the connection with the remote host and then transparently moves data back and forth between the application and the remote machine. The user has no idea that the SOCKS server is even in the loop. (See Figure 2-28.)

The difficulty with using SOCKS is that somebody has to replace the network system calls with the SOCKS versions. (This process is generally referred to as *SOCKS-ification* or *SOCKS-ifying an application*.) Fortunately, most of the common network applications (such as Telnet, FTP, finger, and whois) have already been SOCKS-ified, and many vendors are now including SOCKS support in commercial applications.

Figure 2-28   *The SOCKS Security Model*

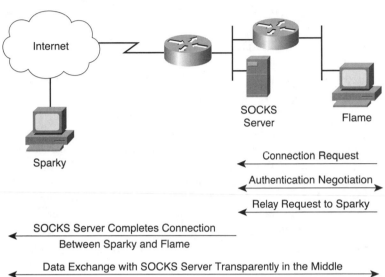

Network Layer Security

Network layer security pertains to security services at the IP layer of the TCP/IP protocol stack. The network layer provides hop-by-hop handling of data packets, where intermediary systems in a network, such as routers, could be involved. At each intermediary system (that is, hop), the data packet is inspected at the IP layer and then forwarded on to the next intermediary system until the final destination is reached. Many years of work have produced a set of standards from the IETF that, collectively, define how to secure services at the IP network layer; these standards are commonly referred to as *IPsec*.

NOTE   Although network layer inspection is done on a hop-by-hop basis, the encryption/ decryption of secured IP network layer packets does not need to happen at each hop.

The IP Security Protocol Suite

The *IP Security* (IPsec) protocol suite comprises a set of standards used to provide privacy and authentication services at the IP layer. The current ratified IPsec standards include four algorithm-independent base specifications:

- RFC 2401, "The IP Security Architecture," defines the overall architecture and specifies elements common to both the IP authentication header (AH) and the IP encapsulating security payload (ESP).

- RFC 2402, "The IP Authentication Header (AH)," defines an algorithm-independent mechanism for providing exportable cryptographic authentication without encryption to IPv4 and IPv6 packets.

- RFC 2406, "The IP Encapsulating Security Payload (ESP)," defines an algorithm-independent mechanism for providing encryption to IPv4 and IPv6 packets.

- RFC 2408, "The Internet Security Association and Key Management Protocol (ISAKMP)," defines procedures and packet formats to establish, negotiate, modify, and delete security associations (SAs). It provides a consistent framework for transferring key and authentication data that is independent of the key generation technique, encryption algorithm, and authentication mechanism. It deliberately separates the details of security association management (and key management) from the details of key exchange. Although this introduces more complexity, it enables the use of different encryption algorithms, authentication mechanisms, and key exchange protocols should more applicable or robust solutions become available for different networking scenarios.

The set of security services IPsec can provide includes access control, connectionless integrity, data origin authentication, rejection of replayed packets (a form of partial sequence integrity), confidentiality (encryption), and limited traffic flow confidentiality. Because these services are provided at the IP layer, they can be used by any higher layer protocol (such as TCP, UDP, ICMP, BGP, and so on).

Authentication and Encryption Services

IPsec uses two protocols, AH and ESP, to provide traffic security, each of which defines a new set of headers to be added to IP datagrams.

The AH protocol is used to ensure the integrity and data origin authentication of the data, including the invariant fields in the outer IP header. It does not provide confidentiality protection. AH provides antireply protection by using sequence numbers and sliding windows to keep track of received packets and packets that are yet to be sent. Replay detection is performed on each IPsec peer by keeping track of the sequence numbers of the packets it has received and advancing a window as it receives newer sequence numbers. It drops any packets with sequence numbers that are outside of the expected window or that are repeated. Note, however, that although the sequence number is always set, replay protection is optional and a receiver may choose to ignore this field.

AH commonly uses a keyed hash function rather than digital signatures, because digital signature technology is too slow and greatly reduces network throughput. HMAC-MD5-96 and HMAC-SHA-96 are required by the protocol specification but keyed MD5 is also commonly supported. AH is an appropriate protocol to use when confidentiality is not required, although in practice it is only rarely deployed. AH has been assigned as IP protocol type 51. Figure 2-29 shows the format of the AH header.

Figure 2-29 *AH Header Format*

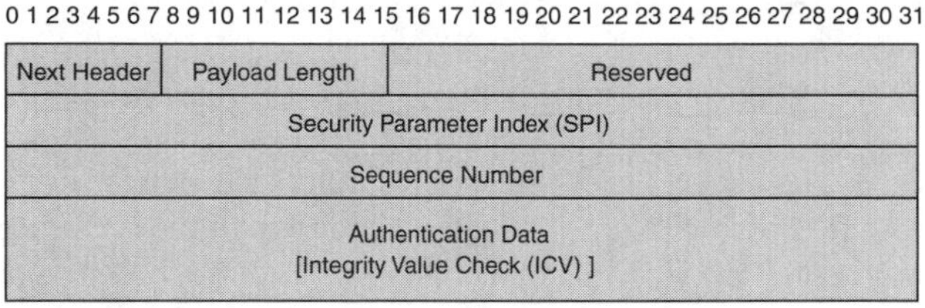

```
0 1 2 3 4 5 6 7 8 9 10 11 12 13 14 15 16 17 18 19 20 21 22 23 24 25 26 27 28 29 30 31
```

Next Header	Payload Length	Reserved
Security Parameter Index (SPI)		
Sequence Number		
Authentication Data [Integrity Value Check (ICV)]		

Next Header: Which higher level protocol is (UDP,TCP, and ESP) next.

Payload Length: Size of AH in 32-bit long words, minus 2.

Reserved: Must be zero.

SPI: Arbitrary 32-bit number that specifies to the receiving device which security association is being used (security protocols, algorithms, keys, times, addresses, and so on).

Sequence Number: Start at 1 and must never repeat. It is always set but receiver may choose to ignore this field.

Authentication Data: ICV is a digital signature over the packet and it varies in length depending on the algorithm used (SHA-1, MD5).

HMAC-MD5-96

HMAC-MD5 is a special kind of keyed hashing. It essentially computes a hash of a hash. The first step is a preparatory step:

- The message is broken down into blocks of 512 bits.

- A shared secret key is XOR'd with a specified 64-byte array to produce result K1.

- The shared secret is XOR'd a second time with another specified 64-byte array to produce result K2.

The first hash is obtained by applying the first block of the message and K1 to the MD5 algorithm to produce hash1. Then hash1 and K2 are used as input for the MD5 algorithm to produce hash2.

Hash2 is used as input to MD5 with the second 512-bit message block to produce hash3. Hash3 is used as input to MD5 with the third 512-bit message block to produce hash4. This process continues until the entire message has been hashed. The resulting final hash is typically truncated to some specified number of bits. MD5 produces a 128-bit output; for HMAC-MD5-96, the number of bits is truncated to 96. HMAC-SHA-96 follows the same principle.

The ESP protocol protects the confidentiality, integrity, and data origin authentication of the data. The original IP headers, protocol headers, and data are all encrypted. Authentication is provided for all fields except the new encapsulation IP header "outside" the ESP Header.

Therefore, the scope of the authentication offered by ESP is narrower than it is for AH. Similar to AH, the ESP protocol provides antireply protection by using sequence numbers and sliding windows to keep track of received packets and packets that are yet to be sent. Replay detection is performed on each IPsec peer by keeping track of the sequence numbers of the packets it has received and advancing a window as it receives newer sequence numbers. It drops any packets with sequence numbers that are outside of the expected window or that are repeated. Note, however, that although the sequence number is always set, replay protection is optional and a receiver may choose to ignore this field.

The ESP standard requires implementing DES for its encryption algorithm, although more current implementation tend to also support 3DES and AES. Other algorithms typically supported include RC5, IDEA, Blowfish, CAST, and NULL. For authentication, the ESP standard requires that both the MD5 and SHA-1 algorithms are supported in compliant implementations. ESP NULL encryption is used for providing only authentication services and not confidentiality. If only the upper-layer protocols must be authenticated, ESP authentication is an appropriate choice and is more space efficient than using AH to encapsulate ESP. ESP has been assigned as IP protocol type 50. Figure 2-30 shows the format of the ESP header.

Figure 2-30 *ESP Header Format*

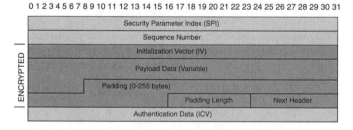

0 1 2 3 4 5 6 7 8 9 10 11 12 13 14 15 16 17 18 19 20 21 22 23 24 25 26 27 28 29 30 31

SPI: Arbitrary 32-bit number that specifies SA to the receiving device.
Seq #: Start at 1 and must never repeat; receiver may choose to ignore.
IV: Used to initialize CBC mode of an encryption algorithm.
Payload Data: Encrypted IP header, TCP, or UDP header and data.
Padding: Used for encryption algorithms that operate in CBC mode.
Padding Length: Number of bytes added to the data stream (may be 0).
Next Header: The type of protocol from the original header that appears in the encrypted part of the packet.
Authentication Header: ICV is a digital signature over the packet and it varies in length depending on the algorithm used (SHA-1, MD5).

AH and ESP can be used independently or in combination to provide a desired set of security services. For both of these protocols, IPsec does not define the specific security algorithms to use; rather, it provides an open framework for implementing industry-standard algorithms. Although certain algorithms are mandated to be supported, it does not require that they be deployed. A rule of thumb to follow is to use the strongest algorithm with the largest key until you run into performance limitations. There is no reason not to deploy strong security if there are no performance impacts.

Each protocol supports two modes of use:

- Transport mode
- Tunnel mode

In *transport mode*, two hosts provide protection primarily for upper-layer protocols; the cryptographic endpoints (where the encryption and decryption take place) are the source and destination of the data packet. In IPv4, a transport mode security protocol header appears immediately after the IP header and before any higher-layer protocols (such as TCP or UDP). Figure 2-31 shows the packet format alterations for AH and ESP in this mode.

Figure 2-31   *Packet Format Alterations in IPsec IPv4 Transport Mode*

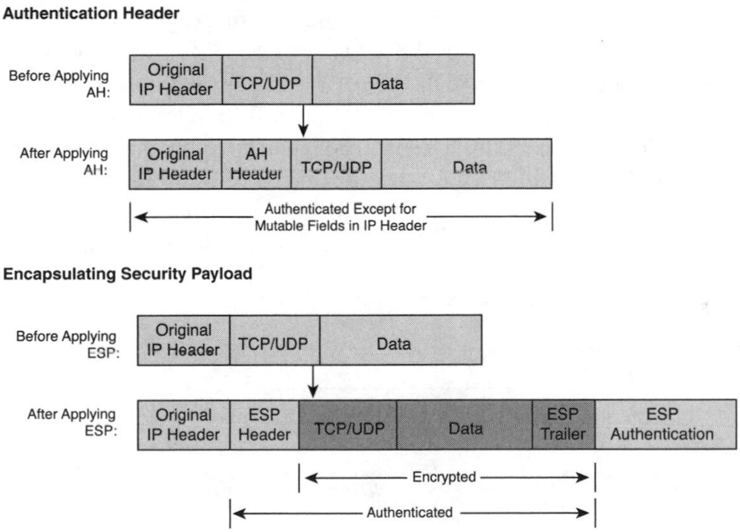

In the case of AH in transport mode, all upper-layer information is protected, and all fields in the IPv4 header excluding the fields that are typically modified in transit. The fields of the IPv4 header that are *not* included are, therefore, set to zero before applying the authentication algorithm. These fields are as follows:

- ToS
- TTL
- Header Checksum
- Offset
- Flags

Notice that the IP addresses in the header are included in the integrity check for AH. This means that if the addresses are altered during transit, as is the case for situations where Network Address Translation (NAT) is deployed, the integrity check will fail at the receiving end. NAT is discussed in more detail in the next chapter in the "VPN Security" section.

In the case of ESP in transport mode, security services are provided only for the higher-layer protocols and the data itself, not for the IP header. The authentication value is also sent in the clear because the integrity check value is computed after the encryption process has taken place.

A *tunnel* is a vehicle for encapsulating packets inside a protocol that is understood at the entry and exit points of a given network. These entry and exit points are defined as *tunnel interfaces*. Tunnel mode can be supported by data packet endpoints and by intermediate security gateways. In *tunnel mode*, an "outer" IP header specifies the IPsec processing destination, and an "inner" IP header specifies the ultimate destination for the packet. The source address in the "outer" IP header is the initiating cryptographic endpoint that will get modified as the packet traverses the network to reach its destination cryptographic endpoint; the source address in the "inner" header is the true source address of the packet. The destination address in the "outer" IP header is the destination cryptographic endpoint; the destination address in the "inner" header is the true destination address of the packet. The protocol fields in the "outer" IP header are set to either AH (51) or ESP (50) depending on the protocol used. The respective AH or ESP security protocol header appears after the "outer" IP header and before the "inner" IP header. (See Figure 2-32.)

Figure 2-32 *Packet Format Alterations in IPsec IPv4 Tunnel Mode*

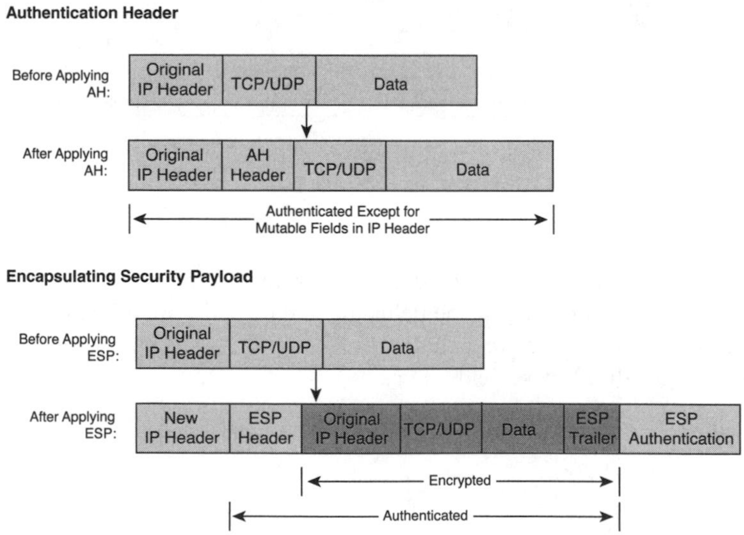

If AH is employed in tunnel mode, portions of the "outer" IP header are given integrity protection (those same fields as for transport mode, described earlier in this section), as well as all of the tunneled IP packet. (That is, all the "inner" IP header is protected as are the higher-layer protocols.) Again, in NAT environments this can be problematic if the IP address translations occur after the IPsec AH services are applied.

If ESP is used, the encryption and authentication protection is afforded only to the tunneled packet, not to the "outer" IP header. The authentication value is also sent in the clear because the integrity check value is computed after the encryption process has taken place.

Security Associations

The concept of a security association (SA) is fundamental to IPsec. An SA is a relationship between two or more entities that describes how the entities will use security services to communicate securely. The SA includes the following:

- The ESP encryption algorithm and key(s)
- The AH authentication algorithm and key
- A shared session key
- Mode, tunnel or transport
- SA source address
- SA lifetime

Because an SA is unidirectional, two SAs (one in each direction) are required to secure typical, bidirectional communication between two entities. The security services associated with an SA can be used for AH or ESP, but not for both. If both AH and ESP protection is applied to a traffic stream, two (or more) SAs are created for each direction to protect the traffic stream.

The SA is uniquely identified by a randomly chosen unique number called the *security parameter index* (SPI), the protocol (AH or ESP), and the destination IP address . SAs can be manually configured, but it is more common and efficient to use Internet Key Exchange (IKE), the key management protocol, to create the SAs.

The concept of selectors is used to define when to create a SA and what the SA will be used for. It classifies the type of traffic requiring IPsec protection and the kind of protection to be applied. Among the elements a selector can contain to identify a particular traffic flow are the following:

- **Source IP address**—This can be a specific host, address range (that is, subnet), or a wildcard, which is typically used when the security policy is the same for all packets.
- **Destination IP address**—This can be a specific host, address range (that is, subnet), or a wildcard, which is typically used when the security policy is the same for all packets. For tunnelled packets, the actual destination is different from the tunnel endpoint, and the IP address of the actual destination is used for policy.

- **Protocol**—It is possible to define separate security services on a per-protocol basis, such as TCP or UDP.

- **Upper-layer protocol ports**—It is possible to define separate security services on a per-protocol port number. This can be used for either source or destination ports, or both. For example, one may want to use ESP with NULL encryption and HMAC-SHA1 for routing updates, but use ESP with 3DES and SHA-1 for Telnet and TFTP access to a router.

When a system sends a packet that requires IPsec protection, it uses a security policy database (SPD) to search for a selector that matches the packet criteria and its associated security policy information. If a pre-established SA does not exist, the SA establishment phase begins assuming IKE is being used. If there exists a pre-established SA, the system finds the SA in its database and applies the specified processing and security protocol (AH/ESP), inserting the SPI from the SA into the IPsec header. When the IPsec peer receives the packet, it looks up the SA in its database by destination address, protocol, and SPI, and then processes the packet as required.

NOTE   The order of rules in a security policy database and how vendors use them is extremely important. Typically, the most specific selector match is used. If there is any ambiguity, however, different vendors may handle processing of the packet differently. How a particular vendor uses its SPD should be clarified and understood.

Key Management

IPsec uses cryptographic keys for authentication/integrity and encryption services. Both manual and automatic distribution of keys is supported.

The lowest (but least desirable) level of key management is *manual keying*, in which a person manually configures each system by keying material and SA management data relevant to secure communication with other systems. Manual techniques are practical in small, static environments, but they do not scale well. If the number of sites using IPsec security services is small, and if all the sites come under a single administrative domain, manual key management techniques may be appropriate. Manual key management may also be appropriate when only selected communications must be secured within an organization for a small number of hosts or gateways. Manual management techniques often employ statically configured, symmetric keys, although other options also exist.

The default automated key management protocol selected for use with IPsec is the Internet Key Management Protocol (IKMP), sometimes just referred to as the *Internet Key Exchange* (IKE). IKE authenticates each peer involved in IPsec, negotiates the security policy, and handles the secure exchange of session keys.

NOTE   Although IKE is specified as the public-key-based approach for automatic key management, other automated key distribution techniques can be used. For example, KDC-based systems such as Kerberos and other public key systems such as SKIP can be employed. There exists some confusion with the interchange of terminology between ISAKMP and IKE. This comes mainly from the fact that ISAKMP (RFC 2408) provides a framework for authentication and key exchange, whereas IKE (RFC 2409) is a protocol that specifically defines the negotiation and keying exchange. It may be easier to think of ISAKMP as providing the frame format and IKE filling in the required details.

IKE is a hybrid protocol, combining parts of the following protocols to negotiate and derive keying material for SAs in a secure and authenticated manner. IKE is derived from the following three protocols, as stated in RFC 2409:

- ISAKMP (Internet Security Association and Key Management Protocol), which provides a framework for authentication and key exchange but does not define them. ISAKMP is designed to be key exchange independent; that is, it is designed to support many different key exchanges.

- Oakley, which describes a series of key exchanges called *modes*, details the services provided by each (for example, perfect forward secrecy for keys, identity protection, and authentication).

- SKEME (Secure Key Exchange Mechanism for the Internet) describes a versatile key exchange technique that provides anonymity, repudiability, and quick key refreshment.

IKE creates an authenticated, secure tunnel between two entities and then negotiates the security association for IPsec. This is performed in two phases. Figure 2-33 shows the two-phase IKE protocol approach.

Figure 2-33   *Overview of IKE*

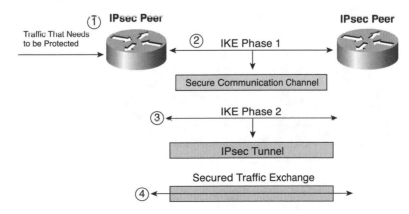

The following steps are carried out:

Step 1 Traffic is generated or received by one of the IPsec peers that is identified to require IPsec protection to its destination.

Step 2 IKE phase 1 uses main mode or aggressive mode, explained in more detail later in the "IKE Phase 1" section, to create an IKE SA between the two IPsec peers, which creates a secure communications channel.

Step 3 IKE phase 2 results in the creation of two IPsec SAs between the two IPsec peers. This pair of unidirectional SAs creates the secure IPsec tunnel.

Step 4 Data starts passing between the IPsec peers over the established secure IPsec tunnel.

Before describing each of these IKE phases in more detail, it's important to consider the ISAKMP message frame formats. There are some specific terms need to be defined first:

- **Domain of interpretation (DOI)**—A DOI defines payload formats, exchange types, and conventions for naming security-relevant information such as security policies or cryptographic algorithms and modes. A DOI identifier is used to interpret the payloads of ISAKMP payloads.

- **Situation**—A situation contains all the security-relevant information that a system considers necessary to decide the security services required to protect the session being negotiated. The situation may include addresses, security classifications, modes of operation (normal versus emergency), and so on.

- **Proposal**—A proposal is a list, in decreasing order of preference, of the protection suites that a system considers acceptable to protect traffic under a given situation.

All ISAKMP messages are carried in a UDP packet with destination port number 500. An ISAKMP message consists of a fixed header followed by a variable number of payloads. Figure 2-34 shows the ISAKMP header.

Figure 2-34 *ISAKMP Header Format*

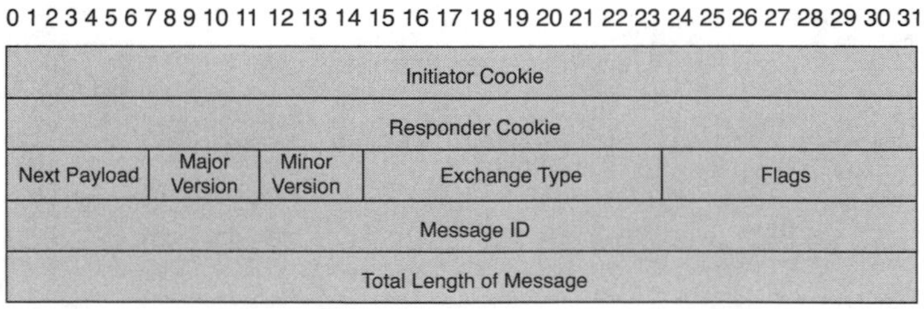

0 1 2 3 4 5 6 7 8 9 10 11 12 13 14 15 16 17 18 19 20 21 22 23 24 25 26 27 28 29 30 31

Initiator Cookie				
Responder Cookie				
Next Payload	Major Version	Minor Version	Exchange Type	Flags
Message ID				
Total Length of Message				

The following fields are included in the header:

- **Initiator Cookie (8 octets)**—Cookie of entity that initiated the SA establishment, SA notification, or SA deletion.

- **Responder Cookie (8 octets)**—Cookie of entity that is responding to an SA establishment request, SA notification, or SA deletion.

- **Next Payload (1 octet)**—Indicates the type of the first payload in the message. Table 2-3 lists the supported payload message types.

Table 2-3   *Next Payload Types*

Next Payload Type	Value	Description
None	0	Indication of last payload in a message.
Security Association	1	Used to negotiate security attributes and to indicate DOI and situation under which negotiation is taking place; a DOI of 0 in phase 1 exchange denotes generic ISAKMP SA, which can be used for any protocol in a phase 2 exchange.
Proposal	2	Specifies the protocol for current negotiation (AH, ESP, and so on) and the number of transforms that will be proposed; also used to send the SPI value.
Transform	3	Consists of a specific security mechanism, or transforms, to be used to secure the communications channel and the SA attributes associated with the specific transform; multiple transform payloads may be specified for a particular proposal.
Key Exchange	4	Used to support a variety of key exchange techniques.
Identification	5	Contains DOI-specific data used to exchange identification information; this information is used for determining the identities of communicating peers and may be used for determining authenticity of information.
Certificate	6	Provides a means to transport certificates or other certificate-related information.
Certificate Request	7	Provides a means to request certificates.
Hash	8	Contains data generated by the hash function selected during the SA establishment exchange; may be used to verify the integrity of the data in an ISAKMP message or for authentication of the negotiating entities.
Signature	9	Contains data generated by the digital signature function selected during the SA establishment exchange; used to verify the integrity of the data in the ISAKMP message, and may be of use for nonrepudiation services.
Nonce	10	Contains random data used to guarantee "freshness" during an exchange and protect against replay attacks.

continues

Table 2-3 *Next Payload Types (Continued)*

Next Payload Type	Value	Description
Notification	11	Used to transmit informational data, such as error conditions, to an ISAKMP peer.
Delete	12	A protocol-specific security association identifier that the sender has removed from its SA database and is, therefore, no longer valid; it is an advisory from the initiator to the responder.
Vendor ID	13	Contains a vendor-defined constant that can be used by vendors to identify and recognize remote instances of their implementations.
Reserved	14–127	Not to be used.
Private Use	128–255	Used for vendor specific use.

- **Major/Minor Version (4 bits each)**—Indicates the major and minor version of the ISAKMP protocol in use.
- **Exchange Type (1 octet)**—Indicates the type of exchange being used for the establishment of SAs and keying material. Exchanges define the payload content and ordering of ISAKMP messages during communications between peers.
- **Flags (1 octet)**—Three flags are specified:
  - Encryption—Indication of whether encryption is used
  - Commit—Used to ensure that encrypted material is not received prior to completion of SA establishment and can also be used to protect against transmission loss over unreliable networks
  - Authentication Only—Intended only for use with an informational exchange using the Notify payload
- **Message ID (4 octets)**—Random value generated by the initiator of the phase 2 negotiation and used to identify protocol state during phase 2 negotiations.
- **Length (4 octets)**—Length of total message (header and payloads) in octets.

NOTE   A "cookie" or anticlogging token (ACT) is used to protect against replay attacks. The two cookie fields in the ISAKMP header are used to uniquely identify ISAKMP SAs. The mechanisms to create the cookies are not specified but a recommendation is made to use a hash over the IP source and destination address, the UDP source and destination ports, a locally generated secret random value, the date, and the time.

The messages themselves are constructed by chaining together a series of payloads. Figure 2-35 shows an example of the ISAKMP message format.

Figure 2-35 *ISAKMP Message Format*

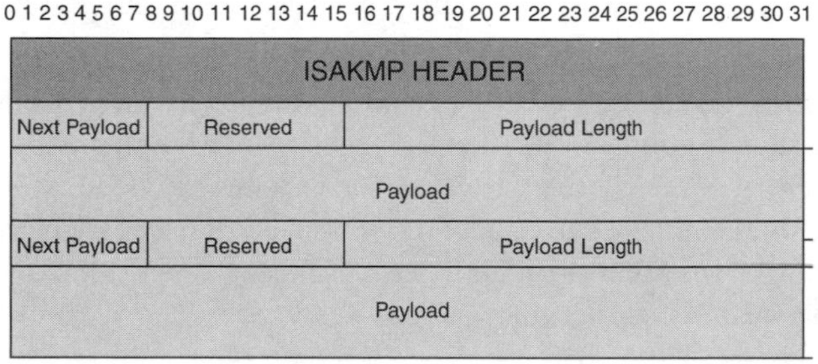

0 1 2 3 4 5 6 7 8 9 10 11 12 13 14 15 16 17 18 19 20 21 22 23 24 25 26 27 28 29 30 31

ISAKMP HEADER		
Next Payload	Reserved	Payload Length
Payload		
Next Payload	Reserved	Payload Length
Payload		

Next Payload: 1 byte; identifier for next payload in message. If it is the last payload, it will be set to 0.

Reserved: 1 byte; set to 0.

Payload Length: 2 bytes; length of payload (in bytes) including the header.

Payload: The actual payload data.

IKE PHASE 1

In an IKE phase 1 exchange, the two ISAKMP peers establish a secure, authenticated channel with which to communicate. This channel is often referred to as an *ISAKMP SA* or also an *IKE SA*. The term IKE SA is used in this text. At the completion of phase 1, only a single SA is established between the two IPsec peers. There are two ways in which this IKE SA can get created: through the use of main mode or aggressive mode, but not both.

NOTE   The terms *SA* and *tunnel* can be confusing and are often misused. In this text, the term *IKE SA* refers to an IKE phase 1 SA that establishes an IKE tunnel. The IKE tunnel is the secure communication channel created upon completion of IKE phase 1. An *IPsec SA* is a unidirectional IKE phase 2 SA. Two IPsec SAs for bidirectional communication will establish an IPsec tunnel by which the IPsec peers will exchange secure data transmissions.

Most implementations use IPsec main mode to establish the IKE SA. Main mode consists of six message types. The following exchanges take place to establish the IKE SA:

- **Negotiate IKE policy (message types 1 and 2).** Information exchanges in these messages contain attributes that will define the security policy to use for the secure communication channel. In both messages, the SA payload is always first, followed by the proposal payload and one or more transform payloads. The transform payloads contain the proposals for the encryption algorithm, hash algorithm, authentication method, and Diffie-Hellman group number. All messages are carried in UDP packets with a destination UDP port number of 500. The UDP header comprises of a header, an SA payload, and one or more proposals. Message type 1 offers many transform proposals, whereas message type 2 contains only a single transform proposal.

- **Perform authenticated DH exchange (message types 3 and 4).** These messages carry out the Diffie-Hellman (DH) exchange. They contain the key exchange payload, which carries the DH public value, and the nonce payload. Message types 3 and 4 also contain the remote peer's public key hash and a hashing algorithm. When these messages are exchanged, both peers use the DH algorithm to create a shared secret and generate three common session keys:

  - **SKEYID_d**—Used to derive non-ISAKMP keying material

  - **SKEYID_a**—Used to provide data integrity and authentication to IKE messages

  - **SKEYID_e**—Used to encrypt IKE messages

- **Protect IKE peer's identity (message types 5 and 6).** Message type 5 allows the responder to authenticate the initiating device. Message type 6 allows the initiator to authenticate the responder. These messages are encrypted using the agreed upon method from message types 1 and 2 and the shared session keys created by message types 3 and 4. IKE supports multiple mechanisms to perform the authenticated DH exchange:

  - **Preshared keys**—The same key is pre-installed on each host. IKE peers authenticate each other by computing and sending a keyed hash of data that includes the preshared key. If the receiving peer can independently create the same hash using its preshared key, it knows that both parties must share the same secret, and therefore, the other party is authenticated. Preshared key authentication in main mode requires that peers use IP addresses as identification, rather than host names. This restriction is not applicable for aggressive mode.

  - **Public key cryptography**—This is sometimes called an *encrypted nonce*. Each party generates a pseudo-random number (a *nonce*) and encrypts it and its ID using the other party's public key. The ability for each party to compute a keyed hash containing the other peer's nonce and ID, decrypted with the local private key, authenticates the parties to each other. This method does not provide nonrepudiation; either side of the exchange could plausibly deny that it took part in the exchange. Currently, only the RSA public key algorithm is supported.

— **Digital signature**—Each device digitally signs a mutually obtainable hash and sends it to the other party. This method is similar to the public key cryptography approach except that it provides nonrepudiation. Currently, both the RSA public key algorithm and the digital signature standard (DSS) are supported.

Figure 2-36 shows the operation of IKE phase 1 main mode.

Figure 2-36   *IKE Phase 1 Main Mode Operation*

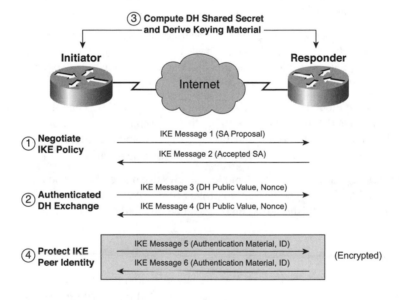

Aggressive mode is rarely used to establish an IKE SA. Aggressive mode uses only three message types. The first two messages negotiate policy, send respective identities, and exchange DH values and any other data necessary for computing keys (depending on which IKE authentication mechanism is chosen). The second message also authenticates the responder. The third message authenticates the initiator and provides proof of participation in the exchange.

The following is an example of aggressive mode phase 1 using preshared key authentication:

1   Initiator sends message type 1. The first message sent by the initiator includes the key payload and nonce payload, which is all the information the responder needs to generate the DH shared secret. This message also includes an ID payload and one or more proposals and transform payloads. Note that there is no opportunity to negotiate the DH group; both parties need to know which group to use or fail IKE phase 1 negotiation. Also, the identity of the initiator is sent in the clear. Upon receipt of message 1, the responder generates the DH shared secret and a hash, hash-R.

2   Responder sends message type 2. The second message, sent by the responder to the initiator, contains the proposal and transform pair to which the responder agreed, the ID payload, the key payload, the nonce payload, and the hash payload, which contains the hash generated by the responder, hash-R. Upon receipt of message 2, the initiator now computes the DH shared secret. It also computes hash-R and compares it to the received hash, which should be equal to validate the responder. Finally, the initiator computes a hash of its own, hash-I.

3   Initiator sends message type 3. The third message is sent by the initiator and contains the hash payload that contains hash-I. Upon receipt of message 3, the responder computes hash-I and compares it to the received hash. If they are equal, the initiator is authenticated and aggressive mode is completed.

Aggressive mode has limited SA negotioation capabilities. The DH group cannot be negotiated and authentication with public key cryptography cannot be negotiated. In addition, none of the communication is encrypted and identities are sent in the clear. It is more common to use main mode for IKE phase 1 negotiation.

The result of a successful main mode or aggressive mode phase produce three authenticated keys and an agreed upon policy to protect further communication. After the IKE tunnel is successfully established, IKE phase 2 can be initiated to establish the IPsec tunnel.

IKE PHASE 2

In phase 2 of the IKE process, SAs are negotiated on behalf of services such as IPsec AH or ESP. In addition, new shared keys are generated for encrypting across the IPsec tunnel. These IPsec shared keys can be derived by using a new DH exchange or by refreshing the shared secret derived from the IKE phase 1 DH exchange by hashing it with a nonce. The first method is slower but provides greater security through perfect forward secrecy. Perfect forward secrecy (PFS) is a property where the compromise of a single key will not compromise subsequent future keys. When used, it forces the IPsec peers to use an additional payload that contain the DH public values during the quick mode exchange. Because there is no mechanism to negotiate a DH group in quick mode, however, the appropriate group must be assumed on both ends for PFS to occur.

NOTE   Diffie-Hellman groups are sometimes referred to as *MODP groups* in configurations because that's what they are referred to in the standard. Two MODP groups are required to be implemented, group 1 and 2. MODP group 2 has a larger prime and is more secure but the trade-off is that it takes more computing cycles to compute the DH shared secret.

IKE phase 2 uses quick mode to establish the IPsec tunnel. Either peer can initiate the phase 2 exchange. All messages in quick mode are encrypted using the encryption key derived from the phase 1 exchange. All messages are authenticated using the hash payload, which must be the first payload following the ISAKMP header. The hashes are computed over the entire ISAKMP payload (including message ID, port, and protocol, but excluding the generic header).

Quick mode has three different message exchanges. Message 1 from initiator to responder includes the following payloads: hash, SA, proposals and transforms, key exchange and nonce (for requesting PFS), and ID. The ID payload contains the identities on whose behalf the initiator does the negotiation (that is, the selector parameters).

When receiving message 1, the responder verifies the hash to ensure integrity/authentication of the received message. It also looks at the IDs offered by the initiator and compares them to its own policy database to ensure validity. Assuming correct verification, it then replies with message 2, which contains the following payloads: hash, SA, proposal and transform (which contain the acceptable values), key payload and nonce (if PFS is used), and ID.

The initiator verifies the hash sent in message 2 to ensure integrity/authentication of the received message. At this time, both peers have the information needed to create new IPsec session keys. Two session keys are generated by both the responder and the initiator, one for each direction of traffic. Remember that an IPsec SA consists of two unidirectional SAs.

Message 3 is the final message sent by the initiator and consists of the hash payload. The hash included is the hash of the latest two nonces that were sent and, when verified by the responder, acts an integrity/authentication check to complete the IPsec tunnel establishment.

NOTE   The responder can also send a message to the initiator similar to message 3, but it is not a requirement in the specification. Also, computing the new session keys may happen after the third (and possibly fourth) messages are sent to ensure against replay attacks.

Figure 2-37 shows the operation of IKE phase 2 quick mode.

Figure 2-37 *IKE Phase 2 Quick Mode Operation*

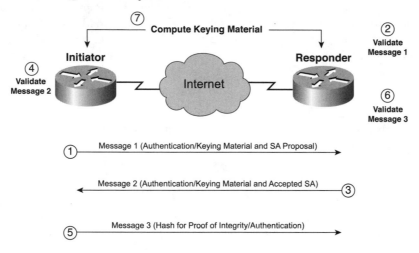

Phase 2 is also used to send reliable and authenticated informational messages.

IKE Extensions

IKE is an extensible protocol that allows new payloads to be easily added to a new message or new exchanges to be defined. Most of the extensions that have been added to IKE are primarily to improve on inefficiencies when it comes to remote access solutions—specifically, to add support for legacy authentication mechanisms to allow for user authentication (as opposed to device authentication) and to add support for variable addressing environments where the IPsec client may have a dynamic IP address or be afflicted by NAT/Port Address Translation (PAT). Because none of the following are proposed standards and it is unclear what their official standard status will be, only a general description of operation is provided. (Readers interested in more specific detail are encouraged to follow the work in the IPsec working group at http://ietf.org/html.charters/ipsec-charter.html.)

NOTE   NAT and PAT are mechanisms by which a packet's IP addresses or protocol port numbers are modified to be something other than what they originally were. Both are covered in more detail in the Chapter 3 in the "VPN Security" section.

- **Challenge Response Authentication for Cryptographic Keys (CRACK)**—
  CRACK is used with either main mode or aggressive mode. The number of messages exchanged depends on the type of legacy authentication method used. The remote

client needs to express interest in performing CRACK authentication, and the VPN gateway replies with its certificate, which autheticates the virtual private network (VPN) gateway to the remote client. The remote client then uses legacy authentication for IKE authentication, whereas the VPN gateway uses certificate-based authentication.

- **Extended Authentication (xauth)**—Xauth occurs after the completion of IKE phase 1 and uses the attribute payload to exchange the remote client authentication information. It is performed on a per-user basis and typically uses a back-end TACACS+ or RADIUS server for scalability. Legacy authentication mechanisms such as username/password, one-time passwords, and CHAP are supported.

- **Pre-IKE Credential Provisioning Protocol (PIC)**—PIC uses legacy authentication methods to retrieve a certified public key before IKE phase 1 begins. The remote client initiates the establishment of a secure connection using an aggressive mode-like exhange. The VPN gateway responds and initiates EAP, which is the protocol used for authentication requests/responses. The remote client requests credentials from the VPN gateway, which in turn responds with its credentials if authentication is successful. This is now followed by the IKE phase 1 exchange, where certificate-based authentication is used to establish IKE authentication.

- **Mode configuration (sometimes called *config mode*)**—Mode configuration is used to allow an IP address to be assigned to a remote client. It occurs after xauth and allows the remote client to request a number of parameters from the VPN gateway (IP address, DNS server address, and so on). The client uses two addresses; the one from the VPN gateway is the source address for packets it inserts into the IPsec tunnel, and the one from the ISP is the source for the tunnel itself.

- **DHCP configuration**—Another mechanism to solve the remote client address problem is to have the gateway peer act as a Dynamic Host Configuration Protocol (DHCP) relay. For this method, an IKE main mode or aggressive mode SA would first be established between the remote client and gateway peer. This is followed by the remote client establishing a DHCP tunnel quick mode IPsec SA to the gateway peer. DHCP messages are exchanged by the remote client and the DHCP server using the gateway as a DHCP relay. After the address is obtained, the client does a quick mode exchange with the peer gateway to establish the IPsec tunnel using its DHCP address. Note that the gateway needs to snoop the DHCP packet to determine the IP address assigned to the client.

- **Dead peer detection**—In cases where an IPsec peer is disconnected without sending a delete notification payload (such as in a peer's system crash or network problems), the dead peer detection acts as a mechanism to detect inactive peers. This is often desirable for quick failover or to recover lost resources. A vendor ID payload is added to the IKE main mode exchange to signify support of this mechanism. A time metric is included to specify the time interval to wait before instigating a notify payload message to see whether a peer is alive. If there is a period of inactivity and the time specified has been exceeded, a peer wanting to send traffic sends a notify message to the other peer to see whether it is still alive. If it is alive, the peer achnowledges the notify payload by sending one of its own. Note that the idle time interval is not a negotiable variable and is implementation-specific.

- **NAT traversal**—NAT is widely deployed in many remote access scenarios and as such there needed to be some way to make IKE work in NAT environments. NAT traversal specifies how to detect the use of NAT and how to handle addressing in those environments. The NAT traversal capability of the remote host is determined by an exchange of vendor ID payloads.

To detect whether the IP address or the port number changes along the path, the peers send the hashes of source/destination IP address and source/destination port numbers to each other. When both ends calculate those hashes and the hashes do not match, it is a good indication that NAT is being used. The hashes are sent as a series of NAT-D (NAT discovery) payloads. Each payload contains one hash, so in the case of multiple hashes, multiple NAT-D payloads are sent. In a normal case, there are only two NAT-D payloads. The NAT-D payloads are included in messages 3 and 4 in main mode and in messages 2 and 3 in aggressive mode. The payload type for the NAT discovery payload is 15.

In main mode, if NAT is detected, the initiator sets both UDP source and destination ports to 4500 for the ID payload. All subsequent packets sent to this peer (including informational notifications) have to be sent on port 4500. If the initiator is behind a NAT, the NAT device maps UDP (4500,4500) to UDP (Y,4500). The responder has to respond with all subsequent IKE packets to this peer using UDP (4500,Y). Aggressive mode uses the same principle.

After IKE phase 1, both ends know whether there is a NAT present between the peers. The decision as to whether to use NAT traversal is negotiated inside the SA payloads of the quick mode. The negotiation of the NAT traversal happens by adding the following two new encapsulation modes:

— UDP-encapsulated tunnel (type 3)

— UDP-encapsulated transport (type 4)

The original IP source and destination addresses are used in transport mode to incrementally update the TCP/IP checksums so that they will match after the NAT transform. (The NAT device cannot do this, because the TCP/IP checksum is inside the UDP-encapsulated IPsec packet.) These original addresses are sent in quick mode using NAT-OA (NAT original address) payloads, which have a type value of 16. The NAT-OA payloads are sent in message 1 and message 2 of quick mode if UDP-encapsulated transport mode is requested.

The use of NAT traversal negates the value of authentication mechanisms based on IP addresses. For IKE main mode, this means that preshared key authentication cannot be used without group shared keys for everybody behind the NAT box, creating a large security risk. If using main mode, another authentication mechanism should be used.

NOTE   Some IPsec-aware NAT devices have deployed proprietary solutions other than NAT traversal. These may not change the IKE source port 500 even if there are multiple clients behind the NAT. A common alternative method is to use IKE cookies to demultiplex traffic instead of using the source port.

For NAT traversal to work with ESP traffic, an additional specification was written. AH was originally also included but was omitted in later versions due to its limited use in actual deployments. The "UDP Encapsulation of IPsec Packets" specification defines methods to encapsulate and decapsulate IPsec ESP packets inside UDP packets. The UDP port numbers are the same as used by IKE traffic. Figure 2-38 shows both transport mode and tunnel mode encapsulation.

Figure 2-38   *UDP Encapsulation of IPsec ESP Packets*

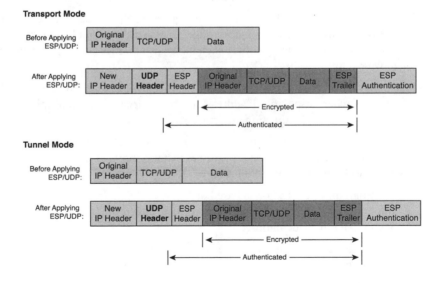

IKE's Future

In the past few years, extensive work has been done to create a successor to the original IKE specification; this successor is named *IKEv2*. IKEv2 intends to preserves most of the features of the original IKE, including identity hiding, PFS, two phases, and cryptographic negotiation, while greatly redesigning the protocol for efficiency, security, robustness, and flexibility. At the time of this writing, the work is still in progress, but the main points that have so far been agreed upon are as follows:

- An initial handshake exchange allows peers to negotiate cryptographic algorithms, mutually authenticate, and establish a session key, creating an IKE SA. This usually consists of two request/response pairs where the first pair negotiates cryptographic algorithms and does a Diffie-Hellman exchange, and the second pair is encrypted and integrity-protected with keys based on the Diffie-Hellman exchange. In the second pair of messages, the peers also send their identities and prove it by using an integrity check based on the secret associated with their identity (private key or shared secret key) and the contents of the first pair of messages in the exchange.

- A first IPsec SA is established during the initial IKE SA creation. The IPsec SAs are referred to as *child SAs*. The exchange to establish a child SA consists of an optional Diffie-Hellman exchange (for PFS), nonces (to establish unique keys), and negotiation of traffic selector values, which indicate what addresses, ports, and protocol types are to be transmitted over that child SA.

- After the initial handshake, additional requests can be initiated by either peer and consist of either informational messages or requests to establish another child SA. Informational messages include such things as null messages for detecting peer aliveness and deletion of SAs.

- An initiator can specify a responder's identity. This enables the use of multiple services where a specific IP address may be associated with multiple identities, each with different authentication credentials.

- Denial-of-service prevention is incorporated using a "stateless cookie." The mechanism deploys two extra messages that are short enough to avoid fragmentation and avoids an attack based on fragmentation.

- Cryptographic negotiation is based on "suites." All parameters are encoded into a single suite number, and negotiation consists of offering one or more suites and having the other side choose.

- Addressing assignment issues are solved by incorporating the mode configuration extension into IKEv2.

- NAT traversal is incorporated into IKEv2 and is based on the NAT traversal extensions for the original IKE.

- Identities hiding from passive attackers is supported for both parties. (This assumes that identities are not based on fixed IP addresses; if they are based on fixed IP addresses, the identity is not hidden.)

- Authentication mechanisms supported are preshared keys and public signature keys. Because with the latter one side has to reveal its identity first, if it is communicating with an active attacker, it will reveal its identity to that attacker. IKEv2 has the initiator reveal its identity first.

- Legacy authentication mechanisms are supported through the use of EAP.

IPsec is designed to protect IP packets from modification or snooping and is an important technology for securing traffic traversing the network. It has been widely implemented and is a vital component in deploying virtual private networks.

Link-Layer Security Technologies

This section discusses security technologies created to address link-layer protocols. Some of the authentication technologies discussed earlier in this chapter are integrated into these solutions. Link-layer security technologies deal primarily with tunnels. *Virtual private dialup networks* (VPDNs) enable large enterprises to extend their private networks across dialup lines. Instead of incurring large costs to ensure security by dialing in to a campus site from anywhere in the world or lessening security by dialing in locally and using the Internet as the transport to get to the main enterprise campus, link-layer tunneling technologies enable remote sites and users to securely connect to the enterprise infrastructure using local dialup access to the Internet.

Three similar protocols currently exist to accomplish this goal:

- The Layer 2 Forwarding (L2F) protocol
- The Point-to-Point Tunneling Protocol (PPTP)
- The Layer 2 Tunneling Protocol (L2TP)

The Layer 2 Forwarding Protocol

The Layer 2 Forwarding (L2F) protocol was created by Cisco Systems. Although it is being replaced by L2TP, it is discussed here because it is still used in some environments. L2F permits the tunneling of the link layer—that is, High-Level Data Link Control (HDLC), async HDLC, or Serial Line Internet Protocol (SLIP) frames—of higher-level protocols. Figure 2-39 shows the format of the tunneled packet.

Figure 2-39 *The Format of a Tunneled Packet*

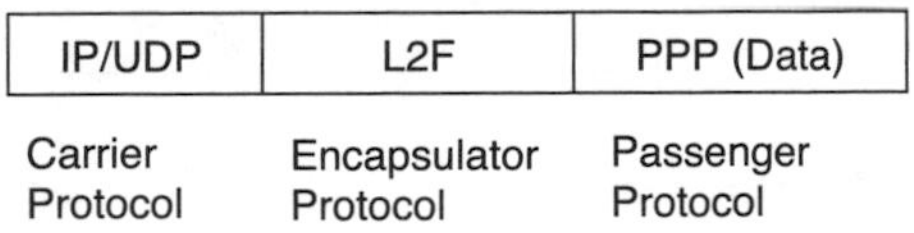

IP/UDP	L2F	PPP (Data)
Carrier Protocol	Encapsulator Protocol	Passenger Protocol

Using such tunnels, it is possible to decouple the location of the initial dialup server from the location at which the dialup protocol connection is terminated and access to the network is provided. These tunnels also enable applications that require support for privately addressed IP, IPX, and AppleTalk dialup using SLIP/PPP across the existing Internet infrastructure.

A Sample Scenario

Figure 2-40 shows a sample virtual dialup scenario for L2F. The following steps are carried out:

Step 1 The remote user initiates a PPP connection to an ISP over the Public Switched Telephone Network (PSTN) (or natively over ISDN).

Step 2 The NAS accepts the connection, and the PPP link is established.

Step 3 The ISP authenticates the end system or user using CHAP or PAP.

NOTE If permitted by the organization's security policy, the authorization of the dial-in user at the NAS can be performed only on a domain name within the Username field and not on every individual username. This setup can substantially reduce the size of the authorization database. If a virtual dialup service is not required, traditional access to the Internet may be provided by the NAS. All address assignment and authentication would be performed locally by the ISP in this situation.

Step 4 NAS initiates the L2F tunnel to the desired corporate gateway.

Step 5 The corporate gateway authenticates the remote user and either accepts or rejects the tunnel.

NOTE The initial setup notification may include the authentication information required to allow the corporate gateway to authenticate the user and decide to accept or decline the connection. In the case of CHAP, the setup packet includes the challenge, username, and raw password; for PAP, the setup packet includes the username and cleartext password. The corporate gateway can be configured to use this information to complete its authentication, avoiding an additional cycle of authentication.

NOTE

Note also that the authentication takes place at the corporate customer, allowing the corporation to impose its own security and corporate policy on the remote users accessing its network. In this way, the organization does not have to fully trust the authentication performed by the ISP.

Step 6 The corporate gateway confirms acceptance of the call and L2F tunnel.

NOTE

If the corporate gateway accepts the connection, it creates a virtual interface for PPP in a manner analogous to what it would use for a direct-dialed connection. With this virtual interface in place, link-layer frames can now pass over this tunnel in both directions. Frames from the remote user are received at the NAS, stripped of any link framing or transparency bytes, encapsulated in L2F, and forwarded over the appropriate tunnel.

The corporate gateway accepts these frames, strips L2F, and processes them as normal incoming frames for the appropriate interface and protocol. The virtual interface behaves very much like a hardware interface, except that the hardware in this case is physically located at the ISP NAS. The reverse traffic direction behaves analogously, with the corporate gateway encapsulating the packet in L2F, and the NAS stripping L2F encapsulation before transmitting it out the physical interface to the remote user.

Step 7 The corporate gateway exchanges PPP negotiations with the remote user. Because the remote user has become just another dialup client of the corporate gateway access server, client connectivity can now be managed using traditional mechanisms with respect to further authorization, address negotiation, protocol access, accounting, and filtering.

Step 8 End-to-end data is tunneled between the remote user and the corporate gateway.

Figure 2-40 *A Sample Scenario for L2F*

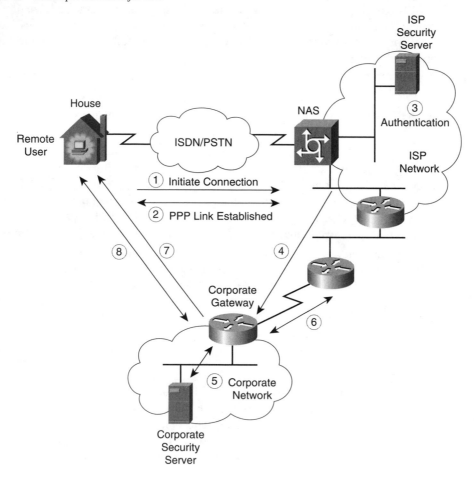

The Point-to-Point Tunneling Protocol

The Point-to-Point Tunneling Protocol (PPTP) was initiated by Microsoft and after additional vendor input became an informational standard in the IETF, RFC 2637. It is a client/server architecture that allows PPP to be tunneled through an IP network and decouples functions that exist in current NASs.

Decoupling Traditional NAS Functionality

Traditionally, the following functions are implemented by a NAS:

- Providing a physical native interface to PSTN or ISDN networks and controlling external modems or terminal adapters
- Providing the logical termination of a PPP LCP session
- Participating in PPP authentication protocols
- Providing channel aggregation and bundle management for PPP multilink protocol
- Performing the logical termination of various PPP network control protocols (NCPs)
- Performing multiprotocol routing and bridging between NAS interfaces

PPTP divides these functions between two entities:

- **PPTP access concentrator (PAC)**—This device is attached to one or more PSTN or ISDN lines capable of PPP operation and of handling the PPTP protocol.
- **PPTP network server (PNS)**—This device handles the server side of the PPTP protocol. Because PPTP relies completely on TCP/IP and is independent of the interface hardware, the PNS may use any combination of IP interface hardware, including LAN and WAN devices.

The PAC is responsible for providing the physical interface to the PSTN and ISDN networks and for providing the logical termination for PPP LCP sessions. Participation in PPP authentication protocols can be part of either the PAC or the PNS. The PNS is responsible for channel aggregation, logical termination of PPP NCPs, and multiprotocol routing and bridging between NAS interfaces. PPTP is the protocol used to carry PPP protocol data units (PDUs) between the PAC and PNS; in addition, call control and management issues are addressed by PPTP.

Protocol Overview

PPTP is connection-oriented. The PNS and PAC maintain connection information for each user attached to a PAC. A session is created when an end-to-end PPP connection is attempted between a dialup user and the PNS. The datagrams related to a session are sent over the tunnel between the PAC and the PNS.

A tunnel is defined by a PNS-PAC pair. The tunnel carries PPP datagrams between the PAC and the PNS. Many sessions are multiplexed on a single tunnel. A control connection operating over TCP manages the establishment, release, and maintenance of sessions and of the tunnel itself.

There are two parallel components of PPTP, as described in the following sections:

- A *control connection* between each PAC-PNS pair operating over TCP.
- An *IP tunnel* operating between the same PAC-PNS pair, which is used to transport Generic Routing Encapsulation (GRE)-encapsulated PPP packets for user sessions between the pair.

The Control Connection

A *control connection* must be established between the PNS-PAC pair before PPP tunneling can occur between them. The control connection is a standard TCP session over which PPTP call control and management information is passed. The TCP session for the control connection is established by initiating a TCP connection to port 1723. The control session is logically associated with, but separate from, the sessions being tunneled through a PPTP tunnel.

The first set of control connection messages is used to maintain the control connection itself. The control connection is initiated by either the PNS or the PAC after they establish the underlying TCP connection. The control connection is responsible for the establishment, management, and release of sessions carried through the tunnel. It is the means by which a PNS is notified of an incoming call at an associated PAC, as well as the means by which a PAC is instructed to place an outgoing dial call. After the control connection is established, the PAC or PNS may initiate sessions by requesting outbound calls or by responding to inbound requests. The control connection itself is maintained by keepalive echo messages.

The IP Tunnel Using GRE

PPTP requires the establishment of a tunnel for each communicating PNS-PAC pair. This tunnel is used to carry all user session PPP packets for sessions involving a given PNS-PAC pair. PPTP uses an extended version of to carry user PPP packets. These enhancements allow for low-level congestion and flow control to be provided on the tunnels used to carry user data between PAC and PNS. Many sessions are multiplexed on a single tunnel. A control connection operating over TCP controls the establishment, release, and maintenance of sessions and of the tunnel itself.

The user data carried by the PPTP protocol is PPP data packets. PPP packets are carried between the PAC and the PNS, encapsulated in GRE packets, which in turn are carried over IP. The encapsulated PPP packets are essentially PPP data packets without any media-specific framing elements.

Figure 2-41 shows the general packet structure that is transmitted over the tunnels between a PAC and a PNS.

Figure 2-41   *The PPTP Tunneled Packet Structure*

Media Header	IP Header	GRE Header	PPP Packet

The GRE header used in PPTP is modified slightly from that specified in RFC 1701. The main difference is the addition of a new Acknowledgment Number field, used to determine whether a particular GRE packet or set of packets has arrived at the remote end of the tunnel. This acknowledgment capability is not used in conjunction with any retransmission of user data packets. It is used instead to determine the rate at which user data packets are to be transmitted over the tunnel for a given user session. Figure 2-42 shows the format of this GRE header.

Figure 2-42   *The PPTP GRE Header Format*

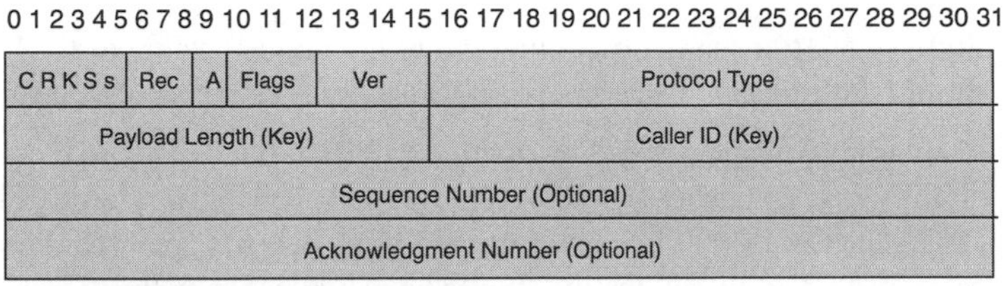

0 1 2 3 4 5 6 7 8 9 10 11 12 13 14 15 16 17 18 19 20 21 22 23 24 25 26 27 28 29 30 31

C R K S s	Rec	A	Flags	Ver	Protocol Type
Payload Length (Key)					Caller ID (Key)
Sequence Number (Optional)					
Acknowledgment Number (Optional)					

C (bit 0): Checksum Present; set to 0.
R (bit 1): Routing Present; set to 0.
K (bit 2): Key Present; set to 1.
S (bit 3): Sequence Number Present. Set to 1 if a data packet is present, otherwise set to 0.
S (bit 4): Strict source route present; set to 0.
Recur (bits 5-7): Recursion control; set to 0.
A (bit 8): Ack sequence number present. Set to 1 if packet contains Ack number to be used for acknowledging previously transmitted data.
Flags (bits 9-12): Must be set to 0.
Ver (bits 13-15): Must contain 1 (denotes modified GRE).
Protocol Type: Set to hex 880B.
Key: Use of the Key field is up to the implementation. PPTP uses 2 octets for payload length (excluding GRE header) and 2 octets for Caller ID.
Sequence Number: Sequence number of the payload.
Acknowledgment Number: Sequence number of the highest numbered GRE packet received by the sending peer for this user session.

NOTE   There currently exist three different GRE specifications in the IETF. RFC 2784 obsoleted RFC 1701, although both implementations are deployed in a variety of networks. There is also a newer version, RFC 2890, which vendors are starting to implement.

The GRE packets forming the tunnel itself are not cryptographically protected and therefore offer no security for the PPTP packets. PPTP control channel messages are neither authenticated nor integrity protected. The security of user data passed over the tunneled PPP connection is addressed by PPP, as is authentication of the PPP peers.

The Layer 2 Tunneling Protocol

Because both L2F and PPTP provide similar functionality, Cisco and Microsoft, along with other vendors, have collaborated on a single standard which is now called *Layer 2 Tunneling Protocol* (L2TP). This protocol is specified in RFC 2661 and is commonly referred to as *L2TPv2*. L2TP has since been adopted for tunneling a number of other layer protocols, and work is in progress to specify a new version of the protocol, L2TPv3, which will provide greater modularity and a clearer separation from PPP. Because the L2TPv3 work is still in progress, however, this discussion focuses on the operational aspects of L2TPv2.

L2TP addresses the following end-user requirements:

- End-system transparency. Neither the remote end system nor the home site hosts should require any special software to use this service in a secure manner.

- Authentication as provided by the dialup PPP CHAP, PAP, EAP, or through other dialogs boxes (such as a textual exchange on V.120 before starting PPP). This includes TACACS+ and RADIUS solutions and also supports smart cards and one-time passwords. The authentication should be manageable by the user independently of the ISP.

- Addressing should be as manageable as dedicated dialup solutions. The address should be assigned by the home site and not by the ISP.

- Authorization should be managed by the home site as it would be in a direct dialup solution.

- Accounting should be performed both by the ISP (for billing purposes) and by the user (for chargeback and auditing purposes).

Protocol Overview

In a way similar to PPTP, L2TP defines two entities:

- **L2TP access concentrator (LAC)**—This device is attached to the switched network fabric (for example, PSTN or ISDN) or co-located with a PPP end system capable of handling L2TP. The LAC only has to implement the media over which L2TP is to operate to pass traffic to one or more LNSs. The LAC may tunnel any protocol carried within PPP. The LAC is the initiator of incoming calls and the receiver of outgoing calls.

- **L2TP network server (LNS)**—This server operates on any platform capable of PPP termination. The LNS handles the server side of the L2TP protocol. Because L2TP relies on only the single media over which L2TP tunnels arrive, the LNS may have only a single LAN or WAN interface yet be able to terminate calls arriving at any LAC's full range of PPP interfaces (async, synchronous ISDN, V.120, and so on). The LNS is the initiator of outgoing calls and the receiver of incoming calls.

To be able to initiate an incoming or outgoing call, an end-to-end PPP connection must first be established between a remote system and the LNS, followed by an exchange of control messages between the LAC-LNS pair to establish the corresponding control connection. When the control connection is in place, sessions can be established as triggered by incoming or outgoing call requests. The sessions carry the L2TP payload packets, which are used to transport L2TP-encapsulated PPP packets between the LAC-LNS pair.

NOTE   For this section, the term *tunnel* is defined as consisting of a control connection and zero or more L2TP sessions. The tunnel carries encapsulated PPP datagrams and control messages between the LAC and the LNS.

Both the control messages and payload packets use the same L2TP header format, as shown in Figure 2-43.

Figure 2-43   *The L2TP Header Format*

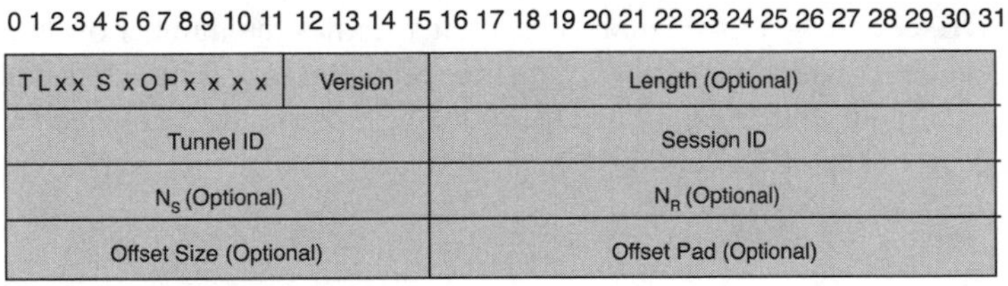

0 1 2 3 4 5 6 7 8 9 10 11 12 13 14 15 16 17 18 19 20 21 22 23 24 25 26 27 28 29 30 31

T L x x S x O P x x x x	Version	Length (Optional)
Tunnel ID		Session ID
N_S (Optional)		N_R (Optional)
Offset Size (Optional)		Offset Pad (Optional)

The fields for the header are as follows:

- **Type (T)**—Indicates the type of message. It is set to 0 for a data message and 1 for a control message.
- **Length (L)**—Set to 1 if the Length field is present; must be 1 for a control message.
- **x bits**—These are reserved for future extensions and are set to 0 on outgoing messages and ignored on incoming messages.
- **Sequence (S)**—If it is set to 1, the Ns and Nr fields are present; must be set to 1 for control messages.
- **Offset (O)**—If it is set to 1, the Offset Size field is present; must be set to 0 for control messages.
- **Priority (P)**—If it is set to 1, this data message should receive preferential treatment in its local queuing and transmission; it is only for use with data messages. The P bit must be set to 0 for all control messages.
- **Version**—Indicates the version of the L2TP data message header.
- **Length**—Indicates the total length of the message in bytes.

- **Tunnel ID**—Indicates the identifier for the control connection. L2TP tunnels are named by identifiers that have local significance only; the tunnel ID in each message is that of the intended recipient, not the sender. Tunnel IDs are selected and exchanged as assigned tunnel ID AVPs (address-value pairs) during the creation of a tunnel.

- **Session ID**—Indicates the identifier for a session within a tunnel; L2TP sessions are named by identifiers that have local significance only. Session ID in each message is that of the intended recipient, not the sender. Session IDs are selected and exchanged as assigned session ID AVPs during the creation of a session.

- **Ns**—Indicates the sequence number for this data or control message, beginning at 0 and incrementing for each message sent.

- **Nr**—Indicates the sequence number expected in the next control message to be received; in data messages, Nr is reserved and, if present (as indicated by the S bit), is ignored upon receipt.

- **Offset Size**—If this field is present, it specifies the number of bytes past the L2TP header at which the payload data is expected to start. The actual data within the offset padding is undefined. If the Offset field is present, the L2TP header ends after the last octet of the offset padding.

The Control Connection

The *control connection* is the initial connection that must be established between a LAC and LNS before sessions can be brought up. Establishment of the control connection includes securing the identity of the peer, as well as identifying the peer's L2TP version, framing, bearer capabilities, and so on. The control messages are responsible for the establishment, management, and release of call sessions, as well as the status of the tunnel itself. Control messages are the means by which an LNS is notified of an incoming call at an associated LAC, as well as the means by which a LAC is instructed to place an outgoing call.

The control connection can be initiated by either the LNS or the LAC. During this phase, an optional CHAP-like mechanism is used for tunnel authentication. To participate in the authentication, a single shared secret must exist between the LAC and LNS.

Following the creating of the control channel, the LNS and LAC configure the tunnel parameters. This is done through a series of AVPs. The control messages include a mechanism to indicate to the receiving peer whether the contents of the AVP are encrypted or present in cleartext. This is accomplished through the combination of an MD5 hash and the XOR function. This feature is useful for hiding sensitive control message data such as user passwords or user IDs. It requires the existence of a shared secret between the LAC and LNS. The shared secret is the same secret used for tunnel authentication.

When the control message exchange is complete, either the LAC may initiate sessions by indicating inbound requests, or the LNS can request outbound calls. If both ends of the tunnel have the capability to act as an LAC and LNS concurrently, nothing prohibits the establishment of incoming or outgoing calls from both sides of the same tunnel.

A keepalive mechanism is employed by L2TP through the use of hello packets to differentiate tunnel outages from extended periods of no control or data activity on a tunnel.

The Data Channel

After a successful L2TP control connection setup, individual sessions can be created to carry user-session PPP packets for sessions involving a given LNS-LAC pair. A session can be established by either a LAC or an LNS. Unlike control connection establishment, session establishment is directional with respect to the LAC and LNS. The LAC requests the LNS to accept a session for an incoming call, and the LNS requests the LAC to accept a session for placing an outgoing call. The Call ID field in the L2TP header indicates the session to which a particular PPP packet belongs. In this manner, PPP packets are multiplexed and demultiplexed over a single tunnel between a given LNS-LAC pair. The Call ID field value is established during the exchange of call setup control messages.

When tunnel establishment is complete, PPP frames from the remote system are received at the LAC, stripped of cyclic redundancy check (CRC), link framing, and transparency bytes, encapsulated in L2TP, and forwarded over the appropriate tunnel. The LNS receives the L2TP packet and processes the encapsulated PPP frame as if it were received on a local PPP interface.

Unlike the L2TP control channel, the L2TP data channel does not use sequence numbers to retransmit lost data messages. Rather, data messages may use sequence numbers to detect lost packets and/or restore the original sequence of packets that may have been reordered during transport.

It is legal for multiple session tunnels to exist between a given LNS-LAC pair. With multiple tunnels, each tunnel can be used for a single user session, and the tunnel media (an SVC, for instance) can have specific quality of service (QoS) attributes dedicated to a given user. L2TP provides a tunnel identifier so that individual tunnels can be identified, even when arriving from a single source LAC or LNS.

L2TP uses the well-known UDP port 1701. The entire L2TP packet, including payload and L2TP header, is sent within a UDP datagram. The initiator of an L2TP tunnel picks an available source UDP port and sends to the desired destination at port 1701. The recipient picks a free port on its own system (which may or may not be port 1701) and sends its reply to the initiator's UDP port, setting its own UDP source port to the free port it found.

It is legal for a peer's IP address or UDP port used for a given tunnel to change over the life of a connection (for example, when a peer with multiple IP interfaces responds to a network topology change). Responses should reflect the last source IP address and the UDP port for that tunnel ID.

A Sample Scenario

Figure 2-44 shows a sample L2TP scenario of a generic Internet arrangement with PSTN
access (that is, async PPP using modems) and ISDN access (synchronous PPP access).
Remote users (either async or ISDN PPP) access the corporate LAN as if they had dialed
in to the LNS, although their physical dialup is through the ISP NAS (acting as the LAC).

Figure 2-44   *A Sample L2TP Scenario*

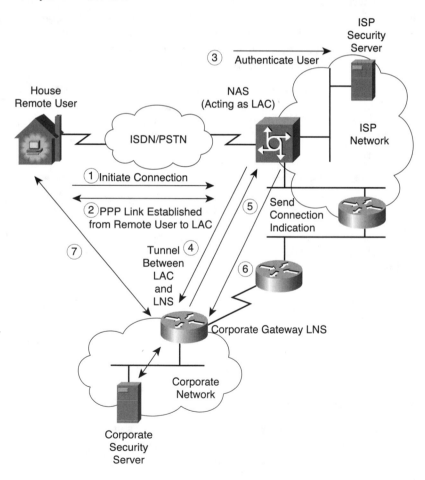

The steps needed to complete the PPP tunnel are as follows:

Step 1   The remote user initiates a PPP connection to an ISP using either the PSTN or ISDN.

Step 2   The LAC accepts the connection, and the PPP link is established. L2TP also permits the LAC to check with an LNS after call indication before accepting the call. This is useful when Dialed Number Information String (DNIS), an indication to the receiver of a call as to what phone number the caller used to reach it or Calling Line Identification (CLID) information is available in the incoming call notification.

Step 3   The ISP can now undertake a partial authentication of the end system or user. Only the Username field is interpreted to determine whether the user requires a virtual dialup service. Alternatively, the ISP may have already determined the target LNS from DNIS. If the LNS is willing to accept tunnel creation without any authentication of the caller, the LAC may tunnel the PPP connection without ever having communicated with the remote user.

Step 4   If no tunnel connection currently exists to the desired LNS, one is initiated. L2TP is designed to be largely insulated from the details of the media over which the tunnel is established; L2TP requires only that the tunnel media provide packet-oriented, point-to-point connectivity. Obvious examples of such media are UDP, Frame Relay PVCs, and X.25 VCs.

Step 5   After the tunnel exists, an unused slot within the tunnel (a call ID), is allocated and a connect indication is sent to notify the LNS of this new dialup session. The LNS either accepts the connection or rejects it.

Step 6   If the LNS accepts the connection, it creates a virtual interface for PPP in a manner analogous to what it would use for a direct-dialed connection. With this virtual interface in place, link-layer frames can now pass through the tunnel in both directions. Frames from the remote user are received at the point of presence (POP); stripped of CRC, link framing, and transparency bytes; encapsulated in L2TP; and forwarded over the appropriate tunnel.

The LNS accepts these frames, strips L2TP, and processes them as normal incoming frames for the appropriate interface and protocol. The virtual interface behaves very much like a hardware interface, with the exception that the hardware in this case is physically located at the ISP POP. The other direction behaves analogously, with the LNS encapsulating the packet in L2TP, and the LAC stripping L2TP before transmitting it out the physical interface to the remote user.

Step 7 At this point, the connectivity is a point-to-point PPP session whose endpoints are the remote user's networking application on one end and the termination of this connectivity into the LNS's PPP support on the other. Because the remote user has become just another dialup client of the LNS, client connectivity can now be managed using traditional mechanisms with respect to further authorization, protocol access, and packet filtering.

L2TP is inherently a link-layer tunneling protocol and has no capability to provide security services to the data being sent across the L2TP tunnel. Although the tunnel endpoints may optionally authenticate each other, the mechanism is not designed to provide an authentication beyond tunnel establishment. Securing L2TP requires that the underlying transport make available encryption, integrity, and authentication services for all L2TP traffic. IPsec in transport mode is used to provide the security services for L2TP over IP traffic and has been standardized in the IETF (RFC 3193).

PPPoE

PPP over Ethernet (PPPoE) is defined in RFC 2516 and provides the means to encapsulate PPP packets over the Ethernet link layer. It enables several hosts on a single subnet to be connected to a remote access concentrator via a simple bridging access device. This model is mostly used in ADSL environments to provide access control, billing, and type of service on a per-user, rather than a per-site, basis.

Protocol Overview

PPPoE has two distinct stages: a discovery stage and a PPP session stage. The discovery process identifies the Ethernet MAC address of the remote access concentrator and establishes a unique PPPoE session identifier. Whereas PPP defines a peer-to-peer relationship, the discovery process is inherently a client/server relationship. Multiple access servers may be discovered, but only one can be selected. Upon completion of a successful discovery process, both the client host and the selected access concentrator have the information they will use to build their PPP connection over Ethernet.

The PPP session can now be established. When the PPPoE session begins, PPP data is sent as in any other PPP encapsulation. The PPPoE payload contains a PPP frame that begins with the PPP protocol ID. All Ethernet packets are unicast.

Figure 2-45 shows the PPPoE frame format.

Figure 2-45 *PPPoE Frame Format*

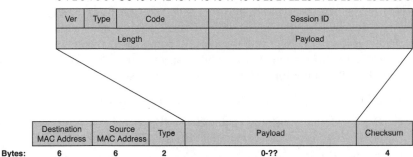

The following fields are defined:

- **Destination MAC Address**—Contains either a unicast Ethernet destination address or the Ethernet broadcast address (0xffffffff). For discovery packets, the value is a unicast or broadcast. For PPP session traffic, this field *must* contain the peer's unicast address as determined from the discovery stage.

- **Source MAC Address**—Contains the Ethernet MAC address of the source device.

- **Type**—Set to either 0x8863 (discovery stage) or 0x8864 (PPP session stage).

- **Version**—Set to 0x1 for the PPPoE specification in RFC 2516.

- **Code**—Used for the discovery and PPP session stages.

- **Session ID**—Set to 0 for discovery packets; for each session, it stays the same (the value assigned in the discovery process).

- **Length**—Indicates the length of the PPPoE payload, excluding the length of the Ethernet or PPPoE headers.

PPPoE is a very simple protocol and only provides a mechanism to tunnel PPP traffic over Ethernet. It does not provide any security services to the traffic that is encapsulated. In addition, PPPoE enables other listeners on the same Ethernet to eavesdrop on the wire and "see" the PPP frames. Therefore, any authentication schemes using cleartext passwords, such as PPP PAP, should be avoided.

Public Key Infrastructure and Distribution Models

Many security protocols rely on public key cryptography to provide services such as confidentiality, data integrity, data origin authentication, and nonrepudiation. The purpose of a Public Key Infrastructure (PKI) is to provide trusted and efficient key and certificate management to support these protocols.

A PKI is defined by the "Internet X.509 Public Key Infrastructure PKIX Roadmap," a work in progress document, as follows:

The set of hardware, software, people, policies, and procedures needed to create, manage, store, distribute, and revoke certificates based on public key cryptography.

A PKI consists of the following five types of components (taken from NIST Special Publication 800-15, "Minimum Interoperability Specification for PKI Components, Version 1," September 1997, by William Burr, Donna Dodson, Noel Nazario, and W. Timothy Polk):

- Certification authorities (CAs) that issue and revoke certificates

- Organizational registration authorities (ORAs) that vouch for the binding between public keys, certificate holder identities, and other attributes

- Certificate holders that are issued certificates and that can sign digital documents

- Clients that validate digital signatures and their certification paths from a known public key of a trusted CA

- Repositories that store and make available certificates and certificate revocation lists (CRLs)

Functions of a PKI

The functions of a PKI can be summarized as follows:

- **Registration**—The process whereby a subject first makes itself known to a CA (directly or through a registration authority [RA]) before that CA issues a certificate or certificates for that subject.

- **Initialization**—The point at which the user or client system gets the values it needs to begin communicating with the PKI. For example, initialization can involve providing the client system with the public key or the certificate of a CA after a client request has been received, or generating the client system's own public/private key pair.

- **Certification**—The process in which a CA issues a certificate for a subject's public key and returns that certificate to the subject (or posts that certificate in a repository).

- **Key pair recovery**—If the CA has generated and issued the key pair, the user's private key can be either backed up by a CA or by a separate key backup system. If a user or his/her employer wants to recover these backed-up key materials, the PKI must provide a system that permits the recovery *without* providing an unacceptable risk of compromise of the private key.

- **Key generation**—Depending on the CA's policy, the private/public key pair can either be generated by the user in his local environment, or be generated by the CA. In the latter case, the key material may be distributed to the user in an encrypted file or on a physical token (such as a smart card or PCMCIA card).

- **Key update**—All key pairs must be updated regularly—that is, replaced with a new key pair—and new certificates must be issued. This happens in two cases: normally, when a key has passed its maximum usable lifetime; and exceptionally, when a key has been compromised and must be replaced.

- **Cross-certification**—A certificate is issued by one CA to another CA; the certificate contains a public CA key associated with the private CA signature key used for issuing certificates. Typically, a cross-certificate is used to allow client systems and end entities in one administrative domain to communicate securely with client systems and end users in another administrative domain.

- **Revocation**—When a certificate is issued, it is expected to be in use for its entire validity period. However, various circumstances may cause a certificate to become invalid before the expiration of the validity period. Such circumstances include change of name, change of association between subject and CA (for example, an employee terminates employment with an organization), and compromise or suspected compromise of the corresponding private key. Under such circumstances, the CA must revoke the certificate.

A Sample Scenario Using a PKI

Figure 2-46 shows an example of two entities communicating with a common CA, using digital certificates to validate public keys.

Figure 2-46   *Digital Certificate Communication*

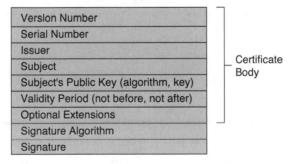

Both routers and the CA have a public/private key pair. Initially, the CA has to enroll an X.509v3 certificate for both routers in a secure manner. Also, both routers must receive a copy of the CA's public key in a secure manner. Now, if the router in New York has traffic to send to the router in Paris and wants authentication, confidential delivery of the data, the following steps must occur:

Step 1   The New York router sends a request to the CA (for example, it makes an LDAP query) to obtain the Paris router's public key.

Step 2   The CA sends the Paris router's certificate, signed with its own private key.

Step 3   The New York router verifies the signature with the CA's public key to validate the Paris router's public key.

Step 4   The Paris router sends a request to the CA to obtain the New York router's public key.

Step 5   The CA sends the New York router's certificate, signed with its own private key.

Step 6   The Paris router verifies the signature with the CA's public key to validate the New York router's public key.

Now, both routers have each other's public key and can use public key encryption to send authenticated, confidential data.

Typically, an authenticated Diffie-Hellman exchange, as explained in Chapter 1, "Basic Cryptography," would take place to derive a shared key for secret key encryption because secret key encryption is usually used for bulk data encryption (it is much faster computationally).

NOTE   The way certificates are exchanged can vary with implementations. For example, in IPsec, IKE allows the certificate to be accessed independently (for instance, through DNSSEC) or by having two devices explicitly exchange certificates as part of IKE.

Certificates

Users of public-key-based systems must be confident that, any time they rely on a public key, the associated private key is owned by the subject with which they are communicating. (This applies whether an encryption or digital signature mechanism is used.) This confidence is obtained through the use of *public key certificates*, which are data structures that bind public key values to subjects. The binding is achieved by having a trusted CA verify the subject's identity and digitally sign each certificate. The purpose of a CA, therefore, is to bind a public key to the common name of the certificate and, thus, assure third parties that some measure of care has been taken to ensure that this binding is valid.

The CA paradigm essentially relies on an authentication chain that ends in a CA that eventually certifies itself. The problem is shifted from a local perspective to a global perspective, with the whole chain depending on one final link.

A certificate has a limited valid lifetime, indicated in its signed contents. Because a certificate's signature and timeliness can be independently checked by a certificate-using client, certificates can be distributed using untrusted communications and server systems and can be cached in unsecured storage in certificate-using systems.

Certificates are used in the process of validating signed data. Specifics vary according to which algorithm is used, but the general process works as follows:

1   The recipient of signed data verifies that the claimed identity of the user is in accordance with the identity contained in the certificate.

2   The recipient validates that no certificate in the path has been revoked (for example, by retrieving a suitably current CRL or querying an online certificate status responder), and that all certificates were within their validity periods at the time the data was signed.

3   The recipient verifies that the data does not claim to have any attributes for which the certificate indicates that the signer is not authorized.

4   The recipient verifies that the data has not been altered since it was signed by using the public key in the certificate.

If all of these checks pass, the recipient can accept that the data was signed by the purported signer. The process for keys used for encryption is similar to the preceding process.

NOTE   It can, of course, be possible that data was signed by someone very different from the signer (for example, if the purported signer's private key was compromised). Security depends on all parts of the certificate-using system, including, but not limited to, the following:

  • The physical security of the place in which the computer resides

  • Personnel security (the trustworthiness of the people who actually develop, install, run, and maintain the system)

  • The security provided by the operating system on which the private key is used

  • The security provided the CA

A failure in any one of these areas can cause the entire security system to fail.

The X.509 Standard

The X.509 standard constitutes a widely accepted basis for a PKI infrastructure, defining data formats and procedures related to the distribution of public keys using certificates digitally signed by CAs. RFC 1422 specified the basis of an X.509-based PKI, targeted primarily at satisfying the needs of Internet privacy-enhanced mail (PEM). Since RFC 1422 was issued, application requirements for an Internet PKI have broadened tremendously, and the capabilities of X.509 have greatly advanced. Much work is being done to use digital certificates in web, e-mail, and IPsec applications. The current standards define the X.509 version 3 certificate and version 2 CRL.

X.509v3 Certificate

The information contained in the certificate must be uniform throughout the PKI. The current proposed standard to provide a common baseline for the Internet uses a X.509v3 certificate format. (See Figure 2-47.)

Figure 2-47 *The X.509v3 Certificate Format*

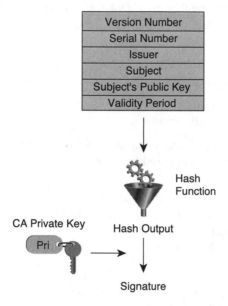

Every certificate contains three main fields:

- The body of the certificate
- The signature algorithm
- The signature itself

The *body* of the certificate contains the version number, the serial number, the names of the issuer and subject, a public key associated with the subject, and an expiration date (not before and not after a specified time/date); some certificate bodies contain *extensions*, which are optional unique identifier fields that associate additional attributes with users or public keys. The *signature algorithm* is the algorithm used by the CA to sign the certificate. The *signature* is created by applying the certificate body as input to a one-way hash function. The output value is encrypted with the CA's private key to form the signature value, as shown in Figure 2-48.

Figure 2-48   *Creating a Digital Signature for an X.509v3 Certificate*

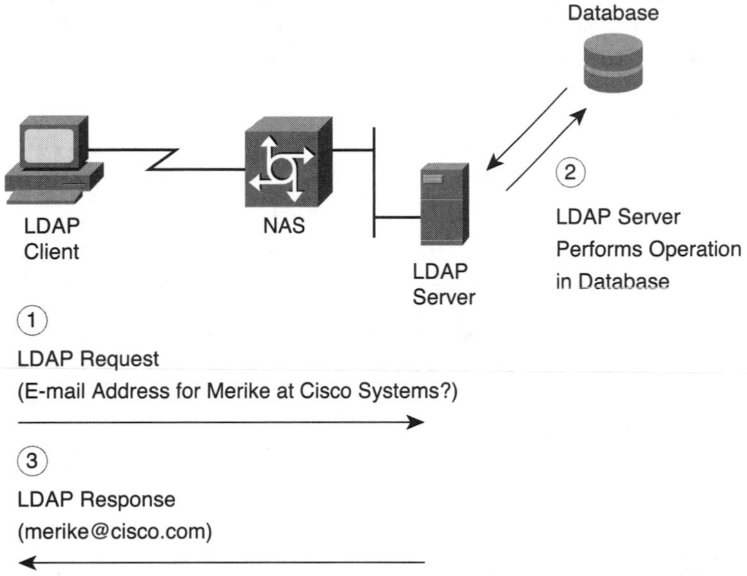

X.509v2 CRL

When a certificate is issued, it is expected to be in use for its entire validity period. However, various circumstances may cause a certificate to become invalid before the validity period expires. Such circumstances might include a change of name, a change of association between the subject and CA (for example, an employee terminates employment with an organization), and the compromise or suspected compromise of the corresponding private key. Under such circumstances, the CA should revoke the certificate.

X.509 defines one method of certificate revocation. This method requires each CA to periodically issue a signed data structure called a *certificate revocation list* (CRL). A CRL is a time-stamped list that identifies revoked certificates. The CRL is signed by a CA and made freely available in a public repository. Each revoked certificate is identified in a CRL by its certificate serial number. When a certificate-using system uses a certificate (for example, to verify a remote user's digital signature), that system not only checks the certificate signature and validity but also acquires a suitably recent CRL and checks that the certificate serial number is *not* on that CRL.

The meaning of "suitably recent" can vary with local policy, but it usually means the most recently issued CRL. A CA issues a new CRL on a regular basis (hourly, daily, or weekly). CAs may also issue CRLs at unpredictable time intervals. (If an important key is deemed compromised, for example, the CA may issue a new CRL to expedite notification of that fact, even if the next CRL does not have to be issued for some time.)

NOTE	A problem of unpredictable CRL issuance is that end entities may not know that a new CRL has been issued and, therefore, may not retrieve it from a repository.

An entry is added to the CRL as part of the next update following notification of revocation. An entry can be removed from the CRL after it appears on one regularly scheduled CRL issued beyond the revoked certificate's validity period.

An advantage of the CRL revocation method is that CRLs can be distributed in exactly the same way as certificates themselves: using untrusted communications and server systems.

One limitation of the CRL revocation method, using untrusted communications and servers, is that the time granularity of revocation is limited to the CRL issue period. For example, if a revocation is reported now, that revocation will not be reliably notified to certificate-using systems until the next CRL is issued—which may be up to 1 hour, 1 day, or 1 week, depending on the frequency at which the CA issues CRLs.

Certificate Distribution

A variety of protocols are under consideration to facilitate the distribution of digital certificates. These include widely used file retrieval mechanisms (such as FTP and HTTP) or specifically designed directory access protocols (such as LDAP). Because FTP and HTTP are assumed to be understood, only LDAP is discussed (in the following section) to give a high-level view of what it is.

Lightweight Directory Access Protocol

The *Lightweight Directory Access Protocol* (LDAP) is used for accessing online directory services. LDAP was developed by the University of Michigan in 1995 to make it easier to access X.500 directories. X.500 was too complicated and required too much computer power for many users, so a simplified version was created. LDAP is specifically targeted at management applications and browser applications that provide read/write interactive access to directories. When used with a directory that supports the X.500 protocols, LDAP is intended to be a complement to the X.500 DAP. The newest version of the LDAP protocol is LDAPv3, which is defined in RFC 3377.

LDAP runs directly over TCP and can be used to access a standalone LDAP directory service or to access a directory service that is back-ended by X.500. The standard defines the following:

- A network protocol for accessing information in the directory
- An information model defining the form and character of the information (called a *schema*)

- A namespace defining how information is referenced and organized
- An emerging distributed operation model defining how data may be distributed and referenced

The general model adopted by LDAP is one of clients performing protocol operations against servers. In this model, a client transmits a protocol request describing the operation to be performed to a server. The server is then responsible for performing the necessary operation(s) in the directory. After completing the operation(s), the server returns a response containing any results or errors to the requesting client.

In LDAP versions 1 and 2, no provision was made for protocol servers returning referrals to clients. Rather, if the LDAP server does not know the answer to a query, it goes to another server for the information instead of sending a message to the user telling the user to go to that other server. For improved performance and distribution, however, this version of the protocol permits servers to return client's referrals to other servers. This approach allows servers to offload the work of contacting other servers to progress operations.

The LDAP protocol assumes that there are one or more servers that jointly provide access to a Directory Information Tree (DIT). Each tree is made up of entries that contain names and one or more attribute values from the entry form its relative distinguished name (RDN), which must be unique among all its siblings. The concatenation of the RDNs of the sequence of entries from a particular entry to an immediate subordinate of the root of the tree forms that entry's distinguished name (DN), which is unique in the tree.

Some servers may hold *cache* or *shadow* copies of entries, which can be used to answer search and comparison queries, but will return referrals or contact other servers if modification operations are requested.

Summary

This chapter detailed many of the current and evolving technologies relating to security; this information should provide a solid background for the remaining chapters of the book. The security protocol you use in a given environment depends on the security services required and on the applications that need protection. One of the most important security considerations is establishing the identity of the entity that wants to access the corporate network. This process usually entails authenticating the entity and subsequently authorizing that entity and establishing access controls. Some protocols are specifically designed to only authenticate end users (people) or end devices (hosts, routers). Frequently, you have to combine the two protocols so that both end users and the end devices they are using to access the network are authenticated.

In addition to establishing identity, you must ensure data integrity and confidentiality; that is, you must protect the data traversing the corporate network. Many technologies exist to provide security services for various TCP/IP layers. Although application layer security protocols provide the most flexibility for application-specific parameters, using a different security protocol for every application is not practical. Transport security protocols, such as SSL/TLS and SSH, are widely deployed. SSL is bundled into many web servers and clients and has become a de facto standard in securing web transactions; SSH is a good all-around protocol for securing transport layer protocols and is most often used for securing Telnet or FTP transactions.

Network layer security through the use of IPsec can define security services at the IP layer. Depending on vendor implementations, security services can be defined based on IP addresses or can be as granular as providing different security services based on a combination of IP address, transport protocol, and application. IPsec has the advantage of hiding transport layer information and can support transport layer protocols other than TCP (such as UDP). However, because it hides transport layer information, if the transport layer header information is required to support other network requirements (such as for QoS, which may have to look at TCP/UDP port numbers), you may have problems.

For dial-in security, protocols such as L2F, PPTP, and L2TP can offer many advantages for corporations. These protocols can provide a way for dial-in users to use the Internet to securely communicate back to the corporate network. However, the packets traversing the secured tunnels are not protected, and it is prudent to add more security with transport or network layer security protocols to protect the traffic.

Many of the security protocols discussed in this chapter require either an exchange of cryptographic keys or digital certificates. A PKI is required to provide trusted and efficient key and certificate management. PKIs are being implemented in corporations or in a more global fashion, but this particular area is still developing and should be watched carefully in the upcoming years.

Many of the technologies discussed in this chapter will keep evolving; those readers interested in additional technical details and the latest developments, should refer to the work performed by the IETF working groups. (See Appendix A.)

Review Questions

The following questions provide you with an opportunity to test your knowledge of the topics covered in this chapter. You can find the answers to these questions in Appendix E, "Answers to Review Questions."

1 What three concepts are encompassed in the term *identity*? Give a brief definition of each.

2 True or false: Passwords can never be compromised if they are easy to guess, if they are not changed often enough, and if they are transmitted in cleartext across a network.

3 Token password authentication schemes are based on the following :

   A PAP authentication

    B   Publicly available encrypted hash function

    C   Challenge-response and time-synchronous authentication

    D   All of the above

4 True or false: The PPP protocol requires that authentication be used to authenticate PPP peers before proceeding to the network layer protocol phase.

5 What is EAP?

6 Which of the following is *not* true?

    A   TACACS+ uses TCP port 49 for its transport.

    B   TACACS+ uses fixed-length and fixed-content authentication exchanges.

    C   In TACACS+, authorization does not merely provide yes or no answers—it can also customize the service for the particular user.

    D   Transactions between the TACACS+ client and TACACS+ server are authenticated through the use of a shared secret, which is never sent over the network.

7 Which transport protocol is used by RADIUS?

8 True or false: Using RADIUS, communication between the client and server is in the clear except for the user passwords, which are encrypted.

9 Fill in the blank. Kerberos is based on the concept of a trusted third party that performs secure verification of users and services. In the Kerberos protocol, this trusted third party is called the _____, sometimes also called the authentication server.

10 What are the three main entities defined in the IEEE 802.1x standard?

11 What are four characteristics of S/MIME that make it a very flexible security solution for a variety of messaging applications?

12 Which of the following is *not* part of the SSL/TLS specification?

    A   Handshake protocol

    B   Hello protocol

    C   Alert protocol

    D   Record protocol

13 What transport protocol is commonly used for SSL? Why?

14 What is the mechanism in IPsec ESP whereby authentication but not confidentiality services is provided?

15 What are five things included as part of an IPsec security association (SA)?

16 In IPsec AH transport mode, which fields in the IP header are not protected?

17 Which of the following statements is *not* true?

    A All ISAKMP messages are carried in a UDP packet with destination port number 500.

    B Through the use of main mode or aggressive mode, an IKE SA is created.

    C Either peer can initiate the IKE phase 2 exchange.

    D IKE supports only the preshared key authentication mechanism to perform the authenticated DH exchange.

18 Which of the following IKE extensions allows an IP address to be assigned to a remote client?

    A Mode configuration and DHCP configuration

    B xauth and mode configuration

    C PIC and xauth

    D DHCP configuration and PIC

19 True or false: For L2TP, the control connection is the initial connection that must be established between a LAC and LNS before sessions can be brought up.

20 A PKI comprises of which five types of components?

21 What are the three main fields in an X.509v3 certificate? Give a brief description of each field.

## CHAPTER 3

Applying Security Technologies to Real Networks

The preceding chapter addressed a number of security technologies that exist to secure corporate networks. Because of the wide range of applicability in different types of networks, this chapter shows how you can use these technologies to secure specific scenarios: virtual private networks (VPNs), wireless networks, and Voice over IP (VoIP) networks. Limitations and areas of evolving technology are highlighted, and specific threats and vulnerabilities are addressed in Chapter 5, "Threats in an Enterprise Network."

Virtual Private Networks (VPNs)

Corporations use VPNs to establish secure, end-to-end private network connections over a public network infrastructure. Many companies have created private and trusted network infrastructures, using internal or outsourced cable plants and wide-area networks, to offer a level of privacy by virtue of physical security. As these companies move from expensive, dedicated, secure connections to the more cost-effective use of the Internet, they require secure communications over what is generally described as an insecure Internet. VPNs can mitigate the security risks of using the Internet as a transport, allowing VPNs to displace the more-expensive dedicated leased lines. From the user's perspective, the nature of the physical network being tunneled is irrelevant because it appears as if the information is being sent over a dedicated private network. A VPN tunnel encapsulates data within IP packets to transport information that requires additional security or does not otherwise conform to Internet addressing standards. The result is that remote users act as virtual nodes on the network into which they have tunneled.

VPN Deployment Models

VPNs exist in a variety of deployment scenarios. Figure 3-1 illustrates a typical corporate VPN scenario.

Figure 3-1 *Corporate VPN*

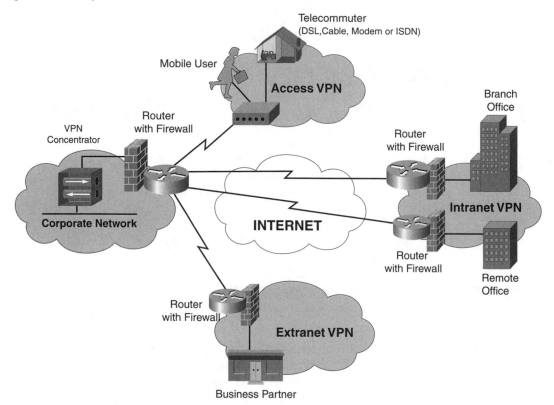

In a corporate network environment, three main types of VPNs exist:

- **Access VPNs**—Access VPNs provide remote access to an enterprise customer's intranet or extranet over a shared infrastructure. Deploying a remote-access VPN enables corporations to reduce communications expenses by leveraging the local dialup infrastructures of Internet service providers. At the same time, VPNs allow mobile workers, telecommuters, and day extenders to take advantage of broadband connectivity. Access VPNs impose security over the analog, dial, ISDN, digital subscriber line (DSL), Mobile IP, and cable technologies that connect mobile users, telecommuters, and branch offices.

- **Intranet VPNs**—Intranet VPNs link enterprise customer headquarters, remote offices, and branch offices in an internal network over a shared infrastructure. Remote and branch offices can use VPNs over existing Internet connections, thus providing a secure connection for remote offices. This eliminates costly dedicated connections and reduces WAN costs. Intranet VPNs allow access only to enterprise customer's employees.

- **Extranet VPNs**—Extranet VPNs link outside customers, partners, or communities of interest to an enterprise customer's network over a shared infrastructure. Extranet VPNs differ from intranet VPNs in that they allow access to users outside the enterprise.

The primary reason for the three distinct classifications is due to security policy variations. A good security policy details corporate infrastructure and information-authentication mechanisms and access privileges, and in many instances these will vary depending on how the corporate resources are accessed. For example, authentication mechanisms may be much more stringent in access VPNs than for either intranet or extranet VPNs.

Many VPNs deploy tunneling mechanisms in the following configurations:

- Secure gateway-to-gateway connections, across the Internet or across private or outsourced networks. These are also sometimes referred to as *site-to-site VPNs* and are typically used for intranet VPNs and some extranet VPNs.

- Secure client-to-gateway connections, either through Internet connections or within private or outsourced networks. These are sometimes referred to as *client-to-site VPNs* and are typically used in access VPNs and some extranet VPNs.

Site-to-Site VPNs

Some office configurations require sharing information across multiple LANs. Routing across a secure VPN tunnel between two office gateway devices allows sites to share information across the LANs without fearing that outsiders could view the content of the data stream. This site-to-site VPN establishes a one-to-one peer relationship between two networks via the VPN tunnel. Figure 3-2 shows an example of such a site-to-site VPN, where a single VPN tunnel protects communication between three separate hosts and a file server.

Figure 3-2   *Site-to-Site VPN*

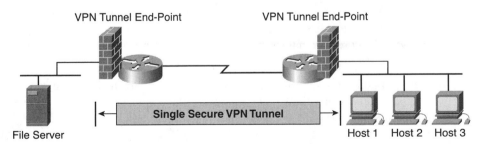

In its simplest form, two servers or routers set up an encrypted IP tunnel to securely pass packets back and forth over the Internet. The VPN tunnel endpoint devices create a logical point-to-point connection over the Internet and routing can be configured on each gateway device to allow packets to route over the VPN link.

Client-to-Site VPNs

When a client requires access to a site's internal data from outside the network's LAN, the client needs to initiate a client-to-site VPN connection. This will secure a path to the site's LAN. The client-to-site VPN is a collection of many tunnels that terminate on a common shared endpoint on the LAN side. Figure 3-3 shows an example of a client-to-site VPN in which two mobile users act as separate VPN tunnel endpoints and establish VPN connections with a VPN concentrator.

Figure 3-3   *Client-to-Site VPN*

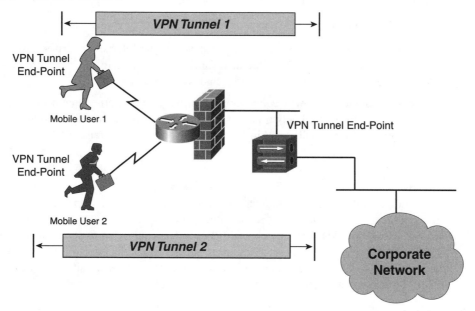

One or more clients can initiate a secure VPN connection to the VPN server, allowing simultaneous secure access of internal data from an insecure remote location. The client receives an IP address from the server and appears as a member on the server's LAN.

Some client-to-site VPN solutions use split tunneling on the client side, which has a number of security ramifications. Split tunneling enables the remote client to send some traffic through a separate data path without forwarding it over the encrypted VPN tunnel. The traffic to be sent in the clear is usually specified through the use of traffic filters. Because split tunneling bypasses the security of a secure VPN, use this functionality with care.

NOTE   Many client-to-site VPNs are used to have a mechanism for laptop users to securely establish connections back to a corporate office. Some of these VPNs do not require a user authentication mechanism and only rely on the device to be authenticated. Special care must be taken to ensure physical security of these laptops to avoid any security compromises.

VPN Security

Securing VPN data streams requires the use of a combination of technologies that provide identification, tunneling, and encryption. IP-based VPNs provide IP tunneling between two network devices, either site-to-site or client-to-site. Data sent between the two devices is encrypted, thus creating a secure network path over the existing IP network. *Tunneling* is a way of creating a virtual path or point-to-point connection between two devices on the Internet. Most VPN implementations use tunneling to create a private network path between two devices.

Tunneling Protocols

There are three widely used VPN tunneling protocols: IP Security (IPsec), Point-to-Point Tunneling Protocol (PPTP), and Layer 2 Tunneling Protocol (L2TP). Although many view these three as competing technologies, these protocols offer different capabilities that are appropriate for different uses. The technical details of these protocols were discussed in Chapter 2, "Security Technologies;" this chapter describes how the three protocols relate to each other to secure VPNs.

NOTE   Some VPNs are also created through the use of Secure Shell (SSH) tunnels, Secure Socket Layer/Transport Layer Security (SSL/TLS), or other security application protocol extensions. These protocols secure communications end-to-end for specific applications and are sometimes used in conjunction with the tunneling protocols discussed here.

IPsec

IPsec provides integrity protection, authentication, and (optional) privacy and replay protection services for IP traffic.

IPsec packets are of two types:

- IP protocol 50, called the *Encapsulating Security Payload* (ESP) format, which provides privacy, authenticity, and integrity.

- IP protocol 51, called the *Authentication Header* (AH) format, which only provides integrity and authenticity for packets, but not privacy.

As discussed in Chapter 2, IPsec can be used in two modes: *transport mode*, which secures an existing IP packet from source to destination; and *tunnel mode*, which puts an existing IP packet inside a new IP packet that is sent to a tunnel endpoint in the IPsec format. Both transport and tunnel mode can be encapsulated in the ESP or AH headers.

IPsec transport mode was designed to provide security for IP traffic end-to-end between two communicating systems—for example, to secure a TCP connection or a UDP datagram. IPsec tunnel mode was designed primarily for network midpoints, routers, or gateways, to secure other IP traffic inside an IPsec tunnel that connects one private IP network to another private IP network over a public or untrusted IP network (for example, the Internet). In both cases, a complex security negotiation is performed between the two computers through the Internet Key Exchange (IKE).

Many implementations of IKE provide a variety of device authentication methods to establish trust between computers. The more common ones include the following:

- Preshared secrets
- Encrypted nonces (a.k.a. raw public keys)
- Signed certificates (X.509)

When configured with an IPsec policy, peer computers negotiate parameters to set up a secure VPN tunnel using IKE phase 1 to establish a main security association for all traffic between the two computers. This involves device authenticating using one of the previously mentioned methods and generating a shared *master key*. The systems then use IKE phase 2 to negotiate another security association for the application traffic they are trying to protect at the moment. This involves generating shared *session keys*. Only the two computers know both sets of keys. The data exchanged using the security association is very well protected against modification or observation by attackers who may be in the network. The keys are automatically refreshed according to IPsec policy settings to provide appropriate protection according to the administrator-defined policy.

The Internet Engineering Task Force (IETF) IPsec tunnel protocol specifications did not include mechanisms suitable for remote-access VPN clients. Omitted features include user authentication options and client IP address configuration. This has been rectified by the addition of Internet drafts that propose to define standard methods for extensible user-based authentication and address assignment. These were discussed in detail in Chapter 2. However, you should ensure interoperability between different vendors before assuming interoperability because all vendors have chosen to extend the protocol in proprietary ways. For example, even if two vendors state that they are supporting the Extended Authentication (Xauth) or Mode Configuration (ModeConfig) Internet drafts, the implementations may not interoperate.

IPsec transport mode for either AH or ESP is applicable to only host implementations where the hosts (that is, IPsec peers) are the initiators and recipients of the traffic to be protected. IPsec tunnel mode for either AH or ESP is applicable to both host and security gateway implementations, although security gateways must use tunnel mode. All site-to-site VPNs and client-to-site VPNs use some sort of security gateway and therefore IPsec tunnel mode is used for most VPN deployments.

NAT/PAT

Network Address Translation (NAT) is often used in environments that have private IP address space as opposed to ownership of a globally unique IP address. The globally unique IP address block is usually obtained from your network service provider, although larger corporations might petition a regional or local Internet registry directly for addressing space. NAT will translate the unregistered IP addresses into legal IP addresses that are routable in the outside public network.

The Internet Assigned Numbers Authority (IANA) has reserved the following three blocks of IP address space for private networks:

10.0.0.0 through 10.255.255.255
172.16.0.0 through 172.31.255.255
192.168.0.0 through 192.168.255.255

If a corporation decides to use private addressing, these blocks of addresses should be used.

In some networks, the number of unregistered IP addresses used can exceed the number of globally unique addresses available for translation. To address this problem (no pun intended), Port Address Translation (PAT) was created. When using NAT/PAT, the source TCP or UDP ports used when the connection is initiated are kept unique and placed in a table along with the translated source IP address. Return traffic is then compared to the NAT/PAT table, and the destination IP address and destination TCP or UDP port numbers are modified to correspond to the entries in the table. Figure 3-4 illustrates the operation of NAT/PAT.

NAT/PAT usage creates a number of challenges for many protocols. Applications that change UDP or TCP source and destination port numbers during the same session can break the PAT mappings. Also, applications that use a control channel to exchange port number and IP address mapping information will mismatch with NAT/PAT (for example, FTP). In addition, if there exist a large number of users behind a NAT/PAT device, the available IP addresses and/or port numbers used for translation purposes can be exhausted rather quickly.

Figure 3-4   *NAT/PAT Operation*

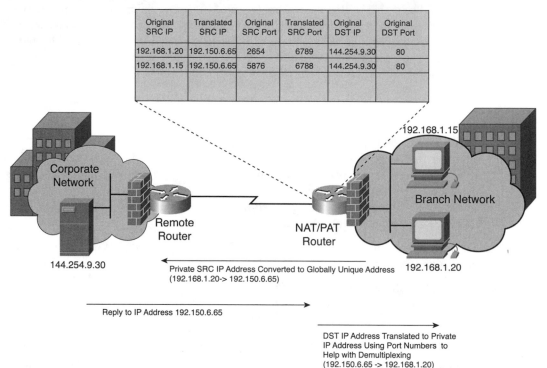

Original SRC IP	Translated SRC IP	Original SRC Port	Translated SRC Port	Original DST IP	Original DST Port
192.168.1.20	192.150.6.65	2654	6789	144.254.9.30	80
192.168.1.15	192.150.6.65	5876	6788	144.254.9.30	80

Using NAT also causes a number of problems when used with IPsec. However, as discussed in Chapter 2, there is a NAT Traversal extension that is being standardized and which will create an interoperable solution for many NAT environments. The following issues are resolved when using NAT Traversal:

- **Upper layer checksum computation**—When the TCP or UDP checksum is encrypted with ESP, a NAT device cannot compute the TCP or UDP checksum. NAT Traversal defines an additional payload in IKE that will send the original IP addresses to appropriately compute the checksum.

- **Multiplexing IPsec data streams**—TCP and UDP headers are not visible with ESP and, therefore, the TCP or UDP port numbers cannot be used to multiplex traffic between different hosts using private network addresses. NAT Traversal encapsulates the ESP packet with a UDP header, and NAT can use the UDP ports in this header to multiplex the IPsec data streams.

- **IKE UDP port number change**—When an IPsec IKE implementation expects both the source and destination UDP port number to be 500, when a NAT device changes the source UDP port number the IKE traffic could be discarded. NAT Traversal allows IKE messages to be received from a source port other than 500.

- **Using IP addresses for identification**—When an embedded IP address is used for peer identification, when NAT changes the source address of the sending node, the embedded address will not match the IP address of the IKE packet and the IKE negotiation fails. NAT Traversal sends the original IP address during phase 2 IKE quick mode negotiation, which can be used to validate the IP address. Note that because this payload is not sent during phase 1 IKE main mode negotiation, the IP address validation cannot be performed and the validation must either not happen or occur by using another mechanism such as using host name validation.

Point-to-Point Tunneling Protocol (PPTP)

PPTP provides authenticated and encrypted communications between a client and a gateway or between two gateways through the use of a user ID and password. In addition to password-based authentication, PPTP can support public key authentication through the Extensible Authentication Protocol (EAP).

The PPTP development was initiated by Microsoft and after additional vendor input became an informational standard in the IETF, RFC 2637. It was first delivered in products in 1996, two years before the availability of IPsec and L2TP. The design goal was simplicity, multiprotocol support, and capability to traverse IP networks. PPTP uses a TCP connection (using TCP port number 1723) for tunnel maintenance and Generic Routing Encapsulation (GRE)-encapsulated PPP frames for tunneled data. The payloads of the encapsulated PPP frames can be encrypted and/or compressed. Although the PPP Encryption Control Protocol (ECP), defined in RFC 1968, and the PPP Compression Control Protocol (CCP), defined in RFC 1962, can be used in conjunction with PPTP to perform the encryption and compression, most implementations use the Microsoft Point-to-Point Encryption (MPPE) Protocol (defined in RFC 3078) and the Microsoft Pint-to-Point Compression (MPPC) Protocol (defined in RFC 2118).

The use of PPP provides the capability to negotiate authentication, encryption, and IP address assignment services. However, the PPP authentication does not provide per-packet authentication, integrity or replay protection, and the encryption mechanism does not address authentication, integrity, replay protection, and key management requirements.

NOTE   PPP ECP does not address key management at all. However, MPPE does address session key generation and management, where the session keys are derived from MS-CHAP or EAP-TLS credentials. The specification can be found in RFC 3079.

Most NAT devices can translate TCP-based traffic for PPTP tunnel maintenance, but PPTP data packets that use the GRE header must typically use additional mappings in the NAT device—the Call ID field in the GRE header is used to ensure that a unique ID is used for each PPTP tunnel and for each PPTP client.

PPTP does not provide very robust encryption because it is based on the RSA RC4 standard and supports 40-bit or 128-bit encryption. It was not developed for LAN-to-LAN tunneling, and some implementations have imposed additional limitations, such as only being capable of providing 255 connections to a server and only one VPN tunnel per client connection.

PPTP is often thought of as the protocol that needs to be used to interoperate with Microsoft software; however, the latest Microsoft products support L2TP, which is a more multivendor interoperable long-term solution.

Layer 2 Tunneling Protocol (L2TP)

The best features of the PPTP protocol were combined with Cisco's L2F (Layer 2 Forwarding) protocol to create L2TP.

L2F was Cisco's proprietary solution, which is being deprecated in favor of L2TP. L2TP is useful for dialup, ADSL, and other remote-access scenarios; this protocol extends the use of PPP to enable VPN access by remote users.

L2TP encapsulates PPP frames to be sent over Layer 3 IP networks or Layer 2 X.25, Frame Relay, or Asynchronous Transfer Mode (ATM) networks. When configured to use IP as its transport, L2TP can be used as a VPN tunneling protocol over the Internet. L2TP over IP uses UDP port 1701 and includes a series of L2TP control messages for tunnel maintenance. L2TP also uses UDP to send L2TP-encapsulated PPP frames as the tunneled data. The encapsulated PPP frames can be encrypted or compressed. L2TP tunnel authentication provides mutual authentication between the L2TP access concentrator (LAC) and the L2TP network server (LNS) tunnel endpoints, but it does not protect control and data traffic on a per-packet basis. Also, the PPP encryption mechanism does not address authentication, integrity, replay protection, and key management requirements.

L2TP was specifically designed for client connections to network access servers, as well as for gateway-to-gateway connections. Through its use of PPP, L2TP gains multiprotocol support for protocols such as Internetwork Packet Exchange (IPX) and AppleTalk. PPP also provides a wide range of user authentication options, including Challenge Handshake Protocol (CHAP), Microsoft Challenge Handshake Protocol (MS-CHAP), MS-CHAPv2, and EAP, which supports token card and smart card authentication mechanisms.

L2TP is a mature IETF standards-track protocol that has been widely implemented by many vendors.

L2TP/IPsec

L2TP does not, by itself, provide any message integrity or data confidentiality because the packets are transported in the clear. To add security, many VPN implementations support a combination commonly referred to as L2TP/Ipsec, in which the L2TP tunnels appear as payloads within IPsec packets. An IPsec transport mode ESP connection is established followed by the L2TP control and data channel establishment.

In this manner, data communications across a VPN benefit from the strong integrity, replay, authenticity, and privacy protection of IPsec, while also receiving a highly interoperable way to accomplish user authentication, tunnel address assignment, multiprotocol support, and multicast support using PPP. It is a good solution for secure remote access and secure gateway-to-gateway connections.

Recently proposed work for L2TP specifies a header compression method for L2TP/IPsec, which helps dramatically reduce protocol overhead while retaining the benefits of the rest of L2TP. In addition, IPsec in remote-access solutions require mechanisms to support the dynamic addressing structure of Dynamic Host Configuration Protocol (DHCP) and NAT as well as legacy user authentication. These were discussed in Chapter 2.

Table 3-1 provides a summary of the key technical differences for the IPsec, L2TP, and PPTP protocols.

Table 3-1   *Key Technical Differences for VPN Tunneling Protocols*

Feature	Description	IPsec (Transport Mode)	IPsec (Tunnel Mode)	L2TP/ IPsec	L2TP/ PPP	PPTP/ PPP
Confidentiality	Can encrypt traffic it carries	Yes	Yes	Yes	Yes[3,4]	Yes[2,4]
Data integrity	Provides an authenticity method to ensure packet content is not changed in transit	Yes	Yes	Yes	No	No
Device authentication	Authenticates the devices involved in the communications	Yes	Yes	Yes	Yes	Yes
User authentication	Can authenticate the user that is initiating the communications	Yes	No	Yes	Yes[3]	Yes[1,2]
Uses PKI	Can use PKI to implement encryption and/or authentication	Yes	Yes	Yes	Yes	Yes
Dynamic Tunnel IP address assignment [5]	Defines a standard way to negotiate an IP address for the tunneled part of the communications	N/A	Work in Progress (Mode Config)	Yes	Yes	Yes
NAT-capable	Can pass through network address translators to hide one or both endpoints of the communications	No	Yes (NAT-Traversal)	No	Yes	Yes
Multicast support	Can carry IP multicast traffic in addition to IP unicast traffic	No	Yes	Yes	Yes	Yes

1 When PPTP/PPP is used as a client VPN connection, it authenticates the user, not the computer. When used as a gateway-to-gateway connection, the computer is assigned a user ID and is authenticated.

2 The PPTP protocol is generally used with either MS-CHAPv2 or EAP-TLS for user authentication and encryption is performed using MPPE.

3 The L2TP protocol generally uses CHAP or EAP-TLS for user authentication and includes the option for encryption through the use of PPP ECP.

4 PPTP and L2TP use a weaker form of encryption than the IPsec protocol uses.

5 Important so that returned packets are routed back through the same session rather than through a nontunneled and unsecured path and to eliminate static, manual end-system configuration.

Authentication

The type of authentication used will depend largely on whether host identity or actual user identity is required. With a user authentication process, a user is typically presented with a login prompt and is required to enter a username and password. This type of mechanism is most widely implemented, and it is important to stress the need to use secure passwords that are changed often. There also exist some alternative authentication technologies that may be incorporated depending on the requirements of the network. Most of these were discussed in Chapter 2 and are part of the legacy authentication mechanisms incorporated into IPsec IKE or can be used with EAP. The list includes, but is not limited to the following:

- One-time passwords
- Generic token cards
- Kerberos
- Digital certificates

It is also common to use RADIUS or TACACS+ to provide a scalable user authentication, authorization, and accounting back-end.

Differences Between IKE and PPP Authentication

L2TP implementations use PPP authentication methods, such as CHAP and EAP. Although this provides initial authentication, it does not provide authentication verification on any subsequently received packet. However, with IPsec, after the asserted entity in IKE has been authenticated, the resulting derived keys are used to provide per-packet authentication, integrity, and replay protection. In addition, the entity is implicitly authenticated on a per-packet basis. The distinction between user and device authentication is very important. For example, if PPP uses user authentication while IPsec uses device authentication, only the device is authenticated on a per-packet basis and there is no way to enforce traffic segregation. When an L2TP/IPsec tunnel is established, any user on a multi-user machine will be able to send traffic down the tunnel. If the IPsec negotiation also includes user authentication, however, the keys that are derived to protect the subsequent L2TP/IPsec traffic will ensure that users are implicitly authenticated on a per-packet basis.

Certificate Authentication

Because in IPsec the key management protocol (IKE) allows for the use of X.509 signed certificates for authentication, it would seem that a PKI could provide for a scalable, distributed authentication scheme. For VPNs, the certificates are more limited because they are used only for authentication and therefore introduce less complexity. However, there aren't large-scale deployments of PKI-enabled IPsec VPNs in use yet. This is largely due to the overall complexity and operational difficulty of creating a public key infrastructure, as well as a lack of interoperable methods, multiple competing protocols, and some missing components. There is currently work under development that addresses these issues. This work addresses the entire lifecycle for PKI usage within IPsec transactions: pre-authorization of certificate issuance, the enrollment process (certificate request and retrieval), certificate renewals and changes, revocation, validation, and repository lookups. When the issues are resolved, the VPN operator will be able to do the following:

- Authorize batches of certificates to be issued based on locally defined criteria
- Provision PKI-based user and/or machine identity to VPN peers on a large scale such that an IPsec peer ends up with a valid public/private key pair and PKIX certificate that is used in the VPN tunnel setup
- Set the corresponding gateway and/or client authorization policy for remote-access and site-to-site connections.
- Establish automatic renewal for certificates
- Ensure timely revocation information is available for certificates used in IKE exchanges

You can find specific information about the work on certificate authentication at http://www.projectdploy.com.

NOTE It is unclear whether Project Dploy will actually be completed, because at the time of this writing the participating vendors have been unable agree on which specific key enrollment protocol to support. Deploying a seamlessly integrating interoperable multivendor PKI solution is a difficult process and may remain a complex issue for a number of years. However, many vendors are aware of the problem and are trying to cooperate at some level to make the deployment issues easier to handle.

VPN Security Application

Large-scale VPNs primarily require the use of the IPsec protocol or the combination of L2TP/IPsec to provide security services. Some organizations choose to use only the PPTP or the L2TP.

However, because IPsec provides comprehensive security services, it should be used in most secure VPN solutions.

Using IPsec, you can provide privacy, integrity, and authenticity for network traffic in the following situations:

- End-to-end security for IP unicast traffic, from end node to VPN concentrator, router-to-router, and end node-to-end node using IPsec transport mode
- Remote-access VPN client and gateway functions using L2TP secured by IPsec transport mode
- Site-to-site VPN connections, across outsourced private WAN or Internet-based connections using L2TP/IPsec or IPsec tunnel mode

Access VPNs

Figure 3-5 illustrates a typical access VPN.

Figure 3-5   *Access VPN*

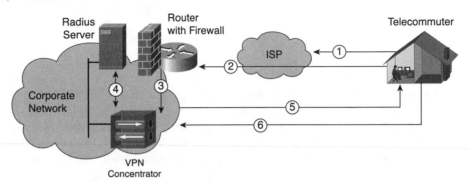

In this example, a telecommuter working from home is accessing the corporate network. The following sequence of events depicts how the secure VPN tunnel gets established:

1 The telecommuter dials his ISP and uses PPP to establish a connection.

2 The telecommuter then initiates IPsec communication. The remote-access VPN traffic is addressed to one specific public address using the IKE protocol (UDP 500) and ESP protocol (IP 50).

3 The IPsec VPN traffic is checked at the corporate network ingress point to ensure that the specific IP addresses and protocols are part of the VPN services before forwarding the traffic to the VPN concentrator.

4 Xauth is used to provide a mechanism for establishing user authentication using a RADIUS server. (The IKE connection is not completed until the correct authentication information is provided and Xauth provides an additional user authentication mechanism before the remote user is assigned any IP parameters. The VPN concentrator communicates with the RADIUS server to accomplish this.)

5 Once authenticated, the remote telecommuter is provided with access by receiving IP parameters (IP address, default gateway, DNS, and WINS server) using another extension of IKE, MODCFG. Some vendors also provide authorization services to control the access of the remote user, which may force the user to use a specific network path through the Internet to access the corporate network.

6 IKE completes the IPsec tunnel, and the secure VPN tunnel is operational.

If the telecommuter were instead a remote dial-in user and the ISP uses L2TP, the scenario is very similar. The traditional dial-in users are terminated on an access router with built-in modems. When the PPP connection is established between the user and the server, three-way CHAP is used to authenticate the user. As in the previous telecommuter remote-access VPN, a AAA server (TACACS+ or RADIUS) is used to authenticate the users. Once authenticated, the users are provided with IP addresses from an IP pool through PPP, and the subsequent IPsec IKE negotiations establish a secure IPsec tunnel. This is then followed by the establishment of the L2TP control and data channels, both protected within the IPsec tunnel.

NOTE   The previous examples described both a voluntary tunnel and a compulsory tunnel. Voluntary tunneling refers to the case where an individual host connects to a remote site using a tunnel originating on the host, with no involvement from intermediate network nodes. Voluntary tunnels are transparent to a provider. When a network node, such as a network access server (NAS), initiates a tunnel to a VPN server, it is referred to as a mandatory (or compulsory) tunnel. Mandatory tunnels are completely transparent to the client.

Intranet/Extranet VPNs

Because both intranet and extranet VPNs primarily deal with site-to-site scenarios, the example given here applies to both. The difference lies mainly in providing more restrictive access to extranet VPNs.

Figure 3-6 shows a typical intranet VPN scenario.

Figure 3-6   *Intranet VPN*

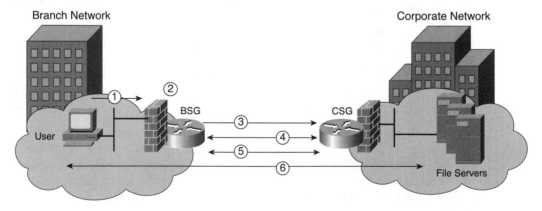

In this example, a branch office and corporate network establish a site-to-site VPN tunnel. The routers in each respective network edge use IPsec tunnel mode to provide a secure

IPsec tunnel between the two networks using IKE for the key management protocol. The following sequence of events depicts how the secure VPN tunnel gets established:

1 A user from the branch office wants to access a corporate file server and initiates traffic, which gets sent to the branch network security gateway (BSG).

2 The BSG sees that the specific IP addresses and protocols are part of the VPN services and requires an IPsec tunnel to the corporate network security gateway (CSG).

3 The BSG proposes an IKE SA to the CSG (if one doesn't already exist).

4 The BSG and CSG negotiate protocols, algorithms, and keys and also exchange encrypted signatures.

5 The BSG and CSG use the established IKE SA to securely create new IPsec SAs.

6 The ensuing traffic exchanged is protected between the client and server.

The examples shown have been very simplistic, but show how many security technologies can be combined to create secure VPNs. For more detailed design architectures, refer to Chapter 12, "Securing VPN, Wireless, and VoIP Networks."

Wireless Networks

In the past few years, wireless LANS (WLANs) have become more widely deployed. These networks provide mobility to network users and have the added benefit of being easy to install without the costly need of pulling physical wires. As laptops become more pervasive in the workplace, laptops are the primary computing device for most users, allowing greater portability in meetings and conferences and during business travel. WLANs offer organizations greater productivity by providing constant connectivity to traditional networks in venues outside the traditional office environment. Numerous wireless Internet service providers are appearing in airports, coffee shops, hotels, and conference and convention centers, enabling enterprise users to connect in public access areas.

Types of Wireless Technology

Wireless local-area networking has existed for many years, providing connectivity to wired infrastructures where mobility was a requirement to specific working environments. These early wireless networks were nonstandard implementations, with speeds ranging between 1 and 2 MB. Without any standards driving WLAN technologies, the early implementations of WLAN were mostly vendor-specific implementations, with no provision for interoperability. The evolution of WLAN technology is shown in Figure 3-7.

Figure 3-7   *WLAN Evolution*

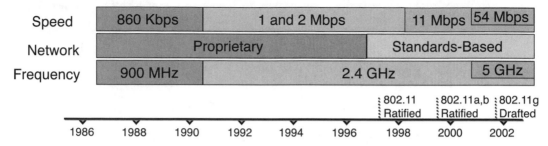

Today, several standards exist for WLAN applications:

- **HiperLAN**—A European Telecommunications Standards Institute (ETSI) standard ratified in 1996. HiperLAN/1 standard operates in the 5-GHz radio band up to 24 Mbps. HiperLAN/2 is a newer standard that operates in the 5-GHz band at up to 54 Mbps using a connection-oriented protocol for sharing access among end-user devices.

- **HomeRF SWAP**—In 1988, the HomeRF SWAP Group published the Shared Wireless Access Protocol (SWAP) standard for wireless digital communication between PCs and consumer electronic devices within the home. SWAP supports voice and data over a common wireless interface at 1- and 2-Mbps data rates from a distance of about 150 feet using frequency-hopping and spread-spectrum techniques in the 2.4-GHz band.

- **Bluetooth**—A personal-area network (PAN) specified by the Bluetooth Special Interest Group for providing low-power and short-range wireless connectivity using frequency-hopping spread spectrum in the 2.4-GHz frequency environment. The specification allows for operation at up to 780 kbps within a 10-meter range although in practice most devices operate in the 2-meter range.

- **802.11**—A wireless standard specified by the IEEE. There are three specifications: 802.11b (sometimes referred to as Wi-Fi), which is currently the most widely deployed WLAN standard and can support speeds of 11 Mbps at 2.4GHz; 802.11a, which is gaining popularity because it allows communication at speeds of up to 54 Mbps at 5.8 GHz; and 802.11g, which extends the capabilities of wireless communications even further by allowing 54-Mbps communication at 2.4 GHz and is backward compatible with 802.11b.

Both the HiperLAN and HomeRF SWAP standards aren't widely deployed and have experienced little real-world adoption. The 802.11 standards are the most commonly deployed interoperable WLAN standards, and therefore the rest of the discussion focuses specifically on the 802.11-based technologies.

Wireless LAN Components

Components of a WLAN are access points (APs), network interface cards (NICs), client adapters, bridges, antennas, and amplifiers:

- **Access point**—An AP operates within a specific frequency spectrum and uses a 802.11 standard specified modulation technique. It also informs the wireless clients of its availability and authenticates and associates wireless clients to the wireless network. An AP also coordinates the wireless client's use of wired resources.

- **Network interface card (NIC)/client adapter**—A PC or workstation uses a wireless NIC to connect to the wireless network. The NIC scans the available frequency spectrum for connectivity and associates it to an AP or another wireless client. The NIC is coupled to the PC/workstation operating system using a software driver.

- **Bridge**—Wireless bridges are used to connect multiple LANs (both wired and wireless) at the Media Access Control (MAC) layer level. Used in building-to-building wireless connections, wireless bridges can cover longer distances than APs. (The IEEE 802.11 standard specifies 1 mile as the maximum coverage range for an AP.)

- **Antenna**—An antenna radiates or receives the modulated signal through the air so that wireless clients can receive it. Characteristics of an antenna are defined by propagation pattern (directional versus omnidirectional), gain, transmit power, and so on. Antennas are needed on both the AP/bridge and the clients.

- **Amplifier**—An amplifier increases the strength of received and transmitted transmissions.

Wireless LAN Deployment Models

WLANs are typically deployed as either ad-hoc peer-to-peer wireless LANs or as infrastructure mode WLANs, in which case the WLAN may becomes an extension of a wired network.

Peer-to-Peer WLAN

In a peer-to-peer WLAN, wireless clients equipped with compatible wireless NICs communicate with each other without the use of an AP, as shown in Figure 3-8.

Figure 3-8   *Peer-to-Peer WLAN*

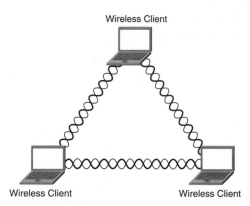

Two or more wireless clients that communicate using ad-hoc mode communication form an independent basic service set (IBSS). Coverage area is limited in an ad-hoc, peer-to-peer LAN, and the range varies, depending on the type of WLAN system. Also, wireless clients do not have access to wired resources.

Infrastructure Mode WLAN

If the WLAN is deployed in infrastructure mode, all wireless clients connect through an AP for all communications. A single wireless AP that supports one or more wireless clients is known as a *basic service set* (BSS). Typically, the infrastructure mode WLAN will extend the use of a corporate wired network, as shown in Figure 3-9.

The AP allows for wireless clients to have access to each other and to wired resources. In addition, with the use of multiple APs, wireless clients may roam between APs if the available physical areas of the wireless APs overlap, as shown in Figure 3-10. This overlap can greatly extend the wireless network coverage throughout a large geographic area. As a wireless client roams across different signal areas, it can associate and re-associate from one wireless AP to another while maintaining network layer connectivity. A set of two or more wireless APs that are connected to the same wired network is known as an *extended service set* (ESS) and is identified by its SSID.

Figure 3-9   *Infrastructure Mode WLAN*

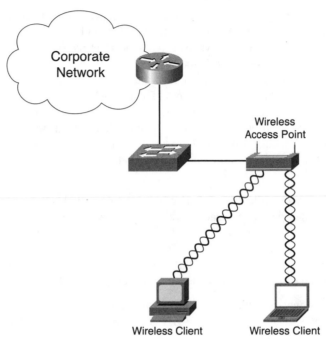

Figure 3-10   *WLAN Roaming*

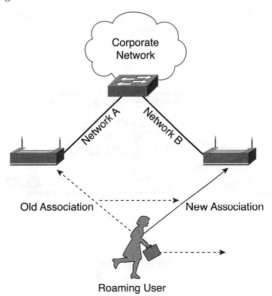

802.11 Physical Layer Basics

The 802.11-based wireless technologies use the spread-spectrum radio technology developed during World War II to protect military and diplomatic communications. Although available for many years, spread-spectrum radio was employed almost exclusively for military use. In 1985, the Federal Communications Commission (FCC) allowed spread-spectrum's unlicensed commercial use in three frequency bands: 902 to 928 MHz, 2.4000 to 2.4835 GHz, and 5.725 to 5.850 GHz, which is known as the ISM (Industrial, Scientific, and Medical) band. The spectrum is classified as unlicensed, meaning there is no one owner of the spectrum, and anyone can use it as long as the use complies with FCC regulations. Some areas the FCC does govern include the maximum transmit power, as measured at the antenna, and the type of encoding and frequency modulations that can be used.

Spread-spectrum radio differs from other commercial radio technologies because it spreads, rather than concentrates, its signal over a wide frequency range within its assigned bands. It camouflages data by mixing the actual signal with a spreading code pattern. Code patterns shift the signal's frequency or phase, making it extremely difficult to intercept an entire message without knowing the specific code used. Transmitting and receiving radios must use the same spreading code, so only they can decode the true signal.

The three signal-spreading techniques commonly used in 802.11-based networks are direct sequencing spread spectrum (DSSS), frequency hopping, and orthogonal frequency-division multiplexing.

Direct Sequencing Spread Spectrum (DSSS)

Direct sequencing modulation spreads the encoded signal over a wide range of frequency channels. The 802.11 specification provides 11 overlapping channels of 83 MHz within the 2.4-GHz spectrum, as shown in Figure 3-11.

Figure 3-11   *Direct Sequencing*

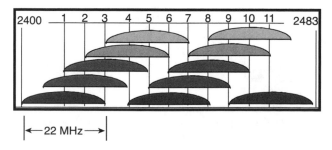

Within the 11 overlapping channels, there are three 22-MHz-wide nonoverlapping channels. Because the three channels do not overlap, three APs can be used simultaneously to provide an aggregate data rate of the combination of the three available channels. Transmitting over an extended bandwidth results in quicker data throughput, but the trade-off is diminished range. Direct sequencing is best suited to high-speed, client/server applications where radio interference is minimal.

Frequency-Hopping Spread Spectrum (FHSS)

For frequency-hopping modulation, during the coded transmission, both transmitter and receiver hop from one frequency to another in synchronization, as shown in Figure 3-12.

Figure 3-12   *Frequency Hopping*

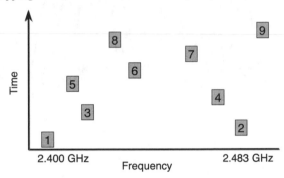

The 2.4-GHz ISM band provides for 83.5 MHz of available spectrum and the frequency-hopping architecture makes use of the available frequency range by creating hopping patterns to transmit on one of 79 1-MHz-wide frequencies for no more than 0.4 seconds at a time. This setup allows for an interference-tolerant network. If any one channel stumbles across an interference, it would be for only a small time slice, because the frequency-hopping radio quickly hops through the band and retransmits data on another frequency. Frequency hopping can overcome interference better than direct sequencing, and it also offers greater range. This is because direct sequencing uses available power to spread the signal very thinly over multiple channels, resulting in a wider signal with less peak power. In contrast, the short signal bursts transmitted in frequency hopping have higher peak power, and therefore greater range.

The major drawback to frequency hopping is that the maximum data rate achievable is 2 Mbps. Although you can place frequency-hopping APs on 79 different hop sets, mitigating the possibility for interference and allowing greater aggregated throughput, scalability of frequency-hopping technologies is poor. Work is being done on wideband frequency hopping, but this concept is not currently standardized with the IEEE. Wideband frequency hopping promises data rates as high as 10 Mbps. Frequency hopping is best suited to environments where the level of interference is high and the amount of data to be transmitted is low.

Orthogonal Frequency-Division Multiplexing (OFDM)

The 802.11a standard uses a type of frequency-division multiplexing (FDM) called orthogonal frequency-division multiplexing (OFDM). In an FDM system, the available bandwidth is divided into multiple data carriers. The data to be transmitted is then divided between these subcarriers. Because each carrier is treated independently of the others, a frequency guard band must be placed around it. This guard band lowers the bandwidth efficiency. In OFDM, multiple carriers (or tones) are used to divide the data across the available spectrum, similar to FDM. This is shown in Figure 3-13.

Figure 3-13   OFDM

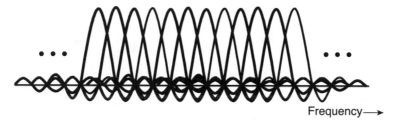

Frequency⟶

However, in an OFDM system, each tone is considered to be orthogonal (independent or unrelated) to the adjacent tones and, therefore, does not require a guard band. Thus, OFDM provides high spectral efficiency compared with FDM, along with resiliency to radio frequency interference and lower multipath distortion.

The FCC has broken the 5-GHz spectrum into three primary noncontiguous bands, as part of the Unlicensed National Information Infrastructure (U-NII). Each of the three U-NII bands has 100 MHz of bandwidth with power restrictions and consists of four nonoverlapping channels that are 20 MHz wide. As a result, each of the 20-MHz channels comprises 52 300-kHz-wide subchannels. Of these subchannels, 48 are used for data transmission, whereas the remaining 4 are used for error correction. Three U-NII bands are available for use:

- U-NII 1 devices operate in the 5.15- to 5.25-GHz frequency range. U-NII 1 devices have a maximum transmit power of 50 mW, a maximum antenna gain of 6 dBi, and the antenna and radio are required to be one complete unit (no removable antennas). U-NII 1 devices can be used only indoors.

- U-NII 2 devices operate in the 5.25- to 5.35-GHz frequency range. U-NII 2 devices have a maximum transmit power of 250 mW and maximum antenna gain of 6 dBi. Unlike U-NII 1 devices, U-NII 2 devices may operate indoors or outdoors, and can have removable antennas. The FCC allows a single device to cover both U-NII 1 and U-NII 2 spectra, but mandates that if used in this manner, the device must comply with U-NII 1 regulations.

- U-NII 3 devices operate in the 5.725- to 5.825-GHz frequency range. These devices have a maximum transmit power of 1W and allow for removable antennas. Unlike U-NII 1 and U-NII 2 devices, U-NII 3 devices can operate only in outdoor environments. As such, the FCC allows up to a 23-dBi directional gain antenna for point-to-point installations, and a 6-dBi omnidirectional gain antenna for point-to-multipoint installations.

Table 3-2 summarizes the three bands and the power restrictions defined for different geographic areas. Note that in some parts of the world, the use of the GHz band will cause contention. Therefore, not all three bands can be used everywhere.

Table 3-2   *Worldwide 5-GHz Spectrum Power Restrictions*

Band	Frequency	USA/Canada	Europe	France	Spain	Japan
U-NII 1	5.150–5.250	50mW	200mW	200mW	200mW	200mW
U-NII 2	5.250–5.350	250mW	200mW	200mW	200mW	
U-NII 3	5.725–5.825	1W				

Figure 3-14 shows the 5-GHz spectrum allocation.

Figure 3-14   *5-GHz Spectrum Allocation*

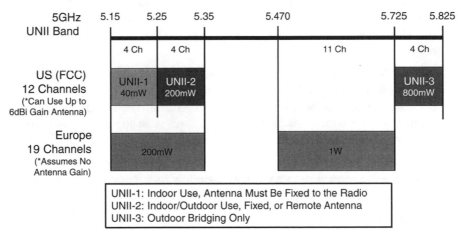

*If You Use a Higher Gain Antenna, You Must Reduce the Transmit Power Accordingly

Table 3-3 summarizes the varying differences in transmission type and speeds for the different 802.11 physical layer standards.

Table 3-3   *Comparison of 802.11 Physical Layer Standards*

Characteristic	802.11	802.11b	802.11a	802.11g
Frequency band	2.4 GHz	2.4 GHz	5 GHz	2.4 GHz
Technology	FHSS/DSSS	DSSS	OFDM	OFDM
Data rate	1 Mbps and 2 Mbps	5.5 Mbps and 11 Mbps	6, 9, 12, 18, 24, 36, 48, and 54 Mbps	20+ Mbps

802.11 Media Access Control

The MAC layer controls how stations gain access to the media to transmit data. 802.11 has many similarities to the standard 802.3-based Ethernet LANs, which use the carrier sense multiple access/collision detect (CSMA/CD) architecture. A station that wants to transmit data to another station first determines whether the medium is in use—the carrier sense function of CSMA/CD. All stations that are connected to the medium have equal access to it—the multiple-access portion of CSMA/CD. If a station verifies that the medium is available for use, it begins transmitting. If two stations sense that the medium is available and begin transmitting at the same time, their frames will "collide" and render the data transmitted on the medium useless. The sending stations are able to detect a collision, the collision-detection function of CSMA/CD, and run through a fallback algorithm to retransmit the frames.

The 802.3 Ethernet architecture was designed for wired networks. The designers placed a certain amount of reliability on the wired medium to carry the frames from a sender station to the desired destination. For that reason, 802.3 has no mechanism to determine whether a frame has reached the destination station. 802.3 relies on upper-layer protocols to deal with frame retransmission. This is not the case for 802.11 networks.

802.11 networks use a MAC layer known as carrier sense multiple access/collision avoidance (CSMA/CA). In CSMA/CA, a wireless node that wants to transmit performs the following sequence of steps:

1 It listens on a desired channel.

2 If the channel has no active transmitters, it sends a packet.

3 If the channel is busy, the node waits until transmission stops plus a contention period (a random period of time after every transmit that statistically allows every node equal access to the media). The contention time is typically 50ms for frequency hopping and 20ms for direct sequencing systems.

4 If the channel is idle at the end of the contention period, the node transmits the packet; otherwise, it repeats Step 3 until it gets a free channel.

Because 802.11 networks transmit across the air, there exist numerous sources of interference. In addition, a transmitting station can't listen for collisions while sending data, mainly because the station can't have its receiver on while transmitting the packet. As a result, 802.11 provides a link-layer acknowledgement function to provide notifications to the sender that the destination has received the frame. The receiving station needs to send an acknowledgment (ACK) if it detects no errors in the received packet. If the sending station doesn't receive an ACK after a specified period of time, the sending station will assume that there was a collision (or RF interference) and retransmit the packet.

Client stations also use the ACK messages as a means of determining how far from the AP they have moved. As the station transmits data, it has a time window in which it expects to receive an ACK message from the destination. When these ACK messages start to time out, the client knows that it is moving far enough away from the AP that communications are starting to deteriorate.

In point-to-multipoint networks, there can exist a condition known as the "hidden-node" problem. This is shown in Figure 3-15.

Figure 3-15   *Hidden-Node Problem*

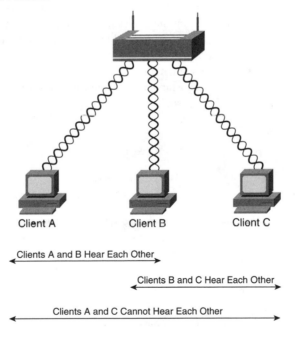

There are three wireless clients associated with an AP. Clients A and B can hear each other, clients C and B can hear each other, but client A cannot hear client C. Therefore, there exists the possibility that both clients A and C would simultaneously transmit a packet. The hidden-node problem is solved by the use of the optional RTS/CTS (Request To Send /

Clear To Send) protocol, which allows an AP to control use of the medium. If client A is using RTS/CTS, for example, it first sends an RTS frame to the AP before sending a data packet. The AP then responds with a CTS frame indicating that client A can transmit its packet. The CTS frame is heard by both client B and C and contains a duration field for which these clients will hold off transmitting their respective packets. This avoids collisions between hidden nodes.

The 802.11 MAC packet format is shown in Figure 3-16.

Figure 3-16 *802.11 MAC Packet Format*

Frame Control	Duration ID	Address 1 (Source)	Address 2 (Destination)	Address 3 (RX Node)	Sequence Control	Address 3 (TX Node)	DATA	FCS
Bytes: 2	2	6	6	6	2	6	0-2312	4

Two forms of authentication are specified in 802.11: open system authentication and shared key authentication. Open system authentication is mandatory, whereas shared key authentication is optional.

When new wireless clients want to associate with an AP, they listen for the periodic management frames that are sent out by APs. These management frames are known as beacons and contain AP information needed by a wireless station to begin the association/ authentication process, such as the SSID, supported data rates, whether the AP supports frequency hopping or direct sequencing, and capacity. Beacon frames are broadcast from the AP at regular intervals, adjustable by the administrator. Figure 3-17 shows a typical scenario for a wireless client association process.

Figure 3-17 *Wireless Client Association*

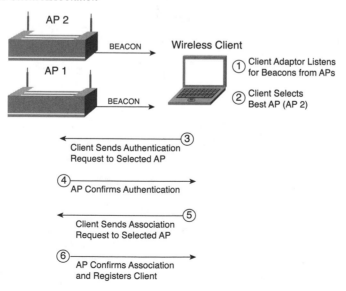

Wireless LAN Roaming

Wireless roaming refers to the capability of a wireless client to connect to multiple APs. ACK frames and beacons provide the client station with a reference point to determine whether a roaming decision needs to be made. If a set number of beacon messages are missed, the client can assume they have roamed out of range of the AP they are associated to. In addition, if expected ACK messages are not received, clients can also make the same assumption.

Usually, the client station tries to connect to another AP if the currently received signal strength is low or the received signal quality is poor and makes it hard to coherently interpret the signal. To find another AP, the client either passively listens or actively probes other channels to solicit a response. When it gets a response, it tries to authenticate and associate to the newly found AP.

The 802.11 specification does not stipulate any particular mechanism for roaming, although there is a draft specification, 802.11f, "Recommended Practice for Inter Access Point Protocol," which addresses roaming issues. IAPP coordinates roaming between APs on the same subnet. Roaming is initiated by the client and executed by the APs through IAPP messaging between the APs. Therefore, it is up to each WLAN vendor to define an algorithm for its WLAN clients to make roaming decisions.

The actual act of roaming can differ from vendor to vendor. The basic act of roaming is making a decision to roam, followed by the act of locating a new AP to roam to. Roaming within a single subnet is fairly straightforward because the APs are in the same IP subnet and therefore the client IP addressing does not change. When crossing subnets, however, roaming becomes a more complex problem. To allow changing subnets while maintaining existing associations requires the use of Mobile IP.

Mobile IP

Mobile IP is a proposed standard specified in RFC 2002. It was designed to solve the subnet roaming problem by allowing the mobile node to use two IP addresses: a fixed home address and a care-of address that changes at each new point of attachment and can be thought of as the mobile node's topologically significant address; it indicates the network number and thus identifies the mobile node's point of attachment with respect to the network topology. The home address makes it appear that the mobile node is continually able to receive data on its *home network*, where Mobile IP requires the existence of a network node known as the *home agent*. Whenever the mobile node is not attached to its home network (and is therefore attached to what is termed a *foreign network*), the home agent gets all the packets destined for the mobile node and arranges to deliver them to the mobile node's current point of attachment.

Whenever the mobile node moves, it *registers* its new care-of address with its home agent. To get a packet to a mobile node from its home network, the home agent delivers the packet from the home network to the care-of address. This requires that the packet be modified so that the care-of address appears as the destination IP address. When the packet arrives at the care-of address, the reverse transformation is applied so that the packet once again appears to have the mobile node's home address as the destination IP address and the packet can be correctly received by the mobile node.

Roaming with the use of Mobile IP is shown in Figure 3-18.

Figure 3-18   *Roaming with Mobile IP*

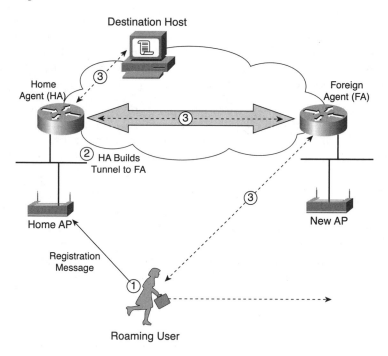

The sequence of steps for roaming with Mobile IP is as follows:

1 The client (mobile node) associates with an AP on a different subnet and sends a registration message to the home network (home agent).

2 The home agent builds a tunnel to the foreign agent and installs a host route pointing to the foreign agent via the tunnel interface.

3 Traffic between the destination host and mobile node is transported via the tunnel between the home agent and foreign agent.

Wireless LAN Security

Wireless security mechanisms are still evolving. The following sections detail what is currently being deployed as well as security functionality that is work in progress but most likely will be available at the time this book comes to press.

Basic Security

Wireless networks require secure access to the AP and the capability to isolate the AP from the internal private network prior to user authentication into the network domain. Minimum network access control can be implemented via the SSID associated with an AP or group of APs. The SSID provides a mechanism to "segment" a wireless network into multiple networks serviced by one or more APs. Each AP is programmed with an SSID corresponding to a specific wireless network. To access this network, client computers must be configured with the correct SSID. Typically, a client computer can be configured with multiple SSIDs for users who require access to the network from a variety of different locations. Because a client computer must present the correct SSID to access the AP, the SSID acts as a simple password and, thus, provides a simple albeit weak measure of security.

NOTE   The minimal security for accessing an AP by using a unique SSID is compromised if the AP is configured to "broadcast" its SSID. When this broadcast feature is enabled, any client computer that is not configured with a specific SSID is allowed to receive the SSID and access the AP. In addition, because users typically configure their own client systems with the appropriate SSIDs, they are widely known and easily shared.

Whereas an AP or group of APs can be identified by an SSID, a client computer can be identified by the unique MAC address of its 802.11 network card. To increase the security of an 802.11 network, each AP can be programmed with a list of MAC addresses associated with the client computers allowed to access the AP. If a client's MAC address is not included in this list, the client is not allowed to associate with the AP.

Using MAC address filtering along with SSIDs provides limited security and is only suited to small networks where the MAC address list can be efficiently managed. Each AP must be manually programmed with a list of MAC addresses, and the list must be kept current (although some vendors have proprietary implementations to use RADIUS to provide for a more scalable means to support MAC address filtering). Many small networks, especially home-office networks, should configure MAC address filtering and SSIDs as a bare minimum. Even though it offers only limited security, it will mitigate a casual rogue wireless client from accessing your wireless network.

NOTE SSIDs were never intended as a security measure and because MAC addresses are sent in the clear over the airwaves, they can easily be spoofed. It is recommended that all wireless networks, whether deployed in a home setting or larger corporate environment, use more stringent security measures, which are discussed in the following sections.

WEP Encryption

The IEEE has specified that Wired Equivalent Privacy (WEP) protocol be used in 802.11 networks to provide link-level encrypted communication between the client and an AP. WEP uses the RC4 encryption algorithm, which is a symmetric stream cipher that supports a variable-length secret key. The way a stream cipher works is shown in Figure 3-19. There is a function (the cipher) that generates a stream of data one byte at a time; this data is called the keystream. The input to the function is the encryption key, which controls exactly what keystream is generated.

Each byte of the keystream is combined with a byte of plaintext to get a byte of cyphertext. RC4 uses the exclusive or (XOR) function to combine the keystream with the plaintext.

Figure 3-19 *Stream Ciphers*

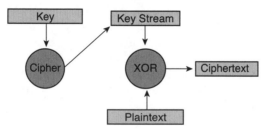

Because RC4 is a symmetric encryption algorithm, the key is the one piece of information that must be shared by both the encrypting and decrypting endpoints. Therefore, everyone on the local wireless network uses the same secret key. The RC4 algorithm uses this key to generate an indefinite, pseudorandom keystream. RC4 allows the key length to be variable, up to 256 bytes, as opposed to requiring the key to be fixed at a certain length. IEEE specifies that 802.11 devices must support 40-bit keys, with the option to use longer key lengths. Many implementations also support 104-bit secret keys.

Because WEP is a stream cipher, a mechanism is required to ensure that the same plaintext will not generate the same ciphertext. The IEEE stipulated the use of an initialization vector (IV) to be concatenated with the symmetric key before generating the stream ciphertext.

The IV is a 24-bit value (ranging from 0 to 16,777,215). The IEEE suggests—but does not mandate—that the IV change per frame. Because the sender generates the IV with no standard scheme or schedule, it must be sent to the receiver unencrypted in the header portion of the 802.11 data frame as shown in Figure 3-20.

Figure 3-20 *Use of Initialization Vector*

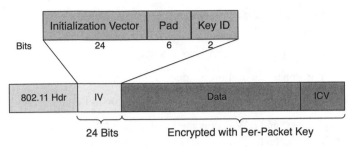

- 802.11 IVs are 24 Bit Integer Values
- Augment 40 Bit Keys to 64 Bits
- Augment 104 Bit Keys to 128 Bits
- Sent in the Clear

The receiver can then concatenate the received IV with the WEP key it has stored locally to decrypt the data frame. As shown in Figure 3-8, the plaintext itself is not run through the RC4 cipher, but rather the RC4 cipher is used to generate a unique keystream for that particular 802.11 frame using the IV and base key as keying material. The resulting unique keystream is then combined with the plaintext and run through a mathematical function called XOR. This produces the ciphertext.

Figure 3-21 shows the steps used to encrypt WEP traffic.

Figure 3-21 *WEP Encryption*

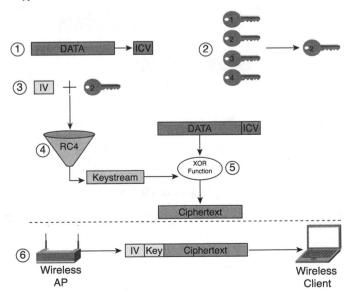

The steps used to encrypt WEP traffic follow:

1 Before a data packet is transmitted, an integrity check value (ICV) is computed of the plaintext, using CRC32.

2 One of four possible secret keys is selected.

3 An IV is generated and prepended to selected the secret key.

4 RC4 generates the keystream from the combined IV and secret key.

5 The plaintext and ICV is concatenated, then XOR'ed with the generated keystream to get the ciphertext.

6 The message sent includes first the IV and key number in plaintext, and then the encrypted data.

Figure 3-22 shows the steps used to decrypt WEP traffic.

Figure 3-22 *WEP Decryption*

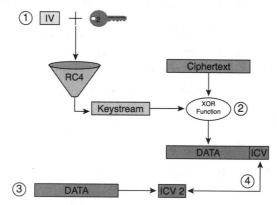

The steps to decrypt WEP traffic follow:

1 The IV and secret key are used to regenerate the RC4 keystream.

2 The data is decrypted by running XOR to get the payload and ICV.

3 The ICV is computed from the decrypted payload.

4 The new ICV is compared with the sent ICV. If they match, the packet is valid.

NOTE   Make sure you understand what a vendor specifies in terms of WEP key length. WEP specifies the use of a 40-bit encryption key and there are also implementations of 104-bit keys. The encryption key is concatenated with a 24-bit "initialization vector," resulting in a 64- or 128-bit key. This key is then input into a pseudorandom number generator with the resulting sequence used to encrypt the data to be transmitted.

Under the original WEP specification, all clients and APs on a wireless network use the same key to encrypt and decrypt data. The key resides in the client computer and in each AP on the network. The 802.11 standard does not specify a key management protocol, so all WEP keys on a network must be managed manually. Support for WEP is standard on most current 802.11 cards and APs. WEP security is not available in ad hoc (or peer-to-peer) 802.11 networks that do not use APs.

WEP encryption has been proven to be vulnerable to attack. Scripting tools exist that can be used to take advantage of weaknesses in the WEP key algorithm to successfully attack a network and discover the WEP key. These are discussed in more detail in Chapter 5. The industry and IEEE are working on solutions to this security problem, which is discussed in the "Security Enhancements" section later in this chapter. Despite the weaknesses of WEP-based security, it can still be a component of the security solution used in small, tightly managed networks with minimal security requirements. In these cases, 128-bit WEP should be implemented in conjunction with MAC address filtering and SSID (with the broadcast feature disabled). Customers should change WEP keys on a regular basis to minimize risk.

For networks with more stringent security requirements, the wireless VPN solutions discussed in the next section should be considered. The VPN solutions are also preferable for large networks, in which the administrative burden of maintaining WEP encryption keys on each client system and AP, as well as MAC addresses on each AP, makes these solutions impractical.

Cryptographic Authentication

The IEEE specified two authentication algorithms for 802.11-based networks: open system authentication and shared key authentication. Open system authentication is the default and is a null authentication algorithm because any station requesting authentication is granted access. Shared key authentication requires that both the requesting and granting stations be configured with matching WEP keys. Figure 3-23 shows the sequence of steps for this type of authentication.

Figure 3-23   *Shared Key Authentication*

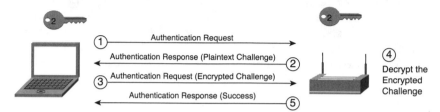

The steps for shared key authentication are as follows:

   1   The client sends an authentication request to the AP.

   2   The AP sends a plaintext challenge frame to the client.

   3   The client encrypts the challenge with the shared WEP key and responds back to the AP.

   4   The AP attempts to decrypt the challenge frame.

   5   If the resulting plaintext matches what the AP originally sent, the client has a valid key and the AP sends a "success" authentication message.

NOTE   Shared key authentication has a known flaw in its concept. Because the challenge packet is sent in the clear to the requesting station and the requesting station replies with the encrypted challenge packet, an attacker can derive the stream cipher by analyzing both the plaintext and the ciphertext. This information can be used to build decryption dictionaries for that particular WEP key.

As mentioned previously, some vendors have implemented proprietary means of supporting scalable MAC address filtering through the use of a AAA server such as RADIUS. In these scenarios, before an AP completes a client association, it presents a PAP request to the RADIUS server with the wireless client's MAC address. If the RADIUS server approves the MAC address, the association between the AP and wireless client is completed.

Security Enhancements

Due to the weak security mechanisms in the original 802.11 specification, the IEEE 802.11i task group was formed to improve wireless LAN security.

Ratification of this standard is expected at the end of 2003 and is expected to provide an interim solution; many vendors have agreed on an interoperable interim standard known as the Wi-Fi Protected Access (WPA). WPA is a subset of the security features proposed in 802.11i and the relevant technologies that will be implemented as part of WPA are described in the following sections.

Temporal Key Integrity Protocol (TKIP)

The Temporal Key Integrity Protocol, being standardized in 802.11i, provides a replacement technology for WEP security and improves upon some of the current WEP problems. TKIP will allow existing hardware to operate with only a firmware upgrade and should be backward compatible with hardware that still uses WEP. It is expected that sometime later, new chip-based security that uses the stronger Advanced Encryption Standard (AES) protocol will replace TKIP, and the new chips will probably be backward compatible with TKIP. In effect, TKIP is a temporary protocol for use until manufacturers implement AES at the hardware level.

TKIP requires dynamic keying using a key management protocol. It has three components: per-packet key mixing, extended IV and sequencing rules, and a message integrity check (MIC):

- **Per-packet key mixing / extended IV and sequencing rules**—The TKIP specification requires the use of a temporal key hash, where the IV and a preconfigured WEP key are hashed to produce a unique key (called a temporal key). This 128-bit temporal key is then combined with the client machine's MAC address and adds a relatively large 16-octet IV, which produces the key that will encrypt the data. Figure 3-24 shows this.

Figure 3-24 *Per-Packet Key Mixing*

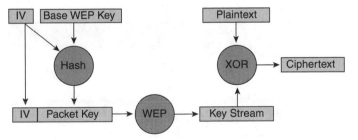

- IV Sequencing—IVs Increment by One
- Per Packet IV is Hashed With Base WEP Key
- Result is a New Packet WEP Key
- The Packet WEP Key Changes Per IV

This procedure ensures that each station uses different keystreams to encrypt the data. TKIP uses RC4 to perform the encryption, which is the same as WEP. A major difference from WEP, however, is that TKIP changes temporal keys every 10,000 packets. This provides a dynamic distribution method that significantly enhances the security of the network. Rekeying is performed more frequently and an authenticated key exchange is added.

- **MIC**—The TKIP message integrity check is based on a seed value, the MAC header, a sequence number, and the payload. The MIC uses a hashing algorithm to derive the resulting value, as shown in Figure 3-25.

Figure 3-25 *TKIP Message Integrity Check*

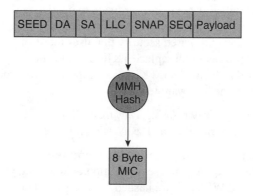

This MIC is included in the WEP-encrypted payload, shown in Figure 3-26.

Figure 3-26 *TKIP MIC-Enhanced WEP Frame*

Standard WEP Frame

MIC Enhanced WEP Frame

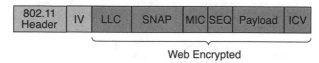

This is a vast improvement from the cyclic redundancy check (CRC-32) function based on standard WEP and mitigates the vulnerability to replay attacks.

802.1X "Network Port Authentication"

802.1X is an IEEE standard approved in June 2001 that enables authentication and key management for IEEE 802 LANs. IEEE 802.1X is not a cipher and therefore is not an alternative to WEP, 3DES, AES, or any other cipher. Because IEEE 802.1X is only focused on authentication and key management, it does not specify how or when security services are to be delivered using the derived keys. However, it can be used to derive authentication and encryption keys for use with any cipher, and can also be used to periodically refresh keys and re-authenticate so as to make sure that the keying material is "fresh."

The specification is general: It applies to both wireless and wired Ethernet networks. IEEE 802.1X is not a single authentication method; instead, it uses EAP as its authentication framework. This means that 802.1X-enabled switches and APs can support a wide variety of authentication methods, including certificate-based authentication, smart cards, token cards, one-time passwords, and so on. However, the 802.1X specification itself does not specify or mandate any authentication methods. Because switches and APs act as a "passthrough" for EAP, new authentication methods can be added without the need to upgrade the switch or AP, by adding software on the host and back-end authentication server.

In the context of an 802.11 wireless network, 802.1X/EAP requires that a wireless client that associates with an AP cannot gain access to the network until the user is appropriately authenticated. After association, the client and an authentication server exchange EAP messages to perform mutual authentication, with the client verifying the authentication server credentials and vice versa.

An EAP supplicant is used on the client machine to obtain the user credentials, which can be in the form of a username/password or digital certificate. Upon successful client and server mutual authentication, the authentication server and client derive a client-specific WEP key to be used by the client for the current logon session. User passwords and session keys are never transmitted in the clear, over the wireless link.

The sequence of events is shown in Figure 3-27. Although a RADIUS server is used in these following steps as the authentication server, the 802.1X specification itself does not mandate any particular authentication server. Note also that the term "authentication server" is a logical entity that may or may not reside external to the physical AP.

Figure 3-27 *802.1X/EAP Authentication*

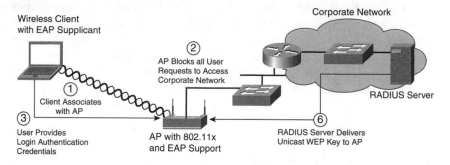

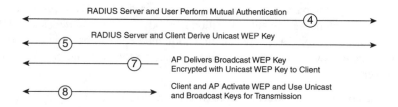

802.1X network port authentication steps are as follows:

1 A wireless client associates with an AP.

2 The AP blocks all attempts by the client to gain access to network resources until the client logs on to the network.

3 The user on the client supplies the network login credentials (username/password or digital certificate).

4 Using 802.1X and EAP, the wireless client and a RADIUS server on the wired LAN perform a mutual authentication through the AP.

5 When mutual authentication is successfully completed, the RADIUS server and the client determine a WEP key that is distinct to the client. The client loads this key and prepares to use it for the logon session.

6 The RADIUS server sends the WEP key, called a session key, over the wired LAN to the AP.

7 The AP encrypts its broadcast key with the session key and sends the encrypted key to the client, which uses the session key to decrypt it.

8 The client and AP activate WEP and use the session and broadcast WEP keys for all communications during the remainder of the session or until a timeout is reached and new WEP keys are generated.

Both the session key and broadcast key are changed at regular intervals. The RADIUS server at the end of EAP authentication specifies session key timeout to the AP and the broadcast key rotation time can be configured on the AP.

Although EAP provides authentication method flexibility, the EAP exchange itself may be sent in the clear because it occurs before wireless frames are encrypted. To provide a secure encrypted channel to be used in conjunction with EAP, a variety of EAP types use a secure TLS channel before completing the EAP authentication process. The following are mechanisms that are implemented in wireless devices and can be deployed today to perform the mutual authentication process.

EAP-Transport Layer Security (EAP-TLS)

Specified in RFC 2716, EAP-TLS is based on TLS and uses digital certificates for both user and server authentication. The RADIUS server sends its digital certificate to the client in the first phase of the EAP authentication sequence (server-side TLS). The client validates the RADIUS server certificate by verifying the issuer of the certificate and the contents of the certificate. Upon completion, the client sends its certificate to the RADIUS server and the RADIUS server proceeds to validate the client's certificate by verifying the issuer of the certificate and the contents. When both the RADIUS server and client are successfully authenticated, an EAP "success" message is sent to the client, and both the client and the RADIUS server derive the dynamic WEP key. EAP-TLS authentication occurs automatically, with no intervention by the user, and provides a strong authentication scheme through the use of certificates. Note, however, that this EAP exchange is sent in the clear.

EAP-Tunneled TLS (EAP-TTLS)

EAP-TTLS is an Internet draft that extends EAP-TLS. In EAP-TLS, a TLS handshake is used to mutually authenticate a client and server. EAP-TTLS extends this authentication negotiation by using the secure connection established by the TLS handshake to exchange additional information between client and server. In EAP-TTLS, the TLS handshake may be mutual; or it may be one-way, in which only the server is authenticated to the client. The secure connection established by the handshake may then be used by the server to authenticate the client using existing, widely deployed authentication infrastructures such as RADIUS.

The authentication of the client may itself be EAP, or it may be another authentication protocol such as PAP, CHAP, MS-CHAP, or MS-CHAP-V2.

EAP-TTLS also allows the client and server to establish keying material for use in the data connection between the client and the AP. The keying material is established implicitly between the client and server based on the TLS handshake.

EAP-Cisco Wireless (LEAP)

LEAP is a Cisco proprietary mechanism where mutual authentication relies on a shared secret, the user's logon password, which is known to both the client and the RADIUS server. At the start of the mutual authentication phase, the RADIUS server sends an authentication challenge to the client. The client uses a one-way hash of the user-supplied password and includes the message digest in its response back to the RADIUS server. The RADIUS server extracts the message digest and performs its own one-way hash using the username's associated password from its local database. If both message digests match, the client is authenticated. Next, the process is repeated in reverse so that the RADIUS server gets authenticated. Upon successful mutual authentication, an EAP "success" message is sent to the client, and both the client and the RADIUS server derive the dynamic WEP key.

Protected EAP (PEAP)

PEAP is an Internet draft co-authored by Cisco, Microsoft, and RSA Security. Server-side authentication is accomplished by using digital certificates, although client-side authentication can support varying EAP-encapsulated methods and is accomplished within a protected TLS tunnel. The PEAP TLS channel is created through the following steps:

1 When a logical link is created, the wireless AP sends an EAP request/identity message to the wireless client.

2 The wireless client responds with an EAP response/identity message that contains either the user or device name of the wireless client.

3 The EAP response/identity message is sent by the AP to the EAP server. In this example, assume that the EAP server used is in fact a RADIUS server.

4 The RADIUS server sends the EAP request/start PEAP message to the wireless client (via the AP).

5 The wireless client and RADIUS server exchange TLS messages where the RADIUS server authenticates itself to the wireless client using a certificate chain and where the cipher suite for the TLS channel is negotiated for mutual encryption and signing keys.

When the PEAP TLS channel is created, the wireless client is authenticated through the following steps:

1 The RADIUS server sends an EAP request/identity message to the wireless client.

2 The wireless client responds with an EAP response/identity message that contains either the user or device name of the client.

3 The RADIUS server sends an EAP request/EAP challenge message (for CHAP or MS-CHAPv2) that contains the challenge.

4 The wireless client responds with an EAP response/EAP challenge-response message that contains both the response to the RADIUS server challenge and a challenge string for the RADIUS server.

5 The RADIUS server sends an EAP request/EAP challenge-success message to indicate that the wireless client response was correct. It also contains the response to the wireless client challenge.

6 The wireless client responds with an EAP response/EAP challenge-ACK message to indicate that the RADIUS server response was correct.

7 The RADIUS server sends an EAP success message to the wireless client.

Wireless VPN Security

VPN solutions, as discussed previously in this chapter, are already widely deployed to provide remote workers with secure access to the network via the Internet. The VPN provides a secure, dedicated path (or "tunnel") over an "untrusted" network—in this case, the Internet. The same VPN technology can also be used to secure wireless access. The "untrusted" network is the wireless network, and all data transmission between a wireless client and an endpoint to a trusted network or end host can be authenticated and encrypted. For example, TLS or some other application security protocol can be used to provide secure communication for specific applications. If IPsec is used, every wireless client must be IPsec-capable and the user is required to establish an IPsec tunnel back to either a VPN concentrator residing at the trusted network ingress point or to another end host. Roaming issues between different subnets will be an issue with a wireless VPN solution to date, and work to resolve the issues is still in progress.

The mechanisms to secure wireless networks are still evolving and readers can follow much of the progress from this unofficial site from Bernard Aboba http://www.drizzle.com/~aboba/IEEE/. Even if the security mechanisms available today aren't totally robust, any risk mitigation that is deployable should be configured.

Voice over IP (VoIP) Networks

IP telephony, known in the industry as *Voice over IP* (VoIP), is the transmission of telephone calls over an IP data network. VoIP networks have in recent years become more prevalent due to enhanced technical standards and solutions that lower the cost of network ownership and enhance business communications.

IP Telephony Network Components

In addition to the underlying IP network, the components of an IP telephony network include the following:

- **IP telephony devices**—This refers to any device that supports placing and receiving calls in an IP telephony network. IP phones can be either separate physical devices or software-based applications installed on user systems with speakers and microphones. IP phones offer services such as user directory lookups and Internet access for stock quotes; these are referred to as IP phone services and are accessed via a proxy server.

- **Call-processing manager**—This server provides call control and configuration management for IP telephony devices; also known as an *IP PBX*. This device provides the core functionality to bootstrap IP telephony devices, register IP phones, provide call setup, perform proxy services, and route calls throughout the network to other voice devices including voice gateways and voice-mail systems.

- **Voice-mail system**—Provides IP-based voice-mail storage and an auto-attendant (an automated attendant providing voice services) for services such as user directory lookup and call forwarding.

- **Voice gateway**—A general term used to refer to any gateway that provides voice services including such features as Public Switched Telephone Network (PSTN) access, IP packet routing, backup call processing, and voice services. This is the device that provides access to legacy voice systems for local calls, toll bypass, and WAN backup in case of failure. Backup call processing allows for the voice gateway to take over call processing in case the primary call-processing manager goes offline for any reason. Typically the voice gateway supports a subset of the call-processing functionality supported by the call-processing manager.

IP Telephony Deployment Models

There are three main models for the deployment of enterprise IP telephony networks:

- **Single-site campus**—A single-site VoIP deployment model is the most basic deployment scenario in which all IP telephony devices, the call-processing mananger, VoIP applications, and the voice gateway reside in a single campus as shown in Figure 3-28. Any external calls are made using the PSTN network.

Figure 3-28 *Single-Site VoIP Deployment Model*

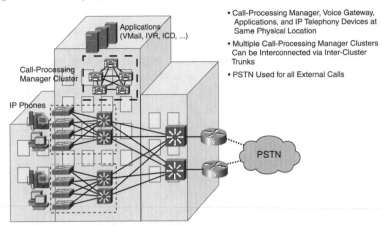

- Call-Processing Manager, Voice Gateway, Applications, and IP Telephony Devices at Same Physical Location
- Multiple Call-Processing Manager Clusters Can be Interconnected via Inter-Cluster Trunks
- PSTN Used for all External Calls

- **WAN centralized call processing**—This is a moderately complex scenario in which multiple sites are connected over a private WAN and the corporate site contains the only call-processing manager cluster. Voice applications can either be centralized or distributed and remote sites may have voice services such as voice-mail.

- **WAN distributed call processing**—This is the most complex scenario, shown in Figure 3-29, in which multiple sites are connected over a private WAN and one or more of the sites contains a call-processing manager cluster. Many of the sites will also have voice application services such as voice-mail. The PSTN is the backup method of placing calls in the event that the WAN IP link goes down.

Figure 3-29 *WAN Distributed Call Processing*

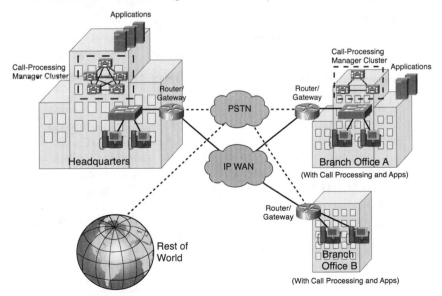

VoIP Protocols

The past few years have seen a major shift in the development of VoIP protocols. This section is not intended as a full detailed description of all the developments because that could easily encompass an entire book by itself. Readers interested in understanding VoIP in its entirety should read *Cisco Voice over Frame Relay, ATM, and IP* (Cisco Press) for a comprehensive description of VoIP networks. Here we concentrate on giving a brief overview of the three protocols that are being deployed in most current VoIP solutions. These are H323, Media Gateway Control Protocol (MGCP), and Session Initiation Protocol (SIP).

H.323

H.323 is a standard created by the International Telecommunications Union (ITU). There currently exist four versions: v1 was approved in 1996, v2 in January 1998, v3 in September 1999, and v4 in November 2000. It provides specifications for real-time, inter-active videoconferencing, data sharing, and audio applications such as IP telephony. The H.323 recommendations cover the IP devices that participate and control H.323 sessions and the elements that interact with the switched-circuit network. H.323 standards do not include the LAN itself, nor the transport layer that interconnects LAN segments. In common with other ITU multimedia teleconferencing standards, H.323 implementation applies to either point-to-point or -multipoint sessions. The H.323 recommendation allows multipoint conferences through a variety of methods and allows for either centralized or decentralized conference technologies.

H.323 Components

In a general H.323 implementation, four logical entities or components are required:

- **Terminal**—A terminal, or a client, is an endpoint where H.323 data streams and signaling originate and terminate. It may be a multimedia PC with a H.323-compliant stack or a standalone device such as a universal serial bus (USB) IP telephone. A terminal must support audio communication; video and data communication support is optional.

- **Gateway**—A gateway is an optional component in an H.323-enabled network. When communication is required between different networks, however, a gateway is needed at the interface. Through the provision of gateways in H.323, it is possible for H.323 terminals to interoperate with other H.32x-compliant conferencing terminals. For example, it is possible for a H.323 terminal to set up a conference with terminals based on H.320 or H.324 through an appropriate gateway. A gateway provides data format translation, control signaling translation, audio and video codec translation, and call setup and termination functionality on both sides of the network. Depending on the type of network for which translation is required, a gateway may support H.310, H.320, H.321, H.322, or H.324 endpoints.

- **Multipoint control unit (MCU)**—The MCU is also an optional component of an H.323-enabled network. It enables conferencing between three or more endpoints and consists of a mandatory multipoint controller (MC) and zero or more multipoint processors (MP). Although the MCU is a separate logical unit it may be combined into a terminal, gateway, or gatekeeper. The multipoint controller provides a centralized location for multipoint call setup. Call and control signaling are routed through the MC so that endpoints capabilities can be determined and communication parameters negotiated. An MC may also be used in a point-to-point call, which can later be extended into a multipoint conference. Another useful job of the MC is to determine whether to unicast or multicast the audio and video streams depending on the capability of the underlying network and the topology of the multipoint conference. The multipoint processor handles the mixing, switching, and processing of the audio, video, and data streams among the conference endpoints.

  The MCU is required in a centralized multipoint conference where each terminal establishes a point-to-point connection with the MCU. The MCU determines the capabilities of each terminal and sends each a mixed media stream. In the decentralized model of multipoint conferencing, an MC ensures communication compatibility but the media streams are multicast and the mixing is performed at each terminal.

- **Gatekeeper**—A gatekeeper is an optional component of an H.323-enabled network. Gatekeepers provide central management and control services and are needed to ensure reliable, commercially feasible communications. When a gatekeeper exists, all endpoints (terminals, gateways, and MCUs) must be registered with it. Registered endpoints' control messages are routed through the gatekeeper. The gatekeeper and the endpoints it administers form a management zone.

The services a gatekeeper provides to all endpoints in its zone include the following:

- **Address translation**—A gatekeeper maintains a database for translation between aliases, such as international phone numbers and network addresses.

- **Admission and access control of endpoints**—This control can be based on bandwidth availability, limitations on the number of simultaneous H.323 calls, or the registration privileges of endpoints.

- **Bandwidth management**—Network administrators can manage bandwidth by specifying limitations on the number of simultaneous calls and by limiting authorization of specific terminals to place calls at specified times.

- **Routing capability**—A gatekeeper can route all calls originating or terminating in its zone. This capability provides numerous advantages. First, accounting information of calls can be maintained for billing and security purposes. Second, a gatekeeper can reroute a call to an appropriate gateway based on bandwidth availability. Third, rerouting can be used to develop advanced services such as mobile addressing, call forwarding, and voice-mail diversion.

Terminals, gateways, and MCUs are collectively known as endpoints. Even though an H.323-enabled network can be established with only terminals, the other components are essential to provide greater practical usefulness of the services.

H.323 Protocol Suite

Actually a suite of protocols, H.323 incorporates many individual protocols that have been developed for specific applications. Figure 3-30 illustrates the relationships of these components in the protocol stack.

Figure 3-30 *The H.323 Protocol Stack*

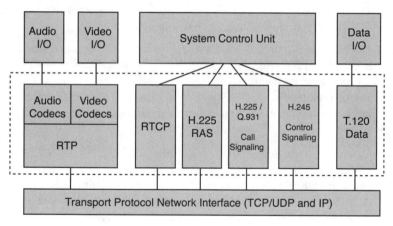

The following core components are part of H.323:

- **Control and signaling**—Control information is essential for call setup and tear down, capability exchange and negotiation, and administrative purposes. H.323 uses three control protocols: H.225 RAS, H.225/Q.931 call signaling, and H.245 media control.

- **H.225.0 RAS**—RAS (registration/authorization/status) messages define communications between endpoints and a gatekeeper. H.225.0 RAS is only needed when a gatekeeper exists. H.225.0 RAS uses unreliable transport for delivery, which in an IP network means using UDP.

- **H.225**—Specifies messages for call control, including signaling, registration and admissions, and packetization/synchronization of media streams. Call signaling is a basic requirement needed to set up and tear down a call between two endpoints. H.225.0 uses a subset of Q.931 signaling protocol for this purpose. Q.931 was initially developed for signaling in Integrated Services Digital Networks (ISDNs). H.225.0 adopts Q.931 signaling by incorporating it in its message format. H.225.0 call signaling is sent directly between the endpoints when no gatekeeper exists. When a gatekeeper exists, it may be routed through the gatekeeper.

- **H.245**—Specifies messages for opening and closing channels for media streams and other commands, requests, and indications. It allows endpoints to negotiate to determine compatible settings before audio, video, and/or data communication links can be established. H.245 is mandatory to implement in all endpoints.

- **Video codecs**—Recommendation H.323 specifies two video codecs: H.261 and H.263. However, H.323 clients are not limited to these codecs only. Other codecs can be used provided both terminals agree on and support it. Video support in H.323 terminals and MCUs is optional.

  The H.261 codec is used for audiovisual services for channels with bandwidths p x 64 kbps, where p can range from 1 to 30. The H.263 codec is a specification for a new video codec for video basic telephone service and is designed for low-bit-rate transmission without loss of quality.

- **Audio codecs**—H.323 specifies a series of audio codecs ranging in bit rates from 5.3 to 64 kbps. The mandatory codec is G.711, which uses pulse code modulation to produce bit rates of 56 and 64 kbps. G.711 is a popular codec designed for telephone networks. However, it is less appropriate for communication over the Internet, where subscriber loop bandwidths are much smaller. Nowadays, most H.323 terminals support G.723.1, which is much more efficient and produces good quality audio at 5.3 kbps and 6.3 kbps. The G.728 and G.729 codecs use advanced linear prediction quantization of digital audio to produce high-quality audio at 16 kbps and 8 kbps, respectively. The following list summarizes the list of audio codecs:

  - G.711—Audio codec, 3.1 kHz at 48, 56, and 64 kbps (normal telephony)
  - G.722—Audio codec, 7 kHz at 48, 56, and 64 kbps
  - G.723—Audio codec for 5.3- and 6.3-kbps modes
  - G.728—Audio codec, 3.1 kHz at 16 kbps
  - G.729—Audio codec

- **Real-time transport**—The Real-Time Transport Protocol (RTP) and the associated control protocol (Real-Time Control Protocol [RTCP]) are used for timely and orderly delivery of audio and video streams. RTP/RTCP is an IETF recommendation that provides logical framing, sequence numbering, time stamping, payload distinction (for instance, between audio and video and between different codecs), and source identification. It may also provide basic error detection and correction. Note that the RTP layer is above the transport layer of the underlying network.

The H.323 protocol stack runs on top of the transport and network IP layers. Reliable transport is for control signals and data, because signals must be received in proper order and cannot be lost. Unreliable transport is used for audio and video streams, which are time sensitive. Delayed audio and video packets are dropped. Consequently, TCP is applied to the H.245 control channel, the T.120 data channels, and the call-signaling channel, whereas UDP applies to audio, video, and registration/authorization/status (RAS) channels. Ports or sockets used for H.245 signaling, audio, video, or data channels are dynamically negotiated between endpoints.

H.323 Protocol Operation

Figure 3-31 shows an example of the H.232 call-signaling flows when a gatekeeper is used.

Figure 3-31 *H.323 Call-Signaling Flows*

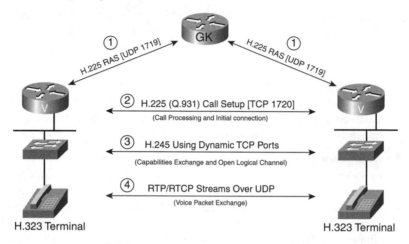

The RAS signaling protocol is used between terminals or gateways and gatekeepers. The RAS channel is opened before any other channel and is independent of the call setup and media transport channels. Initially, the terminals/gateway must discover their zone gatekeepers, which can be accomplished in two ways:

- **Unicast discovery**—This is a manual discovery method that uses UDP port 1718. Endpoints are configured with the gatekeeper IP address and can attempt to begin the registration process by sending gatekeeper request (GRQ) messages. The gatekeeper will reply with a gatekeeper reject (GRJ) message or a gatekeeper confirm (GCF) message, which contains the transport address of the gatekeeper RAS channel.

- **Multicast discovery**—This is an autodiscovery method that uses the UDP multicast address 224.0.1.41 and enables endpoints to discover its gatekeeper through a multicast message. A gatekeeper can be configured to respond only to certain subnets.

If a gatekeeper is not available, the gateway periodically attempts to rediscover a gatekeeper. When a gatekeeper is discovered, the registration process begins. Registration is the process by which gateways, terminals, and/or MCUs join a zone and inform the gatekeeper of their IP and alias addresses. Every gateway can register with only one active gatekeeper because there is only one active gatekeeper per zone. The H.323 gateway registers either with an H.323 ID (e-mail ID) or an E.164 address (telephone number). RAS uses UDP port 1719 for H.225 RAS messages.

The H.225 call control signaling is used to set up connections between H.323 endpoints using Q.931 signaling messages, which connect, maintain, and disconnect calls. The reliable call control channel is set up using TCP port 1720. When a gatekeeper does not exists, the H.225 messages are exchanged directly between the endpoints. When a gatekeeper is present, the H.225 call setup messages are exchanged either via direct call signaling or via gatekeeper-routed call signaling. The method chosen is decided by the gatekeeper during the RAS message exchange.

NOTE   Cisco gatekeepers use direct endpoint call signaling.

The H.245 protocol then establishes logical channels for transmission of audio, video, data, and control channel information. One H.245 session is established for each call. It negotiates channel usage, flow control, and capabilities exchange messages. This is accomplished through the use of dynamically allocated TCP ports.

NOTE   H.323v2 added a fast-connect capability that allows endpoints to establish a basic connection in as little as one round trip. It multiplexes H.245 logical channel proposals in an H.225 call-signaling channel. An endpoint may refuse fast connect and revert to normal H.245 procedures.

Finally, the RTP/RTCP sessions are established; these carry the voice or video data between the two ends. These sessions run over UPD using dynamically allocated UDP ports.

Figure 3-32 shows an example between gateways and gatekeeper interaction during an interzone call setup where two H.323 terminals are located in two different zones.

Figure 3-32   *H.323 Call Setup*

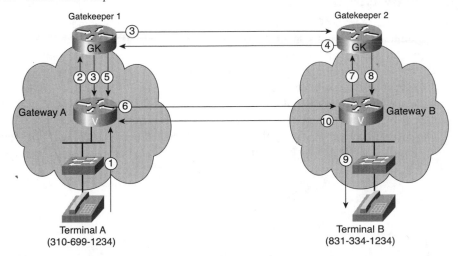

Terminal A
(310-699-1234)

Terminal B
(831-334-1234)

The steps that take place are as follows:

1   Terminal A dials the phone number for terminal B (831-334-1234).

2   Gateway A sends a RAS admission request (ARQ) to gatekeeper 1, asking permission to call terminal B.

3   Gatekeeper 1 does a lookup and does not find terminal B registered; it does a prefix lookup on the phone number and finds a match with gatekeeper 2; gatekeeper 1 sends a RAS location request (LRQ) message to gatekeeper 2 to get the IP address of terminal B; it also sends a RAS request-in-progress (RIP) message to gateway A.

4   Gatekeeper 2 does a lookup and finds terminal B registered; it returns a RAS location confirm message (LCF), which includes the IP address of gateway B.

5   Gatekeeper 1 returns a RAS admission confirm (ACF) message to terminal A, which contains the IP address of gateway B.

6   Gateway A sends a Q.931 call-setup message to gateway B with terminal B's phone number.

7   Gateway B sends gatekeeper 2 a RAS admission request (ARQ) asking permission to answer gateway A's call.

8   Gatekeeper 2 returns a RAS admission confirm (ACF) message, which contains the IP address of gateway A.

9   Gateway B sets up a POTS call to terminal B at 831-334-1234.

10   When terminal B answers, Gateway B sends a Q.931 connect message to gateway A.

This is then followed by the H.245 logical channel setup and RTP/RTCP data transfer.

Media Gateway Control Protocol (MGCP)

The Media Gateway Control Protocol is another VoIP protocol standard and was designed for simplicity. In MGCP, media gateway controllers or call agents provide control, signaling, and the processing skills to control the telephony gateways. A *telephony gateway* is a network device that provides conversion between the audio signals carried on telephone circuits and data packets carried on packet networks. MGCP assumes a call-control architecture wherein the call-control "intelligence" is outside the gateways and is handled by external call-control elements. MGCP is a master/slave protocol, wherein the gateways execute the commands sent by the call agents. The call agent implements the signaling layers of H.323 (listed earlier in the H.323 section) and appears to H.323 devices as an H.323 gateway or one or more H.323 endpoints.

It is possible to build an agent that accepts both H.323 and SIP call setup requests and then uses MGCP to establish calls between MGCP media gateways and H.323 and SIP gateways or endpoints. A basic MGCP-based telephony system involves one or more media gateways and at least one agent, sometimes called a *media gateway controller*. MGCP messages between the call agent and media gateway are sent via UDP/IP. The agent is signaled by all the media gateways that serve it of events such as incoming call, off-hook, and hang-up. The agent, in turn, sends commands to all of these media gateways to ring phones, dial numbers, and establish RTP/RTCP connections.

NOTE   MEGACO (Media Gateway Control)/H.248 is an emerging, incompatible next-generation protocol to MGCP. The IETF group that developed MGCP has joined forces with the ITU and developed MEGACO/H.248 that is standardized by both agencies. It is a master/slave, transaction-oriented protocol in which media gateway controllers (MGCs) control the operation of media gateways (MGs). Most companies that are currently deploying MGCP products plan to move to MEGACO.

Session Initiation Protocol (SIP)

Session Initiation Protocol, defined in RFC 3261, is the principal IETF standard for multimedia conferencing over IP. It is an ASCII-encoded, application layer control protocol that can be used to establish, maintain, and terminate calls between two or more endpoints. Whereas the H.323 protocol uses a more traditional circuit-switched approach to signaling, the SIP protocol is a lightweight, text-based protocol that is based on the HTTP protocol. SIP is becoming the protocol of choice over MGCP due to its simplicity and inherent IP-based architecture. A feature in SIP that records the route traversed has been found to be extremely useful for billing and call-control purposes.

SIP is part of the IETF multimedia data and control architecture, which includes protocols such as the RTP for transporting real-time data and providing quality of service feedback, the Real-Time Streaming Protocol (RTSP) for controlling delivery of streaming media, MEGACO for controlling gateways to the PSTN, the Session Announcement Protocol (SAP), and the Session Description Protocol (SDP) for describing multimedia sessions. The functionality and operation of SIP does not depend on these protocols and it can be used with other call setup and signaling protocols.

SIP is designed to address the functions of signaling and session management within a packet telephony network. Signaling allows call information to be carried across network boundaries. Session management provides the ability to control the attributes of an end-to-end call.

SIP provides the capabilities to do the following:

- **Determine the location of the target endpoint**—SIP supports address resolution, name mapping, and call redirection.

- **Determine the media capabilities of the target endpoint**—Via Session Description Protocol (SDP), SIP determines the "lowest level" of common services between the endpoints. Conferences are established using only the media capabilities that can be supported by all endpoints.

- **Determine the availability of the target endpoint**—If a call cannot be completed because the target endpoint is unavailable, SIP determines whether the called party is already on the phone or did not answer in the allotted number of rings. It then returns a message indicating why the target endpoint was unavailable.

- **Establish a session between the originating and target endpoint**—If the call can be completed, SIP establishes a session between the endpoints. SIP also supports mid-call changes, such as the addition of another endpoint to the conference or the changing of a media characteristic or codec.

- **Handle the transfer and termination of calls**—SIP supports the transfer of calls from one endpoint to another. During a call transfer, SIP just establishes a session between the transferee and a new endpoint (specified by the transferring party) and terminates the session between the transferee and the transferring party. At the end of a call, SIP terminates the sessions between all parties.

SIP Components

SIP uses a client/server model, where the client initiates SIP requests and a server responds to the requests. A SIP architecture consists of user agent clients (UACs) and user agent servers (UASs). The UAC is the client application that initiates SIP requests, and the UAS is the server application that responds to a SIP request on behalf of the user. The SIP user agent applications contain both functionalities, that of the UAC and the UAS.

SIP clients include the following:

- **Phones**—Can act as either a UAC or UAS. Softphones (PCs that have phone capabilities installed) and SIP IP phones can initiate SIP requests and respond to requests.

- **Gateways**—Provide call control. Gateways provide many services, the most common being a translation function between SIP conferencing endpoints and other terminal types. This function includes translation between transmission formats and between communications procedures. In addition, the gateway translates between audio and video codecs and performs call setup and clearing on both the LAN side and the switched-circuit network side.

SIP servers include the following:

- **Proxy server**—The proxy server is an intermediate device that handles the routing of SIP messages. It receives SIP requests from a client and then forwards the requests on the client's behalf. Proxy servers can provide functions such as authentication, authorization, network access control, routing, reliable request retransmission, and security.

- **Redirect server**—Provides the client with information about the next hop or hops that a message should take so that the client can directly contact the next-hop server or user agent (UA).

- **Registrar server**—Processes requests from UAs for registration of their current location. Note that it does not route SIP messages but only handles registrations from SIP UAs. Registrar servers are often co-located with a redirect or proxy server.

SIP Protocol Operation

Users in a SIP network are identified by unique SIP addresses, which are in the form of e-mail-like names such as trixie@venice.com and are used as part of URLs in the format of sip:trixie@venice.com. These are often referred to as SIP Uniform Resource Identifiers (URIs). The user ID can be either a username or an E.164 address. Users register with a registrar server using their assigned SIP addresses. The registrar server provides this information to the location server upon request.

There exist six main SIP signaling message types:

- **REGISTER**—Registers the UA with the registrar server of a domain
- **INVITE**—Invites a user to participate in a call session
- **ACK**—Confirms that a client has received a final response to an INVITE request
- **CANCEL**—Cancels a pending request; does not terminate calls that have been accepted
- **BYE**—Terminates an existing call; can be sent by either UA
- **OPTIONS**—Queries a SIP server for its capabilities

With the exception of the ACK message type, all requests trigger a response. The response messages contain a status code that indicates the result of the server's attempt to process a client's request. SIP response codes are extensible and SIP applications are not required to understand all codes as long as the class of the code is recognized. There are two types of status codes, provisional and final. *Provisional codes* (1xx) are for informational purposes and indicate that the server contacted is performing some further action and does not yet have a definitive response. A server sends a 1xx response if it expects to take more than 200 ms to obtain a final response. All other codes are *final codes* and represent a conclusion to the transaction. A nonfinal response code is always followed by a final code.

SIP messages may be unicast or multicast to their destination(s). When a user initiates a call, a SIP request is sent directly to the IP address of the server, or to a locally configured SIP proxy server.

Figure 3-33 shows an example of SIP UA-to-UA signaling without a server.

Figure 3-33   *SIP UA-to-UA Signaling*

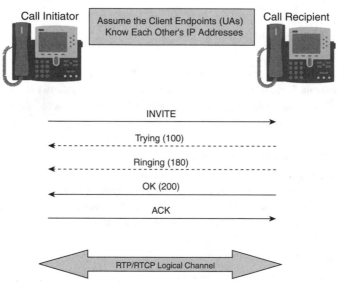

Three mandatory packets are required for the call-establishment handshake: INVITE, INVITE OK, and ACK. It is also common to send the status messages of TRYING (code=100) and RINGING (code=180). When the call recipient picks up the phone, an ACK message is sent, acknowledging the call. When the SIP signaling exchange is completed, the logical channel is set up via RTP/RTCP.

Figure 3-34 shows how SIP operates through use of a proxy server.

Upon initialization, and at periodic intervals, SIP phones send REGISTER messages to a SIP registrar server; these messages contain the addressing information of the phone. The registrar writes this association, also called a *binding*, to a database, called the *location service*, where the addressing information can be used by the proxy. Often, a registrar server for a domain is co-located with the SIP proxy server for that domain. It is an important concept that the distinction between types of SIP servers is logical, not physical.

A user is not limited to registering from a single device. For example, both a phone at home and the one in the office could send registrations. This information is stored together in the location service and allows a proxy to perform various types of searches to locate the user. Similarly, more than one user can be registered on a single device at the same time.

Figure 3-34   *SIP Call Flow with a Proxy Server*

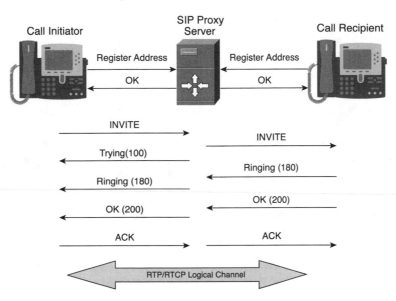

When the caller wants to place a call, the SIP phone initially may not know the location of the destination phone and therefore sends the initial INVITE request to the SIP proxy. The address of the proxy server could be manually configured in the SIP phone or it could have been discovered via DHCP.

In some cases, it may be useful for proxies in the SIP signaling path to see all the messaging between the endpoints for the duration of the session. This would require adding a routing header field known as Record-Route in the SIP messages, which would contain a URI resolving to the host name or IP address of any traversed proxy servers.

NOTE   In SIP, registration is used for routing incoming SIP requests and has no role in authorizing outgoing requests. Authorization and authentication are handled in SIP either on a request-by-request basis with a challenge/response mechanism, or by using a lower-layer scheme (as discussed in the "VoIP Security Protocol" section later in this chapter).

One other interaction is worth mentioning. SIP IP phones support dynamic content services via an HTTP client and Extensible Markup Language (XML) support. The IP phone contains a service locator that is responsible for contacting the call-process manager to determine what authorized services are available. When a service is accessed on the IP phone, it creates an HTTP connection to the proxy server. When the list of services is determined, the phone then creates another HTTP connection to the call-processing manager. In this connection request is included the phone's identification (MAC address). This allows the call-processing manager to check which services the phone has enabled and then notify the phone. At this point, the services available to the user display on the phone.

SIP and H.323 Interaction

SIP and H.323 are competing protocols; however, both protocols can coexist in the same packet telephony network if a device that supports the interoperability is available. The H.323 protocol has been available for many years, and carriers have made significant investment in deploying large H.323-based networks. SIP is growing in popularity due to its capability to easily combine voice and IP-based services. It is expected that both will coexist in the years to come.

Cisco has developed a SIP proxy server that has added capabilities to communicate with an H.323 gatekeeper using the H.323 RAS protocol. The Cisco SIP proxy server acts as an H.323 gateway to the H.323 network. The SIP proxy-to-gateway communication is used only for call signaling and routing and not for any type of protocol translation. Figure 3-35 illustrates an example where a SIP phone establishes a call to an H.323 terminal.

Figure 3-35 *Hybrid SIP and H.323 Call*

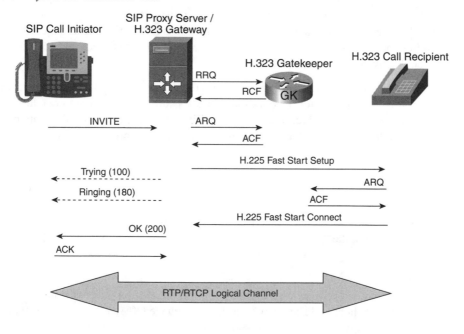

The H.323 gateway and H.323 gatekeeper exchange registration request and registration confirm messages. When the SIP proxy receives an INVITE request from a SIP phone, it interacts with the H.323 gateway to establish a call setup between the H.323 gateway and the H.323 terminal using H.225. Note that this example uses the fast-connect capability to establish an H.245 logical channel. After the H.225 call setup has completed between the H.323 terminal and the H.323 gateway, the SIP proxy completes the call setup with the SIP phone. The RTP/RTCP logical media channels subsequently set up between the SIP phone and the H.323 terminal.

VoIP Security Protocols

Many next-generation VoIP networks will use SIP as the foundation for VoIP deployment. However, because many existing VoIP deployments use H.323, it is expected that SIP and H.323 will co-exist in many environments. As such, this discussion mostly focuses on how to secure H.323 and SIP-based VoIP networks.

H.323 Protocol Security

The ITU-T recommendation H.235 defines security and encryption for H.232 and H.245 multimedia terminals. It includes the capability to negotiate services and functionality in a generic manner, and to be selective concerning cryptographic techniques and capabilities used. There are no specifically mandated algorithms; however, it is strongly suggested that endpoints support as many of the applicable algorithms as possible to achieve interoperability.

RAS Signaling Authentication

The RAS channel used for gateway-to-gatekeeper signaling is not a secure channel. To ensure secure communication, H.235 allows gateways to include an authentication key in their RAS messages. Two types of authentication mechanisms can be used:

- **Symmetric encryption-based authentication**—This method uses public key cryptography and a Diffie-Hellman exchange to obtain a shared secret and requires no prior contact between the endpoint and gatekeeper. At the end of the Diffie-Hellman exchange, both the entities possess a shared secret key along with a chosen algorithm with which to use this key. This shared secret key can then be used on any subsequent request/response exchanges. Typically, the authentication is performed by encrypting the gatekeeper ID using a combination of the negotiated shared secret and the XOR function.

  If the messages are exchanged over an insecure channel, digital signatures (or other message origin authentication method) must be used to authenticate the parties between whom the secret will be shared.

- **Subscription-based authentication**—This authentication exchange assumes that each end possesses some well-known identifier (such as a text identifier) that uniquely identifies it. A mutual two-pass authentication is defined which may be performed only in one direction when the messages originating from the reverse direction do not need to be authenticated. A three-pass authentication procedure uses a randomly generated, unpredictable challenge number as a challenge from the authenticator. Different from the two-pass procedure, the three-pass procedure does not authenticate the first, initial message holding the initiator's challenge.

All RAS messages contain the authentication tokens required by the specific mode of operation. Three different variations may be implemented:

- Password-based with symmetric encryption
- Password-based with hashing
- Certificate-based with signatures

The intent behind the certificate-based exchange is to authenticate the *user* of the endpoint, not just the physical endpoint. Using digital certificates, an authentication protocol proves that the respondents possess the private keys corresponding to the public keys contained in the certificates. For authentication using public key certificates, the endpoints are required to provide digital signatures using the associated private key value.

NOTE   The passwords configured on the H.323 endpoint and gateway authenticate the devices. In addition, many vendors are implementing per-call authentication where specific users are also authenticated. When the gateway receives a call, it prompts the user for a user ID and personal identification number (PIN). These two numbers are included in certain RAS messages sent from the endpoint and are used to authenticate the originator of the call.

Call Setup (H.225/Q.931) Security

The call setup channel operates in the negotiated secured or unsecured mode starting with the first exchange. Because the H.225.0 messages are the first exchanged when establishing H.323 communications, there can be no security negotiations "in band" for H.225, and both parties must know *a priori* that they are using a particular security mode. For H.225 call setup, the TCP port 1300 is used for TLS secured communications.

One purpose of the H.225 exchanges as they relate to H.323 security is to provide a mechanism to set up the secure H.245 channel. The signaling to use TLS, Ipsec, or a proprietary mechanism on the H.245 control channel is done on the secured or unsecured H.225.0 channel during the initial Q.931 message exchange. Optionally, authentication may occur during the exchange of H.225 messages. This authentication may be certificate- or password-based, using encryption and/or hashing (that is, signing) in the same manner as discussed previously for RAS authentication.

Call Control (H.245) Security

The H.245 channel can be secured using any negotiated privacy mechanism. (This includes the option of "none.") The only requirement on all systems is that each shall have some manner in which to negotiate and/or signal that the H.245 channel is to be operated in a particular secured manner before it is actually initiated. H.323 will use the H.225.0 connection signaling messages to accomplish this.

Endpoints exchange capabilities using H.245 messages. These capability sets can contain definitions that indicate security and encryption parameters, including encryption algorithms and keys. The capability to do this, on a logical channel by logical channel basis, allows different media channels to be encrypted by different mechanisms. Each encryption algorithm that is used in conjunction with a particular media codec implies a new capability definition.

Assuming that the connection procedures indicate a secure mode of operation, the negotiated handshake and authentication shall occur for the H.245 logical channel before any other H.245 messages are exchanged. After completing the securing of the H.245 channel, the terminals use the H.245 protocol in the same manner that they would in an insecure mode.

Alternatively, the H.245 channel may operate in an unsecured manner and the two entities open a secure logical channel with which to perform authentication and/or shared-secret derivation. For example TLS or IPsec may be used by opening a logical channel that could then be used to derive a shared secret that protects any media session keys.

Media Stream Privacy

An encrypted H.245 control channel can be used to establish cryptographic keying material and/or set up the logical channels that will carry the encrypted media streams. The H.245 secure channel may be operated with characteristics different from those in the private media channel(s) as long as it provides a mutually acceptable level of privacy. This allows for the security mechanisms protecting media streams and any control channels to operate in a completely independent manner, providing completely different levels of strength and complexity.

If it is required that the H.245 channel be operated in a nonencrypted manner, the specific media encryption keys may be encrypted separately in the manner signaled and agreed to by the participating parties. A separate secure logical channel may be created to accomplish this, using either TLS or IPsec.

The encryption key may be protected by using one of the three possible mechanisms as they are passed between two endpoints.

- If the H.245 channel is secure, no additional protection is applied to the key material.

- If a secret key and algorithm has been established outside the H.245 channel, the shared secret is used to encrypt the key material.

- Certificates may be used when the H.245 channel is not secure, but may also be used in addition to the secure H.245 channel. When certificates are used, the key material is encrypted using the certificate's public key.

RTP streams are encrypted on a packet-by-packet basis. Transport-specific header information is not encrypted (the RTP header as well as the payload header), and the privacy of data is based upon end-to-end encryption.

Whether or not the RTP packets are encrypted, a lightweight packet authentication mechanism is defined, which ensures packet integrity through the use of a message authentication code (MAC). This is referred to as the anti-*spam method* in the H.235 specification. The MAC is computed on selected fields in the RTP header. It is recommended to use the key that is obtained from the H.245 media session key distribution (even if the session key applied is not used for payload encryption).

Synchronization of new keys and encrypted text is based upon a dynamic payload type. The initial encryption key is presented by the sender in conjunction with the dynamic payload number. The receiver(s) of the media stream will start using the key upon receipt of this payload number in the RTP header. New key(s) may be distributed at any time by the sending endpoint. The synchronization of the newer key with the media stream shall be indicated by the changing of the payload type to a new dynamic value. Note that the specific values do not matter, as long as they change for every new key that is distributed.

SIP Protocol Security

The fundamental network-security services required for SIP are preserving the confidentiality and integrity of messaging, preventing replay attacks or message spoofing, providing for the authentication and privacy of the participants in a session, and preventing denial-of-service attacks.

Instead of defining new security mechanisms specific to SIP, SIP reuses existing security models derived from the HTTP and SMTP space. The SIP protocol does not define a specific encryption or authentication technique that must be used with SIP implementations. However, it does specify how HTTP authentication and S/MIME can be used with SIP and also allows for other techniques to be used.

NOTE   Because HTTP basic authentication uses passwords that are sent in the clear and is inherently insecure, this form of authentication has been deprecated in the current SIP standard. Similarly, the Pretty Good Privacy (PGP) mechanism for encrypting the header fields and bodies of SIP messages described in RFC 2543 has been deprecated.

HTTP Digest Authentication

SIP entities have a need to identify one another in a secure fashion. The authentication can take place between the UA and the proxy, where the proxy server requires a UA to authenticate itself before proceeding to process an INVITE message from it. Similarly, a UA can request authentication of a proxy or redirect server. A cryptographic authentication mechanism based on HTTP's digest authentication technique is provided in SIP to address this requirement.

The HTTP digest authentication technique requires a shared secret between the client and the server and is based on a cryptographic hash that includes the username, password, and a challenge provided by the server. The challenge provided by the server is called a *nonce* and is implementation-dependent; the selection and usage of this parameter determines the security of the digest authentication. The nonce should include a server-specific key, a time stamp, the client IP address, and some cryptographically random data to ensure maximum security.

SIP relies on specific response codes as well as specific header fields for carrying challenges and credentials. The *authorization* header contains a signature computed across components of the SIP message. This header does not change in transit between proxies and consists of the nonce, the realm, the request method (the type of request message sent by a user agent client), the request method version, and the authorization type. There is also a *proxy-authorization* header, which is used by a SIP UA to identify itself to a proxy. This contains the type of authentication, credentials of the UA, and/or realm of the resource being requested.

When authentication is achieved, it must be determined whether the authenticated entity is authorized to use the services it is requesting. Despite being securely authenticated, a party may not have permission to use all or some of the services that are being requested, and may require further authorization. This is typically accomplished using RADIUS.

Some extensions to RADIUS have been made to support the HTTP digest authentication so that it can be used with SIP. The UAs authenticate themselves with the proxy by using the HTTP digest authorization header. The proxy, acting as a RADIUS client, sends the username, nonce, and other information required to compute the digest authentication hash value, except the password, along with the hash to the RADIUS server. The server retrieves the password from its database and computes the hash from the password and other values it received. If the computed hash matches the received hash, the client can be authorized.

NOTE   Where a single request URI from a user agent is destined for multiple recipients, the message is forked: The SIP proxy receives a single message from the originating user agent and replicates it to each correspondent destination, having labeled each one with a unique ID. Assuming the recipients are contactable, each responds to the proxy with a SIP message containing a challenge. However, this causes an authentication problem. The proxy forwards on to the user agent only the first challenge response it receives. Subsequent challenges arriving at the proxy from the other destinations are ignored. Therefore, only the first destination to respond is authorized to participate in the SIP-initiated session and the calls to the other destinations are dropped. Because of this, multiple recipients and authorization are currently incompatible.

S/MIME Authentication and Encryption

An independent security mechanism for SIP message bodies supplies an alternative means of end-to-end mutual authentication and provides a limit on the degree to which UAs must trust intermediaries.

SIP messages carry MIME bodies, and the MIME standard includes mechanisms for securing MIME contents to ensure both integrity and confidentiality. Encrypting entire SIP messages end to end for the purpose of confidentiality is not always appropriate because network intermediaries (such as proxy servers) need to view certain header fields in order to route messages correctly; and if these intermediaries are excluded from security associations, SIP messages will essentially be nonroutable. However, S/MIME allows SIP UAs to encrypt MIME bodies within SIP, securing these bodies end to end without affecting message headers. S/MIME can provide end to end confidentiality and integrity for message bodies, as well as mutual authentication. It is also possible to use S/MIME to provide a form of integrity and confidentiality for SIP header fields through SIP message tunneling.

Transport and Network Layer Security

Full encryption of messages provides the best means to preserve the confidentiality of signaling—it can also guarantee that messages are not modified by any malicious intermediaries. However, SIP requests and responses cannot be naively encrypted end-to-end in their entirety because some message fields need to be visible to proxies in most network architectures so that SIP requests are routed correctly. Note that proxy servers need to modify some features of messages as well for SIP to function. Proxy servers must therefore be trusted, to some degree, by SIP UAs. To this purpose, transport and/or network layer security mechanisms for SIP are recommended, which encrypt the entire SIP requests or responses on the wire on a hop-by-hop basis, and that allow endpoints to verify the identity of proxy servers to whom they send requests.

SIP offers various security mechanisms for hop-by-hop and end-to-end encryption of certain sensitive header fields and the message body. Hop-by-hop encryption is needed in instances where proxies need to access the field in the header that allows it to determine how to route a message. For example, a proxy must add itself to the Via field; however, it may first encrypt the rest of the Via fields to hide the previous part of the route. On the return path, the proxy can decrypt the information that it encrypted and pass the rest of the message along. In this manner, each hop only knows about the source and destination of that hop and not the rest of the route.

Transport or network layer security can encrypt SIP signaling traffic, guaranteeing message confidentiality and integrity. Often, certificates are used in the protocols that establish transport or network layer security. These certificates can be used to provide a means of authentication for SIP devices and users. Two popular alternatives for providing security at the transport and network layer are, respectively, TLS and IPsec.

TLS

TLS provides transport layer security over connection-oriented protocols and can be specified as the desired transport protocol for SIP. TLS is most suited to architectures in which hop-by-hop security is required between hosts with no preexisting trust association. For example, Teri trusts her local proxy server, which after a certificate exchange decides to trust Stuart's local proxy server, which Stuart trusts, hence Stuart and Teri can communicate securely.

TLS must be tightly coupled with a SIP application. Note that transport mechanisms are specified on a hop-by-hop basis in SIP; therefore, a UA that sends requests over TLS to a proxy server has no assurance that TLS will be used end-to-end.

The SIP specifications require that TLS implementations support the AES cipher algorithm with 128-bit keys and recommends implementing 3DES with 112-bit keys. SHA is the specified hash algorithm to use for authentication and integrity protection. TLS defers client authentication to something that is widely deployed (for instance, RADIUS).

IPsec

IPsec is a set of network layer protocols that collectively can be used to secure IP traffic. It is most commonly used in architectures in which a set of hosts or administrative domains have an existing trust relationship with one another. As mentioned earlier in this chapter, IPsec creates secure tunnels through untrusted networks. Sites connected by these tunnels form VPNs. VoIP networks can be deployed as VPNs such that security associations can be established between two VoIP entities. Therefore, VoIP traffic flowing across different network components on a shared network can be protected and secured as if it were on a private network.

In many architectures IPsec does not require integration with SIP applications; IPsec is perhaps best suited to deployments in which adding security directly to SIP hosts would be arduous and where UAs already have a preshared keying relationship with their first-hop proxy server. Any deployment of IPsec for SIP would require an IPsec profile that uses traffic selectors specifically designed for SIP.

Many SIP proxy servers support authentication and authorization; IPsec and can be configured to provide authentication either at an external authentication server (for instance, RADIUS) or at the proxy itself. RADIUS functions by exchanging attribute value pairs (AV pairs) between the client and the server. For example, a SIP proxy server acting as a RADIUS client exchanges AV pairs with a RADIUS server to provide authentication functions.

The proxy may support different types of authentication mechanisms in conjunction with the appropriate RADIUS server, such as CHAP and HTTP digest authentication.

NOTE   The IETF Audio/Video Working Group is developing the Secure Real-Time Transport Protocol (sRTP), which is a security profile for RTP that provides confidentiality to RTP data and message authentication to RTP data and headers. It has gained some acceptance and seems to be the up-and-coming encryption scheme for VoIP. One very important reason is that it will support compression and encryption over lower-bandwidth links, which is something IPsec cannot do.

VoIP Security Solution

Deployment of security solutions in VoIP networks is still evolving because the standards to provide security services are fairly new and vendors are still working on providing comprehensive security mechanisms.

For H.323 networks, crypto tokens are generally used in a "password-with-hashing" scheme to authenticate RAS gateway-to-gatekeeper signaling. The gateway will include an authentication key (crypto token) in its RAS message to the gatekeeper. This key is used by the gatekeeper to authenticate the source of the messages, typically by using a RADIUS server and a CHAP challenge containing the crypto token. The crypto tokens are validated by the RADIUS server using the password configured for the gateway. This is shown in Figure 3-36.

Figure 3-36   *H.323 Gateway-to-Gatekeeper Registration Security*

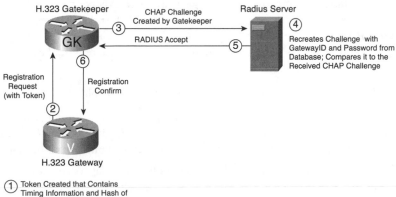

In addition, per-call authentication is generally available. In this case, the user is prompted for a user ID and PIN, which are the items used to authenticate the originator of the call. Both items are included in the RAS messages that are used to initiate a call, namely the admission request (ARQ) and admission confirm (ACF) messages. These messages are sent between the H.323 endpoint and the gateway. When used in conjunction with a gateway crypto token as described previously, all signaling messages provide origin authentication and sender validation.

A complete end-to-end signaling security solution is shown in Figure 3-37. All signaling messages are authenticated, and TLS is used to provide a secure H.225 call setup and H.245 call-control channel.

Figure 3-37   *H.323 End-to-End Call Signaling Security*

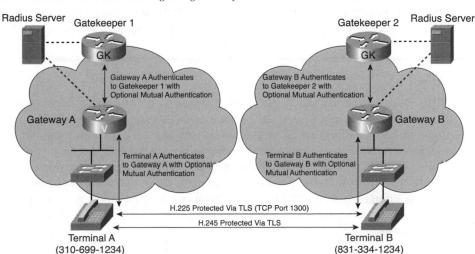

Note that the strength of this authentication, if passwords are used, depends largely on the secrecy of the passwords. Because the gateway-to-gatekeeper passwords are stored on critical infrastructure devices, these passwords should be relatively secure. If a AAA server such as RADIUS is used, the management of these passwords can be greatly simplified. For large enterprise networks looking to deploy a PKI, the use of digital certificates for authentication may be warranted.

For SIP-based VoIP networks, end-to-end security can be obtained as follows:

- UAs authenticate themselves to servers (proxy servers, redirect servers, and registrars) with a digest username and password. Alternatively, TLS can be used, which supports a number of user-based legacy authentication mechanisms.

- Servers authenticate themselves to UAs one hop away, or to another server one hop away (and vice versa), with a site certificate delivered by TLS.

- For SIP implementations running over TCP, TLS or IPsec can be used for confidentiality. All UA-to-server communication runs over TCP.

- For SIP implementations running over UDP, only IPsec can be used for confidentiality. (TLS only runs over TCP.) All UA-to-UA communication runs over UDP.

On a peer-to-peer level, UAs trust the network to authenticate one another; however, S/MIME can also be used to provide direct authentication when the network does not, or if the network itself is not trusted.

There is still ongoing work in the SIP working group of the IETF to resolve issues to effectively secure SIP-based voice traffic over any corporate network infrastructure. NAT environments create a large complication because VoIP traffic embeds IP addresses in the application layer and any mechanism that uses cryptographic means for message integrity and confidentiality will generally be ineffective in NAT environments. Performing encryption/decryption on a hop-by-hop basis is also not a scalable solution due to voice traffic latency considerations. At this time, any capabilities from vendors to secure VoIP traffic should be used and upcoming features and functionalities should be tracked.

Summary

This chapter discussed specific networking scenarios and the protocols that are available to provide effective security services. The networking scenarios included VPNs, wireless networks, and VoIP networks. Virtual private networks have the most robust security solutions because these types of networks have been deployed for a number of years and have gone through their growing pains. Wireless networks and VoIP networks are all still evolving as far as security is concerned. Standards are in the process of being defined to provide comprehensive, scalable security solutions. In some cases, vendors are implementing proprietary security capabilities to address current market needs until standard interoperable solutions are ratified.

Review Questions

1. What is the primary reason for classifying VPNs into access VPNs, intranet VPNs, and extranet VPNs?

2. Which of the following is *not* a link-layer or network layer VPN tunneling solution?

   A   IPsec

   B   L2TP

   C   SSL/TLS

   D   PPTP

3. What is NAT and why is it used?

4. When creating an L2TP/IPsec VPN, what is the problem if user authentication is used for PPP but device authentication is used for IPsec?

5. In a wireless LAN, what mechanism is used to solve the hidden-node problem?

6. True of false: When configuring a wireless access point (AP) with a unique SSID, it provides a good security measure even if the SSID is broadcast out to the rest of the wireless LAN.

7. Why should SSIDs and MAC address filtering be configured in wireless devices even though they offer limited security functionality?

8. Which of the following is *not* a true statement regarding the original WEP encryption specification?

   A   WEP uses the RC4 encryption algorithm.

   B   WEP use different keys to encrypt and decrypt data.

   C   WEP uses a 24-bit initialization vector (IV), which is concatenated with the symmetric key before generating the stream ciphertext.

   D   WEP can use variable-length keys.

9. What protocol is being standardized as a replacement for WEP?

10. In the context of an 802.11 wireless network, which protocol requires a wireless client to authenticate before gaining access to the wireless network through an associated AP?

11. Using the protected EAP (PEAP) protocol, how are clients and servers authenticated?

12. Which ITU-T standard specifies the security services for H.323 networks?

13. True or false: H.225 allows for the negotiation of security algorithms and keys to secure the H.225 call setup channel.

14 What are the three subscription-based authentication mechanisms defined in ITU-T recommendation H.235?

15 Which of the following is *not* a true statement regarding SIP authentication using HTTP digest authentication?

    A The HTTP digest authentication technique requires shared secrets between the client and the server.

    B The HTTP digest authentication is based on a cryptographic hash that includes the username, password, and a challenge provided by the server.

    C The HTTP digest authentication can be used to authenticated SIP user agents to a SIP proxy server as well as the SIP proxy server to the SIP user agent.

    D RADIUS cannot be used with HTTP digest authentication.

16 Why is it problematic to encrypt SIP request and response messages end-to-end?

## CHAPTER 4

Routing Protocol Security

Routing is an essential element in keeping networking infrastructures up and running. Due to the major role that routing protocols play in network infrastructures, this chapter is devoted to detailing some commonly used routing protocols and which built-in functionality exists to effectively secure them (at least to the extent possible today). Most of the mechanisms to provide security have been available for years but have not been widely deployed or are not clearly understood (probably leading to the nondeployment issue). This chapter focuses on most of the routing protocols used in deploying IP routing architectures: RIP, EIGRP, OSPF, IS-IS, and BGP. It is not intended to be a tutorial on routing protocols but rather a brief introduction followed by some explicit details on configurable security provisions built in to each of the protocols.

Routing Basics

Routing is the method by which a host or router decides where to send a datagram. It may be able to send the datagram directly to the destination, if that destination is on one of the networks that is directly connected to the host or router. However, the interesting case is when the destination is not directly reachable. In this case, the host or router attempts to send the datagram to a router that is nearer the destination. The goal of a routing protocol is very simple: to supply the information needed to do routing.

NOTE   In earlier literature, the terms *router* and *gateway* were often interchangeable. In today's networking environment, however, the term gateway is a generic term for a device that joins two or more networks together and can operate at any level of the OSI model from application protocols to low-level signaling. The term router has replaced gateway when used to describe a device that interconnects multiple networks at the Layer 3 (network layer) of the OSI model.

Routers are devices that direct traffic between hosts. Routers collect information on all the paths to all the destinations they know how to reach and build a routing table from this information. They both announce and receive route information from other routers, and each router uses this information to modify its routing tables. Routers use the following four primary mechanisms to create and modify their routing tables:

- **Direct connection**—Any network connection to which the router is directly connected is automatically added to the routing table. Of course, the link must be up.

- **Static routing**—Manual entries can be configured on routers to instruct the router to use a given route to get to a particular destination.

- **Dynamic routing**—Router messages are announced and received. These update messages are used to create routes in the routing table. The routing algorithm associated with a particular routing protocol determines the optimal path to a particular destination and updates the route table. It can automatically adapt to changes in the network.

- **Default routing**—A manually entered route is used as a last-resort method to reach a destination when the route is not known by any other routing mechanism.

NOTE   If a routing table has routes from multiple sources, such as static routes and some dynamic routing protocol routes, there is always a hierarchy of preference defining which route is more preferable if there are two ways to reach a destination. The order of preference can vary depending on router manufacturer, and the order is user configurable. As a default, static routes typically always take precedence over any other routes.

Routing Protocol Classification

Routing protocols can be classified into two separate groups: interior and exterior routing protocols. An Interior Gateway Protocol (IGP) is used for exchanging routing information between gateways within an autonomous system. An Exterior Gateway Protocol (EGP) is used for exchanging routing information between different autonomous systems.

In large nationwide corporate networks such as financial institutions or government facilities, it is very unlikely that a single routing protocol will be used for the whole network. Rather, the network will be organized as a collection of autonomous systems. An *autonomous system* is a group of networking components that will in general be administered by a single entity, or at least will have some reasonable degree of technical and administrative control. Each autonomous system will have its own routing technology. This may well differ for different autonomous systems. The routing protocol used within an autonomous system is referred to as an IGP. A separate protocol is usually used to interface among the autonomous systems.

Interior Gateway Protocols

The four most common routing protocols used as IGPs are as follows:

- **Routing Information Protocol (RIP)**—RIP is a distance vector–based IGP. It maintains a list of distances to other networks measured in *hops*, the number of routers a packet must traverse to reach its destination. It has a maximum hop limitation of 15 hops, which only makes it suitable for smaller-scale networks. Routing updates are broadcast every 30 seconds to all neighboring RIP neighbors. In RIPv1, each update is a full routing table. RIPv2 added many enhancements, including triggered updates and authentication.

- **Enhanced Interior Gateway Routing Protocol (EIGRP)**—EIGRP is a proprietary Cisco IGP. It maintains a complex set of metrics to determine the distance to other networks. It integrates the capabilities of link-state protocols into distance vector protocols and saves not only the least-cost route but up to eight routes to a destination. EIGRP updates are sent only upon a network topology change; updates are not periodic.

- **Open Shortest Past First (OSPF)**—OSPF is a link-state IGP. It uses a link speed-based metric to determine paths to other networks. Each router maintains a simplified map of the entire network. Updates are sent via multicast and are sent only when the network configuration changes. Each update only includes changes to the network.

- **Intermediate System-to-Intermediate System (IS-IS)**—IS-IS is similar to OSPF and is also a link-state IGP. Instead of an area concept like OSPF, IS-IS has two levels: level 1 (areas) and level 2 (backbones). The IS-IS backbone is just a contiguous collection of level 2-capable routers linking level 1 areas together. Most networks use level 2 only because there is little benefit in the extra complexity that running both level 1 and level 2 offers. IS-IS does not use IP for transport; it uses Connectionless Network Service (CLNS). This could make IS-IS harder to attack because CLNS is rarely routed across the Internet.

The decision of which IGP to use depends significantly on both the customer's experience with and the technical capabilities of the routing protocols. Engineers with more experience with IS-IS will always choose IS-IS. Engineers with a strong background in OSPF will always choose OSPF. The rule of thumb seems to be that beginners to interior routing choose RIP or EIGRP because it is easier to get started. However, OSPF is a better choice because it forces good IGP design to ensure that the network will scale. Those who are very experienced tend to choose IS-IS because it allows for better scaling with more configuration options than the other IGPs.

Exterior Gateway Protocols

The Border Gateway Protocol version 4 (BGP-4) is a distance vector–based EGP. It employs a set of sophisticated rules to maintain paths to other networks. Updates are sent over TCP connections between specifically identified peers. BGP-4 supports route aggregation to support very large network. (Most of the Internet core deploys BGP-4.) A large enterprise network comprised of multiple autonomous systems should look at deploying BGP-4 in its backbones.

Routing Protocol Security

The kind of damage that can be done in an unsecured routing infrastructure is discussed in more detail in Chapter 5, "Threats in an Enterprise Network." This chapter focuses on what security mechanisms are available to secure routing updates. Of course, it goes hand-in-hand in protecting the physical routers themselves.

A major concern is to avoid false routing update packets that falsely modify routing tables. Often, this is due more to misconfiguration rather than malicious intent. Two basic approaches for protecting routing table integrity are as follows:

- **Use only static routes**—This works for very small networks but will become an administrative nightmare for networks with more than 5 to 10 entries.
- **Authenticate routing updates**—All dynamic routing protocols have mechanisms to provide some sort of route authentication (that is, ensuring that router updates came from legitimate sources).

NOTE   Currently, there is not a good way to ensure that the routing updates included from the legitimate source were updates the source was authorized to send. This is a difficult problem and still under research in the routing community.

Authenticating Routing Protocol Updates

Most routing protocols incorporate neighbor authentication to protect the integrity of the routing domain. Authentication occurs when two neighboring routers exchange routing information and ensures that the receiving router incorporates into its tables only the route information that the trusted sending neighbor really intends to send. Authentication prevents a legitimate router from accepting and then using unauthorized, malicious, or corrupted routing updates that may compromise the security or availability of the network (for example, having an unauthorized device send a routing update that makes the legitimate router believe that the best route for certain traffic is via an alternative path that may or may not exist). Such a compromise would lead to rerouting of traffic, a denial of service, or just giving access to certain packets of data to an unauthorized person.

When neighbor authentication is configured, the router authenticates the source of each routing update packet it receives. This is accomplished by the exchange of an authentication key (sometimes referred to as a *shared secret*) that is known to both the sending and the receiving routers. Two types of neighbor authentication are typically used: plaintext authentication and cryptographic authentication (typically using the keyed Message Digest 5 [MD5] checksum that was discussed in Chapter 2, "Security Technologies").

Plaintext Authentication

Each participating router must share an authentication key. This key must be specified in each router's configuration. Multiple keys can be specified with some protocols; each key must be identified with a key number. Figure 4-1 illustrates how plaintext authentication is used for routing updates.

Figure 4-1   *Plaintext Neighbor Authentication*

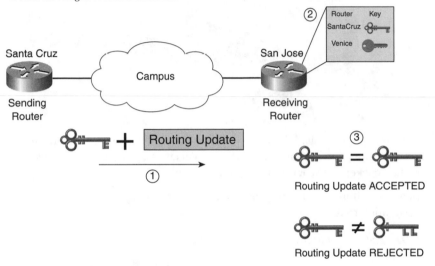

The following steps are carried out:

Step 1   A router sends a routing update with a key and the corresponding key number to the neighbor router. For protocols that can have only one key, the key number is always zero.

Step 2   The receiving (neighbor) router checks the received key against the same key stored in its own memory.

Step 3   If the two keys match, the receiving router accepts the routing update and incorporates the route information into its routing tables. If the two keys do not match, the routing update is rejected.

MD5 Authentication

MD5 authentication works similarly to plaintext authentication, except that the key is never sent over the wire. Instead, the router uses the combination of a shared secret key and the routing update as input to the MD5 algorithm to produce a message digest (also called a *hash*). The shared secret between the sending and receiving routers must typically be manually preconfigured. Figure 4-2 illustrates the sequence of events involved for routing protocol authentication for the originating router.

Figure 4-2 *MD5 Neighbor Authentication: Originating Router*

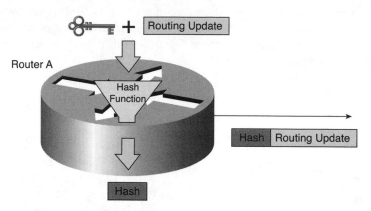

The preconfigured shared secret and the routing update are the input to the MD5 algorithm, which results in a message digest (hash). This message digest is appended to the routing update packet and sent out the appropriate interface.

Figure 4-3 illustrates the sequence of events for routing protocol authentication at the destination router.

Figure 4-3 *MD5 Neighbor Authentication: Destination Router*

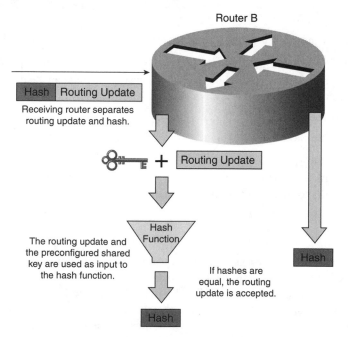

The receiving router takes the routing update and, along with its preconfigured shared secret, uses this as input to the MD5 algorithm to produce a message digest. If this new digest matches the one that was received, the neighbor is authenticated and the routing update is incorporated into the router's routing table.

NOTE	Plaintext authentication is not recommended for use as part of your security strategy. Its primary use is to avoid accidental changes to the routing infrastructure. Keyed MD5 is a more robust authentication mechanism and should be used wherever possible.

IPsec and Routing Protocols

It is possible to use IPsec to protect your routing protocol infrastructure. This would give the added benefits of confidentiality and replay protection. In most cases, the overhead involved in configuring IPsec for routing protocols far outweighs any practical benefits. It is more important that no one sends or spoofs routing updates. Therefore, IPsec is not commonly used to further protect routing updates because all routing protocols have extensions built in to address the authentication piece.

It is widely thought that in current routing infrastructures, confidentiality is not a major issue; and in all routing protocols themselves, there have been no extensions provided for confidentiality. As noted later in this chapter, however, some routing protocols that have working documents for IPv6 specify using IPsec as their inherent security mechanism.

Routing Protocol Security Details

Although all routing protocols generally implement neighbor authentication in a similar manner, there are some differences in each. This section provides more detail on each routing protocol, first describing an overview of the protocol and then detailing how the neighbor authentication is incorporated into each protocol. In addition, it describes the current work in progress for any additional security functionality for the various routing protocols, if it exists. The reader is encouraged to track these ongoing efforts in the particular working groups in the routing area of the Internet Engineering Task Force (IETF), which is located at http://ietf.org/html.charters/wg-dir.html.

RIP

Some people think that RIP is obsolete, given that other IGPs are more robust and flexible. However, RIP does have some advantages over newer IGP routing protocols such as OSPF, IS-IS, and EIGRP. Primarily, in a small network, RIP has very little overhead in terms of bandwidth used and configuration and management time. RIP is also very easy to implement, especially in relation to the newer IGPs. RIP was designed to work with moderate-size networks using reasonably homogeneous technology. Therefore, it is suitable as an IGP for many campuses and for regional networks using serial lines whose speeds do not vary widely. It is not intended for use in more complex environments.

RFC 1058 details the original RIP specification. RIPv1 is a distance vector protocol that uses User Datagram Protocol (UDP), port 520, as its transport protocol. Distance vector algorithms are based on the exchange of only a small amount of information. Each entity (router or host) that participates in the routing protocol is assumed to keep information about all the destinations within the system. Generally, information about all entities connected to one network is summarized by a single entry, which describes the route to all destinations on that network.

Every routing entity keeps a routing database with one entry for every possible destination in the system. Each entry in the RIP routing database includes the following about each destination:

- **Address**—The IP address of the host or network. RIP is used to convey information about routes to destinations, which may be individual hosts, networks, or a special destination used to convey a default route. (The special address 0.0.0.0 is used to describe a default route. A default route is used when it is not convenient to list every possible network in the RIP updates, and when one or more closely connected gateways in the system are prepared to handle traffic to the networks that are not listed explicitly.)

- **Router**—The first next-hop router along the route to the destination.

- **Interface**—The physical network that must be used to reach the first next-hop router.

- **Metric**—A number indicating the distance to the destination. RIP uses a metric referred to as *hop count* that just counts how many routers a message must go through to reach its final destination. For individual hops, this metric is represented as the sum of "costs" for individual hops.

- **Timer**—The amount of time since the entry was last updated.

Information is only exchanged among entities that are adjacent—that is, entities that share a common network. As a default, the routing update exchange occurs every 30 seconds, with provisions to ensure that synchronization does not occur. The exchange can also be triggered by a routing table update.

The RIP protocol makes no formal distinction between networks and hosts. It just describes the exchange of information about destinations, which may be either networks or hosts. If every host on a given network or subnet is accessible through the same routers, there is no reason to mention individual hosts in the routing tables. However, networks that include point-to-point lines sometimes require routers to keep track of routes to certain hosts. Whether this feature is required depends on the addressing and routing approach used in the system. Therefore, some implementations may choose not to support host routes. If host routes are not supported, they are to be dropped when they are received in response messages.

Each entity that participates in the routing scheme sends update messages that describe the routing database as it currently exists in that entity. For the protocol to provide complete information on routing, every router in the system must participate in it. However, provisions in the protocol allow silent RIP processes. A *silent process* is one that normally does not send out any messages. However, it listens to messages sent by others. This would allow for an entity to maintain a routing table without participating in the routing process itself.

Figure 4-4 shows the packet format.

Figure 4-4   *RIPv1 Packet Format*

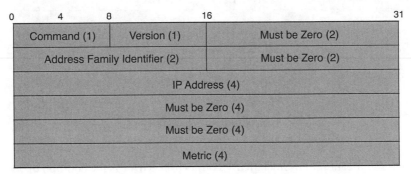

The first four octets of a RIP message contain the RIP header. Several values of the Command field had been defined in the initial implementations, but effectively RIP is supposed to consider only two of them: a request code of value 1 and a response code of value 2. The Version field is set to 1. The remainder of the message is composed of 1 to 25 route entries (20 octets each). The intent of RIPv1 was to carry routing information for several different protocols. Therefore, each entry has an Address Family Identifier to indicate what type of address is specified in that entry. The Address Family Identifier for IP is 2. The IP address is the usual IP address, stored as four octets in network order. The address portion was meant to be extensible for other protocols that used a larger address space; in practice, however, RIP has not been used to support protocols other than IP. The Metric field must contain a value between 1 and 15, inclusive, specifying the current metric for the destination, or the value 16, which indicates that the destination is not reachable. Each route sent by a gateway supersedes any previous route to the same destination from the same gateway.

The maximum datagram size is 512 octets. This includes only the portions of the datagram previously described. It does not count the IP or UDP headers.

Entities that use RIP are assumed to use the most specific information available when routing a datagram. That is, when routing a datagram, its destination address must first be checked against the list of host addresses. Then it must be checked to see whether it matches any known subnet or network number. Finally, if none of these matches, the default route is used.

RIP Authentication

RFC 1723 defines RIPv2, which provides extensions to the message format to allow routers to share important additional information. Because the RIPv1 packet format had a number of Must Be Zero fields, these fields were modified in RIPv2 to add more enhanced routing functionality. Figure 4-5 shows the new RIPv2 packet.

Figure 4-5 *RIPv2 Packet Format*

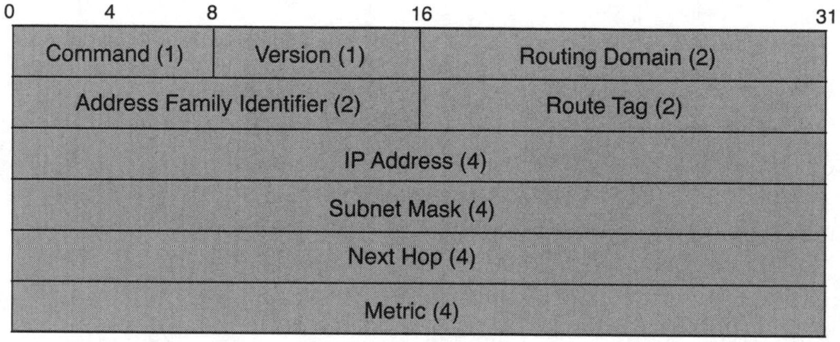

One significant improvement RIPv2 offers over RIPv1 is the addition of an authentication mechanism. Essentially, it is the same extensible mechanism provided by OSPF, described in a later section. In RFC 1723, only a plaintext password is defined for authentication. However, more sophisticated authentication schemes can easily be incorporated into RIPv2 as they are defined. A cryptographic authentication scheme was defined in RFC 2082.

Plaintext Authentication

Because authentication is a per-message function, and because any reasonable authentication scheme requires more than the two-octet field available in the message header, the authentication scheme for RIPv2 uses the space of an entire RIP entry. If the Address Family Identifier of the first (and only the first) entry in the message is 0xFFFF, the remainder of the entry contains the authentication key. This means that there can be, at most, 24 RIP entries in the remainder of the message. If authentication is not in use, no entries in the message should have an Address Family Identifier of 0xFFFF. Figure 4-6 illustrates the RIPv2 packet format when plaintext authentication is used.

The format of the authentication option was carefully chosen to maximize compatibility. Because an authentication entry is marked with an Address Family Identifier of 0xFFFF, a RIPv1 system would skip this entry because it would belong to an address family other than IP, and proceed with the 24 remaining entries. Note, therefore, that use of authentication will not prevent RIPv1 systems from seeing RIPv2 messages.

Figure 4-6   *RIPv2 Plaintext Authentication*

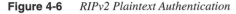

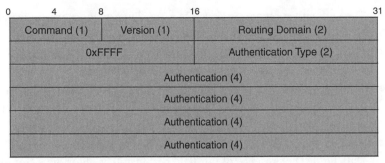

If a router is not configured to authenticate RIPv2 messages, RIPv1 and unauthenticated RIPv2 messages will be accepted; authenticated RIPv2 messages will be discarded. If the router is configured to authenticate RIPv2 messages, RIPv1 messages and RIPv2 messages that pass authentication testing will be accepted; unauthenticated and failed authentication RIPv2 messages will be discarded. In many routers, an administrator can mandate authentication of all packets and request that the RIP process ignore any unauthenticated messages.

Cryptographic Authentication

A cryptographic authentication mechanism for RIPv2 is defined in RFC 2082. Keyed MD5 is proposed as the standard authentication algorithm, but the mechanism is intended to be algorithm independent.

The basic RIPv2 message format provides for an 8-byte header with an array of 20-byte records as its data content. When keyed MD5 is used, the same header and content are used, except that the 16-byte Authentication Key field is reused to describe a Keyed Message Digest trailer, as illustrated in Figure 4-7.

Figure 4-7   *RIPv2 Packet Format Using MD5 Authentication*

RIPv2 MD5 authentication uses the following fields:

- The authentication type is Keyed Message Digest algorithm, indicated by the value 3. (1 and 2 indicate IP route and plaintext password, respectively.)

- A 16-bit offset from the RIPv2 header to the MD5 digest (if no other trailer fields are ever defined; this value equals the RIPv2 data length).

- An unsigned 8-bit field that contains the key identifier or key ID. This identifies the key used to create the authentication data for this RIPv2 message. A key is associated with an interface.

- An unsigned, 8-bit field that contains the length in octets of the trailing Authentication Data field. The presence of this field permits other algorithms (for instance, Keyed Secure Hash Algorithm [SHA]) to be substituted for keyed MD5 if desired.

- An unsigned, 32-bit sequence number. The sequence number is nondecreasing for all messages sent with the same key ID.

- The authentication data, which is the output of the Keyed Message Digest algorithm. When the authentication algorithm is keyed MD5, the output data is 16 bytes.

During digest calculation, the authentication data is effectively followed by a Pad field and a Length field as defined by RFC 1321. The trailing pad is not actually transmitted, because it is entirely predictable from the message length and algorithm in use. Figure 4-8 illustrates the trailer that is kept in memory and is appended by the MD5 algorithm and treated as though it were part of the message.

Figure 4-8   *RIPv2 MD5 Trailer*

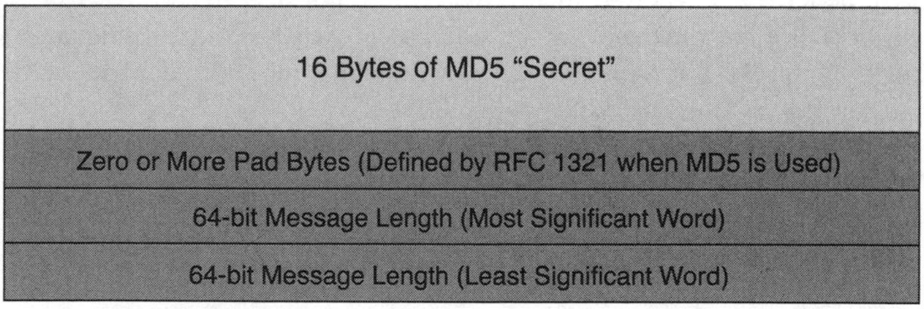

16 Bytes of MD5 "Secret"
Zero or More Pad Bytes (Defined by RFC 1321 when MD5 is Used)
64-bit Message Length (Most Significant Word)
64-bit Message Length (Least Significant Word)

The RIPv2 authentication key is selected by the sender based on the outgoing interface. Each key has a lifetime associated with it, and no key is ever used outside its lifetime. The following steps depict what happens at the sending router to generate an authenticated RIP update:

Step 1   The Authentication Data Offset, Key Identifier, and Authentication Data size fields are appropriately filled in.

Step 2   The 16-byte keyed MD5 RIPv2 authentication key is appended to the data. For all algorithms, the RIPv2 authentication key is never longer than the output of the algorithm in use.

Step 3   The trailing Pad and Length fields are added and the digest calculated using the indicated algorithm. When keyed MD5 is the algorithm in use, these are calculated per RFC 1321.

Step 4   The digest is written over the RIPv2 authentication key. When MD5 is used, this digest is 16 bytes long.

There is also a trailing pad as previously shown. This is not actually transmitted, because it is entirely predictable from the message length and algorithm in use.

When the message is received, the process is reversed:

Step 1   The digest is kept in memory.

Step 2   The appropriate algorithm and key are determined from the value of the Key Identifier field.

Step 3   The RIPv2 authentication key is written into the appropriate number of bytes starting at the indicated offset. With keyed MD5, 16 bytes are used.

Step 4   Appropriate padding is added as needed, and then a new digest is calculated using the indicated algorithm.

If the calculated digest does not match the received digest, the message is not processed and is discarded. If the neighbor has been heard from recently enough to have viable routes in the route table and the received sequence number is less than the last one received, the message is also discarded unprocessed.

The RIPv2 MD5 authentication specification also has a number of key management requirements:

- Storage of more than one key at the same time, although it is recognized that only one key will normally be active on an interface.

- Associate a specific lifetime (that is, date/time first valid and date/time no longer valid) and a key identifier with each key.

- Support manual key distribution (for instance, the privileged user manually typing in the key, key lifetime, and key identifier on the router console).

- Keys that are out of date can be deleted at will by the implementation without requiring human intervention. Manual deletion of active keys can also be supported.

When updating the RIP routers with new keys, a smooth rollover can be ensured if network administrators update all communicating RIPv2 systems with the new key several minutes before the current key expires and several minutes before the new key lifetime begins. The new key should have a lifetime that starts several minutes before the old key expires. This gives time for each system to learn of the new RIPv2 authentication key before that key will be used. It also ensures that the new key will begin being used and the current key will go out of use before the current key's lifetime expires. For the duration of the overlap in key lifetimes, a system may receive messages using either key and authenticate those messages. The key ID in the received message is used to select the appropriate key for authentication.

The specification also recommends that implementations not revert to unauthenticated conditions in the event that the last key associated with an interface expires. It suggests that the router should send a "last authentication key expiration" notification to the network manager and treat the key as having an infinite lifetime until the lifetime is extended, the key is deleted by network management, or a new key is configured.

NOTE   It is prudent to check how a particular vendor actually implements key sequence number rollover and key persistence in the event of device or routing failures.

It is strongly desirable to use a key management protocol to distribute RIPv2 authentication keys among communicating RIPv2 implementations. However, an integrated key management protocol technique was deliberately omitted from the RIPv2 MD5 specification because at the time of the writing of the specification there did not exist a robust enough key management protocol. At the time of this writing, this perception has not changed.

RIPv2 and IPv6

RIPng (RIP next generation) for IPv6 is specified in RFC 2080. The main goal was to make the minimum necessary changes to RIPv2 to support IPv6 networks. With RIPng, a smaller, simpler, distance vector protocol can be used in environments that require authentication or the use of variable-length subnet masks, but that are not of a size or complexity that would require the use of a larger, more complex, link-state protocol.

In essence, the IPv4 address was expanded into an IPv6 address, the IPv4 subnet mask was replaced with an IPv6 prefix length, the Next Hop field was eliminated but the functionality has been preserved, and the Route Tag field has been preserved. Authentication was removed. The maximum diameter of the network (the maximum metric value) is 15; 16 still means infinity (unreachable).

The basic RIP header is unchanged. However, the size of a routing packet is no longer arbitrarily limited. Because routing updates are never forwarded, the routing packet size is now determined by the physical media and the sizes of the headers that precede the routing data (that is, media maximum transmission unit [MTU] minus the combined header lengths). The number of routes that may be included in a routing update is the routing data length divided by the size of a routing entry.

Authentication, which was added to RIPv2 because RIPv1 did not have it, has been dropped from RIPng. It just specifies that because RIPng runs over IPv6, IPsec authentication header (AH) and Encapsulating Security Payload (ESP) will be used to provide the necessary integrity and authentication/confidentiality of routing exchanges.

EIGRP

The Enhanced Interior Gateway Protocol (EIGRP) is a Cisco proprietary routing protocol, referred to as an advanced distance vector protocol. It integrates the capabilities of link-state protocols into distance vector protocols. Traditional distance vector protocols such as RIP exchange periodic routing updates with all their neighbors, saving the best metric and the next hop for each destination. EIGRP differs in that it saves not only the least-cost route but up to eight routes to a destination. Further, EIGRP updates are sent only upon a network topology change; updates are not periodic.

Underlying Technologies

EIGRP uses the following key technologies:

- Neighbor discovery/recovery
- Reliable Transport Protocol (RTP)
- The DUAL finite-state machine

The *neighbor discovery/recovery* mechanism enables routers to dynamically learn about other routers on their directly attached networks and to discover when their neighbors become unreachable or inoperative. This process is achieved by periodically sending small hello packets. As long as a router receives hello packets from a neighboring router, it assumes that the neighbor is functioning, and the two can exchange routing information.

Reliable Transport Protocol (RTP) is used for guaranteed, ordered delivery of EIGRP packets to all neighbors. It supports intermixed transmission of multicast or unicast packets. All transmissions use IP with the protocol type field set to 88. The IP multicast address used is 224.0.0.10. For efficiency, only certain EIGRP packets are transmitted reliably. On a multiaccess network that has multicast capabilities, such as Ethernet, it is not necessary to send hello packets reliably to all neighbors individually. For that reason, EIGRP sends a single multicast hello packet containing an indicator that informs the receivers that the packet need not be acknowledged. Other types of packets, such as updates, indicate in the packet that acknowledgment is required. Neighbors acknowledge the receipt of updates; and if an acknowledgment is not received, EIGRP retransmits the update. RTP contains a provision for sending multicast packets quickly when unacknowledged packets are pending, which helps ensure that convergence time remains low in the presence of varying speed links.

The *Diffusing Update algorithm* (DUAL), developed at SRI International by Dr. J. J. Garcia-Luna-Aceves, embodies the decision process for all route computations by tracking all routes advertised by all neighbors. DUAL uses distance information to select efficient, loop-free paths and selects routes for insertion in a routing table based on feasible successors. A *feasible successor* is a neighboring router used for packet forwarding that is a least-cost path to a destination that is guaranteed not to be part of a routing loop. When a neighbor changes a metric, or when a topology change occurs, DUAL tests for feasible successors. If one is found, DUAL uses it to avoid recomputing the route unnecessarily. When no feasible successors exist but neighbors still advertise the destination, a recomputation (also known as a *diffusing computation*) must occur to determine a new successor. DUAL requires guaranteed and sequenced delivery for some transmissions. This is achieved using acknowledgments and sequence numbers. So, for example, *update packets* (containing routing table data) are delivered reliably (with sequence numbers) to all neighbors using multicast. *Acknowledgment packets*—with the correct sequence number—are expected from every neighbor. If the correct acknowledgment number is not received from a neighbor, the update is retransmitted as a unicast.

EIGRP Routing Concepts

EIGRP relies on neighbor tables, topology tables, route states, and route tagging. Each of these is summarized in the following sections.

Neighbor Tables

When a router discovers a new neighbor, it records the neighbor's address and interface as an entry in the *neighbor table*. One neighbor table exists for each protocol-dependent module. When a neighbor sends a hello packet, it advertises a *hold time*, which is the amount of time that a router treats a neighbor as reachable and operational. If a hello packet is not received within the hold time, the hold time expires and DUAL is informed of the topology change.

The neighbor table entry also includes information required by RTP. Sequence numbers are used to match acknowledgments with data packets, and the last sequence number received from the neighbor is recorded so that out-of-order packets can be detected. A transmission list is used to queue packets for possible retransmission on a per-neighbor basis. Round-trip timers are kept in the neighbor table entry to estimate an optimal retransmission interval.

Topology Tables

The *topology table* contains all destinations advertised by neighboring routers. The protocol-dependent modules populate the table, and the table is acted on by the DUAL finite-state machine. Each entry in the topology table includes the destination address and a list of neighbors that have advertised the destination. For each neighbor, the entry records the advertised metric, which the neighbor stores in its routing table. An important rule that distance vector protocols must follow is that if the neighbor advertises this destination, it must use the route to forward packets.

The metric that the router uses to reach the destination is also associated with the destination. The metric that the router uses in the routing table, and to advertise to other routers, is the sum of the best-advertised metric from all neighbors and the link cost to the best neighbor.

Route States

A topology table entry for a destination can exist in one of two states: active or passive. A destination is in the *passive state* when the router is not performing a recomputation; it is in the *active state* when the router is performing a recomputation. If feasible successors are always available, a destination never has to go into the active state, thereby avoiding a recomputation.

A recomputation occurs when a destination has no feasible successors. The router initiates the recomputation by sending a query packet to each of its neighboring routers. The neighboring router can send a reply packet, indicating that it has a feasible successor for the destination, or it can send a query packet, indicating that it is participating in the recomputation. While a destination is in the active state, a router cannot change the destination's routing table information. After the router has received a reply from each neighboring router, the topology table entry for the destination returns to the passive state, and the router can select a successor.

Route Tagging

EIGRP supports internal and external routes. Internal routes originate within an EIGRP autonomous system. Therefore, a directly attached network that is configured to run EIGRP is considered an internal route and is propagated with this information throughout the EIGRP autonomous system. External routes are learned by another routing protocol or reside in the routing table as static routes. These routes are tagged individually with the identity of their origin.

EIGRP Packet Types

EIGRP uses the following packet types:

- Hello and acknowledgment
- Update
- Query and reply

Hello packets are multicast for neighbor discovery/recovery and do not require acknowledgment. An *acknowledgment* packet is a hello packet that has no data. Acknowledgment packets contain a nonzero acknowledgment number and always are sent by using a unicast address. Neither hellos nor acknowledgments are sent reliably.

Update packets are used to convey reachability of destinations. When a new neighbor is discovered, unicast update packets are sent so that the neighbor can build up its topology table. In other cases, such as a link-cost change, updates are multicast. Updates always are transmitted reliably.

Query and *reply* packets are sent when a destination has no feasible successors. Query packets are always multicast. Reply packets are sent in response to query packets to instruct the originator not to recompute the route because feasible successors exist. Reply packets are unicast to the originator of the query. Both query and reply packets are transmitted reliably.

EIGRP Authentication

EIGRP supports only keyed MD5 cryptographic checksums to provide authentication of routing updates. Each key has its own key identifier, which is stored locally. The combination of the key identifier and the interface associated with the message uniquely identifies the authentication algorithm and MD5 authentication key in use.

EIGRP MD5 authentication supports multiple keys with lifetimes. Only one authentication packet is sent, regardless of how many valid keys exist. The key numbers are examined in order from lowest to highest, and EIGRP MD5 authentication uses the first valid key it encounters.

OSPF

OSPFv2, defined in RFC 2328, is a link-state routing protocol that is designed to be run internal to a single autonomous system. In a link-state routing protocol, each router maintains a database describing the autonomous system's topology. This database is referred to as the *link-state database*. Each participating OSPF router has an identical database. Each individual piece of this database is a particular router's local state (for instance, the router's usable interfaces and reachable neighbors). The router distributes its local state throughout the autonomous system by flooding.

All routers run the exact same algorithm (the Dijkstra algorithm), in parallel. From the link-state database, each router constructs a routing table that is calculated by constructing a shortest-path first (SPF) tree, with itself as root. This SPF tree gives the route to each destination in the autonomous system. When several equal-cost routes to a destination exist, traffic is distributed equally among them. The cost of a route is described by a single dimensionless metric.

OSPF allows sets of networks to be grouped together. Such a grouping is called an *area*. The topology of an area is hidden from the rest of the autonomous system. This information hiding enables a significant reduction in routing traffic. Also, routing within the area is determined only by the area's own topology, lending the area protection from bad routing data. An area is a generalization of an IP subnetted network.

OSPF enables the flexible configuration of IP subnets. Each route distributed by OSPF has a destination and mask. Two different subnets of the same IP network number may have different sizes (that is, different subnet masks). This is commonly referred to as *variable-length subnetting*. A packet is routed to the best (that is, longest or most specific) match. Host routes are considered to be subnets whose masks are "all 1s" (0xffffffff).

All OSPF protocol exchanges are authenticated. This means that only trusted routers can participate in the autonomous system's routing. A variety of authentication schemes can be used; in fact, separate authentication schemes can be configured for each IP subnet.

Externally derived routing data (for example, routes learned from another IGP or an EGP such as BGP) is advertised throughout the autonomous system. This externally derived data is kept separate from the OSPF protocol's link-state data. Each external route can also be tagged by the advertising router, enabling the passing of additional information between routers on the boundary of the autonomous system.

OSPF Authentication

All OSPF protocol exchanges are authenticated. The OSPF packet header illustrated in Figure 4-9 includes an Authentication Type field, and 64 bits of data for use by the appropriate authentication scheme.

Figure 4-9   *OSPF Packet Header*

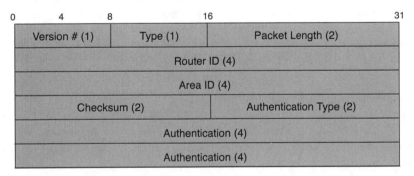

Most fields within this common header have obvious meanings. The version number is set to 2 to indicate OSPFv2 and the type is the OSPF packet type (hello, database description, link-state request, link-state update, and link-state acknowledgment). The packet length is the number of bytes in the packet. The router ID is the IP address selected for identifying the router, and the area ID is the identification of the area. The value zero is reserved for the backbone area. It is common practice to choose an IP network number for identifying an area. The checksum is computed over the whole OSPF packet, excluding the 8-byte Authentication field.

The Authentication Type field identifies the authentication algorithm. Three values are defined in the RFC 2328 standard: null authentication, simple password authentication, and cryptographic authentication. The authentication type is configurable on a per-interface (or equivalently, on a per-network/subnet) basis. Additional authentication data is also configurable on a per-interface basis.

Null Authentication

Use of the null authentication type means that routing exchanges over the network/subnet are not authenticated. The 64-bit Authentication field in the OSPF header can contain anything; it is not examined on packet reception. When null authentication is used, the entire contents of each OSPF packet (other than the 64-bit Authentication field) are checksummed to detect data corruption.

Simple Password Authentication

Using the simple password authentication type, a 64-bit field is configured on a per-network basis. All packets sent on a particular network must have this configured value in their OSPF header 64-bit Authentication field. This essentially serves as a "clear" 64-bit password. In addition, the entire contents of each OSPF packet (other than the 64-bit Authentication field) are checksummed to detect data corruption.

Plaintext authentication uses a shared secret key known to all the routers on the network segment. When a sending router builds an OSPF packet, it signs the packet by placing the key as plaintext in the OSPF header. The receiving router then compares the received key against the key in memory. If the keys match, the router accepts the packet. Otherwise, the router rejects the packet.

NOTE Simple password authentication guards against routers inadvertently joining the routing domain; each router must first be configured with its attached networks' passwords before it can participate in routing. However, simple password authentication is vulnerable to passive attacks where anyone with physical access to the network can learn the password and compromise the security of the OSPF routing domain.

Cryptographic Authentication

In cryptographic authentication, a shared secret key is configured in all routers attached to a common network/subnet. For each OSPF protocol packet, the key is used to generate/verify a "message digest" that is appended to the end of the OSPF packet. The message digest is a one-way function of the OSPF protocol packet and the secret key. Because the secret key is never sent over the network in the clear, protection is provided against passive attacks where intruders can eavesdrop on a network.

The algorithms used to generate and verify the message digest are specified implicitly by the secret key. Most implementations use the MD5 algorithm.

To protect against replay attacks, a nondecreasing sequence number is included in each OSPF protocol packet. This provides long-term protection; however, it is still possible to replay an OSPF packet until the sequence number changes. To implement this feature, each neighbor data structure contains a new field called the *Cryptographic Sequence Number*. This field is initialized to zero, and is also set to zero whenever the neighbor's state transitions to "down." Whenever an OSPF packet is accepted as authentic, the cryptographic sequence number is set to the received packet's sequence number. Because the cryptographic sequence number field is 32 bits in length, rollover issues should not be a problem unless a vendor has a particularly poor implementation.

When cryptographic authentication is used, the 64-bit Authentication field in the standard OSPF packet header is redefined, as illustrated in Figure 4-10.

Figure 4-10   *OSPF Authentication Field When Using Cryptographic Authentication*

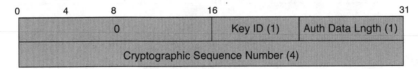

The new field definitions are as follows:

- **Key ID**—Identifies the algorithm and secret key used to create the message digest appended to the OSPF packet. Key identifiers are unique per interface (or equivalently, per subnet).

- **Auth Data Length**—The length in bytes of the message digest appended to the OSPF packet.

- **Cryptographic Sequence Number**—An unsigned, 32-bit nondecreasing sequence number; used to guard against replay attacks.

The message digest is not included in the OSPF header's packet length because it is not considered part of the OSPF protocol packet. However, it is included in the packet's IP header Length field.

Each key is identified by the combination of interface and key ID. An interface may have multiple keys active at any one time to enable smooth transition from one key to another. Each key has four time constants associated with it. These time constants can be expressed in terms of a time-of-day clock or in terms of a router's local clock (for instance, number of seconds since last reboot).

- **KeyStartAccept**—The time that the router will start accepting packets that have been created with the given key.

- **KeyStartGenerate**—The time that the router will start using the key for packet generation.

- **KeyStopGenerate**—The time that the router will stop using the key for packet generation.

- **KeyStopAccept**—The time that the router will stop accepting packets that have been created with the given key.

The OSPFv2 specification states that keys should persist across a system restart, warm or cold, to avoid operational issues. In the event that the last key associated with an interface expires, it is not acceptable to revert to an unauthenticated condition, and not advisable to disrupt routing. Therefore, the router should send a "last authentication key expiration" notification to the network manager and treat the key as having an infinite lifetime until the lifetime is extended, the key is deleted by network management, or a new key is configured.

NOTE	It is prudent to check how a particular vendor actually implements key sequence number rollover and key persistence in the event of device or routing failures.

OSPF and IPv6

The OSPF Working Group in the IETF is working on specifications for using OSPF in IPv6 networks, and their work may at some point evolve into a standard. This work is still in progress, but for completeness, the most recent proposal is detailed in this section. Be aware that some of the information could change; therefore, you should track this effort by referring to the documents in progress in the OSPF Working Group.

OSPFv2 is a specification only for IPv4 networks. OSPFv3 is the protocol defined for IPv6 networks. The current proposal for providing inherent security to OSPFv3 requires the use of the AH/ESP extension headers (that is, IPsec). All OSPFv3 packets must be authenticated using either AH or ESP and confidentiality can be used as an option.

Authentication

OSPFv3 requires transport mode security associations to be used because the protocol packets are exchanged between routers that act like end hosts. ESP with NULL encryption in transport mode is required, which will provide authentication to only higher-layer protocol data and not to the IPv6 header, extension headers, and options. AH in transport mode can optionally be provided and will provide authentication to higher-layer protocols, selected portions of the IPv6 header, selected portions of extension headers, and selected options. OSPF packets received in clear text or received with an incorrect AH integrity check value are required to be dropped when authentication is enabled.

Confidentiality

Providing confidentiality to OSPFv3 in addition to authentication is optional. Confidentiality, if provided, must use the ESP extension header of IPv6. It is required that ESP with non-NULL encryption in transport mode be used when providing confidentiality to OSPFv3.

Authentication and Encryption Algorithms

HMAC-MD5-96 must be implemented as the authentication algorithm and DES-CBC must be implemented as the encryption algorithm.

Key Management

OSPFv3 exchanges both multicast and unicast packets. While running OSPFv3 over a broadcast interface, the authentication/confidentiality required is "one to many." Because Internet Key Exchange (IKE) is based on the Diffie-Hellman key agreement protocol and works only for two communicating parties, it is not possible to use IKE for providing the required "one to many" authentication/confidentiality. Manual keying is required to be used for this purpose. In manual keying, security associations (SAs) are statically installed on the routers, and these static SAs are used to encrypt/authenticate the data.

Because SAs are directional, different security associations are generally used for inbound and outbound processing for providing higher security. To provide the "one-to-many" security, however, the same security associations need to be used for both inbound and outbound processing.

Replay Protection

The current IPsec standards do not provide complete replay protection while using manual keying. Therefore, the proposed solution will not provide protection against replay attacks.

IS-IS

IS-IS for use in TCP/IP environments is defined in RFC 1195. The protocol design is based on the OSI intradomain IS-IS routing protocol defined in "Intermediate System to Intermediate System Intra-Domain Routing Exchange Protocol for Use in Conjunction with the Protocol for Providing the Connectionless-mode Network Service (ISO 8473)," ISO DP 10589, February 1990. In the early 1990s, some people thought that OSI and TCP/IP would coexist and this protocol provided for a means to accomplish "integrated" routing where IS-IS would be the single routing protocol to simultaneously provide an efficient routing protocol for TCP/IP and OSI environments. However, OSI has become a historical artifact, and IS-IS is primarily used as an IGP in TCP/IP only environments.

The integrated IS-IS is a dynamic routing protocol, based on the SPF (Dijkstra) routing algorithm. Similar to OSPF, it is a link-state protocol where each router maintains a database describing the autonomous system's topology. This database is referred to as the *link-state database*. Each participating IS-IS router has an identical database. Each individual piece of this database is a particular router's local state (for instance, the router's usable interfaces and reachable neighbors). The router distributes its local state throughout the autonomous system by flooding.

All routers run the exact same algorithm (the Dijkstra algorithm), in parallel. From the link-state database, each router constructs a routing table that is calculated by constructing a shortest-path tree (SPF) with itself as root. This shortest-path tree gives the route to each destination in the autonomous system. When several equal-cost routes to a destination exist, traffic is distributed equally among them.

The IP address structure allows networks to be partitioned into subnets, and allows subnets to be recursively subdivided into smaller subnets. IS-IS does not require any specific relationship between IP addresses and the area structure. This was a conscious decision on behalf of the protocol designers because in many cases it was believed that the routers would be installed into existing environments, which already had assigned IP addresses. In addition, even if IP addresses were not already pre-assigned, the address limitations of IP constrain what addresses may be assigned. However, greater efficiency and scaling of the routing algorithm can be achieved if there is some correspondence between the IP address assignment structure and the area structure.

IS-IS routing makes use of two-level hierarchical routing. A routing domain is partitioned into areas. Within an area, level 1 routers exchange link-state packets (LSPs), which identify the IP addresses reachable by each router. Specifically, zero or more [IP address, subnet mask, metric] combinations may be included in each LSP. Each level 1 router is manually configured with the [IP address, subnet mask, metric] combinations, which are reachable on each interface. A level 1 router routes as follows:

- If a specified destination address matches an [IP address, subnet mask, metric] combination reachable within the area, the packet is routed via level 1 routing.

- If a specified destination address does not match any [IP address, subnet mask, metric] combination listed as reachable within the area, the packet is routed toward the nearest level 2 router.

An area (and by implication a routing domain) may simultaneously make use of a variety of different address masks for different subnets in the area (or domain). Generally, if a specified destination address matches more than one [IP address, subnet mask] pair, the more specific address is the one routed toward (the one with more 1 bits in the mask; this is known as *best-match routing*).

Level 1 routers maintain the topology within the area, and can route directly to IP destinations within the area. However, IP-capable level 1 routers do not maintain information about destinations outside of the area. Traffic to destinations outside of the area is forwarded to the nearest level 2 router. Because IP routes to subnets, rather than to specific end systems, IP routers do not need to keep nor distribute lists of IP host identifiers. (Note that routes to hosts can be announced by using a subnet mask of all 1s.)

Level 2 routers include in their level 2 LSPs a complete list of [IP address, subnet mask, metric] combinations specifying all IP addresses reachable in their area. This information may be obtained from a combination of the level 1 LSPs (obtained from level 1 routers in the same area), or by manual configuration. In addition, level 2 routers may report external reachability information, corresponding to addresses that can be reached via routers in other routing domains (autonomous systems).

Default routes may be announced by use of a subnet mask containing all 0s. Default routes should be used with great care, because they can result in "black holes." Default routes are permitted only at level 2 as external routes (that is, included in the IP External Reachability Information field). Default routes are not permitted at level 1.

The integrated IS-IS has a provision for carrying authentication information in all IS-IS packets. This is extensible to multiple authentication mechanisms. However, the use of this field is optional.

IS-IS Authentication

An Authentication field in the IS-IS header allows each IS-IS packet to contain information used to authenticate the originator and contents of the packet. This field is used to authenticate the entire packet, including the IP headers. If a router is configured to use authentication and a packet is received that contains invalid authentication information, the entire packet is discarded. If an IS-IS packet is split into multiple packets, each is authenticated independently.

Use of the Authentication field is optional. Routers are not required to be able to interpret authentication information. If a router is not configured to use authentication, it ignores any Authentication field that may be present in an IS-IS packet.

The IS-IS header is shown in Figure 4-11.

Figure 4-11 *IS-IS Header*

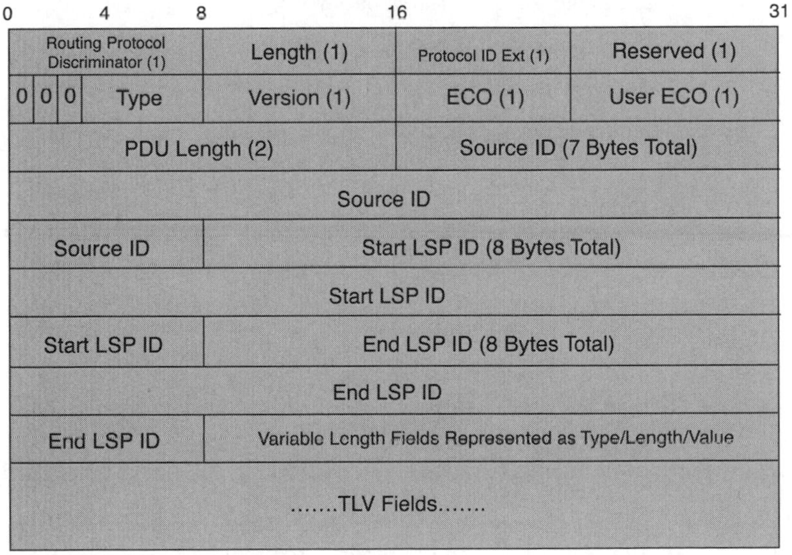

0	4	8	16	31
Routing Protocol Discriminator (1)		Length (1)	Protocol ID Ext (1)	Reserved (1)
0 0 0 Type		Version (1)	ECO (1)	User ECO (1)
PDU Length (2)			Source ID (7 Bytes Total)	
Source ID				
Source ID		Start LSP ID (8 Bytes Total)		
Start LSP ID				
Start LSP ID		End LSP ID (8 Bytes Total)		
End LSP ID				
End LSP ID		Variable Length Fields Represented as Type/Length/Value		
.......TLV Fields.......				

The authentication information is encoded as a type-length-value (TLV) tuple. The type of the TLV is specified as 10. The length of the TLV is variable. The value of the TLV depends on the authentication algorithm and related secrets being used. The first octet of the value is used to specify the authentication type. Type 0 is reserved, type 1 indicates a cleartext password, and type 255 is used for routing domain private authentication methods. The remainder of the TLV value is known as the *authentication value*. Currently, the only defined mechanism in the IS-IS protocol specification is a simple password, transmitted in the clear without encryption.

NOTE   The use of a simple password does not provide useful protection against intentional misbehavior. Rather, this should be thought of as a weak protection against accidental errors such as inadvertent misconfiguration.

Authentication Type 1 - Simple Password

Using this authentication type, a variable-length password is passed in the clear (that is, not encrypted) in the Authentication Information field.

The password can be configured on a per-link, per-area, and per-domain basis. Specifically, when the simple password form of authentication is used

- IS-IS hello packets contain the per-link password.
- Level 1 LSPs contain the per-area password.
- Level 2 LSPs contain the per-domain password.
- Level 1 sequence number packets contain the per-area password.
- Level 2 Sequence number packets contain the per-domain password.

Each of the three passwords is configured with a transmit password, whose value is a single password, and receive passwords, whose value is a set of passwords. The transmit password value is always transmitted. However, any password contained in the receive password set will be accepted on receipt. This method allows the graceful changing of passwords without temporary loss of connectivity.

Cryptographic Authentication

Because the use of cleartext passwords is not very secure, there is work in progress to define a more secure form of cryptographic authentication using the HMAC-MD5 algorithm.

Some of the following details could change, so you should keep up with any ongoing work in this area by following the work in the IS-IS Working Group in the IETF.

In this particular specification, which is widely implemented in many routers, the authentication type used for HMAC-MD5 is 54, the length of the authentication value for HMAC-MD5 is 16, and the Length field in the TLV is 17.

The HMAC-MD5 algorithm requires two parameters as input: a key K, which is the password for the packet type as specified in ISO 10589, and text T, which is the IS-IS packet to be authenticated (with the Authentication Value field inside the authentication information TLV set to 0). Before authentication is computed, the authentication type is set to 54 and the length of the TLV is set to 17. When LSPs are authenticated, the Checksum and Remaining Lifetime fields are set to zero before authentication is computed. The result of the algorithm is placed in the Authentication Value field.

If a router is configured to use the HMAC-MD5 authentication and receives authentication information, the router will not accept the IS-IS packet if the authentication value is incorrect. Also, to provide a mechanism to incrementally change passwords in a network, a set of passwords can be defined when verifying the authentication value, similar to the plaintext authentication scheme. This specification also has restrictions for implementations that prevent malicious users from initiating purges without knowing the authentication password.

NOTE	It is prudent to check how a particular vendor actually implements key sequence number rollover and key persistence in the event of device or routing failures.

This authentication mechanism does not prevent replay attacks; however, such attacks would trigger existing mechanisms in the IS-IS protocol that would effectively reject old information.

The HMAC-MD5 proposal is widely implemented in many routers. Changes to the authentication mechanism were considered, primarily to add a Key ID field such as in OSPFv2 and RIPv2. However, these were ultimately rejected because the improvement provided was not great enough to justify the change, given the installed base and lack of interest in deploying the proposed revised mechanism.

Future considerations for securing IS-IS include the following:

- A different authentication mechanism that is designed for use with a key management protocol could be added if and when a key management protocol appears that is both widely implemented and easily deployed to secure routing protocols.

- The use of a full digital signature if a stronger authentication were believed to be required. At this time, it is believed that the computational burden of full digital signatures is much higher than is reasonable given the current threat environment in operational commercial networks.

BGP-4

The Border Gateway Protocol version 4 (BGP-4) is specified in RFC 1771. It is a complex EGP whose primary function is to allow the exchange network reachability information with all BGP-speaking systems.

BGP uses TCP as its transport protocol, which eliminates the need to implement explicit update fragmentation, retransmission, acknowledgment, and sequencing. Any authentication scheme used by the transport protocol may be used in addition to BGP's own authentication mechanisms. The error notification mechanism used in BGP assumes that the transport protocol supports a "graceful" close—that is, all outstanding data will be delivered before the connection is closed.

Two BGP systems that want to communicate form a transport protocol connection (using TCP port 179) between one another. They exchange messages to open and confirm the connection parameters. The initial data flow is the entire BGP routing table. Incremental updates are sent as the routing tables change. BGP does not require periodic refresh of the entire BGP routing table. Therefore, a BGP speaker must retain the current version of the entire BGP routing tables of all of its peers for the duration of the connection. Keepalive messages are sent periodically to ensure the liveness of the connection. Notification messages are sent in response to errors or special conditions. If a connection encounters an error condition, a notification message is sent, and the connection is closed.

A BGP speaker advertises to its peers (other BGP speakers which it communicates with) in neighboring autonomous systems only those routes that it uses itself. Routing information exchanged via BGP supports only the destination-based forwarding paradigm, which assumes that a router forwards a packet based solely on the destination address carried in the IP header of the packet.

A peer in a different autonomous system is referred to as an *external peer*, whereas a peer in the same autonomous system is referred to as an *internal peer*. Internal BGP and external BGP are commonly abbreviated IBGP and EBGP.

BGP is primarily used for routing in the Internet. Due to its complexity, more detailed specification is beyond the scope of this chapter. For a more complete description of BGP, refer to the book *Internet Routing Architectures*, Second Edition, by Sam Halabi (Cisco Press, 2000).

BGP-4 Authentication

Authentication for BGP-4 is specified in RFC 2385, *Protection of BGP Sessions via the TCP MD5 Signature Option.*

Every BGP-4 packet sent on a TCP connection to be protected against spoofing will contain the 16-byte MD5 digest produced by applying the MD5 algorithm to these items in the following order:

Step 1 The TCP pseudo-header (in the order of source IP address, destination IP address, zero-padded protocol number, and segment length)

Step 2 The TCP header, excluding options, and assuming a checksum of zero

Step 3 The TCP segment data (if any)

Step 4 An independently specified key or password, known to both BGP speakers and presumably connection-specific

It is up to the TCP implementation in the BGP-speaking router to determine what the application can specify as the key.

Upon receiving a signed packet, the receiver must validate it by calculating its own MD5 digest from the same data (using its own key) and comparing the two digests. If the two digests match, the packet is processed; if they don't match, the packet is just dropped. The specification does remark that logging the failure is advisable.

NOTE Key configuration mechanism of routers may restrict the possible keys that may be used between peers. It is prudent to check how a particular vendor actually implements key configuration, key sequence number rollover, and key persistence in the event of device or routing failures.

BGP Security Futures

In response to the increasing requirement of securing network infrastructures and the security limitations in existing routing protocols, the IETF has formed the Routing Protocols Security Requirements Working Group, to analyze security in routing systems, including BGP.

Several methods of securing the information carried within BGP have been proposed. Secure BGP (S-BGP) is based on work that was started as early as 1999 to produce a more secure BGP protocol. The Internet drafts produced in the ensuing years have since expired, although there are still some strong proponents for this protocol.

One of the major obstacles with S-BGP is that it requires the use of a public key infrastructure (PKI). This PKI is used to support the authentication of ownership of IP address blocks, ownership of autonomous system numbers, an autonomous system's identity, and a BGP router's identity and its authorization to represent an autonomous system. Although the intent is that the PKI parallels the IP address and autonomous system number assignment system and takes advantage of the existing infrastructure (Internet registries and so forth), in practice there are still many operational obstacles to overcome to create this trusted PKI.

S-BGP defines a new, optional, BGP transitive path attribute to carry digital signatures covering the routing information in a BGP routing update. These signatures along with certificates from the S-BGP PKI would enable the receiver of a BGP routing update to verify the address prefixes and path information that it contains. Also, S-BGP specifies that IPsec be used to provide data and partial sequence integrity, and to enable BGP routers to authenticate each other for exchanges of BGP control traffic.

S-BGP has not been widely deployed or implemented, and analysis on S-BGP has been limited. Keep in mind that the efforts to define this protocol are principally done with large Internet service provider networks in mind. To track ongoing efforts with S-BGP, go to http://www.net-tech.bbn.com/sbgp/sbgp-index.html.

In recent years, there has been another proposal to secure BGP, named Secure Origin BGP (SOBGP). Rather than require a huge infrastructure change, as with S-BGP, SOBGP only requires incremental changes to the BGP infrastructure. Unlike S-BGP, SOBGP mainly focuses on the origin of a route and not the entire BGP path. Signatures and certificates still need to be generated in the same way as for S-BGP, but the propagation of information differs. For SOBGP, instead of relying on an out-of-band database, the certificates are advertised using a new type of BGP message, the BGP security message.

How BGP and other routing protocols will be secured in the future and which proposals might become eventual Internet standards is still very much work in progress. Interested readers should follow the work in the IETF working group at http://www.ietf.org/html.charters/rpsec-charter.html.

Summary

This chapter covered some commonly used routing protocols and the built-in functionality that exists within each protocol to provide some measure of security. Each of the routing protocols discussed—RIP, EIGRP, OSPF, IS-IS, and BGP-4—has incorporated neighbor authentication that uses either a plaintext password or a cryptographic authentication scheme. The plaintext authentication should be avoided because it is inherently insecure. All protocols support a keyed MD5 algorithm for their cryptographic neighbor authentication scheme, and all users are encouraged to configure this feature in their routers. Because privacy is not thought to be a great concern in routing infrastructures, confidentiality concerns are not addressed. Most routing protocols that have work in progress to address IPv6 networks are relying on the inherent IPsec capabilities to provide for routing protocol authentication, integrity, and confidentiality.

Review Questions

The following questions provide you with an opportunity to test your knowledge of the topics covered in this chapter. You can find the answers to these questions in Appendix E, "Answers to Review Questions."

1 What are the four primary mechanisms routers use to create and modify their routing tables?

2 How do you define an Interior Gateway Protocol?

3 Name four commonly used interior gateway protocols.

4 What are the two basic approaches for protecting routing table integrity?

5 Describe the general steps used for plaintext neighbor authentication.

6 True or false: For keyed MD5 neighbor authentication, a digital signature is appended to the routing updates.

7 What field in the RIPv2 packet indicates the use of authentication?

8 How many authentication schemes does EIGRP support?

9 What authentication mechanisms are supported in the OSPFv2 protocol?

10 True or false: All OSPFv3 packets must be authenticated using either AH or ESP in tunnel mode.

11 Why is simple password authentication not very secure?

12 True or false: In the IS-IS protocol, the use of authentication is mandatory.

13 What is used as input to the BGP-4 MD5 authentication algorithm?

14 Why are there no confidentiality mechanisms for routing security?

The Corporate Security Policy

## CHAPTER 5

Threats in an Enterprise Network

Today, there is an ever-growing dependency on computer networks for business transactions. With the free flow of information and the high availability of many resources, managers of enterprise networks have to understand all the possible threats to their networks. These threats take many forms, but all result in loss of privacy to some degree and possibly malicious destruction of information or resources that can lead to large monetary losses.

Knowing which areas of the network are more susceptible to network intruders and who is the common attacker is useful. The common trend in the past has been to trust users internal to the corporate network and to distrust connections originating from the Internet or from remote access networks using virtual private networks (VPNs), dial-in modems, and Integrated Services Digital Network (ISDN) lines. It is important to place trust in the employees internal to the network and in authorized people trying to use internal network resources from outside the corporation. However, trust must also be weighed with reality. According to some sources, at least 60 percent or more attacks are perpretrated by corporate insiders, and there is an increasing trend not to trust internal users and have stricter security measures in place. Wireless networks are becoming in more wide-spread use, and more stringent security considerations are often required in these instances. Restricted use of network infrastructure equipment and critical resources is necessary. Limiting network access to only those who require access is a smart way to deter many threats that breach computer network security.

Not all threats are intended to be malicious, but they can exhibit the same behavior and can cause as much harm—whether intended or not. Unfortunately, many networking infrastructures have to deal with the increasing issue of viruses and malware that can be found on compromised computing resources and pose unintentional security threats from unsuspecting employees. It is important to understand what types of attacks and vulnerabilities are common and what you can do at a policy level to guarantee some degree of safe networking.

This book does not address the many common host application vulnerabilities in detail; instead, it is more concerned with securing the networking infrastructure. In discussions of areas in which host vulnerabilities can be deterred or constrained in the network infrastructure, more details are given.

Types of Threats

Many different types of threats exist, but many threats fall into three basic categories:

- Unauthorized access
- Impersonation
- Denial of service

Unauthorized Access

Unauthorized access is when an unauthorized entity gains access to an asset and has the possibility to tamper with that asset. Gaining access is usually the result of intercepting some information in transit over an insecure channel or exploiting an inherent weakness in a technology or a product.

Getting access to corporate network resources is usually accomplished by doing some reconnaissance work. Most likely, the corporate network will be accessed through the Internet, tapping into the physical wire, remote modem dial-in access, or wireless network access. Also, a very common component to reconnaissance work is social engineering of information, which is discussed later in this chapter in the section "Social Engineering."

Internet Access

If an intruder is trying to gain unauthorized access via the Internet, he must do some information-gathering work to first figure out which networks or resources are susceptible to vulnerabilities. Some common methods used to identify potential targets follow.

Reachability Checks

A reachability check uses tools that verify that a given network or device exists and is reachable. For example, DNS queries can reveal such information as who owns a particular domain and what addresses have been assigned to that domain. This can then be followed by the **ping** command, which is an easy way to verify whether a potential target is reachable.

Other network utilities can also locate a reachable target, such as Finger, Whois, Telnet, and NSLOOKUP.

Port Scanning

When live systems are discovered, an attacker will usually attempt to discover which services are available for exploitation. This is accomplished by a technique commonly known as *port scanning*. The sections in this chapter titled "The TCP/IP Protocol" and "The

UDP Protocol" respectively detail both the TCP and UDP protocol and clarify how ports are used; suffice to say, however, that every application has a specific port number associated with it that identifies that application. Through the use of port scanners, intruders can gain access to information on which applications and network services are available to be exploited.

Figure 5-1 shows an example of a reconnaissance attempt.

Figure 5-1   *Example Reconnaissance Attempt*

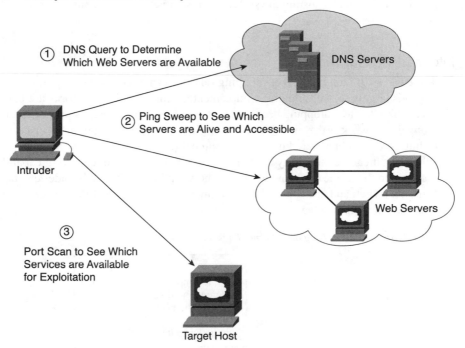

The intruder may follow these steps to gain unauthorized access to a web server:

1 DNS query to figure out which web servers are available.

2 Ping sweep to see which servers are alive and accessible.

3 Port scan to see which services are available for exploitation.

NOTE   Network reconnaissance cannot be prevented entirely. If Internet Control Message Protocol (ICMP) echo and echo-reply is turned off on edge routers, ping sweeps can be stopped, but at the expense of network diagnostic data. However, port scans can easily be run without full ping sweeps; they just take longer because they need to scan IP addresses that might not be live. Intrusion detection systems (IDSs) at the network and host levels can usually notify an administrator when a reconnaissance attack is underway. This enables the administrator to better prepare for the coming attack or to notify the Internet service provider (ISP) that is hosting the system that is launching the reconnaissance probe.

Tapping into the Physical Wire

The ease or difficulty of packet snooping (also known as *eavesdropping*) on networks depends largely on the technology implemented. Shared media networks are particularly susceptible to eavesdropping because this type of network transmits packets everywhere along the network as they travel from the origin to the final destination. When concentrators or hubs are used in a shared media environment (such as FDDI, 10BASE-T, or 100-Mbps Ethernet), it can be fairly easy to insert a new node with packet-capturing capability and then snoop the traffic on the network. As shown in Figure 5-2, an intruder can tap into an Ethernet switch and, using a packet-decoding program, such as EtherPeek or TCPDump, read the data crossing the Ethernet.

Figure 5-2   *Unauthorized Access Using an Ethernet Packet Decoder*

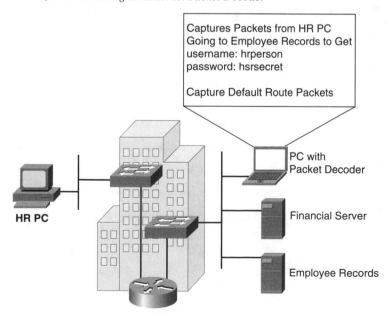

Captures Packets from HR PC
Going to Employee Records to Get
username: hrperson
password: hsrsecret

Capture Default Route Packets

PC with
Packet Decoder

HR PC

Financial Server

Employee Records

In this example, the intruder gains access to username/password information and sensitive routing protocol data using an Ethernet packet decoder such as EtherPeek. The data packets being sent are captured by the laptop running EtherPeek; the program decodes the hex data into human-readable form. After obtaining access to information, the intruder can use this information to gain access to a machine and then possibly copy-restricted, private information and programs. The intruder may also subsequently have the capability to tamper with an asset; that is, the intruder may modify records on a server or change the content of the routing information.

In recent years, it has been getting much easier for anyone with a portable laptop to acquire software that can capture data crossing data networks. Many vendors have created user-friendly (read *easy-to-use*) packet decoders that can be installed with minimal cost. These decoders were intended for troubleshooting purposes but can easily become tools for malicious intent.

Packet snooping by using these decoding programs has another effect: The technique can be used in impersonation attacks, which are discussed in the next section.

Packet snooping can be detected in certain instances, but it usually occurs without anyone knowing. For packet snooping to occur, a device must be inserted between the sending and receiving machines. This task is more difficult with point-to-point technologies such as serial line connections, but it can be fairly easy with shared media environments. If hubs or concentrators are used, it can be relatively easy to insert a new node. However, some devices are coming out with features that remember MAC addresses and can detect whether a new node is on the network. This feature can aid the network manager in noticing whether any suspicious devices have been added to the internal network. In addition, using 802.1x, which is discussed in Chapter 2, "Security Technologies," can provide an effective security measure against MAC address spoofing.

Figure 5-3 shows an example of a switch that has the capability to learn MAC addresses and provide some measure of port security. The 10BASE-T Ethernet switch provides connectivity to several hosts. The switch learns the source MAC addresses of the connecting hosts and keeps an internal table representing the MAC address and associated ports. When a port receives a packet, the switch compares the source address of that packet to the source address learned by the port. When a source address change occurs, a notification is sent to a management station, and the port may be automatically disabled until the conflict is resolved.

Figure 5-3   *Port Security on Ethernet Switches*

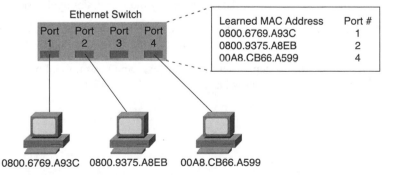

Remote Dial-In Access

As surprising as it sounds, there are still people out there who use well-known exploits, such as war dialing, to gain unauthorized access. This term became popular with the film *War Games* and refers to a technique that involves the exploitation of an organization's telephone, dial, and private branch exchange (PBX) systems to penetrate internal network and computing resources. All the attacker has to do is find a user within the organization with an open connection through a modem unknown to the IT staff or a modem that has minimal or, at worst, no security services enabled. It is important to note that all unknown modems bypass any IT security measures—firewalls, virus checkers, authentication servers, and so on—and the use of unauthorized modems should be considered a severe security breach.

Many corporations still set up modems to auto-answer and will allow unauthenticated access from the Public Switched Telephone Network (PSTN) directly into your protected infrastructure. Many war-dialer programs are freely available on the Internet (for example, Modemscan, PhoneTag, ToneLoc, and so on), which greatly simplify the attack methodology and decrease the time required for the discovery of a vulnerability. Most programs automatically dial a defined range of phone numbers and log and enter into a database those numbers that successfully connect to the modem. Some programs can also identify the particular modem manufacturer and, if the modem is attached to a computer, can identify the operating system and may also conduct automated penetration testing. In such cases, the war dialer runs through a predetermined list of common usernames and passwords in an attempt to gain access to the system. If the program does not provide automated penetration testing, the intruder may attempt to break into a modem with unprotected logins or easily cracked passwords. Figure 5-4 illustrates a typical war-dialing scenario.

The steps to gain unauthorized access in a war-dialing scenario are as follows:

1   The intruder chooses a target and finds a list of phone numbers associated with this target. Phone numbers are easy to obtain via your handy phone book or even through corporate web pages.

2   The intruder uses the target's phone number block (usually a group of sequential numbers) and initiates the war-dialer application.

3   When the war-dialer application finishes, the intruder accesses the answered numbers from either a log file or database kept by the war-dialer application.

4   The intruder then tries to dial up and connect to the devices that answered. This is usually done via a deceptive path that hides the intruder's actual location.

5   Assuming the modem is set to auto-answer and has minimal password protection (if any), the intruder now has unauthorized access into the corporate network.

Figure 5-4   *War Dialing*

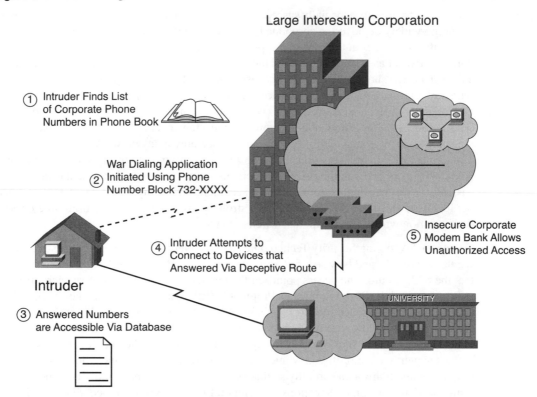

An interesting paper was presented in spring 2001 by Peter Shipley and Simson Garfinkel. Refer to http://www.dis.org/filez/WardialShipleyGarfinkel.pdf. This paper formally presents the results of the first large-scale survey of dialup modems. The survey dialed approximately 5.7 million telephone numbers in the 510, 415, 408, 650, and parts of the 707 area codes, and the subsequent analysis of the 46,192 responding modems that were detected.

NOTE   To mitigate this threat, war dialers, also sometimes referred to as *modem scanners*, should be used by system administrators to identify unauthorized and insecure modems deployed in an enterprise network. Also, an effective method to block war-dialing attacks is to use phone numbers in a range completely different from the corporation's internal PBX numbers. Make sure to keep these numbers secret and limit access to vital staff members.

Wireless Access

Wireless networks are especially susceptible to unauthorized access. Wireless access points are being widely deployed in corporate LANs because they easily extend connectivity to corporate users without the time and expense of installing wiring. These wireless access points (APs) act as bridges and extend the network up to 300 yards. Many airports, hotels, and even coffee shops make wireless access available for free, and therefore most anyone with a wirelss card on his mobile device is an authorized user. However, many wireless networks only want to allow restricted access and may not be aware of how easily someone can gain access to these networks. (I know of quite a few instances where people have made it a sport to drive around their neighborhoods to see how many networks they can access.) The number of wireless networks that have zero security measures enabled is astounding. A majority of people run their APs in effectively open mode, which means they are basically wide open and have no encryption enabled. A majority also run in default Service Set Identifier (SSID) and IP ranges, which strongly implies that they've used little or no configuration when they set up their wireless LAN.

Chapter 3, "Applying Security Technologies to Real Networks," extensively discusses wireless networks and how security technologies apply. Remember from that discussion that the 802.11 cards and access points on the market implement a wireless encryption standard, called the Wired Equivalent Protocol (WEP), which in theory makes it difficult to access someone's wireless network without authorization, or to passively eavesdrop on communications. However, WEP has many inherent weaknesses that enable intruders to crack the crypto with sophisticated software, and ordinary off-the-shelf equipment. Later in this chapter, vulnerabilities in wireless networks are discussed in more detail. Follow the developments in this area carefully so that as better security functionality becomes available—such as implementations for Temporal Key Integrity Protocol (TKIP), Light Extensible Authentication Protocol (LEAP), Protected Extensible Authentication Protocol (PEAP), and so on—you can deploy it. For now, it still makes sense to enable WEP and to ensure that all defaults have been changed so that some reasonable authentication and confidentiality services are being used. This will go a long way in reducing unauthorized access from just the random drive-by intruder.

Figure 5-5 shows an example of an intruder gaining access to a wireless network.

No matter which method is used for initial unauthorized access—reconnaisance work, access through the Internet, tapping into the physical wire, remote modem dial-in access, or wireless network access—the best way to deter unauthorized access is by using confidentiality and integrity security services to ensure that traffic crossing the insecure channel is scrambled and that it cannot be modified during transit.

Figure 5-5   *Gaining Unauthorized Access to a Wireless Network*

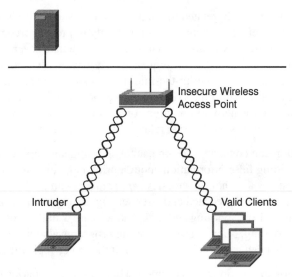

Table 5-1 lists some of the more common access breaches and how they are a threat to corporate networks.

Table 5-1   *Common Unauthorized Access Scenarios*

Ways of Obtaining Unauthorized Access	Ways to Use Unauthorized Access
Establishing false identity with false credentials	Sending e-mail that authorizes money transfers or terminating an employee
Physical access to network devices	Modifying records to establish a better credit rating
Eavesdropping on shared media networks	Retrieving confidential records, such as salary for all employees or medical histories
Reachability checks and port scanning to determine access to vulnerable hosts	Exploiting host vulnerabilities to perpetrate websites and modify the content
Using a wireless modem card and sitting in a car by a high office building to see whether there's a network to which it can connect	Using this "free access" to the Internet to misuse bandwidth or instigate malicious denial-of-service attacks

Impersonation

Impersonation is closely related to unauthorized access but is significant enough to be discussed separately. *Impersonation* is the ability to present credentials as if you are something or someone you are not. These attacks can take several forms: stealing a private key or recording an authorization sequence to replay at a later time. These attacks are commonly referred to as man-in-the-middle attacks, where an intruder is able to intercept traffic and can as a result hijack an existing session, alter the transmitted data, or inject bogus traffic into the network. In large corporate networks, impersonation can be devastating because it bypasses the trust relationships created for structured authorized access.

Impersonation can come about from packet spoofing and replay attacks. *Spoofing attacks* involve providing false information about a principal's identity to obtain unauthorized access to systems and their services. A *replay attack* can be a kind of spoofing attack because messages are recorded and later sent again, usually to exploit flaws in authentication schemes. Both spoofing and replay attacks are usually a result of information gained from eavesdropping. Many packet-snooping programs also have packet-generating capabilities that can capture data packets and then later replay them.

Impersonation of individuals is common. Most of these scenarios pertain to gaining access to authentication sequences and then using this information to obtain unauthorized access. Once the access is obtained, the damage created depends on the intruder's motives. If you're lucky, the intruder is just a curious individual roaming about cyberspace. However, most of us will not be that lucky and will find our confidential information compromised and possibly damaged.

With the aid of cryptographic authentication mechanisms, impersonation attacks can be prevented. An added benefit of these authentication mechanisms is that, in some cases, nonrepudiation is also achieved. A user participating in an electronic communication exchange cannot later falsely deny having sent a message. This verification is critical for situations involving electronic financial transactions or electronic contractual agreements because these are the areas in which people most often try to deny involvement in illegal practices.

Impersonation of devices is largely an issue of sending data packets that are believed to be valid but that may have been spoofed. Typically, this attack causes unwanted behavior in the network. The example in Figure 5-6 shows how the unexpected modified behavior changes the routing information. By impersonating a router and sending modified routing information, an impostor was able to gain better connectivity for a certain user.

Figure 5-6   *Impersonation of Routing Updates*

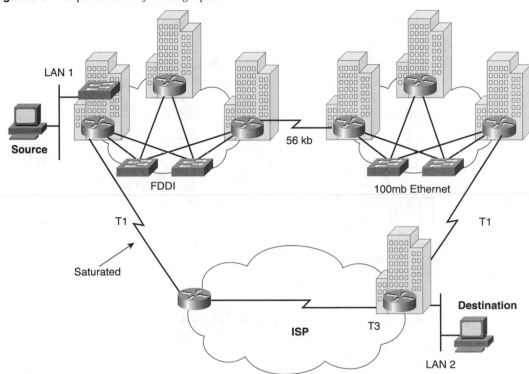

Original path: FDDI →56 kb →100mb Ethernet →T1 → destination
Altered path: T1 →T3 → destination

In this example, the intruder was connected to a corporate LAN and did a lot of work with another researcher on a different LAN. The backbone was set up in such a way that it took five hops and a 56-kbps line to get to the other research machines. By capturing routing information and having enough knowledge to change the routing metric information, the intruder altered the path so that his access became seemingly better through a backdoor connection. However, this modification resulted in all traffic from the intruder's LAN being rerouted, saturating the backdoor link, and causing much of the traffic to be dropped.

This is an extreme and premeditated example of impersonation. However, impersonation can also occur as an accident through unknown protocol and software behavior. For example, old versions of some operating systems have the innocuous behavior of acting as routers if more than one interface is connected; the OS sends out RIP (Routing Information Protocol) updates pointing to itself as the default. Figure 5-7 shows an example of this behavior.

Figure 5-7 *Default Route Impersonation*

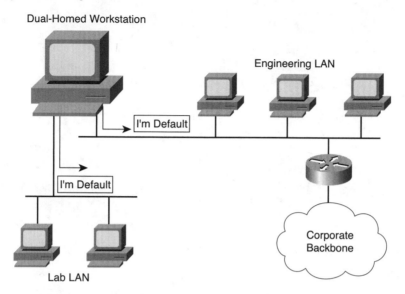

The routed network running RIP is set up to source a default RIP advertisement to all the hosts connected to the engineering lab's LAN. Hosts running RIP typically send all traffic destined to other IP subnets to the default router. If one of the workstations connected to this LAN has a second interface connected to another LAN segment, it advertises itself as the default router. This would cause all hosts on the engineering LAN to send traffic destined to other IP subnets to the misguided workstation. It can also cause many wasted hours troubleshooting routing behavior that can be avoided through the use of route authentication or the configuration of trusted sources for accepting routing updates. In the network infrastructure, you have to protect yourself from malicious impersonations and accidental ones.

NOTE   Many current networks use the Dynamic Host Configuration Protocol (DHCP), which provides a host with an IP address and an explicit default router. RIP is not used in these environments.

Impersonations of programs in a network infrastructure can pertain to wrong images or configurations being downloaded onto a network infrastructure device (such as a switch, router, or firewall) and, therefore, running unauthorized features and configurations. Many large corporate networks rely on storing configurations on a secure machine and making changes on that machine before downloading the new configuration to the device. If the secure machine is compromised, and modifications are made to device access passwords, downloading this altered configuration to a router, switch, or firewall results in an intruder being able to present false credentials—the modified password—and thereby gain access to critical network infrastructure equipment.

Impersonation can be deterred to some degree by using authentication and integrity security services such as digital signatures. A *digital signature* confirms the identity of the sender and the integrity of the contents of the data being sent.

Denial of Service

Denial of Service (DoS) is an interruption of service either because the system is destroyed or because it is temporarily unavailable. Examples include destroying a computer's hard disk, severing the physical infrastructure, and using up all available memory on a resource.

Many common DoS attacks are instigated from network protocols such as IP. Table 5-2 lists the more common DoS attacks.

Table 5-2   *Common Denial of Service Attacks*

Name of DoS Attack	Vulnerability Exploited
TCP SYN attack	Memory is allocated for TCP connections such that not enough memory is left for other functions.
Ping of Death	Fragmentation implementation of IP whereby large packets are reassembled and can cause machines to crash.
Land.c attack	TCP connection establishment.
Teardrop.c attack	Fragmentation implementation of IP whereby reassembly problems can cause machines to crash.
Smurf attack	Flooding networks with broadcast traffic (ICMP echo requests) such that the network is congested.
Fraggle attack	Flooding networks with broadcast traffic (UDP echo requests) such that the network is congested.

Some DoS attacks can be avoided by applying vendor patches to affected software. For example, many vendors have patched their IP implementations to prevent intruders from taking advantage of the IP reassembly bugs. A few DoS attacks cannot be stopped, but their scope of affected areas can be constrained.

TCP SYN flooding attack effects can be reduced or eliminated by limiting the number of TCP connections a system accepts and by shortening the amount of time a connection stays half open (that is, the time during which the TCP three-way handshake has been initiated but not completed). Typically, limiting the number of TCP connections is performed at the entry and exit points of corporate network infrastructures. Some corporations are terminating TCP connections on devices that front servers to protect them. When the TCP handshake is completed with the protecting device, the TCP connection is started with the server and, when complete, the protecting device is transparent to the connection. The section "Common Protocol Vulnerabilities," later in this chapter, provides a more detailed explanation of the most common DoS attacks.

DDoS

In recent years, a variant of a DoS attack has caused even more problems. This is the *Distributed Denial of Service* (DDoS) attack, where multiple machines are used to launch a DoS attack. The basics of a DDoS attack is shown in Figure 5-8.

Figure 5-8   *Basics of a DDoS Attack*

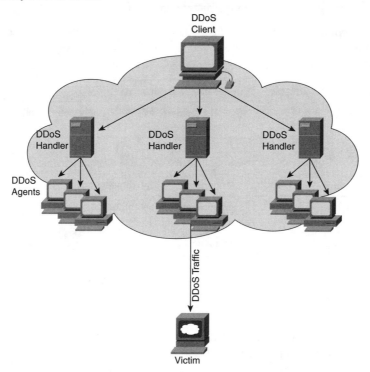

The *DDoS client* is used by the person who orchestrates an attack as the initial starting point. The *handler* is a compromised host with a special program running on it. Each handler is capable of controlling multiple agents. An *agent* is a compromised host that is also running a special program. Each agent is responsible for generating a stream of packets that is directed toward the intended victim.

Many of these attacks are now either semiautomatic or completely automatic. In semiautomatic DDoS attacks, the intruder typically uses automatic tools to scan and compromise vulnerable machines and infect these machines with the attack code. At some later time, the machines with the attack code are used to launch a widely distributed attack. Even more problematic are the completely automatic attacks, where the need for later communication with attack machines is bypassed. The attack code used to infect machines already contains the time the attack will be launched, the type of attack, and preprogrammed attack duration and destinations.

To facilitate DDoS, the attackers need to have several hundred to several thousand compromised hosts. Because often an automated process is used, attackers can compromise and install the tool on a single host in less than 5 seconds. In other words, several thousand hosts can be compromised in less than 1 hour. Figure 5-9 shows an example of such an attack.

Figure 5-9   *Automated DDoS Attack*

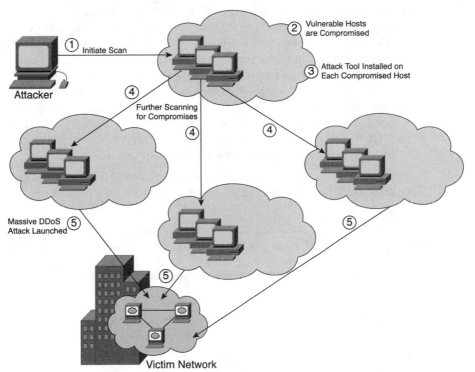

The steps taken to launch this automated attack are as follows:

1   The attacker initiates a scan phase in which a large number of hosts (on the order of 100,000 or more) are probed for a known vulnerability.

2   The vulnerable hosts are compromised to gain unauthorized access.

3   The attack tool is installed on each host.

4   The compromised hosts are used for further scanning and compromises.

5   The attack is launched and causes major disruption for corporate business.

The following are common programs that intruders use to facilitate DDoS attacks. Detailed information about these programs can be found at the websites listed:

- **Trinoo** (http://staff.washington.edu/dittrich/misc/trinoo.analysis)—Trinoo is an attack tool released in late December 1999 that performs a DDoS attack. Trinoo's master (handler) component is typically installed on a compromised computer. Mostly, the compromise stemmed from exploiting buffer overflow bugs in varying UNIX systems, although now this tool is also available on compromised Windows platforms. Trinoo's master component identifies potential targets, creates a script that performs the exploit, and installs the Trinoo daemons (agents). The master then performs the attack. It is capable of broadcasting many UDP packets to a designated or targeted computer via its handlers. The targeted computer tries to process and respond to these invalid UDP packets with "ICMP port unreachable" messages for each UDP packet. Because it has to respond to so many of them, it eventually runs out of network bandwidth, which results in a denial of service.

  Trinoo also has a client component that is used to control the master component. This enables the intruder to control multiple master components remotely.

NOTE   The port numbers listed here are the *default* ports for these tools. Use these ports for orientation and example only, because the port numbers can easily be changed.

Clients, handlers, and agents use the following ports to communicate:

- 1524 TCP
- Client to handler: destination port TCP 27665
- Handler to agent: destination port UDP 27444
- Agent to handler: destination port UDP 31335

- **TFN** (http://staff.washington.edu/dittrich/misc/tfn.analysis)—The Tribal Flood Network, or TFN, is made up of client and daemon programs that implement a DDoS tool capable of causing ICMP flood, SYN flood, UDP flood, and Smurf-style attacks. Communication between clients, handlers, and agents use ICMP echo and ICMP echo-reply packets. The handler can manipulate the IP identification number and payload of the ICMP echo-reply to identify the type of attack to be launched. TFN can also spoof the source IP address to hide the origin of the attack.

- **TFN2K**—This is a newer variant of the TFN tool. Communication between clients, handlers, and agents does not use any specific port (it may be supplied on runtime or may be chosen randomly by a program), but is a combination of UDP, ICMP, and TCP packets.

- **Stacheldraht**—Stacheldraht is a DDoS tool that combines features from Trinoo and the original TFN tool. In addition, it can encrypt communication between the attacker client and Stacheldraht masters and provides automated updates of the agents.

  clients, handlers, and agents use the following ports to communicate:

  — Client to handler: TCP port 16660 or 60001

  — Handler to agent: TCP port 65000 or ICMP echo-reply

  — Agent to handler: TCP port 65000 or ICMP echo-reply

You can find a comprehensive list of DDoS tools and their variants at http://packetstormsecurity.nl/distributed/.

DDoS attacks are extremely hard to trace; and due to the variety of mechanisms used to perform this type of attack, these attacks are continuing to be an interesting problem for the research community but a never-ending source of pain for people running networks. However, the first rule of thumb is don't panic! This threat is real and it is a difficult one to mitigate. Yet, you can deploy mechanisms to thwart many attemps. Due to the exceptional nature of these attacks, Appendix D, "Mitigating DDoS Attacks," is solely devoted to a discussion of DDoS attack mitigation techniques in a corporate network infrastructure.

You might also want to refer to a comprehensive paper describing DDoS attacks and DDoS defense mechanisms authored by Jelena Mirkovic, Janice Martin, and Peter Reicher from UCLA at http://lasr.cs.ucla.edu/ddos/ucla_tech_report_020018.pdf.

Motivation of Threat

Understanding some of the motivations for an attack can give you some insight about which areas of the network are vulnerable and what actions an intruder will most likely take. The perception is that, in many cases, the attacks occur from the external Internet. Therefore, a firewall between the Internet and the trusted corporate network is a key element in limiting where the attacks can originate. Firewalls are important elements in network security, but securing a network requires looking at the entire system as a whole.

Some of the more common motivations for attacks include the following:

- **Greed**—The intruder is hired by someone to break into a corporate network to steal or alter information for the exchange of large sums of money.

- **Prank**—The intruder is bored and computer savvy and tries to gain access to any interesting sites.

- **Notoriety**—The intruder is very computer savvy and tries to break into known hard-to-penetrate areas to prove his competence. Success in an attack can then gain the intruder the respect and acceptance of his peers.

- **Revenge**—The intruder has been laid off, fired, demoted, or in some way treated unfairly. The more common of these kinds of attacks result in damaging valuable information or causing disruption of services.

- **Ignorance**—The intruder is learning about computers and networking and stumbles on some weakness, possibly causing harm by destroying data or performing an illegal act.

There is a large range of motivations for attacks. When looking to secure your corporate infrastructure, consider all these motivations as possible threats.

Common Protocol Vulnerabilities

Attacks exploit weaknesses in systems. These weaknesses can be caused by poorly designed networks or by poor planning. A good practice is to prevent any unauthorized system or user from gaining access to the network where weaknesses in products and technologies can be exploited.

Spoofing attacks are well known on the Internet side of the world. *Spoofing* involves providing false information about a person's or host's identity to obtain unauthorized access to a system. Spoofing can be done by just generating packets with bogus source addresses or by exploiting a known behavior of a protocol's weakness. Some of the more common attacks are described in this section. Because understanding the IP protocol suite is a key element in most attacks, this section describes the protocol suite along with the weaknesses of each protocol (such as TCP, ICMP, UDP, DNS, NNTP, HTTP, SMTP, FTP, NFS/NIS, and X Windows). You can find a more thorough study of these protocol weaknesses in *Firewalls and Internet Security: Repelling the Wily Hacker, Second Edition* by William Cheswick and Steven Bellovin (Addison Wesley Professional, 2003).

The TCP/IP Protocol

Internet Protocol (IP) is a packet-based protocol used to exchange data over computer networks. IP handles addressing, fragmentation, reassembly, and protocol demultiplexing. It is the foundation on which all other IP protocols (collectively referred to as the *IP protocol suite*) are built. As a network layer protocol, IP handles the addressing and controls information to allow data packets to move around the network (commonly referred to as *IP routing*). Figure 5-10 shows the IP header format.

Figure 5-10 *The IP Header Format*

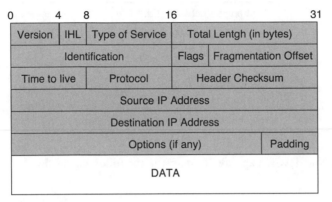

The *Transmission Control Protocol* (TCP) is built on the IP layer. TCP is a connection-oriented protocol that specifies the format of data and acknowledgments used in the transfer of data. TCP also specifies the procedures that the computers use to ensure that the data arrives reliably. TCP allows multiple applications on a system to communicate concurrently because it handles all demultiplexing of the incoming traffic among the application programs. Figure 5-11 shows the TCP header format, which starts at the data portion immediately following the IP header.

Figure 5-11 *The TCP Header Format*

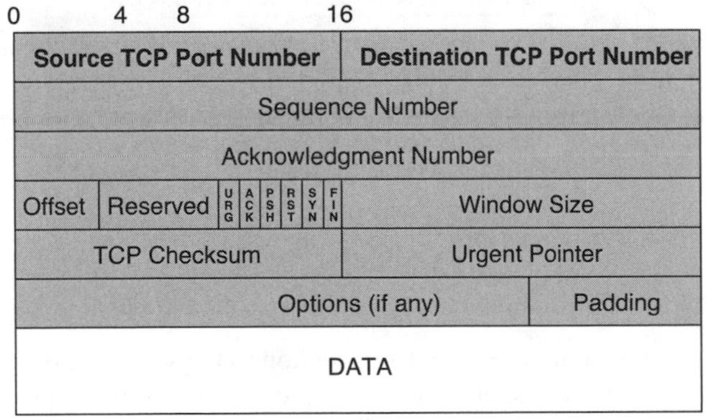

Six bits (flags) in the TCP header tell how to interpret other fields in the header. Table 5-3 lists these flags.

Table 5-3   *TCP Flags*

Flag	Meaning
URG	Urgent pointer field is valid.
ACK	Acknowledgment field is valid.
PSH	This segment requests a push.
RST	Resets the connection.
SYN	Synchronizes sequence numbers.
FIN	Sender has reached the end of its byte stream.

The SYN and ACK flags are of interest in the following section.

TCP/IP Connection Establishment

To establish a TCP/IP connection, a three-way handshake must occur between the two communicating machines. Each packet of the three-way handshake contains a sequence number; sequence numbers are unique to the connection between the two communicating machines. Figure 5-12 shows a sample three-way handshake scenario.

Figure 5-12   *Establishing a TCP/IP Connection*

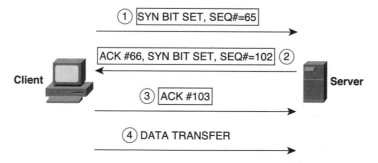

The steps for establishing the initial TCP connection are as follows:

Step 1   The client initiates a TCP connection to the server. This packet has the SYN bit set. The client is telling the server that the Sequence Number field is valid and should be checked. The client sets the Sequence Number field in the TCP header to its initial sequence number.

Step 2   The server responds by sending a packet to the client. This packet also has the SYN bit turned on; the server's initial sequence number is the client's initial sequence number plus 1.

Step 3   The client acknowledges the server's initial sequence number by sending the server's initial sequence number plus 1.

Step 4   The connection is established, and data transfer takes place.

TCP uses a sequence number for every byte transferred and requires an acknowledgment of the bytes received from the other end upon receipt. The request for acknowledgment enables TCP to guarantee reliable delivery. The receiving end uses the sequence numbers to ensure that the data is in proper order and to eliminate duplicate data bytes.

You can think of TCP sequence numbers as 32-bit counters. These counters range from 0 to 4,294,967,295. Every byte of data exchanged across a TCP connection (as well as certain flags) is sequenced. The Sequence Number field in the TCP header contains the sequence number of the first byte of data in the TCP segment. The Acknowledgment (ACK) field in the TCP header holds the value of next expected sequence number, and also acknowledges all data up through this ACK number minus 1.

TCP uses the concept of *window advertisement* for flow control. That is, TCP uses a sliding window to tell the other end how much data it can buffer. Because the window size is 16 bits, a receiving TCP can advertise up to a maximum of 65,535 bytes. Window advertisement can be thought of as an advertisement from one TCP implementation to the other of how high acceptable sequence numbers can be.

Many TCP/IP implementations follow a predictable pattern for picking sequence numbers. When a host is bootstrapped, the initial sequence number is 1. The initial sequence number is incremented by 128,000 every second, which causes the 32-bit initial sequence number counter to wrap every 9.32 hours if no connections occur. Each time a connection is initiated, however, the counter is incremented by 64,000.

If sequence numbers were chosen at random when a connection arrived, no guarantees could be made that the sequence numbers would be different from a previous incarnation.

If an attacker wants to determine the sequencing pattern, all she has to do is establish a number of legitimate connections to a machine and track the sequence numbers used.

TCP/IP Sequence Number Attack

When an attacker knows the pattern for a sequence number, it is fairly easy to impersonate another host. Figure 5-13 shows such a scenario.

Figure 5-13 *TCP/IP Sequence Number Spoofing*

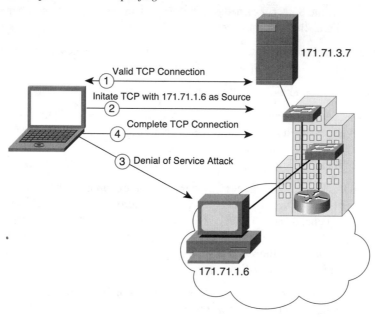

The steps for impersonating a host are as follows:

Step 1 The intruder establishes a valid TCP connection to the server to figure out the sequence number pattern.

Step 2 The intruder starts the attack by generating a TCP connection request using a spoofed source address. Often, the intruder picks a trusted host's address and initiates a DoS attack on that host to render it incapacitated.

Step 3 The server responds to the connection request. However, because the trusted host is under a DoS attack, it cannot reply. If it actually could process the SYN/ACK packet, it would consider it an error and send a reset for the TCP connection.

Step 4 The intruder waits a certain amount of time to ensure that the server has sent its reply and then responds with the correctly guessed sequence number.

Step 5 If the intruder is correct in guessing the sequence number, the server is compromised and illegal data transfer can begin.

Because the sequence numbers are not chosen randomly (or incremented randomly), this attack works—although it does take some skill to carry out. Steven M. Bellovin, coauthor of *Firewalls and Internet Security*, describes a fix for TCP in RFC 1948 that involves partitioning the sequence number space. Each connection has its own separate sequence number space. The sequence numbers are still incremented as before; however, there is no obvious or implied relationship between the numbering in these spaces.

The best defense against spoofing is to enable packet filters at the entry and exit points of your networks. The external entry point filters should explicitly deny any inbound packets (packets coming in from the external Internet) that claim to originate from a host within the internal network. The internal exit point filters should permit only outbound packets (packets destined from the internal network to the Internet) that originate from a host within the internal network.

TCP/IP Session Hijacking

Session hijacking is a special case of TCP/IP spoofing, and the hijacking is much easier than sequence number spoofing. An intruder monitors a session between two communicating hosts and injects traffic that appears to come from one of those hosts, effectively stealing the session from one of the hosts. The legitimate host is dropped from the connection, and the intruder continues the session with the same access privileges as the legitimate host.

Session hijacking is very difficult to detect. The best defense is to use confidentiality security services and encrypt the data for securing sessions.

TCP SYN Attack

When a normal TCP connection starts, a destination host receives a SYN (synchronize/start) packet from a source host and sends back a SYN/ACK (synchronize acknowledge) packet. The destination host must then hear an ACK (acknowledge) of the SYN/ACK before the connection is established. This exchange is the TCP three-way handshake, described earlier in this chapter.

While waiting for the ACK to the SYN/ACK, a connection queue of finite size on the destination host keeps track of connections waiting to be completed. This queue typically empties quickly because the ACK is expected to arrive a few milliseconds after the SYN/ACK is sent.

The TCP SYN attack exploits this design by having an attacking source host generate TCP SYN packets with random source addresses toward a victim host. The victim destination host sends a SYN/ACK back to the random source address and adds an entry to the connection queue. Because the SYN/ACK is destined for an incorrect or nonexistent host, the last part of the three-way handshake is never completed, and the entry remains in the connection queue until a timer expires—typically in about 1 minute. By generating phony TCP SYN packets from random IP addresses at a rapid rate, an intruder can fill up the connection queue and deny TCP services (such as e-mail, file transfer, or WWW service) to legitimate users.

There is no easy way to trace the originator of the attack because the IP address of the source is forged. In the network infrastructure, the attack can be constrained to a limited area if a router or firewall intercepts the TCP connection and proxies on behalf of the connection-initiating host to make sure that the connection is valid.

NOTE   A *proxy* is a device that performs a function on behalf of another device. For example, if the firewall proxies TCP connections on behalf of a web server, the firewall intercepts the TCP connections from a host trying to access the web server and ensures that valid connection requests are made. After it validates the connection requests (usually by completing the connection by proxy), it initiates its own TCP connection request to the web server on behalf of the host. The connection is established, and normal data transfer between the client and server can start without further interference from the proxy. If a TCP SYN attack occurs, the proxy is attacked but not the actual server. Multiple proxies are typically used to mediate communication between the outside world and one or more web servers, to avoid having a TCP SYN attack that cripples the proxy/firewall from disrupting all web server access.

The Land.c Attack

The *land.c attack* is used to launch DoS attacks against various TCP implementations. The land.c program sends a TCP SYN packet (a connection initiation), giving the target host's address as both the source and destination and using the same port on the target host as both the source and destination. This can cause many operating systems to hang in some way.

In all cases, the TCP ports reached by the attack must be ports on which services are actually being provided (such as the Telnet port on most systems). Because the attack requires spoofing the target's own address, systems behind effective antispoofing firewalls are safe.

The UDP Protocol

Like TCP, the *User Datagram Protocol* (UDP) is a transport layer protocol. However, UDP provides an unreliable, connectionless delivery service to transport messages between machines. It does not offer error correction, retransmission, or protection from lost and duplicated packets. UDP was designed for simplicity and speed and to avoid costly overhead associated with connection establishment and teardown. Figure5-14 shows the UDP header format.

Figure 5-14   *The UDP Header Format*

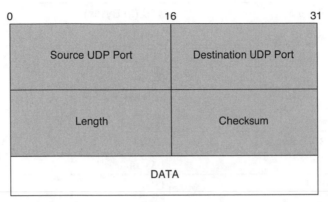

Because there is no control over how fast UDP messages are sent, and there are no connection establishment handshakes or sequence numbers, UDP packets are much easier to spoof than TCP packets. Therefore, it is wise to set up packet filters at the entry and exit points of a campus network to specifically permit and deny UDP-based applications.

The ICMP Protocol

The *Internet Control Message Protocol* (ICMP) is used by the IP layer to exchange control messages. ICMP is also used for some popular diagnostic tools such as ping and traceroute. Figure 5-15 shows an example of an ICMP packet.

Figure 5-15   *An ICMP Packet*

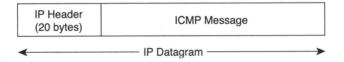

The ICMP message is encapsulated within the IP packet. As provided by RFC 791, IP packets can be up to $65,535$ ($2^{16} - 1$) octets long; this packet length includes the header length (typically 20 octets if no IP options are specified). Packets bigger than the maximum transmission unit (MTU) are fragmented by the transmitter into smaller packets, which are later reassembled by the receiver. The MTU varies for different media types. Table 5-4 shows sample MTUs for different media types.

Table 5-4   *MTUs for Various Media Types*

Media Type	MTU (in Bytes)
ISDN BRI/PRI	1500
10-Mbps/100-Mbps Ethernet	1500
HYPERchannel	65,535
FDDI	4352
X.25	576
16MB IBM Token Ring	17,914
SLIP	1006
Point-to-Point	1500
Gigabit Ethernet	1500 (proposal of 9180, which is currently nonstandard)

The Ping of Death

The Ping of Death is an attack that exploits the fragmentation vulnerability of large ICMP echo request (that is, "ping") packets. Figure 5-16 shows a sample ICMP echo request packet.

Figure 5-16   *An ICMP Echo Request Packet*

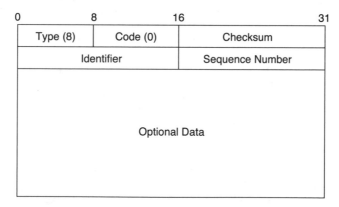

The ICMP echo request packet consists of eight octets of ICMP header information followed by the number of data octets in the ping request. The maximum allowable size of the data area is therefore calculated this way:

$(65{,}535 - 20 - 8) = 65{,}507$ octets

The problem is that it is possible to send an illegal ICMP echo packet with more than 65,507 octets of data because of the way the fragmentation is performed. The fragmentation relies on an offset value in each fragment to determine where the individual fragment goes when it is reassembled. Therefore, on the last fragment, it is possible to combine a valid offset with a suitable fragment size so that the following is true:

$$(\text{Offset} + \text{Size}) > 65,535$$

Because typical machines don't process the packet until they have all the fragments and have tried to reassemble them, there is the possibility of the overflow of 16-bit internal variables, which can lead to system crashes, reboots, kernel dumps, and other unwarranted behavior.

NOTE   This vulnerability is not restricted to the ping packet. The problem can be exploited by sending any large IP datagram packet.

A temporary fix to prevent the Ping of Death is to block ping packets at the ingress points to the corporate network. The ideal solution is to secure the TCP/IP implementation against overflow when reconstructing IP fragments.

Smurf Attack

The Smurf attack starts with a perpetrator sending a large number of spoofed ICMP echo requests to broadcast addresses, hoping that these packets will be magnified and sent to the spoofed addresses. If the routing device delivering traffic to those broadcast addresses performs the Layer 3 broadcast to Layer 2 broadcast function, most hosts on that IP network will reply to the ICMP echo request with an ICMP echo-reply each, multiplying the traffic by the number of hosts responding. On a multiaccess broadcast network, there could potentially be hundreds of machines replying to each echo packet.

Turning off directed broadcast capability in the network infrastructure is one way to deter this kind of attack.

The Teardrop.c Attack

Teardrop.c is a program that results in another fragmentation attack. It works by exploiting a reassembly bug with overlapping fragments and causes the targeted system to crash or hang. A specific instance of a teardrop program is newtear.c, which is just a specific case in which the first fragment starts at offset 0 and the second fragment is within the TCP header.

The original teardrop.c program used fragmented ICMP packets, but people seem to have created all kinds of variants. The basic attack works for any IP protocol type because it hits the IP layer itself.

If broadcast addresses are used, turning off directed broadcast capability in the network infrastructure is one way to deter this kind of attack. However, the ideal solution is to secure the TCP/IP implementation against problems when reassembling overlapping IP fragments.

NOTE   Fragmenting the IP packets in the middle of the TCP header has often been used to evade firewall port filtering.

The DNS Protocol

The *Domain Name System* (DNS) protocol is used to resolve host names and IP addresses. DNS servers are probably one of the most common targets for gathering reconnaissance information about hosts for later exploit efforts. DNS differs from a normal client/server application in that there may be interactions with other intermediaries before a response is obtained. When a client issues a DNS query, a DNS server accepts the query, possibly interacts with one or more additional DNS servers, and when it finally receives the response to the query, it forwards it to the client.

DNS is a globally distributed database system that depends on the coopertaive interaction of many DNS servers to store records about domains and to communicate with each other. A domain is a subset of DNS records associated with a logical grouping, such as illustrated in Figure 5-17.

Figure 5-17   *DNS Hierarchy*

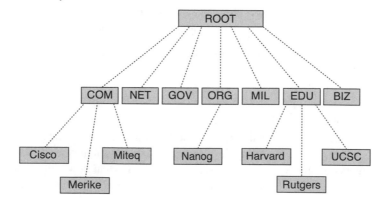

The domain names have a hierarchical structure where the "top-level" domains correspond to classes of users or countries. Thirteen root servers, distributed around the world, are at the top of the domain tree. These top-level domains register "subdomains" and check that the name is unique. They also keep track of the authoritative name servers for subdomains. An authoritative name server is a DNS server that owns and maintains DNS records for a given subdomain. Each domain must have a primary domain server; however, for redundancy, one or more secondary servers are usually created. These secondary servers can be used to load share in responding to DNS queries. DNS servers cache (that is, save) responses that they receive to make the resolution process more efficient. Each response of a DNS record has a time-to-live (TTL) value that is set by the responding DNS server. DNS servers that update records more often are more likely to have lower TTL values than relatively static servers have.

UDP is the protocol used for the majority of the DNS traffic because the queries and responses are often short and the application itself can tolerate lost data. When anticipated data is not received, a new DNS query is issued. Both source and destination ports are UDP 53.

DNS information is maintained on the primary server in flat text files. The secondary server periodically contacts the primary name server to see whether any updates have been made for a particular domain. If so, the updated DNS records are transferred using zone transfers. Zone transfers are done via TCP because there is usually a large amount of data and the transfer needs to be reliable. Zone information is valuable data that a malicious user could easily misuse. To prevent unauthorized zone transfers, newer releases of BIND have configurable parameters that enable an administrator to specify IP numbers or subnets authorized to do zone transfers. Additionally, a network administrator could block inbound traffic to TCP port 53. However, this may block other legitimate traffic as discussed later.

Generally a default name server is configured on every client machine. The gethostbyname call is sent from the client machine to the default DNS server. Assuming that the default server has no knowledge of the host's associated domain, it must contact a root name server. Root name servers maintain a mapping between the domain names and their respective authoritative servers. When the root name server returns a referral, the configured default DNS server then queries the authoritative name server and receives an authoritative answer, the IP address.

Figure 5-18 illustrates the steps for resolving a typical DNS query.

Figure 5-18 *DNS Resolving*

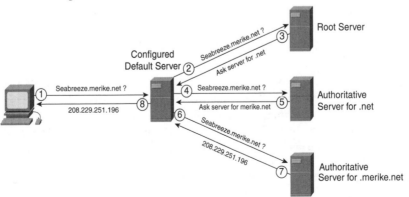

The following steps are carried out for the initial query to find the IP address for seabreeze.merike.net:

Step 1 The querying host (aka resolver) asks the question to the configured default DNS server.

Step 2 The default DNS server does not know the answer, and forwards the request to a root name server.

Step 3 The root server answers with the name (and the address) of the authoritative DNS server for .net.

Step 4 The default DNS server now queries the authoritative .net server.

Step 5 The authoritative .net server replies with a referral to for the authoritative .merike.net server.

Step 6 The default DNS server repeats the query to the authoritative .merike.net server.

Step 7 The authoritative .merike.net server gives the IP address.

Step 8 The default DNS server forwards the reply to the querying host.

DNS queries can be recursive or iterative. If a DNS server is configured to be recursive, it tries and queries all known referrences of name servers that could possibly have the answer to a query. The name server must follow all the references until it finds a name server that has the answer and then respond back to the original requester. In an iterative query, if the name server doesn't have the answer, it returns to the querying server a reference of another name server that possibly has the answer to the query. The queried name server does not pursue finding the answer.

NOTE Recursive DNS queries can lead to DNS cache poisoning. Because DNS uses UDP, it is trivial to determine the sequence number and create an invalid entry. Because many DNS servers are configured with recursive lookups, malicious user can make a DNS query and inject a bogus entry while the query recipient does a recursive DNS lookup. It is recommended not to allow recursive lookups.

How to secure your DNS infrastructure is beyond the scope of this book. However, you do need to be aware that a number of DNS vulnerabilities exist, including corrupting the data, unauthorized updates, impersonating a primary name server, cache pollution by data spoofing, and cache impersonation. DNS data can be spoofed and corrupted on its way between server and resolver or forwarder because the current DNS protocol does not enable you to check the validity of DNS data. Many of these vulneranilities are addressed in the DNS Security (DNSSEC) standard, described in RFC 2535. It provides better authentication mechanisms based on cryptographic signatures to validate the integrity and origin of the DNS data. Currently, the work has not yet been widely adopted; however, it is going through some modifications, and the hope is that it will become widely adopted by the community.

At the network infrastructure level, some filtering can be done to provide some small measure of security. The maximum size of a UDP DNS response is 512 bytes. Of these, a minumum of 20 bytes must be reserved for the IP header, and 8 bytes must be reserved for the UDP header. Therefore, the maximum DNS message can only be 484 bytes. If a DNS resource record exceeds this size, it will be truncated and rather than send UDP fragments, the information is sent via TCP. If inbound traffic to TCP port 53 is blocked (both source and destination port) to prevent unauthorized zone transfers, you also block any external host from resolving large responses. To avoid this problem, block traffic to destination port 53 only and allow traffic to source port 53 that already has an established connection.

The NNTP Protocol

Most Usenet traffic uses the *Network News Transfer Protocol* (NNTP) to send messages between news servers and between servers and newsreaders. Because the control protocol used for NNTP does not provide for any authentication, it can be easy to cancel messages before they are posted, create new unauthorized newsgroups, or delete existing newsgroups from the server.

Servers exist that can provide restrictions on who can post to a group based on their user ID or network address. These servers can be used for authenticated access to read and receive news. Local newsgroups should be placed on an internal secure news server; updates from other news services should be received through packet filters that can restrict which machines communicate to it from outside the corporate infrastructure.

The SMTP Protocol

All electronic mail on the Internet is based on the *Simple Mail Transfer Protocol* (SMTP). Most email programs lack authentication, integrity, and confidentiality services unless special programs such as S/MIME or Pretty Good Privacy (PGP) programs are used. If these programs are not used, authentication, integrity, and confidentiality services can still be provided by using IP Security (IPsec, RFC 2401–2410) on routers and firewalls and by specifying that all e-mail traffic be authenticated and encrypted. Although the security services provided by IPsec are not equivalent to those provided by either PGP or S/MIME, they provide some security controls at the network infrastructure level.

Spam Attack

A large contingency of e-mail attacks are based on e-mail bombing or spamming. E-mail *bombing* is characterized by abusers repeatedly sending an identical e-mail message to a particular address. E-mail *spamming* is a variant of bombing; it refers to sending e-mail to hundreds or thousands of users (or to lists that expand to that many users). E-mail spamming can be made worse if recipients reply to the e-mail, causing all the original addresses to receive the reply.

When large amounts of e-mail are directed to or through a single site, the site may suffer a denial of service through loss of network connectivity, system crashes, or failure of a service because of these factors:

- Overloading network connections
- Using all available system resources
- Filling the disk as a result of multiple postings and resulting syslog entries

A recent mass-mailing, network-aware worm named W32.Sobig.F infected thousands of machines in August 2003. The worm used its own SMTP engine to propagate and sent itself to multiple addresses. The spoofed From addresses and the Send To addresses were both taken from the files found on the compromised computer.

Spamming or bombing attacks cannot be prevented, but you can minimize the number of machines available to an intruder for an SMTP-based attack. If your site uses a small number of e-mail servers, you may want to configure your *ingress* (entry from the Internet to the corporate network) and *egress* (exit from the corporate network to the Internet) points to ensure that SMTP connections from the outside can be made only to your central e-mail hubs and to none of your other systems. Additionally, you may want to configure your email server to block or remove email that contains file attachments that are commonly used to spread viruses, such as .vbs, .bat, .exe, .pif, and .scr files.

You can find more detailed information on SPAM attacks and deterrents at the following addresses: http://spam.abuse.net/ and http://www.cauce.org/.

The FTP Protocol

The *File Transfer Protocol* (FTP) is a TCP-based application program often used to transmit and receive large data files. The protocol uses two TCP connections, as shown in Figure 5-19:

- One connection for the initial FTP control connection, which is initiated by the client to the server
- The other connection for the FTP data connection, which is initiated from the server back to the client

Figure 5-19 *FTP Operation*

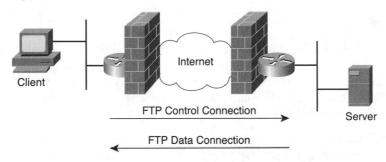

FTP Control Connection

FTP Data Connection

Most common FTP implementations create a new FTP data connection for each file transfer and also require a new port number to be used for each of these new FTP data connections. These requirements can cause problems for restricted environments that want to block externally initiated FTP connections. The packet filters block the incoming data connection back from the server so that file transfer no longer works.

To circumvent this problem, passive mode FTP was developed. With *passive mode FTP*, the client initiates both the control connection and the data connection so that a packet-filtering firewall can provide some protection and not block data transfers.

Be aware that FTP is an insecure protocol and that passwords are sent as plaintext between your user sessions and any FTP server you are likely to run. Even if you insist that users connect to your servers using Secure Shell (SSH), if their FTP and shell login passwords are the same (which is the default), someone snooping around can gain access to your system via SSH by sniffing FTP user sessions for passwords.

It is best to try and avoid FTP completely. Where possible, use the Secure Copy Protocol (SCP), which is built in to many SSH daemons.

The Remote Procedure Call (RPC) Service

The Remote Procedure Call (RPC) service is a programming interface for a client/server relationship between two interfaces which allows a program running on one computer to seamlessly execute code on a remote system. It can utilize either TCP or UDP as its transport protocol. RPC is widely used for many distributed network services and is often the culprit for security breaches since in UNIX environments many RPC services execute with root privileges and can provide an attacker with unauthorized root access. RPC programs do not perform sufficient error checking or input validation services and are often exploited through buffer overflow attacks. The UNIX portmap service, which uses TCP or UDP port 111 keeps track of the location of various RPC services by port and potential attackers often use the portmap service to locate the procedures they want to attack. A secure version of portmapper is available and should be used. To mitigate reconnaissance attempts using portmap, blocking TCP and UDP port 111 at network edges can avert many potential attacks. In addition, it is advisable to block RPC loopback ports 32770 through 32789 (TCP and UDP).

More recent and widespread worms involving RPC are the notorious Blaster.D and Nachi worms which infected devices running the Microsoft operating system. These worms exploit the DCOM RPC vulnerability which is described in Microsoft Security Bulletin MS03-026 at http://www.microsoft.com/technet/treeview/default.asp?url=/technet/ security/bulletin/MS03-026.asp.

Similar to the UNIX RPC issues, the Microsoft vulnerability results because the Windows RPC service does not properly check message inputs under certain circumstances. Both Blaster.D and Nachi exploit the RPC DCOM vulnerability to gain access to a system. After a vulnerable system is compromised, the worms use TFTP to download the rest of its operating components and attempts to spread themselves across the network. While Blaster.D blindly attempts to reach addresses on the compromised hosts' network, the Nachi worm first sends out a series of pings to verify that target hosts are actually online and subsequently results in an ICMP DoS on the compromised hosts' network. To mitigate attacks based on Blaster.D and Nachi, it is recommended to block outbound traffic of the following ports at enterprise network perimeters:

- 135 (UDP and TCP)
- 137 (UDP and TCP)
- 139 (UDP and TCP)
- 445 (UDP and TCP)
- 593 (TCP)
- 69 (UDP): TFTP traffic to prevent the worm version of the exploit from downloading code to a newly infected host
- 4444 (TCP): The exploit uses this to provide command line access to a Windows target host

NOTE   To avert exploits which may make use of any host vulnerability it is extremely important to understand the services, which need to be made accessible to the Internet. The best defense is to apply filters at network perimeters (edges), which deny everything and permit only the services, which are required. However, this can be too restrictive in many circumstances and needs careful consideration. The following URL lists the common TCP and UDP ports used for Windows services, and it is listed here to help you make appropriate decisions in enterprise networks that largely use the Microsoft operating system:

http://www.microsoft.com/technet/treeview/default.asp?url=/technet/prodtechnol/ windows2000serv/reskit/tcpip/part4/tcpappc.asp

The NFS/NIS Services

The *Network File System* (NFS) and the *Network Information System* (NIS) are commonly used services in UNIX environments. NFS is used to access remote file systems by allowing users to mount remote file systems so that they can be accessed locally. NIS is used to establish central services and databases in client/server relationships. (Typically, these services include user account information and passwords.) NIS and NFS are often used together to help enforce file permissions on mounted systems.

Both NFS and NIS use UDP as their underlying protocol. In typical configurations, there is limited authentication on either end of the connection. These services are extremely insecure; this kind of traffic should never be allowed through the entrance or exit points of the corporate network.

X Window System

X Window System is one of the most commonly used windowing systems. The X server offers resources such as the keyboard, the mouse, and the windows on the screen to X clients. The server accepts requests from the client for keyboard input, screen output, or mouse movement and returns the results of these requests. The X11 protocol has been adopted by many of the major workstation vendors for displaying network graphics and is the common element upon which each vendor's graphical user interface is based.

X Window System requires a reliable bidirectional stream protocol such as TCP. The communication between the client and the server consists of 8-bit bytes exchanged across a TCP connection.

Because of limited authentication inherent in the X11 protocol, it is possible for someone with access to the network to connect directly to the X server and either view or modify ongoing communication between the server and the X client.

In a network infrastructure, limiting X11 traffic to only internal hosts is one way to limit these kinds of attacks.

Common Network Scenario Threats and Vulnerabilities

This section covers attacks that exploit weaknesses in poorly designed networks, detailing threats to specific networking scenarios pertaining to VPNs, wireless networks, and Voice over IP (VoIP) networks to emphasize vulnerabilities in these network designs. In addition, some threats to routing protocols are discussed. Implementation details for building secure VPN, wireless, and VoIP networks are discussed in Chapter 12, "Securing VPN, Wireless, and VoIP Networks."

Virtual Private Networks

When discussing vulnerabilities specific to deploying VPNs, the main issue revolves around understanding where the VPN tunnel starts and ends and where the traffic is exposed. In an ideal situation, the VPN tunnel will be created end-to-end; in many cases, however, the tunnel endpoints are both intermediary gateways or a VPN concentrator.

Unauthorized Access

Unauthorized access via VPNs would likely result from obtaining credentials, such as a username/password, for a given user or device. Typically, more robust authentication and authorization mechanisms would be used to make it harder to get access to the credentials used. Laptops being used for remote secure access can compromise a corporate VPN if they are not sufficiently protected. Often, the credentials used to authenticate the device are saved on the laptop via a VPN software package. If the laptop is stolen and the VPN software is not adequately protected on the laptop, a malicious user could easily gain access to the corporate VPN. To provide more protection, any remote user VPN scenario should obtain credentials to authenticate both a given device and individual user before allowing access to the corporate network.

Look at a situation where Layer 2 Tunneling Protocol (L2TP)/IPsec is deployed to create a secure VPN tunnel. Assume that the identity claimed in PPP is a user identity, whereas the identity claimed within Internet Key Exchange (IKE) is a device identity. Although PPP provides initial authentication, it does not provide per-packet authentication, integrity, or replay protection. For IPsec, when the identity asserted in IKE is authenticated, the resulting derived keys are used to provide per-packet authentication, integrity, and replay protection. As a result, the identity verified in the IKE conversation is subsequently verified on reception of each packet. So, in this scenario, because only the device identity is verified on a per-packet basis, there is no way to verify that only the user authenticated within PPP is using the tunnel. In fact, IPsec implementations that only support device authentication typically have no way to enforce traffic segregation. As a result, where device authentication is used, after an L2TP/IPsec tunnel is opened, any user on a multi-user machine will typically be able to send traffic down the tunnel.

If the IPsec implementation supports user authentication, this problem can be averted. When using IPsec with user authentication, the user identity asserted within IKE will be verified on a per-packet basis. To provide segregation of traffic between users when user authentication is used, the client can ensure that only traffic from that particular user is sent down the L2TP tunnel.

Impersonation

Impersonation could be accomplished if the actual key material gets compromised. If a company uses a group shared key for all employees, the shared key is more susceptible to getting compromised and can have a larger impact. It is best to avoid a group shared key whenever possible.

When using IPsec to deploy VPNs, it is still common to use preshared keys for authentication. Use of preshared keys in IKE phase 1 main mode increases vulnerability to man-in-the-middle attacks in remote access situations. In main mode, it is necessary for the derived encryption key to be used prior to the receipt of the identification payload. Therefore, the selection of the preshared key can only be based on information contained in the IP header. However, in remote access situations, dynamic IP address assignment is typical, so it is often not possible to identify the required preshared key based on the IP address.

When preshared keys are used in remote access scenarios, the same preshared key is shared by a group of users and is no longer able to function as an effective shared secret. In this situation, neither the client nor the server identifies itself during IKE phase 1; it is only known that both parties are members of the group with knowledge of the preshared key. This permits anyone with access to the group preshared key to act as a man in the middle.

This vulnerability does not occur in IKE phase 1 aggressive mode because the identity payload is sent earlier in the exchange, and therefore the preshared key can be selected based on the identity. When aggressive mode is used, however, the user identity is exposed and this is often considered undesirable.

As a result, where IKE phase 1 main mode is used with preshared keys, unless PPP performs mutual authentication, the server is not authenticated. This enables a rogue server in possession of the group preshared key to successfully masquerade as the L2TP network server (LNS) and mount a dictionary attack on legacy authentication methods such as Challenge Handshake Authentication Protocol (CHAP). Such an attack could potentially compromise many passwords at a time. This vulnerability is present in some existing IPsec tunnel mode implementations.

To avoid this problem, L2TP/IPsec implementations often do not use a group preshared key for Internet Key Exchange (IKE) authentication to the LNS.

Denial of Service

DoS attacks may be directed at critical components in the VPN path, such as a VPN concentrator that could potentially terminates hundreds of VPN connections. If the VPN is created such that certain protocols that are part of the VPN (such as SSL/TLS, SSH, and IPsec) are inherently trusted and could bypass any firewall controls, a malicious user could potentially spoof these types of packets using trusted IP addresses and then use these spoofed packets to launch a DoS attack against internal corporate resources. Never assume that traffic, just by being transported as part of a VPN solution, is secure and can be trusted. How to make appropriate secure VPN design decisions is discussed in more detail in Chapter 12.

Wireless Networks

Wireless networks have become one of the most interesting targets for security breaches. Most wireless LAN devices ship with all security features disabled, and several websites are documenting all the freely available wireless connections nationwide, giving potential intruders a choice of which site to go tamper with. Although many intruders just exploit these "free" connections as a means to get free Internet access or to hide their identity, others might see this situation as an opportunity to break into networks that otherwise might have been difficult to attack from the Internet because unlike a wired network, wireless networks send data over the air and usually extend beyond the physical boundary of an organization.

Unauthorized Access

Unauthorized access to wireless LANs can be obtained in a number of ways. When strong directional antennas are used, a wireless LAN can reach well outside the buildings that it is designed for, and if WEP is not enabled it is easy to create an environment where traditional physical security controls are ineffective because the packets can be viewed by anyone within radio frequency range.

Most wireless LANs deployed by organizations operate in a mode called "infrastructure." In this mode, all wireless clients connect through an AP for all communications. You can, however, deploy wireless LAN technology in a way that forms an independent peer-to-peer network, which is more commonly called an ad hoc wireless LAN. In an ad hoc wireless LAN, laptop or desktop computers that are equipped with compatible wireless LAN adapters and are within range of one another can share files directly, without the use of an AP. The range varies, depending on the type of wireless LAN system. Laptop and desktop computers equipped with 802.11b wireless LAN cards can create ad hoc networks if they are within at least 500 feet of one another. Many wireless cards, including some shipped as a default item by PC manufacturers, ship with ad hoc mode enabled by default. Any person who is also configured for ad hoc mode is immediately connected to PCs using these cards and could attempt to gain unauthorized access. In most environments, it would be prudent to disable ad hoc mode wireless LANs.

In the hands of a determined malicious intruder, a rogue AP can be a valuable asset in the attempted compromise of network resources. The principal threat is installing an AP into a network after gaining unauthorized access to a building. The user typically gains access to the building by following behind a user with a valid access badge or by obtaining a guest badge for some other reason. Because APs are relatively small and can be purchased at many electronics outlets worldwide, it is easy for the intruder not only to obtain the AP but also to install it discreetly. Attaching the AP to the underside of a conference-room table and plugging into the live network enables the intruder to break into a network from the relative security of his car in the parking lot. Man-in-the-middle attacks are also easy to carry out. Using a device that can masquerade as a trusted AP, an intruder can easily intercept and manipulate wireless packets.

NOTE   An organization should have a complete wireless network policy in addition to its overall security policy. (Refer to Chapter 6, "Considerations for a Site Security Policy," and Chapter 7, "Design and Implementation of the Corporate Security Policy," for more detail on how to create a security policy.) This wireless policy should, at a minimum, disallow the connection of non-IT supported APs into the network. In addition, the IT department needs to conduct regular scans of its office space to check for rogue APs. This includes both physical searches and wireless scans. Several vendors offer tools designed to discover the presence of the wireless APs in a certain area.

Impersonation

The wireless LAN access points can identify every wireless card by its unique Media Access Control (MAC) address. Some APs have MAC address filtering capabilities that require that the cards be registered before the wireless services can be used. However, this introduces administrative nightmares because every AP needs to have this list configured. In addition, all MAC addresses are sent in the clear and there exist programs such as Network Stumbler that a malicious user can use to eavesdrop on a wireless network and to obtain valid MAC addresses. The eavesdropper could then use a wireless LAN card that can be loaded with firmware to define its MAC address. Using this spoofed MAC address, the malicious user can attempt to inject network traffic or spoof legitimate users.

Denial of Service

It is easy to interfere with wireless communications. A simple jamming transmitter can easily cause a DoS attack and render communications impossible. For example, consistently sending access requests to an AP, whether successful or not, will eventually exhaust its available radio frequency spectrum and make it unavailable. Other wireless services in the same frequency range can also reduce the range and usable bandwidth of wireless LAN technology, as illustrated in Figure 5-20.

Although by no means a malicious denial of service, those deploying wireless networks need to be aware of other obstructions that could potentially render a network unusable if they are added in an office environment. These include microwave ovens near kitchens, metal file cabinets, and possibly large industrial equipment.

Figure 5-20 *Wireless LAN Interference Considerations*

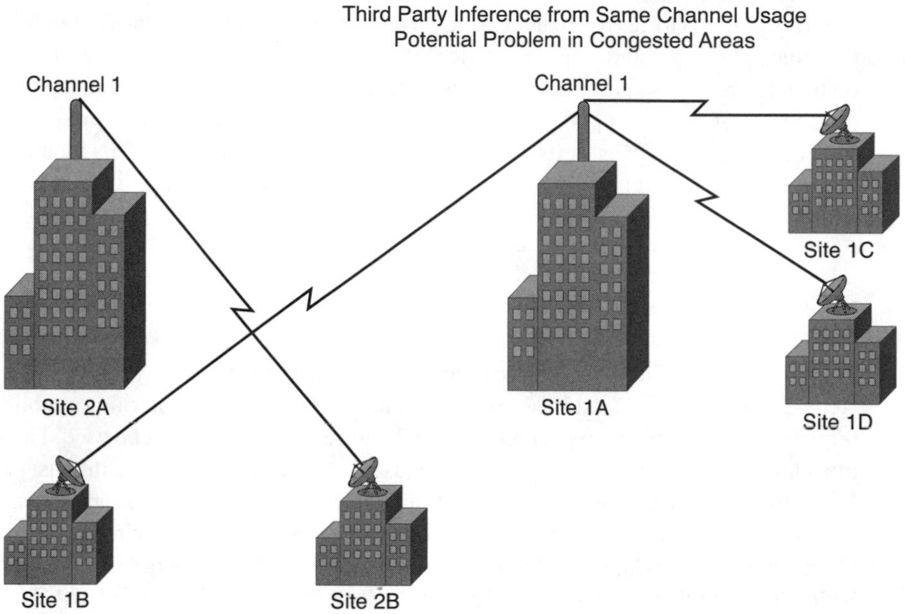

WEP Insecurity

The operation of WEP is described in Chapter 3. The 802.11 standards define WEP as a simple mechanism to protect the communication between wireless LAN APs and network interface cards (NICs). WEP uses the RC-4 encryption algorithm and requires that the same secret key be shared by all communicating parties. To avoid conflicting with U.S. export controls that were in effect at the time the standard was developed, 40-bit encryption keys were required by IEEE 802.11b, although many vendors now support the optional 128-bit standard. These key lengths are not very robust, and WEP can be easily cracked in both 40- and 128-bit variants by using off-the-shelf tools readily available on the Internet.

The IEEE 802.11 standard describes the use of the RC-4 algorithm and key in WEP, but does not specify specific methods for key distribution. Without an automated method for key distribution, any encryption protocol will have implementation problems due to the potential for human error in key input, escrow, and management. As discussed in Chapter 3, 802.1x is being embraced by the wireless LAN vendor community as a potential solution for this key distribution problem.

WEP's biggest problem came with the publication of weaknesses in RC-4 that were discovered by cryptanalysts Fluhrer, Mantin, and Shamir. The first weakness is in the Key Scheduling Algorithm (KSA), which derives the initial state from a variable key size. There exists a large class of keys (weak keys) in which a small part of the secret key determines a large number of bits in the KSA output. This weakness is known as the *invariance weakness*. The weakness can be exploited by what is termed the *FMS attack* (Fluhrer, Mantin, Shamir attack), which is illustrated in Figure 5-21 and is described in a paper found at http://www.cs.umd.edu/~waa/class-pubs/rc4_ksaproc.ps.

The paper discusses the theoretical derivation of a WEP key in a range of 100,000 to 1,000,000 packets encrypted using the same key. Recent practical implementations of the FMS attack have been able to derive a static WEP key by capturing about a million packets. This is demonstrated in a paper by AT&T Labs and Rice University at http://www.cs.rice.edu/~astubble/wep/wep_attack.pdf. Several independent developers then released their own implementations of the FMS attack; the most popular of these is AirSnort, which can be downloaded at http://airsnort.sourceforge.net/.

Figure 5-21   *WEP Weak Key Attack*

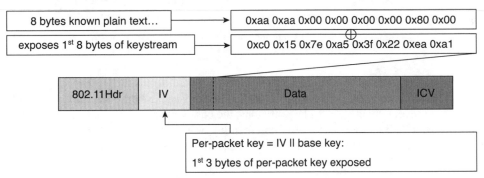

- Class of RC4 *weak keys* exists where patterns in the 1st 3 bytes of key causes corresponding patterns in 1st few bytes of the generated RC4 key stream.

- For each packet, use IV and exposed key stream to identify potential weak keys.

- Iterate over potential weak keys from a sequence of packets until the RC4 base key is found.

The second weakness is related to the first and occurs when part of the key presented to the KSA is exposed to the attacker. Because the initialization vector (IV) for RC-4 is transmitted as plaintext and placed in the 802.11 header, anyone eavesdropping on a wireless LAN can see it. Because the IV is 24 bits long, it provides a range of 16,777,216 possible values. A University of California at Berkeley paper found that when the same IV is used with the same key on an encrypted packet, an eavesdropper can capture the data frames and derive information about the data as well as the network. This is also known as the *IV Collision attack* and is illustrated in Figure 5-22.

Figure 5-22 *WEP IV Collision Attack*

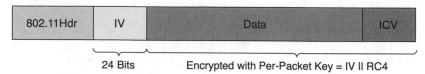

24 Bits   Encrypted with Per-Packet Key = IV || RC4

- WEP expands each RC4 key into 2^{24} per-packet keys $\Rightarrow$ data can be recovered if IV is ever repeated with same key $\Rightarrow$ RC4 key must be changed at least every 2^{24} packets or data is exposed through IV collisions!

  Some implemented IV selection strategies:

- Random: Collision probability P_n two packets will share same IV after n packets is $P_2 = 1/2^{24}$ for $n = 2$ and $P_n = P_{n-1}+(n-1)(1-P_{n-1})/2^{24}$ for $n > 2$.

  50% chance of a collision exists already after only 4823 packets!

- Increment from 0: Collision probability = 100% after **two** devices transmit.

For more information, refer to the University of California at Berkeley paper titled "Security of the WEP Algorithm" at http://www.isaac.cs.berkeley.edu/isaac/wep-faq.html. To prevent attacks due to IV collisions, the base key should be changed before the IVs repeat, and many vendors are implementing proprietary mechanisms to address this issue until newer 802.11 standards incorporating Temporal Key Integrity Protocol (TKIP) and the Advanced Encryption Standard (AES) encryption algorithm are available.

Another concern with WEP is its vulnerability to replay attacks. This is due to the use of the cyclic redundancy check (CRC)-32 checksum function performed by standards-based WEP, as illustrated in Figure 5-23.

As the previously mentioned paper "Security of the WEP Algorithm" indicates, with CRC-32, it is, "possible to compute the bit difference of two CRCs based on the bit difference of the messages over which they are taken. In other words, flipping bit *n* in the message results in a deterministic set of bits in the CRC that must be flipped to produce a correct checksum on the modified message. Because flipping bits carries through after an RC-4 decryption, this allows the attacker to flip arbitrary bits in an encrypted message and correctly adjust the checksum so that the resulting message appears valid."

Wireless networks are being deployed quite rapidly and although the standards work still needs to be completed to make these networks more secure, knowing which threats and vulnerabilites exist can help in deploying a reasonably secure wireless network, as discussed in Chapter 12.

Figure 5-23 *WEP Bit-Flipping Vulnerability*

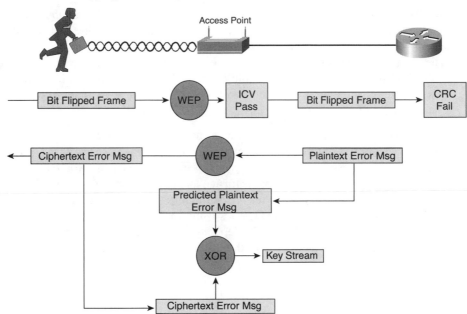

Voice over IP Networks

The main issue with voice networks today is that they are generally wide open and require little or no authentication to gain access. The reason for this is that the model chosen for IP voice networks parallels that chosen for legacy voice systems. It is expected that going forward the traditional security features such as strong authentication and encryption will integrate with IP telephony standards. Here we outline some threats to be aware of when deploying VoIP networks.

Unauthorized Access

Voice transport mechanisms generally don't use encryption, which makes it easy to use packet sniffers so that the voice steams can be saved and reassembled for listening. The tool "voice over misconfigured Internet telephones" (also known as vomit), takes an IP phone conversation trace captured by the UNIX tool tcpdump, and reassembles it into a WAV file for easy listening. The phones are not actually misconfigured. Rather, if someone were able to obtain access to the IP data stream at any point in the network, they could eavesdrop.

Another threat constitutes theft of service, and there are numerous methods an intruder could use to accomplish this task. In its most basic form, toll fraud includes an unauthorized user accessing an unattended IP phone to place calls. A more complex scenario might include placing a rogue IP phone or gateway on the network to place unauthorized calls.

Impersonation

Caller identity spoofing can occur when an intruder is able to trick a remote user into believing she is talking to someone when in fact she is really talking to the intruder. This type of attack typically occurs with the intruder assuming the identity of someone who is not familiar to the target. A complex attack would be to first place a rogue IP phone in the network and then via a secondary exploit assume the identity of a valid IP phone (assuming the identity that you want your target to see). It could also be as simple as a bypassing physical building security and using an unattended IP phone!

An IP spoofing attack can occur when an intruder inside or outside a network impersonates the conversations of a trusted computer. An intruder can do this in one of two ways. He uses either an IP address that is within the range of trusted IP addresses for a network or an authorized external IP address that is trusted and to which access is provided to specified resources on a network. IP spoofing attacks are often a launch point for other attacks. The classic example is to launch a DoS attack using spoofed source addresses to hide the intruder's identity. As it relates to IP telephony, without spoof mitigation filters the intruder might be able to spoof the address of the call-processing manager and UDP flood the entire voice segment.

Denial of Service

Certainly the most publicized form of attack, DoS attacks are also among the most difficult to completely eliminate. These attacks include the following, all of which were discussed earlier in this chapter:

- TCP SYN flood
- Ping of Death
- UDP fragment flood
- ICMP fragment flood

If not properly mitigated, all of these sample DoS attacks could render a voice segment unusable.

SIP Application Layer Insecurity

This section lists a few inherent insecurities to be aware of when using Session Initiation Protocol (SIP)-based networks. Most of these can be found in the discussion in the security considerations section of the SIP protocol (RFC 3261).

HTTP Digest

One of the primary limitations of using HTTP Digest in SIP is that the integrity mechanisms in the digest do not work very well for SIP. Specifically, they offer protection of the Request-URI and the method of a message, but not for any of the header fields that user agents would most likely want to secure.

Another limitation of HTTP Digest is the scope of realms. The digest is valuable when a user wants to authenticate himself to a resource with which he has a preexisting association, such as a service provider of which the user is a customer (which is quite a common scenario and thus HTTP Digest provides an extremely useful function).

S/MIME

The largest outstanding defect with the S/MIME mechanism is the lack of a prevalent public key infrastructure for end users. If self-signed certificates (or certificates that cannot be verified by one of the participants in a dialogue) are used, the SIP-based key exchange is susceptible to a man-in-the-middle attack with which an attacker can potentially inspect and modify S/MIME bodies. The attacker needs to intercept the first exchange of keys between the two parties in a dialogue, remove the existing CMS-detached signatures from the request and response, and insert a different CMS-detached signature containing a certificate supplied by the attacker (but which seems to be a certificate for the proper address of record). Each party will think he has exchanged keys with the other, when in fact each has the public key of the attacker.

It is important to note that the attacker can only leverage this vulnerability on the first exchange of keys between two parties; on subsequent occasions, the alteration of the key would be noticeable to the user agents. It would also be difficult for the attacker to remain in the path of all future dialogues between the two parties over time (as potentially days, weeks, or years pass). The S/MIME mechanism allows user agents to send encrypted requests without preamble if they possess a certificate for the destination address of record on their keyring. However, it is possible that any particular device registered for an address of record will not hold the certificate that has been previously used by the device's current user, and that it will therefore be unable to process an encrypted request properly, which could lead to some avoidable error signaling. This is especially likely when an encrypted request is forked.

The keys associated with S/MIME prove most useful when associated with a particular user (an address of record) rather than a device (a user agent). When users move between devices, it may be difficult to transport private keys securely between user agents; how such keys might be acquired by a device is beyond the scope of this discussion.

Transport Layer Security (TLS)

The most commonly voiced concern about TLS is that it cannot run over UDP; TLS requires a connection-oriented underlying transport protocol and therefore can only be used with TCP for SIP-based networks. It can be problematic for a local outbound proxy server and registrar to maintain many simultaneous long-lived TLS connections with numerous user agents, which introduces scalability concerns for intensive ciphersuites and allows for susceptibility for DoS attacks.

TLS only allows SIP entities to authenticate servers to which they are adjacent; TLS offers strictly hop-by-hop security. Neither TLS, nor any other mechanism specified in the SIP standard, allows clients to authenticate proxy servers to whom they cannot form a direct TCP connection.

NOTE   When SIP is used in a mode where resources can specify that they should be reached securely, the term SIPS is used to designate this secure mode. The SIPS URI scheme adheres to the syntax of the SIP URI, although the scheme string is "sips" rather than "sip."

Using TLS on every segment of a request path entails that the terminating user agents must be reachable over TLS (perhaps registering with a SIPS URI as a contact address). This is the preferred use of SIPS. Many valid architectures, however, use TLS to secure part of the request path, but rely on some other mechanism for the final hop to a user agent, for example. Therefore, SIPS cannot guarantee that TLS usage will be truly end to end. Note that because many user agents will not accept incoming TLS connections, even those user agents that do support TLS may be required to maintain persistent TLS connections as discussed earlier in this chapter to receive requests over TLS as a user agent.

Ensuring that TLS will be used for all of the request segments up to the target domain is somewhat complex. It is possible that cryptographically authenticated proxy servers along the way that are noncompliant or compromised may choose to disregard the forwarding rules associated with SIPS. Such malicious intermediaries could, for example, retarget a request from a SIPS URI to a SIP URI in an attempt to downgrade security.

Alternatively, an intermediary might legitimately retarget a request from a SIP to a SIPS URI. Recipients of a request whose Request-URI uses the SIPS URI scheme therefore cannot assume on the basis of the Request-URI alone that SIPS was used for the entire request path (from the client onward).

If an attacker corrupts a DNS cache, inserting a fake record set that effectively removes all SIPS records for a proxy server, any SIPS requests that traverse this proxy server may fail. When a user sees that repeated calls to a SIPS address of record (AOR) are failing, however, he could on some devices manually convert the scheme from SIPS to SIP and retry. Of course, there are some safeguards against this (if the destination user agent is truly paranoid it could refuse all non-SIPS requests), but it is a limitation worth noting. On the bright side, users might also divine that "SIPS" would be valid even when they are presented only with a SIP URI.

Privacy

SIP messages frequently contain sensitive information about their senders—not just what they have to say, but with whom they communicate, when they communicate, and for how long, and from where they participate in sessions. Many applications and their users require that this sort of private information be hidden from any parties that do not need to know it.

There are also less direct ways in which private information can be divulged. If a user or service chooses to be reachable at an address that is guessable from the person's name and organizational affiliation (which describes most AORs), the traditional method of ensuring privacy by having an unlisted "phone number" is compromised. A user location service can infringe on the privacy of the recipient of a session invitation by divulging the user's specific whereabouts to the caller. Therefore, it is important to be able to restrict, on a per-user basis, what kind of location and availability information is given out to certain classes of callers. Note that this is a whole class of problem that is expected to be studied further in ongoing SIP work.

In some cases, users may want to conceal personal information in header fields that convey identity. This can apply not only to the From and related headers representing the originator of the request, but also the To—it may not be appropriate to convey to the final destination a speed-dialing nickname, or an unexpanded identifier for a group of targets, either of which would be removed from the Request-URI as the request is routed, but not changed in the To header field if the two were initially identical. Therefore, check whether the SIP implementation you are using creates a To header field that differs from the Request-URI.

VoIP is being deployed in numerous configurations. Even though the standards work still needs to be completed to make these networks more secure, knowing which threats and vulnerabilites exist can you deploy a reasonably secure VoIP network. as shown in Chapter 12.

Routing Protocols

Routing protocols have all adopted peer neighbor authentication mechanisms, as discussed in Chapter 4, "Routing Protocol Security." However, routing infrastructures are still subject to threats involving eavesdropping because no privacy is provided. Also, DoS attacks can be launched with spoofed addresses or invalid routing protocol updates. Using a combination of filtering techniques, neighbor authentication, and IPsec, it is possible to gain more security; however, it is often not thought that the risk in routing update spoofing warrants the added administrative costs of implementing IPsec in current networks.

NOTE   The attacks and weaknesses described in this chapter are only some of the more common vulnerabilities to which current networks are susceptible. For current listings of vulnerabilities and technical tips, refer to the many advisories available on the Internet:

- ftp://info.cert.org/pub/cert_advisories

- www.rootshell.com

- www.secnet.com/advisories

- www.cert.dfn.de/eng

Social Engineering

Finally, it is important to remember the importance of social engineering when considering threats to the corporate network. Consider a scenario in which a financial administrator in a large corporate network gets a phone call from someone saying she is part of the IS department and wants to verify users and passwords. An unwitting employee may think this is a valid request and submit his username and password over the phone to the intruder impersonating someone from the IS department. The intruder can now impersonate the financial administrator and gain access to very confidential data and possibly alter it for her personal gain.

Although some threats to network security are quite sophisticated, it can be very simple to gain access to networks through seemingly innocent social means. Corporate employees should be educated about the company security policy procedures and the importance of authentication methodologies. Employees must understand the ramifications of security breaches so that they are aware of the importance of security procedures. It is the responsibility of the corporation to establish a network security policy and then establish a way to implement that policy.

Summary

This chapter examined the various threats to a corporate network by detailing which types of attacks and vulnerabilities are common and what you can do at a policy level to guarantee some degree of safe networking. The types of threats usually come in the form of unauthorized access, impersonation, or DoS. Understanding some of the motivations for an attack can give you insight about which areas of the network are vulnerable and what actions an intruder may take. The more common vulnerabilities were detailed to help you evaluate your susceptibility—this can be invaluable in determining which steps you should take to safeguard your most exposed areas.

Review Questions

The following questions provide you with an opportunity to test your knowledge of the topics covered in this chapter. You can find the answers to these questions in Appendix E, "Answers to Review Questions."

1 What are three basic categories of threats?

2 True or false: Network reconnaissance attempts can be completely avoided with appropriate security measures in place.

3 What technique is commonly used to gain unauthorized access to networks that use modems?

4 True or false: For wireless networks, it doesn't make sense to enable WEP because it is inherently insecure.

5 What is a man-in-the-middle attack?

6 Which of the following are well-known denial-of-service attacks?

   A Smurf, TCP SYN, Stacheldraht

   B Land.c, Ping of Death, wizard.c

   C Both a and b

   D Neither a nor b

7 What are four common motivations for a computer network attack?

8 What is a TCP SYN attack?

9 What are two common DoS attacks that exploit fragmentation vulnerabilities?

10 True or false: To effectively stop invalid DNS zone transfers but still allow valid DNS traffic, it is best to block traffic to destination port 53 only and allow traffic to source port 53 that already has an established connection.

11 What enhancement does passive mode FTP offer over the original FTP?

12 Why is MAC address filtering in wireless LANs not an effective security control?

13 True or false: In WEP, the initialization vector is encrypted, so anyone eavesdropping on a wireless LAN cannot see what it is.

14 What is the main issue today that makes Voice over IP networks insecure?

## CHAPTER 6

Considerations for a Site Security Policy

Defining a site security policy is one of the basic building blocks of designing an enterprise network. It is as critical as defining bandwidth requirements or redundancy needs. RFC 2196, *The Site Security Handbook*, defines a site security policy as follows:

A security policy is a formal statement of rules by which people who are given access to an organization's technology and information assets must abide.

The policy should be formed with representation from key corporate individuals: management members who have budget and policy authority, technical staff who know what can and cannot be supported, and legal personnel who know the legal ramifications of various policy choices.

Benefits of creating a corporate security policy include the following:

- Providing a framework for implementing security features in the network infrastructure
- Providing a process by which you can audit existing network security
- Identifying procedures that are considered expedient, prudent, advantageous, and productive
- Enabling global security implementation and enforcement
- Creating a basis for legal action if necessary

A successful security policy must be committed to paper and show that the issues have been well thought out. Following are some key characteristics of a good security policy:

- It must be capable of being implemented technically.
- It must be capable of being implemented organizationally.
- It must be enforceable with security tools where appropriate and with sanctions where prevention is not technically feasible.
- It must clearly define the areas of responsibility for the users, administrators, and management.
- It must be flexible and adaptable to changing environments.

A security policy should not determine how a business operates; the nature of the business should dictate the security policy. Defining a company's security policy can seem difficult, but by defining the policy before choosing security methods, organizations can avoid having to redesign security methodologies after they are implemented.

This chapter focuses on how to start the process of defining a corporate security policy. Risk assessment and asset identification are reviewed, along with other considerations for forming a policy. After identifying the global corporate security considerations, you can define a security policy specific to the corporate network and determine the implementation details.

Where to Begin

Many companies have existing guidelines for security procedures in a corporate environment. These can be in the form of a statement of conduct rules for employees— which, to some extent, outlines how employees are to deal with confidential technology, intellectual property rights, and other confidential corporate information. These guidelines can be a basis for establishing a strategy for an enterprise network security policy because they establish corporate rules for what information is valuable to the company from a business point of view. The following is an example of a corporate statement of conduct.

Sample Corporate Standard of Conduct

Scope

Clearly articulated and consistently administered standards of conduct form the basis for behavioral expectations within a corporate community. The enforcement of such standards should be accomplished in a manner that protects the rights, health, and safety of the corporate members so that they can pursue their goals without undue interference.

As a way of supporting our individual commitments to fairness, honesty, equity, and responsibility, the members of this corporation subscribe to the following ethical principles and standards of conduct in their professional practice. Acceptance of employment signifies that the individual member agrees to adhere to the principles in this statement.

Use of This Statement

The purpose of this statement is to assist corporate personnel in regulating their own behavior by providing them with standards commonly held by practitioners in the industry. Self-regulation is preferred. If an individual observes conduct that may be contrary to established principles, however, she or he is obligated to bring the matter to the attention of the person allegedly committing the breach of ethics. If unethical conduct continues, the matter may be referred to the offender's superiors for appropriate action.

Signing this document implies agreement with and adherence to the following ethical principles and standards of conduct:

1 *Professional Responsibility.* Corporate employees have a responsibility to support both the general mission and goals of the employing company. All employees shall make every effort to balance the developmental and professional needs of employees with the obligation of the company to protect the safety and welfare of the corporate community.

2 *Legal Authority.* Employees respect and acknowledge all lawful authority. Employees refrain from conduct involving dishonesty, fraud, deceit, misrepresentation, or unlawful discrimination.

3 *Conflict of Interest.* Employees shall seek to avoid private interests, obligations, and transactions that are, or appear to be, in conflict of interest with the mission, goals, policies, or regulations of this company. Members shall clearly distinguish between those public and private statements and actions that represent their personal views and those that represent the views of this company. Further, if employees are unable to perform their duties and responsibilities in a fair and just manner because of previous involvement with a party or parties, they shall remove themselves from the decision-making process.

4 *Confidentiality.* Employees ensure that confidentiality is maintained with respect to all privileged communications and confidential corporate information and professional records. Employees inform all parties of the nature and limits of confidentiality.

For existing computer networks, in addition to the corporate statement of conduct, an anonymous user survey can be conducted to gather information on the possible circumvention of security procedures. This survey can result in invaluable information from people who may be circumventing security procedures for productivity reasons without any malicious intent. The circumvented security procedures can then be re-evaluated to determine how the policy can reflect security measures that can practically be implemented. Following is a sample survey questionnaire you can use.

It is important to recognize that the business opportunities are what drive the need for security procedures in the first place. If a corporation does not have many secrets to guard—perhaps because all the information and data available on the network is nonconfidential and freely available—security procedures may be minimal. However, the more likely it is that a security breach will have negative business implications resulting in lost revenues, the more stringent the security policies should be.

Sample Security Survey Questionnaire

The corporate information systems (IS) department is currently conducting a review of current security procedures to identify areas that may need improvement. Please answer the following questions to the best of your knowledge. All information will be kept confidential to the IS task force performing this survey. Please drop completed forms into the box marked "IS Survey" in the building lobby. Thank you for your participation.

1 I use the following systems (circle all that apply):

Windows   UNIX   Macintosh   Other (specify):_____

2 Rate the percentage of time spent accessing the corporate network using the following mechanisms:

Corporate LAN: _____

Corporate Frame Relay (remote branch office): _____

Internet: _____

Modem dial-in: _____

ISDN: _____

Wireless remote access: _____

VPN: _____

3 The applications I use most often are (circle all that apply):

Web browsers   E-mail   Other (specify): _____

4 Rate the existing security measures:

Too restrictive   Just right   Too loose

5 Have you discovered any security problems in the past 12 months? If so, what?

_____

_____

_____

6 Are you aware of any backdoor accesses to the corporate network? If so, what?

_____

_____

_____

7 Any additional comments on security issues:

_____

_____

_____

Name (optional): _____

_____

Risk Management

Risk management is a systematic approach to determine appropriate corporate security measures. How to address security, where to address security, and the type and strength of security controls requires considerable thought.

Before the proliferation of computer networks, confidential data was kept under lock and key, and people were trusted to keep confidential documents in a safe place. In extremely secure environments of the past, such as where classified work for the Department of Defense (DoD) was carried out, your briefcase, purse, and so on were inspected every night on the way out the door. You could not leave the building with *any* magnetic media or classified computer printouts. (The printers attached to secured machines used specially colored paper.)

In today's environments, all those physical security checks are made obsolete by the computer network. Why try to smuggle a magnetic tape out of the building when you can encrypt it and send it out in e-mail? Computer networks have created an environment in which data can be accessed, moved, or destroyed electronically if there are no electronic lock-and-key mechanisms in place to safeguard the corporation's secrets. New avenues of risk are created and must be managed.

Risk Assessment

Risk assessment is a combination of identifying critical assets, placing a value on the asset, and determining the likelihood of security breaches. When the critical resources have been identified and the likelihood and costs associated with the compromise, destruction, or unavailability of these critical resources have been assessed, a decision can be made as to what level of risk is acceptable to the company. The result of the risk assessment is unique to the organization because it depends on the business needs, trustworthiness of its users, and the location of critical assets.

Identify Network Assets

It is impossible to know who might be an organization's potential enemy. A better approach is for the organization to know itself. Companies must understand what they want to protect, what access is needed to those assets, and how these considerations work together. Companies should be more concerned about their assets and their associated value than about an attacker's motivation.

The corporation must identify the things that require protection. Table 6-1 lists some possible network assets to take into consideration.

Table 6-1   *Network Assets*

Asset	Description
Hardware	Workstations, personal computers, printers, routers, switches, modems, terminal servers, firewalls, remote access servers, and application-specific servers
Software	Source programs, object programs, utilities, diagnostic programs, operating systems, and communication programs
Data	Data stored online and archived offline, backups, audit logs, databases, and data in transit over communication media
People	Users, administrators, and hardware maintainers
Documentation	Software programs, internal hardware and software evaluations, systems, and local administrative procedures

The inventory of the corporation's assets should be conducted globally to ensure consistent handling and evaluation of corporate assets.

Value of Assets

Placing values on corporate assets can be a very subjective process. For intangible assets— usually some form of software, data, or documentation—it can be useful to represent the value in terms of importance or criticality. In this way, the relative loss of the asset becomes more important than placing a "correct" value on it. The value of tangible assets can be based on replacement value and, as in the case of intangible assets, the immediate impact of the loss and the consequences of a loss.

The *replacement value* can encompass the monetary cost of purchasing security hardware (such as firewalls and encrypting devices) and software (such as one-time password generators and audit tools) and the cost of retraining security personnel. For data loss, the immediate impact caused by inaccessible or corrupt data may be a missed presentation deadline that consequently results in the account being lost.

Estimating the worth of data can be difficult in some situations—especially when an established research environment has to evolve to meet changing business needs. Business needs may place a higher value on some data because of its potential patent royalty or other monetary gains. Classifying data according to varying levels of criticality can be a preliminary step in establishing its value. A simple rating system of *high*, *medium*, and *low* can be the starting point for evaluating the relative criticality of data. The data can take many forms, including the following:

- **Administrative data**—Correspondence and such information as property records and personnel information that is generally available to the public.

- **Financial data**—Budgeting and expenditure information relating to corporate operations.

- **Client data**—Information relating to the client that is of a personal nature, or information developed as a result of tests, observations, or counseling.

- **Research data**—Information resulting from, or used to support, any corporate research activity.

- **Proprietary data**—Information that cannot be released to the public without the permission of the owner.

Table 6-2 shows an example of how you can classify different types of data and apply a criticality rating.

Table 6-2   *Data Classification*

Type of Data	Classification	Criticality
Clinical trial result	Research	High
Market trends	Research	Low
Pending patents	Proprietary	High
Corporate memos	Administrative	Low
Employee locator file	Administrative	Low
New product features	Proprietary	Medium
Trade secrets	Proprietary	High
Acquisition data	Financial	High
Employee salaries	Financial	Medium

NOTE   Some data is more critical because of its time sensitivity. For example, impending patent data and new product data are highly sensitive either until the patent is applied for or until the product is announced.

When the assets have been identified and valued, it is time to start looking at the likelihood of security breaches.

Threats and Vulnerability

After identifying the network assets, you have to determine the possible threats to the assets and the likelihood that the asset is vulnerable to a given threat. A *threat* can be any person, object, or event that, if realized, can potentially cause damage to the network or networked device. Threats can be malicious (such as the intentional modification of sensitive information) or accidental (such as an error in a calculation or the accidental deletion of a file).

A *vulnerability* is a weakness in a network that can be exploited by a threat. For example, unauthorized access (the threat) to the network can occur by an outsider guessing an obvious password. The vulnerability exploited is the poor password choice made by a user. Reducing or eliminating the vulnerable aspects of the network can reduce or eliminate the risk of threats to the network. For example, a tool that can help users choose robust passwords may reduce the chance that users will select poor passwords and, thus, reduce the threat of unauthorized network access.

The threats, as discussed in Chapter 5, "Threats in an Enterprise Network," are usually in the following forms:

- Eavesdropping and information theft

- Disabling access to network resources (denial-of-service attacks)

- Unauthorized access to resources

- Data manipulation

If these threats are realized and networking devices or data is compromised, what are the immediate impacts and further consequences? Will it result in embarrassment or bankruptcy? The greater the possibility of bankruptcy, the more stringent the security measures should be.

The following sections consider corporate impacts and consequences in the event of data compromise, loss of data integrity, and unavailability of networked resources.

Data Compromise

Any information stored or transferred electronically can potentially be stolen. Data can be stolen if an intruder has unauthorized access to a system or can eavesdrop on confidential data exchanges. Depending on the type of information disclosed, the results can range from inconsequential to catastrophic. In financial institutions, monetary transactions can cause great loss to the institution itself or to customers who may represent loss of revenue if they take their business elsewhere.

You should create a priority list of the information that is most valuable to the corporation. Data pertaining to customer accounts, personnel data, and data related to finances is almost always extremely sensitive and, therefore, valuable. The security policy should reflect where different classes of sensitive data are stored, how the data is stored, and who has access to the different classes of data.

Loss of Data Integrity

Loss of data integrity can be extremely costly to many corporations. Loss of integrity can result in negative press and, therefore, loss of reputation—which translates into loss of customers and revenue. An obvious example is in the financial environment: A bank or other financial institution would have a large probability of bankruptcy if it were to become publicly known that any account data had been compromised. The public would be hard-pressed to place trust in that institution to reliably handle its financial business.

In addition to the losses incurred from a negative reputation, the costs are extremely high to investigate and restore the compromised data. The data has to be restored from a backup, if a backup exists, and an investigation must be performed to determine whether, when, and how the data was compromised. The hours of work required to analyze and restore any compromised data can be quite numerous.

When determining possible security risks, the corporation should take into account all the ways that integrity can be compromised. Data integrity goes right to the heart of your operation:

- How you perform backups
- Where you store the backups
- How you physically secure live data
- Who has physical access to the media that contains your data

Insurance underwriters, for example, confirm that four out of five companies that lose files in a fire go out of business because they cannot recover from the loss. Because so many businesses are now running with all their "actual" data on magnetic media, imagine what someone could do to your business just by noting that you don't make regular backups and that you leave your computers out in the open where he can crash your disks? The security policy should clearly state how to best preserve data integrity for its valuable assets.

Unavailability of Resources

When networked resources become unavailable, the resulting business losses can be catastrophic. In today's environment, in which businesses rely more and more on business transactions over computer networks, if critical systems are inaccessible, losses can be tallied in the millions of dollars.

Businesses must estimate the costs of possible system downtime caused by equipment failure, acts of nature (such as flooding, fire, and lightning), or some denial-of-service (DoS) attack. Network resources can become unavailable because of system upgrades that introduce new software bugs, faulty configurations, or inadequate capacity planning. This area is closely coupled with system reliability and redundancy, which is why a security policy should be established while the network is being designed.

Evaluating Risk

For all possible threats, you must evaluate the risk. Many methodologies are available to measure risk. The common approaches are to define risk in quantitative terms, qualitative terms, or a combination of both. *Quantitative* risk evaluation uses empirical data and known probabilities and statistics. *Qualitative* risk analysis uses an intuitive assessment. Regardless of the mechanism you use, the important aspect is that how you quantify the loss and the likelihood of the loss occurring should be consistent and meaningful to the people who make the decisions about how to guard against the risks.

NOTE   Automatic risk analysis tools are available in many sophisticated spreadsheet software packages. Because of a lack of standards in how to perform risk analysis, however, the manner in which most losses and the likelihood of the losses are quantified and are represented should be clearly understood. If the methodology is fully understood and acceptable, an automatic risk analysis tool may be an adequate solution for evaluating risk.

Figure 6-1 shows a simple example of calculating risk by using the relative likelihood that the threat can occur and the value of the expected incurred loss.

Figure 6-1   *A Simple Risk Calculation*

Likelihood of Threat (T_L)   Expected Incurred Loss (L_E)   Risk= T_L x L_E

1 = Least Likely   1 = Low Loss   1,2 = Low Risk
2 = Probably Likely   2 = Moderate Loss   3,4 = Moderate Risk
3 = Very Likely   3 = Critical Loss   6-9 = High Risk

T_L	L_E	RISK
1	1	1 → Low
1	2	2 → Low
1	3	3 → Moderate
2	1	2 → Low
2	2	4 → Moderate
2	3	6 → High
3	1	3 → Moderate
3	2	6 → High
3	3	9 → High

A more specific example (taken from an existing LAN administration guide used at the National Institutes of Health) is given in Table 6-3. This table tries to determine how critical security considerations are for different LANs using a combination of network importance, the probability of a harmful occurrence, and the probability that a degradation of LAN performance will occur after the harmful occurrence is in effect.

Table 6-3   *Relative Risk Calculation for LANs*

LAN	A[1]	I[1]	C[1]	NI[2]	PO[3]	PD[4]	RR[5]
Admin	2	3	1	6	Very low 0.1	Low 0.3	3.8
Eng	2	3	2	8	Moderate 0.5	Moderate 0.5	2.0
Finance	2	3	3	18	Low 0.3	Low 0.3	8.8

[1] A = Availability, I = Integrity, and C = Confidentiality

[2] NI = Network Importance. NI is the value of A multiplied by the value of I multiplied by the value of C.

[3] PO= Prevent an Occurrence. PO is determined by considering the number of users, previous accreditation, frequency of backups, and compliance with mandatory safeguards requirements.

[4] PD = Prevent Degradation. The capability to PD of A, I, and C for a LAN in the event of a harmful occurrence is determined using the relative need to protect the LAN's availability, integrity, and confidentiality with regard to the sensitivity of data and the criticality of the data-processing capability.

[5] RR = Relative Risk. RR equals NI multiplied by (1–PO) multiplied by (1–PD).

Establishing network importance is significant to managers because doing so facilitates the allocation of resources (to implement additional security services) to protect the assets that are part of the LAN. In terms of potential vulnerability, the more important a network is to a corporation, the greater the percentage of available resources that should be devoted to its protection.

Network importance is a term used to describe the relative importance of a LAN with regard to other corporate LANs. A measure of the RR associated with a harmful occurrence can be expressed as follows:

$$RR = NI \times [(1 - PO) \times (1 - PD)]$$

In this expression, NI is network importance, $(1 - PO)$ is proportional to the probability of a harmful occurrence, and $(1 - PD)$ is proportional to the probability that a degradation in LAN performance will result after an occurrence has been initiated.

The importance of the RR calculation is that it provides management with the information required to rank the risk associated with the various corporate networks relative to one another. This ranking of network importance can facilitate the allocation of resources for the implementation of additional safeguards.

In Table 6-3, the left column identifies the evaluated LANs. The next three columns record the ratings for availability, integrity, and confidentiality. The NI column is completed by multiplying the values in the previous three columns. This number establishes the relative importance of each LAN based on the need to protect the LAN. The numbers recorded under both the PO and PD columns are determined using those qualitative ratings (very low, low, moderate, high, very high) and the following scale:

Very low	0.1
Low	0.3
Moderate	0.5
High	0.7
Very high	0.9

The RR column is calculated using the following equation:

$$RR = NI \times [(1 - PO) \times (1 - PD)]$$

Note that the magnitude of the difference in RR between the various LANs is not important. What is important is the relative value. The number reflected in the right column of Table 6-3 represents relative risk such that the higher the number, the greater the relative risk. Thus, the LAN with the highest number represents the greatest relative risk to the corporation.

For the LANs listed in Table 6-3, the financial LAN has the most risk and the engineering LAN has the least risk. Under normal circumstances, the higher the position of the LAN on the relative scale, the higher its priority should be for allocation of protection resources to implement additional safeguards. In some cases, however, resources are not available to implement all the needed upgrades. So, a balance must be achieved in which the resources available are applied to achieve the greatest risk reduction.

Risk Mitigation and the Cost of Security

After assessing all the risks, the corporation must determine how much risk it is willing to accept and to what degree the assets should be protected. *Risk mitigation* is the process of selecting appropriate controls to reduce risk to an acceptable level. The *level of acceptable risk* is determined by comparing the risk of security hole exposure to the cost of implementing and enforcing the security policy. If some threats are highly unlikely, it may not be worth the cost of creating a tight security policy to protect the assets. A good rule to follow is to assess the cost of certain losses and not to spend more to protect something than it is actually worth.

To develop an acceptable security policy, you must consider a number of costs to ensure that the policy is enforceable. There are performance costs to be considered because both encryption and decryption take time and processing power. An offhand decision to encrypt *all* traffic may result in severely degraded performance everywhere; that policy may have to be re-evaluated. There are also opportunity costs to be considered. What are the lost opportunities if your company moves more slowly than the competition because of hampered communication and the increased overhead that security procedures—not to mention security audits—impose?

The costs of implementing and managing security procedures must be weighed against the cost of potential benefits. It must be understood that security measures do not make it impossible for an unauthorized user to access information and perform unauthorized tasks on a network computer system; security measures can only make it harder for unauthorized access to occur. A very simplistic example is that of packet filters. Even if the corporation simply implemented packet filters to accept outside data traffic from specified networks, the intruder must first find out which IP network addresses were accepted before attempting to gain access to the internal corporate network through those addresses. Perhaps this may not be very difficult, but it can be a deterrent to some random, bored intruders looking for something to do in their spare time.

A more sophisticated example is that of trying to crack encrypted traffic. Even a weak algorithm and a short key can stop some attackers from gaining access to valued information. A stronger algorithm and a longer key takes more sophisticated machines and more time to break. The point is to slow down the attack and increase the cost of the attack until it becomes too expensive to be worthwhile for the intruder.

Need-to-Know Policy

Consider the costs associated with the need-to-know policy that are common in the military and defense industries. In these cases, you are given only the information required to accomplish your job. You don't get to see the "big picture" unless you are a project leader or a higher-level manager in the company working on the project in question.

Highly secret facts, issues, and details are compartmentalized so that the left hand literally doesn't know what the right hand is doing. Although this level of classification and compartmentalization certainly increases security, it also results in some huge cost overruns on projects: Consider the situation in which one engineer finally sees his design mated with the results of another engineer, and they both realize that a little communication 2 years ago would have eliminated some obvious incompatibilities and resulted in a more efficient overall design, but now it is too late to remedy this situation in the final stages of the project. Was security maintained? Yes, but at an enormous cost.

Those who violate security policy in a defense shop face *serious* consequences—starting with being fired and possibly ending with criminal prosecution and incarceration.

Consider a private company in a highly competitive market that pursues the same level of compartmentalization and need-to-know policy as the DoD. The results are also most likely unfavorable: late products that don't take into account a change in market requirements and a great deal of wasted effort and duplication. The costs for a need-to-know policy in a corporate environment are largely negative; in this case, the policy itself is extremely hard to enforce largely because people violate the policy for all the right reasons at the wrong times.

Consider an example of a salesperson and an engineer who have become friends. The engineer tells the salesperson the results of a highly secret project. Now we all know that people in sales will go to great lengths to close a sale. Ten minutes into a highly competitive sale, out of the salesperson's mouth comes the statement, "Why yes, I have it on good authority that we will be coming out with a product to do XYZ later this year." Your competitor, who might be able to deliver the same product in half the time, now has from the prospective sales account the information they need to effectively compete against you in other accounts.

Is your company going to fire the salesperson? Most likely not: He closed the sale and booked millions in business. Is your company going to fire the engineer? Probably not, because he didn't violate security, and he didn't reveal proprietary information to anyone outside the company. Yet the company just lost a big competitive advantage in the marketplace: *market timing*.

It is hard to enforce a need-to-know policy, but there are instances where specific information does need to be closely guarded. For example, acquisition or potential partnership discussions represent areas where information dissemination is usually on a need-to-know basis. Also, vulnerability disclosures should be need-to-know policy and are discussed in more detail in Chapter 8, "Incident Handling."

Need-to-know policies in corporate environments are very difficult and should be selective to make sure that it is an appropriate policy in a specific instance.

A Security Policy Framework

Now that you have learned to deal with risk management, it is time to start looking at additional issues that relate to creating the security policy for an enterprise network infrastructure. Special areas of more stringent security needs are places most vulnerable to attacks, such as network interconnections, remote dialup access points, remote wireless access points, and critical network infrastructure devices and servers.

It is helpful to divide the corporate network into separate components that can be addressed separately. You also need a framework for the security policy that addresses all the elements of a security architecture. The framework must be adhered to by all areas of the corporation to ensure a consistent security approach throughout the enterprise environment.

Components of an Enterprise Network

Traditionally, in the days when network environments consisted primarily of a centralized point-to-point architecture with predetermined information paths, security was fairly straightforward. Securing the link itself provided reasonable assurance of maintaining the integrity, access, and privacy of the information.

Modern enterprise internetworks provide a tremendous opportunity for corporations to remain competitive while increasing overall efficiency. This opportunity comes with a cost. Today's open networking technologies pose a threat to the overall security of the enterprise. This openness can mean that a corporation has little control over who accesses its information resources and the path over which that information flows. Traditional security systems based on point-to-point, nonpacketized transmission media simply were not designed to address the evolving WAN and LAN technologies at the heart of today's enterprise network in which data travels across public networks.

When creating a security policy, you must balance easy accessibility of information with adequate mechanisms of identifying authorized users, ensuring data integrity, and confidentiality. A security policy must be enforceable, both technically and organizationally. It is usually easiest to break an enterprise network into three distinct components, as shown in Figure 6-2:

- The main campus infrastructure
- Remote access connectivity (this includes dial-in, wireless, and virtual private networking)
- Internet connectivity

Figure 6-2   *The Components of an Enterprise Network*

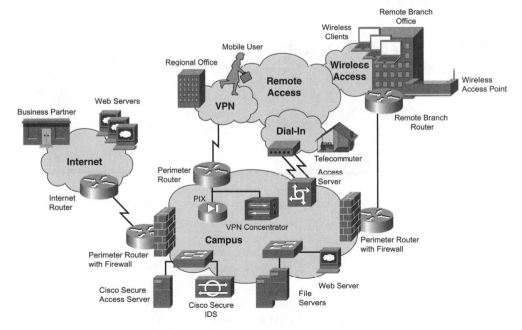

The *main campus infrastructure* typically is located within a constrained geographic area and is the core of the enterprise network. Remote access is a broad concept that comprises of all the methods that may be used to connect remote branches, telecommuters, and mobile dialup users to the corporate infrastructure. Therefore, remote access consists of Public Switched Telephone Network (PSTN) or Integrated Services Digital Network (ISDN) services, wireless LANs, or virtual private networks (VPNs). The *Internet access* connects the main campus through a local Internet service provider (ISP) to the Internet.

NOTE   The astute reader may be wondering how remote access and Internet access actually differ. Remote access typically deals with providing inbound connectivity to the corporate network resources, whereas Internet connectivity deals with providing outbound connectivity to resources outside the corporate network. Both can be referred to as the *network edge*.

Each of these three components may have different security needs. It is important to have a global corporate security framework in place that addresses all the elements of a security architecture so that individual policies can be consistent with the overall site security architecture. For example, having a strong policy with regard to Internet access and having weak restrictions on modem usage is inconsistent with an overall philosophy of strong security restrictions on external access.

Elements of a Security Architecture

The global framework must include the following elements of a security architecture:

- Identity
- Integrity
- Confidentiality
- Availability
- Audit

Each of these elements must be taken into consideration when determining the corporate policy.

Identity

In this book, *identity* is defined as the element of the security architecture that encompasses both authentication and authorization. *Authentication* answers the question, "Who are you and where are you?" *Authorization* answers the question, "What are you allowed to access?" Identity mechanisms must be carefully deployed because even the most careful of security policies can be circumvented if the implementations are hard to use. A classic example is that of passwords or *personal identification code* (PIN) numbers scribbled on a sticky pad and attached to the computer monitor or telephone—a real solution for the user who has to remember a multitude of passwords.

Another example of poorly implemented security is when employees use an easily guessed password so that they don't have to write it down. An ad hoc study at Bell Labs some years ago found that a surprisingly high percentage of the people logging on to systems chose a password that was a child's name, dog's name, wife's name, and so on. Corporations can install systems that ensure that the passwords selected by its employees are not proper names, words found in the dictionary, or other logical sequences of characters. However, verification and authorization systems that are cumbersome or unnecessarily redundant can frustrate users and should be avoided.

Companies must create appropriate barriers inside their systems so that if intruders do access one part of the corporate environment, they do not automatically have access to the rest of it. Just as the creation of security barriers applies to physical buildings (access to the building itself does not let you access every room in the building), it should also apply to network access. That is, the computer network infrastructure should be partitioned to provide as much protection as necessary for specific components of the network. Although maintaining a high level of security on the entire corporate environment is difficult, it is often possible to do so for a smaller sensitive component.

Integrity

In this book, *integrity* is the element of the security architecture that encompasses network infrastructure device security (physical and logical access) to protect against undesirable changes in the network infrastructure and perimeter security to ensure that any traffic traversing the network is valid.

Physical access to a computer (or router or switch or firewall) usually gives a sufficiently sophisticated user total control over that device. Physical access to a network link usually allows a person to tap into that link, jam it, or inject traffic into it. Software security measures can often be circumvented when physical access to the hardware is not controlled. Therefore, for corporate facilities, physical security should be based on security guards, closed-circuit television, and card-key entry systems. With these measures in place, organizations can feel confident that within their physical facilities, assets are protected and high user productivity is maintained.

Logical access security refers to providing identity mechanisms (authentication and authorization) that must be satisfied before the user is allowed access to integral network infrastructure components (such as routers and firewalls). The logical access can be obtained in any number of ways, including access via console ports, virtual terminal ports (Telnet or Secure Shell [SSH]), auxiliary ports, Simple Network Management Protocol (SNMP), or web-based access. *Perimeter security* deals with firewall-type functionality, determining which traffic is permitted or denied from various areas of the network. Often, firewalls are placed between the Internet and the main campus or between the dialup connection and the main campus.

Confidentiality

Confidentiality is the element of the security architecture that ensures that data communication is kept private between the sender and receiver of information. A strong policy statement should dictate to users the types of information deemed sensitive enough to warrant encryption. A program-level policy may dictate the broad categories of information that must be stringently protected, whereas a system-level policy may detail the specific types of information and the specific environments that warrant encryption protection.

At whatever level the policy is dictated, the decision to use encryption should be made by the authority within the organization charged with ensuring protection of sensitive information. If a strong policy that defines what information to encrypt does not exist, the owner of the data should ultimately make the decision about whether to encrypt information.

Availability

Availability is the process of ensuring that all critical resources are accessible when needed. Keeping data available means that you must have planned system upgrades and configuration changes that are fully tested to avoid catastrophic surprises caused by software bugs or misconfigurations.

Physical security and logical security are also part of ensuring availability. *Physical security* ensures that no malicious tampering can take place and that acts of nature will not cause systems to be inaccessible. It also ensures that hardware failures are handled in a timely manner. *Logical security* ensures that traffic can be rerouted and that malicious software threats can be deterred.

Audit

The *audit* element of the security architecture is necessary to verify and monitor the corporate security policy. A software audit verifies the correct implementation of the security policy in the corporate network infrastructure. Subsequent logging and monitoring of events can help detect any unusual behavior and possible intrusions.

To test the effectiveness of the security infrastructure, security auditing should occur frequently and at regular intervals. Auditing should include new system installation checks, methods to discover possible malicious insider activity, possible presence of a specific class of problems (DoS attacks), and overall compliance with the site security policy.

An audit log, generated by all the various operating systems running in your infrastructure, can be used to determine the extent of the damage from a successful attack. Audit trails are most often put to use after the fact to reconstruct what happened during damage assessment. The problem to avoid is logging *every* event such that the amount of data to sift through becomes insurmountable. If you log too much data and an intrusion does occur, that intrusion will definitely be logged—along with hundreds of other insignificant events. The intrusion will most likely remain undetected by the people responsible for detecting such things because the intrusion is hidden under a mountain of other data being generated by the system.

NOTE	If your network or system is designed and implemented well, think about logging the kinds of activity that would most likely indicate a first-stage attack. Don't log every event—just the unusual ones. This information can give you a warning that something is amiss without burying you in too much inconsequential detail. When creating data log files, consider the following points: • Use a program to filter through the audit data and bring to your attention the truly serious issues. • Do not audit every little issue in your network or system.

Understanding how a system normally functions, knowing what is expected and unexpected behavior, and being familiar with how devices are usually used can help the organization detect security problems. Noticing unusual events can help catch intruders before they can damage the system. Software auditing tools can help companies detect, log, and track those unusual events. In addition, sophisticated intrusion detection systems (IDSs) may be deployed.

Additional Considerations

The security policy should address personnel security considerations as well. Personnel security issues include processes and procedures for establishing identity confirmation, privilege rights required to access certain information, accountability for the proper use and security of the systems being accessed, and proper training to make sure that employees understand and fulfill their security responsibilities.

The most serious breaches of corporate security come from the inside (for example, a disgruntled employee). Internal security breaches can take the form of intellectual property being leaked or disseminated to competitors, employees quitting and going to competitors with proprietary material, or a consultant simply selling off your company's materials for fiscal gain. A serious example of the last scenario happened in the mid-1980s. A consultant sold off proprietary details of IBM's then latest storage management system to Fujitsu. IBM sued Fujitsu and won a considerable sum of money as a result. Yet the amount IBM won in the settlement could not come close to the estimated $1 billion in lost revenue as a result of Fujitsu stealing IBM's technology.

Disgruntled employee problems are the hardest for corporate management to handle in this litigious age because there are so many lawyers who will take the flimsiest of employee termination cases on contingency in hopes of obtaining a tidy out-of-court settlement from the company. Companies know that it costs more to fight the suit in court than to pay the malcontent $25K to get rid of him, so the majority of companies will pay some sum of money to get rid of a problem employee who makes a legal threat. Sadly, the disgruntled employee is now loose on the job market again—without the public record of a court case for future employers to find in any background check.

Are background checks even performed? Not every company does them. This brings us to the topic of personnel security audits, a controversial topic because it can infringe on a person's right to privacy. Procedures for background checks should be included in the security policy—the level of screening required may vary from minimal to full background checks, depending on the sensitivity of the information the individual will handle or the risk and magnitude of loss that can be caused by the individual. Beyond that, any subsequent personal auditing is a sensitive area.

In some industry sectors, such as the financial and legal sectors, it is widely accepted that phone conversations are recorded to deter insider trading or client confidentiality infringements. Employees sign a waiver accepting this policy. A corporation should get legal advice about the latest rulings for personal privacy legislation, because it relates to the workplace, before putting any auditing mechanisms in place.

Another significant issue that needs to be addressed in a corporate security policy definition is the internal misuse of corporate resources. File sharing in particular is a large target because of its potential financial and legal risk to the corporation employing users of such software. Obtaining and sharing pirated or copyright-violated materials is expressly forbidden in many corporate statements of conduct. In many instances, the security architecture is increasingly being used to track these types of corporate misuse.

Companies must be firmer in handling insider security breaches and take corrective action on what is uncovered in a policy or personnel audit. The security policy must be reflected in corporate human resources policies. It is not enough to say, "Our proprietary information is ours, and you can't go around disclosing it." The company must give explicit examples with explicit consequences, putting a clause in an employment agreement that reads, "Give away even one corporate secret to an outsider, and you will be summarily fired." By doing this, a problem employee can be dealt with more quickly, with more confidence that most lawyers won't accept the case. Establish a clear standard of behavior as well as penalties for violations of that standard and make them part of the employee handbook. If employees then violate the standard, they can't claim that they didn't know about the standard or the penalties.

Summary

This chapter detailed the process of defining a corporate security policy. The first step is identifying the global corporate security considerations. Second, critical resources need to be identified and the likelihood and costs associated with the compromise, destruction, or unavailability of these critical resources have to be assessed. Third, a decision can be made as to what level of risk is acceptable to the company. After the acceptable risk has been determined for given vulnerabilities, a security policy specific to the corporation can be defined that includes the security services of identity, integrity, confidentiality, availability, and auditing.

Review Questions

The following questions provide you with an opportunity to test your knowledge of the topics covered in this chapter. You can find the answers to these questions in Appendix E, "Answers to Review Questions."

1 What are three characteristics of a good security policy?

2 What is the purpose of an anonymous user survey?

3 Which of the following form part of a risk assessment?

   A   Critical asset identification

   B   Asset valuation

   C   Asset vulnerability assessment

   D   All of the above

4 What are the two ways of evaluating risk?

5 What are the five elements of a security architecture?

6 Can a weak algorithm and short key stop attackers from gaining access to valued information?

7 Why must identity mechanisms be carefully deployed?

8 Define confidentiality.

9 When logging networking events, should you log everything?

## CHAPTER 7

Design and Implementation of the Corporate Security Policy

The design and implementation of a corporate security policy is site specific. After you have identified the critical assets and analyzed the risks, it is time to design the policy by defining the guidelines and procedures to be followed by corporate personnel.

To be effective, the procedures should be concise and to the point. Don't write a large cumbersome document few people will actually read. A short document of fewer than 10 pages should suffice as a start. Technical implementation details should not be included because they can change over time. If a corporate network infrastructure is already in place, you might have to modify the existing *ad-hoc* security procedures to align more closely with the newly created policy. The design of the policy takes careful planning to ensure that all security-related issues are adequately addressed.

This chapter discusses the following areas that you must consider before you can design a security policy for the corporate networking environment:

- Defining the physical security controls
- Defining the logical security controls
- Ensuring system and data integrity
- Ensuring data confidentiality
- Defining mechanisms to verify and monitor security controls
- Developing policies and procedures for the staff that is responsible for the corporate network
- Developing appropriate security awareness training for users of the corporate network

Some implementation details are given as examples of how to carry out part of the policy. Most of the implementation details are found in Chapter 9, "Securing the Corporate Network Infrastructure," Chapter 10, "Securing Internet Access," and Chapter 11, "Securing Remote Dial-in Access," which detail specific features and considerations.

NOTE   Incidence response handling is also part of the planning and implementation phase, but, because of its importance and breadth, it is detailed separately in Chapter 8, "Incident Handling."

Physical Security Controls

Physical security controls are those controls pertaining to the physical infrastructure, physical device security, and physical access. Do you expect intruders to tap into your infrastructure to eavesdrop on transmitting data? How easy or difficult is it for intruders to gain physical access to the important network infrastructure devices? If the corporate network has not yet been created at an existing site, you should consider the physical security controls available in its planning phase.

For existing networks, if a security policy is being created or modified to accommodate changing environments, it might be necessary to change the physical infrastructure or the locations of some critical pieces of equipment to ensure an easier security policy implementation. After you have incorporated the physical security controls into the policy, as the corporation grows and new sites are added, you should consider the network physical security controls as the site is constructed.

Physical Network Infrastructure

The physical network infrastructure encompasses both the selection of the appropriate media type and the path of the physical cabling (the network topography). You want to ensure that no intruder is able to eavesdrop on the data traversing the network and that all critical systems have a high degree of availability. For wireless networks, it is clear that eavesdropping must always be a consideration because anyone with a wireless networking card has potential access to any existing wireless network. Wireless networks require specific security considerations, which are described in subsequent appropriate sections.

Physical Media Selection

From a security point of view, the type of cable chosen for various parts of the network can depend on the sensitivity of the information traveling over that cable. The three most common cable types used in networking infrastructures are twisted pair, coax, and optical fiber. Optical fiber is most often used in high-bandwidth and long-haul environments. Unlike either twisted pair or coax, optical fiber does not radiate any energy and, therefore, provides a very high degree of security against eavesdropping. Optical fiber is also much more difficult to tap into than either twisted pair or coax cable.

Wiretaps can sometimes be detected by using tools to measure physical attenuation of cable. Typically, a time domain reflectometer (TDR) tool is used to check coax cable, and an optical time domain reflectometer (OTDR) tool is used for optical fiber cable. These devices are used mainly to measure signal attenuation and the length of an installed cable base; sometimes, however, they can also detect illegal wiretaps.

Let's take a look at how you can detect taps in fiber-optic cable using an OTDR. One of the things an eavesdropper needs when tapping into an optical cable is an *optical splitter*. The insertion of an optical splitter into an optical cable allows the tap to be made, but it also affects the signal level in the media. This level can be measured. If a benchmark optical signal level is observed at several points along the topology of an optical media network, any conventional optical tap inserted into the network should be observable. Figure 7-1 shows an initial OTDR fiber-optic cable trace between two buildings.

Figure 7-1   *A Baseline OTDR Measurement*

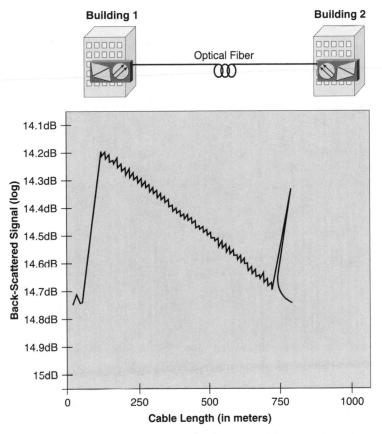

Figure 7-2 shows the fiber-optic trace taken after an optical splitter was inserted into the length of the fiber cable.

Figure 7-2 *The OTDR Measurement After the Fiber-Optic Splitter is Inserted*

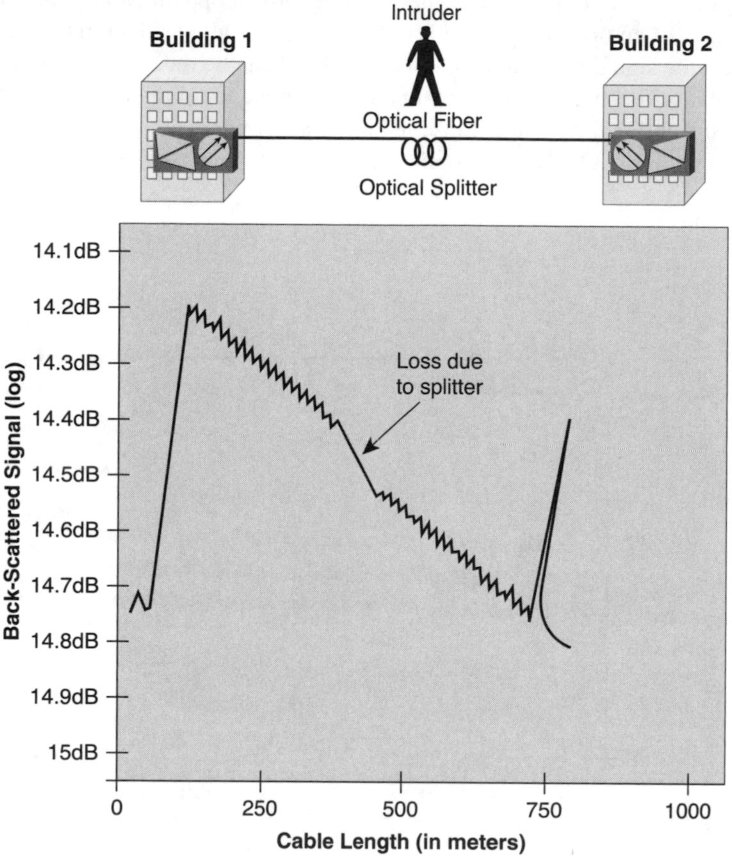

Although these types of traces can be an indication that an illegal tap might be in place, they are most useful in detecting cable degradation problems.

NOTE An expert can insert a tap in a way that isn't easily detectable by a TDR or OTDR. However, it is good practice to initially take a baseline signal level of the physical cable infrastructure and periodically verify the integrity of the physical cable plant. Even if it doesn't detect unauthorized media taps, the measurement will provide you with some confidence in the integrity of the cable infrastructure.

When choosing the transmission media to install for various segments of the network infra-structure, it is important to ensure that eavesdropping on the physical wire is proportionally more difficult as the data on that wire becomes more sensitive. In addition, if it is important that the transmission media be secure, the entire data path must be secure. (See Figure 7-3.)

Figure 7-3   *An Example of Consistent Transmission Media Use*

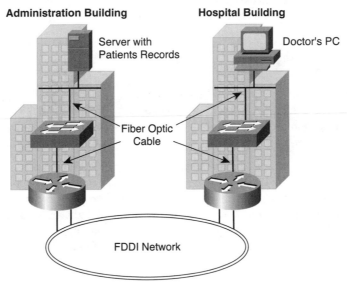

Administration Building   **Hospital Building**

Server with Patients Records   Doctor's PC

Fiber Optic Cable

FDDI Network

Figure 7-3 shows a large medical facility with two buildings connected by an FDDI ring. Because the server holding the patient records is located in the administrative building, and the doctor retrieving the information is located in the hospital building, both the backbone segment and the LAN segments of the network use optical fiber. It is very difficult for someone to gain access to patient information by tapping into optical fiber.

NOTE   Although it is useful to keep the possibility of tapping in mind, in today's typical corporate network, there is very little need to use an "unauthorized" tap. Why bother with all the cloak-and-dagger stuff when there are all these PCs and workstations already attached to the network? All the thief has to do is run a program on any authorized workstation/PC to put its network controller into promiscuous mode; then the thief can "sniff" the network at his or her lcisure.

Several shareware programs can do this now; they are available for Windows, Linux, Solaris, and others. There is no need for a thief to set up an actual sniffer on the network anymore. Because there is no way to prevent anyone from running such a program on a Macintosh or a PC running Windows 98/2000/XP, there isn't much point in actually worrying about restricting the ability to sniff. Even a policy stating that anyone caught sniffing the corporate network will be fired probably won't be very helpful because this is very hard to detect, although having the policy is still a good idea because it reinforces to the users that this is unacceptable behavior.

The issue therefore is reversed: The question you ask now is, "How do we prevent people who *are* sniffing the network from reading the contents of the packets they've sniffed?" The answer is obviously some form of encryption.

Network Topography

The physical path of the media, also known as the *network topography*, is a concern for the availability of the network and its attached devices. It touches on the reliability and security of the infrastructure. It is important to have a structured cabling system that minimizes the risk of downtime.

Imagine a large campus environment with multiple buildings. If the topography of the backbone network infrastructure is not a true starred network with common conduits at the base of the star, a construction worker with a backhoe could bring down large portions of the network. (See Figure 7-4.) If alternative physical paths are made available (that is, if you create a true starred network), however, only small portions of the network might become inaccessible if the physical cable fails. (See Figure 7-5.)

Figure 7-4   *A Sample Physical Topography*

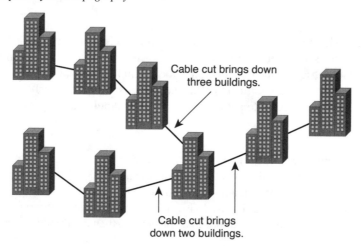

Figure 7-5    *A True Starred Physical Topography*

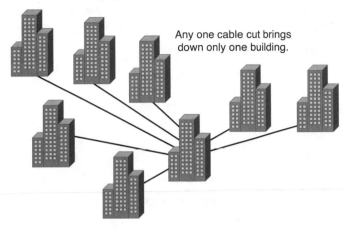

Any one cable cut brings
down only one building.

The cable infrastructure should also be well secured to prevent access to any part of it. If cables installed between buildings are buried underground, they must be buried a minimum of 40 inches, although local regulations might dictate other guidelines. Sometimes, cables can be encased in concrete to provide maximum protection. The International Telecommunication Union has a number of recommendations (the Series L Recommendations) that cover the construction, installation, and protection of cable plants. You can access these guidelines at http://online.vsi.ru/library/ITU-T/.

Physical Device Security

Physical device security is sometimes understated. Intruders with enough incentive will think of anything to get at what they want. Physical device security includes identifying the location of the devices, limiting physical access, and having appropriate environmental safeguards in place.

Physical Location

The location of critical network resources is extremely important. All network infrastructure equipment should be physically located in restricted-access areas to eliminate the possibility of unauthorized access by physical proximity. Facility issues can be a horrific nightmare, but when it comes to creating space for wiring closets that house critical infrastructure equipment, such as switches, firewalls, modems, and routers, it is imperative that you fight for whatever autonomous space there is. Don't overlook any aspect of the physical facility. Having a secure lock on a wiring closet does not provide much protection if you can go through the ceiling panels to get into the room.

The infrastructure equipment includes more than just the networks and the routers, firewalls, switches, and network access servers that interconnect the networks. Infrastructure equipment also includes the servers that provide the various network services:

- Network management (SNMP)
- Domain Name Service (DNS)
- Network Time (NTP)
- Network File System (NFS)
- Hypertext Transfer Protocol (HTTP)
- User authentication and authorization (TACACS+, RADIUS, Kerberos)
- Network audit and intrusion detection
- Multimedia conferencing server (NetMeeting)
- Voice over IP gateway

Most of these servers can be segmented into a common area to provide easier access control measures. However, you must also be sure that adequate redundancy needs are met to ensure the availability of these critical services, especially when a single LAN may get segmented from the rest of the network.

NOTE   Whenever possible, incorporate security controls for cases in which physical access might be compromised. Protect console access using authentication mechanisms, for example, and use screen savers with authentication mechanisms for critical servers.

Here is another area of concern that is sometimes overlooked. When printing confidential configuration files or faxing configurations, there is the possibility that the printouts from printers or fax machines might fall into the wrong hands. You might want to make it a requirement to put all sensitive printers and fax machines on a LAN segment that is physically located in a room with controlled access. Also, you must have a way to dispose of the printouts and documents securely. Shredding is not out of the question.

Physical Access

Who has access to the wiring closets and restricted locations? The physical access requirements of controlled areas are determined largely by the results of the risk analysis or a physical security survey. It is good practice to restrict physical access to wiring closets and locations of critical network infrastructure equipment. Access to these areas should not be permitted unless the person is specifically authorized or requires access to perform his or her job.

Wireless access servers require special consideration because the nature of the technology requires that they be deployed in open spaces. A possible solution could be to put wireless access servers under video surveillance to deter physical tampering.

Not all physical security tampering is malicious, but it can have the same effect of causing network resources to be unavailable. The following incident is a true story and although it might represent a rare occurrence, it is nevertheless something to keep in mind. After countless hours of troubleshooting an unavailable network connection, analyzing all potential switch and routing problems, the equipment closet was inspected. It turned out that the cable connecting the LAN to the router had been disconnected. A maintenance worker had been working in another part of the closet, found the wire to be in the way, and disconnected it. When his work was finished, he forgot to reconnect it. Needless to say, this incident caused any subsequent maintenance work to be more closely supervised.

Part of the physical security policy should be to have contract maintenance personnel or others who are not authorized with unrestricted access, but who are required to be in the controlled area, to be escorted by an authorized person or to sign in before accessing the controlled area.

To ensure an enforceable physical security policy, it is essential to ensure that people's work areas mesh well with access restrictions. If these conditions are not met, well-meaning employees will find ways to circumvent your physical security. (For example, they will jam doors open rather than lock and unlock them 15 times per hour.)

If your facility is providing temporary network access for visitors to connect back to their home networks (for example, to read e-mail), plan the service carefully. Define precisely where you will provide it so that you can ensure the necessary physical access security. A typical example is at large industry meetings; if these meetings are hosted at a corporate facility, the host corporation usually has a separate network solely for guest privileges. This network should reside in a single area and access should be given only to conference attendees.

Environmental Safeguards

Adequate environmental safeguards must be installed and implemented to protect critical networked resources. The sensitivity or criticality of the system determines whether security is "adequate." The more critical a system, the more safeguards must be put in place to ensure that the resource is available at all costs. At a minimum, consider the following environmental safeguards:

- Fire prevention, detection, suppression, and protection
- Water hazard prevention, detection, and correction

- Electric power-supply protection
- Temperature control
- Humidity control
- Natural disaster protection from earthquakes, lightning, windstorms, and so on
- Protection from excessive magnetic fields
- Good housekeeping procedures for protection against dust and dirt

The last item might seem a little extreme, but anyone who has worked with fiber-optic equipment knows that is has been prone to network degradation and downtime caused by dust particles and will recognize the usefulness of this seemingly inane point.

Sample Physical Security Control Policy

The following is a sample physical security control policy.

Construction and Location of Premises:

- All university buildings must have network closets built in accordance with relevant fire and safety standards.
- All network closets must be protected from potential sources of man-made or natural hazards, such as floods, earthquakes, and lightning.

Maintenance of Equipment:

- All network infrastructure equipment must be connected to backup power supplies.
- All network infrastructure equipment must be in locked cabinets with keys that only maintenance staff can access.

Physical Access:

- Access to network closets and equipment racks is authorized only for people in the network infrastructure operations group.
- Other personnel may access network closets only in the company of a member of the network infrastructure operations group.
- Surveillance cameras must be installed in all network closets.
- In the event of personnel changes, the locks to the network closets must be changed.

Logical Security Controls

Logical security controls create boundaries between network segments. As such, they control the flow of traffic between different cable segments. When traffic is logically filtered between networks, logical access controls provide security.

The example in Figure 7-6 shows three university buildings each connected by a router. The administration building has a LAN that allows only specific IP addresses from the engineering building (144.254.3.3 and 144.254.3.4) and the liberal arts building (144.254.7.3 and 144.254.7.4) to access the LAN. These addresses are permitted access because they are known to belong to hosts in the faculty room, to which only faculty members have access.

Figure 7-6   *Security Through Logical Access Controls*

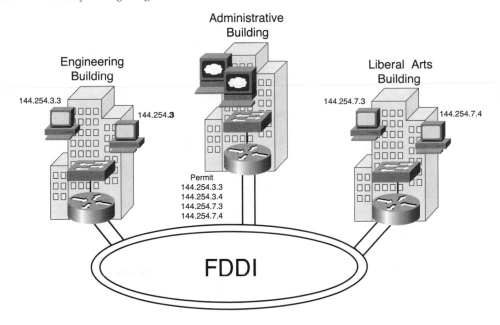

NOTE   Although traffic filtering provides some measure of security, it is easy to spoof IP addresses. Filtering should be used in conjunction with other security measures.

Because logical boundaries are not as secure as physical boundaries, you must fully understand the path the data is taking from one point to another. Although logical boundaries usually exist between separate subnets, routing policies and virtual local-area networks (VLANs) can obfuscate the logical traffic flow.

TIP   The only way to detect unauthorized traffic on the network is through the use of a packet analyzer or an intrusion detection system. It is prudent to place intrusion detection systems at critical network access points.

Subnet Boundaries

A characterization is sometimes made that traffic on different subnets is secure because the traffic is constrained to a single subnet domain. The thinking is that there is a logical separation between different groups of addresses that make up the different network access domains. You can provide filters to permit or deny traffic based on subnet addresses. As pointed out in the preceding section, however, IP addresses are easy to spoof; other security measures should always be used in conjunction with filtering mechanisms. (Readers not familiar with IP addressing and subnetting can refer to the following sidebar.)

IP Addressing

An *IP address* is a 32-bit binary number written in a series of 4 decimal digits (octets), known as dotted decimal, of the form X.Y.Z.K (for example, 66.128.252.6). Each of the 4 period-delimited octets can have the range of 0 thru 255. The following chart lists how the IP address space is divided by function.

Address Range	Functionality
1.0.0.0–223.255.255.255	IP unicast address
244.0.0.0–239.255.255.255	IP multicast address
240.0.0.0–255.255.255.254	Reserved for future use
0.0.0.0	An unknown IP address
255.255.255.255	Local segment broadcast

The IP unicast addresses are divided into three classes.

Class	Address Range	Number of Networks	Approximate Number of Hosts per Single Network
A	1.0.0.0–126.255.255.255	127	16 million
B	128.0.0.0–191.255.255.255	64	65,000
C	192.0.0.0–223.255.255.255	32	254

Class A is used for large networks and the first octet values range from 1 to 126. These networks have an 8-bit network prefix and are commonly referred to as /8s (pronounced slash eights).

Class B is mainly used for medium-sized networks and the first octet values range from 128 to 191. These network addresses have a 16-bit network prefix and are commonly referred to as /16s.

Class C is reserved for smaller networks and can be identified by their first octet, which ranges from 192 to 223. Class C networks have a 24-bit network prefix and are commonly referred to as /24s.

The 32-bit IP address contains a network portion (the network prefix) and a host portion, as shown in Figure 7-7.

Figure 7-7   *A Bitmap of Class A, Class B, and Class C Addresses*

n = Network Portion
h = Host Portion

A *network mask* is used to separate the network information from the host information. The mask is represented in binary notation as a series of contiguous 1s followed by a series of contiguous 0s. The network mask of the Class A, Class B, and Class C networks in their binary and dotted-decimal format is shown in Figure 7-8.

Figure 7-8   *An Example of Natural Network Masks*

	IP Address	**Network Mask**
Class A		
Decimal Notion	11.0.0.0	255.0.0.0
Binary Notion	00001011 00000000 00000000 00000000	11111111 00000000 00000000 00000000
Class B		
Decimal Notion	128.1.0.0	255.255.0.0.
Binary Notion	10000000 00000001 00000000 00000000	11111111 11111111 00000000 00000000
Class C		
Decimal Notion	192.1.0.0	255.255.255.0
Binary Notion	11000000 00000001 00000000 00000000	11111111 11111111 11111111 00000000

A *subnet* is a subset of the Class A, Class B, or Class C network. Subnets are created by further extending the network portion of the address into the host portion. The use of subnets increases the number of subnetworks and reduces the number of hosts on each subnetwork. The following chart shows an example of a Class C network 192.150.42.0 and the possible ways you can create subnetworks with contiguous subnet masks.

Bits in Subnet Mask	Dotted-Decimal Format	Number of Networks	Number of Hosts in Each Network
0	255.255.255.0	1	254
1	255.255.255.128	2	126
2	255.255.255.192	4	62
3	255.255.255.224	8	30
4	255.255.255.240	16	14
5	255.255.255.248	32	6
6	255.255.255.252	64	2

Consider the specific example of a 3-bit subnet mask used on the 192.150.42.0 network. This network yields 8 separate subnetworks with 30 hosts on each network, as listed here.

Subnet	Network Address	Broadcast Address	Host Address Range
0	192.150.42.0	192.150.42.31	192.150.42.1–192.150.42.30
1	192.150.42.32	192.150.42.63	192.150.42.33–192.150.42.62
2	192.150.42.64	192.150.42.95	192.150.42.65–192.150.42.94
3	192.150.42.96	192.150.42.127	192.150.42.97–192.150.42.126
4	192.150.42.128	192.150.42.159	192.150.42.129–192.150.42.158
5	192.150.42.160	192.150.42.191	192.150.42.161–192.150.42.190
6	192.150.42.192	192.150.42.223	192.150.42.193–192.150.42.222
7	192.150.42.224	192.150.42.255	192.150.42.225–192.150.42.254

Subnetting gives the network administrator several benefits: It provides extra flexibility, makes more efficient use of network address utilization, and contains broadcast traffic because a broadcast does not cross a router.

Because subnets are under local administration, the outside world sees an organization as a single network and has no detailed knowledge of the organization's internal structure. However, internally, each subnet constitutes a separate LAN, possibly on a separate physical cable segment. (See Figure 7-9.)

Figure 7-9   *An Example of Subnet Boundaries*

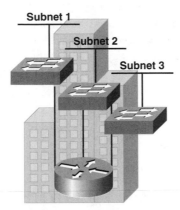

Corporate Building

The logical infrastructure of any network depends largely on how networks are logically separated into groups using subnets and how traffic is controlled between these subnets. Routing (also known as *Layer 3 switching*) is how traffic is controlled between subnets. Where routing information is distributed and accepted plays a large role in how you gain access to data on various networks. VLANs can also modify traditional subnet physical boundaries.

Routing Boundaries

Routing involves two basic activities:

- Determining optimal routing paths
- Transporting *packets* through an internetwork

The latter activity is typically referred to as *Layer 3 switching*. Switching is relatively straightforward: It involves looking up the destination address in a table that specifies where to send the packet. The table is created as a result of determining the optimal path to a given destination. If the table entry for a given destination is not there, the optimal path must be computed. The computation of the optimal path depends on the routing protocol used and can be a very complex process.

NOTE   Routing fundamentals are beyond the scope of this book. Read *Internet Routing Architectures*, Second Edition (Cisco Press, 2000) for a more detailed discussion on routing.

A security policy can incorporate detailed routing policies, where routes for separate networks and subnets are announced and accepted on an as-needed basis. Most routers, regardless of the routing protocol used, have features that suppress the announcement of specified routes and can ignore certain received routes and not incorporate them into their tables. Usually, there are many ways to accomplish the same goal. It is best to first design the logical boundaries, decide how open or closed an environment you want, and then implement the policy accordingly.

Filtering routes is one way of exerting some control over who can source traffic and to what destination. Filtering does not protect you from spoofing attacks, but it can make spoofing attacks harder to carry out.

Figure 7-10 shows a common scenario of creating logical routing boundaries.

Figure 7-10 *An Example of Logical Routing Boundaries*

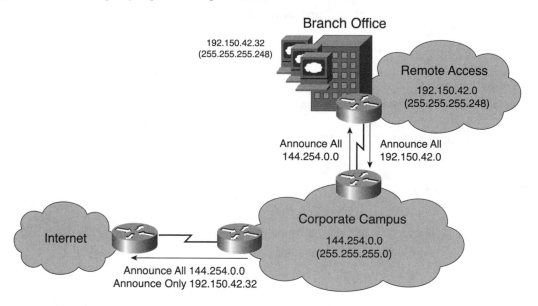

In this scenario, the corporate network is divided into three distinct components:

- Corporate campus network
- Internet access
- Remote access

The campus network has a Class B address of 144.254.0.0, which is subnetted into 256 distinct networks using an 8-bit subnet mask of 255.255.255.0. The Internet access is provided by an unnumbered interface. An unnumbered interface refers to a point-to-point connection that is configured without using an IP address. The remote access for a branch office is provided by a subnetted Class C address of 192.150.42.0 with a 5-bit subnet mask of 255.255.255.248. This branch office is mainly used for taking orders via the web and carrying out the corporation's financial transactions. The web servers used to collect the order information are all located on the 192.150.42.32 network. The corporation's routing policy allows free access to all corporate campus servers but allows only the branch office web server network, 192.150.42.32, to access the Internet through the campus network. The policy can be implemented as follows:

- Allow all 144.254.0.0 routes to be announced everywhere.
- Announce all 192.150.42.0 networks to the main campus.
- Announce the 192.150.42.32 network to the Internet.
- Suppress all other 192.150.42.0 network announcements.

Static routing protocols offer the ultimate control of routes. However, the management of static routes in environments that exceed 10 or more entries can become an administrative nightmare. A dynamic routing protocol is much more flexible and can offer similar control for larger environments.

In some remote access scenarios, it may also be useful to further subdivide wireless network access, VPN network access, and dial-in access into separate subnets. If you have different authentication and access control policies for these remote access networks, these policies are easier to control and enforce using separate subnets.

NOTE	Routing can be a very complex subject; it is strongly recommended that you fully understand the routing protocols used in a given corporate environment and draw out the logical infrastructure before implementing any filtering commands. Where possible, use a modeling tool as a sanity check to verify the assumed logical path of network traffic.

VLAN Boundaries

A VLAN is a group of hosts or network devices—such as routers (running transparent bridging) and bridges—that form a single bridging domain. Layer 2 bridging protocols, such as IEEE 802.10 and Inter-Switch Link (ISL), allow a VLAN to exist across a variety of equipment, such as LAN switches.

VLANs are formed to group related users regardless of the physical locations of their hosts to the network. The users can be spread across a campus network or even across geographically dispersed locations. A variety of strategies can be used to group users. For example, the users can be grouped according to their department or functional team. In general, the goal is to group users into VLANs so that most of the user traffic stays within the VLAN. If you do not include a router in a VLAN, no users outside that VLAN can communicate with the users in the VLAN and vice versa.

Typically, although not necessarily, a VLAN corresponds to a particular subnet. Because a VLAN enables you to group end stations even if they are not located physically on the same LAN segment, you must ensure that the VLAN boundaries are properly understood and configured.

NOTE   Avoid using VLANs as the sole method of securing access between two subnets. The possibility for human error, combined with the understanding that VLANs and VLAN tagging protocols were not designed with security in mind, makes their use in sensitive environments inadvisable.

Within an existing VLAN, private VLANs provide some added security to specific network applications. Private VLANs work by limiting which ports within a VLAN can communicate with other ports in the same VLAN. Isolated ports within a VLAN can communicate only with promiscuous ports. Community ports can communicate only with other members of the same community and promiscuous ports. Promiscuous ports can communicate with any port. This is an effective way to mitigate the effects of a single compromised host.

Logical Access Control

Access to equipment and network segments should be restricted to individuals who require access. Two types of controls should be implemented:

- **Preventative controls**, which are designed to uniquely identify every authorized user and to deny access to unauthorized users

- **Detective controls**, which are designed to log and report the activities of authorized users and to log and report unauthorized access or attempted access to systems, programs, and data

Providing a policy for administrative access to the network devices depends directly on the size of the network and the number of administrators required to maintain it. Local authentication on the network infrastructure device can be performed, but may not be scalable. The use of network management tools can help in large networks; if local authentication is used on each device, however, the policy usually consists of a single login, which does not promote adequate device security. In these cases, an access control server should be considered, which allows for a centralized administrator database, and administrators can be added or deleted at one location.

The type of access is also an important consideration. It is usually prudent to consider using different administrative access levels to the network infrastructure device such that specific commands have specific privilege levels and that these privilege levels are defined for individual user logins.

The three most common types of users are as follows:

- **Administrators**—All levels of access privileges
- **Privileged**—Troubleshooting access privileges
- **Staff**—General monitoring access privileges

The correct technical solution is one that will be followed and not circumvented. You must strive to strike a balance between what authentication methods users will actually use and the methods that provide adequate security for a given system.

Control and Limit Secrets

When providing access control, it never works to have a different password for every router, switch, firewall, and other network device. Probably the easiest approach is to use one password for console access and another for logical Telnet or Secure Shell (SSH) access to the devices. These passwords should be changed on a monthly basis (or whatever timetable is comfortable). The passwords should definitely change when a person leaves the group.

Better access control can be achieved by avoiding common group passwords and instead, having passwords per individual user needing access to a given device. Using a AAA protocol such as RADIUS or TACACS+, per-user authentication, authorization, and accounting can be achieved in a scalable manner. This is extremely important as networks become larger, because individual password management of network devices only scales in small installations. As the number of routers, switches, and so on grows, it may be time to consider using a specific set of hosts as jumphosts to access the network devices. An administrator would be required to strongly authenticate to the jumphost and then from the jumphost leverage an authentication service to access network devices. The authentication service can be accomplished using RADIUS, TACACS+, or Kerberos where there typically exists machine-level trust to the network elements.

Authentication Assurance

Some organizations still base their authentication mechanisms on standard, reusable passwords. Any reusable password is subject to eavesdropping attacks from sniffer programs. It is recommended that, if possible, these environments change to a more robust authentication scheme, such as any of the one-time passwords described in Chapter 2, "Security Technologies." If this is not possible, however, here are some recommendations for using traditional passwords:

- Choose passwords that cannot be guessed easily. Many automated password-cracking programs use a very large dictionary and can crack passwords in a matter of seconds. Passwords should also be as long as the system supports and as users can tolerate.
- Change default passwords immediately when you install new network infrastructure equipment. Don't forget to change the passwords for console access and passwords used for maintenance purposes. For any product you buy, find out from the manufacturer whether there are ways to recover passwords and whether there are any ways to access configurations using these passwords (usually through undocumented means).

- Restrict access to the password when possible. Many vendors now have features that encrypt the password portion of configuration files. Use these features whenever they are available.

- Provide guidelines for how often users should change their password. It is recommended that passwords be changed at least whenever a privileged account is compromised or when there is a critical change in personnel.

Choosing Passwords

Here are some guidelines for choosing appropriate passwords:

- Do not use your logon name in any form (as-is, reversed, capitalized, doubled, and so on).
- Do not use your first, middle, or last (current or former) name in any form.
- Do not use any of your immediate family's names (spouse, offspring, parents, pets, and so on).
- Do not use other information easily obtained about you, including license plate numbers, telephone numbers, social security numbers, the brand of automobile you drive, the name of the street you live on, and so on.
- Do not use a password of all digits or of all the same letter. These types of passwords significantly decrease the search time for a cracker.
- Do not use a word contained in any English or foreign language dictionaries, spelling lists, or other lists of words.
- Do not use a password with fewer than six characters.
- Never give your network password to anyone. Securing your password is *your* responsibility. The whole purpose of having a password in the first place is to ensure that no one other than you can use your logons. Remember that the best-kept secrets are those you keep to yourself.
- Never e-mail your password to anyone.
- Use a password with mixed-case alphabetics, if possible. (Some systems use passwords that are case sensitive.)
- Use a password that includes some nonalphabetic characters, such as digits or punctuation marks.
- Use a password that is easy to remember, because you don't want to write it down.
- Use a password you can type quickly without having to look at the keyboard. This makes it harder for someone to steal your password by watching over your shoulder. Be wary of typing passwords in front of others.
- Change your password on a regular basis. Try to change it every 3 months.

NOTE Many authentication mechanisms have automated password protocol enforcement. For instance, an initial password is marked as expired in the account record, either forcing the user to change the password when he or she logs in, or disabling the account if the user doesn't change the password. Users can be forced to change their passwords at regular intervals. If your authentication mechanism has these provisions (many TACACS+ and RADIUS implementations do), use them.

System Greeting Messages

Many systems offer the capability to configure a greeting or banner message when accessing the system. Never include location information or the type of system in greeting or login banner messages. The system announcement messages must not welcome the user or identify the company, neither must it identify the equipment vendor or the type of operating system in use. Savvy intruders can easily reference databases of vendor or system hacks and bugs that they then can exploit. Make intruders work to get into the system before they learn what type of system it is; this gives you an additional chance to detect them breaking in. In addition, governments are creating legislature requiring specific language to aid in prosecution of any network infiltrators. It is always best to discuss the use and language of a banner message with your corporate legal department to ensure that the message is appropriate for your environment.

Example 7-1 shows a sample of a good banner message.

Example 7-1   *Sample Banner Message*

```
**WARNING**WARNING**WARNING**WARNING**WARNING**

YOU HAVE ACCESSED A RESTRICTED DEVICE. USE OF THIS DEVICE WITHOUT AUTHORIZATION
OR FOR PURPOSES FOR WHICH AUTHORIZATION HAS NOT BEEN EXTENDED IS PROHIBITED.
LOG OFF IMMEDIATELY. VIOLATORS WILL BE PROSECUTED TO THE FULL EXTENT OF THE LAW.

**WARNING**WARNING**WARNING**WARNING**WARNING**
```

Remember the Human Factor

Any security implementation is only as secure as its weakest link. If the security mechanisms you put in place are too complex for the users, they will find a way to circumvent the security practices, thereby creating more vulnerabilities.

Sample Logical Security Control Policy

The following is an example of a logical security control policy for a university.

Logical Network Layout:

- All connections to which students have easy access (student housing, classrooms, labs, and libraries) will be on VLANs.

- The VLANs a student can access will be determined by the curriculum in which the student is enrolled.

- The faculty rooms in each building will be connected to subnets specified solely for faculty use.

- The administration building will be on its own subnet.

- All infrastructure devices and critical services will be on their own subnets.

Access to Networks:

- All VLAN traffic will be cross-routed to each other so that all students have access to all classroom, housing, and lab computing facilities.

- Only faculty members will be allowed access to the faculty subnets.

- Only faculty and administrative personnel will be allowed access to the administration building LAN.

Access to Infrastructure Devices:

- Telnet, SSH, and modem access to network infrastructure equipment is allowed only for network infrastructure operations personnel. (This equipment includes routers, firewalls, switches, remote access servers, and critical application servers.)

- SSH will be the primary mechanism to access network infrastructure equipment. Telnet will only be allowed if it is used from a specified set of hosts.

- All infrastructure device access will be based on one-time password authentication technology.

- All infrastructure devices will have a generic login prompt with no information pertaining to system type or vendor name.

- All activity on infrastructure devices will be logged (such as configuration changes or new image loading).

Infrastructure and Data Integrity

On the network infrastructure, you want to ensure as best you can that any traffic on the network is valid traffic. *Valid traffic* can be categorized as expected network traffic, such as the following:

- Supported services
- Unspoofed traffic
- Data that has not been altered

Firewalls control the flow of traffic between networks and are often used to control the flow of supported network services. Authenticating data in the network infrastructure gives reasonable security against altered packets. Putting safeguards in place to deploy methods to deter attacks might help deter spoofed traffic.

Firewalls

A common way to ensure infrastructure integrity is with firewalls. A firewall, in its most simplistic sense, controls the flow of traffic. Rules are created to permit or deny various types of traffic and parallel any routing decisions made. The permission or denial of traffic can include specific network services. Many books have been written on firewalls and firewall design; some are referenced at the end of this chapter. Typically, firewalls are deployed at critical ingress and egress points of the network infrastructure, as shown in Figure 7-11.

Figure 7-11 *Firewall Deployment*

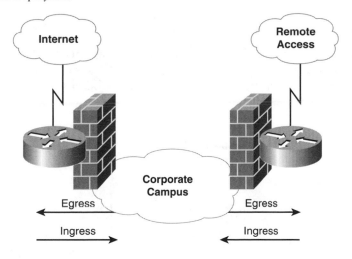

Currently, there are three classifications of firewalls that encompass different filtering characteristics:

- **Packet filtering**—These firewalls rely solely on the TCP, UDP, ICMP, and IP headers of individual packets to permit or deny traffic. The packet filter looks at a combination of traffic direction (inbound or outbound), IP source and destination address, and TCP or UDP source and destination port numbers.

- **Circuit filtering**—These firewalls control access by keeping state information and reconstructing the flow of data associated with the traffic. A circuit filter won't pass a packet from one side to the other unless it is part of an established connection.

- **Application gateway**—These firewalls process messages specific to particular IP applications. These gateways are tailored to specific protocols and cannot easily protect traffic using newer protocols.

Before determining which classifications best fit your environment, examine the traffic flow control you can exert in your environment. Most of the control is based on a combination of the following characteristics:

- Direction of traffic
- Traffic origin
- IP address
- Port numbers
- Authentication
- Application content

Direction of Traffic

Traffic can be filtered in either the inbound or outbound direction. Generally, *inbound* traffic comes from an outside untrusted source to the inside trusted network. *Outbound* traffic comes from inside the trusted network to an outside untrusted network. (See Figure 7-12.)

Figure 7-12 *Traffic Direction*

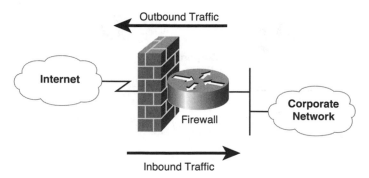

Traffic Origin

Whether traffic was initiated from the inside (trusted) network or the outside (untrusted) can be a factor in managing traffic flow. For example, you might want to allow certain UDP packets to originate from inside the trusted network (DNS), but might not allow DNS requests to come in from the outside untrusted network. Alternatively, you might want to restrict TCP traffic to outside untrusted networks if the TCP session was initiated from the inside trusted network.

IP Address

The source or destination address can be used to filter certain traffic. This approach is useful for implementing precursory controls to help avoid spoofing attacks. Specifically, inbound filters should be configured that block source addresses that should be internal and to block destinations that are not internal.

Port Numbers

TCP and UDP source and destination port numbers are used to recognize and filter different types of services. Which services you support is a key question and is discussed in more detail in the "Network Services" section later in this chapter.

Authentication

At all ingress points to trusted networks, you should authenticate users before they can access particular services, such as Telnet, FTP, or HTTP. Available authentication mechanisms vary, but they all aid in controlling use and auditing who is accessing which services. As an aside, authentication can also help service providers with billing and accounting information.

Application Content

It can be useful to look at applications and determine certain controls. You might want to look into filtering certain URLs or filtering specific content types (such as Java applets).

Network Services

Choosing which services and protocols you support can be a daunting task. An easy approach is to permit all and deny as needed. This policy is easy to implement because all you have to do is turn on all services and allow all protocols to travel across network boundaries. As security holes become apparent, you restrict or patch those services at either the host or network level.

This approach is fairly simple, but it is also vulnerable to a multitude of attacks and not recommended. A more secure approach is to deny all and permit as needed. With this method, you turn off all services and selectively enable services on a case-by-case basis as they are needed. The deny-all model is generally more secure than the permit-all model, but it requires more work to successfully implement. It also requires a better understanding of the services. If you allow only known services, you provide for a better analysis of a particular service or protocol and you can design a security mechanism suited to the security level of the site.

NOTE   Security complexity can grow exponentially with the number of services provided. Evaluate all new services with a skeptical attitude to determine whether they are actually needed.

It is beyond the scope of this book to provide a detailed list of all the network services available. However, the books recommended in Appendix A, "Sources of Technical Information," provide you with all the detail necessary to choose the services appropriate for your specific environment. To summarize, the services most commonly required in environments include SNMP, DNS, NTP, WWW, Telnet, FTP, NNTP, and SMTP. Additionally, a good way to understand what traffic exists (and thus what filters need to be defined) is just to snoop the network for traffic. A table can be constructed of common data flows based on these observations. That table can then be verified with the users of the resources being accessed to determine legitimacy of the data.

It can be a daunting task to figure out which services to filter. At a minimum, you should follow the CERT recommendations, which strongly suggest that you filter the services listed in Table 7-1. The Computer Emergency Response Team (CERT) from Carnegie Mellon University collects reports of computer crime, provides this information to vendors, and distributes information from vendors regarding vulnerabilities of their systems.

Table 7-1   *CERT-Recommended Services to Filter*

Protocol	Port Number	Description
TCP	53	DNS Zone Transfer
UDP	69	Tftpd
TCP	87	Link (commonly used by intruders)
TCP	111	SunRPC
UDP	111	SunRPC
TCP	2049	NFS
UDP	2049	NFS

Table 7-1   *CERT-Recommended Services to Filter (Continued)*

Protocol	Port Number	Description
TCP	512	BSD UNIX R-command
TCP	513	BSD UNIX R-command
TCP	514	BSD UNIX R-command
TCP	515	lpd
TCP	540	uucpd
TCP	2000	OpenWindows
UDP	2000	OpenWindows
TCP	6000+	X Windows
UDP	6000+	X Windows

The services a site provides will, in most cases, have different levels of access needs and models of trust. Services essential to the security or smooth operation of a site are better off on a dedicated machine with very limited access.

Services provided on the same machine can interact in catastrophic ways. For example, allowing anonymous FTP on the same machine as the World Wide Web server might permit an intruder to place a file in the anonymous FTP area and cause the HTTP server to execute it. If possible, each service should run on a different machine. This arrangement helps isolate intruders and limit potential harm.

Authenticated Data

To ensure a reasonable amount of data integrity, you should authenticate most traffic traversing the network. For network infrastructure integrity, traffic specific to the operation of a secure infrastructure (such as routing updates) should also be authenticated.

Routing Updates

If you do not authenticate routing updates, unauthorized or deliberately malicious routing updates can compromise the security of your network traffic. A security compromise can occur if an unfriendly party diverts or analyzes your network traffic. For example, an unauthorized router could send a fictitious routing update to convince your router to send traffic to an incorrect destination. This diverted traffic could be analyzed to learn confidential information about your organization, or merely to disrupt your organization's ability to effectively communicate using the network.

NOTE   The need to authenticate network traffic also applies to bridging spanning-tree and VLAN protocols. If you can spoof a routing update or bridge topology change, you can black-hole various portions of the network, causing denial-of-service (DoS) attacks that can be very, very difficult to detect because routing protocols don't keep much information about the device that sent them a routing packet. Bridges and switches keep even less information.

Checksums protect against the injection of spurious packets, even if the intruder has direct access to the physical network. Combined with a sequence number or other unique identifier, a checksum can also protect against *replay attacks*, wherein an old (but once valid) routing update is retransmitted by either an intruder or a misbehaving router. The most security is provided by complete encryption of sequenced, or uniquely identified, routing updates. This approach prevents an intruder from determining the topology of the network. The disadvantage to encryption is the overhead involved in processing the updates.

NOTE   At a minimum, it is recommended that you authenticate routing updates with a checksum.

Common Attack Deterrents

Most common networking attacks can be made more difficult with firewall-type products.

Attacks Against Any Random Host Behind the Firewall

In many cases, attacks against random hosts behind the firewall can be completely prevented, depending on how you've configured the firewall. The most conservative configuration allows no traffic at all to reach internal hosts unless those hosts initiate an outgoing connection of some kind. If you're set up this way, a number of attacks can be deterred.

Attacks Against Exposed Services

Web servers, mail servers, FTP servers, and so on behind the firewall are at the most risk because any host on the network can send at least some kinds of packets to them at any time. You are generally better off putting those exposed services on a demilitarized zone (DMZ) network, rather than on your internal network. You must also make sure that application server itself is protected. Firewalls do some things to protect exposed services, but that's still where the biggest risks lie.

Attacks Against Internal Client Hosts

If internal client hosts have formed outgoing connections, they are exposing themselves to some return traffic. In general, attacks against internal clients can be conducted only by the server to which the client has connected—which includes someone impersonating that server using IP spoofing. To impersonate the server, the attacker obviously has to know which server the client has connected to.

For any given attack, protection is generally complete for hosts that aren't actively talking to the net, partial for hosts that are actively talking to the net, and minimal for exposed services. However, security depends on how the system is configured.

Spoofing Attacks

No product, even if properly configured, can protect you completely against outside hosts assuming the addresses of your inside hosts. There is no way a firewall, or any other device, can determine whether the source address given in an unauthenticated IP packet is valid—other than to look at the interface on which that packet arrived. Therefore, no firewall can protect against the general case of one outside host spoofing another. If something has to rely on the address of an outside host, you must have control over the *entire* network path to that host, not just a single access point.

Any internetworking product can make spoofing attacks more difficult by making it harder for the attacker to guess which nodes it's profitable to spoof at any given moment. This protection is not complete; an attacker who can sniff the network at strategic points, or who can make good guesses based on knowledge of the traffic patterns, can get around the internetworking product.

Sample Infrastructure and Data Integrity Policy

The following is an example of the infrastructure and data integrity section of a sample university security policy.

Infrastructure Security:

- Access to switch LAN ports and router interfaces will be disabled when not in use.
- Firewall functionality will be used at egress points; *egress points* are defined as any connections that provide access anywhere outside the main university campus.
- Only necessary network services will be supported. These services will be defined by the network operations steering group.
- The infrastructure will be addressed from a well-defined block of IP addresses so that the edge filters at egress points may block inbound traffic to the infrastructure.

Data Integrity:

- Software not related to work will not be used on any computer that is part of the network infrastructure and critical services.

- All software images and operating systems should use a checksum verification scheme before installation to confirm their integrity.

- All routing updates and VLAN updates must be authenticated between sending and receiving devices.

Data Confidentiality

Data confidentiality pertains to encryption. The hardest aspect of this endeavor is deciding which data to encrypt and which to keep as cleartext. This decision should be made using the *risk assessment procedure*, in which data is classified according to various sensitivity levels. It is usually prudent to take a careful look at your data and to encrypt the data that would pose the greatest risk if it should ever be compromised.

Network Address Translation

Network Address Translation (NAT) is often falsely regarded as a security feature. NAT was originally created to help solve the problem of a large corporation having to renumber its thousands of hosts when it connected to the Internet with an illegal address (an *illegal address* being one that is either nonpublic or not assigned by the NIC and might therefore already be in use).

The only way NAT serves as a security feature is if no one knows the internal corporate network address being translated into a valid legal address. If the corporate office were the target for an attack, some forms of attacks would be harder to carry out because the corporate network address is unknown. However, in most cases, the network addresses are well known, even if they are illegal. An RFC recommends specific Class A, Class B, and Class C network numbers to be used illegally (that is, three legal, illegal addresses). These addresses, as specified in RFC 1918, are listed here:

- 10.0.0.0 through 10.255.255.255
- 172.16.0.0 through 172.31.255.255
- 192.168.0.0 through 192.168.255.255

If a corporation is using an illegal network address, it is recommended that it go through the grueling process of renumbering to prevent the many Band-Aid solutions it will otherwise encounter with future features and applications that might not be NAT friendly.

There are, of course, some situations in which an illegal network address cannot be changed. For more details on using legal versus illegal network addresses, refer to the section on NAT in Chapter 10.

Sample Data Confidentiality Policy

The following is an example of the data confidentiality section of a university security policy.

Data Confidentiality:

- All information regarding student grades and transcripts must be encrypted when transmitted across the network.

- All information regarding student financial information must be encrypted when transmitted across the network.

- All employee salary and benefits information must be encrypted when transmitted across the network.

Security Policy Verification and Monitoring

To ensure that a security policy is being adhered to, proper controls need to be put in place to verify and monitor authentication, access controls, and the data traversing your network. Mainly this requires the use of vulnerability scanners, accounting procedures, secure management, and intrusion detection controls.

Vulnerability Scanners

Vulnerability scanners provide mechanism to both check and validate system-level security controls. It is prudent to audit the network infrastructure on a recurring basis to ensure that the security policy is being enforced appropriately and that no irregularities have developed as the network has evolved. The following are some of the capabilities needed for a useful vulnerability scanner to help users stay appraised of their network security status:

- **Network mapping**—Compiles an electronic inventory of the systems and the services on your network

- **Security vulnerability assessment**—Identifies security holes by probing for and confirming vulnerabilities

- **Risk management**—Enables effective management of vulnerability data through innovative data browsing technology

- **Decision support**—Communicates results through comprehensive reports and charts and enables you to effective decisions to improve the organization's security posture

- **Security policies validation**—Defines and enforces valid security policies when used during security device installation and certification

Accounting

Accounting provides the method for collecting and sending security server information used for billing, auditing, and reporting, such as user identities, start and stop times, executed commands (such as PPP), number of packets, and number of bytes. Accounting enables you to track the services users are accessing and the amount of network resources they are consuming.

Logging and reading accounting information from the numerous network infrastructure devices can prove to be a challenging proposition. Which accounting logs are most important? How do you separate important messages from mere notifications? How do you ensure that logs are not tampered with in transit? How do you ensure your time stamps match each other when multiple devices report the same event? What information is needed if log data is required for a criminal investigation? How do you deal with the volume of messages that can be generated by a large network? You must address all these questions when considering managing accounting files effectively.

Secure Management

From a device-management standpoint, a different set of questions needs to be asked: How do you securely manage a device? How can you track changes on devices to troubleshoot when attacks or network failures occur?

Many larger networks opt for an out-of-band (OOB) management system, which refers to a network on which no production traffic resides. Devices would have a direct local connection to the OOB network where possible. If geographic or system-related issues make such an OOB connection impossible, the device should connect in-band via a private encrypted tunnel over the production network. The private encrypted tunnel should be preconfigured to communicate only across the specific ports required for management and reporting and should only allow specific hosts to initiate and terminate tunnels.

An OOB management network can make dealing with logging and reporting much more straightforward. Most networking devices can send syslog data, which can be invaluable when troubleshooting network problems or security threats. Depending on the device involved, various logging levels can be chosen to ensure that the correct type and amount of data is sent to the logging devices. For many attacks, it is important to identify the order in which specific events occurred. Therefore, it is critical that clocks on hosts and network devices are in sync so that all log messages are time synchronized to one another. For devices that support it, Network Time Protocol (NTP) provides a way to ensure that accurate time is kept on all devices.

OOB management is not always the best solution and largely depends on the type of management application you are running and the protocols that are required. If you are using a management tool that periodically determines the reachability of all devices on the network, for example, an OOB management system may not detect a critical failure between core devices because all devices appear to be attached to a single network. With these types of management applications, in-band management through an encrypted private tunnel is preferred.

When deploying in-band management of a device, you should consider several factors. First, what security and/or management protocols does the device support? If IP Security (IPsec) is supported, devices can be managed by creating IPsec tunnels from the management network to the device and sending all the management traffic across this secure tunnel. When IPsec is not feasible because it is not supported on a device, you can use other alternatives such as SSH or Secure Socket Layer (SSL) to configure devices and access management data securely.

The use of SNMP should be carefully considered because the underlying protocol has its own set of security vulnerabilities. If required, consider providing read-only access to devices via SNMP and treat the SNMP community string with the same care you might treat a privileged (that is, enable or root) password on a critical router or UNIX host.

Configuration change management is another issue related to secure management. Sometimes routine checks on when the last configuration change occurred and what was modified can lead to detecting unwanted security vulnerabilities. In addition, when a network is under attack, it is important to know the state of critical network devices and when the last known modifications took place. This helps identify where compromises could have occurred and to later restore the network to its original state (of course fixing any newly discovered security vulnerabilities). Creating a plan for change management should be a part of any comprehensive security policy. At a minimum, configuration changes should be securely recorded and archived. Many devices support AAA functionality, which allows for RADIUS or TACACS+ to be used to authenticate, authorize, and keep accounting data for any configuration modifications.

Intrusion Detection

An intrusion detection system (IDS) acts like an alarm system in the physical world. When an IDS detects something that it considers an attack, it can either take corrective action itself or notify a management system, which would alert a network administrator to take some action. A host-based IDS (HIDS) intercepts operating system and application calls on an individual host and can also operate by after-the-fact analysis of local log files. The former approach allows better attack prevention, whereas the latter approach dictates a more passive attack-response role. Because of the specificity of their role, a HIDS is often better at preventing specific attacks than a network IDS (NIDS), which usually issues an alert only upon discovery of an attack. However, that specificity causes a loss of perspective to the overall network.

When an IDS is deployed, you must tailor its implementation to your specific environment to increase its effectiveness and remove "false positives." *False positives* are defined as alarms caused by legitimate traffic or activity. False negatives are attacks that the IDS fails to see. Many IDSs have the capability to learn the normal traffic patterns in a given environment and automate configuring the system to more specifically act in its threat-mitigation role. An effective strategy would be to use a combination of host and network IDSs. The NIDS would provide an overall perspective of your network and is useful for identifying distributed attacks, whereas the HIDS would stop most valid threats at the host level because it is well prepared to determine that certain activity is, indeed, a threat.

When deciding on automated attack-mitigation roles for a NIDS, you have two primary options:

- Shun traffic through the use of access control filters on routers and firewalls.
- Use TCP resets.

The first option—and potentially the most damaging if improperly deployed—is to shun traffic through the use of access control filters on routers and firewalls. When a NIDS detects an attack from a particular host over a particular protocol, it can block that host from coming into the network for a predetermined amount of time. Although on the surface this might seem like a great aid to a security administrator, in reality it must be very carefully implemented, if at all. The main problem is that of spoofed addresses. If traffic that matches an attack is seen by the NIDS, and that particular alarm triggers a shun situation, the NIDS will deploy an access list to the device to effectively lock out traffic from the troublesome address. If the attack that caused the alarm used a spoofed address, however, the NIDS has now locked out an address that never initiated an attack. If the spoofed IP address happens to be the IP address of a major ISP's outbound HTTP proxy server, a huge number of users could be locked out. This by itself could be an interesting DoS threat in the hands of a creative hacker.

To mitigate the risks of having a NIDS use automated filtering to shun traffic, you should generally use it only on TCP traffic, which is much more difficult to successfully spoof than UDP. Use it only in cases where the threat level is high and the chance that the attack is a false positive is very low. Also consider setting the shun length to a very short time interval. The automated filter should block the user long enough to allow the administrator to decide what permanent action (if any) he/she wants to take against that IP address.

The second option for automated attack mitigation using a NIDS is the use of TCP resets. As the name implies, TCP resets operate only on TCP traffic and terminate an active attack by sending TCP reset messages to the attacking and attacked host. Keep in mind that TCP resets in a switched environment are more challenging than when a standard hub is used, because all ports don't see all traffic without the use of a Switched Port Analyzer (SPAN) or mirror port. Make sure this mirror port supports bidirectional traffic flows and can have SPAN port MAC learning disabled.

IDSs are a critical piece of deploying secure network infrastructures. Understand the limitations of your system to effectively deploy and use it. Too often it becomes a device that loses its effectiveness due to improper setup, resulting in a flurry of false positives that are too hard to deal with. An IDS will not be effective in an asymmetric routing environment.

Packets sent out from one set of routers and switches and returning through another will cause the IDS to see only half the traffic, causing false positives. Also, ensure that the performance capability of the NIDS is sufficient to meet the traffic requirements in your network.

Sample Verification and Monitoring Section

The following is an example of the verification and monitoring section of a university security policy.

Security Policy Verification and Monitoring:

- All Internet and remote-access activity must be logged. These logs are to include user identities, resources accessed, and the duration of the connection.
- All activity logs must be stored in an encrypted fashion for at least 5 years.
- All network infrastructure device access and configuration changes must be logged.
- Network intrusion detection systems must be deployed at corporate network ingress points.
- The network infrastructure must be audited every 6 months to ascertain adherence to the existing security policy.

Policies and Procedures for Staff

The people responsible for maintaining and upgrading the network infrastructure should have specific guidelines to aid them in carrying out their tasks in accordance with the corporate security policies.

Secure Backups

The procedure of creating backups is an integral part of running a computer environment. For the network infrastructure, backups of all network service servers, as well as backups of the configurations and images of networking infrastructure equipment, are critical. The following list should be included in your backup policy:

- Ensure that your site is creating backups for all network infrastructure equipment configurations and software images.
- Ensure that your site is creating backups for all servers that provide network services.
- Ensure that your site is using offsite storage for backups. The storage site should be carefully selected for both its security and its availability.

- Consider encrypting your backups to provide additional protection for when the information is offsite. However, be aware that you will need a good key management scheme so that you'll be able to recover data at any point in the future. Also, make sure that you will have access to the necessary decryption programs in the future when you might need to perform the decryption.

- Don't always assume that your backups are good. There have been many instances of computer security incidents that have gone on for long periods of time before a site has noticed the incident. In such cases, backups of the affected systems are also tainted.

- Periodically verify the correctness and completeness of your backups.

Keep original and backup copies of data and programs safe. Apart from keeping them in good condition for recovery purposes, you must protect the backups from theft. It is important to keep backups in a separate location from the originals, not only for damage considerations but also to guard against theft. Media used to record and store sensitive software or data should be externally identified, protected, controlled, and secured when not in actual use.

Equipment Certification

All new equipment to be added to the network infrastructure should adhere to specified security requirements. Each specific site must determine which security features and functionality are necessary to support its security policy. These features can be as simple as providing TACACS+ or RADIUS support and can progress to the more specific requirements of providing TACACS+ and RADIUS support with token-card authentication integration and time-of-day support.

Use of Portable Tools

Portable hosts pose some risk. Make sure that the theft of one of your staff's portable computers won't cause problems. Consider developing guidelines for the kinds of data allowed to reside on the hard disks of portable computers, as well as how the data should be protected (for example, whether encryption should be used) when it is on a portable computer.

Audit Trails

Keeping logs of traffic patterns and noting any deviation from normal behavior can be your first clue to a security breach. Cliff Stoll relayed his experience in *The Cuckoo's Egg*, in which he helped catch some cyberspies by noting a 2-cent discrepancy in some accounting data.

What to Collect

The actual data you collect for your logs will differ for different sites and for different types of access changes within a site. In general, the information you want to collect includes the following:

- Username
- Host name
- Source and destination IP address
- Source and destination port numbers
- Time stamp

Of course, you can gather much more information, depending on what the system makes available and how much space is available to store that information.

NOTE   Do not record passwords that might be sent in cleartext. Doing so creates an enormous potential security breach if the audit records should be improperly accessed.

Storing the Data

Depending on the importance of the data and the need to have it local in instances in which services are being denied, data could be kept local to the resource until needed or be transmitted to storage after each event. Consider how secure the path is between the device generating the log and the actual logging device (the file server, tape or CD-ROM drive, printer, and so on). If that path is compromised, logging can be stopped or spoofed or both.

In an ideal world, the logging device would be directly attached to the device generating the log by a single, simple, point-to-point cable. Because that is usually impractical, the data path should pass through the minimum number of networks and routers. Even if logs can be blocked, spoofing can be prevented with cryptographic checksums. (It probably isn't necessary to encrypt the logs because they should not contain sensitive information in the first place.)

The storage device should also be carefully selected. Consider write-once, read many (WORM) drives for storing audit data. With these drives, even if attackers can get to the data (with the exception of the physical media), they cannot change or destroy the data.

Because collecting audit data can result in a rapid accumulation of bytes, you must consider the availability of storage for this information in advance. By compressing data or keeping data for a short period of time, you can reduce the required storage space. It is useful to determine a time frame with which everyone is comfortable and for which you will keep detailed audit logs for incident response purposes.

Audit data should be some of the most carefully secured data at the site and in the backups. If an intruder were to gain access to audit logs, the systems themselves—in addition to the data—would be at risk. Audit data can also become the key to the investigation, apprehension, and prosecution of the perpetrator of an incident. For this reason, it is advisable to seek the advice of legal counsel when deciding how you will treat audit data. Get legal counsel *before* an incident occurs. If your data-handling plan is not adequately defined before an incident occurs, it might mean that there is no recourse in the aftermath of an event, and it might create a liability resulting from the improper treatment of the data.

Legal Considerations

Because of the nature of the content of audit data, a number of legal questions arise that you might want to bring to the attention of your legal counsel. These legal considerations often differ from country to country. If you collect and save audit data, be prepared for consequences resulting from both its existence and its content. One area of concern is the privacy of individuals. In certain instances, audit data might contain personal information. Searching through the data, even for a routine check of the system's security, might represent an invasion of privacy. If you collect sensitive data, you should probably encrypt the stored data.

A second area of concern involves your having knowledge of intrusive behavior originating from your site. If an organization keeps audit data, is it responsible for examining it to search for incidents? If a host in one organization is used as a launching point for an attack against another organization, can the second organization use the audit data of the first organization to prove negligence on the part of that organization?

Sample Policies and Procedures for Staff

The following is an example of the policies and procedures for the staff aspect of a university security policy.

Personnel Security Controls:

- Key positions must be identified, and potential successors should always be identified.

- Employee recruitment for positions in the implementation and operation of the network infrastructure must require a thorough background check.

- All personnel involved with implementing and supporting the network infrastructure must attend a 2-day security seminar, which has been developed internally.

Equipment Acquisition and Maintenance:

- All infrastructure equipment must pass the acquisition certification process before purchase.
- All new images and configurations must be modeled in a test facility before deployment.
- All major scheduled network outages and interruptions of services must be announced to those affected.

Backup Procedures:

- All software images and configurations will be backed up in infrastructure devices when modified.
- The previous image and configuration file will be kept until another change is made. Therefore, there should always be available the current and the previous image and configuration.
- All backups will be stored in a dedicated locked area.

Security Awareness Training

Users are typically not aware of security ramifications caused by certain actions. People who use computer networks as a tool to get their job done want to perform their job functions as efficiently as possible—and security measures often are more of a nuisance than a help. It is imperative for every corporation to provide employees with adequate training to educate them about the many problems and ramifications of security-related issues.

The security training should be provided to all personnel who design, implement, or maintain network systems. This training should include information regarding the types of security and internal control techniques that should be incorporated into the network system development, operations, and maintenance aspects.

Individuals assigned responsibilities for network security should be provided with in-depth training regarding the following issues:

- Security techniques
- Methodologies for evaluating threats and vulnerabilities
- Selection criteria and implementation of controls
- The importance of what is at risk if security is not maintained

For large corporate networks, it is good practice to have a LAN administrator for each LAN that connects to the corporate backbone. These LAN administrators can be the focal point for disseminating information regarding activities affecting the LAN.

Rules to abide by typically should exist before connecting a LAN to the corporate backbone. Some of these rules are as follows:

- Provide documentation on network infrastructure layout.
- Provide controlled software downloads.
- Provide adequate user training.

Training is also necessary for personnel in charge of giving out passwords. This personnel should ensure that proper credentials are shown before reinstating a "forgotten" password. There have been many publicized incidents in which people received new passwords just by acting aggravated enough but without presenting adequate credentials. Giving out passwords in this fashion can have serious-enough ramifications that the person who bypasses known regulations should be terminated.

Social Engineering

Many intruders are far more successful using social engineering than they are with a technical hack. A critical training requirement should be that employees and users are not to believe anyone who calls them on the phone and asks them to do something that might compromise security. Would you give any caller your personal financial information and accept a new PIN number over the phone? Hopefully not—you have not absolutely established the inquirer's identification. The same is true for passwords and any kind of confidential corporate information requested over the phone. Before divulging any kind of confidential information, you must positively identify the person to whom you are talking.

Summary

This chapter covered what is needed to create the guidelines and procedures that are part of a corporate security policy. To be effective, the procedures should be concise and to the point. They should encompass rules that define physical security controls—these pertain to the physical infrastructure, physical device security, and physical access. These security policy rules should also promote infrastructure and data integrity as well as data transmission confidentiality to ensure that data has not been altered in transit and is only understandable by the sender and intended receiver of information. In addition, a security policy should have clearly defined rules for security policy verification and monitoring to ensure that the security policy is being effectively implemented and enforced. It also is imperative for every corporation to provide employees with adequate training to educate them about the many problems and ramifications of security-related issues.

Review Questions

The following questions provide you with an opportunity to test your knowledge of the topics covered in this chapter. You can find the answers to these questions in Appendix E, "Answers to Review Questions."

1 Why do you want physical security controls?

2 What are two factors to consider for physical device security?

3 Is traffic filtering an adequate security control?

4 What are five characteristics of choosing a good password?

5 Why should security mechanisms not be overly complex?

6 What is a common way to ensure infrastructure integrity?

7 Name and describe the three common classifications of firewalls.

8 What needs to be combined with checksums to protect against replay attacks?

9 Name three attacks that can be made more difficult with firewall-type products.

10 Why is Network Address Translation not a security feature?

11 Why should cleartext passwords not be recorded in audit trails?

12 Who should receive security awareness training?

## CHAPTER 8

Incident Handling

A *security breach* is often referred to as an incident. An *incident* is any breach that results from an external intruder attack, unintentional damage, an employee testing some new program and inadvertently exploiting a software vulnerability, or a disgruntled employee causing intentional damage. Each of these possible events should be addressed in advance by adequate contingency plans.

The time to think about how to handle a security incident is *not* after an intrusion has occurred. When a security breach hits, it can cause widespread panic for unprepared corporations where a flurry of disorganized activity can cause even more disruption as impatient managers try to ascertain the damage while defensive administrators and engineers try and figure out a reasoned course of action. Planning and developing procedures to handle incidents before they occur is a critical piece of any security policy. The procedures should be detailed enough to encompass the practical steps in recognizing that a breach has occurred, evaluating the breach, and restoring and recovering from your losses.

NOTE   Acceptable use policy violations—for example, employees who are using corporate computing resources to trade pirated music or software—may also be handled similarly to a security breach. With the continuing pursuit of digital rights management legislation, this issue is becoming increasingly relevant to large corporations who may be held liable for their employees' actions.

Fearing unknown intrusion threats to their computer systems, some corporations restrict access to their systems and networks. Consequently, these organizations spend far too much time reacting to recurring incidents at costs to convenience and productivity. What is needed is a form of computer security response that can quickly detect and respond to incidents in a way that is both cost-efficient and cost-effective.

Several factors have contributed to the growing presence of computer network security incidents:

- **Reliance on computers**—An increasing number of corporations rely on computers and networks for communications and critical business transactions. Consequently, many corporations would suffer great losses to productivity should their systems become unavailable. Because of system complexity, reliance on computer networks often presents unanticipated risks and vulnerabilities.

- **Use of large networks**—Large networks that link governments, businesses, and academia are growing by leaps and bounds. Efficient response to computer security incidents is very important for anyone relying on a large network. Compromise of one computer network can affect a significant number of other systems connected to the network but located in different organizations—with resulting legal and financial ramifications. Incident response teams note that intruder attempts to penetrate systems occur daily at numerous sites throughout the United States, and that many corporations are often unaware that their systems have been penetrated or have been used as springboards for attacks on other systems.

How bad is the problem? Table 8-1 summarizes some major security incidences in a timeline.

Table 8-1   *Timeline of Major Security Incidences*

Year	Incident
1988	The first major publicized incident, the Internet Worm caused shutdowns and denial-of-service (DoS) problems for weeks to more than 6000 sites.
1989	The NASA WANK (Worms Against Nuclear Killers) worm caused a major loss of availability on two large government networks, resulting in significant expense and investigations by the U.S. Government Accounting Office (GAO) into network management and security.
1995	Attacks became more specific and intentional, such as Kevin Mitnick's theft of numerous credit card numbers in California from 1992 to 1995 (http://kevinmitnick.com/ indictment.html) and the widely publicized attempted attack against a telecommunications infrastructure initiated by the Chaos Computer Club (CCC) in Germany in September 1995. The CCC called for a DoS attack against the French telecommunications systems to protest French nuclear testing in the Pacific (Chaos Computer Club, "Stop the Test," http://www.zerberus.de/texte/aktion/atom/, September 1, 1995).
1998	Intruders infiltrate and take control of more than 500 military, government, and private-sector computer systems. Although originally this incident was thought to have originated from operatives in Iraq, it was later learned that two California teenagers were behind the attacks.
1999	The infamous Melissa virus infects thousands of computers worldwide, causing at least an estimated $80 million in damage.

Table 8-1   *Timeline of Major Security Incidences (Continued)*

Year	Incident
2000	The I Love You virus infects millions of computers virtually overnight and authorities trace the virus to a young Filipino computer student. However, the Philippine government cannot prosecute him because the country has no laws against hacking and spreading computer viruses. A distributed denial of service (DDoS) attack causes Yahoo!, e-Bay, Amazon, Datek, and dozens of other high-profile websites to be offline for up to several hours. These attacks were traced back to violated computers at the University of California, Santa Barbara.
2001	The Code Red and Code Red II viruses, or "worms," infect tens of thousands of systems running Microsoft Windows NT and Windows 2000 Server software, causing an estimated $2 billion in damages. The Nimda virus infects hundreds of thousands of computers around the world.
2002	A Danish antiglobalization group warned that protesters unable to get to Copenhagen to demonstrate in person against a European Union (EU) summit discussing enlargement of the union would attempt to shut down an EU website by having more than 10,000 people simultaneously launch a WebScript program to overload the EU presidency home page and block access to the site. Someone broke into a U.S. Department of Defense contractor HMO's server farm and stole all the drives. This organized identity theft got the names, medical records, and social security numbers of half a million U.S. soldiers and their families.
2003	The Sapphire worm (also called Slammer) was the fastest computer worm in history and provided the first incident demonstrating the capabilities of a high-speed worm. As the worm began spreading throughout the Internet, it doubled in size every 8.5 seconds and infected more than 90 percent of vulnerable hosts within 10 minutes. In comparison, the Code Red worm doubled in size about every 37 minutes. The slammer worm infected at least 75,000 hosts, and although it did not contain a malicious payload, it caused considerable harm just by overloading networks and taking database servers out of operation, causing significant disruption of financial, transportation, and government institutions.

The problem of security incidences is very real, and as malicious intruders get more creative, the impact of the resulting attacks can be devastating to businesses. E-mail spam has been exploding in the past year, and corporations have been battling to thwart attacks based on e-mail bombardment. Multiple variations of DDoS attacks can cause major disruptions in business services by making unavailable critical resources. Intruders also break into computer networks and steal, among other information, credit card numbers, social security numbers, private medical records, passwords, and proprietary business information.

In a survey conducted in 2001 by the Computer Security Institute and the FBI, security experts from a variety of corporations, government agencies, financial institutions, and universities were questioned. Of 538 respondents, 85 percent detected security breaches over the previous year, and 64 percent experienced financial losses as a result. Of the 186 respondents willing to detail how much they lost, the deficits totaled nearly $378 million. In 2000, 249 respondents said they lost about $265 million. Seventy percent of those surveyed in 2001 cited the Internet as a frequent point of attack, compared to 59 percent in 2000.

It is interesting to note that a research study conducted by Jupiter Media Metrix in July 2001 reported that IT and web managers were more concerned about the impact a security breach could have on customer confidence rather than direct financial loss. More than 40 percent of the 471 IT managers surveyed by Jupiter said they are concerned about the impact online security break-ins would have on consumer trust and confidence, while only 12.1 percent cited financial loss as a top concern. Jupiter analysts said this data suggests a dramatic undervaluing of assets, especially in the wake of the rampant spread of the Code Red worm throughout the Internet in the summer of 2001 and other highly publicized security breaches.

Accurate accounting costs and profit losses caused by security incidents are rather difficult to obtain, yet it is clear that the threat of security incidences and the resulting losses in business dollars is increasing very dramatically each year. This information is extremely sensitive to corporations whose business relies more and more on reliable computing services. Many times, computer incidents are kept under cover and are not even reported, although that trend also seems to be shifting as new legislation is put into place to prosecute the perpetrators The problem is very real; corporations should have procedures in place to recover from a security breach should one occur.

Building an Incident Response Team

An organization must first create a centralized group to be the primary focus when an incident happens. This group is usually a small core team whose responsibilities include the following:

- Keeping current with the latest threats and incidents
- Being the main point of contact for incident reporting
- Notifying others of the incident
- Assessing the damage and impact of the incident
- Finding out how to avoid further exploitation of the same vulnerability
- Recovering from the incident

This centralized group should map into the organizational structure of the company to make sure that someone is responsible for representing each particular area of the organization. This also helps ensure that incidents and exposures are communicated and followed up throughout the corporate hierarchy.

Establishing the Core Team

The core incident response team should consist of a well-rounded representation from the corporation. Essential are people who can diagnose and understand technical problems; therefore, technical knowledge is a primary qualification. Good communication skills are equally important. Because computer security incidents can provoke emotionally charged situations, a skilled communicator must know how to resolve technical problems without fueling emotions or adding complications. For example, it is not effective to call someone a moron for not having adequate access control filters in place, the lack of which may have inadvertently led to outages due to some DoS attack. In addition, the individuals on the response team may spend much of their time communicating with affected users and managers, either directly or by preparing alert information, bulletins, and other guidance.

News about computer security incidents can be extremely damaging to an organization's stature among current or potential clients. Therefore, a company spokesperson is also needed to interact with the media. If the incident is significant, the corporation will want to represent itself clearly without worrying its customers or the stock market and causing negative business repercussions. You must find personnel who have the correct mix of technical, communication, and political skills.

A member of the core incident response team should have many of the following qualifications:

- Comprehensive networking knowledge
- Good communication skills
- Good interpersonal skills
- Understanding of company business
- Good analytical skills
- Even temperament

Detecting an Incident

Determining whether some suspicious system or user behavior is really an incident is tricky. When looking for signs of a security breach, some of the areas to look for from a network viewpoint include the following:

- Accounting discrepancies
- Data modification and deletion
- Users complaining of poor system performance
- Atypical traffic patterns
- Atypical time of system use
- Large numbers of failed login attempts

Detecting any anomalies in normal network behavior requires a knowledge of what is "normal" behavior. Using auditing tools that keep track of traffic patterns and historical trends can be one of the many ways you can determine normal behavior. Realistically, a corporation should not delude itself in thinking it can detect and stop all intrusions from occurring. Rather, it should put procedures in place that limit any impact of an intrusion.

Keeping Track of Important Information

It is important to have the capability to collect as much evidence as you can when a security incident has occurred. This means you should make sure you have full auditing and logging enabled on systems making up your network infrastructure. This includes switches, routers, and critical servers. In addition, it may be prudent to use packet sniffers to capture trace files and save them to regularly archived disks.

It is also critical to save all log files in a tamper-proof way, because the first thing most intruders try to do is to hide any evidence of the break-in. You can significantly diminish the threat of tampering by using a "write-once" storage system whereby once data is written, it can never be altered.

How to gather additional data when a host is suspected of being compromised can be tricky. In some instances, you may want to isolate the device to avoid any further modification to data or worse damage and try to ascertain any attack-trail information left on the device. However, you risk not having enough information to catch the attacker; therefore, some people choose to observe the attack in progress, as long as the damage created is manageable and not catastrophic. Observing the attack in progress sometimes enables you to capture a great deal of evidence on the device before the cleanup process has been able to occur, where the attacker tries to erase any trail that could potentially lead to him.

Many of the considerations for keeping track of important information when dealing with a security breach were described in the preceding chapter in the section "Audit Trails." One of the biggest problems facing people who run large networks is correlating all the information that can be obtained from myriad networking devices. This is where the use of intrusion detection systems can be invaluable.

Intrusion Detection Systems

Because of the multitude of existing known attacks and new ones cropping up on a regular basis, the use of automated tools is essential. Intrusion detection systems are designed to detect known attack signatures and network anomalies, and these should be used at critical network access points to signal appropriate alarms that a security breach may have occurred.

Many intrusion detection systems are based on a combination of statistical analysis methods and rule-based methods:

- **Statistical analysis**—The statistical analysis method maintains historical statistical profiles for each user or system that is monitored. The method raises an alarm when observed activity departs from established patterns of use. This type of analysis is intended to detect intruders masquerading as legitimate users. Statistical analysis may also detect intruders who exploit previously unknown vulnerabilities that cannot be detected by any other means.

- **Rule-based analysis**—The rule-based analysis method uses rules that characterize known security attack scenarios and raise an alarm if observed activity matches any of its encoded rules. This type of analysis is intended to detect attempts to exploit known security vulnerabilities of the monitored systems. This analysis can also detect intruders who exhibit specific patterns of behavior known to be suspicious or in violation of site security policy. Most rule-based systems are user configurable so that you can define your own rules based on your own corporate environment.

Although intrusion detection is discussed in the preceding chapter, it is important to emphasize in the context of incident handling some of the issues to be aware of when deploying intrusion systems within your network infrastructure.

Intrusion Detection Issues in Switched Networks

Switched networks (such as 100-Mbps and Gigabit Ethernet switches) can pose problems to network intrusion detection systems because there is no easy place to "plug in" a sensor to see all the traffic. The problem is illustrated in Figure 8-1, which shows hub versus switch functionality. Hubs differ from switches in how they transmit data from port to port. If two computers are connected to ports on a hub and computer A wants to send information to computer B, the packet is sent, the hub receives it, and then sends the packet out to all the ports on the hub. Because all traffic is sent to every port, a network intrusion detection system (NIDS) connected to port 12 can detect traffic no matter where it is being sent across the hub.

Figure 8-1   *Hub vs. Switch Functionality*

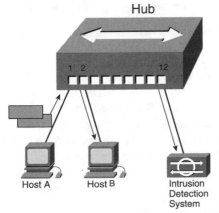

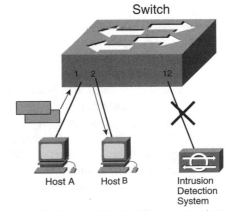

Traffic from host A to host B gets sent to the hub ports so the IDS can effectively monitor the traffic.

Traffic from host A to host B gets sent only to the port that connects host B, and the IDS does not see any traffic.

If a switch were used rather than a hub, however, data destined for computer B would only be sent to port 12. This increases efficiency by reducing packet collision, and optimizes bandwidth by reducing unnecessary transmissions. The problem is that the NIDS connected to port 12 also does not receive any data unless traffic is explicitly sent to that port.

To overcome the limitations of placing a NIDS in a switched environment, consider the following solutions:

- **Embed IDS within the switch**—Some vendors embed intrusion detection capabilities directly into switches. This gives administrators the flexibility to tag certain frames for inspection that will be pulled directly off the switch's backplane. The functionality of these systems needs to be ascertained because many of these intrusion detection systems do not have the full range of detection as a dedicated standalone-device NIDS.

- **Monitor/span/mirror port**—Many switches have a monitor (also sometimes referred to as a span or mirror) port for attaching devices such as network analyzers or a NIDS. A spanning port configures the switch to behave like a hub for a specific port and thus will echo every packet to the dedicated span port in addition to delivering it to the intended recipient. This raises a few issues, the most obvious of which is that of packet loss to the mirror/span port. Make sure that the NIDS used will have the capability to see all the traffic on a heavily loaded switch and that the switch itself can be relied on to pass 100 percent of the traffic to the spanned port; otherwise, attacks could go unnoticed even when the IDS is configured properly to look for a specific attack. If the switch enables you to mirror more than one port at a time, you also need to be aware of your traffic loads. If the switch enables you to simultaneously mirror ports 1 through 11 by copying the traffic to port 12, and the combined traffic of ports 1 through 12 exceeds that available via port 12, for instance, your IDS sensor is going to start missing a significant amount of traffic. Be aware also of an increase in packet collisions, because all ports on the switch will be continually sending packets to the mirror/span port. Often, port mirroring presents additional problems because it does not receive VLAN information and only presents one side of a full-duplex connection.

- **Cable taps**—A NIDS can also be connected directly to the cable via inline taps to monitor the traffic. This is illustrated in Figure 8-2 using a NIDS with cable taps. Passive Ethernet taps can be used, where "copies" of the frames are sent to a second switch dedicated to IDS sensors. The tap is able to give a NIDS the capability to view both sides of a full-duplex conversation, reduce packet loss due to collisions, and view all packets transmitted across the line. Taps can effectively increase the security of an IDS installation in a switched environment. Because the tap takes all data off the line and sends it directly to the NIDS, the NIDS behind a tap does not require an address; therefore, no traffic can be directed specifically toward the NIDS. This prevents directed attacks against the NIDS, and can actually make attackers believe that no NIDS is present to identify and track their attacks.

Honey pots may also provide a useful tool. These are locations to send suspected traffic to/
from an attack. For example, all traffic destined to a certain protocol that is known to be
characteristic of an attack is sent to a collection host or NIDS. The data can then be
collectively analyzed to mitigate some possible attacks.

Figure 8-2   *Using a NIDS with Cable Taps*

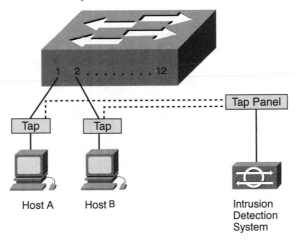

Network Intrusion Detection System Limitations

Network intrusion detection systems reside at critical and often centralized locations on the
network. Therefore, they must be able to keep up with, analyze, and store information about
potentially thousands of hosts. The following are some of the more common limitations to
be aware of:

- **Traffic loads**—Some network intrusion detection systems have trouble keeping up
with fully loaded networking segments. An intruder can attack the sensor by just
saturating the link. If the sensor cannot keep up with the high traffic rate, it starts
dropping packets that it cannot process or, in the worst case, it can completely shut
down the sensor. Keep in mind that frame reception and frame analysis are two
different activities. Most architectures require the system to capture the packet even
when it is too busy to analyze it, which takes even more time away from analysis. The
key factor is in how many packets per second the system can handle capturing while
simultaneously being able to analyze the captured traffic. Most vendors can handle
100-Mbps traffic using 1518-byte packets; few can handle 100-Mbps traffic using 64-byte

packets. In addition, some network intrusion detection systems are capable of receiving only one direction of two-way communication, which greatly misrepresents the traffic characteristics.

- **State information**—State information, such as TCP connection information, IP fragmentation, and Address Resolution Protocol (ARP) tables, requires an extensive amount of memory. Make sure the system is capable of handling many simultaneous TCP connections and that it can keep track of state for a long enough time to detect slow scans (ping sweeps or port scans) where intruders scan one port/address every hour.

- **Attacks against a NIDS**—The IDS itself can be attacked in several ways. The system must be able to withstand the vulnerabilities discussed in Chapter 5, "Threats in an Enterprise Network," including traffic directed at the IDS, which encompasses TCP SYN attacks, fragmentation attacks, and attacks where unexpected protocol traffic is seen.

- **Bypassing a NIDS**—Some clever intruders can direct their traffic in such a way as to bypass the IDS. Exploitations often relate to how varying TCP/IP stacks behave to slightly invalid input. Typical ways of causing different traffic to be accepted/rejected is to send TCP options, cause timeouts to occur for IP fragments or TCP segments, overlap fragments/segments, or send slightly wrong values in TCP flags or sequence numbers. If overlapping fragments are sent with different data, for example, some systems prefer the data from the first fragment (Windows NT, Solaris), whereas others keep the data from the last fragment (Linux, BSD). The NIDS has no way of knowing which the end node will accept, and may guess wrong.

For readers who are interested in more detail about how NIDS can be bypassed, the following two papers offer an excellent analysis of the problem:

- Vern Paxon's USENIX presentation in 1998 on "Bro: A System for Detecting Network Intruders in Real-Time" (ftp://ftp.ee.lbl.gov/papers/bro-usenix98-revised.ps.Z)

- Thomas H. Ptacek and Timothy N. Newsham, "Insertion, Evasion, and Denial Of Service: Eluding Network Intrusion Detection," Technical Report, Secure Networks, Inc., January 1998 (http://citeseer.nj.nec.com/ptacek98insertion.html)

The previous information on NIDS limitations is not meant to cause undue skepticism when making the decision to use network-based intrusion detection systems. Rather, it is meant to highlight some issues that have been problematic in the past and which should be taken into consideration when shopping around for a more robust system to handle current networking security needs. A system that only gives the illusion of security should be avoided. As the limitations of these systems have become apparent—many issues were raised as early as 1998 when papers were first being written on the subject—many evolutionary improvements have been made in this area in the past few years.

Handling an Incident 365

Keep the previously discussed limitations in mind when looking for an IDS to deploy in your environment, and consider the following characteristics indicative of a good system. (You can find a complete list at http://www.cs.purdue.edu/coast/intrusion-detection/detection.html.)

- It must run continually without human supervision. The system must be reliable enough to allow it to run in the background of the system being observed. However, it should not be a black box—that is, its internal workings should be verifiable from the outside.

- It must be fault tolerant. The system must survive a system crash without rebuilding its knowledge base at restart.

- It must impose minimal overhead on the system. An IDS that slows a computer to a crawl will simply not be used.

- It must observe deviations from normal behavior and have timely alerting mechanisms.

- It must be easily tailored to fit into various corporate environments. Every network has a different usage pattern, and the statistical analysis database or rule database should adapt easily to these patterns.

- It must cope with changing system behavior over time as new applications are added.

- It must be difficult to bypass. The IDS should itself be secure and not open to compromise in any way.

NOTE Intrusion detection systems that meet all of the preceding requirements are few; those that do exist are expensive. Before spending a lot of money on any IDS, make sure you understand what the system can detect and how easy the software is to modify to handle new attack scenarios.

Handling an Incident

You must follow certain steps when you handle an incident. These steps should be clearly defined in security policies to ensure that all actions have a clear focus. The goals for handling any security breaches should be defined by management and legal counsel in advance.

One of the most fundamental objectives is to restore control of the affected systems and to limit the impact and damage. In the worst-case scenario, shutting down the system, or disconnecting the system from the network, may be the only practical solution.

Prioritizing Actions

Prioritizing actions to be taken during incident handling is necessary to avoid confusion about where to start. Priorities should correspond to the organization's security policy and may be influenced by government regulations and business plans. The following are things to be considered:

- Protecting human life and people's safety. Systems should be implemented that control plant processes, medical procedures, transportation safety, or other critical functions that affect human life and safety and are required by law to be operational (as per Occupational Safety & Health Administration [OSHA] and other governmental safety regulations).

- Protecting sensitive or classified data.

- Protecting data that is costly in terms of resources. With any security incident, you want to reduce the loss as much as possible.

- Preventing damage to systems.

- Minimizing the disruption of computing resources. You want to reduce the spread of any damage across additional parts of the network.

Assessing Incident Damage

A very time-consuming task is initially determining the impact of the attack and assessing the extent of any damages. When a breach has occurred, all parts of the network become suspect. You should start the process of a systematic check through the network infrastructure to see how many systems could have been impacted. Check all router, switch, network access server, and firewall configurations as well as all servers that have services that support the core network infrastructure. Traffic logs must be analyzed to detect unusual behavior patterns. The following checklist is a useful starting point:

- Check log statistics for unusual activity on corporate perimeter network access points, such as Internet access or dial-in access.

- Verify infrastructure device checksum or operating system checksum on critical servers to see whether operating system software has been compromised.

- Verify configuration changes on infrastructure devices and servers to ensure that no one has tampered with them.

- Check sensitive data to see whether it was accessed or changed.

- Check traffic logs for unusually large traffic streams from a single source or streams going to a single destination.

- Run a check on the network for any new or unknown devices.

- Check passwords on critical systems to ensure that they have not been modified. (It would be prudent to change them at this point.)

Reporting and Alerting Procedures

You should establish a systematic approach for reporting incidents and subsequently notifying affected areas. Effective incident response depends on the corporate constituency's ability to quickly and conveniently communicate with the incident response team. Essential communications mechanisms include a central telephone "hotline" monitored on a 24-hour basis, a central e-mail address, or a pager arrangement. To make it easy for users to report an incident, an easy-to-remember phone number such as XXX-HELP (where XXX is the company internal extension) should be used. Users should have to remember only this one number; technology can handle the issues of call forwarding and sending out e-mail and pager alerts.

Who to alert largely depends on the scope and impact of the incident. Because of the widespread use of worldwide networks, most incidents are not restricted to a single site. In some cases, vulnerabilities apply to several million systems, and many vulnerabilities are exploited within the network itself. Therefore, it is vital that all sites with involved parties be informed as soon as possible. The incident response team should be able to quickly reach all users by sending to a central mailing list or, alternatively, sending telephone voice mailbox messages or management points-of-contact lists.

Although you want to inform all affected people, it is prudent to make a list of points of contacts and decide how much information will be shared with each class of contact. The classes of contact include people within your own organization (management, users, network staff), vendors and service providers, other sites, and other incident response teams. Here is an example of a message that can be sent to corporate employees in some situations:

> We are currently experiencing a possible security breach and have disconnected all outside corporate connections. Please review the current status at http://corporate/security.info. We will let you know as soon as connectivity is restored.

Efficient incident handling minimizes the potential for negative exposure. Some guidelines for the level of detail to provide are given here (taken from RFC 2196):

- **Keep the technical level of detail low.** Detailed information about the incident may provide enough information for others to launch similar attacks on other sites, or even damage the site's ability to prosecute the guilty party after the event has ended.

- **Work with law enforcement officials to ensure that evidence is protected.** Many times, you may have to show law enforcement officials why they should be involved in your case—they are not yet equipped to handle an initial response to an electronic security incident. If prosecution is involved, ensure that the evidence collected is not divulged to the public.

- **Delegate all handling of the public to in-house PR people who know how to handle the press.** These PR people should be trained professionals who know how to handle the public diplomatically.

Incident Vulnerability Mitigation

When a security vulnerability is disclosed by a vendor without an explicit security breach occurring in your network, what are the appropriate steps for applying the appropriate system updates (patches) to the affected system? This is a very controversial subject but one which requires careful consideration for any corporation. It is imperative that a risk assessment be carried out to determine what potential effect the vulnerability of a particular device will have on your corporate network. If it is determined that a patch must be applied, all operating system updates for critical infrastructure devices should be thoroughly tested under the same guidelines and procedures as set forth by the infrastructure equipment certification process prior to initial deployment. Also, procedures must be in place to restore the system to its original state as soon as it is determined that the new software is causing added network issues and/or outages that may not have been uncovered during the certification process.

NOTE   Although outside of the scope of this book, I'd like to make a point regarding patch management of hosts in general. It is very difficult today to control corporate employee host machines that may consist of a myriad of operating systems and that have essentially no cohesive patch management control. You must carefully consider any corporate policy that may call for automated patch management in the event of a major disclosed vulnerability.

Can you trust your users to apply the appropriate patches themselves once they are educated on the risk they can cause if they don't use patches? How do you verify that the hosts are patched? If you decide that automation is the way to go, would you apply this automation directly from the vendor or have your IT department do a thorough test and then make the applicable software patch(es) available from the corporate network? At this time, patch management is a headache, but there is work in progress that may help IT departments more easily assess their corporate hosts (regardless of operating system) and in the future apply software patches in a more cohesive and controlled manner.

- **Do not break or halt lines of communication with the public.** Bad PR can result if the public doesn't hear anything or is speculating on its own.

- **Keep the speculation out of public statements.** Speculation of who is causing the incident or the motives behind the incident are very likely to be in error and can give a poor impression of the people handling the incident (for example, that they are given to speculation rather than to factual analysis).

- **Do not allow the public attention to detract from the handling of the event.** Always remember that the successful closure of an incident is of primary importance.

WARNING *Never* allow anyone within the organization who is not properly trained to talk to the public. The most embarrassing leaks and stories typically originate from employees who are cornered by a persistent press person. Employees are usually instructed not to talk to the public concerning contracts, mergers, financial reports, and so on for the same reasons, so the typical corporate policy need only be extended to include security incidents.

Governements are starting to become much more aware and responsive to security incident needs. The following links are good sources of information for reporting security breaches and give guidelines on how to structure reporting procedures in a corporate environment:

- A general source of government information regarding cybercrime from the Computer Crime and Intellectual Property Section (CCIPS) of the Criminal Division of the U.S. Department of Justice: http://www.cybercrime.gov

- An example of incident reporting procedure from the U.S. Department of Energy: http://www.ciac.org/ciac/CIAC_incident_reporting_procs.html

- How to report Internet crimes as specified by the CCIPS of the Criminal Division of the U.S. Department of Justice: http://www.cybercrime.gov/reporting.htm

Responding to the Incident

One of the most fundamental objectives is to restore control of the affected systems and to limit the impact and damage. In the worst-case scenario, whether it is an inside or outside attacker, you can usually shut off the attacker's access point. Doing so limits the potential for further loss, damage, or disruption but can have some adverse effects:

- It can be disruptive to legitimate users.
- You cannot obtain more legal evidence against the attacker.
- You may not have enough information to find out who the attacker is or what motivated the attack.

An alternative is to wait and monitor the intruder's activities. This may provide evidence about who the intruder is and what the intruder is up to. This alternative must be considered very carefully because delays in stopping the intruder can cause further damage. Although monitoring an intruder's activities can be useful, it may not be worth the risk of further damage.

Keep Accurate Documentation

Documenting all details relating to the incident is crucial because doing so provides the information necessary to later analyze any cause-and-effect scenarios. Details recorded should include who was notified and what actions were taken—all with the proper date and time. A logbook for incident response should be kept that will make it easier to sort through all the details later to reconstruct events in their proper chronological order. For legal purposes, all documentation should be signed and dated to avoid the invalidation of any piece of data that could later be used as evidence if legal action is taken.

Real-World Example Scenarios

The following sections cover three example scenarios of real-world problems.

Scenario 1: Maliciously Internal Compromised Hosts

The Internet connection mysteriously collapses a number of different times. By looking at the corporate network traffic charts, we see that there is a huge disparity between incoming and outgoing traffic. A huge number of outgoing packets are heading out to the Internet without any responses. Looks like we are generating a significant number of User Datagram Protrocol (UDP) packets. What is going on? Using our cool RMON probes and data, we see that 3 million packets per minute are being generated from an internal computer to some Internet Relay Chat (IRC) site in Russia. We block out the IRC site thinking that it is the problem. Later that night, it happens again to an IRC site in the Netherlands. The corporation again loses connectivity to the Internet.

This time, we are ready and watching for the perpetrator. We catch the intruder in the act: It turns out that she is using one of the corporate computers to attack the IRC sites! The intruder was running a version of a spray program that floods UDP packets to the victim. A check of the computer being used as the attack launch site finds that its password file has more than 200 compromised accounts, so there is little chance of being able to lock out the intruder.

We have a significant dilemma. This computer is a critical corporate resource for thousands of users. Do we take down the machine, notify all users, and create new passwords? Do we take down the Internet connection and lock out everyone working on the Internet?

The answer depends largely on the corporation's decision about how to handle this and other types of scenarios. How would you handle this scenario in your environment? The answer should be obvious if you have gone through the process of doing a risk analysis and created a comprehensive corporate security policy that also includes rules and procedures for incident handling.

Scenario 2: Violation of Acceptble-Use Policy

Some internal intrusions may be completely harmless yet still violate an acceptable-use policy. Consider the following scenario.

You notice that traffic from an unusual IP address is on the engineering network and is connecting to privileged machines. Instead of hastily turning off the Internet connection and locking out 1000 users, you take some time to trace the connection. You find no entry for the IP address in DNS, and it's not a new corporate IP address (which you probably would have known about). It turns out that the supposed intruder is an engineer who has a separate account at home and has dialed in to the modem he set up on the workstation in his office at work. Once logged on to the workstation, the engineer was able to continue gaining access to the rest of the engineering network. (See Figure 8-3.)

Figure 8-3   *An Unintentional Breach*

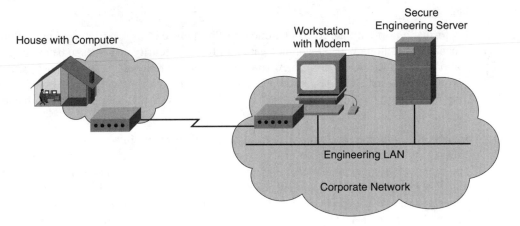

Assuming that the employee was just working overtime, you should put in place procedures about the proper usage of network access. Most likely, the corporation would mandate that all access to the corporate network be achieved through legitimate connections.

Scenario 3: Random Network Interloping

As an administrator of a corporate network, you suddenly notice a significant increase in traffic use from one of the remote office sites. This remote office uses a wireless network within the building and connects to the corporate office via a high-speed Digital Subscriber Line (DSL) line. Because this remote office has approximately 20 users who primarily use the network for e-mail and web-based order processing with the corporate servers, usual traffic loads are minimal. Now all of a sudden, the DSL line is saturated and you wonder whether it is worth getting a more expensive higher-bandwidth service.

Upon closer investigation, however, you see that the number of users sending/receiving traffic exceeds the number of employees at the remote office. It turns out that there is a bartending school next door and some savvy employees there have discovered "free"

Interent access via the wireless network of the remote office and are using it to blast music from some avant-garde Internet music site while teaching students the trade of mixology.

The best way to discourage random interloping on wireless networks is to place simple authentication mechanisms in place before allowing access to a wireless network.

Recovering from an Incident

Recovering from an incident involves a post-mortem analysis of what happened, how it happened, and what steps should be taken to prevent a similar incident from occurring again.

A formal report with the correct chronological sequence of events should be presented to management along with a recommendation of further security measures to be put in place. It may be prudent to perform a new risk analysis at this time and to change past security policies if the incident was caused by a poor or ineffective policy. It is good practice to periodically review your corporate security policy to ensure that it is up-to-date with current corporate direction and new threats.

It is not very productive to turn your computing environment into a virtual fortress after surviving a security breach. Instead, re-evaluate current procedures and prepare yourself before another incident occurs so that you can respond quickly. Having procedures formulated before an incident happens enables the system operators to tell management what is expected should an incident occur. This arrangement aids in setting expectations about how quickly the incident can be handled and which one of many possible outcomes results from a security incident.

Summary

This chapter focused on how to deal with security incidents. Planning and developing procedures to handle incidents before they occur is a critical part of any security policy. With these procedures in place, it will be easier for the group responsible for dealing with security incidents to prioritize its actions. All organizations should create a centralized group to be the primary focus when an incident happens.

The hardest part is actually determining whether some suspicious system or user behavior is really an incident. In many corporate environments, myriad traffic information must be correlated. Intrusion detection systems are designed to detect known attack signatures and network anomolies, and these should be used at critical network access points to signal appropriate alarms that a security breach may have occurred.

After it has been determined that a security breach has indeed occurred, one of the most fundamental objectives is to restore control of the affected systems and to limit the impact and damage. Only when control is restored can the recovery process begin. Recovering from an incident involves a post-mortem analysis of what happened, how it happened, and what steps should be taken to prevent a similar incident from occurring again.

Review Questions

The following questions provide you with an opportunity to test your knowledge of the topics covered in this chapter. You can find the answers to these questions in Appendix E, "Answers to Review Questions."

1 What are three causes of a security breach?

2 What was the first major publicized security incident?

3 What are four possible signs of a security breach?

4 Many intrusion detection systems are based on what two methods?

5 Name three methods to overcome limitations when using a NIDS in a switched environment.

6 What is the fundamental objective of handling a security breach?

7 What are three considerations when prioritizing actions to be taken during incident handling?

8 True or false: When a security incident occurs, anyone who inquires about the incident should be informed in full detail as to what happened.

9 What are some things to be included in a post-mortem analysis?

PART III

Practical Implementation

## CHAPTER 9

Securing the Corporate Network Infrastructure

This chapter explains how to secure the corporate campus networking infrastructure. It looks at features specific to equipment provided by Cisco Systems, Inc. and explains how to configure specific devices to incorporate the following elements of a security architecture:

- Identity
- Integrity
- Data confidentiality
- Network availability
- Audit

Many of these functions can also be used from other products if they are available. Many examples are given with references to commands used for the various devices most commonly found as part of the corporate network infrastructure:

- Routers
- Switches
- Network access servers
- Firewalls

The configuration examples are guidelines; in many instances, you will have to modify them to fit your specific environment. At the end of the chapter are sample configurations for Cisco IOS routers, switches, and the PIX firewall which can be used as sample templates for securing these infrastructure devices. The sample main corporate infrastructure shown in Figure 9-1 is the basis for all configuration examples in this chapter.

Figure 9-1 *The Main Corporate Infrastructure*

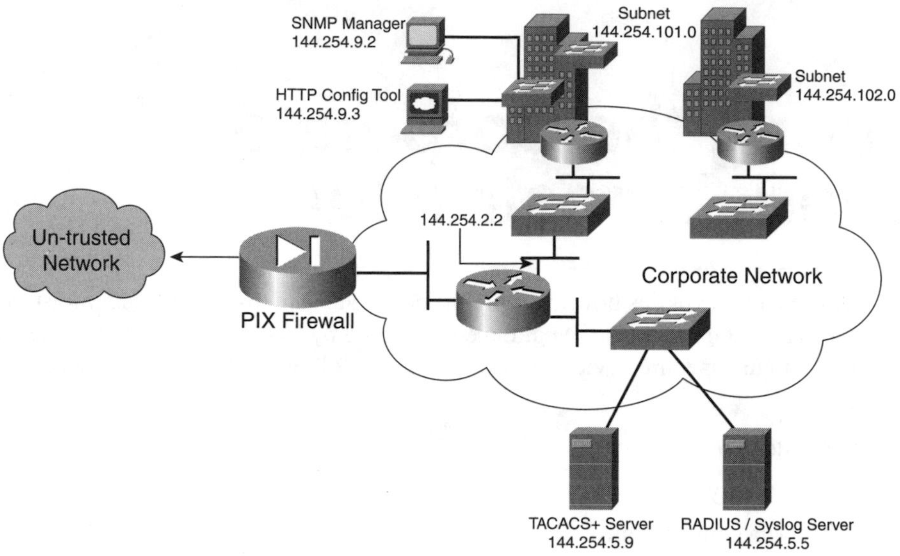

NOTE	A number of Cisco Press books specifically detail security configuration information for routers, switches, the PIX firewall, intrusion detection systems, and so on. Chapters 9-12 are intended to enable the reader to become familiar with the fundamental features Cisco offers with respect to security. The commands may vary slightly depending on the software version used, and readers are encouraged to verify the Command Reference documents for their specific hardware and software release for the features detailed in Chapters 9-12.

Identity - Controlling Network Device Access

Authentication and authorization are considered together under the heading "Identity," which in this section relates to designated personnel who have the right to access the network devices that comprise the corporate network infratsructure. *Authentication* pertains to users identifying themselves with specified credentials, such as a username and a password. *Authorization* refers to the subsequent access rights to which the successfully identified person has privileges. Many times, these processes can be taken as separate entities. In most of the cases considered in this chapter, however, authorization and access privileges are a natural second step after a person has been successfully authenticated. The two processes are therefore considered together under the topic of identity.

NOTE	Keep in mind that controlling physical access to any infrastructure device is critical. All network infrastructure equipment should be in areas accessible only by authorized personnel. Without physical access control, the rest of the control measures are useless.

Basic Versus Privileged Access

Most network devices have the capability to provide for multiple levels of administartive privileges. They typically have two modes of operation:

- Basic
- Privileged

Both modes are password protected. The basic mode commands are used for everyday system monitoring and some basic troubleshooting. The privileged commands are used for system configuration, system maintenence, and more in-depth troubleshooting capabilities. The passwords used should be different for basic and privileged modes. For all Cisco devices, after you access the system and enter an initial login sequence, the system enters basic mode, which gives you access to only basic mode commands. You can enter privileged mode by entering the **enable** command followed by the privilege mode password.

NOTE	The basic mode is commonly referred to as "login" mode, and the privilege mode is commonly called "enable" mode by many network administrators.

Cisco IOS Devices

For Cisco IOS devices, basic access mode is denoted by the > prompt after the host name; privileged access is denoted by the # prompt after the host name. Table 9-1 shows the commands accessible for basic access; Table 9-2 shows the commands for privileged access (that is, enable mode). The basic access commands are just a subset of the privileged access commands.

Table 9-1   *Cisco IOS Basic Access Commands*

Command	Description
Router>?	
<1-99>	Session number to resume.
access-enable	Create a temporary access list entry.
access-profile	Apply user profile to interface.
clear	Reset functions.
connect	Open a terminal connection.

continues

Table 9-1   *Cisco IOS Basic Access Commands (Continued)*

Command	Description
disable	Turn off privileged commands.
disconnect	Disconnect an existing network connection.
enable	Turn on privileged commands.
exit	Exit from the EXEC.
help	Description of the interactive help system.
lock	Lock the terminal.
login	Log in as a particular user.
logout	Exit from the EXEC.
modemui	Start a modem-like user interface.
mrinfo	Request neighbor and version information from a multicast router.
mstat	Show statistics after multiple, multicast traceroutes.
mtrace	Trace reverse multicast path from destination to source.
name-connection	Name an existing network connection.
pad	Open an X.29 PAD connection.
ping	Send echo messages.
ppp	Start IETF Point-to-Point Protocol (PPP).
radio	Radio commands.
resume	Resume an active network connection.
rlogin	Open an rlogin connection.
show	Show running system information.
slip	Start Serial-Line IP (SLIP).
ssh	Open a Secure Shell client connection.
systat	Display information about terminal lines.
telnet	Open a Telnet connection.
terminal	Set terminal line parameters.
traceroute	Trace the route to destination.
tunnel	Open a tunnel connection.
udptn	Open a UDPTN connection.
voice	Voice commands.
where	List active connections.
x3	Set X.3 parameters on PAD.

Table 9-2   *Cisco IOS Privileged Access Commands*

Command	Description
Router#?	
<1-99>	Session number to resume.
access-enable	Create a temporary access list entry.
Access-profile	Apply user profile to interface.
access-template	Create a temporary access list entry template.
alps	ALPS EXEC commands.
archive	Manage archive files.
audio-prompt	Load IVR prompt.
bfe	For manual emergency mode settings.
call	Load IVR call application.
ccm-manager	Call Manager application EXEC commands.
cd	Change current directory.
clear	Reset functions.
clock	Manage the system clock.
cns	CNS subsystem.
configure	Enter configuration mode.
connect	Open a terminal connection.
copy	Copy configuration or image data.
debug	Debugging functions (*see also* **undebug**).
delete	Delete a file.
dir	List a file on a file system.
disable	Turn off privileged commands.
disconnect	Disconnect an existing network connection.
enable	Turn on privileged commands.
erase	Erase Flash or configuration memory.
exit	Exit from the EXEC.
help	Description of the interactive help system.
isdn	Run an ISDN EXEC command on a BRI interface.
lat	Open a LAT connection.
lock	Lock the terminal.

continues

Table 9-2   *Cisco IOS Privileged Access Commands (Continued)*

Command	Description
login	Log in as a particular user.
logout	Exit from the EXEC.
microcode	Microcode commands.
modemui	Start a modem-like user interaface.
monitor	Monitor different system events.
more	Display the contents of a file.
mpoa	MPOA EXEC commands.
mrinfo	Request neighbor and version information from a multicast router.
mrm	IP multicast routing monitor test.
mstat	Show statistics after multiple multicast traceroutes.
mtrace	Trace reverse multicast path from destination to source.
name-connection	Name an existing network connection.
ncia	Start/stop NCIA server.
no	Disable debugging functions.
ping	Send echo messages.
ppp	Start IETF Point-to-Point Protocol (PPP).
pwd	Display current working directory.
radio	Radio commands.
reload	Halt and perform a cold restart.
rename	Rename a file.
restart	Restart a connection.
resume	Resume an active network connection.
rlogin	Open an rlogin connection.
rsh	Execute a remote command.
sdlc	Send SDLC test frames.
send	Send a message to other tty lines.
setup	Run the SETUP command facility.
show	Show running system information.
slip	Start Serial-Line IP (SLIP).
squeeze	Squeeze a file system.

Table 9-2   *Cisco IOS Privileged Access Commands (Continued)*

Command	Description
start-chat	Start a chat script on a line.
systat	Display information about terminal lines.
telnet	Open a Telnet connection.
terminal	Set terminal line parameters.
test	Test subsystems, memory, and interfaces.
traceroute	Trace the route to destination.
tunnel	Open a tunnel connection.
udptn	Open an udptn connection.
undebug	Disable debugging functions.
verify	Verify checksum of a Flash file.
voice	Voice commands.
where	List active connections.
write	Write running configuration to memory, network, or terminal.

How to get initial basic level access is discussed in the section, "Line Access Controls."
Here, take a closer look at how to allow privileged level (that is, enable mode) access. The
authentication of enable mode in Cisco IOS devices can take one of these forms:

- A password
- An encrypted password (secret)
- TACACS/XTACACS
- AAA

Example 9-1 is taken from a router in configuration mode to see the options for configuring
authentication for enable mode.

Example 9-1   *Output from the* **enable ?** *Command*

```
Router(config)#enable ?
  last-resort      Define enable action if no TACACS servers respond
  password         Assign the privileged level password
  secret           Assign the privileged level secret
  use-tacacs       Use TACACS to check enable passwords
```

Passwords

Both the **enable password** and **enable secret** commands enable you to establish an unencrypted or encrypted password that users must enter to access the privileged enable mode.

The difference between the **enable password** and the **enable secret** commands lies in the encryption algorithm used to encrypt the password or secret. The **enable password** command uses a reversible encryption algorithm (denoted by the number **7** in the configuration option and sometimes referred to as type 7 encryption). This reversible algorithm is necessary to support certain authentication protocols (notably CHAP), where the system needs access to the cleartext of user passwords. However, **enable secret** is encrypted using the MD5 algorithm (denoted by the number **5** in the configuration option and sometimes referred to as type 5 encryption). This algorithm is not reversible and is more secure. The strength of the encryption used is the most significant difference between the two commands. It is recommended that you use the **enable secret** command because it has an improved encryption algorithm over the **enable password** command.

NOTE	The command **service password-encryption** encrypts all passwords that support the type 7 password algorithm. It should be enabled on all routers to ensure that none of these passwords are stored in readable text form in configuration files. Depending on which release of software you are running, all passwords may not be encrypted by this command. The passwords to consider include username passwords, RADIUS and TACACS+ keys, SNMP community strings, peer router authentication keys, and NTP authentication keys.

Example 9-2 shows the configuration options for **enable password** and **enable secret**.

Example 9-2   **enable password** *and* **enable secret** *Command Options*

```
Router(config)#enable password ?
0       Specifies that an unencrypted password will follow
7       Specifies that a hidden password will follow
LINE    The unencrypted (cleartext) enable password
level   Set exec level password
Router(config)#enable secret ?
0       Specifies that an unencrypted password will follow
5       Specifies that an encrypted secret will follow
LINE    The unencrypted (cleartext) enable secret
level   Set exec level password
```

You can enter **enable password** or **enable secret** in unencrypted form as follows:

```
Router(config)#enable secret 0 thisisasecret
```

Should you do so, however, **enable password** or **enable secret** is shown in the configuration file as follows:

```
enable secret 5 $1$dLOD$QR.onv68q3326pzM.Zexj1
```

You can also enter the secret in encrypted form, as in this example:

```
Router(config)#enable secret 5 $1$dLOD$QR.onv68q3326pzM.Zexj1
```

To do so, however, the encrypted secret would have to be copied from a previously encrypted secret. For this example, the (unencrypted) secret the user would type is thisisasecret.

WARNING   You cannot recover a lost encrypted password. You must clear nonvolatile random-access memory (NVRAM) and set a new password. Entering **enable password** or **enable secret** in encrypted form should be done with caution.

Example 9-3 shows the configuration file after both **enable secret** and **enable password** have been configured.

Example 9-3   *Sample Configuration File Using* **enable secret** *and* **enable password**

```
Router# show configuration
hostname Tallinn
!
enable secret 5 $1$dLOD$QR.onv68q3326pzM.Zexj1
enable password 7 047E050200335C465817
```

TIP   If you configure both the **enable secret** and the **enable password** commands, the **enable secret** command takes precedence.

It is recommended that you use **enable secret** rather than **enable password** because the former command provides a more secure encryption algorithm for the secret in the configuration. The **enable secret** command provides more security for your configuration files should they be stored remotely on a TFTP server. Passwords should never be seen in cleartext when you view any configuration files.

Scalable Password Management

The **use-tacacs** command is a command that allows for TACACS and Extended TACACS authentication to be used. If this authentication method is chosen for enable mode, you can specify a backup authentication mechanism in the event that connection to the TACACS server is not available, via the **tacacs-server last resort** command. However, this method is not widely used because TACACS and Extended TACACS have been depracated by Cisco and it is more common to use AAA authentication mechanisms that allow for the use of either RADIUS or TACACS+.

WARNING   If you use the **enable use-tacacs** command, you must also specify **tacacs-server authentication enable**; otherwise, you will be locked out of the privileged enable mode.

AAA authentication is the more scalable way to handle password management and can be used to specify enable mode authentication. To use AAA authentication, you must use the configuration commands in Table 9-3.

Table 9-3   *AAA Authentication Commands*

Command	Purpose
aaa new-model	Enables the use of AAA (RADIUS or TACACS+)
aaa authentication enable default *method 1* [*method2…*]	Enables user ID and password checking for users requesting priviledged-level access

The supported login authentication methods are shown in Example 9-4.

Example 9-4   *AAA Login Authentication Methods for Enable Mode*

```
Router(config)#aaa authentication enable default ?
enable      Use enable password for authentication
group       Use server-group
line        Use line password for authentication
none        NO authentication
```

The keyword **group** allows the configuration of multiple TACACS+ or RADIUS servers, as shown in Example 9-5.

Example 9-5   *Configuring Multiple TACACS+ or RADIUS Servers*

```
Router(config)#aaa authentication enable default group?
WORD        Server-group name
radius      Use list of all radius hosts
tacacs+     Use list of all tacacs+ hosts
```

Multiple Privilege Levels

The Cisco IOS Software has incorporated additional user controls through which privilege levels can be assigned to various commands to further limit administrative access. Many times, you may want to assign particular members of the staff only a subset of the privileged **enable** commands. Cisco IOS allows 16 privilege levels, numbered 0 through 15. Level 1 is the current basic mode, and level 15 is the current privileged mode accessible through the **enable** command.

NOTE	Five commands are associated with privilege level 0: **disable**, **enable**, **exit**, **help**, and **logout**. If you configure AAA authorization for a privilege level greater than 0, these five commands are not included.

Both **enable password** and **enable secret** can be configured to provide for the privilege-level authentication. Example 9-6 shows how to configure either **enable password** or **enable secret** to gain access to a specific privilege level.

Example 9-6   *Configuring Privilege Levels with* **enable password** *or* **enable secret** *Commands*

```
Router(config)#enable password level 10 ?
0          Specifies that an unencrypted password will follow
7          Specifies that a hidden password will follow
LINE       The unencrypted (cleartext) enable password
Router(config)# enable secret level 10 ?
0          Specifies that an unencrypted password will follow
5          Specifies that an encrypted secret will follow
LINE       The unencrypted (cleartext) enable secret
```

Here is a specific example of the **privilege level** command used in conjunction with **enable secret** to assign different commands to different privilege levels. In this case, network operators can log in with a secret configured for level 9 privilege access; once properly authenticated, these operators are allowed to reload the routers and look at statistics using the **show** command. Example 9-7 shows what such a configuration would look like.

Example 9-7   *Assigining Different Commands to Different Privilege Levels*

```
Hostname Tallinn
!
privilege exec level 9 show
privilege exec level 9 reload
enable secret level 9 5 $1$dLOD$QR.onv68q3326pzM.Zexj1
```

The network operators are given the secret; then, they can access the appropriate commands using the following command at the router prompt:

```
router> enable 9
password: <secret for level 9>
```

NOTE	The **write terminal** and **show running-config** commands display all the commands the current user can modify (that is, all the commands at or below the user's current privilege level). The commands do not display commands above the user's current privilege level because of security considerations.

The **show config** and **show startup-config** command does not really show the configuration. It just prints out the contents of NVRAM, which just happens to be the configuration of the router at the time the user does a **write memory**.

To enable a privileged user to view the entire configuration in memory, the user must modify the privileges for all commands configured on the router. This approach is not recommended because it is quite cumbersome. Instead, the following alternative configuration is suggested:

```
username showconfig password foo
username showconfig priv 15 autocommand write terminal
```

With this approach, users with lower priviledge levels can view the configuration without any other additional priviledges. Anyone who knows the foo password can show the configuration by doing an extra login on a spare vty.

AAA Authorization

AAA authorization mechanisms can be used to achieve a similar result as with the **privilege level** command and define varying command privileges. AAA authorization mechanisms are much more granular and provide more extensive and scalable controls. The following is a sample of what can be defined:

```
Router(config)#aaa authorization ?
auth proxy              For authentication proxy services
commands                For exec (shell) commands
config-commands         For configuration mode commands
configuration           For downloading configurations from AAA server
exec                    For starting and exec (shell)
ipmobile                For mobile IP services
network                 For network services (PPP, SLIP, ARAP)
reverse-access          For reverse-access connections
```

Here is the example when using TACACS+ authorization to deny access to configuration commands which relate to **crypto**, **aaa**, and **tacacs** commands. On the router, you would use the following command:

```
aaa authorization command 15 tacacs+ none
```

On the TACACS+ server, you have this:

```
group=partner_company {
    default service = permit
    cmd = crypto {
        deny .*
    }
    cmd = aaa {
        deny .*
    }
    cmd = tacacs-server {
        deny .*
```

```
        }
        cmd = no {
            deny crypto.*
            deny aaa.*
            deny tacacs.*
        }
    }
    user = luser {
        login = des slslkdfjse
        member=partner_company
    }
```

The first portion of the **cmd = crypto …** statement denies any **crypto**, **aaa**, and **tacacs** configuration commands. The second portion of the statement beginning with **cmd=no** does not allow the group to remove the **crypto**, **aaa**, or **tacacs** commands.

Cisco Switches

The Catalyst family of switches (Catalyst 4000, Catalyst 5000, and Catalyst 6000 running CatOS) also has a basic and more privileged access mode. The privileged mode has supported some form of authentication, beginning in the 2.2 code. Enhancements have been added with later versions, and listed here are the most basic commands to get started. For Cisco Catalyst switches, basic access mode is denoted by the > prompt after the system prompt; privileged access is indicated by the word (enable) in the system prompt. Table 9-4 displays the basic mode commands; Table 9-5 shows the privileged mode commands. (Both tables list the commands available when your system is equipped with a Supervisor Engine I or II module.)

Table 9-4   *Cisco Switch Basic Access Commands*

Command	Description
Switch> ?	
enable	Enable privileged mode.
help	Show this message.
history	Show contents of history substitution buffer.
ping	Send echo packets to hosts.
quit	Exit from the administration session.
session	Tunnel to ATM or router module.
set	Set, use **set help** for more information.
show	Show, use **show help** for more information.
wait	Wait for *x* seconds.

Table 9-5   *Cisco Switch Privilege Access Commands*

Command	Description
Switch> (enable) **?**	
clear	Clear, use **clear help** for more information.
configure	Configure system from terminal/network.
disable	Disable privileged mode.
disconnect	Disconnect user session.
download	Download code to a processor.
enable	Enable privileged mode.
help	Show this message.
history	Show contents of history substitution buffer.
ping	Send echo packets to hosts.
quit	Exit from the administration session.
reconfirm	Reconfirm VMPS.
reset	Reset system or module.
session	Tunnel to ATM or router module.
set	Set, use **set help** for more information.
show	Show, use **show help** for more information.
slip	Attach/detach Serial Line IP (SLIP) interface.
switch	Switch to **standby** *<clock\supervisor>*.
telnet	Telnet to a remote host.
test	Test, use **test help** for more information.
upload	Upload code from a processor.
wait	Wait for *x* seconds.
write	Write system configuration to terminal/network.

To authenticate a user for privileged access on Cisco switches, multiple forms of authentication are possible:

- Using a AAA server (either TACACS+ or RADIUS)
- Using Kerberos
- Using a locally defined password

The commands required to specify the authentication are as follows:

```
set authentication enable {radius I tacacs I kerberos} {enable I disable}
    [console I telnet I http I all] {primary}
set authentication enable local {enable I disable}
    [console I telnet I http I all]
set authentication enable attempt {count} [console I remote]
set authentication enable lockout {time} [console I remote]
```

The default is that local authentication is enabled for console and Telnet sessions. When the keyword **primary** is used, it specifies which authetication method is tried first. If a primary method is not specified, the authentication is tried in the order in which the authentication methods were enabled. In addition, it is possible to specify the number of login attempts and the period of time a user is locked out of the switch after unsuccessfully attempting to log in. The keyword **remote** applies to remote logins such as Telnet, Secure Shell (SSH), Kerberos, and HTTP.

The locally defined enable password is configured using the **set enablepass** command. The command prompts you for the old password. If the password you enter is valid, you are prompted to enter a new password and to verify the new password. A zero-length password is allowed. Example 9-8 shows how you would configure a locally defined enable password.

Example 9-8   *Configuring a Locally Defined Enable Password*

```
Console> (enable) set enablepass
Enter old password: <old_password>
Enter new password: <new_password>
Retype new password: <new_password>
Password changed.
Console> (enable)
```

TIP

In some older versions of CatOS, the passwords on the switch are not encrypted. Take care when changing or viewing configurations to ensure that no unauthorized person can view the password.

If TACACS+ is used as the enable authentication method, the switch also has the capability to authorize privileged mode session events. This is accomplished with the following command:

```
set authorization enable enable {option} {fallbackoption}
    [console I telnet I both]
```

The option can be one of three values:

- **tacacs+** enables you to proceed with your actions if you have authorization.

- **if-authenticated** enables you to proceed with your action if you have been authenticated.

- **none** enables you to proceed without further authorization in case the TACACS+ server does not respond.

Example 9-9 shows the commands required to provide enable authentication and authorization using TACACS+ .

Example 9-9 *Switch Privileged Mode Authentication and Authorization with TACACS+*

```
! Make sure there is a back door available in case the TACACS+
! server is unavailable.

set authentication enable local enable

! Enable TACACS+ authentication and TACACS+ server parameters.

set authentication enable tacacs enable primary
set tacacs server 144.254.5.9
set tacacs key LetMeIn

! Set the number of console and remote login enable mode attempts to 3.

set authentication enable attempt 3

! Set the enable mode lockout time to 5 minutes for console login.

set authentication enable lockout 300 console

! Set the enable mode lockout time to 10 minutes for remote login.

set authentication enable lockout 600 remote

! Configure the switch to require enable authorization.  Allow for
! no authorization if the server is down.


set authorization enable enable tacacs+ none both
```

Starting in CatOS version 7.5.1, local user authentication is possible where a username/password combination can be used to authenticate/authorize users. This is accomplished using the following commands:

```
set localuser user username password userpassword privilege [0 | 15]
set localuser authentication enable
```

There are only two privilege levels for local user authentication, 0 or 15. Level 0 is the nonprivileged EXEC level. Level 15 is the privileged enable level. Note that if a user is set as using privilege level 0 but knows the enable mode password, that user can continue to authenticate for enable mode. A maximum of 25 local users can be configured on each switch. The defined user password is encrypted in the configuration file.

Cisco PIX Firewall

The Private Internet Exchange (PIX) firewall contains a command set based on Cisco IOS technologies. The unprivileged basic mode is available when you first access the PIX firewall; this mode displays the > prompt and specifies commands with privilege level 0. The basic mode enables you to view restricted settings. Privileged mode displays the # prompt and enables you to change current settings—these commands are at privilege level 15. Any unprivileged command also works in privileged mode. To show the privilege levels settings for all commands, issue the command **show privilege all**. Tables 9-6 and 9-7 display the basic mode and privileged mode commands for the PIX firewall.

Table 9-6   *Cisco PIX Firewall Basic Access Commands*

Command	Description
pixfirewall>?	
enable	Enter privileged mode or change privileged mode password.
quit	Quit.
uptime	Show system uptime.
who	Show active administration sessions on PIX.

Table 9-7   *Cisco PIX Firewall Privileged Access Commands*

Command	Description
pixfirewall# ?	
configure	Configure from terminal, floppy, or memory.
debug	Enable debugging ICMP trace.
disable	Exit from privileged mode.
enable	Modify enable password.
groom	Groom the Flash by rewriting it.
http	Add authorized IP addresses for HTTP access to PIX.
kill	Terminate a Telnet session.
passwd	Change Telnet and HTTP console access password.
ping	Test connectivity from specified interface to an IP.
quit	Quit.
radius-server	Configure a RADIUS server.
reload	Halt and reload system.
session	Internal router console.
syslog	Log messages to syslog server.

continues

Table 9-7 *Cisco PIX Firewall Privileged Access Commands (Continued)*

Command	Description
tacacs-server	Configure a TACACS+ server.
telnet	Add authorized IP addresses for Telnet access to PIX.
uptime	Show system uptime.
who	Show active administration sessions on PIX.
write	Write configuration to Flash, floppy disk, or terminal; or, erase the Flash memory.

To authenticate a user for privileged access on PIX firewalls, you can use either a privileged mode password or a AAA authentication. The privileged mode password can be specified with this command:

```
enable password <password> [encrypted]
```

The *password* is encrypted in the configuration file using MD5. If you use the word **encrypted** during configuration, you are specifying that the password you enter is already encrypted. The encrypted password must be 16 characters in length.

Example 9-10 shows an example of entering the **enable password** command unencrypted.

Example 9-10 *Entering the Enable Password Unencrypted*

```
enable password thisisasecret
show enable password
enable password feCkwUGktTCAgIbD encrypted
```

Example 9-11 shows an example of entering the **enable password** command encrypted.

Example 9-11 *Entering the Enable Password Encrypted*

```
enable password thisisgibberish encrypted
show enable password
enable password thisisgibberish encrypted
```

A more scalable authentication method is to use AAA, which is accomplished using the following command:

```
aaa authentication [serial | enable | telnet | ssh | http] console group_tag
```

When used with the console option, it enables authentication service for access to the PIX firewall console over Telnet or from the console connector on the PIX firewall unit. TACACS+, RADIUS, or a locally defined user authentication database can be specified. To use a locally defined user authentication base, the word **local** is specified as the group tag.

Example 9-12 shows a configuration in which enable access is authenticated using a locally defined user database.

Example 9-12 *PIX Firewall Privileged Mode Access Using a Locally Defined Database*

```
! Set up the local database with user merike with enable-mode privilege level.

username merike password ThisIsASecret privilege 15

! Set up the AAA mechanism to use the local user database.

aaa-server LOCAL protocol local
aaa authentication enable console LOCAL
```

Multiple Privilege Levels

It is possible to assign different privilege levels for certain commands and then assign users to only have privilege levels to use those commands. This is done with the following command:

Privilege [**show** | **clear** | **configure**] **level** *level* **mode** [**enable** | **configure**]
    command *command*

Example 9-13 shows a configuration where privilege level 6 is assigned to user Cathy to perform only a specified set of **show** commands.

Example 9-13 *Setting Up a Specified Privilege Level for Specific Commands*

```
! Define the username with associated privilege level.

username Cathy password MySecret privilege 6

! Set up the specified commands to correspond to privilege level 6.

privilege show level 6 command alias
privilege show level 6 command arp
privilege show level 6 command conn
privilege show level 6 command block
```

Line Access Controls

A number of mechanisms enable users to gain basic access to a network device. Most devices have console ports that allow a physical connection to a given device. The console port is a terminal line port (tty port). A console port is extremely useful in cases where the network is down; it is often a last-resort method of communicating with the device. The virtual terminal (vty) ports are usually for remote console access. Administrators can remotely Telnet, SSH, or rlogin into a device to access and perform all commands as if they were attached to the device with a physical console connection. Auxiliary ports can be used for modem support and asynchronous connections.

Authentication and authorization capabilities for console ports, vty ports, or auxiliary lines vary by product. At a minimum, users should be authenticated before gaining device access. Consistent authentication mechanisms should be used if possible to simplify keeping track of passwords. In addition, login banners can be configured on most devices. These are essential for legal prosecution, should you ever need to prosecute an intruder for unauthorized access. Keep the following important points in mind when wording this banner:

- Do *not* include any wording that even remotely can be construed as an invitation to access the device (such as using the word "welcome").

- Do *not* include any information that can divulge which operating system is being used, what the hardware is, or what logical interface has been accessed.

- Include statements that advertise that unauthorized access is prohibited and violators will be prosecuted under the full extent of the law.

- Include statements that advertize that access to the device will be logged and monitored.

To ensure that any legal requirements are met, it is best to consult with your corporate lawyers when constructing these device banners.

Cisco IOS

Cisco IOS devices can be accessed via console ports, auxiliary ports, and virtual terminal ports. The following sections detail how to effectively secure them.

Console Ports

Console ports typically provide access via a physical connection, but sometimes users connect a terminal server to this port to provide remote console access through the use of reverse Telnet. The following steps will secure console access:

Step 1   Restrict access to only protocols that will be used to connect to the console port.

Cisco routers do not accept incoming network connections to asynchronous ports (tty lines) by default. You have to specify an incoming transport protocol, or specify transport input all before the line will accept incoming connections. The only protocols that should be configured to access console ports are Telnet and SSH. Telnet is not a secure mechanism and unless used in conjunction with IPsec, it should not be used. Note, however, that Cisco IOS Software currently uses only SSH version 1 and will at some future date support SSH version 2.

Example 9-14 shows the commands needed to set up SSH console access.

Example 9-14 *Setting Up Console Access with SSH*

```
! The following two commands define the router's host name and domain name.
! The RSA keys used for SSH are named using these parameters.

hostname SantaCruz
ip domain-name cisco.com

! The next command is used to generate a default 1024-bit RSA key pair.

crypto key generate rsa

! Only allow SSH access for console access.

line console 0
   transport input ssh

! You can also configure the time period when idle  SSH connections get
! cleared and the number of retry attempts.

ip ssh time-out 60
ip ssh authentication-retires 3
```

Step 2   Set the session timeout for unattended console ports.

By default, the timeout is 10 minutes and can be modified with the **exec-timeout** command. Example 9-15 sets the timeout to 1 minute and 30 seconds.

Example 9-15 *Setting Up Timeouts for Console Access*

```
line console 0
   exec-timeout 1 30
```

Step 3   Set up authentication for console access.

Anyone accessing the console port needs to be authenticated. The authentication mechanism used can consist of several methods, which include setting up passwords, using a local username/password database, or using AAA.

By using passwords, where no username has to be entered, the passwords are either cleartext or encrypted in the configuration file. Example 9-16 shows the configuration commands used to set up a password for console access.

Example 9-16 *Setting Up a Password for Console Access*

```
Router# Configure terminal
Router(config)# line console 0
Router(config-lin)# password ?
0         Specifies that an unencrypted password will follow
7         Specifies that a hidden password will follow
LINE      The unencrypted (cleartext) line password
```

For more restricted access control, authentication with a username and a corresponding password can be configured. The username can be set either from a database local to the Cisco IOS device or using a TACACS server. TACACS has the advantage of more flexibility and an easier database management control mechanism; however, it is being deprecated for the more flexible AAA method. If you have *not* yet configured the command **aaa new-model**, you will see what is in Example 9-17.

Example 9-17 *Configuring Console Access with a Username and Corresponding Password*

```
Router# Configure terminal
Router(config# line console 0
Router(config-lin)# login ?
local               Local password checking
tacacs              Use TACACS server for password checking
```

The **local** keyword designates using the local database for authentication. Therefore, a local database must be configured on the router. This is done by creating a list of usernames and passwords by using the commands in Example 9-18.

Example 9-18 *Configuring a Local User Login Database*

```
Router# Configure terminal
Router(config)# username staff password ?
0         Specifies that an unencrypted password will follow
7         Specifies that a hidden password will follow
LINE      The unencrypted (cleartext) line password
```

The most scalable mechanism is to use AAA authentication. After you have configured the command **aaa new-model**, the router expects to use either RADIUS or TACACS+ for authentication and Example 9-19 can be configured.

Example 9-19 *Configuring Console Access with AAA Authentication*

```
Router# Configure terminal
Router(config# line console 0
Router(config-lin)# login ?
authentication          Authentication parameters

Router(config-lin)# login authentication?
WORD                    Use an authentication list with this name
Default                 Use the default authentication list
```

The **login authentication** command for console access must be used with the **aaa authentication login** command to configure the default or specified word authentication method(s). If this command is not used for console login, the login will succeed without any authentication checks.

The AAA authentication login methods can be any of the ones listed in Table 9-8.

Table 9-8   *AAA Authentication Login Methods*

Keyword	Description
enable	Use the enable password for authentication.
krb5	Use Kerberos 5 for authentication.
line	Use the line password for authentication.
local	Use the local username database for authentication.
none	Use no authentication.
radius	Use RADIUS authentication.
tacacs+	Use TACACS+ authentication.
krb5-telnet	Use Kerberos 5 Telnet authentication protocol when using Telnet to connect to the router.

Example 9-20 shows a sample configuration in which the console access is secured using AAA authentication. Note that specific RADIUS commands may vary a little depending on software versions used. (Specifically, the keyword **group**, which allows for a list of multiple servers to be defined, did not exist in older software versions, but this feature is backward compatible if the word is not used.)

Example 9-20 *Console Connection Authentication Using AAA*

```
! The following command turns on AAA.

aaa new-model

! The username and password that follow constitute the local
! authentication database.

username merike  password 7 082C495C0012001E010F02
username cathy   password 7 0574837212001E010F0296

! The next commands define a radius server and key.

radius-server host  144.254.5.5
radius server key LetMeIn

! The following commands define the default authentication login  method list.
! If the RADIUS server
! fails, the local database is used for authentication.

aaa authentication login default group radius local

! The following are the console-specific commands where authentication
! is specified as requiring a login
! username/password as defined by AAA authentication.

line console 0
    transport input ssh
    exec-timeout 1 30
    login authentication default
```

It is good practice to have the local database contain specific users' names and passwords instead of creating a group username and password. The fewer passwords that are shared, the better.

Auxiliary Ports

The auxiliary port should generally be disabled. If there is an absolute need to connect this port to a modem, similar mechanisms to secure this port should be used as were discussed for the console port. Interactive access can be completely prevented by applying the configuration command **no exec** to any asynchronous line. This command allows only an outgoing connection for a line. When a user tries to Telnet to a line with the **no exec** command configured, the user gets no response when he presses the Return (Enter) key at the login screen. To define which protocols to use to connect to a specific line of the router, use the **transport input** line configuration command:

```
transport input {all | lat | mop | nasi | none | pad | rlogin | telnet | v120}
```

NOTE   The **none** option became the default in Cisco IOS Software Release 11.1. Before Release 11.1, the default was **all**.

Example 9-21 shows a configuration where the auxiliary port does not accept any incoming connections and will not even give a login prompt.

Example 9-21 *Auxiliary Port, which is Disabled*

```
line aux 0
 no exec
 transport input none
```

Virtual Terminal Ports

Most versions of IOS have five virtual terminal ports, numbered 0 through 4. Some Cisco IOS Software versions may have more, and it is important to know how many vty ports you have and to configure them all securely. You can list them using the **show line vty** command.

The same steps for securing console ports should be used with securing the vty lines with one added step. It is possible to configure a specific access list (that is, filter) that allows vty access from only a specific network or host(s). This functionality should be used if login to vty terminals is always from a known set of IP addresses. Example 9-22 shows the commands used to restrict vty access.

Example 9-22 *Restricting vty Access to Cisco IOS Routers*

```
access-list 3 permit 144.254.9.0 0.0.0.255
access-list 3 permit 144.254.19.0 0.0.0.255
!
line vty 0 4
 access-class 3 in
```

Cisco Switches

You can access the **switch** command-line interface (CLI) from a console terminal connected to an EIA/TIA-232 port or through remote methods including Telnet, HTTP, or SSH sessions. The **set authentication login** command enables you to designate the authentication mechanism to use for either console or remote login access:

```
set authentication login {radius | tacacs | kerberos} {enable | disable}
    [console | telnet | http | all]
```

The deafult is local authentication and a maximum of three login attempts are permitted. If TACACS+ is used as the authentication method, the switch also has the capability to authorize session events. This is accomplished with the following command:

```
set authorization commands enable {config | enable | all} {option}
    {fallbackoption} [console | telnet | both]
```

This is similar to the authorization commands specifically for privileged access (enable mode). However, it does not replace it.

The Cisco switches also have the capability to restrict access to specified hosts through the **set ip permit** command. When you enable this feature, Telnet access, SSH access, and SNMP services are authorized only for the IP addresses of the hosts configured on the permit list. Up to 100 entries can be configured. The IP permit list is the first level of security for the Telnet and SNMP protocols. All other Transmission Control Protocol/Internet Protocol (TCP/IP) services continue to work for any hosts when you enable the IP permit list. Outbound Telnet, Trivial File Transfer Protocol (TFTP), and other IP-based services remain unaffected by the IP permit list. SNMP from nonpermitted IP addresses have no response—that is, the request times out. Notifications of unauthorized access attempts are available through SNMP traps and syslog options.

Before enabling the IP permit feature, be sure that you configure your IP address in the permit list, especially when configuring through SNMP. Failure to do so results in immediate disconnection from the system being configured. (I recommend that you disable the IP permit feature before clearing the IP permit entries or host addresses.)

Example 9-23 shows a configuration for allowing a switch to accept SSH connections from network 144.254.9.0 and network 144.254.19.0.

Example 9-23 *Switch with SSH Access*

```
! First generate the 1024-bit RSA public/private key pair used for SSH.

 set crypto key rsa 1024

! Define the range of ip addresses from where to allow connections.

set ip permit 144.254.9.0 0.0.0.255
set ip permit 144.254.19.0 0.0.0.255

! Restrict IP access to only allow remote login SSH connections.

set ip permit enable ssh
```

Cisco PIX Firewall

The PIX firewall CLI can be accessed using the serial console connector or over remote login using Telnet or SSH. The following command enables authentication using either TACACS+ or RADIUS:

```
aaa authentication [serial | enable | telnet | ssh | http] console group_tag
```

When used with the **console** option, this command enables authentication service for access to the PIX firewall console over Telnet or from the serial console connector on the PIX firewall unit. This command is used together with the **aaa-server** command:

```
aaa-server group-tag (interface_name) host server-IP-address shared-key
    timeout seconds
aaa-server group_tag protocol [tacacs+ | radius]
```

You can define 14 groups of servers with a maximum of 14 servers each. Certain types of AAA services can be directed to different servers; such as TACACS+ servers for inbound traffic and another for outbound traffic. Services can also be set up to fail over to multiple servers. The interface name defines on which interface the authentication server resides.

Telnet access to the PIX firewall console is available for both the inside and outside interface. For Telnet access to work from the outside interface, however, an IPsec client needs to be set up to initiate a VPN connection to the PIX using IPsec. *Inside interface* refers to the interface connected to the corporate network, whereas *outside interface* refers to the interface connected to the Internet, as shown in Figure 9-2.

Figure 9-2   *The Inside and Outside Interfaces of the PIX Firewall*

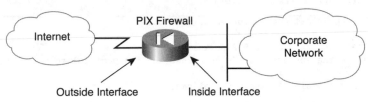

Telnet access requires use of the **telnet** command:

```
telnet ip-address [netmask] [inside | outside]
```

The **telnet** command enables you to decide who can access the PIX firewall with Telnet. Up to 16 hosts or networks are allowed access to the PIX firewall console with Telnet, five simultaneously.

To set up a password for Telnet access to the console, you must configure the **passwd** command:

```
passwd password [encrypted]
```

The default password is cisco. The **passwd** command sets a password for Telnet and gives the PIX Firewall Manager access to the firewall console. An empty password can be used and is also changed into an encrypted string. Any use of a **write** command displays or writes the password in encrypted form. After passwords are encrypted, they cannot be changed back to plaintext. Consider Example 9-24.

Example 9-24   *Configuring a PIX Telnet Password*

```
passwd secretforpix
show passwd


passwd jMorNbK0514fadBh encrypted
```

NOTE   Default password or passwords should be changed before any network infrastructure device is put into production use.

WARNING	Authentication of the serial console creates a potential deadlock situation if the authentication server requests are not answered and you must access the console to attempt diagnosis. If the console login request to authentication times out, you can gain access to the PIX firewall from the serial console by entering the username "pix" and the enable password.

It is much more scalable to set up AAA mechanisms to authenticate Telnet access. Example 9-25 shows a configuration where Telnet access is authenticated using AAA.

Example 9-25 *Restricted Telnet Access Using AAA*

```
! Set up Telnet access for specified hosts.

telnet 144.254.9.0 0.0.0.255  inside
!Define the server group TelnetAccess and the protocol to use, RADIUS.

aaa-server TelnetAccess protocol radius

! Set up the AAA server parameters which includes IP address of RADIUS
! server and shared key.

aaa-server TelnetAccess (inside) host 144.254.5.5 ThisIsASecret timeout 60
! Configure AAA authentication for Telnet access.
aaa authentication telnet console TelnetAccess
```

SSH access to the PIX firewall console is available from any interface without IPsec configured, and requires use of the **ssh** command. Older software that does not support AAA authentication requires that the Telnet password be used to authenticate SSH access. Example 9-26 illustrates the use of SSH for secure and authenticated access using AAA.

Example 9-26 *Authenticated SSH Access to the PIX Firewall*

```
! The following two commands define the PIX host name and domain name.
! The RSA keys used for SSH
! are named using these parameters.

hostname PIX-Venice
domain-name cisco.com

! The next command is used to generate a default 1024-bit RSA key pair.

ca generate rsa key 1024

! Save the key to Flash memory.

ca save all
! Accept SSH connections from the outside interface from any host
! from a particular network and specify
```

Example 9-26 *Authenticated SSH Access to the PIX Firewall (Continued)*

```
! that the connection will timeout after 5 minutes of inactivity.

ssh 208.251.229.0 0.0.0.255 outside
ssh timeout 5

! Set up the AAA server parameters using a TACACS+ server.

aaa-server SSHAccess protocol tacacs+
aaa-server SSHAccess (inside) host 144.254.5.9 ThisIsAKey  timeout 10
! Configure AAA authentication for SSH access.
aaa authentication ssh console SSHAccess
```

NOTE   Similar to the Telnet model, if an **aaa authentication ssh console** [*group_tag*] command statement is not defined, you can gain access to the PIX firewall console with the username "pix" and with the PIX firewall Telnet password. If the **aaa** command is defined but the SSH authentication requests times out, you can gain access to the PIX firewall using username "pix" and the enable password. By default, the Telnet password is cisco and the enable password is not set.

If the console login request times out, you can gain access to the PIX firewall from the serial console by entering the username "pix" and the enable password.

Password Management

With the variety of configurable passwords for different devices, password management can be a nightmare. The use of AAA mechanisms can greatly reduce the administrative headaches and because many current software releases support AAA authentication and authorization, it is highly recommended that this method be used. In addition, the following rules dictate good security paractices:

- Privileged-level passwords should be unique from any other password.
- Username/password privileges should be configured on a per-user basis and group shared keys should be avoided.
- Create passwords that avoid dictionary words, dates, phone numbers, and names.
- Always change any default passwords.
- Change passwords on a regular basis.

SNMP Security

The Simple Network Management Protocol (SNMP) is often used to gather statistics and remotely monitor network infrastructure devices. It is a very simplistic protocol and therefore has virtually no security built in to its original version. In SNMP version 1

(SNMPv1), *community strings* (passwords) are sent in cleartext. These community strings are used to authenticate messages sent between the SNMP manager and the agent. These community strings can easily be stolen by someone eavesdropping on the wire.

SNMPv2 addresses some of the known security weaknesses of SNMPv1. Specifically, version 2 uses the MD5 algorithm to authenticate messages between the SNMP server and the agent.

In most devices, SNMP has two options:

- The read-only (**ro**) option specifies that you can only read any SNMP MIB objects.
- The read-write (**rw**) option specifies that the SNMP manager can read and/or modify SNMP MIB objects.

Whenever possible, configure filters to allow only specified hosts to have SNMP access to devices. In addition, use just the read-only option to gather statistics because the read-write option is rarely used and creates additional security risks.

SNMPv3 has recently been added to some Cisco products. This version of SNMP added authentication through the use of the HMAC-MD5 or HMAC-SHA algorithms, as well as confidentiality through the use of 56-bit DES encryption. Specific details on how to set up SNMPv3 are available at http://www.cisco.com/en/US/products/sw/iosswrel/ps1830/products_feature_guide09186a00800878fa.html.

HTTP Security

To facilitate configuration and management of network devices, many manufacturers are implementing HTTP servers into devices to create cross-platform, easy management solutions. Keep in mind that the communication between the HTTP client and the HTTP server embedded into the network infrastructure devices should be secured (that is, encrypted). This means that you must use some of the technologies (such as HTTPS, SSL, SSH, or possibly even IPsec) discussed in Chapter 2, "Security Technologies."

Most Cisco IOS routers, catalyst switches, and PIX firewalls have incorporated mechanisms to authenticate and restrict access for HTTP remote access. It is extremely important that these be configured. Some versions of software will have HTTP access turned off by default. It is recommended that if there is no need for HTTP access, that the HTTP server be explicitly disabled.

Cisco IOS Devices

You can issue most of the Cisco IOS commands using a web browser. The Cisco IOS feature is accessed by using the Cisco web browser interface, which is accessed from the router's home page. All Cisco routers and access servers running Cisco IOS Software Release 11.0(6) or later have an HTTP server, which is an embedded subcomponent of the

Cisco Cisco IOS Software. The HTTP server allows users with a privilege level of 15 (or any other configured privilege level) to access the Cisco web browser interface.

```
Router(config)#access-class        Restrict access by access class
authentication       Set HTTP authentication method
port                 HTTP port
server               Enable HTTP server
```

NOTE   Before Cisco IOS Software Release 11.3, only users with privilege level 15 could use this feature, and the only authentication mechanism was the enable password.

You can use three different methods to authenticate HTTP:

```
Router(config)#ip http authentication ?
enable        Use enable passwords
local         Use local username and passwords
tacacs        Use TACACS+ to authorize user
```

To permit users to have access to the HTTP server, you must enable the Cisco web browser interface with the following command:

```
ip http server
```

After you have enabled the Cisco web browser interface, users can use a web browser to access web pages associated with the router and to issue commands. Cisco IOS Software currently allows only users with a privilege level of 15 to access the predefined home page for a router or access server. If you have a privilege level other than 15, you can issue Cisco IOS Software commands from a web page where the commands defined for your specific user privilege level are displayed.

To request a router web page for a privilege level other than the default of 15, perform the following steps:

Step 1   Type the following command in the URL field of your web browser and press Enter (where *mode* refers to the user privilege level):

http://*router-name*/**level**/*mode*/*command*

The browser prompts you for the password.

Step 2   Type the password and press Enter. The web browser should display a web page specific to your user privilege level, mode, and the command you have requested.

The following example shows what you would type in the URL field of your web browser to request a user privilege level of **9** on a Cisco router named Tallinn:

```
http://Tallinn/level/9/exec
```

Example 9-27 shows a configuration in which HTTP access is allowed only from specific hosts and in which the enable password is the method of authenticating HTTP server users.

Example 9-27 *Sample Configuration for Securing HTTP Access in Cisco IOS Software*

```
access-list 6 permit 144.254.5.0 0.0.0.255
!
ip http server
ip http  access-class 6
ip http authentication enable
```

You can find more detailed configuration examples for local authentication for HTTP server users at the Cisco web site at http://www.cisco.com/en/US/tech/tk583/tk642/technologies_configuration_example09186a0080178a51.shtml.

Cisco PIX Firewall

The PIX firewall can also be accessed using a web-based configuration tool. The commands required on the PIX are as follows:

```
http ip_address [netmask] [if_name]
passwd password
```

After you have enabled the Cisco PIX web browser interface by specifying a host IP address, users can use a web browser on the specified host to access web pages associated with the PIX firewall console HTML management interface.

Integrity

Integrity in the campus infrastructure requires that any software image (where *image* is the executable binary images of programs) running on a device must be valid, and that none of the configurations have been altered by any person other than permitted personnel. You want to ensure that only permitted devices are connected to the network, and that no one is injecting any unwanted data. Integrity is largely available through the use of data-authentication methods, such as checksums and hash functions.

Image Authentication

When downloading images onto any network infrastructure device, you may want to ensure that the images have not been modified or changed in transit. Most devices have a checksum verification to ensure that the image will load correctly when the device is rebooted. Any time the checksum does not verify correctly, the image should be erased and replaced with an image containing a successful checksum.

All Cisco Software releases on Cisco Connection Online (CCO) and all floppy disk-based Cisco IOS Software releases subsequent to and including 10.2(5) are protected by MD5 image authentication. MD5, defined in RFC 1321, scans the image and produces a unique 128-bit checksum. The mathematics of the MD5 algorithm give you a checksum mechanism that makes it computationally not feasible to create a substitute file with the same checksum as a chosen target file and therefore helps prevent a specific, targeted attack on a specific file (in this case, the router image).

MD5 allows Cisco Connection Online users to verify that no bits in the image were corrupted during file transfer, reducing the possibility of loading corrupted software onto their routers. MD5 floppy disk verification ensures image integrity on disk-based shipments.

Secure Workgroup

In corporate campus networks, there are increasingly more requests to provide integrity at the workgroup level. On the Catalyst series switches, the *port security* feature allows the switch to block input traffic to an Ethernet or Fast Ethernet port when the MAC address of a station attempting to access the port differs from the configured MAC address. (See Figure 9-3.)

Figure 9-3   *Port Security on a Switch*

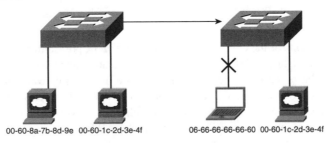

00-60-8a-7b-8d-9e 00-60-1c-2d-3e-4f   06-66-66-66-66-60 00-60-1c-2d-3e-4f

The Port is Disabled When Unexpected MAC Address is Seen

When a port receives a packet, the module compares the source address of that packet to the secure source address learned by the port. When a source address change occurs, the port is disabled, and the LED for that port turns orange. When the port is re-enabled, the port LED turns green.

Secure port filtering does not apply to trunk ports, where the source addresses change frequently.

MAC address security is configured with the following command:

```
set port security modNum/portNum(s) {enable | disable} [mac_addr]
```

If the MAC address is not given, the address is learned. After the address is learned, the address remains unchanged until the system relearns it when you reenter the command. The

MAC address is stored in NVRAM and is maintained even after a reset. When a packet's source address does not match the allowed address, the port through which the packet came is disabled, and a link-down trap is sent to the SNMP manager.

Example 9-28 shows a port security configuration where two critical web servers are connected to ports 2/1 and 2/2 on a switch. In case of a violation, the ports shut down for 1 hour (60 minutes). Although the example only shows the use of a single MAC address per port, multiple MAC addresses (up to 1024) can be used with port security on some switches.

Example 9-28 *Port Security on a Catalyst Switch*

```
! Enable the port security feature on both ports.

 set port security 2/1 enable
Set port seecurity 2/2 enable

! Specify the MAC addresses.

set port security 2/1 enable 00-60-8a-7b-8d-9e
set port security 2/2 enable 00-60-1c-2d-3e-4f

! Configure the time the port shuts down in case of violation.

set port security 2/1 shutdown 60
set port security 2/2 shutdown 60
```

Newer versions of the Cisco switches support 802.1x port authentication. 802.1x was discussed in detail in Chapter 2. 802.1x authenticates each user device that is connected to a switch port and assigns the port to a VLAN before making available any services that are offered by the switch or the LAN. In Catalyst switches, TACACS+, RADIUS, or Kerberos can be used as the authentication protocol, although RADIUS is generally recommended because it has built-in extensions that support EAP frames.

A thorough description and configuration guide for 802.1x port authentication is available from the Cisco website, titled "Configuring 802.1x Authentication." You can find it at http://www.cisco.com/en/US/products/hw/switches/ps708/products_configuration_guide_chapter09186a0080121d12.html.

Routing Authentication

Secure routing encompasses all areas that ensure routing integrity. The simplest way to create complete havoc in a network is to inadvertently inject bogus routes into the core network. This problem can be minimized through the use of route authentication and route filtering.

Route authentication ensures that routing updates come from a trusted source and that none of the data has been tampered with. It uses a *cryptographic checksum*, the one-way hash function, to ensure the authentication of a peer and the integrity of the contents of the routing update.

All peer routers must be configured with a specific key and encryption algorithm. The typical hash algorithms used are MD5, SHA-1, and IDEA. Cisco routers use MD5. The IP routing protocols that currently support route authentication include the following:

- Routing Information Protocol version 2 (RIPv2)
- Border Gateway Protocol (BGP)
- Open Shortest Path First (OSPF)
- Enhanced Interior Gateway Routing Protocol (EIGRP)
- Intermediate System-to-Intermediate System (IS-IS)

For the IP routing protocols in Cisco routers that do not support MD5 route authentication, RIPv1, or IGRP, the command **validate-update-source** enables you to ensure that the source IP address of incoming routing updates is on the same IP network as one of the addresses defined for the receiving interface. This feature is on by default.

Example 9-29 shows a sample configuration for two routers using EIGRP and route authentication. (See Figure 9-4.)

Example 9-29 *Sample Configuration for EIGRP Route Authentication*

```
Hostname Building1
!
key chain To-Bldg2
key 1
key-string secretkey
accept-lifetime 08:30:00 June 6 1998 infinite
send-lifetime 08:30:00 June 6 1998 infinite
!
interface FE 1
ip address 144.254.2.2 255.255.255.0
ip authentication mode eigrp 109 md5
ip authentication key-chain eigrp 109 toBuilding1
!
router eigrp 109
network 144.254.0.0

Hostname Building2
!
key chain To-Bldg1
key 1
key-string secretkey
accept-lifetime 08:30:00 June 6 1998 infinite
send-lifetime 08:30:00 June 6 1998 infinite
!
interface FE 1
ip address 144.254.2.3 255.255.255.0
ip authentication mode eigrp 109 md5
ip authentication key-chain eigrp 109 toBuilding2
!
router eigrp 109
network 144.254.0.0
```

Figure 9-4 *Route Authentication*

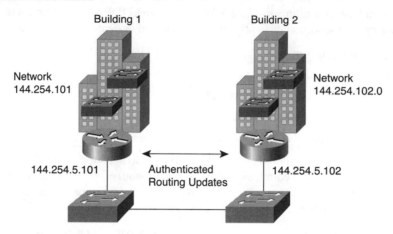

NOTE   Router clocks should be synchronized with Network Time Protocol (NTP) if route authentication is to work properly.

Route Filters and Routing Believability

By default, all dynamic routing protocols propagate routing information. At times, you may not want certain other devices or portions of your network to learn your network topology from the routing protocol. If this is the case, you must take explicit steps to prevent route propagation.

To prevent routing updates through a specified router interface, use the following command in router configuration mode:

passive interface [*interface type and number*]

To prevent other routers from learning one or more routes, you can suppress routes from being advertised in routing updates. You do this to prevent other routers from learning a particular device's interpretation of one or more routes. To suppress routes from being advertised in routing updates, use the following command in router configuration mode:

distribute-list {*access-list-number | name*} **out** [*interface-name*]

You may want to avoid processing certain routes listed in incoming updates. This feature does not apply to OSPF or IS-IS. To avoid processing certain routes, configure the following command in router configuration mode:

distribute-list {*access-list-number | name*} **in** [*interface-name*]

It is also possible to filter sources of routing information. You can do this to prioritize routing information from different sources, because some pieces of routing information may be more accurate than others. For Cisco IOS routers, an administrative distance enables you to rate the trustworthiness of a routing information source, such as an individual router or a group of routers. In a large network, some routing protocols and some routers can be more reliable than others as sources of routing information. Also, when multiple routing processes are running in the same router for IP, it is possible for the same route to be advertised by more than one routing process. By specifying administrative distance values, you enable the router to intelligently discriminate between sources of routing information. The router will always pick the route with a routing protocol that has the lowest administrative distance. To filter sources of routing information, give the following command in router configuration mode:

```
distance weight [address mask [access-list-number | name]] [ip]
```

The *weight* argument can be an integer from 10 to 255. (The values 0 to 9 are reserved for internal use.) Used alone, the *weight* argument specifies a default administrative distance that the Cisco IOS Software uses when no other specification exists for a routing information source. Routes with a distance of 255 are not installed in the routing table.

WARNING   None of the preceding commands with the distribution and attributes attached to distributed routes should be played with lightly. In nontrivial networks, unpredictable and disruptive behavior can result.

Figure 9-5 shows a sample scenario in which the core network is comprised of 100BASE-T switches connected to routers. 10 BASE-T interfaces are used to connect the local LANs using the RIP routing protocol. Route filtering enables you to ensure that only default routes are announced on the local LANs and that no inadvertent, misbehaving host can source a default route to the backbone.

Figure 9-5   *Controlling Routing Information*

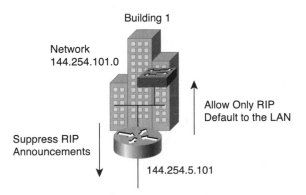

NOTE   If you are using DHCP on the LAN, the hosts on the LAN have a default router configured and there is no need to use RIP. In fact, by configuring default routes and using HSRP (HSRP is discussed later in this chapter in the section "Redundancy Features"), the need for running any routing protocols on hosts, even just to listen to updates, is no longer necessary.

Example 9-30 shows a sample router configuration illustrating the use of the **passive interface**, **distance**, and **distribute list** commands.

Example 9-30   *Sample Configuration for Route Filtering and Route Believability*

```
router eigrp 109
network 144.254.0.0
distance 255
distance 100 144.254.5.0 0.0.0.255
!
router rip
network 144.254.0.0
passive interface FE 1/0
distribute list 11 out
distance 255
!
access-list 11 permit 0.0.0.0
```

In the configuration in Example 9-30, the **passive interface** command is not required for the LAN interface for EIGRP because EIGRP requires a neighbor before sending out routing updates. Because no other EIGRP neighbors exist on the LAN, no routing updates will be sent out.

Data Confidentiality

Data confidentiality pertains to encryption. Whether you encrypt traffic within the main corporate infrastructure depends largely on how sensitive the information is and how likely it is that the data can be intercepted. In many environments, encryption of sensitive data occurs mostly between dial-in access points and Internet access points.

Within the corporate network infrastructure, confidentiality is important when accessing device information. Typically, it is prudent to encrypt the following:

- Telnet sessions to devices
- TFTP configuration downloads
- SNMP transactions to and from network devices
- HTTP access to device information

Kerberos-encrypted Telnet can be used to provide confidential Telnet access. (The Cisco IOS Software has included this feature since Cisco IOS Software Release 11.2.) Figure 9-6 shows some likely traffic that would require confidentiality for corporate infrastructure devices: Telnet sessions, SNMP sessions, TFTP sessions, and HTTP sessions. SSH and IPsec offer such support. The choice of which technology to use depends largely on what is currently supported in various products. Most recent software versions of Cisco IOS routers, Catalyst switches, and the PIX firewall all have SSH and IPsec capability. IPsec configuration is discussed in more detail in Chapter 11, "Securing Remote Dial-In Access," and Chapter 12, "Securing VPN, Wireless, and VoIP Networks."

Figure 9-6   *Secure Access to Corporate Infrastructure Devices*

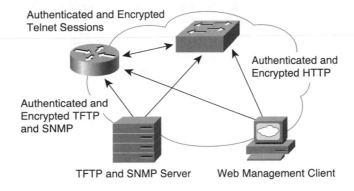

Network Availability

Network availability ensures that redundancy measures are in place and that features arc configured to deter most common attacks. For critical devices, redundant power supplies are a must. (Don't forget to put them on separate circuits—not just separate power outlets—leading to a distinctly separate circuit breaker at the distribution panel.) There are two reasons for incurring the expense of this kind of redundant power supply:

- Should a power supply fail, it might cause the circuit to go dead. (That is, it will cause the breaker back at the distribution panel to blow open.)

- The startup inrush current of two supplies in parallel can cause a breaker to open up.

You also may want to consider uninterruptable power supplies (UPSs) as insurance against catastrophic power outages. The UPSs should be rated to carry the maximum load for at least 10 minutes, and the UPS should be able to deliver a notification or warning to the operator when the UPS senses that the primary power has failed for more than approximately 30 seconds. If there is a possibility of severe electrical outages, you may want to consider a backup generator if your network requires continuous uptime.

NOTE	To determine whether the additional cost of a UPS makes sense, consider the impact of a power loss or downtime for each piece of equipment. If a 100BASE-T switch goes down in a building and is on the same power supply as most of the building's users, it may not make sense to keep the switch operational. However, if a router is on the same power supply, and the design of the network is such that the router must stay up to continue giving valid routing information to other routers, a UPS for the router would be necessary.

Redundancy Features

Equipment redundancy is largely an issue of how quickly the outage of a piece of equipment can be resolved. Any network infrastructure device that must be available 100 percent of the time is an obvious candidate for complete redundancy to cover the worst possible scenario. Many devices have incorporated redundant processor cards in high-performance equipment to ensure a smooth, dynamic failover in the event of single-card failures. In addition, new protocols or enhancements to existing protocols have been developed to ensure that redundancy with multiple boxes have failover capability without user intervention. To have redundant coverage, make sure that failover to the backup system happens automatically.

Cisco IOS

For critical network segments that cannot have any routing outages, the Cisco IOS devices supporting these segments should be configured with the Hot Standby Router Protocol (HSRP). HSRP provides high network availability because it routes IP traffic from hosts on Ethernet, FDDI, or Token Ring networks without relying on the availability of any single router.

When HSRP is configured on a network segment, it provides a virtual MAC address and an IP address that is shared among routers in a group of routers that is running the HSRP. One of these devices is selected by the protocol to be the active router. The active router receives and routes packets destined for the group's MAC address. For n routers running the HSRP, there are $n + 1$ IP and MAC addresses assigned.

The HSRP detects when the designated active router fails, at which point a selected standby router assumes control of the hot standby group's MAC and IP addresses. A new standby router is also selected at that time.

Devices running the HSRP send and receive multicast UDP-based hello packets to detect router failure and to designate active and standby routers.

NOTE	When the HSRP is configured on an interface, ICMP redirect messages are disabled by default for the interface.

The HSRP feature is configured with the following interface command:

```
standby [group-number] ip [ip-address [secondary]]
```

You can configure a number of group attributes to affect how the local router participates in the HSRP. Here is an example of these attributes:

```
Router(config)#int e 0
Router(config-if)#standby ?
<0-255>              Group number
authentication      Authentication string
ip                  Enable hot standby protocol for IP
mac-address         Specify virtual MAC address for the virtual router
preempt             Overthrow lower priority designated routers
priority            Priority level
timers              Hot standby timers
track               Priority tracks this interface state
use-bia             Hot standby uses interface's burned-in address
```

Consider the scenario shown in Figure 9-7.

Figure 9-7   *An Example of HSRP Implementation*

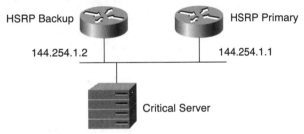

The configuration of a primary router is shown in Example 9-31.

Example 9-31 *Primary Router HSRP Configuration*

```
hostname Primary
!
interface Ethernet1
  ip address 144.254.1.1 255.255.255.0
  no ip redirects
  standby priority 200
  standby preempt
  standby ip 144.254.1.3
```

The configuration of a standby router is shown in Example 9-32.

Example 9-32 *Standby Router HSRP Configuration*

```
hostname Standby
!
interface Ethernet1
  ip address 144.254.1.2 255.255.255.0
  no ip redirects
  standby priority 101
  standby ip 144.254.1.3
```

Cisco Switches

Switches are normally connected hierarchically, as shown in Figure 9-8. Although there still exist large flat networks built with switches, a hierarchtical architecture is much more manageable and can use features to address security issues, such as the ones discussed in this section.

Figure 9-8   *An Example of Switch Hierarchy*

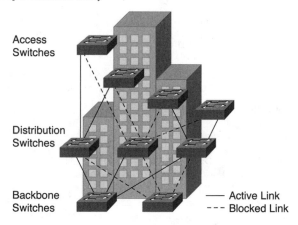

In simple networks, the upper two levels of the hierarchy can be collapsed into a single backbone layer. Figure 9-8 shows the network topology after the spanning tree converges into a loop-free topology. The spanning tree has blocked the redundant links to avoid loops. Every access switch and distribution switch in the figure has a redundant uplink.

The Spanning Tree Protocol

The Spanning Tree Protocol (STP; IEEE 802.1D bridge protocol) is a link-management protocol that provides path redundancy while preventing undesirable loops in the network. For an Ethernet network to function properly, only one active path must exist between two stations. In STP, an algorithm calculates the best loop-free path through a switched network. Switches send and receive spanning-tree packets at regular intervals. The switches do not forward the packets, but use the packets to identify a loop-free path.

To provide path redundancy, STP defines a tree that spans all switches in an extended network. STP forces certain redundant data paths into a standby (blocked) state. If one network segment in the STP becomes unreachable, or if STP costs change, the spanning-tree algorithm reconfigures the spanning-tree topology and reestablishes the link by activating the standby path.

STP operation is transparent to end stations, which do not detect whether they are connected to a single LAN segment or to a switched LAN of multiple segments.

Election of the Root Switch

All switches in an extended LAN participating in STP gather information on other switches in the network through an exchange of data messages called *bridge protocol data units* (BPDUs). This exchange of messages results in the following actions:

- The election of a unique root switch for the stable spanning-tree network topology
- The election of a designated switch for every switched LAN segment
- The removal of loops in the switched network by placing redundant switch ports in a backup state

The STP root switch is the logical center of the spanning-tree topology in a switched network. All paths that are not needed to reach the root switch from anywhere in the switched network are placed in STP blocked mode.

Bridge Protocol Data Units

BPDUs contain information about the transmitting switch and its ports, including switch and port Media Access Control (MAC) addresses, switch priority, port priority, and port cost. The STP uses this information to elect the root switch and root port for the switched network, as well as the root port and designated port for each switched segment.

The stable active topology of a switched network is determined by the following:

- The unique switch identifier (MAC address) associated with each switch
- The path cost to the root associated with each switch port
- The port identifier (MAC address) associated with each switch port

Each configuration BPDU contains the following minimal information:

- The unique identifier of the switch that the transmitting switch believes to be the root switch
- The cost of the path to the root from the transmitting port
- The identifier of the transmitting port

The switch sends configuration BPDUs to communicate with and compute the spanning-tree topology. A MAC frame conveying a BPDU sends the switch group address to the destination address field. All switches connected to the LAN on which the frame is transmitted receive the BPDU. BPDUs are not directly forwarded by the switch, but the receiving switch uses the information in the frame to calculate a BPDU, and, if the topology changes, to initiate a BPDU transmission.

A BPDU exchange results in the following:

- One switch is elected as the root switch.
- The shortest distance to the root switch is calculated for each switch.

- A designated switch is selected. This is the switch closest to the root switch through which frames will be forwarded to the root.

- A port for each switch is selected. This is the port providing the best path from the switch to the root switch.

- Ports included in the STP are selected.

Creating a Stable STP Topology

If all switches are enabled with default settings, the switch with the lowest MAC address in the network becomes the root switch. In some cases, however (because of traffic patterns, the number of forwarding ports, or line types), the switch picked as the root may not be the ideal root switch. By increasing the priority (that is, by lowering the numeric priority number) of the ideal switch so that it becomes the root switch, you force an STP recalculation to form a new, stable topology.

The time it takes to detect and correct failures is important. For Cisco switches, the Spanning Tree Protocol UPlinkFast and BackboneFast features reduce spanning-tree convergence times. *UPlinkFast* provides fast convergence after a spanning-tree topology change and achieves load balancing between redundant links using uplink groups. An *uplink group* is a set of ports (per VLAN), only one of which is forwarding at any given time. Specifically, an uplink group consists of the root port (which is forwarding) and a set of blocked ports, except for self-looping ports. The uplink group provides an alternative path in case the currently forwarding link fails. Be warned that the topology must not allow loops during a change. The topology must be architected so that one can turn off spanning tree's normal behavior and make the link transition without creating any loops.

NOTE   The UPlinkFast feature is most useful in wiring-closet switches. This feature may not be useful for other types of applications.

To configure a switch as the primary root switch, enter this command:

```
set spantree root vlans [diameter network_diameter] [hello hello_time]
```

This command reduces the bridge priority (the value associated with the switch) from the default (32,768) to a significantly lower value, which allows the switch to become the root switch.

NOTE   Run the **set spantree root** command on backbone switches or distribution switches only; do not run it on access switches.

To configure a switch as the secondary root switch, enter this command:

```
set spantree root [secondary] vlans [dia network_diameter] [hello hello_time]
```

You can run this command on more than one switch to create multiple backup switches in case the primary root switch fails.

The *BackboneFast Convergence feature* reduces the time needed for the spanning tree to converge after experiencing a topology change caused by indirect link failures. This feature complements the UPlinkFast feature just described. However, the BackboneFast Convergence feature is designed for all switches that experience indirect link failures.

NOTE   For the BackboneFast feature to work, you must enable it on all switches in the network.

To configure the BackboneFast Convergence feature, enter this command:

```
set spantree backbonefast enable
```

The *Multiple Default IP Gateways feature* enables you to configure up to three default IP gateways. Defining multiple default IP gateways provides redundancy. In the event that the primary gateway cannot be reached, the switch uses the secondary default IP gateways in the order in which they are configured. This feature is configured with the following command:

```
set ip route destination gateway [metric] [primary]
```

Use the **primary** keyword to give a default IP gateway higher priority than the other default IP gateway(s). If you do not designate a primary default IP gateway, the system chooses the default IP gateway based on the order in which the gateways were configured. If two or more gateways are designated as primary gateways, the system chooses the *last* primary gateway configured to be the default IP gateway.

Cisco PIX Firewall

The Cisco PIX firewall is usually a critical device in most corporate infrastructures. To eliminate it being a single point of failure, it is prudent to install a redundant PIX firewall and to use the **failover** command to ensure fast dynamic recovery in the event that the primary PIX has a power failure or some other type of failure. There are two modes of failover:

- **Stateless**—When the active PIX firewall fails and the standby PIX becomes active, all connections are lost and the client applications must initiate new connections.

- **Stateful**—When the active PIX firewall fails and the standby PIX becomes available, connection information is available at the new PIX and client applications retain their communication sessions. The TCP connection table is synchronized with the secondary PIX over an interface configured for stateful failover. The interface must be a dedicated 100-Mbps Ethernet interaface. (For the PIX 535, it can also be a Gigabit interface.) Some information that is not included and needs to be rebuilt includes IPsec SA tables, ARP tables, and routing information.

The default failover setup uses serial cable failover, where the serial failover cable is a cross-over cable. For serial cable failover, use the **failover** command without an argument after you connect the optional failover cable between your primary PIX firewall and a secondary PIX firewall. The default configuration has failover enabled. Enter **no failover** in the configuration file for the PIX firewall if you will not be using the failover feature. Use the **show failover** command to verify the status of the connection and to determine which unit is active.

LAN-based failover requires explicit LAN-based failover configuration using the **failover lan** commands. The **show failover lan** command displays LAN-based failover information. In addition, for LAN-based failover, you must install a dedicated 100-Mbps or Gigabit Ethernet, full-duplex VLAN switch connection for failover operations. Failover is not supported using a crossover Ethernet cable between two PIX firewall units. Although the same dedicated interface can also be used for stateful failover, it is recommended to use two separate interfaces because many times the dedicated interface does not have enough capacity to handle both the LAN-based failover and stateful failover traffic.

NOTE   The PIX 506/506E cannot be used for failover in any configuration. The primary unit in the PIX 515/515E, PIX 525, or PIX 535 failover pair must have an unrestricted (UR) license. The secondary unit can have failover (FO) or UR license. However, the failover pair must be two otherwise identical units with the same PIX firewall hardware and software.

It is possible to force a failover by using the **failover active** command to initiate a failover switch from the standby unit, or the **no failover active** command from the active unit to initiate a failover switch. This proves useful when returning a previously failed unit to service, or to force an active unit off line for maintenance.

Failover IP addresses must be configured on each interface card. The active unit of the failover pair uses the system IP addresses and the primary unit's MAC address; the standby unit uses the failover IP addresses and the secondary unit's MAC address. The system IP addresses and the failover IP addresses must be on the same subnet with no router between them.

The **failover mac address** command is used to configure a virtual MAC address for a PIX firewall failover pair. It sets the PIX firewall to use the virtual MAC address stored in the PIX firewall configuration after failover, instead of obtaining a MAC address by contacting its failover peer. This enables the PIX firewall failover pair to maintain the correct MAC addresses after failover. If a virtual MAC address is not specified, the PIX firewall failover pair uses the burned-in network interface card (NIC) address as the MAC address. For LAN-based failover, this command is not needed because the IP and MAC addresses do not change when a failover occurs.

NOTE	Both PIX firewall units in a failover pair must have the same configuration. To accomplish this, always enter configuration changes on the active unit in a PIX firewall failover configuration. Use the **write memory** command on the active unit to save configuration changes to Flash memory (nonvolatile memory) on both the active and the standby units. Changes made on the standby unit are not replicated on the active unit.

Both units in a failover pair communicate through the failover cable. The two units send special failover hello packets to each other over all network interfaces and the failover cable every 15 seconds. The failover feature in PIX firewall monitors failover communication, the power status of the other unit, and the hello packets received at each interface. If two consecutive hello packets are not received within a time determined by the failover feature, failover starts testing the interfaces to determine which unit has failed and transfers active control to the standby unit.

Common Attack Deterrents

A multitude of types of attacks can bring a network to its knees. Many can be avoided or constrained with features that have been specifically developed to deter some of the better-known attacks. Appendix D, "Mitigating Distributed Denial-of-Service Attacks," specifically describes some filtering techniques to use for mitigating distributed denial-of-service (DDoS) attacks. Filtering and logging any violations are by far the most effective ways to mitigate and trace many attacks. The following sections describe some additional features that you may find useful to deploy.

Spoofed Packets

Although it is very difficult to actually recognize spoofed packets, you can use some mechanisms to help prevent some more obvious spoofs. Some of these packets may be caused by simple misconfigurations and routing loops. Whenever possible, filters should be put into place to ensure that only valid network addresses are permitted past the routers. All corporate infrastructure routers should have filters in place to disallow any obviously bogus traffic. For example, any edge router should deny traffic whose source address is one of the RFC reserved addresses shown in Table 9-9.

Table 9-9   *RFC Reserved Addresses*

Network IP Address	Mask
127.0.0.0	0.255.255.255
10.0.0.0	0.255.255.255
172.16.0.0	0.15.255.255
192.168.0.0	0.0.255.255

These IP addresses are specified for special use and are therefore designated as nonroutable in the Internet infrastructure. (That is, no Internet service provider will route these networks; therefore, no edge routers connecting to the Internet should receive packets with these addresses as a source.)

Some devices also have features to assist in tracking down the source of packets with invalid source addresses. For Cisco IOS devices, this is an extension of the access list logging feature that will show the input interface for packets. (For a detailed discussion on Cisco IOS access lists, refer to Chapter 10, "Securing Internet Access.") It is enabled by adding **log-input** to an access list entry:

```
access-list 100 permit ip any host 171.69.233.3 log-input
```

The output from this command looks like this:

```
%SEC-6-IPACCESSLOGP: list 100 permitted udp 171.69.2.132(53)
(Ethernet0/0)-> 171.69.233.3(5775), 1 packet
%SEC-6-IPACCESSLOGDP: list 100 permitted icmp 171.69.2.75
(Ethernet0/0) -> 171.69.233.3 (0/0), 1 packet
```

Fragmentation Attacks

To deter any attack based on fragments, the device must have an option to reassemble the original packet, ensure that the packet is valid, and then fragment the packet again before forwarding it. This check can severely limit system performance; think carefully before rushing off to implement this feature on every device. It is best to determine the most critical, vulnerable area and then place the deterrent there. In most instances in a large corporate network, the most vulnerable areas are at the network access points, such as Internet access or dial-in access.

Broadcast Attacks

Some attacks are based on flooding networks with traffic based on directed broadcast addresses, such as the Smurf and Fraggle attacks discussed in Chapter 5, " Threats in an Enterprise Network." The Cisco IOS command **no ip directed-broadcast** should be configured on every interface to avoid traffic being broadcast out.

An effective mechanism to be alerted to these types of attacks is to configure filters that would permit ICMP echo requests/replies (for Smurf attacks) or UDP echo requests (for Fraggle attacks). By logging and monitoring this traffic, it is possible to detect whether such an attack is in progress. The source addresses are the addresses of the Smurf or Fraggle reflectors. By looking up the owners of these address blocks in the appropriate Internet "whois" databases, the administrators of these networks can be located and asked for their help in dealing with the attack.

It's important to remember that these reflectors are fellow victims, *not* attackers. It's extremely rare for attackers to use their own source addresses on IP packets in any DoS flood, and impossible for them to do so in a working Smurf attack. Any address in a flood packet should be assumed to be either completely falsified, or the address of a compromised victim. The most productive approach for the ultimate target of a Smurf attack is to contact the reflectors, either to ask them to reconfigure their networks to shut down the attack, or to ask for their assistance in tracing the attack stream.

NOTE   Temporary filters can be put in place to filter out all attack traffic or the attack traffic from specified hosts. This sort of filter shouldn't usually be left in place permanently. Temporary filters are very often used when large streams of DoS traffic is causing severe network outages. It is good practice to have a template already configured which can then be modified depending on the attack and applied to the appropriate device interface.

TCP SYN Attack

It is important to recognize that it is nearly impossible to stop a TCP SYN flooding attack. What can be done, however, is to constrain its impact on critical parts of the network.

Typically, a firewall is set up to act as a proxy when a TCP connection is established. A TCP proxy is a server that acts as an intermediary between a client and a destination server. Clients establish connections to the TCP proxy server, which then establishes a connection to the destination server. The proxy server sends data received from the client to the destination server and forwards data received from the destination server to the client. The TCP proxy server acts as both a server and a client.

The firewall checks for incoming TCP connection requests and then acts as the TCP proxy. (See Figure 9-9.)

Figure 9-9 *A TCP Proxy*

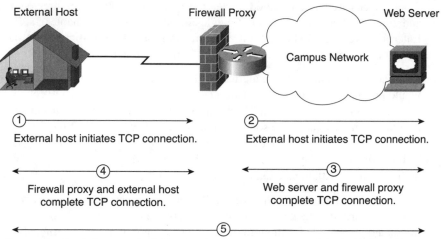

In the case of bogus requests, the firewall usually also has parameters to set very aggressive timeouts on half-open connections; it also has parameters to set threshold levels for the number of both outstanding connections and the incoming rate of TCP-connection requests.

WARNING Be careful when changing any TCP timer parameters. You don't want them so short that valid connections from slower links time out.

On the Cisco IOS devices, the command to use against TCP SYN attacks is this one:

```
ip tcp intercept access-list-number
ip tcp intercept mode watch
```

This command keeps track of the following information:

- How many session requests were there in the last one minute?

- How many incomplete sessions are there?

- How long is the wait for the final acknowledgment?

For the PIX firewall, you can issue the following command to limit the number of half-open TCP connections and total number of TCP connections allowed:

```
static 172.17.1.12 10.1.1.2 [max_conns] [em_limit]
```

In this syntax, *max_conns* is the maximum number of TCP connections allowed, and *em_limit* is the embryonic connection (half-open connection) limit. Refer to Chapter 10 for a more complete description.

Audit

The audit element is necessary to verify that the security policy is being adhered to. This includes making sure that the network infrastructure is configured as expected and that networking activity is effectively monitored to detect any unusual behavior and possible intrusions.

WARNING   All communication between auditing servers and network infrastructure devices should be authenticated and confidential (that is, encrypted) whenever possible. Audit logs should also be saved on write-once media (for example, WORM drives) or should be sent over a network to a trusted system that is inaccessible by the administrators of the system being audited. This way, if a break-in occurs, the intruder cannot erase his tracks.

Configuration Verification

It is important to verify that network infrastructure device configurations are valid to ensure proper implementation behavior. Verification of configurations is usually performed with some kind of modeling or simulation tool that can access all the infrastructure device configurations and then provide a simulation model that can be tested. Here is a list of some areas to be modeled:

- Mapping current network topology
- Identifying services on hosts
- Performing "what-if" scenarios to detect filtering problems
- Performing sample attack scenarios to find vulnerabilities

In addition, a variety of available tools can launch well-known attacks. These are either available from vendors or as free software. Using these tools on a regular basis, usually after significant configuration changes or software upgrades, can be a proactive way to avoid finding configuration mistakes while a security breach is in progress.

Monitoring and Logging Network Activity

This area intersects with network management; you can monitor system usage and traffic patterns to help determine what normal behavior is. There are numerous ways to accomplish this, but the main focus should be what to monitor and log. At the very least, you want to keep track of network usage and any high volumes of data traffic.

Event logging is very important in keeping track of various system information. Event logging automatically logs output from system error messages and other events to the console terminal. You may want to redirect these messages to another destination (such as syslog servers that can be used as a single destination point for all infrastructure system information). You should be able to specify the severity of the event to be logged; you also want to configure the logged output to be timestamped. The logged output can be used to assist real-time debugging and management and to track potential security breaches or other nonstandard activities throughout a network. The time stamps need to be accurate and synchronized. All Cisco devices have the capability to configure the standardized Network Time Protocol (NTP), which enables you to distribute accurate time. Many publicly available time servers can be used as sources. Refer to http://www.eecis.udel.edu/~mills/ntp/servers.html to get a complete list of them. In addition, Cisco IOS Software provides the capability to be a time source. For large networks, this should be used so as not to overly burden any publicly available NTP source. It is then also possible to set up MD5 authentication between the Cisco IOS Software time source and the other routers, switches, and firewalls that use it.

It is good security practice to use the syslog facility as well as keep a local log on the device itself, if the device supports it. This keeps some logging information available should the network be inaccessible or the syslog server itself be compromised. Once configured, verify that the time stamps match on both logs to avoid any later confusion. It is common to use the same NTP time source(s) across infrastructure devices.

NOTE   If you are using Cisco IOS routers, features such as NetFlow and IP accounting may prove useful to keep traffic statistics information. The IP accounting support also provides information identifying IP traffic that fails IP access lists. Identifying IP source addresses that violate IP access lists alerts you to possible attempts to breach security. To use this feature, you must enable IP accounting of access list violations using the **ip accounting access-violations** command. Users can then display the number of bytes and packets from a single source that attempted to breach security against the access list for the source-destination pair.

Syslog Management

Syslog messages are based on the User Datagram Protocol (UDP) and are received on UDP port 514. The message text is kept under 512 bytes to ensure that the UDP packet is smaller than 576 bytes—the smallest packet that must be accepted by a host without packet fragmentation.

Syslog messages are categorized by eight priority levels, shown in Table 9-10.

Table 9-10   *Syslog Priority Codes*

Priority	Code	Description
LOG_EMERG	0	Emergency or panic condition messages
LOG_ALERT	1	Conditions that should be corrected immediately
LOG_CRIT	2	Critical conditions
LOG_ERR	3	Errors
LOG_WARNIN G	4	Warnings
LOG_NOTICE	5	Not error conditions, but may require special handling
LOG_INFO	6	Informational messages
LOG_DEBUG	7	Debugging messages

Syslog messages generated by various devices can be logged locally or redirected to a log file or syslog management server. A syslog management server can be used to collect all syslog information that is deemed critical as part of the corporate network for auditing purposes.

Example 9-33, Example 9-34, and Example 9-35 illustrate how to configure syslog logging on a Cisco IOS router, Catalyst switch, and PIX firewall, respectively.

Example 9-33   *Syslog Logging and Accurate Time Stamps Using NTP on a Cisco IOS Router*

```
! These commands configure the granularity of the time stamps.

service timestamps debug datetime localtime show-timezone
service timestamps log datetime localtime show-timezone

! Allow an internal buffer to log up to 32000 bytes of data.
! When the maximum is reached, the older data will be overwritten.

logging buffered 32000 informational

! Do not allow for logging on the console interface.

no logging console

! Set up all messages with a severity of up to 6 (informational) to be
! sent to the syslog server.

logging trap informational

! Specify the facility expected by the syslog server in the messages sent to it.

logging facility local1
```

continues

Example 9-33 *Syslog Logging and Accurate Time Stamps Using NTP on a Cisco IOS Router (Continued)*

```
! Specify the syslog server IP address.

logging 144.254.5.5

! Configure multiple NTP time sources for redundancy.

ntp server 192.5.41.40
ntp server 192.36.143.150
```

NOTE   By default, a Cisco router will act as an NTP server if one or more NTP servers are configured. If the router is not responsible for providing time service to other networking devices, NTP should be disabled on all interfaces except for the one from where the NTP time is obtained.

Example 9-34 *Syslog Logging and Accurate Time Stamps Using NTP on a Catalyst Switch*

```
! Turn logging on.

set logging server enable

! Specify the facility expected by the syslog server in the messages sent to it.

set logging server facility local 2

! Set up all messages with a severity of up to 6 (informational) to
! be sent to the syslog server.

set logging server severity 6

! Specify the syslog server IP address.

set logging server 144.254.5.5

! Turn on NTP in client mode so that it interacts with an NTP master device.

set ntp client enable

! Configure multiple NTP master devices for redundancy.

ntp server 192.5.41.40
ntp server 192.36.143.150
```

Example 9-35 *Syslog Logging and Accurate Time Stamps Using NTP on a PIX Firewall*

```
! Turn logging on.

logging on

! Specify the facility expected by the syslog server in the messages sent to it.

logging  facility 3

! Set up all messages with a severity of up to 6 (informational)
! to be sent to the syslog server.

logging trap informational

! Specify the syslog server IP address.

logging host inside 144.254.5.5

! Configure multiple NTP master devices for redundancy.

ntp server 192.5.41.40
ntp server 192.36.143.150
```

Intrusion Detection

Intrusion detection refers to the real-time monitoring of network activity and the analyzing of data for potential vulnerabilities and attacks in progress. Internal, authorized users conducting unauthorized activity on the network—such as trying to transmit confidential documents over the Internet or illegally modifying network access privileges—can be detected in real time and stopped immediately. An external intruder trying to break into the network can be handled in the same manner.

Real-time capability (as opposed to a periodic review of log files) can significantly reduce potential damage and recovery costs of an attack by eliminating the intruder from the network.

As mentioned in Chapter 8, "Incident Handling," a good intrusion system should have the following characteristics:

- It must run continuously without human supervision. The system must be reliable enough to allow it to run in the background of the system being observed.

- It must be fault tolerant in the sense that it must survive a system crash and not require its knowledge base to be rebuilt at restart.

- It must resist subversion. The system can monitor itself to ensure that it has not been subverted.

- It must impose minimal overhead on the system. A system that slows a computer to a crawl will simply not be used.

- It must observe deviations from normal behavior and immediately alert someone in the event of abnormal behavior.

- It must cope with changing system behavior over time as new applications are being added.

The ability to write customized detection rules for proprietary purposes is also of interest. You may want to write customized detection rules to prevent a document labeled "confidential" from being e-mailed outside the network or to address vulnerabilities for custom or legacy systems. Such customization allows the system to be modified for use in almost any environment, even if those uses are not common enough to be included as standard features of a commercial product.

Cisco has a number of products and features that provide intrusion detection functions. The standalone IDS 4200 series sensors along with the Cisco Secure Policy Manager provide extensive capabilities to implement a robust network surveillance system. Rather than attempt a suboptimal brief summary of such an important function, the reader is referred to the Cisco Press book *Cisco Secure Intrusion Detection Systems*, which provides in-depth coverage of the standalone system. For many networks, a standalone network intrusion detection system should be an integral part of any secure network architecture.

In addition, Cisco IOS Software, the Catalyst 6000 IDSM (Intrusion Detection System Module) sensor, and the PIX firewall provide limited capabilities to identify and log attack signatures but can be used effectively in some environments where the cost of standalone intrusion detection systems is prohibitive. Take extreme care when configuring this functionality to ensure that the device can handle the potential traffic processing. The Cisco IOS Software and PIX firewall configurations are shown in this chapter. However, the Catalyst 6000 IDSM requires a more in-depth understanding; an excellent document titled "Catalyst 6000 IDSM Installation and Configuration Note 2.5," on the Cisco web site provides a thorough description of its use. You can find this document at http://www.cisco.com/en/US/products/sw/secursw/ps2113/products_installation_ and_configuration_guide09186a00800f24fe.html.

Cisco IOS

The Cisco IOS Image needs to include the Cisco Secure Integrated (that is, the firewall/intrusion detection system [IDS]) Software to use it as an IDS sensor. It has so far incorporated 59 of the most common attack signatures that are used to detect patterns of misuse in network traffic. They are categorized as information signatures, such as port scans and echo requests, or as attack signatures, such as common DoS attacks. The router can be configured to send an alarm, drop traffic, or perform TCP resets for any traffic it considers malicious. In addition, the router has the capability to disable the use of a specific signature if it causes too many false alarms.

NOTE	When using the IDS capability, the packets are only scanned if they are actually being routed and therefore will not detect attacks that occur between hosts on the same LAN.

Routers log the alarm events via syslog. The router can also interact with a management system using the Post Office Protocol (UDP port 45000) such as the Cisco Secure Policy Manager or the Cisco Secure IDS Director (also called Netranger Director) to receive alarm information. This communication is not confidential, and IPsec should be used to provide authentication and confidentiality for the management communication.

Configuration of the router IDS sensor requires the use of the **ip audit** commands. Example 9-36 illustrates a sample configuration where the logs are sent to a syslog server. Only the relevant IDS commands are shown.

Example 9-36 *Cisco IOS IDS Configuration*

```
! Specify the syslog server IP address.

logging 144.254.5.5

! Initialize the IDS facility with the following command.
! It denotes the maximum number of e-mail recipients
! in a given mail message before the mail is categorized as spam.

ip audit smtp spam 200

! Configure the IDS alerts to be sent to syslog and a buffered log.

ip audit notify log

! Define the audit rule that will be used to take action on informational
! signatures and attack signatures.
! For informational signatures only an alarm will be logged but for attack
! signatures an alarm will
! be logged and the traffic will be dropped and the TCP connection will be reset.

ip audit name E10Audit info action alarm
ip audit name E10Audit attack action alarm drop reset

! Apply the rule to the Ethernet 1/0 interface.

interface Ethernet 1/0
   description Connection to Branch Office
   ip audit E10Audit in
```

PIX Firewall

You can make the PIX firewall act as an IDS sensor by using the **ip audit** commands. The PIX does not communicate with a management console, but all alarms can be logged via syslog. Because the sensing module sits on the packet path, it inspects the packets inline. The PIX can be configured to send an alarm, drop traffic, or perform TCP resets for any traffic it considers malicious. Example 9-37 illustrates a sample configuration showing only the relevant IDS commands.

Example 9-37 *PIX IDS Configuration*

```
! Specify the syslog server IP address.

logging host inside 144.254.5.5

! Define the audit rule that will be used to take action
! on informational signatures.
! In this case, only an alarm will be logged.

ip audit name InfoAudit info action alarm

! Define the audit rule that will be used to take action on
! attack signatures - offending packets
! will be dropped and the connections will be reset.
! An alarm will also be logged.

ip audit name AttackAudit attack action alarm drop reset

! The rules are now applied to an interface.  Up to two rules can be
! applied per interface.

ip audit interface outside InfoAudit
ip audit interface outside AttackAudit
```

Network Forensics

Although you may have taken every conceivable precaution to prevent security breaches, you must not be fooled into thinking that they will never occur. It is quite probable that at some point and time you may be the victim of an attack. The hope is that your corporate security policy has included the procedures for handling a security incident once it is detected.

As far as the corporate infrastructure goes, it is extremely important to keep track of all available information. Do *not* reboot any device because you may lose valuable information. Instead, access any potentially affected devices through console ports (assuming this is very tightly controlled) and record the entire console session. Record all volatile information, which is typically available through a variety of **show** commands and can include the following:

- Configuration information
- Routing information
- ARP information

- Interface statistics
- NAT translation statistics
- Routing cache statistics
- Switching cache statistics
- SNMP statistics
- Logging statistics

The more information you collect in a controlled orderly manner, the more success you will have in possibly tracking down the intruder. In the unfortunate circumstances of having lost device access due to compromised passwords, port scans, and SNMP scans may provide some alternative mechanisms to obtain information pertaining to the device compromise.

Implementation Examples

Securing network infrastructure devices can seem like a daunting task with the slew of configuration options available. This section provides configuration templates for a router, switch, and PIX firewall, which show the commands that were discussed in this chapter and which should be used for most Cisco infrastructure equipment to ensure security in the devices and the network infrastructure itself. This includes providing authenticated access for any mechanism used to access the device (console ports or remote access via Telnet, SSH, SNMP or HTTP), logging data to a syslog server, and making sure you have accurate time stamps available. Some commands are shown that have not been discussed in detail in this chapter; they mostly relate to network services that are being disabled because they are not often used and can cause some security risks.

The authentication method for device access uses AAA wherever available to take advantage of a single centralized authentication database. This has the following benefits:

- Passwords are stored in a single database, which is easier to modify than changing passwords on all devices on a regular basis (to follow good security practices).
- All accesses are logged to the AAA server; and in some AAA software, the actions performed on the device are also logged. This provides a useful audit function.

Many freeware AAA servers are available, so cost should not be a prohibitive factor. You should use a commercial AAA server, however, because they can be more feature-rich and are supported.

The examples use the addressing shown in Figure 9-1 with the following:

- The backbone network is on 144.254.2.0.
- The network operators are on two networks: 144.254.9.0 and 144.254.19.0.
- The TACACS+ server has the IP address 144.254.5.9.
- The RADIUS and syslog servers reside on one machine with the IP address 144.254.5.5.

- The SNMP manager has IP address 144.254.9.3.
- The HTTP manager has IP address 144.254.9.2.

Example 9-38 shows a template for securing a Cisco router. This assumes that the router is running a software release that supports SSH authentication. Some commands may not be valid if you are using older software releases. Filters listed in Appendix D should be used in conjunction with the following template.

Example 9-38 *Cisco Router Security Template*

```
! Configure the host name and domain name.

hostname Router
domain name my.domain

! Configure password encryption to ensure that all type 7 passwords
! are stored in nonreadable form.

service password encryption

! Configure enable password and enable secret - the enable secret takes
! precedence.

enable password 0 ThisIsEnablePassword
enable secret 0 ThisIsEnableSecret

! Set local database authentication.

username merike secret 0 LetMeIn
username cathy secret 0 MeToo

! Configure ssh parameters: 1024-bit key, a 60 second timeout, and
! a maximum of 3 login attempts.

crypto key generate rsa
ip ssh time-out 60
ip ssh authentication-retries 3

! Turn off uneccessary services.

no service finger
no service pad
no service udp-small-servers
no service tcp-small-servers
no ip bootp server
no ip source route
no ip source-route

! Configure logging.

service timestamps debug datetime localtime show-timezone
service timestamps log datetime localtime show-timezone
logging buffered 32000 informational
```

Example 9-38 *Cisco Router Security Template (Continued)*

```
no logging console
logging trap informational
logging facility local1
logging 144.254.5.5

! Configure NTP.  This router will get time from an external source but will
! then act as an NTP master for the rest of the corporate network. Therefore
! authentication parameters will also be configured with the key number of 665.

ntp server 192.5.41.40
ntp server 192.36.143.150
ntp master
ntp authenticate
ntp authenticate-key 665 md5 ThisIsAKey
ntp trusted-key 665

! Configure access lists to limit access to specific functions. Access list  2
! is for HTTP access, access list 3 is for SNMP access, and access list 9 is
! for all machines on the NOC network.

access-list 2 permit host 144.254.9.2
access-list 2 deny any log

access-list 3 permit host 144.254.9.3
access-list 3 deny any log

access-list 9  permit 144.254.9.0 0.0.0.255
access-list 9  permit 144.254.19.0 0.0.0.255
access-list 9 deny any log

! snmp configuration
! SNMP access is read-only and can only be accessed by devices
! associated with access-list 3

snmp-server community public RO 3

! Http configuration
! HTTP access can only be accessed by devices associated with access list 2 and
! access must be authenticated with the enable secret.

ip http server
ip http access class 2
ip http authentication enable

! Configure TACACS+ authentication as default login with enable secret as backup.
! For users logging in as merike or cathy (members of staff set up in the TACACS+
server)
! the local database will be used as backup if the TACACS+ server is unavailable.
! The enable mode authentication also uses TACACS+ and then the enable
! secret as backup.

aaa new-model
```

continues

Example 9-38 *Cisco Router Security Template (Continued)*

```
aaa authentication login default tacacs+ enable
aaa authentication login staff  tacacs+ local
aaa authentication enable default tacacs+ enable

! Authorize running EXEC shell when authenticated - if TACACS+
! server is not available, commands associated with privilege
! levels 0 and 1 don't require authentication while commands associated.
! With privilege level 15, require local authentication.

aaa authorization exec tacacs+  local
aaa authorization commands 0 tacacs+ none
aaa authorization commands 1 tacacs+ none
aaa authorization commands 15 tacacs+ local

! Interim accounting records will be sent every time there is
! new information to report.
! Accounting for all EXEC terminal sessions

aaa accounting update newinfo
aaa accounting exec start-stop tacacs+

! Configure TACACS+ server and encryption key.

tacacs-server host 144.254.5.9
tacacs-server key thisisakey

! Configure console, aux, and vty port access.
! Physical console access accessible via merike and cathy login and
! appropriate local password - the session times out after
! 2 minutes and 30 seconds of idle time.

line con 0
  exec-timeout 2 30
  login authentication staff
  transport input telnet ssh

! No login prompt and no input access allowed through auxiliary port

line aux 0
  no exec
  transport input none

! Telnet or SSH access requires default authentication (TACACS+) and
! only hosts on the NOC network are allowed access. The session
!  times out after 2 minutes and 30 seconds of inactivity.

line vty 0 4
  exec-timeout 2 30
  access-class 9 in
  login authentication staff
  transport input telnet ssh
```

Example 9-38 *Cisco Router Security Template (Continued)*

```
! Set up a banner message for remote login access to the router.

banner login #
You are not authorized to access this device.  Any violators will
be prosecuted to the full extent of the law!  All access is being
monitored and logged.
#

! Configure all interafces to disable unneccessary services. This is a sample
! for a single interaface.

interface ethernet 0/0

! The router uses proxy ARP (defined in RFC 1027) to help hosts with
! no knowledge of routing determine the MAC addresses of hosts on other
! networks or subnets. This feature can cause a potential security
! hole and should be disabled.

no ip proxy arp

! Disable the forwarding of directed broadcasts to avoid
! unnecessary denial-of-service attacks.

no ip directed broadcast

! Disable the Cisco Discovery Protocol (CDP) for this interface.
! CDP could provide sensitive information such as configuration
! and routing tables to a potential attacker.

no cdp enable
```

Example 9-39 shows a template for securing a Catalyst switch. This again assumes that the software used will support SSH. If not, substitute the word **telnet** for **ssh** in the **ip permit** commands. Also, the console password (**set password** command) and enable password (**set enable** command) are not shown because they require user interaction. These also need to be configured.

Example 9-39 *Catalyst Switch Security Template*

```
:
! Configure the host name and domain name.

hostname Switch
domain name my.domain

! set local database authentication
set localuser user merike password LetMeIn  privilege 0
set localuser user cathy password MeToo privilege 0
set localuser authentication enable

! Configure login access -  remote access capability only from console and
```

continues

Example 9-39 *Catalyst Switch Security Template (Continued)*

```
! is authenticated with TACACS+. The local database is used as the backup in case the
! server is unavailable. Telnet and HTTP access are not allowed.

set authentication login local enable console
set authentication login tacacs enable console primary

! Configure enable mode access - all privileged mode access is authenticated with
TACACS+ with local authentication as a backup.

set authentication enable local enable console
set authenticationenable tacacs enable console primary

! Configure SSH parameters: 1024-bit key and access control list.

set crypto key  rsa 1024
set ip permit 144.254.9.0 0.0.0.255 ssh
set ip permit 144.254.19.0 0.0.0.255 ssh
set ip permit enable ssh

! Turn off uneccessary services.

set cdp disable
set ip http server disable

! Configure logging.

set logging server enable
set logging server facility local2
set logging server severity 6
set logging server 144.254.5.5

! Configure NTP. The time source will be a router with IP address
! 144.254.2.2 and use the key number 665. Note that the key is stored
! in the configuration file using MD5 encryption.

set ntp client enable
set ntp authenticate enable
set ntp key 665 trusted md5 ThisIsAKey
set ntp server 144.254.5.2 key 665

! SNMP configuration
! SNMP access is read-only and can only be accessed by devices
! that are used as SNMP managers (in this case, only 144.254.9.3).

set snmp community read-only ThisIsACommunityString
set ip permit 144.254.9.3 255.255.255.255 snmp
set ip permit enable snmp

! Configure TACACS+ server and encryption key.

set tacacs-server  144.254.5.9
set tacacs key thisisakey
```

Example 9-39 *Catalyst Switch Security Template (Continued)*

```
! Configure accounting parameters.

set accounting exec enable start-stop tacacs+
set accounting connect enable start-stop tacacs+

! Set up a banner message for remote login access to the router.

banner login #
You are not authorized to access this device.  Any violators will
be prosecuted to the full extent of the law!  All access is being
monitored and logged.
#
```

Example 9-40 shows a template for securing a PIX firewall. This again assumes that the software used will support SSH.

Example 9-40 *PIX Firewall Security Template*

```
! The following two commands define the PIX host name and domain name.

hostname PIX-Firewall
domain-name my.domain

! Configure the SSH parameters - only SSH access is allowed to the device.

ca generate rsa key 1024
ssh 144.254.9.0 0.0.0.255 inside
ssh 144.254.19.0 0.0.0.255 inside
ssh timeout 5
aaa-server SSHAccess protocol tacacs+
aaa-server SSHAccess (inside) host 144.254.5.9 ThisIsAKey  timeout 10
aaa authentication ssh console SSHAccess
! Define enable password and Telnet password - although Telnet will
! not be allowed you want to change the default password.

enable password CanYouGuessMe encrypted
passwd IAmSecure encrypted

! Set up the local database with staff users with enable mode privilege level.

username merike password ThisIsASecret privilege 15
username cathy password YetAnotherSecret privilege 15

! Set up the aaa mechanism to use the local user database for console
! authentication.

aaa-server LOCAL protocol local
aaa authentication enable console LOCAL

! Disable SNMP.
```

continues

Example 9-40 *PIX Firewall Security Template (Continued)*

```
no snmp-server location
no snmp-server contact

! Set up logging capabilities.

logging on
logging  facility 3
logging trap informational
logging host inside 144.254.5.5

! Configure NTP.

ntp authenticate
ntp authentication key 665 md5 ThisIsAKey
ntp server 144.254.2.2 key 665 source inside
ntp trusted key 665
```

Summary

This chapter explained what you should consider to secure your networking infrastructure. It is important to control all device access—both physical and logical—to ensure that no one can tamper with the network by reconfiguring the devices. General concepts and specific features used in Cisco devices were shown to incorporate additional elements of a security architecture, including integrity, confidentiality, availability, and audit. You must use all these concepts together to obtain the most effective security controls for your network infrastructure.

Review Questions

The following questions provide you with an opportunity to test your knowledge of the topics covered in this chapter. You can find the answers to these questions in Appendix E, "Answers to Review Questions."

1 True or False: If network infrastructure devices have strict security features and functionality configured, physical access does not have to be taken into consideration.

2 What is the difference between the Cisco IOS enable password and enable secret?

3 Which Cisco IOS command encrypts passwords with type 7 encryption?

4 Which four forms of authentication modes are possible to access enable mode in Cisco Catalyst switches?

5 What are three important points to keep in mind when crating a device login banner?

6 What is required for Telnet to be used on a PIX outside interface?

7 What are the trade-offs in using SSH versus Telnet access?

8 What are four good password management rules?

9 What security functionality differences are there between SNMPv1, v2, and v3?

10 Why is RADIUS the recommended mechanism for a Catalyst switch 802.1x port authentication?

11 What kind of traffic should be encrypted and be kept confidential for network infrastructure devices? Name three specific examples.

12 Why is the audit element necessary when implementing a secure network infrastructure?

13 True or false: Syslog messages are typically 1500 bytes to enable as much information as possible to be sent in a single packet.

14 Which of the following statements is *not* true when gathering data from network devices that are under a suspected security breach?

    A Access the device through the console port.

    B Immediately reboot the device.

    C Gather all volatile information via **show** commands.

    D Initiate a port scan or SNMP scan if you cannot access the device due to password compromise.

## CHAPTER 10

Securing Internet Access

This chapter examines how to secure Internet access to the corporate network. You can create such security by using some type of firewall functionality and securing the infrastructure devices, as discussed in the previous chapter, that interface with the Internet. Firewalls have become an integral component of perimeter network access, such as the boundary between the trusted corporate network and the less-trusted Internet. On this perimeter, traffic can be analyzed and controlled according to parameters such as specific applications, addresses, and users for both incoming traffic from remote users and outgoing traffic to the Internet.

NOTE   Constructing a firewall policy for your corporate environment was discussed in Chapter 7, "Design and Implementation of the Corporate Security Policy." If you are new to firewalls, turn to Appendix A, "Sources of Technical Information," and read the books listed under "Firewall Books" to get a good understanding of firewalls and their function.

A firewall device should be as impenetrable as possible; therefore, it should be one of the most secure devices in your infrastructure. This chapter contains sample firewall design implementations to control Internet access and refers to features specific to equipment provided by Cisco Systems. The chapter explains how to configure Cisco IOS devices and the Cisco (Private Internet Exchange [PIX]) firewall to provide necessary security controls for Internet access. You also can use many of the functions of other products mentioned in this chapter if they are available. You should use the controls described in Chapter 9, "Securing the Corporate Network Infrastructure," in these devices to provide appropriate security controls.

Internet Access Architecture

When the decision is made to connect the corporate network to the Internet, it is important to recognize the additional security exposures. In most cases, you make a decision about how open an environment you can tolerate. In a very open environment, you may impose limited restrictions on access; in a more secure environment, you may impose more stringent access controls for traffic entering or leaving the main corporate network.

There are many variations on how to design access to the Internet. A common scenario is to construct a firewall between the internal corporate network and the external Internet connection, as shown in Figure 10-1.

Figure 10-1   *Internet Access with a Firewall*

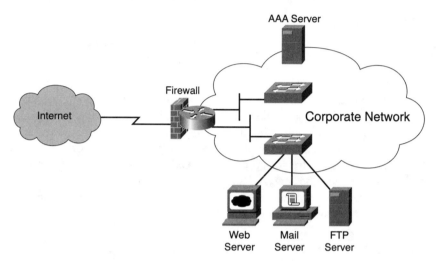

The firewall can be a single device, such as a screening router with limited firewall capabilities. Often, the firewall has at least three interfaces. One of these interfaces is used as a perimeter network to isolate services (such as e-mail, FTP, Domain Name System [DNS], and HTTP) offered to Internet users. Internet connections may be restricted solely to these services, which reside on a single subnet. Restricting the services offered to Internet users to a single subnet, if possible, is a good strategy to use to simplify the administration of access control filter lists. The filter lists would typically be much shorter if you only have to worry about a single subnet. The single-firewall-device Internet access architecture may be a sufficient model for a small corporation. However, the downfall is that if this single device is compromised, the entire network is open to exposure.

Another scenario, used most often in high-traffic environments, uses an exterior screening router along with a more robust firewall, as shown in Figure 10-2.

This second model is much more secure because it offers multiple levels of security to the corporation. The exterior screening router acts as a first-level filter to permit or deny traffic coming in from the Internet to the internal campus. It validates most incoming traffic before passing it on to the firewall. The firewall then provides the more CPU-intensive function of packet-by-packet inspection. In this scenario, it is also effective to include an *active audit device* that includes network traffic monitoring and intrusion detection on the network segment connecting the firewall to the exterior router. This device can verify adherence to the corporate security policy and can pinpoint and isolate any attacks from the Internet to the corporate network—or any attacks instigated from your internal network out to the Internet.

Figure 10-2   *Internet Access with a Screening Router and a Firewall*

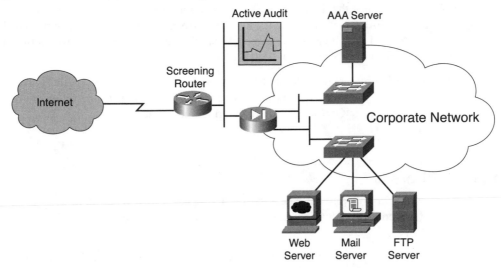

NOTE	Intrusion detection and active audit capabilities should be incorporated at network perimeter points to provide added security measures and to verify proper traffic behavior. A combination of intrusion detection, active audit, and a firewall at the network perimeter is the best defense against most known attacks.

External Screening Router Architecture

If your corporate network is small, the screening router model may be a sufficient solution to providing secure access to the Internet. It is possible that the security measures used will not always catch spoofed traffic, but at least they should provide a reasonable level of a basic buffer from the Internet.

You can also use the screening router solution in larger networks to define a logical separation internally between some sensitive areas of your network—for example, using a firewall between the finance building and the rest of a large campus, or using firewalls at all network perimeter points (including dial-in points and branch-office connections).

One common variant of the screening router architecture is to place a subnet immediately behind the screening router and have this external LAN be used for all externally available services. A corporate web server, e-mail relay, or application host would be placed on this external LAN. In addition, a second router attached to this subnet can be configured such that administrative access to the servers supplying the externally available services is only allowed from internal corporate hosts. This scenario is often implemented for security policies that dictate that inbound data is allowed only for internally initiated connections and all Internet-destined data from the internal network is proxied through servers residing on the external LAN. It creates a physical separation and also a logical layer between the internal corporate LAN and the Internet.

Most screening routers use filtering capabilities to act as a firewall. How filters are created and to what extent they look at traffic is largely vendor dependent. The following sections examine how Cisco IOS routers provide filtering; most other vendors' devices have similar capabilities.

Cisco IOS Filters

The Cisco IOS Software has an extended filtering capability to permit or deny specific traffic from entering or leaving the corporate network. These filters are called *access control lists* (ACLs).

Access control lists filter network traffic by controlling whether routed packets are forwarded or blocked at the router's interfaces. Your router examines each packet to determine whether to forward or drop the packet, based on the criteria specified within the ACLs. The ACL criteria can include the source address of the traffic, the destination address of the traffic, the upper-layer protocol, or other information.

NOTE   Sophisticated users can sometimes successfully evade or fool basic ACLs because the filters are typically based on spoofed or illegal addresses and well-known used services. However, it takes a little more effort to figure out valid IP addresses and services that a corporation may allow, so a minimal set of filtering should always be performed. Refer to Appendix D, "Mitigating Distributed Denial of Service Attacks," for more information.

If the ACL is inbound, the Cisco IOS Software checks the ACL's criteria statements for a match when the router receives a packet. If the packet is permitted, the software continues to process the packet. If the packet is denied, the software discards the packet.

If the ACL is outbound, the software checks the ACL's criteria statements for a match after receiving and routing a packet to the outbound interface. If the packet is permitted, the software transmits the packet. If the packet is denied, the software discards the packet.

WARNING Cisco IOS Software Release 11.1 and later releases introduced substantial changes to IP ACLs. These extensions are backward compatible; migrating from a release earlier than Release 11.1 to the current image will convert your ACLs automatically. However, previous releases are not upwardly compatible with these changes. Therefore, if you save an ACL with the current image and then use older software, the resulting ACL may not be interpreted correctly. This error can cause severe security problems. Save your old configuration file before booting Release 11.1 or later images.

You can specify ACLs for a number of different protocols. This example shows the output on a Cisco IOS device when performing an **access-list**:

```
Router(config)#access-list ?
<1-99>        IP standard access list
<100-199>     IP extended access list
<200-299>     Protocol type-code access list
<300-399>     DECnet access list
<600-699>     Appletalk access list
<700-799>     48-bit MAC address access list
<800-899>     IPX standard access list
<900-999>     IPX extended access list
<1000-1099>   IPX SAP access list
<1100-1199>   Extended 48-bit MAC address access
              list
<1200-1299>   IPX summary address access list
```

Because we deal mainly with the IP protocol for Internet access, this discussion is restricted to the IP standard and IP extended ACLs. For details on other protocols, refer to the Cisco online documentation.

Standard IP Access Control Lists

Standard IP access control lists use the source IP addresses for matching operations. The configuration command takes the following syntax:

```
access-list access-list-number {deny ¦ permit} source [source-wildcard] [log]
```

NOTE You can use the abbreviation **any** to specify a source and source mask of 0.0.0.0 through 255.255.255.255.

In Example 10-1, a standard ACL is created and applied to the incoming Internet traffic interface. The ACL denies all inbound traffic from the Internet that contains a source address from known reserved RFC addresses and permits any other traffic from the Internet to the corporate campus. Only the invalid traffic is logged, because there should be minimal logging unless a potential attack is in progress. It is also good practice to precede any access list configuration with the **no access-list** *access-list-number* command to clear out any previously defined commands.

Example 10-1 *Standard Access List Configuration Commands on Incoming Interface*

```
! clear out any previously defined list
no access-list 9
! source addresses from reserved address space defined in RFC 1918
access-list 9 deny  127.0.0.0 0.255.255.255 log
access-list 9 deny  10.0.0.0 0.255.255.255 log
access-list 9 deny  172.16.0.0 0.15.255.255 log
access-list 9 deny  192.168.0.0 0.0.255.255 log
access-list 9 permit any
! apply  access-list 9 to the incoming Internet interface
interface Serial 0/0
description to the Internet
ip address 161.71.73.33 255.255.255.248
ip access-list 9 in
```

Figure 10-3 shows the algorithm used to process a standard ACL. As a packet reaches an interface, a process occurs to determine whether an access list should be checked. If the answer is no, the packet is forwarded for processing. If the answer is yes, the list is sequentially checked to determine whether there is a source address match. When there is a match, the appropriate condition is applied (to drop the packet and send an Internet Control Message Protocol [ICMP] unreachable message or to forward the packet). The last entry of an ACL is always an implicit **deny all**.

Figure 10-3 *Processing of a Standard Access List*

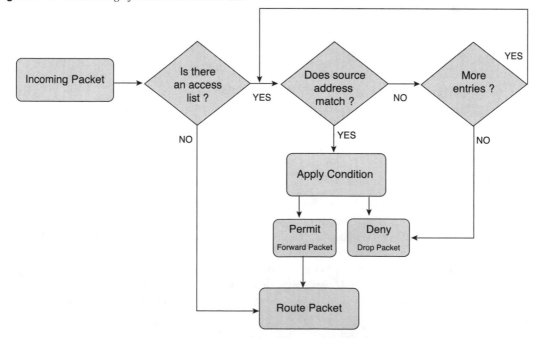

Extended Access Control Lists

Extended IP ACLs provide finer granularity of control for the type of traffic that is permitted or denied. They use a combination of source and destination IP addresses and optional protocol-type information for matching operations.

The following command defines an extended IP ACL number and its access conditions:

```
access-list access-list-number {deny | permit} protocol source source-wildcard
destination destination-wildcard [operator] [operand][precedence precedence]
[tos tos] [established] [log | log-input]
```

NOTE	You can use the abbreviation **host** for a specific source and for a specific destination without having to include the source wildcard or the destination wildcard. The *log-input* parameter will include the interface that the packet applies to and is the recommended logging parameter.

For IP extended ACLs, you can define a number of well-known protocols:

```
Router(config)#access-list 101 permit ?
<0-255>    An IP protocol number
eigrp      Cisco's Enhanced IGRP routing protocol
gre        Cisco's GRE tunneling
icmp       Internet Control Message Protocol
igmp       Internet Gateway Message Protocol
igrp       Cisco's IGRP routing protocol
ip         Any Internet protocol
ipinip     IP in IP tunneling
nos        KA9Q NOS-compatible IP over IP tunneling
ospf       OSPF routing protocol
tcp        Transmission Control Protocol
udp        User Datagram Protocol
```

The most common protocols to filter are the TCP and UDP protocols. For the TCP protocol, you can filter on the following parameters (operators):

```
Router(config)#access-list 101 permit tcp any any ?
eq            Match only packets on a given port number established
established   Match established connections
gt            Match only packets with a greater port number
log           Log matches against this entry
lt            Match only packets with a lower port number
neq           Match only packets not on a given port number
precedence    Match packets with a given precedence value
range         Match only packets in the given range of port numbers
tos           Match packets with the given TOS value
```

Here is a list of the more commonly used TCP port numbers (operands):

```
Router(config)#access-list 101 permit tcp any any eq ?
<0-65535>  Port number
bgp        Border Gateway Protocol (179)
chargen    Character generator (19)
cmd        Remote commands (rcmd, 514)
```

```
daytime     Daytime (13)
discard     Discard (9)
domain      Domain Name Service (53)
echo        Echo (7)
exec        Exec (rsh, 512)
finger      Finger (79)
ftp         File Transfer Protocol (21)
ftp-data    FTP data connections (used infrequently, 20)
gopher      Gopher (70)
hostname    NIC hostname server (101)
ident       Ident Protocol (113)
irc         Internet Relay Chat (194)
klogin      Kerberos login (543)
kshell      Kerberos shell (544)
login       Login (rlogin, 513)
lpd         Printer service (515)
nntp        Network News Transport Protocol (119)
pop2        Post Office Protocol v2 (109)
pop3        Post Office Protocol v3 (110)
smtp        Simple Mail Transport Protocol (25)
sunrpc      Sun Remote Procedure Call (111)
syslog      Syslog (514)
tacacs      TAC Access Control System (49)
talk        Talk (517)
telnet      Telnet (23)
time        Time (37)
uucp        UNIX-to-UNIX Copy Program (540)
whois       Nicname (43)
www         World Wide Web (HTTP, 80)
```

For UDP, here is a list of the more commonly used port numbers:

```
Router(config)#access-list 101 permit udp any any eq ?
<0-65535>      Port number
biff           Biff (mail notification, comsat, 512)
bootpc         Bootstrap Protocol (BOOTP) client (68)
bootps         Bootstrap Protocol (BOOTP) server (67)
discard        Discard (9)
dnsix          DNSIX security protocol auditing (195)
domain         Domain Name Service (DNS, 53)
echo           Echo (7)
mobile-ip      Mobile IP registration (434)
nameserver     IEN116 name service (obsolete, 42)
netbios-dgm    NetBios datagram service (138)
netbios-ns     NetBios name service (137)
ntp            Network Time Protocol (123)
rip            Routing Information Protocol (router, in.routed, 520)
snmp           Simple Network Management Protocol (161)
snmptrap       SNMP Traps (162)
sunrpc         Sun Remote Procedure Call (111)
syslog         System Logger (514)
tacacs         TAC Access Control System (49)
talk           Talk (517)
tftp           Trivial File Transfer Protocol (69)
time           Time (37)
who            Who service (rwho, 513)
xdmcp          X Display Manager Control Protocol (177)
```

NOTE   When dealing with TCP or UDP port numbers, remember that these commonly known port numbers are always used as the *destination* port number. The *source* port number is more or less arbitrarily picked by the originating host from the range of numbers 0 to 65,535.

Keep in mind the following few things when configuring ACLs on Cisco IOS devices:

- By default, the end of the ACL contains an implicit **deny** statement for everything if it does not find a match before reaching the end.

- After the ACL has been created on the router, any subsequent additions (possibly entered from the terminal) are placed at the end of the list. In other words, you cannot selectively add or remove ACL command lines from a specific ACL.

- The order of ACLs is important. The entries are searched in sequential order; the first match is the one acted on.

Figure 10-4 shows the algorithm used for an IP extended ACL.

Figure 10-4   *Processing of an IP Extended Access List*

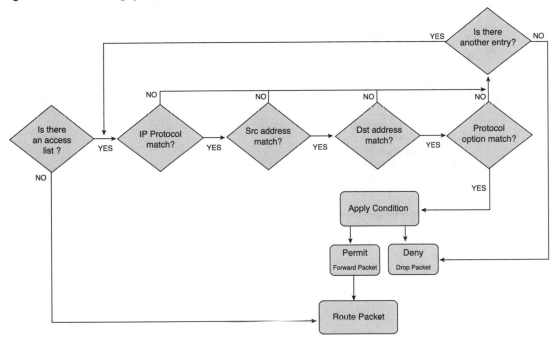

NOTE	It is recommended that you create your ACLs on a secure FTP or Secure Copy Protocol (SCP) server and then download the ACLs to your router. This approach can considerably simplify maintenance of your ACLs because the order of ACL criteria statements is important and because you cannot reorder or delete criteria statements on your router. The secure FTP or SCP server should be well protected from both read and write access to ensure that only authorized personnel have access to the files. Also, remove references to the access lists on interfaces before changing or updating the access list. After completing the editing, you should again configure the interface to apply the access list. Although this opens a small window of potential exposure while the interfaces are without ACLs, this procedure is the "cleanest" way to update ACLs.

Example 10-2 shows the configuration commands of an extended IP ACL. It meets the following criteria:

- It allows all incoming TCP traffic if the session was initiated within the internal corporate network.

- It allows FTP control and FTP data traffic to the FTP server with the address 144.254.1.4.

- It allows HTTP traffic to the web server with the address 144.254.1.3.

- It denies all other traffic from entering the corporate network.

- It logs all ACL violations.

Example 10-2 *Configuration of an Extended Access List*

```
! start with clearing out any previously established list
no access list 101
! create the access list
access-list 101 permit tcp any any established
access-list 101 permit tcp any host 144.254.1.4 eq ftp
access-list 101 permit tcp any host 144.254.1.4 eq ftp-data
access-list 101 permit tcp any host 144.254.1.3 eq www
access-list 101 deny ip any any log-input

! configure the Internet interface and apply the inbound access-list 101

interface Serial 0/0
description to the Internet
ip address 161.71.73.33 255.255.255.248
ip access-group 101 in
```

The order in which you create your ACL entries is important in Cisco IOS devices. When the router is deciding whether to forward or block a packet, the Cisco IOS Software tests the packet against each criteria statement in the order the statements were created. After a match is found, no more criteria statements are checked. From a performance standpoint, if you have the need for very long lists (for example, more than 100 entries), you should place the more common scenarios at the beginning of the list. If most of your incoming traffic is web related, for instance, you should place the criteria for web traffic at the top of the list. The other ordering criteria for statements is to go from the specific to the general. You need to be careful about reordering statements if the granularity differs for newer entries.

NOTE	You can use the **established** keyword only for the TCP upper-layer protocol filters. The expectation is that a session has been started from an internal source to an external source and this permitted traffic is the reply; therefore, it is an "established" session. The manner in which the **established** keyword filters TCP packets is based on whether the ACK or RST bit is set. (Set ACK and RST bits indicate that the packet is not the first in the session and, therefore, that the packet belongs to an established session.) Reflexive ACLs provide a more robust session-filtering mechanism and are described later in this chapter.

Turbo Access Control Lists

Turbo ACLs were introduced in Cisco IOS Software Release 12.1(6). A Turbo ACL is configured with the **access-list compiled** command. It is a technique that takes a standard or extended ACL, creates a set of data tables, and compiles them into fast lookup tables. The matching semantics are preserved while reducing the number of CPU operations to find a match. This allows for very large filter lists to be used without an increase in packet latency. The processing of Turbo ACLs takes a maximum of five steps, no matter what the size of the filter. This feature proves useful if you have filters that contain a large number of entries. (I recommend using it if you exceed 20 entries on any ACL.)

NOTE	Application-specific integrated circuit (ASIC)-based access control functionality is also available on some higher-end router platforms such as the Cisco 12000. This hardware-based filter processing greatly enhances the processing performance of large filter lists. Large corporations that have such requirements should follow the latest Cisco developments for this capability. So far, I have heard that Turbo lists are most effective on higher-end router platforms with access lists with more than 128 entries (448 entries for hardware-assisted Turbo).

Named Access Lists

Named ACLs were introduced in Cisco IOS Software Release 11.0. You can identify IP ACLs with an alphanumeric string (a name) rather than a number (1 to 199). Named ACLs enable you to configure more than 99 standard IP (and 100 extended IP) ACLs in a router. Currently, only packet and route filters can use a named list.

The advantage of using a named ACL is that you can selectively remove entries. However, you still cannot selectively add ACL command lines to a specific ACL—subsequent additions are still placed at the end of the list.

Consider the following before configuring named ACLs:

- Access lists specified by name are not compatible with older releases.
- Not all ACLs that accept a number will accept a name. Access lists for packet filters and route filters on interfaces can use a name.
- A standard ACL and an extended ACL cannot have the same name.

An example of a named ACL is shown in the next section. (Reflexive ACLs *require* the use of extended named ACLs.)

NOTE   As of Cisco IOS Software Release 12.0 (2)T, it is possible to include comments (remarks) about entries in any IP ACL. This includes standard, extended, and named ACLs. The remarks make the ACL easier for the network administrator to understand. Each remark is limited to 100 characters.

Reflexive Access Lists

Reflexive ACLs were introduced in Cisco IOS Software Release 11.3. They allow IP packets to be filtered based on upper-layer session information.

A common requirement for filtering is to permit IP traffic for sessions originating from within your network but to deny IP traffic for sessions originating from outside your network. Using basic extended ACLs, you can approximate session filtering by using the **established** keyword with the **permit** command. The **established** keyword filters TCP packets based on whether the ACK or RST bits are set. This method of using the **established** keyword is available only for the TCP upper-layer protocol. For the other upper-layer protocols (such as UDP, ICMP, and so forth), you have to either permit all incoming traffic or define all possible permissible source/destination host/port address pairs for each protocol.

Reflexive ACLs are much more suitable for true session filtering. After it has been configured, a reflexive ACL is triggered when a new IP upper-layer session (such as TCP or UDP) is initiated from inside your network, with a packet traveling to the external network. When triggered, the reflexive ACL generates a new, temporary entry. This entry permits traffic to enter your network if the traffic is part of the session, but does not permit traffic to enter your network if the traffic is not part of the session. The filter criterion is based on the ACK and RST bits as well as the source and destination addresses and port numbers. Session filtering uses temporary filters that are removed when a session is over, limiting the hacker's attack opportunity to a smaller time frame.

Temporary reflexive ACL entries are removed at the end of the session. For TCP sessions, the entry is removed 5 seconds after two set FIN bits are detected, or immediately after matching a TCP packet with the RST bit set. (Two set FIN bits in a session indicate that the session is about to end; the 5-second window allows the session to close gracefully. A set RST bit indicates an abrupt session close.) Alternatively, the temporary entry is removed after no packets of the session have been detected for a configurable length of time (called the *timeout period*).

For UDP and other protocols, the end of the session is determined differently than it is for TCP. Because other protocols are considered to be connectionless (sessionless) services, they have no session-tracking information embedded in their packets. Therefore, the end of a session is considered to be when no packets of the session have been detected for a configurable length of time (the timeout period).

Two restrictions apply to using the reflexive ACL feature:

- Reflexive ACLs can be defined with extended named IP ACLs only. You cannot define reflexive ACLs with numbered or standard named IP ACLs or with other protocol ACLs.

- Reflexive ACLs do not work with some applications that use port numbers that change during a session. If the port numbers for a return packet differ from those of the originating packet, the return packet will be denied, even if the packet is actually part of the same session.

The TCP-based application FTP is an example of an application with changing port numbers. With reflexive ACLs, if you start an FTP request from within your network, the request will not complete. Instead, you must use passive FTP when originating requests from within your network.

Figure 10-5 shows an example of how to use reflexive ACLs. Notice that the Ethernet interface connects to the internal corporate networks, and that the serial interface connects to the Internet. The configuration example permits both inbound and outbound TCP traffic on the serial interface—but only if the first packet in a given session originated from inside your corporate network.

Figure 10-5   *Reflexive Access Lists*

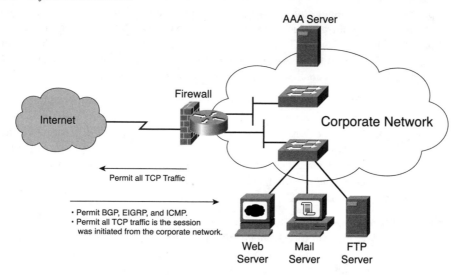

Example 10-3 shows the configuration commands for a reflexive ACL.

Example 10-3   *Configuring a Reflexive Access List*

```
! Define the global idle timeout value for all reflexive access lists.
! If for 120 seconds there is no TCP traffic that is part of an
! established session, the corresponding reflexive access list
! entry will be removed.

ip reflexive-list timeout 120

! Define the outbound access list. This is the access list that
! evaluates all outbound traffic on interface Serial 1.

ip access-list extended outboundfilters
remark permit all outbound TCP traffic

! Define the reflexive access list tcptraffic. This entry permits all
! outbound TCP traffic and creates a new access list named tcptraffic.

permit tcp any any reflect tcptraffic

! Define the inbound access list. This is the access list
! that evaluates all inbound traffic on interface Serial 1.

ip access-list extended inboundfilters
remark permit routing but deny ICMP and check all TCP traffic

! Define the inbound access list entries. Permit BGP and EIGRP
! but deny ICMP. The last entry points to the reflexive access list.
! If a packet does not match the first three entries, the packet will
```

Example 10-3 *Configuring a Reflexive Access List (Continued)*

```
! be evaluated against all the entries in the reflexive access list
! named tcptraffic.

permit bgp any any
permit eigrp any any
deny icmp any any
evaluate tcptraffic

! Define the interface where the session-filtering configuration is
! to be applied and apply access lists to the interface, for inbound
! traffic and for outbound traffic.
interface Serial 1
 description Access to the Internet
 ip access-group inboundfilters in
 ip access-group outboundfilters out
```

Advanced Firewall Architecture

Although a screening router is a good first step toward providing Internet access security, a more secure solution relies on a more robust firewall architecture. Typically, this is accomplished with both a screening router and more intense firewall capabilities. In addition to primitive filtering capabilities, a firewall typically has the capability to provide the following:

- Advanced packet-by-packet inspection
- Application content filtering
- Application authentication/authorization
- Encryption technology
- Network Address Translation (NAT)

The traffic-filtering capabilities must incorporate state information and often must also be able to filter on application content. E-mail virus scanning, Java applet filtering, and URL logging or blocking are some of the commonly implemented advanced functions in a firewall. Sometimes these application-specific functions are offloaded to separate devices to save CPU processing cycles on the firewall device itself.

Packet authentication and confidentiality using encryption is becoming a strong requirement. Implementing this functionality in a multivendor-interoperable way has become much easier with the emergence of IPsec products. IPsec authentication and confidentiality capabilities can be applied to many Internet access architectures to provide for authenticated, confidential traffic flow.

NAT is also commonly used but, as mentioned in Chapter 6, "Considerations for a Site Security Policy," a legitimate network interface card (NIC)-assigned address should be used whenever possible to avoid any application or feature restrictions in the future. (This is strictly the author's opinion and mileage may vary depending on specific requirements.)

Advanced Packet Session Filtering

A robust firewall must have the capability to perform packet-by-packet inspection and filtering on specific packet session information. The firewall should inspect traffic that travels through it to discover and manage state information for TCP and UDP sessions. For many corporate environments, FTP, Telnet, HTTP traffic, Java applets, e-mail, DNS, and some popular voice and video applications must be supported. Controls must be in place to ensure as best as possible that any such traffic is valid traffic.

Most advanced session filters keep information relating to the following questions:

- How long ago was the last packet in this session transmitted?
- Are the sequence/acknowledgment numbers climbing as expected?
- Was the session initiated from the inside or outside?
- Is the session still open or has it been closed?
- What port or ports are the return data channels using?

TCP Protocol Traffic

For IP traffic using the TCP protocol, advanced packet session filtering inspects all IP and TCP headers in every packet based on a combination of the following fields:

- IP Destination Address
- IP Source Address
- IP Protocol
- TCP Source Port
- TCP Destination Port
- TCP Flags:
  - SYN alone for a request to open a connection
  - SYN/ACK for a connection confirmation
  - ACK for a session in progress
  - FIN for session termination

These fields allow the monitoring of connection state information and provide a reasonable amount of certainty about when valid connections are in progress.

UDP Protocol Traffic

For IP traffic using the UDP protocol, advanced packet session filtering inspects all IP and UDP headers in every packet based on a combination of the following fields:

- IP Destination Address
- IP Source Address
- IP Protocol
- UDP Source Port
- UDP Destination Port

Because UDP is a connectionless service, there are no actual UDP "sessions" *per se*. Most systems approximate sessions by examining UDP packet information and determining whether the packet is similar to other UDP packets recently seen.

Application Content Filtering

Application content filtering refers to examining packet content in more detail to ensure validity of the content. Some of the more common applications whose content you may want to control or examine are described in the following sections.

World Wide Web

The World Wide Web has played a large role in making the Internet a place to conduct business. Chapter 2, "Security Technologies," described technologies such as S-HTTP and SSL that enable you to secure web transactions. However, program languages, such as Java and JavaScript, that are used to write interactive programs for web applications remain a security issue. Some corporations also want to restrict specific URL sites from their employees because of the sites' possibly illegal content.

Java Applets

When World Wide Web users download a web page with embedded Java or JavaScript programs (called *applets*), there is no control over whether the applet has approved content or whether it contains a virus or malicious program. You must prevent users from inadvertently downloading destructive Java applets into your network. To protect against this risk, you could require all users to disable Java in their browser. If this is not an agreeable solution, you can use methods to filter Java applets at the firewall, allowing users to download only those applets residing within the firewall and trusted applets from outside the firewall.

Many firewalls do not detect or block encapsulated Java applets. Therefore, Java applets that are wrapped or encapsulated (for example, those in .zip or .jar format) are usually not blocked at the firewall. In addition, some firewalls may not detect or block applets loaded using FTP, Gopher, or HTTP on a nonstandard port.

URL Filtering/Blocking

Some corporations may want to restrict access to certain URLs because of the sites' inappropriate content (for example, pornographic material). By providing URL-filtering and blocking capabilities, the firewall can be used to restrict access to specified websites.

E-mail and SMTP

Simple Mail Transfer Protocol (SMTP) is used to handle e-mail exchange between mail servers on the Internet. Many firewalls have the capability to check SMTP messages for illegal commands. Any packets with illegal commands are usually dropped, and the SMTP session will hang and eventually time out.

In a Cisco PIX firewall, for example, an *illegal command* is any command except for the following legal commands:

DATA
EHLO
EXPN
HELO
HELP
MAIL
NOOP
QUIT
RCPT
RSET
SAML
SEND
SOML
VRFY

Other Common Application Protocols

Many multimedia applications used for videoconferencing—for example, CUseeMe, H.323 (for NetMeeting and ProShare), and RealAudio—use the TCP control channel to establish media channels. This control channel contains information that opens new media channels. Firewalls should have the capability to watch these control channels, to identify those ports that media channels use, and the capability to open additional channels on a dynamic basis.

Table 10-1 lists the most common applications that should be supported in firewalls if they are to have extensive application control support.

Table 10-1   *Common Application Protocols*

Protocol	Description
Audio/Video Streaming	
CuseeMe Networks formerly White Pine Software	Application that supports live audio/ videoconferencing and text chat across the Internet.
H.323	New standard in audio/videoconferencing.
Internet Phone by Intel	Voice communication application above H.323 protocol stack.
NetMeeting by Microsoft	Audio, video, and application sharing implemented over T.120 and H.323.
RealAudio and RealVideo by Progressive Networks	Protocol for the transmission of high-quality streaming sound and video on the Internet.
StreamWorks by Xing	Protocol for the transmission of high-quality streaming sound and video on the Internet.
VDOLive by VDOnet	Application for transmitting high-quality video over the Internet.
Information Seeking	
Archie	Standard tool for searching Internet file servers.
Gopher	Application that provides a menu-driven front end to Internet services.
HTTP	Primary protocol used to implement the World Wide Web.
Network News Transfer Protocol (NNTP)	Protocol used to transmit and receive network news.
Pointcast by Pointcast (HTTP)	Protocol for viewing news in TV-like fashion.
Wide Area Information Servers (WAIS)	Tool for keyword searches (based on database content) of databases on the Internet.
Security and Authentication	
HTTPS	Secured (that is, encrypted) HTTP; an implementation of Secure Socket Layer (SSL). (Note that this is different from S-HTTP, which is an extension of the HTTP protocol.)
TACACS+	Authentication protocol.
Kerberos	Authentication service.

continues

Table 10-1 *Common Application Protocols (Continued)*

Protocol	Description
RADIUS	Widely adopted authentication protocol.
LDAP (Lightweight Directory Access Protocol)	Standard for Internet directory services.
Secure ID	Protocol used by an authentication service product of Security Dynamics Technologies, Inc.
Databases	
Lotus Notes	Proprietary protocol developed by Lotus to implement its Notes application.
SQL Server by Microsoft	A data replication server.
SQL*Net version 1	Oracle protocol for transmission of SQL queries.
SQL*Net version 2	Extension of SQL*Net version 1; adds support for port redirection.
Mail	
Comsat	Mail notification protocol.
Imap	Internet mail access protocol.
POP (Post Office Protocol) version 2	Mail protocol that allows a remote mail client to read mail from a server.
POP version 3	Modified version of POP version 2.
SMTP (Simple Mail Transfer Protocol)	Protocol widely used for the transmission of e-mail.
Other TCP and UDP Services	
Chargen	TCP Chargen server sends a continual stream of characters until the client terminates the connection; UPD Chargen servers send a datagram containing a random number of characters in response to each datagram sent by a client.
Daytime	Daytime server returns the date and the time of day in text format; can be run over TCP or UDP.
Discard	Discard server discards whatever is sent to it by a client; can be run over TCP or UDP.
DNS	Distributed database used by TCP/IP to map names to IP addresses.
Finger	Protocol that provides information about users on a specified host.

Table 10-1   *Common Application Protocols (Continued)*

Protocol	Description
FTP	Protocol for copying files between hosts.
Identd (auth)	Protocol used for user identification.
Internet Relay Chat (IRC)	Protocol for online "chat" conversations over the Internet.
NetBIOS over TCP/IP (NBT)	NetBIOS name, datagram, and session services encapsulated within TCP/IP.
Network Time Protocol (NTP)	Protocol providing time synchronization across a network with precise clocks; implemented over TCP and UDP.
RAS	Remote access service.
Rexec	Protocol that provides remote execution facilities.
Rlogin	Protocol that enables remote login between hosts.
Rsh	Protocol that allows commands to be executed on another system.
Simple Network Management Protocol(SNMP)	Protocol used for managing network resources.
SNMP Trap	Notification by SNMP to the manager of some event of interest.
Syslog	Protocol that allows a computer to send logs to another computer.
Telnet (Telecommunications Network Protocol)	Remote terminal protocol enabling any terminal to log in to any host.
TFTP	Small, simple FTP used primarily in booting diskless systems.
Time	Service that returns the time of day as a binary number.
UNIX-to-UNIX Copy Program (UUCP)	UNIX file-copying protocol.
Who	Service that uses local broadcasts to provide information about who is logged on to the local network.
X11	Windowing system protocol.
Remote Procedure Call Services	
Lockmanager (nlockmgr)	Protocol used for the transmission of lock requests.
Mountd	Protocol used for the transmission of file mount requests.

continues

Table 10-1   *Common Application Protocols (Continued)*

Protocol	Description
Network File System (NFS)	Protocol that provides transparent file access over a network.
Network Information Service (NIS)	Protocol that provides a network-accessible system administration database, widely known as the Yellow Pages.
Rstat	Protocol used to obtain performance data from a remote kernel.
Rwall	Protocol used to write to all users in a network.

Application Authentication/Authorization

You should configure authentication and authorization controls for device access on all infrastructure devices, including the routers and firewalls that provide Internet access. These controls were discussed in Chapter 9. In addition, there may be a requirement to authenticate based on application access. For example, you may have a policy in place that requires all incoming HTTP sessions to be authenticated before they can access a specific web server.

Figure 10-6 shows a sample scenario.

Figure 10-6   *HTTP Authentication Through a Firewall*

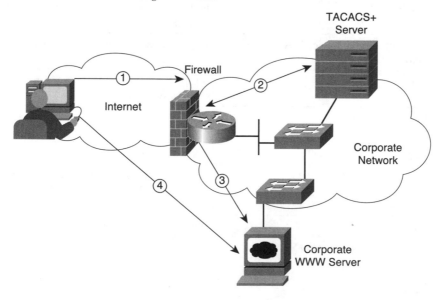

In this figure, the following steps are carried out:

Step 1   The user from the Internet initiates an HTTP request to a specified corporate web server.

Step 2   The firewall intercepts the connection and initiates the authentication process (shown here using TACACS+).

Step 3   If the user authenticates successfully, the firewall completes the HTTP connection to the corporate web server.

Step 4   The firewall forwards requests and responses without further intervention.

In addition to authentication, if you are using TACACS+ or RADIUS (which also include authorization methods), you can usually configure the firewall to permit access to specific hosts or services depending on user or host identity. It is up to the corporation to determine which users can access the network, which services those individuals can use, and which hosts they can access.

Encryption

With the emergence of IPsec in many products, it is easier for corporate networks to implement authenticated and confidential data transfer sessions. Ideally, encrypted traffic (encrypted for the sake of authentication and confidentiality) should stay encrypted from the sender to the recipient. Because of the complexity and difficulty of deploying encryption for all hosts on the network, however, many companies use the network infrastructure to encrypt the traffic traversing untrusted networks.

NOTE   When talking about authentication in IPsec, it relates to data integrity and data origin authentication. Most other authentication (such as application layer authentication) relates to a user actually having to enter credentials to provide identification that allows access to a specific application or service.

Because IPsec allows for authenticated traffic, confidential traffic, or both, you must make a variety of decisions about where to provide authentication and where to provide confidentiality measures. Figure 10-7 shows the network, and Table 10-2 lists the various combinations to be considered for traffic passing to or from the Internet and the corporate network. The traffic from/to the Internet is outside the firewall (the external network), and the traffic to/from the corporate network is inside the firewall (the internal network). Often, the policy chosen with regard to authentication and confidentiality will vary for traffic that traverses the external or internal network.

Figure 10-7 *Using IPsec Through a Firewall*

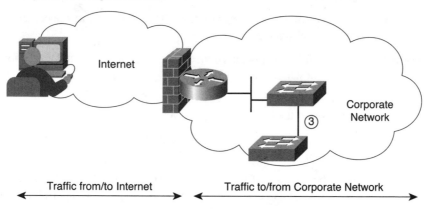

Table 10-2 *Possible IPsec Use Through a Firewall*

Policy Choices for Traffic from/ to Internet	Policy Choices for Traffic to/from Corporate Network
Authentication and confidentiality	Authentication and confidentiality
Authentication and confidentiality	Authentication
Authentication and confidentiality	No IPsec
Authentication	Authentication
Authentication	Authentication
No IPsec	No IPsec

In all cases for Table 10-2, the firewall is an IPsec endpoint that can operate in either IPsec transport or tunnel mode.

Refer to Chapter 2 for a more detailed explanation of IPsec.

NOTE   When using IPsec, authentication is always recommended and is in practice usually deployed using IPsec ESP with NULL encryption. Authentication ensures a high probability of data origin validation and that the data has not been altered in transit. Confidentiality measures should be used in addition to authentication for very sensitive data as determined by risk analysis.

If traffic remains encrypted for confidentiality from sender to recipient, in many cases this means that the corporate Internet access firewall will have to be bypassed, which is commonly referred to as "crating a hole in the firewall." By its very nature, encrypted traffic is kept confidential and the only filtering that can be done is on IP addresses and the destination protocol being used (IPsec Internet Key Exchange [IKE], IPsec ESP, SSL, and so on). This is usually not sufficient. Smaller corporations might want to use a scenario such as the one shown in Figure 10-8, in which a single device handles the routing and firewall functionality.

Figure 10-8   *Internet Access with a Single Router/Firewall Device*

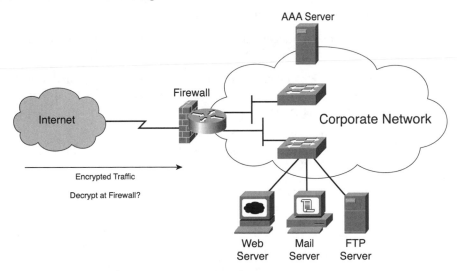

The considerations here for outside-encrypted traffic coming in to the corporate network takes two forms: The router/firewall can decrypt the traffic, or the assumption is made that the traffic is valid and therefore just forwarded to the destination within the network. If you decide on the latter, you will effectively bypass any security policy that mandates that all incoming traffic should be statefully inspected for potential security violations. It is much better to decrypt the traffic at the Internet access ingress point and perform a stateful firewall inspection. In addition, if you have decrypted the traffic, the router/firewall could take advantage of added functionality when certain application traffic may need to be authenticated by users before it is forwarded.

NOTE	Many current implementations that use SSL for secure web traffic tunnel SSL through the firewall. Future secure web transactions may use IPsec, where firewalls will not be bypassed.

Figure 10-9 shows a sample scenario in which web traffic is encrypted using IPsec, but the firewall can still enforce user-authenticated web transactions.

In the figure, the following steps are carried out:

Step 1   The user from the Internet initiates an encrypted HTTP request to a specified corporate web server.

Step 2   The firewall decrypts the packet and recognizes that it is an HTTP request.

Step 3   The firewall intercepts the connection and initiates the authentication process (shown here using TACACS+).

Step 4   If the user authenticates successfully, the firewall completes the HTTP connection to the corporate web server.

Step 5   The firewall subsequently decrypts all incoming web traffic and forwards the unencrypted packet to the internal corporate host. (All new web sessions are authenticated.)

Step 6   The firewall takes all responses from the web server going to the host on the Internet and encrypts them before forwarding them to the Internet host.

Figure 10-9   *Encrypted HTTP Authentication Through a Firewall*

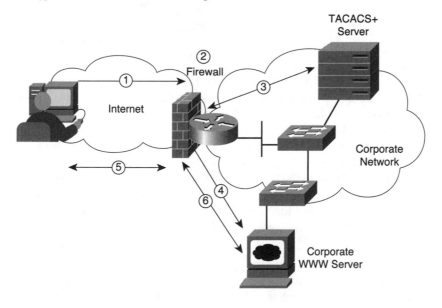

If a requirement exists to encrypt the web traffic from the firewall to the internal web server, it can be accomplished at the expense of more CPU cycles. The firewall must first decrypt the incoming data, perform the firewall functionality (and possible user authentication), and then encrypt the data again before forwarding it to the internal web server. This is not necessarily an optimal solution, but it can provide for end-to-end encryption if you do not trust even your internal network.

Larger networks are more likely to have a scenario such as the one illustrated in Figure 10-10, where Internet access uses a combination of a screening router and a firewall. For this sort of architecture, the considerations are a bit more complex, as follows:

- Encrypt/decrypt only between outside hosts and the screening router.

  This approach allows the screening router to decrypt a packet coming from an untrusted outside network and perform a precursory filter check before passing the packet to the firewall for more complete inspection. This approach assumes that the internal network is secure and that no encryption is required within the corporate network.

- Encrypt/decrypt only between outside hosts and the firewall.

  After an initial filter check is performed using only IP addresses, the packet is sent to the firewall for inspection. Most likely the filter will permit any traffic through that uses IPsec and adheres to certain IP address constraints. The firewall then decrypts the packet and performs a stateful inspection (and possible user authentication). When the packet is declared valid, it is forwarded to its intended recipient within the corporate network.

- Encrypt/decrypt on both the screening router and the firewall.

  This approach allows the screening router to decrypt a packet coming from an untrusted outside network and perform a precursory filter check before passing the packet to the firewall for more complete inspection. When the firewall has completed its task, the firewall then encrypts the packet and forwards it to its intended recipient. The assumption here is that the corporate network is insecure and that the CPU cycles spent are necessary to protect the packet end to end (with the exception of when the packet gets passed from the screening router to the firewall, which is expected to be a secure connection).

- Do not encrypt/decrypt.

  This approach will bypass any stateful firewall inspection, and the assumption is made that all encrypted traffic can be trusted.

The decision as to which is the best approach in your environment can vary greatly and very much depends on the conclusions you came to when creating your corporate security policy. (The approach I prefer is to use the screening router to perform an initial filter check and then let the firewall decrypt the traffic and do a stateful analysis on the packet.) Whether or not to encrypt the traffic again depends on how much you trust the internal network and whether there are more firewalls to traverse before the packet actually reaches its intended destination.

Network Address Translation

Network Address Translation (NAT) is often used in environments that have private address space as opposed to a globally unique address. Private address space is not a security feature because, more often than not, the private address will be known. The Internet Assigned Numbers Authority (IANA) has reserved the following three blocks of IP address space for private networks:

> 10.0.0.0 through 10.255.255.255
> 172.16.0.0 through 172.31.255.255
> 192.168.0.0 through 192.168.255.255

The first block is a single Class A network number, the second block is a set of 16 contiguous Class B network numbers, and the third block is a set of 256 contiguous Class C network numbers. IANA has reserved these address blocks for private use because they were specified by RFC 1918.

If a corporation decides to use private addressing, these blocks of addresses should be used—unless, of course, there is a historical reason why some other private address space is being used. The more common reason is the infamous, "We'll never need to connect to the Internet!"

Public Versus Private IP Addresses

The question of whether to use private addressing is becoming a part of network design for many corporate TCP/IP application users. The Internet has grown beyond anyone's expectations. With this growth came concerns about Internet address depletion and, more importantly, address-allocation procedures and their impact on the Internet routing system. There are a few reasons why private address space could and should be used (such as for environments where external connectivity may not be required or is extremely limited). Some examples include the following:

- A large organization where only a small number of specific hosts are allowed access to the Internet.

- A large organization where outside Internet access is allowed only to a few specified hosts, such as web servers.

- An organization that may have had to switch Internet service providers and received a new block of address space. It may have been too cost prohibitive or disruptive to change to the new address space at the time.

The cost of using private Internet address space is the potentially costly effort to renumber hosts and networks between public and private. If the company has any thought about opening up to global Internet access, it is recommended that the corporation start a transition plan for renumbering to a globally unique address if it is currently using private address space. The widespread use of Dynamic Host Configuration Protocol (DHCP) is making this process much easier and may help avoid possible future issues with non-NAT-able and non-proxy-able protocols.

If you decide to use private address space, however, you don't have to coordinate with IANA or an Internet registry. Addresses within this private address space are unique only within your network.

NOTE   Remember, if you need globally unique address space, you must obtain addresses from an Internet registry or your service provider. This is necessary if any part of your network is connected to the Internet. The trend in the past few years has been to get a block of globally unique addresses from your network service provider, with only larger corporations petitioning a regional or local Internet registry directly for addressing.

To use private address space, determine which hosts do not need to have network layer connectivity to the outside. These hosts are private hosts and will use private address space. *Private hosts* can communicate with all other hosts within the corporate network, both public and private, assuming that all addressing within the corporate network is unique. However, the private hosts cannot have IP connectivity to any host external to the corporate network without the use of NAT or proxies.

All public hosts use the globally unique address space assigned by an Internet registry. *Public hosts* can communicate with other hosts within the network and can have IP connectivity to external public hosts. Figure 10-10 shows the differences between public and private address spaces (assuming that NAT is not being used).

Figure 10-10 *Private and Public Address Spaces*

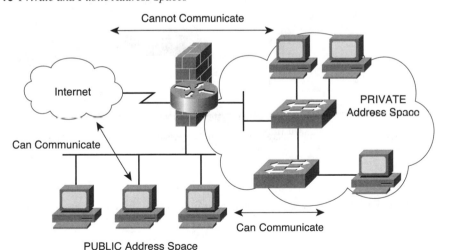

Because private addresses have no global meaning, routing information about private networks is not propagated on outside links, and packets with private source or destination addresses should not be forwarded across such links. Routers in networks that don't use private address space—especially those of Internet service providers—should be configured to reject (filter out) routing information about private networks.

With this scheme, many large networks need only a relatively small block of addresses from the globally unique IP address space. The Internet at large benefits through conservation of globally unique address space, and the corporate networks benefit from the increased flexibility provided by a relatively large private address space.

NAT Functionality

In its simplest configuration, NAT is performed in both directions on only one end of the communication and operates on the router or firewall connecting the inside corporate network to the outside Internet, as shown in Figure 10-11.

Figure 10-11 *NAT on a Router or Firewall*

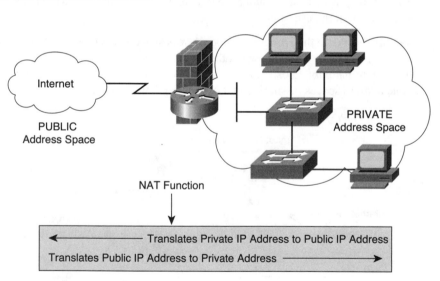

The inside corporate network is addressed with private addresses that must be converted into legal addresses before packets can be forwarded to the outside Internet.

NAT functionality can become quite complex, depending on the applications it has to support. Here are some of the functionalities you should consider when opting for NAT for Internet access:

- **Static address translation**—The user can establish a one-to-one mapping between the inside local addresses and the global addresses.

- **Dynamic source address translation**—The user can establish dynamic mapping between the inside local addresses and the global addresses. This is done by describing the local addresses to be translated and the pool of addresses from which to allocate global addresses, and then associating the two.

- **Dynamic port translation**—The user can conserve addresses in the global address pool by allowing source ports in TCP connections or UDP conversations to be translated. Different local addresses then map to the same global address, with port translation providing the necessary uniqueness. When translation is required, the new port number is picked out of the same range as the original, following the convention of Berkeley Standard Distribution (BSD):

  (1–511, 512–1023, 1024–4999, 5000–65,535)

- **Destination address rotary translation**—A dynamic form of destination translation can be configured for some outside-to-inside traffic. After a mapping is set up, a destination address matching one of those addresses on an ACL is replaced with an address from a rotary pool. Allocation is done on a round-robin basis, performed only when a new connection is opened from the outside to the inside. All non-TCP traffic is passed untranslated (unless other translations are in effect).

When using NAT, you should *always* ensure that all corporate applications that require Internet access are supported through the firewall. Typically, the following protocols and applications are supported:

- Any TCP-based protocol that does not carry the source or destination IP address in the data portion of the segment. These protocols include ICMP, HTTP, SMTP, and others.

- Any UDP-based protocol that does not carry the source or destination IP address in the data portion of the datagram. These protocols include TFTP, NTP, and others.

NOTE   Many applications embed IP addresses into the data portion of the packet. If you are using NAT, ensure that the firewall you are using supports the translation of IP addresses within the specific applications you are using.

Implementation Examples

Now it's time to consider two scenarios:

- A Cisco IOS firewall
- A PIX firewall used in conjunction with a screening Cisco IOS router

In both cases, you should use an intrusion detection system to help get more information in case an attack is attempted and to keep active audit logs of traffic coming into or leaving the corporate network.

NOTE   The intent of the following sections is to point out practical design examples for implementing robust firewall designs. Sample scenarios are given with configuration commands that may not have been covered in detail in this text. Refer to Appendix A under "Cisco Security Product Information" for places to get more detailed configuration command information.

Cisco IOS Firewall

The Cisco IOS firewall includes features that enable the required functionality of a robust firewall. The advanced traffic session filtering is performed using the Content-Based Access Control (CBAC) mechanism.

Content-Based Access Control

Advanced packet session filtering in Cisco IOS Software is supported as of Release 11.2 with the CBAC feature. By default, Cisco routers pass all routable traffic between all router interfaces.

CBAC not only examines network layer and transport layer information, it also examines the application layer protocol information (such as FTP connection information) to learn about the state of the TCP or UDP session. In this way, CBAC allows support of protocols that involve multiple channels created as a result of negotiations in the control channel. Most of the multimedia protocols—and some other protocols (such as FTP, remote-procedure call [RPC], and SQL*Net)—involve multiple channels.

CBAC inspects traffic that travels through the firewall to discover and manage state information for TCP and UDP sessions. This state information is used to create temporary openings in the firewall's ACLs to allow return traffic and additional data connections for permissible sessions (sessions that originated from within the protected internal network).

In many cases, you will configure CBAC in one direction only at a single interface. This arrangement causes traffic to be permitted back into the internal network only if the traffic is part of a permissible (valid, existing) session.

To define a set of inspection rules, use the **ip inspect name** global configuration command:

```
ip inspect name inspection-name protocol [timeout seconds]
```

You can configure CBAC to inspect the following types of transport and application layer protocols:

- All TCP sessions, regardless of the application layer protocol (sometimes called *single-channel* or *generic* TCP inspection). This includes applications such as HTTP, Telnet, SSL, POP3, and so on. Generic TCP transport inspection works only for protocols that use a single TCP connection and are initiated from the client inside the trusted network.

- All UDP sessions, regardless of the application layer protocol (sometimes called *single-channel* or *generic* UDP inspection). This includes applications such as IPsec IKE, DNS, TFTP, NTP, SNMP, and so on. Generic UDP transport inspection works only for protocols that use a single client host/port pair and a single server host/port pair.

- CUseeMe (only the White Pine version).

- FTP. CBAC watches the FTP authentication exchange and also prevents use of nonstandard ports for FTP data.

- H.323 (such as NetMeeting, ProShare). Generic UDP must also be configured for NetMeeting because it uses additional nonstandard UDP ports.

- Java.

- UNIX R commands (such as **rlogin**, **rexec**, and **rsh**).

- RealAudio. CBAC will automatically track the RealAudio port assignments.

- RPC (Sun RPC, not DCE RPC or Microsoft RPC).

- SMTP. Only RFC 821 standard SMTP commands are permitted when using CBAC.

- SQL*Net.

- StreamWorks.

- TFTP.

- VDOLive.

When a protocol is configured for CBAC, the protocol's traffic is inspected, state information is maintained, and, in general, packets are allowed back through the firewall only if they belong to a permissible session.

NOTE Before you configure Java inspection, you must configure a standard ACL that defines "friendly" and "hostile" external sites. You configure this ACL to permit traffic from friendly sites and to deny traffic from hostile sites. If you do not configure an ACL but use a "placeholder" ACL in the **ip inspect name** *inspection-name* **http** command, all Java applets are blocked.

Create a standard ACL that permits traffic only from friendly sites and that denies traffic from hostile sites. Block all Java applets except for applets from the friendly sites defined in the ACL. Java blocking works only with standard ACLs.

```
access-list access-list-number {deny | permit} source [source-wildcard]
ip inspect name inspection-name http [java-list access-list] [timeout
seconds]
```

CBAC does not provide intelligent filtering for all protocols; it works only for the protocols you specify. If you don't specify a certain protocol for CBAC, the existing ACLs determine how that protocol is filtered. No temporary openings are created for protocols that have not been specified for CBAC inspection.

CBAC also has mechanisms that can protect against denial-of-service (DoS) attacks. A number of commands control timeout and threshold values to manage session state information and help determine when to drop sessions that do not become fully established. Table 10-3 lists the configurable parameters and their associated default values.

Table 10-3 *CBAC Default Timeout and Threshold Values*

Timeout/Threshold Value	Description	Default Value
max-incomplete high	The number of existing half-open sessions that will cause the software to start deleting half-open sessions	500
max-incomplete low	The number of existing half-open sessions that will cause the software to stop deleting half-open sessions	400
one-minute high	The rate of new unestablished sessions that will cause the software to start deleting half-open sessions	500
one-minute low	The rate of new unestablished TCP sessions that will cause the software to stop deleting half-open sessions	400
tcp finwait-time	How long a TCP session will still be managed after the firewall detects a FIN exchange	5 seconds

Table 10-3   *CBAC Default Timeout and Threshold Values (Continued)*

Timeout/Threshold Value	Description	Default Value
tcp idle-time	The length of time a TCP session will still be managed while there is no activity	3600 seconds
tcp synwait-time	How long the software will wait for a TCP session to reach the established state before dropping the session	30 seconds
udp idle-time	The length of time for which a UDP "session" will still be managed while there is no activity	30 seconds

In some instances, it may be necessary to modify the default values, but that will depend on what speeds your links are and how conservative you want to be.

There is also a command you can use to protect a specific host and set a maximum threshold for half-open TCP sessions. This can protect critical web servers explicitly. The command is as follows:

```
ip inspect max-incomplete host number block-time minutes
```

The default values are 50 half-open sessions and 0 minutes.

NOTE	A half-open session for TCP means that the three-way handshake has not yet completed, and for UDP means that the firewall has not detected any return traffic.

You can also address fragmentation attacks using CBAC by using the following command:

```
ip inspect name inspect-name fragment [max number timeout seconds]
```

Without this command, the first packet fragment is verified against any application layer CBAC checks, but any subsequent fragment can only be checked for IP layer information. When the fragment CBAC functionality is enabled, the Cisco IOS firewall maintains state information and checks the fragment sequence number, Offset field, and length to ensure that it is a valid fragment. The amount of memory dedicated to maintain the fragment state is limited by the max parameter to reduce the router becoming a victim of a potential DoS attack. To override the global timeouts for the specified protocol, specify the number of seconds for a different idle timeout.

Sample Cisco IOS Firewall Configuration

Example 10-4 shows a sample firewall configuration that implements the following policy:

- Device access is limited to the username security_geeks.
- Device authentication is performed from the local database.
- Antispoofing filters are in place for Internet connections.
- Only services initiated within the corporate environment are allowed, except for FTP and World Wide Web services to the FTP server and World Wide Web server.
- Some special debugging tools are allowed to be initiated from the Internet to the corporate network to make troubleshooting available for traveling staff.
- SNMP access is allowed only from specified internal corporate SNMP servers.

NOTE   The filters that allow incoming IP traffic are constructed in such a way that specified services are denied unless specifically permitted. This arrangement allows for more control of traffic coming into the corporate network and is the recommended method for environments with severe security concerns.

Example 10-4 *The IOS CBAC Firewall Configuration*

```
! Ensure all vty login, line, and username passwords are encrypted
! with minimal encryption (7) unless configured as a secret
! that uses MD5 encryption.

service password-encryption

! Disable access to minor TCP services such as echo,
! chargen, discard, and daytime.

no service udp-small-servers

! Disable access to minor UDP services such as echo,
! chargen, and discard.

no service tcp-small-servers

hostname imafirewall

! The enable secret

enable secret 5 $1$dLOD$QR.onv68q3326pzM.Zexj1

! Disable other unnecessary services.

no service finger
no service pad
```

Example 10-4 *The IOS CBAC Firewall Configuration (Continued)*

```
no ip bootp server

! Set local database authentication.

username security_geeks  password 7 082C495C0012001E010F02

! Allow for subnet zero networks

ip subnet-zero

! Don't need source routing.

no ip source-route

! The following commands define the inspection rule "primaryfw",
! allowing the specified protocols to be inspected. Note that Java
! applets will be permitted according to access list 66, defined later
! in this configuration.

ip inspect name primaryfw cuseeme timeout 3600
ip inspect name primaryfw ftp timeout 3600
ip inspect name primaryfw http java-list 66 timeout 3600
ip inspect name primaryfw rcmd timeout 3600
ip inspect name primaryfw realaudio timeout 3600
ip inspect name primaryfw smtp timeout 3600
ip inspect name primaryfw tftp timeout 30
ip inspect name primaryfw udp timeout 15
ip inspect name primaryfw tcp timeout 3600

! The following interface configuration applies the "primaryfw"
! inspection rule to inbound traffic at Ethernet 0. Since this interface
! is connected to the internal corporate network side of the firewall,
! traffic entering Ethernet 0 is actually exiting the trusted internal
! network. Applying the inspection rule to this interface causes all
! traffic going from the corporate network to the
! Internet to be inspected; return traffic will only be
! permitted back through the firewall if it is part of a session that
! began from within the corporate network. Also note that access list
! 101 is applied to inbound traffic at Ethernet 0. Any traffic that
! passes the access list will be inspected by CBAC. (Traffic blocked by
! the access list will not be inspected.)
!
! Access list 108 prevents spoofing by allowing only the traffic destined to
! the corporate network to go out the Ethernet 0 interface.
interface Ethernet0
 description To Corporate Network
 ip address 144.254.1.1 255.255.255.0
 no ip directed-broadcast
 no ip proxy-arp
 ip inspect primaryfw in
 ip access-group 101 in
 ip access-group 108 out
```

continues

Example 10-4 *The IOS CBAC Firewall Configuration (Continued)*

```
 no ip route-cache
 no cdp enable

interface Ethernet 1
description DMZ for ftp and www servers
ip address 144.254.2.1 255.255.255.0
no ip directed broadcast
ip access-group 102 in
no ip route-cache
no cdp enable

interface Serial0
 description Frame Relay to Internet
 no ip address
 ip broadcast-address 0.0.0.0
 encapsulation frame-relay IETF
 no ip route-cache
 no arp frame-relay
 bandwidth 56
 service-module 56k clock source line
 service-module 56k network-type dds
 frame-relay lmi-type ansi

! Note that the following interface configuration applies access list
! 111 to inbound traffic at the external serial interface. (Inbound
! traffic is entering the network.) When CBAC inspection occurs on
! traffic exiting the network, temporary openings will be added to
! access list 111 to allow returning traffic that is part of existing
! sessions.

interface Serial0.1 point-to-point
 ip unnumbered Ethernet0
 ip access-group 111 in
 no ip route-cache
 bandwidth 56
 no cdp enable
 frame-relay interface-dlci 16

! set up default route.

ip classless
ip route 0.0.0.0 0.0.0.0 Serial0.1

! Filter such that only devices on this network have SNMP access.

access-list 6 permit 144.254.9.0 0.0.0.255



! The following access list defines "friendly" and "hostile" sites for
! Java applet blocking. Because Java applet blocking is defined in the
! inspection rule "primaryfw" and references access list 66, applets
```

Example 10-4 *The IOS CBAC Firewall Configuration (Continued)*

```
! will be actively denied if they are from any of the "deny" addresses
! and allowed only if they are from either of the two "permit" networks.

access-list 66 deny    172.19.1.203
access-list 66 deny    172.19.2.147
access-list 66 permit 172.18.0.0 0.1.255.255
access-list 66 permit 192.168.1.0 0.0.0.255
access-list 66 deny    any

! The following access list 101 is applied to interface Ethernet 0
! above. This access list permits all traffic that should be CBAC
! inspected, and also provides antispoofing. The access list is
! deliberately set up to deny unknown IP protocols because no such
! unknown protocols will be in legitimate use.

access-list 101 permit tcp 144.254.0.0 0.0.255.255 any
access-list 101 permit udp 144.254.0.0 0.0.255.255 any
access-list 101 permit icmp 144.254.0.0 0.0.255.255 any
access-list 101 deny    ip any any

! Anti-spoof filters for my own network address

access-list 102 permit ip 144.254.2.0 0.0.0.255 any
access-list 108 permit ip any 144.254.0.0 0.0.255.255

! The following access list 111 is applied to interface Serial 0.1
! above. This access list filters traffic coming in from the external
! Internet side. When CBAC inspection occurs, temporary openings will be
! added to the beginning of this access list to allow return traffic
! back into the internal network. This access list should restrict
! traffic that will be inspected by CBAC.

! Antispoofing filters rfc1918 and my own network address

access-list 111 deny ip 127.0.0.0.0 0.255.255.255 any
access-list 111 deny ip 10.0.0.0 0.255.255.255 any
access-list 111 deny ip 172.16.0.0 0.15.255.255 any
access-list 111 deny ip 192.168.0.0 0.0.255.255 any
access-list 111 deny ip 144.254.0.0 0.0.255.255 any

! Allow Internet traffic for ftp, ftp-data and www to ftp server
! and www server on dmz.

access-list 111 permit ip any host 144.254.2.2   eq ftp
access-list 111 permit ip any host 144.254.2.2   eq ftp-data
access-list 111 permit ip any host 144.254.2.3   eq http

! Port 22 is used for SSH, i.e.encrypted, RSA-authenticated remote login. Can be
! used to securely access specified corporate host(s) from the Internet.

access-list 111 permit tcp any   144.254.9.0 0.0.0.255 eq 22
```

continues

Example 10-4 *The IOS CBAC Firewall Configuration (Continued)*

```
! Sometimes Enhanced IGRP is run on the Internet link. When you use
! an input access list, you have to explicitly allow control
! traffic. This could be more restrictive, but there would have to be
! entries for the Enhanced IGRP multicast as well as for the corporation's
! own unicast address.

access-list 111 permit eigrp any any

! These are the ICMP types actually used...
! administratively-prohibited is useful when you're trying to figure out
! why you can't reach something you think you should be able to reach.

access-list 111 permit icmp any 144.254.0.0 0.0.255.255 administratively-prohibited

! This allows network admins who may be traveling or otherwise coming
! in through the Internet to ping hosts at the corporate
! office.

access-list 111 permit icmp any 144.254.0.0 0.0.255.255 echo

! This allows outgoing pings

access-list 111 permit icmp any 144.254.0.0 0.0.255.255 echo-reply

! Path MTU discovery requires too-big messages

access-list 111 permit icmp any 144.254.0.0 0.0.255.255 packet-too-big

! Outgoing traceroute requires time-exceeded messages to come back

access-list 111 permit icmp any 144.254.0.0 0.0.255.255 time-exceeded

! Incoming traceroute

access-list 111 permit icmp any 144.254.0.0 0.0.255.255 traceroute

! Permits all unreachables because if you are trying to debug
! things from the corporate network, you want to see them.
! If no debugging was ever done from the network, it would be more
! appropriate to permit only port unreachables or no unreachables at
! all.

access-list 111 permit icmp any 144.254.0.0 0.0.255.255 unreachable


! Final deny all which logs all access list violations via syslog

access-list 111 deny ip any any log


no cdp run
snmp-server community public RO 6
```

Example 10-4 *The IOS CBAC Firewall Configuration (Continued)*

```
! device access controls

line con 0
  exec-timeout 2 30
  login authentication security_geeks
line aux 0
  no exec
  transport input none
line vty 0 4
  exec-timeout 2 30
  login authentication security_geeks

! Logging commands
service timestamps log datetime localtime show-timezone

logging on
logging 144.254.5.5
logging console information
```

PIX Firewall

The PIX (Private Internet Exchange) firewall is a standalone device that is totally dedicated for secure stateful packet inspection. Its logic is engineered around the Adaptive Security Algorithm (ASA), and every inbound packet is checked against the ASA and the connection state information.

Security levels are assigned to various interfaces on the PIX firewall to help identify the default behavior in a multi-interface unit. Different variants of PIX firewalls can support from 2 to 10 interfaces. The numeric security-level value can range from 0 to 100 and is configured with the following command:

  nameif *hardware_id if_name security_level*

The default behavior between the PIX firewall interfaces is as follows:

- **Traffic coming in from an interface with a higher security level and going to a destination interface with a lower security level**—Allow all IP-based traffic unless specifically restricted by ACLs.

- **Traffic coming in from an interface with a lower security level and going to a destination interface with a higher security level**—Drop all packets unless specifically allowed.

- **Traffic coming in from an interface with same security level as the destination interface security level**—No communication between the two networks.

In addition, there are some further considerations:

- The first interface has a default security level of 100 and is named inside.
- The second interface has a security level of 0 and is named outside.

- Only one network should have a security level of 100.
- Only one network should have a security level of 0.
- Multiple perimeter networks can exist.
- If a command requires two interface names, always specify the more secure name first and the less secure name second (for example, Static [inside, outside]).

Figure 10-12 shows how you can deploy different security levels on a PIX firewall with multiple interfaces.

Figure 10-12 *PIX Firewall Security Levels*

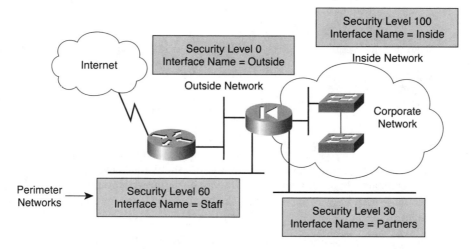

The inside network has a security level of 100; the outside interface has a security level of 0. In addition, there are two separate perimeter networks: one with a security level of 60, and another with a security level of 30. Example 10-5 shows the configuration.

Example 10-5 *Sample Security-Level Configuration*

```
nameif ethernet0 outside security0
nameif ethernet1 inside security100
nameif ethernet2 staff security60
nameif ethernet3 partners security30
```

Controlling Inbound Access

In many corporate environments, internal users are allowed access to all Internet resources, but traffic coming in from the Internet undergoes closer scrutiny. If your security policy requires that outside users access inside hosts and servers, use the **static** command to specify which IP addresses are visible on the outside interfaces. The command creates a permanent mapping (sometimes referred to as a *translation slot* or *xlate*) between a local IP address and a global IP address.

NOTE	NAT is the mechanism by which a PIX firewall allows communication between its interfaces. By default, the PIX firewall protects corporate network addresses from being visible to an external network. The **nat** command is used to enable or disable address translation for one or more internal addresses. As a rule of thumb, for access from a higher security level interface to a lower security level interface, use the **nat** command. From a lower security level interface to a higher security level interface, use the **static** command.

The **static** command must be followed by the **conduit** command (or **access-list** command in newer software versions) to specify which services outside users can access on the internal servers. These commands take the following form:

```
static [(internal_if_name, external_if_name)] global_ip local_ip
  [netmask network_mask] [max_conns [em_limit]] [norandomseq]

conduit permit¦deny protocol global_ip global_mask [operator port [port]]
  foreign_ip foreign_mask [operator port [port]]
```

Together, a **static** and **conduit** (or **access-list**) statement pair create an exception to the PIX firewall adaptive security mechanism by permitting connections from one firewall network interface to access hosts on another.

The **conduit** command is being phased out in favor of the **access-list** command, which can take the following form:

```
access-list acl-ID permit¦deny protocol {source_addr ¦ local_addr}
  {source_mask ¦ local_mask} [operator port [port]]
  {destination_addr ¦ remote_addr} {destination_mask ¦ remote_mask}
  [operator port [port]]
```

It is very similar to the Cisco IOS **access-list** command with one extremely important exception. The netmask is defined in the opposite way. For Cisco IOS ACLs, the netmask is represented by using 0s to represent the network number and 1s to represent the host number. For PIX firewall ACLs, the netmask is represented by what's referred to as the *natural mask*, where 1s are used to represent the network number and 0s are used to represent the host number. The following example shows the difference:

- Cisco IOS: **access-list dontbeconfused permit tcp any 144.254.0.0 0.0.255.255**

- PIX firewall: **access-list dontbeconfused permit tcp any 144.254.0.0 255.255.0.0**

With the **access-list** command, greater functionality will be introduced in future PIX products; it would, therefore, be wise for you to convert to using them now. If you have more than 19 access list entries, you can use the command **access-list compiled** to more efficiently process ACLs. Note that this command is supported only for PIX firewall platforms that have 16 MB of Flash memory.

Controlling Outbound Access

Outbound access control is accomplished using ACLs. The ACLs are created with the **outbound** command and are based on the following information:

- IP source address
- IP destination address
- IP protocol type
- Destination port number

An **outbound** command requires the use of the **apply** command. The **apply** command enables you to specify whether the ACL applies to inside users' ability to start outbound connections with the **apply** command's **outgoing_src** option, or whether the ACL applies to inside users' ability to access servers on the outside network with the **apply** command's **outgoing_dest** option.

The commands take the following form:

```
outbound list_ID permit¦deny ip_address [netmask [java¦port[-port]]] [protocol]
outbound list_ID except ip_address [netmask [java¦port[-port]]] [protocol]
apply [(if_name)] list_ID outgoing_src¦outgoing_dest
```

The outbound controls are typically used for the following situations:

- Whether one or more inside users can create outbound connections (single IP address, single subnet, or all IP addresses)
- Whether inside users can access specific outside servers
- Which services inside users can use for outbound connections and to access outside servers
- Whether outbound connections can execute Java applets on the inside network

Example 10-6 shows a configuration that permits only outbound HTTP traffic from a specified source address.

Example 10-6 *Controlling Outbound Traffic on a PIX Firewall*

```
outbound 1 deny    0.0.0.0       0.0.0.0        0    tcp
outbound 1 except 192.168.0.2  255.255.255.255    http
apply (inside)   1    outgoing_src
```

Cut-Thru-Proxy Feature

Whenever you permit outside users access to your network, you should establish a user authentication and authorization system. The PIX has a feature called *Cut-Thru-Proxy* that enables authentication based on FTP, HTTP, or Telnet traffic and subsequent authorization for any allowed application traffic. The example in Figure 10-13 shows the use of this feature.

In the figure, any outbound FTP or HTTP traffic must be successfully authenticated before the connection is established, as illustrated in Example 10-7.

Example 10-7 *PIX Firewall Cut-Thru-Proxy Configuration*

```
aaa authentication ftp, http inbound 0.0.0.0 0.0.0.0 tacacs+
aaa authorization ftp, http inbound 0.0.0.0 0.0.0.0
tacacs-server host 144.254.5.9 sharedsecret
```

When an outside user tries to access the corporate FTP server, the following sequence of steps occur:

Step 1   The user from the Internet initiates an HTTP or FTP request to a specified corporate server.

Step 2   The firewall intercepts the connection and initiates the authentication process (in this case, using TACACS+).

Step 3   If the user authenticates successfully, the firewall completes the HTTP or FTP connection to the specified corporate server.

Step 4   The firewall forwards requests and responses without further intervention.

Figure 10-13 *The PIX Cut-Thru Proxy Feature (FTP and HTTP)*

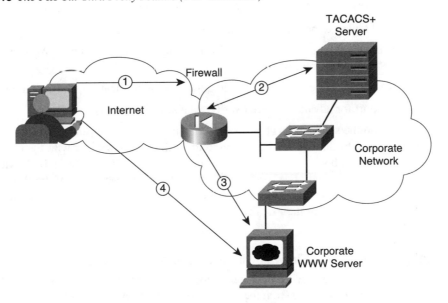

Example 10-8 shows a corresponding sample user profile on the TACACS+ server that authorizes an authenticated user to use FTP on 144.254.1.4 and HTTP on 144.254.1.3.

Example 10-8 *TACACS+ User Profile to Match Cut-Thru-Proxy Configuration*

```
{
Profile_cycle = 11
Profile_id = 8
Password = clear "abcd"
Set Server current failed_login = 0
Service = Shell {
cmd = ftp {
permit 144.254.1.4
}
cmd = http {
permit 144.254.1.3
}
}
}
```

Advanced Features

The PIX firewall has numerous advanced features, including the following:

- Support for IPsec and L2TP/PPTP-based virtual private networks (VPNs)
- Flood Guard and Fragmentation Guard to protect against DoS attacks
- Mail Guard to protect against attacks on a mail server
- Support for high-performance URL filtering via integration with WebSense-based URL filtering solutions
- AAA capabilities for scalable authentication, authorization, and accounting
- Support for advanced Voice over IP standards

It is beyond the scope of this book to describe the PIX firewall functionality in detail, and only a brief introduction has been offered to familiarize the reader with the most basic commands. The book *Cisco Secure PIX Firewalls* (Cisco Press, 2001), by David W. Chapman, Jr. and Andy Fox, provides a comprehensive description of the PIX firewall. Chapter 12 in this book describes VPN scenarios and shows configuration examples using IPsec that also include the PIX firewall.

Sample Configuration of PIX Firewall with Screening IOS Router

In this scenario, the Cisco IOS router is used as the screening router to provide basic filtering of traffic coming from the Internet. The PIX firewall provides the more robust firewall features, as shown in Figure 10-14.

Figure 10-14 *Sample Cisco PIX Firewall with Cisco IOS Screening Router*

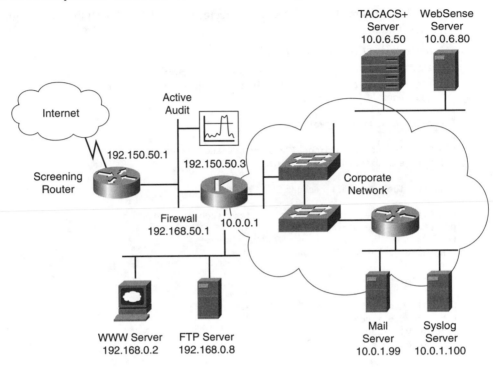

The sample configurations in Examples 10-9 and 10-10 depict the implementation of the following Internet access security policy:

- Device (screening router and firewall) access is through TACACS+ authentication and authorization.

- The screening router has simple antispoofing filters.

- Two illegal networks (192.168.0.0 and 10.0.0.0) must make use of NAT to convert to the legal address given by the ISP of 192.150.50.0.

- Hosts on the 10.0.0.0 network can access everything.

- Hosts on the 192.168.0.0 network can access the Internet but cannot access hosts on the 10.0.0.0 network.

- Only Internet traffic from 144.254.0.0 can access the FTP server whose illegal 192.168.0.6 address must be assigned the legal address 192.150.50.6.

- The FTP traffic must be authenticated using TACACS+.

- All Internet web (HTTP) traffic is directed to host 192.168.0.2. (It must be assigned the legal address of 192.150.50.9.)

- All outbound web traffic is sent to do a URL check by way of the WebSense server.
- All Internet mail (SMTP) traffic is directed to host 10.0.1.99. (It must be assigned the legal address of 192.150.50.7.)

Example 10-9 *Configuration of Cisco IOS Screening Router*

```
! Ensure all vty login, line, and username passwords are encrypted
! with minimal encryption (7) unless configured as a secret
! that uses MD5 encryption.

service password-encryption

! Disable access to minor TCP services such as echo,
! chargen, discard, and daytime.

no service udp-small-servers

! Disable access to minor UDP services such as echo,
! chargen, and discard.

no service tcp-small-servers

hostname screen

enable secret 5 $1$dLOD$QR.onv68q3326pzM.Zexj1
no service finger
no service pad
no ip bootp server

no ip source-route

! Configure TACACS+ authentication as default - for users logging in as
! staff, there is a local database authentication in the event that the
! TACACS+ server is unavailable.

aaa new-model
aaa authentication login default tacacs+
aaa authentication login staff tacacs+ local
aaa authorization exec tacacs+  local

! Interim accounting records will be sent every time there is
! new information to report
! accounting for all exec terminal sessions.

aaa accounting update newinfo
aaa accounting exec start-stop tacacs+

! Set local database authentication.

username staff password 7 082C495C0012001E010F02

! Configure the interfaces.
```

Example 10-9 *Configuration of Cisco IOS Screening Router (Continued)*

```
interface Serial 0/0
description to the Internet
ip address 161.71.73.33 255.255.255.248
ip access-group 109 in

interface Ethernet1/0

 description To Corporate Network
 ip address 192.150.50.1 255.255.255.0
 no ip directed-broadcast
 no ip proxy-arp
 ip access-group 108 in
 no ip route-cache
 no cdp enable

! Antispoof filter for internal network

access-list 108 permit ip  192.150.50.0  0.0.0.255 any

! Antispoof filters for rfc1918 addresses.

access-list 109 deny ip 127.0.0.0 0.255.255.255 any
access-list 109 deny ip 10.0.0.0 0.255.255.255 any
access-list 109 deny ip 172.16.0.0 0.15.255.255 any
access-list 109 deny ip 192.168.0.0 0.0.255.255 any

! Allow any tcp traffic that has been established from the corporate network.

access-list 109 permit tcp any any established

! allow Internet traffic for ftp and ftp-data only from network 144.254.0.0

access-list 109 permit tcp 144.254.0.0 0.0.255.255  host 192.150.50.8  eq ftp
access-list 109 permit tcp 144.254.0.0 0.0.255.255  host 192.150.50.8  eq ftp-data

! Allow Internet traffic for smtp and www server to specific servers.

access-list 109 permit tcp any host 192.150.50.9  eq http
access-list 109 permit tcp any host 192.150.50.7  eq smtp

! Sometimes Enhanced IGRP is run on the Internet link. When you use
! an input access list, you have to explicitly allow control
! traffic. This could be more restrictive, but there would have to be
! entries for the Enhanced IGRP multicast as well as for the corporation's
! own unicast address.

access-list 109 permit eigrp any any

! These are the ICMP types actually used...
! administratively-prohibited is useful when you're trying to figure out
! why you can't reach something you think you should be able to reach.
```

continues

Example 10-9 *Configuration of Cisco IOS Screening Router (Continued)*

```
access-list 109 permit icmp any 192.150.50.0 0.0.0.255 administratively-prohibited

! This allows network admins who may be traveling or otherwise coming
! in through the Internet to ping hosts at the corporate
! office:

access-list 109 permit icmp any 192.150.50.0 0.0.0.255 echo

! This allows outgoing pings.

access-list 109 permit icmp any 192.150.50.0 0.0.0.255 echo-reply

! Path MTU discovery requires too-big messages.

access-list 109 permit icmp any 192.150.50.0 0.0.0.255 packet-too-big

! Outgoing traceroute requires time-exceeded messages to come back.

access-list 109 permit icmp any 192.150.50.0 0.0.0.255 time-exceeded

! Incoming traceroute

access-list 109 permit icmp any 192.150.50.0 0.0.0.255 traceroute

! Permits all unreachables because if you are trying to debug
! things from the corporate network, you want to see them.
! If no debugging was ever done from the network, it would be more
! appropriate to permit only port unreachables or no unreachables at
! all.

access-list 109 permit icmp any 192.150.50.0 0.0.0.255 unreachable

! Final deny all which logs all access list violations via syslog

access-list 109 deny ip any any log

no cdp run

! configure tacacs+ parameters

tacacs-server host 192.150.50.10
tacacs-server key thisisakey

! configure device access.

line con 0
  exec-timeout 2 30
  login authentication staff

line aux 0
  no exec
  transport input none
```

Example 10-9 *Configuration of Cisco IOS Screening Router (Continued)*

```
line vty 0 4
  exec-timeout 2 30
  login authentication default

! Configure logging.
service timestamps log datetime localtime show-timezone

logging on
logging 192.150.50.11
logging console information
```

Example 10-10 *Configuration of PIX Firewall*

```
! Sets the security levels for each interface, specifies that each
! interface uses Ethernet, and assigns IP addresses and network
! masks.

nameif ethernet0 outside security0
nameif ethernet1 inside security100
nameif ethernet2 dmz security50
interface ethernet0 auto
interface ethernet1 auto
interface ethernet2 auto

ip address outside 192.150.50.3 255.255.255.255
ip address inside 10.0.0.1 255.255.255.0
ip address dmz 192.168.0.1 255.255.255.0

! Specifies the host name for the PIX firewall.

hostname pixfirewall

! Define enable password and Telnet password.

enable password BjeuCKspwqCc94Ss encrypted
passwd nU3DFZzS7jF1jYc5 encrypted


! The following performs defined protocol security checks.

fixup protocol ftp 21
fixup protocol http 80
fixup protocol h323 1720
fixup protocol rsh 514
fixup protocol smtp 25
fixup protocol sqlnet 1521
!
! Enables use of text strings instead of IP addresses. This makes your
! configuration files more readable.
```

continues

Example 10-10   *Configuration of PIX Firewall (Continued)*

```
names

! Enables paging so that if 24 lines of information
! display, PIX firewall pauses the listing and prompts you
! to continue.

pager lines 24

! The logging host command specifies which host runs a syslog server.
! This command also causes the PIX firewall to start sending syslog
! messages to that host. The logging trap command sets syslog to send
! all possible messages to the syslog host. The no logging console
! command disables displaying messages to the console.

logging on
logging host 10.0.1.100
logging trap 7
logging facility 20
no logging console

! Sets the ARP timeout to 14,400 seconds (four hours).
! Entries are kept in the ARP table for four hours before
! they are flushed. Four hours is the standard default value
! for ARP timeouts.

arp timeout 14400

! Create a pool of addresses to be used with NAT.

global (outside) 1 192.150.50.15-192.150.50.250 netmask 255.255.255.0

! Enable IP communications between hosts on the 10.0.0.0 network and host on
! either the Internet or the 192.168.0.0 network. For communication to the
! Internet, the source IP address gets substituted with an address from the
! global pool.

nat (inside) 1 10.0.0.0 255.0.0.0 0 0

! Enables IP communications between hosts on the 192.168.0.0 network and
! the Internet. Any address starting with 192.168.0 will be substituted
! with an address from the global pool

nat (dmz) 1 192.168.0.0 255.255.255.0 0 0

! Define static translations for the FTP server, web server, SMTP server,
! TACACS+ server, and syslog server.

static (dmz, outside) 192.150.50.6 192.168.0.6 netmask 255.255.255.255 0 0
static (dmz, outside) 192.150.50.9 192.168.0.2 netmask 255.255.255.255 0 0
static (inside, outside) 192.150.50.7 10.0.1.99 netmask 255.255.255.255 0 0

static (inside, outside) 192.150.50.10 10.0.0.100 netmask 255.255.255.255 0 0
```

Example 10-10 *Configuration of PIX Firewall (Continued)*

```
static (inside, outside) 192.150.50.11 10.0.6.50 netmask 255.255.255.255 0 0

! Allows packets from 10.0.0.0 network to go to the 192.168.0.0 network.

statix (inside, dmz) 10.0.0.0 192.168.0.0 netmask 255.0.0.0 0 0


! Enables www access to 192.168.0.2 - this command requires the static command
! above to know proper translated address.

conduit permit tcp host 192.150.50.9 eq www any

! Enables SMTP access to 10.0.1.99 - this command requires the static command
! above to know proper translated address.

conduit permit tcp host 192.150.50.7 eq smtp any

! Allow FTP access from hosts from 144.254.0.0 network.

conduit permit tcp host 192.150.50.6 eq ftp 144.254.0.0 255.255.0.0

! Sets RIP listening attributes. The three no rip interface passive lines
! cause the PIX firewall to not listen to RIP broadcasts on each interface.
! The no rip interface default lines causes PIX firewall to not
! broadcast a default route on any interface.

no rip inside passive
no rip outside passive
no rip dmz passive
no rip inside default
no rip outside default
no rip dmz default

! Sets the outside default route to the router attached to the Internet.

route outside 0.0.0.0 0.0.0.0 192.150.50.1 1

! Default values for the maximum duration that PIX firewall resources
! can remain idle until being freed. To improve system performance,
! you can set the xlate and conn timers from 24 hours to 1 hour.

timeout xlate 24:00:00 conn 12:00:00 udp 0:02:00
timeout rpc 0:10:00 h323 0:05:00 uauth 0:05:00

! Use WebSense server which has address 10.0.6.80 - all outbound URL requests are
! sent to the WebSense server.

url-server (inside) host 10.0.6.80 timeout 5
filter url http 0.0.0.0 0.0.0.0 0.0.0.0 0.0.0.0

! Authenticate FTP traffic via TACACS+.
```

continues

Example 10-10 *Configuration of PIX Firewall (Continued)*

```
tacacs--server host 10.0.6.50 thisisakey
aaa authentication ftp inbound 192.168.0.6 255.255.255.255 144.254.0.0 255.255.0.0

! Give Telnet access to PIX firewall console to inside hosts on 10.0.8.0 subnet.

telnet 10.0.8.0 255.255.255.0

! Sets the maximum transmission unit value for Ethernet access.

mtu outside 1500
mtu inside 1500
mtu dmz 1500
```

Summary

This chapter discussed general architectures for securing Internet access to the corporate network and showed two specific implementations that illustrate some configurations when using Cisco devices. Many variants are possible, depending on how open or restrictive your corporate environment is. It is often best to permit only IP services that are supported in the corporation and to deny all others. This arrangement allows for fairly strict control of traffic entering or leaving the corporate network through the Internet connection. For more robust Internet access monitoring and control, it is usually a good idea to include some kind of intrusion detection system and active audit component into the Internet access implementation architecture.

Review Questions

1 In a firewall strategy that includes an external screening router, what is the role of this router?

2 Which of the following is a good strategy to adhere to for providing services such as DNS, HTTP, and e-mail to outside users?

   A   Distribute all services to different subnets.

   B   Place all services on a single subnet.

   C   Do not offer any services to outside users.

   D   Interview all users before allowing access.

3 Why can it be more important to create filter lists based on destination UDP/TCP ports rather than source UDP/TCP ports?

4 What are three characteristics of Cisco IOS standard and extended access lists?

5 What is one of the important characteristics of Cisco IOS named access lists?

6 True of false: A robust firewall must have the capability to do packet-by-packet inspection and filtering on specific packet session information.

7 Why can encrypted confidential traffic pose a problem for firewalls?

8 True or false: The use of NAT provides a security feature because private addresses are kept private.

9 Identify the Class A, Class B, and Class C networks that have been reserved by IANA for private address space use (that is, NAT).

10 Which of the following is not true?

  A   CBAC examines the application layer protocol information to learn about the state of a TCP or UDP session.

  B   CBAC does not provide intelligent filtering for all protocols; it works only for the protocols you specify.

  C   CBAC has mechanisms that can protect against DoS attacks.

  D   None of the above; they are all true statements.

11 True or false: The default behavior on a PIX firewall for traffic coming in from an interface with a lower security level and going to a destination interface with a higher security level is to allow all IP-based traffic unless specifically restricted by access control lists.

12 What is the one significant difference between how Cisco IOS IP addresses are defined and how they are defined on a PIX firewall?

## CHAPTER 11

Securing Remote Dial-In Access

Remote access environments include VPN networks, wireless networks, and dial-in connections. VPN networks and wireless networking scenarios are covered in the next chapter. This chapter examines how to secure the remote dial-in connections coming into the corporate network. Often, corporate networks encompass both privately connected dial-in infrastructures (direct dial-in) and public data infrastructures (virtual private dial-in networks). Virtual private dial-in networks (VPDNs) refer to outsourced services from Internet service providers (ISPs) to deliver remote access to corporate users. The ISP recognizes that a particular client belongs to an enterprise and handles the client such that the network has a "private" feel to it. Dial-in access for a corporate network usually includes access between corporate branches located in different geographic regions, telecommuters, and mobile users.

The direct dial-in access can be by way of Public Switched Telephone Networks (PSTNs)—for example, modem lines or ISDN. VPDN network access is usually provided using Frame Relay, ATM, T1/T3 circuits, DSL, or cable modems. Figure 11-1 shows a sample dial-in environment; notice that there are branch offices connected with T1 lines, mobile users dialing in with modems, and telecommuters dialing in using ISDN BRI.

Figure 11-1 *A Sample Dial-In Access Environment*

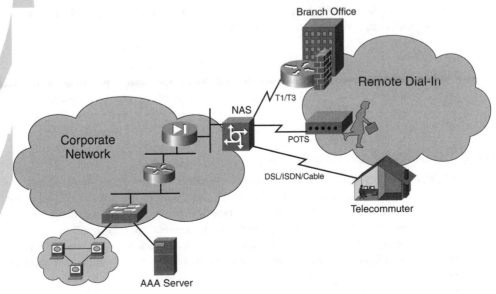

Another way corporations provide dial-in access is by partnering with an ISP and using the ISP's public infrastructure to provide network access. This concept of virtual private dial-in is shown in Figure 11-2. For this model to work in a secure manner, tunneling technologies, such as GRE, L2F, L2TP, or IPsec, must be used to provide secure access back to the corporate network.

Figure 11-2   *Dial-In Access Using the Internet*

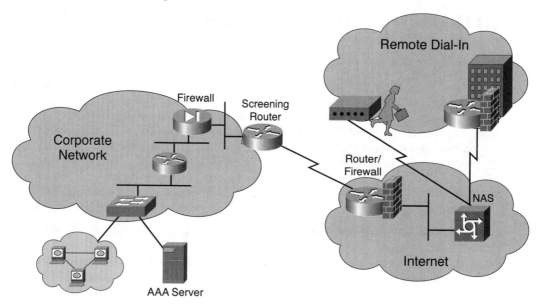

The following sections look at both the direct dial-in and the virtual dial-in scenarios and examine ways that various protocols can be applied.

NOTE   The example configurations given are specific to Cisco Systems equipment; however, many of the functions shown can also be used with other vendors' products if they are available.

Dial-In Security Concerns

The dial-in environment has security considerations similar to those involved in securing a corporation's Internet access, discussed in the preceding chapter. It may be necessary to restrict access to certain areas of the corporate network depending on who the remote user is and from where the user is trying to obtain the connection. It is usually a good idea to incorporate firewall functionality into the dial-in access perimeters and to implement some kind of auditing and intrusion detection system to keep accurate connection and traffic statistics.

Regardless of how dial-in access is provided to the corporate network (as an extension using leased lines, ISDN, or plain old telephone service [POTS] networks, or as a connection from remote parts of the Internet), the main security concerns lie in the following areas:

- Identifying the caller
- Identifying the location of the caller
- Identifying the destination of the call
- Keeping track of accessed applications and data
- Keeping track of the duration of a connection
- Ensuring authenticated communication
- Ensuring private communication

NOTE   For all equipment that is part of the dial-in infrastructure, the same security precautions should be used on the devices composing the corporate dial-in infrastructure as described in Chapter 9, "Securing the Corporate Network Infrastructure."

Authenticating Dial-In Users and Devices

A key element in allowing dial-in connectivity is to know who is accessing your corporate network by establishing an initial authentication mechanism. Authentication can be performed at the device level or at the user level.

Serial Line Internet Protocol (SLIP) and Point-to-Point Protocol (PPP) are two common methods of sending IP packets over standard asynchronous serial lines with minimum line speeds of 1200 baud. Using SLIP or PPP encapsulation over asynchronous lines is an inexpensive way to connect PCs to a network. SLIP and PPP over asynchronous dialup modems allow a home computer to be connected to a network without the cost of a leased line. Dialup SLIP and PPP links can also be used for remote sites that need only occasional remote node or backup connectivity. Both public-domain and vendor-supported SLIP and PPP implementations are available for a variety of computer applications.

NOTE   PPP is a newer, more robust protocol than SLIP and provides more built-in security mechanisms. PPP is much more prevalent than SLIP in modern networks.

Simple Dial-In Environments

Most serial line connections make use of PPP encapsulation, which can use a variety of authentication mechanisms to establish the identity of a peer device. (Refer to Chapter 2, "Security Technologies.") Figure 11-3 shows an example of a simple dial-in environment. Notice that only two remote branch offices need nonpermanent low-bandwidth or variable-bandwidth connections to the corporate network (and can therefore connect to the corporate campus using ISDN). The corporate network also accommodates a few mobile users dialing in with modem connections. Challenge Handshake Authentication Protocol (CHAP) is used as the primary authentication method with PAP as the fallback method. Examples 11-1 and 11-2 show the configurations of these routers.

Figure 11-3 *An Example of a Small Company's Dial-In Environment*

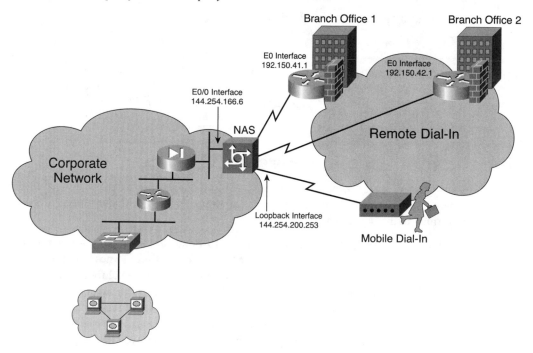

Example 11-1 *Configuration of the Corporate Access Router*

```
hostname CORPORATE-NAS
!
! Ensure all vty, login, line, and username passwords are encrypted.
! In the configuration file using minimal encryption (type 7)
! unless configured as a secret which uses MD5 encryption (type 5).
!
service password-encryption
!
```

Example 11-1 *Configuration of the Corporate Access Router (Continued)*

```
! Disables access to minor TCP services such as echo,
! chargen, discard, and daytime.
!
no service tcp-small-servers
!
! Disables access to minor UDP services such as echo,
! chargen, and discard.
!
no service udp-small-servers
!
!Define privileged access password.
!
enable secret letmedostuff
!
! Define modem usernames and passwords.
!
username merike password ilikeAbsolut
username toivo password joekeg
username staff password iamincontrol
!
! Define shared passwords for CHAP authentication with branch routers.
!
username BRANCH1 password letmein
username BRANCH2 password knockknock
!
! Define ISDN switch type.
!
isdn switch-type primary-5ess
!
! Loopback interface is 'logical' subnet to which
! all dial-in users belong.
!
interface loopback 0
ip address 144.254.200.253 255.255.255.0
!
! Define local LAN interface.
!
interface Ethernet 0/0
description Corporation LAN
ip address 144.254.166.6 255.255.255.0
!
! Configure framing commands.
!
controller T1 1/0
  framing esf
  clock source line primary
  linecode b8zs
  pri-group timeslots 1-24
!
! Configure PRI.
!
interface Serial1/0:23
```

continues

Example 11-1 *Configuration of the Corporate Access Router (Continued)*

```
  description To Branch Routers
  no ip address
encapsulation ppp
!
! Route incoming ISDN modem calls to the modem module.
!
isdn incoming-voice modem
!
! To use dialer profiles just in case we expand to
! another PRI in the future
!
dialer rotary-group 0
dialer-group 1
!
no fair-queue
no cdp enable
!
! Set up a dialer profile.
!
interface Dialer0
!
!Users will be on subnet defined under loopback 0.
!
ip unnumbered Loopback0
no ip mroute-cache
encapsulation ppp
!
! Assign IP addresses from pool named dialup.
!
peer default ip address pool dialup
dialer in-band
!
! Define which packets keep link up as defined by dialer list.
!
dialer-group 1
no fair-queue
no cdp enable
!
! Define CHAP authentication with PAP as fallback.
!
ppp authentication chap pap
ppp multilink
!
! Modem access configuration.
!
interface Group-Async1
!
! Users will be on subnet defined by loopback 0.
!
ip unnumbered loopback0
encapsulation ppp
!
```

Example 11-1 *Configuration of the Corporate Access Router (Continued)*

```
! User interactively selects to use box as a
! terminal server or a PPP router.
!
async mode interactive
!
! Assign IP address from pool named dialup.
!
peer default ip address pool dialup
no cdp enable
!
! Define CHAP authentication with PAP as fallback.
!
ppp authentication chap pap
!
!Define all async lines to belong to this interface.
!
group-range 1 16
!
! Address pool for dial-in users
!
ip local pool dialup 144.254.200.20 144.254.200.50
!
!configure routing
!
router eigrp 109
redistribute static
passive-interface Dialer0
network 144.254.0.0
no auto-summary
!
ip route 192.150.41.0  255.255.255.0 Dialer0
ip route 192.150.42.0  255.255.255.0 Dialer0
!
! Permit dialing and keep line up for IP traffic.
!
dialer-list 1 protocol ip permit
!
! Physical console access accessible with any login name
! but requires correct password.
!
line con 0
login
password igetfullcontrol
!
! Modem RS-232 interface configuration
!
  line 1 16
!
! Use local database to authenticate users.
!
  login local
! Present a login prompt but monitor packets.
```

continues

Example 11-1 *Configuration of the Corporate Access Router (Continued)*

```
!
  autoselect during-login
!
! If PPP packet detected, shift automatically into PPP mode.
!
  autoselect ppp
!
! Selects state machine for CD and DTR modem signals.
!
  modem InOut
!
! Allow connections to modem using any transport.
!
  transport input all
!
! No login prompt and no input access allowed through auxiliary port.
!
  line aux 0
  no exec
  transport input none
!
! Virtual terminal line (Telnet) access using any login name
! but requires correct password.
!
  line vty 0 4
  exec-timeout 20 0
  login
  password letmein
!
```

Example 11-2 *Configuration of the Branch Routers*

```
hostname BRANCH1
!  BRANCH2: hostname BRANCH2
!
service password-encryption
no service udp-small-servers
no service tcp-small-servers
!
!Define shared passwords for CHAP authentication with Corporate NAS.
! For BRANCH2 router it would be: username CORPORATE-NAS password knockknock.
!
username CORPORATE-NAS password letmein


!
isdn switch-type basic-5ess
!
! Configure Ethernet interface.
! For BRANCH2 router IP address would be 192.150.42.1  255.255.255.0.
!
interface Ethernet0
```

Example 11-2   *Configuration of the Branch Routers (Continued)*

```
ip address 192.150.41.1   255.255.255.0

!
! Configure BRI interface.
!
interface BRI0
description ISDN TO CORPORATE
ip unnumbered Ethernet0
encapsulation ppp
dialer wait-for-carrier-time 60
dialer map IP 144.254.166.6   name CORPORATE-NAS speed 56 5551234
dialer load-threshold 100 either
dialer-group 1
ppp authentication chap pap
!
! Configure routing.
!
ip classless
ip route 0.0.0.0 0.0.0.0 144.254.166.6
ip route 144.254.166.6 255.255.255.255 BRI0
!
dialer-list 1 list protocol ip permit
!
! Physical console access accessible using any login name
! but requires correct password.
!
line con 0
  login
  password igetfullcontrol
!
! No login prompt and no input access allowed through auxiliary port.
!
  line aux 0
  no exec
  transport input none
!
! Virtual terminal line (Telnet) access using any login name
! but requires correct password.
!
  line vty 0 4
  exec-timeout 20 0
  login
  password letmein
!
```

NOTE	Because the branch routers connect to the same device at the corporate office and provide the same functionality, their configurations are nearly identical. Only one configuration is given for the branch routers; differences to show what should be configured on the BRANCH2 router were shown in the comments.

Complex Dial-In Environments

Configuring PAP or CHAP authentication on individual devices is manageable in simple environments. In corporations with hundreds or thousands of dial-in connections, however, a more scalable approach must be used. To scale to a large number of users, consider incorporating either TACACS+ or RADIUS as a better way to provide a manageable database of users. Although CHAP and PAP can be used with RADIUS and TACACS+, a more flexible PPP authentication method would be to use EAP. Both TACACS+ and RADIUS provide for separate authentication, authorization, and accounting facilities. When you use either TACACS+ or RADIUS with EAP, the authentication mechanisms can take multiple forms, including these:

- Static password
- Changeable password
- One-time password
- NT database authentication
- UNIX /etc/password authentication
- Kerberos
- Digital certificates

TACACS+ and RADIUS Authentication

To enable TACACS+ on a Cisco network access server (NAS), enter the following commands:

```
aaa new-model
tacacs-server host ip-address-of-tacacs-server
tacacs-server key key
```

The *key* must be specified both here and in the TACACS+ server configuration file if you want the packets to be encrypted between the server and the client (the NAS).

To enable RADIUS on a Cisco NAS, enter the following commands:

```
aaa new-model
radius-server host ip-address-of-radius-server
radius-server key key
```

The *key* must be specified both here and in the RADIUS server configuration file if you want the password in the packet to be encrypted between the server and the client (the NAS).

Two steps are required to configure the actual authentication mechanisms: defining a method list and applying the method list to an appropriate interface.

Defining a Method List

The first step in configuring either TACACS+ or RADIUS authentication is to define a method list. A *method list* is just a list describing the authentication methods to be queried, in sequence, to authenticate a user. Method lists enable you to designate one or more security protocols to be used for authentication, thus ensuring a backup system for authentication in case the initial method fails. Cisco IOS Software uses the first method listed to authenticate users; if that method fails to respond, the Cisco IOS Software selects the next authentication method listed in the method list. This process continues until there is successful communication with a listed authentication method—or until all methods defined are exhausted. The method list must be applied to an interface before any of the defined authentication methods are performed.

NOTE	The Cisco IOS Software attempts authentication with the next-listed authentication method only when there is no response from the previous method. If authentication fails at any point in this cycle—meaning that the security server or local username database responds by denying the user access—the authentication process stops, and no other authentication methods are attempted.

The syntax for specifying a method list on the access server is as follows:

```
aaa authentication service {default | list-name} method-type1
    method-type2 method-type3 method-type4
```

Table 11-1 lists the definable authentication services.

Table 11-1   *AAA Authentication Services*

Service	Description
arap	Sets authentication list for AppleTalk Remote Access (ARA) users' attempts to log in to the router.
nasi	Sets authentication list for NetWare Asynchronous Services Interface (NASI) users' attempts to log in to the router.
enable	Sets authentication list for enable mode.
login	Sets authentication lists for character mode connections.
ppp	Sets authentication lists for PPP connections.

You can specify up to four different authentication methods per method list for backup purposes. Table 11-2 lists the methods that you can use to authenticate a user for the defined service. Although all supported methods are listed, this discussion concentrates specifically on TACACS+ and RADIUS as the primary authentication methods.

Table 11-2 *AAA Authentication Methods*

Method Type	Description
enable	Use the enable password for authentication.
line	Use the line password for authentication.
local	Use the local database for authentication.
none	No authentication.
tacacs+	Use TACACS+ for authentication.
radius	Use RADIUS for authentication
krb5	Use Kerberos 5 for authentication.
krb5-telnet	Use Kerberos 5 Telnet authentication protocol when using Telnet to connect to the router. If selected, this keyword must be listed as the first method in the method list.
auth-guest	Allow guest logins only if the user has already logged in to EXEC.
guest	Allow guest logins.
if-needed	Do not authenticate if the user has already been authenticated on a tty line.

Not all services can use all methods. Table 11-3 shows which authentication methods can be defined for which services in Cisco IOS Software devices.

NOTE   In more recent versions of Cisco IOS Software, the keyword group was added to support a list of TACACS+ and RADIUS servers.

Table 11-3 *Authentication Methods and Their Corresponding Services*

Method	ARAP	NASI	Enable	Login	PPP
enable	N/A	X	X	X	N/A
line	X	X	X	X	N/A
local	X	X	N/A	X	X
none	N/A	X	X	X	X
tacacs+	X	X	X	X	X

Table 11-3   *Authentication Methods and Their Corresponding Services (Continued)*

Method	ARAP	NASI	Enable	Login	PPP
radius	X	N/A	X	X	X
krb5	N/A	N/A	N/A	X	X
krb5-telnet	N/A	N/A	N/A	X	N/A
auth-guest	X	N/A	N/A	N/A	N/A
guest	X	N/A	N/A	N/A	N/A
if-needed	N/A	N/A	N/A	N/A	X

After defining the authentication method list, you must apply it to the appropriate interface or line.

Although you can use any name to define a method list, there is a reserved name known as *default*. The authentication methods defined within default are applied to any interface or line that does not have any other list linked to it. However, any named list overrides the default method list.

NOTE   To configure the Cisco IOS Software to check the local user database for authentication before attempting another form of authentication, use the **aaa authentication local-override** command. This command proves useful when you want to configure an override to the normal authentication process for certain personnel (such as system administrators).

The following examples show some typical uses of the **aaa authentication** command:

- The following command specifies that a user trying to make a character mode login to the router must be authenticated by the TACACS+ server; if that server fails to respond, use the local database instead:

  `aaa authentication login ADMIN tacacs+ local`

NOTE   The local database is checked only if the TACACS+ server fails to respond, not if the user fails authentication with the TACACS+ server.

- The following command specifies that a user attempting a PPP connection to the router must authenticate with the RADIUS server; if that fails, the user must provide the enable password:

  `aaa authentication ppp USER radius enable`

- The following command specifies that the default for character mode access is to use RADIUS unless otherwise stated:

  ```
  aaa authentication login default radius
  ```

- The following command specifies that the default for packet mode access is to use TACACS+ authentication:

  ```
  aaa authentication ppp default tacacs+
  ```

Linking the Method List to a Line or Interface

After a method list has been created, the next step is to link the method list to a line or interface. The following examples provide some typical uses.

Example 11-3 configures TACACS+ as the security protocol to be used for PPP authentication using the method list dialusers.

Example 11-3   *PPP Authentication Using TACACS+*

```
! Define a local user database.
username merike secret LetMeIn
username cathy secret MeToo
!
! Turn on aaa.
!
aaa new-model
!
! Defines a method list, dialusers, to be used on serial interfaces running PPP.
! The keyword tacacs+ means that authentication will be done through TACACS+.
! If TACACS+ returns an ERROR of some sort during authentication, the keyword
! local indicates that authentication will be attempted using the local database
! on the network access server.
!
aaa authentication ppp dialusers tacacs+ local
tacacs-server host 144.254.9.5
tacacs-server key iamasecret
!
! Select line and apply the test method list to this line.
!
interface serial 0
ppp authentication chap pap dialusers
```

Example 11-4 configures RADIUS as the security protocol to be used for PPP authentication using the method list default.

Example 11-4   *PPP Authentication Using RADIUS*

```
! Define a local user database.
username merike secret LetMeIn
username cathy secret MeToo
!
! turn on aaa
```

Example 11-4 *PPP Authentication Using RADIUS (Continued)*

```
!
aaa new-model
!
! Defines a method list, default, to be used on serial interfaces running PPP.
! The keyword default means that PPP authentication is applied by default to all
! interfaces. The if-needed keyword means that if the user has already
! authenticated by going through the ASCII login procedure, then PPP
! authentication is not necessary and can be skipped.
! If authentication is needed, the keyword radius means that authentication
! will be done through RADIUS. If RADIUS returns an ERROR of some sort during
! authentication, the keyword local indicates that authentication will be
! attempted using the local database on the network access server.
!
aaa authentication ppp default if-needed radius local
radius-server host 144.254.9.5
radius-server key iamasecret
!
! Select line and apply the default method list to this line.
!
interface serial 0
ppp authentication default
```

WARNING   I have seen documentation that recommends using the keyword **none** as a backup
authentication method in the event that the NAS cannot contact the TACACS+ or RADIUS
server. Because **none** specifies that no authentication is required, it would create a large
security risk. Instead, it is better to configure a backup mechanism that either uses a locally
defined database or the enable password/secret.

Authorization

Authorization is the process by which you can control what users can and cannot do. Often
it is not enough to just establish a link connection on authentication. After the device or user
has been authenticated, a subsequent authorization step may be required to permit access
to a specified area of the network. Many corporate environments restrict access to some
company branches or limit certain users to only particular areas of the network or particular
applications.

Here are some reasons to use authorization requests:

- If you choose to assign a particular IP address or an access list to a particular user or
  group of users
- If you choose to allow a particular user or group of users to use Telnet but not to use
  rlogin
- If you want a user to get his or her IP address from an address pool on the NAS
- If you want to add callback functionality for added security and accounting

Any and all of these reasons require authorization for the particular service to be configured on the NAS; you must also configure the appropriate profile in the TACACS+ or RADIUS configuration file.

TACACS+ and RADIUS Authorization

When either TACACS+ or RADIUS authorization is enabled, the NAS uses information retrieved from the user's profile (located either in the local user database or on the security server) to configure the user's session. After this is done, the user is granted access to a requested service only if the information in the user's profile allows it.

Much like configuring authentication, the first step in configuring either TACACS+ or RADIUS authorization is to define a method list. The method list defines the sequence in which the ways to authorize will be performed. If the initial method to authorize users fails, the next method listed in the method list is used. This process continues until there is successful communication with a listed authorization method, or until all defined methods are exhausted.

The syntax for specifying a named authorization method list on the access server is as follows:

```
aaa authorization service-type {default | list-name} method-list
```

NOTE	Authorization is bypassed for authenticated users who log in using the console line, even if authorization has been configured.

Service Types

Table 11-4 lists the authorization service types supported.

Table 11-4   *AAA Authorization Service Types*

Service	Description
Network	Checks authorization for all network activities, including SLIP, PPP, and ARAP.
EXEC	Determines whether the user is allowed to run an EXEC shell when logging in to the NAS. This keyword may cause the TACACS+ or RADIUS daemon to return user profile information such as autocommand, ACL, and so on.
Commands	Checks authorization for all commands at the specified privilege level. Command authorization attempts authorization for all EXEC mode commands (including global configuration commands) associated with a specific privilege level. Valid levels are 0 through 15. Level 1 is normal user EXEC commands; level 15 is the privileged level.
Reverse-Access	Applies to reverse-access connections, such as reverse Telnet sessions.

Reverse Telnet

Telnet is a standard terminal emulation protocol used for remote terminal connection. Normally, you log in to a NAS through a dialup connection and then use Telnet to access other network devices from that NAS. Sometimes, however, it is necessary to establish the Telnet connection in the opposite direction—from inside a network to a NAS on the network periphery—to gain access to modems or other devices connected to that NAS. *Reverse Telnet* enables users with dial-out capability to Telnet to modem ports attached to a NAS.

NOTE	It is important to control access to ports accessible through Reverse Telnet. Failure to do so exposes a security hole through which unauthorized users can gain free access to modems, from which they can trap and divert incoming calls or make outgoing calls to unauthorized destinations.

Authentication during Reverse Telnet is performed through the standard authenticated login procedure for Telnet. Typically, the user has to provide a username and password to establish either a Telnet or a Reverse Telnet session. Reverse Telnet authorization provides an additional (optional) level of security by requiring authorization in addition to authentication. When enabled, Reverse Telnet can use RADIUS or TACACS+ to authorize whether this user is allowed Reverse Telnet access to specific asynchronous ports (after the user successfully authenticates through the standard Telnet login procedure).

Reverse Telnet authorization offers the following benefits:

* An additional level of protection by ensuring that users engaged in Reverse Telnet activities are indeed authorized to access a specific asynchronous port using Reverse Telnet

* An alternative method to using only access lists on an interface to manage Reverse Telnet authorization

Authorization Methods

You can specify a variety of methods to carry out the authorization for the specified service type. Table 11-5 lists the supported methods.

Table 11-5 *AAA Authorization Methods*

Method	Description
tacacs+	The NAS exchanges authorization information with the TACACS+ security daemon. TACACS+ authorization defines specific rights for users by associating attribute-value pairs (stored in a database on the TACACS+ security server) with the appropriate user.

continues

Table 11-5   *AAA Authorization Methods (Continued)*

Method	Description
If-Authenticated	The user is allowed to access the requested function provided that the user has been authenticated successfully.
local	The router or access server consults its local database, as defined by the **username** command, to authorize specific rights for users. Only a limited set of functions can be controlled from the local database.
radius	The NAS requests authorization information from the RADIUS security server. RADIUS authorization defines specific rights for users by associating attributes (stored in a database on the RADIUS server) with the appropriate user.
krb5-instance	The NAS uses the instance defined by the **kerberos instance map** *map* command for authorization.
none	No authorization is performed.

NOTE   In more recent versions of Cisco IOS Software, the keyword **group** was added to support a list of TACACS+ and RADIUS servers.

Once defined, method lists must be applied to specific lines or interfaces before any of the defined methods are performed. The only exception is the default method list (named default). If the **aaa authorization** command for a particular authorization type is issued without specifying a named method list, the default method list automatically applies to all interfaces or lines except those that have a named method list explicitly defined. (A defined method list overrides the default method list.) If no default method list is defined, no authorization takes place.

WARNING   If authorization is not explicitly configured on the access server, everything is permitted by default. If authorization is configured, however, the default behavior is to deny everything. Before configuring authorization on the access server, be sure that you have configured an authenticated user who is authorized to do everything, or you may lock yourself out of the NAS.

Example 11-5 shows the configuration on a Cisco IOS NAS for authentication and authorization services to be provided by a RADIUS server. If the RADIUS server fails to respond, the local database is queried for authentication and authorization information.

Example 11-5 *Authentication and Authorization with RADIUS*

```
! Turn on aaa.
!
aaa new-model
!
! Command defines a method list, staff, for login authentication.
!
aaa authentication login staff local
!
! Defines the authentication method list dialup, which
! specifies that RADIUS authentication then (if the RADIUS server
! does not respond) local authentication will be used on
! serial lines using PPP.
!
aaa authentication ppp dialup radius local
!
! Defines the network authorization method list named
! dialup2, which specifies that RADIUS authorization will be used
! on serial lines using PPP. If the RADIUS server fails
! to respond, then local network authorization will be performed.
!
aaa authorization network dialup2 radius local
!
! Username and password to be used for the PPP CHAP
!
username staff password letmein
!
! Set RADIUS parameters.
!
radius-server host 144.254.9.6
radius-server key myRaDiUSpassWoRd
!
! Define and configure asynchronous interface group.
!
interface group-async 1
  group-range 1 16
  encapsulation ppp
!
! Selects CHAP as the method of PPP authentication and applies
! the dialup method list to the specified interfaces.
!
  ppp authentication chap dialup
!
! Applies the dialup2 network authorization method list to the
! specified interfaces.
!
  ppp authorization dialup2
  line 1 16
!
```

continues

Example 11-5 *Authentication and Authorization with RADIUS (Continued)*

```
! Command used to allow a PPP session to start up automatically.
!
   autoselect ppp
!
! Command used to display the username and password prompt without
! pressing the Enter key. After the user logs in, the autoselect
! function (in this case, PPP) begins.
!
   autoselect during-login
!
! Command used to apply the staff method list for login authentication.
!
   login authentication staff
!
! Command to configure modems attached to the selected lines to accept
! only incoming calls.
!
   modem dialin
```

Sample TACACS+ Database Syntax

Example 11-6 shows the syntax used in CiscoSecure, the Cisco TACACS+ Access Control Server, for its TACACS+ database. The syntax may change as more functionality is added; this example is given to show what you can configure on the TACACS+ server side. Most TACACS+ servers use similar functionality and often also have a simple-to-use graphical user interface that creates the appropriate database for you.

Example 11-6 *The Syntax for the CiscoSecure Server*

```
[unknown_user] = {
[user | group] = [<user name> | <group name>] {
password = [clear | chap | arap | pap | des] ["password"]
 [from "dd mmm yy" until "dd mmm yy" | until "dd mmm yy"]
password = [skey | system | no_password] [from "dd mmm
  yy" until "dd mmm yy" | until "dd mmm yy"]
password = file <"file name"> [from "dd mmm yy" until "dd
  mmm yy" | until "dd mmm yy"]
privilege = [clear | des ] "<password>" [0-15]
privilege = [skey] [0-15]
default service = [permit | deny]
prohibit service = <service name>
default attribute = [permit | deny]
allow <"nas name"> <"port name"> <"rem_addr">
refuse <"nas name"> <"port name"> <"rem_addr">
expires = [<"month day year"> | <"dd mmm yy">]
valid = [<"month day year"> | < "dd mmm yy">]
member = <group name>
 service = shell {
  default attribute = [permit | deny]
  default cmd = [permit | deny]
  prohibit cmd = <command>
```

Example 11-6 *The Syntax for the CiscoSecure Server (Continued)*

```
          set acl = <access-class number>
          set autocmd = <"command">
          set noescape = [ true | false]
          set nohangup = [ true | false]
          set priv-lvl = [ 0-15 ]
          set timeout = <minutes>
          set callback-dialstring = <phone number>
          set callback-line = <line number>
          set callback-rotary = <rotary number>
          set nocallback-verify = 1
          cmd = <command> {
            [deny | permit]  <"command arg">
            default attribute = permit
          }
          time = [<Mo, Tu, We, Th, Fr, Sa, Su  0000 - 2359> | <Any 0000 - 2359>]
        }
      service = ppp {
        default protocol = [permit | deny]
        prohibit protocol = <protocol>
        protocol = lcp {
          default attribute = [permit | deny]
          set callback-dialstring = <phone number>
          set callback-line = <line number>
          set callback-rotary = <rotary number>
          set nocallback-verify = 1
          time = [<Mo, Tu, We, Th, Fr, Sa, Su  0000 - 2359> | <Any 0000 - 2359>]
        }
        protocol = vpdn {
          set tunnel-id = <NAS name>
          set ip-addresses = <"x.x.x.x x.x.x.x">
        }
        protocol = ip {
          default attribute = [permit | deny]
          set addr = <ip address>
          set addr-pool = <ip local pool name>
          set inacl = <input access-list number>
          set outacl = <output access-list number>
          set route = <"destination_address mask gateway">
          set routing = [ true | false ]
          time = [<Mo, Tu, We, Th, Fr, Sa, Su  0000 - 2359> | <Any 0000 - 2359>]
        }
        protocol = ipx {
          default attribute = [permit | deny]
      set acl = <access-list number>
          time = [<Mo, Tu, We, Th, Fr, Sa, Su  0000 - 2359> | <Any 0000 - 2359>]
        }
        protocol = atalk {
          default attribute = [permit | deny]
          set zonelist = <zonelist>
          time = [<Mo, Tu, We, Th, Fr, Sa, Su  0000 - 2359> | <Any 0000 - 2359>]
        }
      }
```

Accounting and Billing

In large corporations, accounting and billing are essential for keeping track of who is accessing which corporate resources. Although it is mostly a network management function, keeping a historical database of dial-in usage patterns can alert the network administrator to any unusual activity and can serve as a historical paper trail when an intrusion does occur. The important parameters to keep track of include the following:

- Origin of connection
- Destination of connection
- Duration of connection

TACACS+ and RADIUS Accounting

When AAA accounting is enabled, the NAS reports user activity to the TACACS+ or RADIUS security server (depending on which security method you have implemented) in the form of *accounting records*. Each accounting record contains accounting attribute-value (AV) pairs and is stored on the security server. This data can be analyzed for network management, client billing, and auditing purposes.

Like authentication and authorization method lists, method lists for accounting define the way accounting is performed. Named accounting method lists enable you to designate a particular security protocol to be used on specific lines or interfaces for accounting services.

```
aaa accounting event-type {default | list-name} {start-stop | wait-start
| stop-only | none} [broadcast][ method1 [method2]]
```

Table 11-6 lists the six different event types supported.

Table 11-6   *AAA Accounting Event Types*

Event	Description
system	Enables accounting for all system-level events not associated with users (such as reloads).
network	Enables accounting (including packet and byte counts) for all network-related requests, including SLIP, PPP, and ARAP sessions.
connection	Provides information about all outbound connections made from the NAS, such as Telnet, local-area transport (LAT), TN3270, packet assembler/disassembler (PAD), and rlogin.
exec	Enables accounting for EXEC processes (user shells).
commands	Applies to the EXEC mode commands a user issues. Command authorization attempts authorization for all EXEC mode commands, including global configuration commands associated with a specific privilege level.
auth-proxy	Provides information about all the authentication-proxy user events.

You can specify when accounting records are to be sent by using one of the keywords in Table 11-7.

Table 11-7 *AAA Accounting Records – Keywords Specifying When They Are to Be Sent*

Keyword	Description
start-stop	An accounting start record is sent to the server as soon as the session begins. (It does not wait for an acknowledgment from the server.) A stop record is sent when the session ends and includes the session statistics.
wait-start	An accounting start record is not sent until an acknowledgment is received from the server that the session has started. A stop record is sent when the session ends and includes the session statistics.
stop-only	The NAS sends only an accounting stop at the end of the session; the stop record includes the session statistics.
none	Stops all accounting activities on a line or interface.
broadcast	Enables accounting records to be sent to multiple AAA servers.

Cisco IOS Software supports the two methods for accounting described in Table 11-8.

Table 11-8 *AAA Accounting Methods*

Method	Description
TACACS+	The NAS reports user activity to the TACACS+ security server in the form of accounting records. Each accounting record contains accounting AV pairs and is stored on the security server.
RADIUS	The NAS reports user activity to the RADIUS security server in the form of accounting records. Each accounting record contains accounting AV pairs and is stored on the security server.

In the following sample configuration, RADIUS-style accounting is used to track all usage of EXEC commands and network services such as SLIP, PPP, and ARAP:

```
aaa accounting exec start-stop radius
aaa accounting network start-stop radius
```

Accounting records are text lines containing tab-separated fields. The first six fields are always the same:

- Time stamp
- NAS name
- Username
- Port
- Address
- Record type

Centralized Billing

For central control of dial-in use and a centralized billing strategy, it is often the requirement of large corporations to use a callback mechanism. (See Figure 11-4.)

Figure 11-4 *A Callback Example*

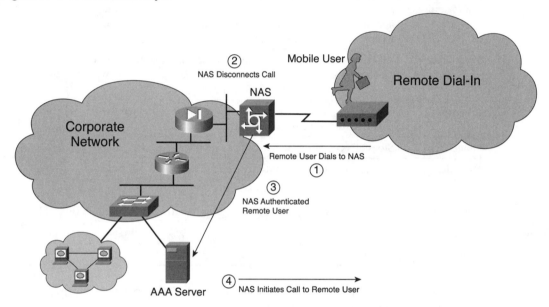

The steps for a callback are as follows:

Step 1 Remote user dials into network access server.

Step 2 The NAS disconnects the call.

Step 3 The NAS authenticates the remote user.

Step 4 If the user is authenticated, the NAS initiates a call to the remote user and a connection is established.

Configurations for both the NAS and the TACACS+ servers are shown in Examples 11-7 and 11-8.

Example 11-7 *Configuration for NAS Server*

```
NAS(config)# aaa new-model
NAS(config)# tacacs-server host 144.254.5.9
NAS(config)# tacacs-server key secretkey
NAS(config)# aaa accounting exec wait-start tacacs+
NAS(config)# aaa accounting network wait-start tacacs+
NAS(config)# service exec-callback
NAS(config)# arap callback
```

Example 11-7 *Configuration for NAS Server (Continued)*

```
!
NAS(config)# aaa authentication login EXECCHECK tacacs+
NAS(config)# aaa authorization network tacacs+
NAS(config)# aaa authentication arap ARAPCHECK tacacs+
NAS(config)# aaa authorization network tacacs+
NAS(config)# aaa authentication ppp PPPCHECK tacacs+
NAS(config)# aaa authorization network tacacs+
!
NAS(config)# line 4
NAS(config-line)# login authentication EXECCHECK
NAS(config-line)# arap authentication ARAPCHECK
!
NAS(config)# int async 6
NAS(config-if)# ppp authentication chap PPPCHECK
NAS(config-if)# ppp callback accept
```

Example 11-8 *Configuration for TACACS+ Server*

```
user = merike {
    arap = cleartext AAAA
    login = cleartext LLLL
    chap = cleartext CCCC
    pap = cleartext PPPP
    opap = cleartext OOOO
    service = ppp protocol = lcp {
        callback-dialstring=67150
    }
    service = arap {
        callback-dialstring=2345678
    }
    service = exec {
        callback-dialstring=3456789
        callback-line=7
        nocallback-verify=1
    }
}
```

Using AAA with Specific Features

AAA is the most scalable way of providing authentication, authorization, and accounting services for many remote dial-in scenarios. Cisco IOS Software has incorporated the use of AAA into two features:

- Lock and key
- Double authentication/authorization

The Lock-and-Key Feature

Lock and key is a traffic-filtering security feature in Cisco IOS Software devices that dynamically filters IP protocol traffic. It can be used to authorize temporary access to specified areas of a corporate network. Lock and key is configured using IP dynamic extended access lists and can be used in conjunction with other standard access lists and static extended access lists.

When triggered, lock and key reconfigures the interface's existing IP access list to permit designated users to reach specified areas of the network. When it is finished, lock and key reconfigures the interface back to its original state.

For a user to gain access to a host through a router with lock and key configured, the user must first Telnet to the router. When a user initiates a standard Telnet session to the router, lock and key automatically attempts to authenticate the user. If the user is authenticated, he or she then gains temporary access through the router and can reach the destination host.

Lock-and-Key Authentication

There are three possible ways to configure an authentication query process:

- Configure a security server. Use a network access security server such as a TACACS+ server. This method allows for stricter authentication queries and more sophisticated tracking capabilities.

```
Router# login tacacs
```

- Configure the **username** command. This method allows authentication from a local database on a per-user basis.

```
Router# username merike password LetMeIn
```

- Configure the **password** and **login** commands. This method is less effective than the first method because the password is configured for the port, not for the user. Therefore, any user who knows the password can authenticate successfully.

```
Router# password IAmAPassword
Router# login local
```

NOTE   It is recommended that you use the TACACS+ server for your authentication query process. TACACS+ provides authentication, authorization, and accounting services. It also provides protocol support, protocol specification, and a centralized security database.

Lock-and-Key Operation

A user at a remote site can use WAN technology—such as Asynchronous Transfer Mode (ATM), dial-on-demand routing (DDR), Frame Relay, ISDN, PPP, or X.25—to connect to the corporate office using lock and key. The WAN infrastrucure is presumed to be private due to being either a direct connection between corporate sites or through a trusted service provider network. Keep in mind that Telnet sends its passwords in the clear.

The following steps, also shown in Figure 11-5, describe the lock-and-key access operation:

Step 1   A user opens a Telnet session to a border (firewall) router configured for lock and key. The user connects using the virtual terminal port on the router.

Step 2   The Cisco IOS Software receives the Telnet packet, opens a Telnet session, prompts for a password, and performs a user authentication process. The user must pass authentication before access through the router is allowed. The authentication process can be done by the router or by a central access security server, such as a TACACS+ or RADIUS server.

Step 3   When the user passes authentication, he or she is logged out of the Telnet session, and the software creates a temporary entry in the dynamic access list. (Per your configuration, this temporary entry can limit the range of networks to which the user is given temporary access.)

Step 4   The user exchanges data through the router/firewall.

Figure 11-5   *A Lock-and-Key Operation*

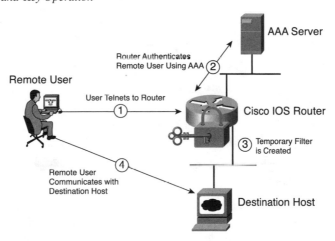

The software deletes the temporary access list entry when a configured timeout is reached or when the system administrator manually clears the entry. The configured timeout can either be an idle timeout or an absolute timeout.

NOTE   The temporary access list entry is not automatically deleted when the user terminates a session. The temporary access list entry remains until a configured timeout is reached or until the entry is cleared by the system administrator.

When lock and key is triggered, it creates a dynamic opening in the firewall by temporarily reconfiguring an interface to allow user access. While this opening exists, another host can spoof the authenticated user's address to gain access behind the firewall. Lock and key does not cause the address spoofing problem; the problem is only identified here as a concern to the user. Spoofing is a problem inherent to all access lists, and lock and key does not specifically address this problem.

To prevent spoofing, you can configure network data encryption as described in the last section of this chapter. Configure encryption so that traffic from the remote host is encrypted at a secured remote router and is decrypted locally at the router interface that provides the lock-and-key service. You want to ensure that all traffic using lock and key is encrypted when entering the router. In this way, no hackers can spoof the source address because they are unable to duplicate the encryption or to be authenticated (a required part of the encryption setup process).

Lock-and-Key Examples

The first lock-and-key example is shown in Figure 11-6. This figure shows how to configure lock-and-key access from a telecommuter to a NAS, with authentication occurring locally at the campus NAS. Lock and key is configured on the BRI 0 interface of the NAS.

Figure 11-6   *Lock and Key for Telecommuter Access*

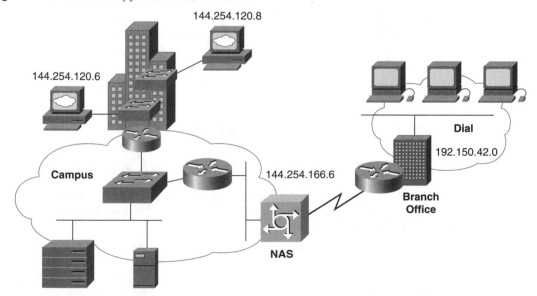

Example 11-9 shows the configuration.

Example 11-9 *Lock-and-Key Configuration*

```
! Telecommuter who will come in using lock-and-key.
!
username telecommuter password 7 0758364708452A
!
! Define ISDN switch type.
!
isdn switch-type basic-dms100
!
! Configure interfaces.
!
interface ethernet 0
  ip address 144.254.166.6 255.255.255.0
interface BRI0
  ip unnumbered ethernet 0
  encapsulation ppp
  dialer idle-timeout 3600
  dialer wait-for-carrier-time 100
  dialer map ip 171.73.34.33  name merike
  dialer-group 1
  isdn spid1 8316333715291
  isdn spid2 8316339371566
  ppp authentication chap
  ip access-group 101 in
!

! Configure routing.
!
ip classless
ip route 0.0.0.0 0.0.0.0 144.254.166.6
ip route 144.254.166.6  255.255.255.255 BRI0
!
! Allows Telnet from telecommuter to this router.
!
access-list 101 permit tcp any host 144.254.166.6 eq telnet
!
! Allows telecommuter to have access anywhere inside campus after Telneting
! to router and successful authentication.
!
access-list 101 dynamic telecommuter timeout 120 permit ip any any
!
dialer-list 1 protocol ip permit
line vty 0
login local
autocommand access-enable timeout 5
```

The first **access-list** entry allows only Telnet sessions into the router. The second **access-list** entry is always ignored until lock and key is triggered.

After a user Telnets into the router, the router attempts to authenticate the user. If authentication is successful, **autocommand** executes and the Telnet session terminates. The **autocommand** command creates a temporary inbound access list entry at the BRI 0 interface, based on the second **access-list** entry (**telecommuter**). This temporary entry expires after 5 minutes, as specified by the timeout value.

NOTE   Although the preceding example uses an Ethernet interface to provide the unnumbered address to the BRI, in many cases you would instead use a loopback. A loopback interface is usually configured on devices that have multiple exit interfaces, and WAN links will typically use the IP address assigned to the loopback interface to provide the unnumbered address. This alleviates the potential problem of having an unreachable device should any single exit interface become unavailable.

The second lock-and-key example is shown in Figure 11-7. This example shows how to configure lock-and-key access for a branch router, with authentication on a TACACS+ server. Lock-and-key access is configured on the BRI 0 interface of the NAS.

Figure 11-7   *Lock and Key for Branch Router Access*

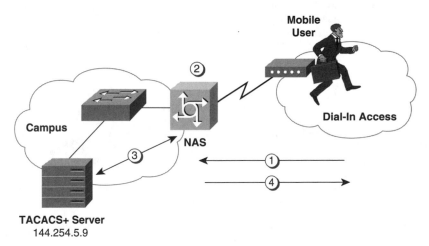

Example 11-10 shows the configuration on the NAS.

Example 11-10   *Lock-and-Key Example Using AAA*

```
aaa new-model
aaa authentication login lockkey tacacs+ enable
aaa authorization exec  tacacs+
!
isdn switch-type basic-dms100
!
interface Ethernet0
```

Example 11-10 *Lock-and-Key Example Using AAA (Continued)*

```
 ip address 144.254.166.6  255.255.255.0
 !
interface BRI0
 ip unnumbered Ethernet0
 ip access-group 101 in
 no ip mroute-cache
 encapsulation ppp
 dialer idle-timeout 300
 dialer map ip 192.150.42.1 name Branchrouter 97328866
 dialer-group 1
 isdn spid1 8316333715291
 isdn spid2 8316339371566
 no fair-queue
 compress stac
 ppp multilink
 !
router eigrp 100
network 144.254.0.0
 !
ip classless
ip route 0.0.0.0 0.0.0.0 192.150.42.1
ip route 192.150.42.1 255.255.255.255 BRI0
 !
! Allows Telnet from the branch hosts to this router.
 !
access-list 101 permit tcp any host 144.254.166.6 eq telnet
 !
! Allows anybody inside campus to have access to the branch resources.
 !
access-list 101 permit tcp any 144.254.0.0 0.0.255.255 established
 !
! Allows certain hosts inside to be accessed from the branch without authentication.
 !
access-list 101 permit ip any host 144.254.120.6
access-list 101 permit ip any host 144.254.120.8
 !
! Allows for branch to have access anywhere inside campus after Telneting
! to router and successful authentication.
 !
access-list 101 dynamic Branch timeout 5 permit ip any any
 !
tacacs-server host 144.254.5.9
tacacs-server key secretkey
 !
dialer-list 1 protocol ip permit
 !
line con 0
 exec-timeout 2 30
 password letmein
 line vty 0 4
 exec-timeout 15 0
! Once user logs in, authentication is by way of TACACS+.
login authentication lockkey
```

The configuration on TACACS+ is illustrated in Example 11-11.

Example 11-11 *TACACS+ Server Configuration*

```
user = lockkeyuser {
  password = clear "secretword"
    service = shell {
      ! following turns on the dynamic access-list
      set autocmd = "access-enable"
      }
}
```

Example 11-12 shows the third lock-and-key example. This example shows a configuration in which two users can have different lock-and-key dynamic access list configurations and different access privileges. If these two users access the device from the same interface, only the first configured dynamic access control list is activated.

Example 11-12 *Lock and Key with Multiple Access Privileges*

```
interface Ethernet0/0
ip address 144.254.163.2 255.255.255.0
ip access-group 161 in
no ip directed-broadcast
no ip mroute-cache
!
interface Ethernet0/1
ip address 144.254.166.8  255.255.255.0
ip access-group 141 in
no ip directed-broadcast
no ip mroute-cache
!
access-list 141 dynamic genesis permit ip any any log
access-list 141 permit ip any host 224.0.0.10
access-list 141 permit ip any any
access-list 161 dynamic new permit tcp any any log
access-list 161 permit ip any any
```

Double Authentication/Authorization

When a remote user dials in to a local corporate perimeter host (a NAS or router) over PPP, CHAP or PAP is often used to authenticate the user. However, both of these authentication methods rely on a secret password (the "secret") that must be stored on the local host and either remembered by a user or saved on the remote host. If either host ever comes under the control of a network attacker, the secret password is compromised.

Consider a corporate user who often uses a laptop computer to log in to the corporate enterprise network, which uses only CHAP for authentication. If the laptop computer is stolen, the computer can still connect to the corporate network if the correct dial-in script is executed. For this reason alone, passwords should never be stored in dial-in scripts.

With the double-authentication feature, there are two authentication/authorization stages. These two stages occur after a remote user dials in and a PPP session is initiated.

In the first stage, the user logs in using the remote host name. CHAP (or PAP) authenticates the remote host, and then PPP negotiates with RADIUS or TACACS+ to authorize the remote host. In this process, the network access privileges associated with the remote host are assigned to the user.

NOTE   You should restrict authorization at this first stage to allow only Telnet connections to the local host. This arrangement prevents an attacker from using the device authentication to access the NAS and to then Telnet from the NAS to other parts of the network.

In the second stage, the remote user must Telnet to the NAS to be authenticated. When the remote user logs in, the user must be authenticated with the specified login authentication. The user then must enter the **access-profile** command to be re-authorized. When this authorization is complete, the user has been double authenticated and can access the network according to per-user network privileges.

WARNING   Double authentication can cause certain undesirable events if multiple hosts share a PPP connection to a NAS. If user Aiki initiates a PPP session and activates double authentication at the NAS, any other user automatically has the same network privileges as Aiki until Aiki's PPP session terminates. This happens because Aiki's authorization profile is applied to the NAS's interface during the PPP session; any PPP traffic from other users uses the PPP session that has already been established.

Another undesirable event can occur if, in the middle of Aiki's PPP session, another user, Jim, executes the **access-profile** command. This action results in a re-authorization; Jim's authorization profile is applied to the interface, replacing Aiki's profile. This replacement can disrupt or halt Aiki's PPP traffic or grant Aiki additional authorization privileges she should not have.

Example 11-13 shows the configuration on a Cisco NAS. The first three lines configure a TACACS+ server. The next two lines configure PPP and login authentication, and the last two lines configure network and EXEC authorization. The last line is necessary only if the **access-profile** command will be executed as an autocommand.

Example 11-13 *Double-Authentication Configuration on a Cisco NAS*

```
aaa new-model
tacacs-server  host 144.254.5.9
tacacs-server  key mytacacskey
aaa authentication ppp default tacacs+
aaa authentication login default tacacs+
aaa authorization network tacacs+
aaa authorization exec tacacs+
```

The sample configuration in Example 11-14 shows authentication/authorization profiles on the TACACS+ server for the remote host psycho and for three users (usernames Merike-default, Aiki-merge, and Tom-replace). The configurations for these three usernames show different configurations that correspond to the three different forms of the **access-profile** command. The three user configurations also show how to set up autocommand for each form of the **access-profile** command.

Example 11-14 *Authentication/Authorization Profiles on the TACACS+ Server*

```
key = "mytacacskey"
default authorization = permit
#
# This allows the remote host to be authenticated by the local host
# during fist-stage authentication, and provides the remote host
# authorization profile.
#
user = psycho
{
    login = cleartext "welcome"
    chap = cleartext "welcome"
        service = ppp protocol = lcp {
          interface-config="ip unnumbered ethernet 0"
        }
        service = ppp protocol = ip {
          # It is important to have the hash sign
          # and some string after it.  This indicates
          # to the NAS that you have a per-user config.
          inacl#3="permit tcp any 192.150.42.0  0.0.0.255 eq telnet"
          inacl#4="deny icmp any any"
          route#5="192.150.42.0 255.255.255.0"
          route#6="192.150.41.0 255.255.255.0"
        }
}


# - Without arguments access-profile removes any access-lists it can find
#   in the old configuration (both per-user and per-interface), and makes sure
#   that the new profile contains ONLY access-list definitions.
```

Example 11-14 *Authentication/Authorization Profiles on the TACACS+ Server (Continued)*

```
#
user = Merike-default
{
        login = cleartext "welcome"
        chap = cleartext "welcome"
        service = exec
        {
                # this is the autocommand that
                # executes when Merike-default logs in
                autocmd = "access-profile"
        }
        service = ppp protocol = ip {
                # Put whatever access-lists, static routes, and so on here
                # If you leave this blank, the user will have NO IP
                # access-lists (not even the ones installed prior to
                # this)
                inacl#3="permit tcp any host 144.254.166.10 eq telnet"
                inacl#4="deny icmp any any"
        }
}


# With the 'merge' option, all old access-lists are removed (as before),
#   but then (almost) all AV pairs are uploaded and installed. This
#   will allow for uploading any custom static routes, filters, and so on,
#   that the user may need in his or her profile. This needs to be used with
#   care, as it leaves open the possibility of conflicting configurations.
#
user = Aiki-merge
{
        login = cleartext "welcome"
        chap = cleartext "welcome"
        service = exec
        {
                # this is the autocommand that executes when Aiki-merge logs in
                autocmd = "access-profile merge"
        }
        service = ppp protocol = ip
                {
                # Put whatever access-lists, static routes, and so on here
                # If you leave this blank, the user will have NO IP
                # access-lists (not even the ones installed prior to
                # this)
                                inacl#3="permit tcp any any"
                                route#2="144.254.0.0  255.255.0.0"
        }
}
#- With the 'replace' option,
#   ALL old configuration is removed and ALL new configuration is installed.
#
# One caveat: access-profile checks the new configuration for address-pool and
```

continues

Example 11-14 *Authentication/Authorization Profiles on the TACACS+ Server (Continued)*

```
# address AV pairs. As addresses cannot be renegotiated at this point, the
# command will fail (and complain) when it encounters such an AV pair.
# Such AV pairs are considered to be "invalid" for this context.
#------------------------------------------------------------------------
user = Tom-replace
{
        login = cleartext "welcome"
        chap = cleartext "welcome"
        service = exec
              {
              # this is the autocommand that executes when Tom-replace logs in
              autocmd = "access-profile replace"
        }
        service = ppp protocol = ip
              {
              # Put whatever access-lists, static routes, and so on here
              # If you leave this blank, the user will have NO IP
              # access-lists (not even the ones installed prior to
              # this)
              inacl#3="permit tcp any any"
              inacl#4="permit icmp any any"
              route#2="171.71.73.0  255.255.255.0"
              }
}
```

Automated Double Authentication

You can make the double-authentication process easier for users by implementing automated double authentication. *Automated double authentication* provides all the security benefits of double authentication, but offers a simpler, more user-friendly interface for remote users. With double authentication, a second level of user authentication is achieved when the user Telnets to the NAS or router and enters a username and password. With automated double authentication, the user does not have to Telnet to the NAS; instead, the user responds to a dialog box that requests a username and password or personal identification number (PIN).

Automated double authentication is configured with the following command:

```
ip trigger-authentication [timeout seconds] [port number]
```

The default timeout is 90 seconds, and the default UDP port number is 7500.

NOTE   To use the automated double-authentication feature, the remote user hosts must be running a companion client application. As of Cisco IOS Software Release 12.0, the only client application software available is the Glacier Bay application server software for PCs.

Example 11-15 shows a complete configuration file for a Cisco IOS Software router with automated double authentication.

Example 11-15   *Complete Configuration File for Automated Double Authentication*

```
hostname myrouter
!
no service password-encryption
!
! Set up local user database access.
!
username merike secret LetMeIn
username cathy secret MeToo
!
!  The following command enables AAA:
!
aaa new-model
!
!  The following command enables user authentication via the TACACS+  server:
!
aaa authentication login default tacacs+ local
aaa authentication login console enable
!
!  The following command enables device authentication via the TACACS+  server:
!
aaa authentication ppp default tacacs+
!
!  The following command causes the remote user's authorization profile
!   to be downloaded from the TACACS+ server to the Cisco router when required:
!
aaa authorization exec tacacs+
!
!  The following command causes the remote device's authorization profile
!    to be downloaded from the TACACS+ server to the Cisco router when required:
!
aaa authorization network tacacs+
!
enable secret thisisasecret
!
ip host twiggy 192.150.42.101
ip host  minky  192.150.42.103
ip host  itchy 192.150.42.105
ip domain-name mycompany.com
ip name-server  144.254.5.27
!
! The next command globally enables automated double authentication:
!
ip trigger-authentication timeout 60 port 7500
!
isdn switch-type basic-5ess
!
!
interface Ethernet0
  ip address 144.254.166.10
```

continues

Example 11-15 *Complete Configuration File for Automated Double Authentication (Continued)*

```
  no ip route-cache
  no ip mroute-cache
  no keepalive
  ntp disable
  no cdp enable
!
interface Virtual-Template1
  ip unnumbered Ethernet0
  no ip route-cache
  no ip mroute-cache
!
! Automated double authentication occurs via the ISDN BRI interface BRI0:
!
interface BRI0
  ip unnumbered Ethernet0
!
! The following command turns on automated double authentication at this
! interface:
!
  ip trigger-authentication
!
! PPP encapsulation is required:
  encapsulation ppp
  no ip route-cache
  no ip mroute-cache
  dialer idle-timeout 500
  dialer map ip 192.150.42.1 name Branch2  5554768
  dialer-group 1
  no cdp enable
!
! **The following command specifies that device authentication occurs via PPP
! CHAP:
  ppp authentication chap
!
router eigrp 109
  redistribute static
  network 144.254.0.0
  no auto-summary
!
ip default-gateway 172.18.1.1
no ip classless
ip route 192.150.42.0  255.255.255.0 Bri0
!
! Virtual profiles are required for double authentication to work:
!
virtual-profile virtual-template 1
dialer-list 1 protocol ip permit
no cdp run
!
! configure TACACS+ server
!
tacacs-server host 144.254.5.9 port 1049
```

Example 11-15   *Complete Configuration File for Automated Double Authentication (Continued)*

```
tacacs-server timeout 90
tacacs-server key mytacacskey
!
line con 0
  exec-timeout 10 0
  login authentication console
line aux 0
  no exec
  transport input none
line vty 0 4
  exec-timeout 10 0
  login authentication default
!
```

Encryption for Virtual Dial-In Environments

When using a virtual dial-in environment in which dial-in access is provided by using an ISP's public infrastructure, you must take additional security measures to ensure that the data traversing the public network is not modified in transit and is kept private. You can implement these additional security measures using a combination of various tunneling techniques, including GRE, L2F, L2TP, IPsec, and CET. (CET is a proprietary Cisco encryption mechanism and is not used very often in favor of IPsec. The end of life for CET has been announced and Cisco IOS Software 12.1 is the last version to support it; however, because it exists, it is briefly discussed here.)

NOTE   The PPTP, L2F, and L2TP tunneling technologies were discussed in Chapter 2. These techniques were specifically designed to add more security services to virtual dial-in environments. They all accomplish nearly the same functions of providing flexibility of authenticating dial-in clients with an ISP NAS (using either local or remote security servers), creating a virtual tunnel between the ISP NAS and a corporate home gateway, and finally negotiating a virtual PPP session between the originating client and the home gateway. Because extensions for multiprotocol PPP environments exist, using these mechanisms allows for native routing of non-IP protocols such as AppleTalk and IPX. If you want to add IP packet authentication and confidentiality on top of the multiprotocol data tunnel, however, you must encapsulate these protocols in an IPsec tunnel.

GRE Tunneling and CET

Although CET is a Cisco proprietary IP encryption technology that is not widely used, some details are discussed here. IPsec should be the protocol used to provide security services for IP-based networks.

GRE Tunneling

The Generic Routing Encapsulation (GRE) protocol encapsulates various network protocols inside IP tunnels. With GRE tunneling, a router at each site encapsulates protocol-specific packets in an IP header, creating a virtual point-to-point link to routers at other ends of an IP cloud, where the IP header is stripped off. GRE is capable of handling the transportation of multiprotocol and IP multicast traffic between two sites that have only IP unicast connectivity. GRE tunneling does not provide any security services but is required in instances where the IP encryption technology does not support IP multicast traffic and there is a requirement to support it, such as for certain routing protocols. If data origin authentication and confidentiality is required when using GRE, however, the packets can be protected using IPsec.

WARNING   Use GRE tunneling with care because it can disguise the nature of a link, making it look slower, faster, or more or less costly than it may actually be in reality. This change can cause problems with routing behavior. It also takes up more CPU cycles than does routing a protocol natively.

GRE packets using IPv4 headers use the IP protocol type 47. If the packet encapsulated within GRE is also IPv4, the GRE header's protocol type field is set to 0x800. This may be important for filtering considerations. Some firewalls (such as the PIX firewall) do not have the capability to support GRE, but it could be set up to allow GRE traffic to pass through it.

Cisco Encryption Technology (CET)

CET is a proprietary security solution introduced in Cisco IOS Software Release 11.2. It provides network data encryption at the IP packet level and implements the following standards:

- Digital Signature Standard (DSS)
- Diffie-Hellman (DH) public-key algorithm
- Data Encryption Standard (DES)

The following is a simple configuration example of two routers that use CET to encrypt/decrypt Telnet and World Wide Web traffic between the branch office and the corporate campus network. Example 11-16 shows the configuration of the branch router configuration commands, and Example 11-17 shows the configuration commands on the campus NAS.

Example 11-16   *Branch Router Configuration Commands*

```
hostname Branch_router
!
! Define encryption algorithm.
```

Example 11-16   *Branch Router Configuration Commands (Continued)*

```
!
crypto map toNAS 10
set algorithm 56-bit des cfb-64
!
! Encryption peer is device named NAS.
!
set peer NAS
!
! Encrypt/decrypt what is defined in this access list.
!
match address 101
!
interface Ethernet 0
ip address 192.150.42.1 255.255.255.0
!
! Configure branch interface to NAS which will
! use encrypted communication.
!
interface Bri 0
ip address unnumbered Ethernet 0
encapsulation ppp
dialer map ip 144.254.5.20 name NAS
dialer-group 1
ppp authentication chap
crypto map toNAS
!
! Define traffic to start dial or keep isdn line up.
!
dialer-list 1 protocol ip permit
!
! encrypt/decrypt telnet traffic between branch and campus
!
access-list 101 permit ip 144.254.0.0 0.0.255.255 192.150.42.0 0.0.0.255 eq telnet
!
! Encrypt/decrypt WWW traffic between branch and campus.
!
access-list 101 permit ip 144.254.0.0 0.0.255.255 192.150.42.0 0.0.0.255 eq http
```

Example 11-17   *NAS Configuration Commands*

```
hostname NAS
! Define encryption algorithm.
!
crypto map toBranch 10
set algorithm 56-bit des cfb-64
!
! Encryption peer is device named Branch_router.
!
set peer Branch-router
! Encrypt/decrypt what is defined in this access list.
!
```

continues

Example 11-17 *NAS Configuration Commands (Continued)*

```
match address 101
!
interface Ethernet 0
ip address 144.254.5.20 255.255.255.0
!
! Configuring PRI, which will use encrypted communication
!
interface Serial0:23
description to the Branch
crypto map toBranch
!
! Encrypt/decrypt Telnet traffic between branch and campus.
!
access-list 101 permit ip 192.150.42.0 0.0.0.255 144.254.0.0 0.0.0.255 eq telnet
!
! Encrypt/decrypt WWW traffic between branch and campus.
!
access-list 101 permit ip 192.150.42.0 0.0.0.255 144.254.0.0 0.0.0.255 eq http
```

Figure 11-8 shows a more complex scenario in which a branch router located in Estonia is connecting to the corporate network in Vancouver over the Internet.

Figure 11-8 *Virtual Dial-In Using GRE with CET*

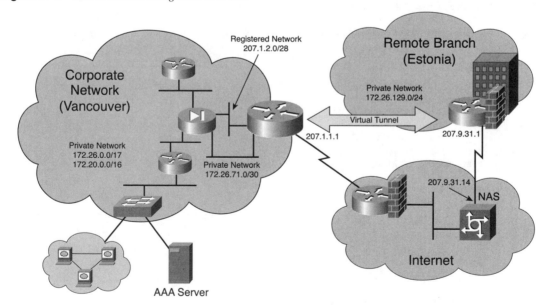

The following security policy is defined for this scenario:

- Private addresses are used for the remote branch router and the corporate network.

- Communications from the remote branch to the corporate network must be private and must be encrypted.

- All infrastructure devices should have authenticated access.

The policy is implemented as follows:

- A tunnel is constructed between the home gateway and the remote branch router. The function of the tunnel is to provide connectivity from the branch office private network address space into the corporate network private address space.

- When configuring the tunnel interface between the two routers, the source and destination of the tunnel must be registered IP addresses.

- The remote router runs NAT so that communications from the remote router to the Internet are routed locally, and only communications to the corporate network go across the encrypted tunnel.

- The corporate home gateway router has two separate links to the firewall: one over a network that has a registered IP address, and the other over a network with the private network address.

- A filter is placed on the corporate home gateway router to ensure that only VPN routes are passed on the private network link to the firewall (**access list 120**).

- Device authentication is by way of a local database. Passwords are the same (because this scenario deals with only a limited number of devices) but are changed every 2 months.

Example 11-18 and Example 11-19 show the configurations of the Vancouver home gateway and the Estonia branch router, respectively.

Example 11-18 *Vancouver Home Gateway Configuration*

```
hostname Vancouver-gw
!
! Ensure all vty, login, line, and username passwords are encrypted
! using minimal encryption (type 7) unless configured as a secret
! which t uses MD5 encryption (type 5).
!
service password-encryption
!
! Disable access to minor TCP services such as echo,
! chargen, discard, and daytime.
!
no service tcp-small-servers
!
! Disable access to minor UDP services such as echo,
! chargen, and discard.
!
no service udp-small-servers
```

continues

Example 11-18 *Vancouver Home Gateway Configuration (Continued)*

```
!
!Define privileged access password.
!
enable secret letmedostuff
!
! Local database for device authentication access
!
username admin password ComeOnIN
!
! Change the encryption key every 24 hours.
!
crypto cisco key-timeout 1440
!
! Public key for the remote router Eesti
!
crypto key pubkey-chain dss
 named-key Eesti signature
  serial-number 07124346
  key-string
   44EF0246 9EF0E99E 79BA3629 142D4C0E 923D02EF 5B358A1C 089468CE 8B3562F8
   398692A8 A38D99F8 0703913C 2F51F7B6 9217128C 29BA6251 AA77E442 2EE00A63
  quit
!
! Crypto map for the connection between Vancouver-gw and Eesti;
! this defines the remote crypto peer, what traffic to encrypt.
! It is applied to the tunnel and physical interfaces.
!
 crypto map Vancouver-to-Eesti 10
set peer Eesti
 match address 140
!
! Tunnel interface from Vancouver-gw to remote branch router (Eesti).
! The tunnel interface is unnumbered to preserve address space; it could also
! use IP addresses from the private network space.
! The source of the tunnel and the destination of the tunnel are ISP registered
! addresses because the tunnel end points must be reachable across the Internet.
!
interface Tunnel100
 description tunnel to branch router Eesti
 ip unnumbered FastEthernet5/0
 no ip directed- broadcast
 tunnel source Serial2/0
 tunnel destination 207.9.31.1
 crypto map Vancouver-to-Eesti
!
! Apply the crypto map to the serial interface.
!
interface Serial2/0
 description connection to ISP1 - DS3
 ip address 207.1.1.1 255.255.255.252
 no ip directed-broadcast
 framing c-bit
```

Example 11-18 *Vancouver Home Gateway Configuration (Continued)*

```
 cablelength 50
 dsu bandwidth 44210
 crypto map Vancouver-to-Eesti
!
interface FastEthernet3/0
 description network for Internet traffic
 ip address 207.1.2.1 255.255.255.240
 no ip directed-broadcast
 full-duplex
!
interface FastEthernet5/0
 description network for private network traffic
 ip address 172.26.71.1 255.255.255.252
 no ip directed-broadcast
 full-duplex
!
! Apply acccess list for this interface so that only private network
! traffic traverses this link.
!
 ip access-group 120 in
!
! configure routing
ip classless
!
! Default route to ISP
ip route 0.0.0.0 0.0.0.0 207.1.1.2
!
! Routes for the corporate intranet for use by the VPN routers:
  ip route 172.20.0.0 255.255.0.0 172.26.71.2
  ip route 172.26.0.0 255.255.128.0 172.26.71.2
! Route to the remote branch network on router Eesti:
  ip route 172.26.129.0 255.255.255.0 Tunnel100
! Route to the NAT pool on the firewall:
ip route 207.1.2.16 255.255.255.248 207.1.2.2
! ACL list to only allow VPN traffic through the VPN DMZ interface:
  access-list 120 permit ip 172.26.129.0 0.0.0.255 any
  access-list 120 permit ip 172.26.130.0 0.0.0.255 any
! ACL to determine what to be encrypted, packets between
! the two tunnel endpoints which are GRE encapsulated.
  access-list 140 permit gre host 207.1.1.1 host 207.9.31.1
!
line con 0
  exec-timeout 2 30
  login authentication admin
!
line aux 0
no exec
transport input none
!
line vty 0 4
  exec-timeout 2 30
  login authentication admin
  transport input telnet
```

Example 11-19 *Estonia Remote Branch Router Configuration*

```
hostname Eesti
!
! Ensure all vty, login, line and username passwords are encrypted
! with minimal encryption (7) unless configured as a secret
! that uses MD5 encryption.
!
service password-encryption
!
! Disable access to minor TCP services such as echo,
! chargen, discard, and daytime.
!
no service tcp-small-servers
!
! Disable access to minor UDP services such as echo,
! chargen, and discard.
!
no service udp-small-servers
!
!Define privileged access password.
!
enable secret letmedostuff
!
! Local database for device authentication access:
!
username admin password ComeOnIN
!
! Change the encryption key every 24 hours.
!
crypto cisco key-timeout 1440
!
! Public key for the home gateway Vancouver-gw:
!
crypto key pubkey-chain dss
  named-key VancouverESA signature
  serial-number 007462E4
  key-string
   17C11157 CC640BF3 3DC5B608 C5C60963 C0421A67 D2D7AF70 97728A9A BACA0E07
   35288070 AD90A20F 56F1BFE7 D8A4BB68 2C2419E0 26CF8E17 B09CA9A0 3090942E
  quit
!
! Crypto map for the connection from Eesti to Vancouver-gw;
! this defines the remote
! peer, and what traffic to encrypt, which is determined by access list 140
! This gets applied to the tunnel and physical interfaces.
!
crypto map Eesti-to-Vancouver 10
 set peer VancouverESA
 match address 140
!
! Tunnel interface from remote branch (Eesti) to home gateway (Vancouver-gw):
!
interface Tunnel100
```

Example 11-19 *Estonia Remote Branch Router Configuration (Continued)*

```
 description network connection back to headquarters (Vancouver)
 ip unnumbered Ethernet1/0
 no ip directed-broadcast
 tunnel source 207.9.31.1
 tunnel destination 207.1.1.1
 crypto map Eesti-to-Vancouver
!
! Apply the crypto map to the physical interface;
! this is also the outside NAT interface.
!
interface Serial0/0
 description frame relay connection to ISP
 ip address 207.9.31.1 255.255.255.240
 no ip directed-broadcast
 ip nat outside
 encapsulation frame-relay
 frame-relay lmi-type ansi
 crypto map Eesti-to-Vancouver
!
! NAT inside interface:
!
interface Ethernet1/0
 description private IP address for remote site
 ip address 172.26.129.1 255.255.255.0
 no ip directed-broadcast
 ip nat inside
!
! Translate IP addresses matching access list 150 into the IP address
! given to serial interface connected to the ISP.
 ip nat inside source list 150 interface Serial0/0 overload
 ip classless
! default route to ISP
 ip route 0.0.0.0 0.0.0.0 207.9.31.14
!
! Routes for the networks inside the corporate intranet that
! the remote needs to access:
!
ip route 172.26.0.0 255.255.128.0 Tunnel100
ip route 172.20.0.0 255.255.0.0 Tunnel100
!
! Traffic going to any other destination will take the default route and be
! translated by NAT, access list 150 tells NAT what to translate.
!
access-list 150 permit ip 172.26.129.0 0.0.0.255 any
!
! ACL to determine what is to be encrypted,
! which are all packets between the two tunnel endpoints:

!
access-list 140 permit gre host 207.9.31.1 host 207.1.1.1
!
line con 0
```

continues

Example 11-19   *Estonia Remote Branch Router Configuration (Continued)*

```
   exec-timeout 2 30
   login authentication admin
 !
line aux 0
   no exec
   transport input none
 !
line vty 0 4
   exec-timeout 2 30
   login authentication admin
   transport input telnet
```

IPsec

IPsec is a framework of open standards developed by the IETF that provides security services at the IP level. (Refer to Chapter 2 for details.) IPsec shares the same benefits as CET: Both technologies offer authenticated and confidential IP packet transport. IPsec, however, offers a standards-based solution that provides multivendor interoperability.

NOTE   GRE tunneling is required in an IPsec environment if there is a requirement to encrypt an IP routing protocol that uses multicast packets to distribute its routing information (for example, Open Shortest Path First [OSPF] or Enhanced Interior Gateway Routing Protocol [EIGRP]). In its current form, the IPsec standard supports only unicast IP packets. For small environments, static routes should suffice, and GRE tunnels are not necessary.

Configuring IPsec

Configuring IPsec on Cisco IOS Software devices requires a number of steps, as described here. Internet Key Exchange (IKE) is on by default and is the recommended mechanism to negotiate IPsec keys. It is possible to use manual keying, but this is highly discouraged because it provides limited scalability and an administrative nightmare. This discussion is limited to IPsec using IKE.

Step 1   Configure the IKE Phase 1 policy (ISAKMP policy).

Cisco literature refers to IKE Phase 1 as the ISAKMP policy. It is configured using the following command:

```
crypto isakmp policy priority
```

You can configure multiple policies and the priority number, which ranges from 1 to 10,000, which denotes the order of preference that a given policy is negotiated with an ISAKMP peer. The lower value has the higher priority.

When in the ISAKMP configuration mode, you can specify the following parameters:

- Encryption algorithm: Configurable options are **des** or **3des**; the default is 56-bit DES CBC.

- Hash algorithm: Configurable options are **sha** (specified HMAC-SHA-1) or **md5** (specifies HMAC-MD5); the default is SHA-1.

- Authentication: Configurable options are **rsa-sig** (digital signature), **rsa-encr** (public key cryptography) or **pre-share** (preshared keys); the default is RSA signatures.

- Group: Configurable options are group 1 (the 768-bit Diffie-Hellman group) and group 2 (the 1024-bit Diffie-Hellman group); the default is group 1.

- Lifetime: the default is 86,400 seconds.

Step 2 Set the ISAKMP identity.

The ISAKMP identity specifies how the IKE Phase 1 peer is identified, which can be either by IP address or host name. Use the following command:

```
crypto isakmp identity {ip-address | hostname}
```

By default, a peer's ISAKMP identity is the peer's IP address. If you decide to change the default, just keep in mind that it is best to always be consistent across your entire IPsec-protected network when you choose to define a peer's identity.

Step 3 Configure the IPsec AH and ESP parameters.

The AH and ESP parameters are configured with the following commands:

```
crypto ipsec transform-set transform-set-name transform 1 transform 2
mode [tunnel | transport]
crypto ipsec security-association lifetime seconds seconds
```

A transform set represents a certain combination of security protocols and algorithms. Depending on the version of Cisco IOS Software you are running, the transform sets offered may vary because deployment of IPsec is still somewhat new and the standard was still being modified when Cisco first started offering IPsec. The transforms offered on Cisco IOS Software 12.2 are as follows:

- **ah-md5-hmac**: AH using the HMAC-MD5 hash function

- **ah-sha-hmac**: AH using the HMAC-SHA-1 hash function

- **comp-lzs**: IP compression using the LZS compression algorithm

— **esp-3des**: ESP encryption using 3DES

— **esp-des**: ESP encryption using DES

— **esp-md5-hmac**: ESP hash function using the HMAC-MD5

— **esp-null**: ESP encryption without a cipher (that is, no encryption)

— **esp-sha-hmac**: ESP hash function using the HMAC-SHA-1 function

When there are no interoperability constraints on which algorithms to use, you should use the **<esp-3des>** and **<esp-sha-hmac>** transforms to provide the authenticated and encrypted traffic exchange.

Tunnel mode is used for most IPsec traffic traversing through the IPsec routers. If the routers are the IPsec source and destination endpoints, transport mode should be specified.

Step 4 Configure the IPsec traffic selectors.

The traffic selectors are configured by defining extended access lists. The **permit** keyword causes all IP traffic that matches the specified conditions to be protected by IPsec

Step 5 Configure the IKE Phase 2 (IPsec SA) policy.

This step sets up a crypto map, which specifies all the necessary paramters to negotiate the IPsec SA policy. The following commands are required:

```
crypto map crypto-map-name seq-num ipsec-isakmp
match address access-list-id
set peer [ip-address | hostname]
set transfrom-set transform-set-name
set security-association lifetime seconds seconds
set pfs [group1 | group2]
```

It is possible to configure multiple transform sets and then apply up to six different transform sets to a specific crypto map. The transform set in the crypto map entry will be used in the IPsec SA negotiation to find a match between both peers.

Step 6 Apply the IPsec policy to an interface.

The configured crypto map is then applied to the appropriate interface using the **crypto map** *crypto-map-name* command. It is possible to apply the same crypto map to multiple interfaces. This case requires the use of the following command:

```
crypto map crypto-map-name local-address interface-id
```

If you use this command, the identifying interface is used as the local address for IPsec traffic originating from or destined to those interfaces sharing the same crypto map. A loopback interface should be used as the identifying interface.

NOTE   The syntax for configuring IPsec will vary slightly depending on the Cisco IOS Software version you are using. There are also more configuration options, but they are optional and not always used. It is always good practice to review the Command Reference for your software version before starting any configurations. Sometimes the optional configuration commands are required for interoperability reasons if you have a multivendor IPsec environment.

Figure 11-9 illustrates a scenario for two routers that use IPsec to encrypt/decrypt Telnet and World Wide Web traffic between the branch office and the corporate campus network.

Figure 11-9   *IPsec Between Two Routers*

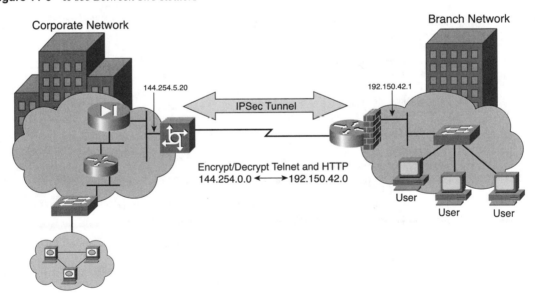

The IPsec parameters are as follows:

- IKE Phase 1
  - Encryption algorithm: 3DES
  - Hash algorithm: SHA-1

        — MODP group 2 (the Diffie-Hellman group)

        — Authentication using preshared keys (key is iamapresharedkey)

        — IKE SA lifetime 28,800 seconds (8 hours)

- IPsec SA

        — Encryption algorithm: 3DES

        — Hash algorithm: SHA-1

        — Only use ESP

        — ESP tunnel mode

        — Use perfect forward secrecy with MODP group 2

        — IPsec SA lifetime of 3600 seconds (1 hour)

Example 11-20 shows the configuration commands for the branch router, and Example 11-21 shows the configuration commands for the corporate NAS.

Example 11-20 *IPsec Branch Router Configuration*

```
! Define the hostname.
hostname Branch_router
!
! Configure IKE Phase 1 policy.  In this example the
! policy is to use 3DES for the encryption algorithm
! and SHA-1 for the hash algorithm.  Preshared
! authentication is used and MODP group 2.  The
! ISAKMP (IKE) SA lifetime is 8 hours (28,800 seconds).
!
crypto isakmp policy 6
  encryption 3des
  hash sha
  group 2
  lifetime 28800
  authentication pre-share
crypto isakmp key iamasharedkey address 144.254.5.20
!
! Configures the IPsec AH or ESP parameters.  In this example
! the policy is to use ESP with 3DES and SHA1 in tunnel mode.
!
crypto ipsec transform-set secureDES esp-3des esp-sha-hmac
  mode tunnel
!
! Configure the IP traffic selectors which are to encrypt
! Telnet and WWW traffic.
!

access-list 106 permit ip 192.150.42.0  0.0.0.255  144.254.0.0
    0.0.255.255 eq telnet
access-list 106 permit ip 192.150.42.0  0.0.0.255  144.254.0.0
    0.0.255.255 eq http
!
```

Example 11-20 *IPsec Branch Router Configuration (Continued)*

```
! Configure IKE Phase 2 (IPsec SA)  policy.
! PFS is used and MODP group 2 is always used
! The SA lifetime is 1 hour (3600 seconds).  Define
! the transform set secureDES to be used.
!
crypto map toNAS 12 ipsec-isakmp
  set peer 144.254.5.20
  set transfrom-set secureDES
  match address 106
  set pfs group 2
  set security-association lifetime seconds 3600
!
! Configure internal network.
!
! interface Ethernet 0
  ip address 192.150.42.1 255.255.255.0
!
! Configure the ISDN interface which connects to
! the corporate network and will have the crypto
! map applied to it.
interface Bri 0
ip address unnumbered Ethernet 0
encapsulation ppp
dialer map ip 144.254.5.20  name NAS
dialer-group 1
ppp authentication chap
crypto map toNAS
!
```

Example 11-21 *IPsec Corporate NAS Configuration*

```
! Define the hostname.
!
hostname NAS
!
! Configure IKE Phase 1 policy.  In this example the
! policy is to use 3DES for the encryption algorithm
! and SHA 1 for the hash algorithm.  Preshared
! authentication is used and MODP group 2.  The
! ISAKMP (IKE) SA lifetime is 8 hours (28,800 seconds).
!
crypto isakmp policy 6
  encryption 3des
  hash sha
  group 2
  lifetime 20000
  authentication pre-share
crypto isakmp key iamasharedkey address 192.150.42.1
!
! Configures the IPsec AH or ESP parameters.  In this example
! the policy is to use ESP with 3DES and SHA1 in tunnel mode.
```

continues

Example 11-21 *IPsec Corporate NAS Configuration (Continued)*

```
!
crypto ipsec transform-set secureDES esp-3des esp-sha-hmac
  mode tunnel
!
! Configure the IP traffic selectors which are to encrypt
! Telnet and WWW traffic.
!

access-list 106 permit ip 144.254.0.0  0.0.255.255 192.150.42.0
    0.0.0.255 eq telnet
access-list 106 permit ip 144.254.0.0  0.0.255.255 192.150.42.0
    0.0.0.255 eq http


!
! Configure IKE Phase 2 (IPsec SA)  policy.
! PFS is used and MODP group 2 is always used.
! The SA lifetime is 1 hour (3600 seconds).  Define
! the transform set secureDES to be used.
!
crypto map toBranch 12 ipsec-isakmp
  set peer 192.150.42.1
  set transfrom-set secureDES
  match address 106
  set pfs group 2
  set security-association lifetime seconds 3600
!
! Configure internal network.
!
interface Ethernet 0
ip address 144.254.5.20 255.255.255.0
!
!Configuring PRI.
interface Serial0:23
description to the Branch
crypto map toBranch
!
```

L2TP with IPsec

L2TP can be used to carry IP unicast, IP multicast, and non-IP protocols, and IPsec transport mode can be used to protect the L2TP-encapsulated traffic. The scenario in Figure 11-10 illustrates the remote connection of a remote branch office in Toronto and a remote branch office in New York connecting back to the corporate network in Denver. Both connections are done through local ISPs and use the Internet as the way to transport the data back to the corporate network in Denver. Mobile users also have access to the corporate network using local ISP dialup connections. Example 11-22, Example 11-23, Example 11-24, and Example 11-25 show the configurations for the home gateway router in Denver, the remote branch router in Toronto, the remote branch router in New York, and a relevant ISP NAS in Figure 11-10, respectively.

Figure 11-10 *Virtual Dial-In Using L2TP with IPsec*

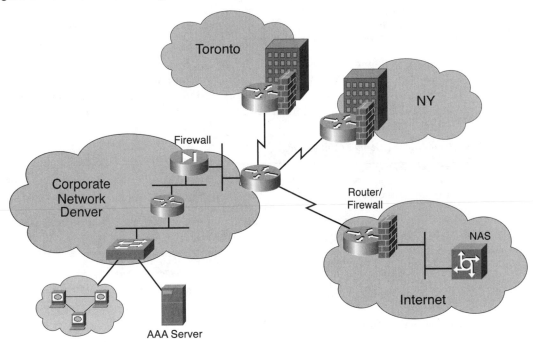

The following security policy is defined for this example:

- The branch office in Toronto is allowed to communicate directly to the Internet but must encrypt all traffic going to the corporate network in Denver.

- All New York branch office traffic must go through the Denver corporate office firewall.

- All mobile users use authenticated and private data connections back to the corporate network through ISP collaborative agreements.

- Corporate infrastructure device access is required to be authenticated and authorized for limited access.

The policy is implemented as follows:

- The branch office router in Toronto allows the users to talk directly to the Internet while using an IPsec-encrypted tunnel to access the corporate network. The serial interface on the router has been assigned an IP address from the ISP's address space. The Ethernet interface uses a private network address, and NAT is used to translate traffic going to the Internet. This router uses static routing.

- The branch router in New York requires that all traffic, even traffic to the Internet, must go through the corporate firewall. The serial interface on the router has been assigned an IP address from the ISP's address space; the Ethernet interface uses a private network address. This router uses OSPF routing.

- There is an agreement between the ISP and the corporation that if a mobile user presents the ISP's NAS with a username in the format username@mkos.name, the PPP session will be transported to the corporation's home gateway for termination. By using L2TP tunneling with IPsec, a secure tunnel is provided from the NAS (isp-nas) to the home gateway (Denver-gw).

Example 11-22 *Home Gateway Router Configuration*

```
hostname Denver-gw
!
! In IOS firewall IPsec images "no service tcp & no udp small servers" is the
! default so it does not have to be explicitly defined.
! Turn on time stamps for log and debug information, set to the local time with
! time zone information displayed.
!
service timestamps debug datetime msec localtime show-timezone
service timestamps log datetime msec localtime show-timezone
!
service password-encryption
!
no logging console
!
! Enable TACACS+ to authenticate login, enable any PPP sessions, also enable
! accounting start-stop records for EXEC and PPP sessions.
!
aaa new-model
aaa authentication login default tacacs+ enable
aaa authentication login console none
aaa authentication enable default tacacs+ enable
aaa authentication ppp default tacacs+
aaa authorization network default tacacs+
aaa accounting exec default start-stop tacacs+
aaa accounting network default start-stop tacacs+
!
enable secret 5 $1$xDvT$sT/TGeGrAwfAKbMr4N1NZ1
enable password 7 02050D480809
!
no ip finger
ip domain-name mkos.com
!
! Enable VPDN and tell it to use L2TP. The PPP name of the remote NAS will be
! isp-nas and the local PPP name is Denver-gw. Also for the VPDN, use an
! alternative tacacs+ server. Connections inbound will use virtual-template 1
! as the basis to create to the actual virtual-access interface.
!
vpdn enable
!
vpdn aaa override-server 172.20.24.47
```

Example 11-22   *Home Gateway Router Configuration (Continued)*

```
vpdn-group 1
 accept dialin l2tp virtual-template 1 remote isp-nas
 local name Denver-gw
 !
 ! Define the IPsec transform policy set,
 ! (esp-3des) ESP with triple DES encryption algorithm,
 ! (esp-sha-hmac) ESP with SHA authentication algorithm. Because a GRE is used,
 ! run IPsec in transport rather than tunnel mode.
 !
crypto ipsec transform-set auth2 esp-3des esp-sha-hmac
 mode transport
 !
 ! IPsec using certificates: The routers must first obtain certificates from
 ! the Certificate Authority (CA) server. When both peers have valid certificates,
 ! they automatically exchange RSA public keys as part of the ISAKMP negotiation.
 ! All that is required is that the routers register with the CA and obtain
 ! a certificate. A router does not have to keep public RSA keys for all peers
 ! in the network.
 !
crypto ca identity vpnnetwork
  enrollment url http://mkosca
  crl optional
cryto ca certificate chain vpnnetwork
  certificate 44FC6C531FC3446927E4EE307A806B20
 ! Certificate is multiple lines of hex digits
 quit
  certificate ca 3051DF7169BEE31B821DFE4B3A338E5F
 ! Certificate of the CA, multiple of lines hex digits
 quit
  certificate 52A46D5D10B18A6F51E6BC735A36508C
 ! Certificate is multiple lines of hex digits
 quit
 !
 ! The crypto map determines what to encrypt and to what peer to send the traffic.
 ! An interface can have only one crypto map applied to it. The crypto map below
 ! is structured into sections, which apply for the different destinations,
 ! while still being a single crypto map entity.
 !
crypto map Denver-to-remotes local-address Serial2/0
crypto map Denver-to-remotes 100 ipsec-isakmp
  set peer 207.9.31.1
  set transform-set auth2
  match address Denver_gre_Toronto
crypto map Denver-to-remotes 200 ipsec-isakmp
  set peer 207.10.31.1
  set transform-set auth2
  match address Denver_gre_NewYork
crypto map Denver-to-remotes 500 ipsec-isakmp
  set peer 201.1.1.1
  set transform-set auth2
  match address ISP1_VPDN
 !
```

continues

Example 11-22 *Home Gateway Router Configuration (Continued)*

```
! Set the time zone and daylight savings time for this router.
!
clock timezone PST -8
clock summer-time PDT recurring
!
! Tunnel interface to router Toronto. The tunnel source is specified as an
! interface with a registered IP address. The crypto map is applied to both
! the tunnel and physical interfaces. The IP precedence of packets being
! tunneled are copied into the IP header of the outbound frame.
! This example uses an IP unnumbered tunnel interface. Only packets destined
! for the intranet arrive on this interface because NAT is used at the remote
! for packets destined for the Internet.
!
interface Tunnel100
 description tunnel to branch router Toronto
 ip unnumbered FastEthernet5/0
 no ip directed-broadcast
 tunnel source Serial2/0
 tunnel destination 207.9.31.1
 crypto map Denver-to-remotes
!
! Tunnel interface to router New York. The crypto map is applied to both the
! tunnel and physical interfaces. Note that the same crypto map has been used
! on both the tunnels, with different sections of the crypto map applying to each
! tunnel. The IP precedence of packets being tunneled are copied into the IP
! header of the outbound frame. This example uses an IP-numbered tunnel interface
! with OSPF as the routing protocol and routing information authentication
! enabled. The policy for this remote site is that all packets destined to the
! Internet must go through the corporate firewall. This is achieved by using
! policy routing (route-map VPN_InBound).
!
interface Tunnel101
 description tunnel to branch router NewYork
 ip address 172.26.123.1 255.255.255.252
 no ip directed-broadcast
 ip ospf message-digest-key 1 md5 7 00071A15075434101F2F
 ip policy route-map VPN_InBound
 tunnel source Serial2/0
 tunnel destination 207.10.31.1
 crypto map Denver-to-remotes
!
! DS3 connection to ISP. Two ACLS are applied here. The inbound ACL stops
! some common protocols and network addresses known to be invalid or harmful.
! The outbound security ACL prevents packets from private network addresses
! that have not been through NAT from leaving. The crypto map is applied
! to the interface.
!
interface Serial2/0
 description connection to ISP1 - DS3
 ip address 207.1.1.1 255.255.255.252
 ip access-group IntSecurity in
 ip access-group IntSecurityOut out
```

Example 11-22 *Home Gateway Router Configuration (Continued)*

```
  no ip directed-broadcast
  framing c-bit
  cablelength 50
  dsu bandwidth 44210
  crypto map Denver-to-remotes
 !
 ! This interface is connected to the corporate network Web server and to the
 ! firewall, which is doing NAT for the corporate network's access to the
 ! Internet.
 !
 interface FastEthernet3/0
  description network for Internet traffic
  ip address 207.1.2.1 255.255.255.240
  no ip directed-broadcast
  full-duplex
 !
 ! This interface is connected to the firewall, is treated as an inside interface,
 ! is for the VPN traffic to access the corporate network, and is using NAT
 ! on the firewall to the Internet. This route-map on the interface is responsible
 ! for setting the correct precedence on the IP packets destined for the VPN,
 ! to gain the QoS agreement with the service provider. The ACL is used to allow
 ! only known VPN networks on the link.
 !
 interface FastEthernet5/0
  description network for VPN traffic
  ip address 172.26.71.1 255.255.255.252
  ip access-group 120 out
  no ip directed-broadcast
  ip policy route-map VPN_QoS
  full-duplex
 !
 ! The virtual template is used by the VPDN code as the basis to create the
 ! virtual-access interface on which the L2TP connections terminate.
 !
 interface Virtual-Template1
   ip unnumbered FastEthernet5/0
   no ip directed-broadcast
   peer default ip address pool vpn_users
 !
 ! OSPF for the VPN network, remote branch NewYork is running OSPF.
 ! The OSPF process is set to redistribute static routes that match
 ! route-map VPN_ROUTES_OUT, and originate the default route for the
 ! remote VPN sites running OSPF. Authentication is enabled for routing
 ! information so that only remotes with the correct key can participate.
 !
 router ospf 100
  redistribute static subnets route-map VPN_ROUTES_OUT
  passive-interface FastEthernet5/0
  passive-interface Tunnel100
  network 172.26.71.0 0.0.0.3 area 0
  network 172.26.120.0 0.0.3.255 area 172.26.120.0
  default-information originate
```

continues

Example 11-22 *Home Gateway Router Configuration (Continued)*

```
 area 172.26.120.0 authentication message-digest
!
ip classless
!
! Default route to ISP:
ip route 0.0.0.0 0.0.0.0 207.1.1.2
!
! Corporate network uses 172.20/24 and 172.26/24.
ip route 172.20.0.0 255.255.0.0 172.26.71.2
ip route 172.26.0.0 255.255.0.0 172.26.71.2
!
! Static route to branch in Toronto (Ethernet 0):
ip route 172.26.120.0 255.255.255.0 Tunnel100
!
! Route to the NAT pool on the firewall:
ip route 207.1.2.16 255.255.255.248 207.1.2.2
!
! ACL to determine what frames get set specified QoS for ISP1:
ip access-list extended Bronze_ISP1_QoS
 permit ip 172.26.0.0 0.0.255.255 172.26.120.0 0.0.0.255
 permit ip 172.20.0.0 0.0.255.255 172.26.120.0 0.0.0.255
!
! ACL to determine the traffic to encrypt for the VPDN L2TP tunnel:
! from ISP NAS "isp-nas"
ip access-list extended ISP1_VPDN
  permit ip host 207.1.1.1 host 201.1.1.1
!
! ACL to block any traffic inbound from private addresses
! and some common troublesome services:
ip access-list extended IntSecurity
 permit tcp any any established
 deny    ip 127.0.0.0 0.255.255.255 any
 deny    ip 10.0.0.0 0.255.255.255 any
 deny    ip 172.16.0.0 0.15.255.255 any
 deny    ip 192.168.0.0 0.0.255.255 any
 deny    udp any any eq snmp
 deny    udp any any eq 2000
 deny    udp any any gt 6000
 deny    tcp any any gt 6000
 deny    tcp any any eq 2000
 deny    udp any any eq tftp
 deny    udp any any eq sunrpc
 deny    udp any any eq 2049
 deny    tcp any any eq 2049
 deny    tcp any any eq sunrpc
 deny    tcp any any eq 87
 deny    tcp any any eq exec
 deny    tcp any any eq login
 deny    tcp any any eq cmd
 deny    tcp any any eq lpd
 deny    tcp any any eq uucp
 permit ip any any
```

Example 11-22 *Home Gateway Router Configuration (Continued)*

```
!
! ACL to prevent any packets from private addresses being sent to the Internet.
ip access-list extended IntSecurityOut
 deny   ip 127.0.0.0 0.255.255.255 any
 deny   ip 10.0.0.0 0.255.255.255 any
 deny   ip 172.16.0.0 0.15.255.255 any
 deny   ip 192.168.0.0 0.0.255.255 any
 permit ip 207.0.0.0 0.255.255.255 any
!
! ACL to determine which frames are set to Silver QoS for ISP1:
ip access-list extended Silver_ISP1_QoS
  permit ip 172.26.0.0 0.0.255.255 172.26.121.0 0.0.0.255
  permit ip 172.20.0.0 0.0.255.255 172.26.121.0 0.0.0.255
!
! ACL determines which packets IPsec will look at for tunnel100:
ip access-list extended Denver_gre_Torornto
 permit gre host 207.1.1.1 host 207.9.31.1
!
! ACL determines which packets IPsec looks at for tunnel101:
ip access-list extended Denver_gre_NewYork
 permit gre host 207.1.1.1 host 207.10.31.1
!
! Turn on syslog and point it at the management station.
logging 172.20.18.5
!
! ACL determines which static routes are redistributed into the OSPF VPN process:
access-list 18 permit 172.26.0.0 0.0.255.255
access-list 18 permit 172.20.0.0 0.0.255.255
!
! ACL only allows Telnet to the router from particular subnets:
access-list 70 permit 172.20.18.0 0.0.0.192
access-list 70 permit 172.20.24.0 0.0.0.255
!
! ACL determines which management stations can access this device using SNMP:
access-list 75 permit 172.20.18.0 0.0.0.255
!
! ACL only allows particular networks on the VPN interface to the firewall:
access-list 120 permit ip 172.26.120.0 0.0.0.255 any
access-list 120 permit ip 172.26.121.0 0.0.0.255 any
access-list 120 permit ip 172.26.122.0 0.0.0.255 any
access-list 120 permit ip 172.26.123.0 0.0.0.255 any
!
! ACL for route map to policy route all packets to the firewall.
access-list 195 permit ip 172.26.121.0 0.0.0.255 any
access-list 195 permit ip 172.26.123.0 0.0.0.3 any
!
! Route map determines which routes to distribute into OSPF VPN process.
route-map VPN_ROUTES_OUT permit 20
 match ip address 18
set metric 1000
  set metric-type type-1
!
```

continues

Example 11-22 *Home Gateway Router Configuration (Continued)*

```
! Route map used to policy route all specified packets to the corporate firewall.
route-map VPN_InBound permit 100
 match ip address 195
  set ip next-hop 172.26.71.2
!
! Route map used to set the precedence bits on outbound VPN network packets.
route-map VPN_QoS permit 100
 match ip address Bronze_ISP1_QoS
  set ip precedence priority
route-map VPN_QoS permit 200
 match ip address Silver_ISP1_QoS
  set ip precedence immediate
!
! Configure SNMP, only allow management stations matching access list 75
! to manage this router.
snmp-server community public RO 75
snmp-server community private RW 75
snmp-server trap-source Ethernet1/0
snmp-server packetsize 4096
snmp-server enable traps snmp
snmp-server enable traps frame-relay
snmp-server host 172.20.18.5 traps public
snmp-server tftp-server-list 75
!
! Configure which TACACS server to use and the key.
tacacs-server host 172.20.18.5
tacacs-server key SECRET12345
!
! Console and vty are secured using TACACS+.
line con 0
 exec-timeout 5 0
 transport input none
line aux 0
!
! Only allow Telnet to this router if the source address is in access list 70.
line vty 0 4
 access-class 70 in
 password 7 1511021F0725
 transport input telnet
!
! Configure NTP so that all the routers have the same time in the network.
ntp clock-period 17179770
ntp server 172.26.71.2
end
```

Example 11-23 *Remote Branch Router in Toronto Configuration*

```
hostname Toronto
!
! In IOS firewall IPsec images "no service tcp & no udp small servers" is the
! default. Turn on time stamps for log and debug information and set to the local
```

Example 11-23   *Remote Branch Router in Toronto Configuration (Continued)*

```
! time with time zone information displayed.
!
service timestamps debug datetime msec localtime show-timezone
service timestamps log datetime msec localtime show-timezone
service password-encryption
!
logging buffered 32000 debugging
no logging console
!
! Enable TACACS+ to authenticate login and enable passwords,
! also enable accounting start-stop records for exec sessions.
!
aaa new-model
aaa authentication login default tacacs+ enable
aaa authentication enable default tacacs+ enable
aaa accounting exec default start-stop tacacs+
!
enable secret 5 $1$SKkd$qbTmOJ9dyffjccNUB0cvn0
enable password 7 02050D480809
!
no ip finger
ip domain-name mkos.com
!
! Define the IPsec transform policy set; because a GRE is used, run IPsec in
! transport rather than tunnel mode.
!
crypto ipsec transform-set auth2  esp-3des esp-sha-hmac
 mode transport
!
crypto ca identity vpnnetwork
 enrollment url http://mkosca
 crl optional
cryto ca certificate chain vpnnetwork
  certificate 44FC6C531FC3446927E4EE307A806B20
! Certificate is multiple lines hex digits
 quit
  certificate ca 3051DF7169BEE31B821DFE4B3A338E5F
! Certificate is multiple lines hex digits
 quit
  certificate 52A46D5D10B18A6F51E6BC735A36508C
! Certificate is multiple lines hex digits
 quit
!
! The crypto map determines what packets should be encrypted as determined by
! access list 140, and the crypto peer that is the IP address of Denver-gw,
! along with the transforms that will be allowed. The setting of the local-address
! ensures that if there are multiple paths, the same IP address is always used
! for this crypto pair, no matter what interface a packet arrives on.
!
crypto map ipsec-Toronto-to-Denver local-address Serial0/0
crypto map ipsec-Toronto-to-Denver 10 ipsec-isakmp
 set peer 207.1.1.1
```

continues

Example 11-23 *Remote Branch Router in Toronto Configuration (Continued)*

```
 set transform-set auth2
 match address 140
!
! Set the time zone and daylight savings time for this router.
!
clock timezone EST -5
clock summer-time EDT recurring
!
! Tunnel interface to transport traffic to Denver-gw, the tunnel source is
! specified as an interface with a registered IP address. The IP address of
! the Ethernet is used, which is a private address; an unnumbered interface
! is used here to show that you do not have to address the tunnel interface.
! The IP precedence of the packets being tunneled are copied into the IP header
! of the outbound frame.
!
interface Tunnel100
 description VPN connection back to headquarters (Denver)
 ip unnumbered Ethernet1/0
 no ip directed-broadcast
 tunnel source Serial0/0
 tunnel destination 207.1.1.1
 crypto map ipsec-Toronto-to-Denver
!
! Serial 0/0 is the connection to the ISP; it has one of the ISP's registered
! addresses. Two access lists are applied to the interface: one inbound and
! one outbound. These are explained where the access list is defined below.
! This interface is specified as the outside interface for NAT.
! Finally, the crypto map is applied to the interface to determine what
! should be encrypted.
!
interface Serial0/0
 description frame relay connection to ISP
 ip address 207.9.31.1 255.255.255.240
 ip access-group IntSecurity in
 ip access-group IntSecurityOut out
 no ip directed-broadcast
 ip nat outside
 encapsulation frame-relay IETF
 no ip mroute-cache
 frame-relay lmi-type ansi
 crypto map ipsec-Toronto-to-Denver
!
! Ethernet 1/0 is the remote LAN interface; it is assigned a private IP address
! and is a NAT inside interface. A route-map is applied to the interface to set
! the IP precedence to get the ISP Bronze offering of QoS.
!
interface Ethernet1/0
 description private IP address for remote site
 ip address 172.26.120.1 255.255.255.0
 no ip directed-broadcast
 ip nat inside
 ip policy route-map Bronze_ISP1_QoS
```

Example 11-23   *Remote Branch Router in Toronto Configuration (Continued)*

```
!
! Configure NAT: Any source address matching access list 150,
! translate to the IP address of interface serial 0/0. The overload options
! mean that many IP addresses will be translated to serial 0/0 IP addresses
! on different ports.
!
ip nat inside source list 150 interface Serial0/0 overload
ip classless
!
! Static routes: The default is to send all traffic to the ISP. The corporation
! uses networks 172.20/24 and 172.26/24 for its networks, so any traffic
! destined to these addresses should go across the tunnel interface.
!
ip route 0.0.0.0 0.0.0.0 207.9.31.14
ip route 172.20.0.0 255.255.0.0 Tunnel100
ip route 172.26.0.0 255.255.0.0 Tunnel100
!
! ACL to block particular services and networks, inbound from the ISP.
ip access-list extended IntSecurity
 permit tcp any any established
 deny    ip 127.0.0.0 0.255.255.255 any
 deny    ip 10.0.0.0 0.255.255.255 any
 deny    ip 172.16.0.0 0.15.255.255 any
 deny    ip 192.168.0.0 0.0.255.255 any
 deny    udp any any eq snmp
 deny    udp any any eq 2000
 deny    udp any any gt 6000
 deny    tcp any any gt 6000
 deny    tcp any any eq 2000
 deny    udp any any eq tftp
 deny    udp any any eq sunrpc
 deny    udp any any eq 2049
 deny    tcp any any eq 2049
 deny    tcp any any eq sunrpc
 deny    tcp any any eq 87
 deny    tcp any any eq exec
 deny    tcp any any eq login
 deny    tcp any any eq cmd
 deny    tcp any any eq lpd
 deny    tcp any any eq uucp
 permit ip any any
!
! ACL to prevent packets from private networks leaving by the ISP interface.
ip access-list extended IntSecurityOut
 deny    ip 127.0.0.0 0.255.255.255 any
 deny    ip 10.0.0.0 0.255.255.255 any
 deny    ip 172.16.0.0 0.15.255.255 any
 deny    ip 192.168.0.0 0.0.255.255 any
 permit ip 207.9.31.0 0.0.0.255 any
!
! Turn on syslog and point it at the management station.
logging 172.20.18.5
```

continues

Example 11-23 *Remote Branch Router in Toronto Configuration (Continued)*

```
!
! ACL to secure why can Telnet to the router:
access-list 70 permit 207.1.1.1
access-list 70 permit 172.20.18.0 0.0.0.192
access-list 70 permit 172.20.24.0 0.0.0.255
!
! ACL to determine which management stations can access this device using SNMP:
access-list 75 permit 172.20.18.0 0.0.0.255
!
! ACL to determine which frames should be protected (encrypted) with Ipsec:
access-list 140 permit gre host 207.9.31.1 host 207.1.1.1
!
! What packets are eligible sourced from NAT inside networks for
! address translation.
access-list 150 permit ip any any
!
! Access list used in route map to set IP precedence to get specified
! QoS level from ISP.
access-list 175 permit ip any any
!
! Route map used on Ethernet 1/0 to set the precedence bits of all IP frames
! to priority (1).
route-map Bronze_ISP1_QoS permit 10
 match ip address 175
 set ip precedence priority
!
! Configure which TACACS server to use and the key.
tacacs-server host 172.20.18.5
tacacs-server key SECRET12345
!
! Configure SNMP for network management. Because only the corporation's
! management stations will manage this router, the trap source is set to use
! Ethernet 1/0.
!
snmp-server community public RO 75
snmp-server community private RW 75
snmp-server trap-source Ethernet1/0
snmp-server packetsize 4096
snmp-server enable traps snmp
snmp-server enable traps frame-relay
snmp-server enable traps syslog
snmp-server host 172.20.18.5 traps public
snmp-server tftp-server-list 75
!
! Console and vty are secured using TACACS+.
!
line con 0
 exec-timeout 5 0
 transport input none
line aux 0
!
! Only allow Telnet to this router if the source address is in access list 70:
```

Example 11-23   *Remote Branch Router in Toronto Configuration (Continued)*

```
line vty 0 4
 access-class 70 in
 password 7 1511021F0725
 transport input telnet
!
! Configure NTP so that all the routers have the same time in the network.
ntp clock-period 17179770
ntp server 172.26.71.2
end
!
```

Example 11-24   *Remote Branch Router in New York Configuration*

```
Hostname NewYork
!
! In IOS firewall IPsec images "no service tcp & no udp small servers" is the
! default. Turn on time stamps for log and debug information, set to the
! local time with time zone information displayed.
!
service timestamps debug datetime msec localtime show-timezone
service timestamps log datetime msec localtime show-timezone
service password-encryption
!
logging buffered 32000 debugging
no logging console
!
! Enable TACACS+ to authenticate login and enable passwords, also enable
! accounting start-stop records for exec sessions.
!
aaa new-model
aaa authentication login default tacacs+ enable
aaa authentication enable default tacacs+ enable
aaa accounting exec default start-stop tacacs+
!
enable secret 5 $1$z1c.$vLAcnZ849epT8xLHNeTT0/
enable password 7 110A1016141D
!
ip domain-name mkos.com
!
! Define the IPsec transform policy set; because a GRE is used, run IPsec in
! transport rather than tunnel mode.
!
crypto ipsec transform-set auth2 esp-3des esp-sha-hmac
 mode transport
!
crypto ca identity vpnnetwork
 enrollment url http://mkosca
 crl optional
cryto ca certificate chain vpnnetwork
   certificate 44FC6C531FC3446927E4EE307A806B20
! Certificate is multiple lines of hex digits
```

continues

Example 11-24 *Remote Branch Router in New York Configuration (Continued)*

```
 quit
  certificate ca 3051DF7169BEE31B821DFE4B3A338E5F
 ! Certificate is multiple lines of hex digits
 quit
  certificate 52A46D5D10B18A6F51E6BC735A36508C
 ! Certificate is multiple lines of hex digits
 quit
 !
 ! The crypto map determines which packets should be encrypted as determined
 ! by access list 141, and the crypto peer, which is the IP address of Denver-gw,
 ! along with the transforms that will be allowed. The setting of the
 ! local-address ensures that if there are multiple paths, the same IP address
 ! is always used for this crypto pair, no matter what interface a packet arrives ! on.
 !
 crypto map NewYork-to-Denver local-address Serial0/0
 crypto map NewYork-to-Denver 20 ipsec-isakmp
 set peer 207.1.1.1
set transform-set auth2
 match address 141
 !
 ! Set the time zone and daylight savings time for this router.
 !
clock timezone est -8
clock summer-time EST recurring
 !
 ! Tunnel interface to transport traffic to Denver-gw, the tunnel source is
 ! specified as an interface with a registered IP address. The router is
 ! configured to run OSPF with the home gateway across the tunnel interface.
 ! OSPF is using message digest 5 to authenticate routing updates.
 ! The crypto map is applied to both the tunnel and the physical interfaces.
 ! The IP precedence of packets being tunneled are copied into the IP header
 ! of the outbound frame.
 !
interface Tunnel101
 ip address 172.26.123.2 255.255.255.252
 no ip directed-broadcast
 ip ospf authentication-key 7 104D000A06182D1D1C
 ip ospf message-digest-key 1 md5 7 045802150C2E73581917
 tunnel source Serial0/0
 tunnel destination 207.1.1.1
 crypto map NewYork-to-Denver
 !
 ! Serial 0/0 is the connection to the ISP; it has one of the ISP's registered
 ! addresses. Two ACLs are applied to the interface: one inbound and one outbound.
 ! The crypto map is applied to the interface to determine what should
 ! be encrypted.
 !
interface Serial0/0
 ip address 207.10.31.1 255.255.255.240
 ip access-group IntSecurity in
 ip access-group IntSecurityOut out
 no ip directed-broadcast
```

Example 11-24 *Remote Branch Router in New York Configuration (Continued)*

```
 encapsulation frame-relay IETF
 frame-relay lmi-type ansi
 crypto map NewYork-to-Denver
!
! Ethernet 1/0 is the remote LAN interface; it is assigned a private IP address.
! A route map is applied to the interface to set the IP precedence
! level to get the ISP Silver offering of QoS.
interface Ethernet1/0
 ip address 172.26.121.1 255.255.255.0
 no ip directed-broadcast
 ip policy route-map Silver_ISP1_QoS
!
! Configure OSPF for IP routing and authenticate routing updates.
router ospf 100
 network 172.26.120.0 0.0.3.255 area 172.26.120.0
 area 172.26.120.0 authentication message-digest
!
ip classless
!
! Because all traffic from the remote router must go through the firewall at
! corporate headquarters, a static default route is not used but an explicit
! route for the tunnel destination end point is used. This router gets its
! default route from OSPF.
!
ip route 207.1.1.1 255.255.255.255 207.10.31.14
!
! ACL to block particular services and networks, inbound from the ISP.
ip access-list extended IntSecurity
 permit tcp any any established
 deny    ip 127.0.0.0 0.255.255.255 any
 deny    ip 10.0.0.0 0.255.255.255 any
 deny    ip 172.16.0.0 0.15.255.255 any
 deny    ip 192.168.0.0 0.0.255.255 any
 deny    udp any any eq snmp
 deny    udp any any eq 2000
 deny    udp any any gt 6000
 deny    tcp any any gt 6000
 deny    tcp any any eq 2000
 deny    udp any any eq tftp
 deny    udp any any eq sunrpc
 deny    udp any any eq 2049
 deny    tcp any any eq 2049
 deny    tcp any any eq sunrpc
 deny    tcp any any eq 87
 deny    tcp any any eq exec
 deny    tcp any any eq login
 deny    tcp any any eq cmd
 deny    tcp any any eq lpd
 permit ip any any
!
! ACL prevents packets from private networks from leaving by the ISP interface.
ip access-list extended IntSecurityOut
```

continues

Example 11-24 *Remote Branch Router in New York Configuration (Continued)*

```
deny   ip 127.0.0.0 0.255.255.255 any
deny   ip 10.0.0.0 0.255.255.255 any
deny   ip 172.16.0.0 0.15.255.255 any
deny   ip 192.168.0.0 0.0.255.255 any
permit ip 207.0.0.0 0.255.255.255 any
!
! Turn on syslog and point it at the management station.
logging 172.20.18.5
!
! ACL secures who can Telnet to the router.
access-list 70 permit 207.1.1.1
access-list 70 permit 172.20.18.0 0.0.0.255
!
! ACL determines which management stations can access this device using SNMP.
access-list 75 permit 172.20.18.0 0.0.0.255
!
! ACL determines which frames should be protected (encrypted) with IPsec
access list 141 permit gre host 207.10.31.1 host 207.1.1.1.
!
! ACL used in route map to set IP precedence to get specified QoS level from ISP.
access-list 175 permit ip 172.26.121.0 0.0.0.255 any
!
! Route map used on Ethernet 1/0 to set the precedence bits of all IP frames
! to immediate (2).
route-map Silver_ISP1_QoS permit 10
 match ip address 175
 set ip precedence immediate
!
! Configure which TACACS server to use and the key.
tacacs-server host 172.20.18.5
tacacs-server key SECRET12345
!
! Configure SNMP for network management. Because only the corporation's
! management stations will manage this router, the trap source is set to
! use Ethernet 1/0.
!
snmp-server community public RO 75
snmp-server community private RW 75
snmp-server trap-source Ethernet1/0
snmp-server packetsize 4096
snmp-server enable traps snmp
snmp-server enable traps frame-relay
snmp-server enable traps syslog
snmp-server host 172.20.18.5 traps public
snmp-server tftp-server-list 75
!
! Console and vty are secured using TACACS+.
!
line con 0
 exec-timeout 5 0
 transport input none
 login authentication default
```

Example 11-24 *Remote Branch Router in New York Configuration (Continued)*

```
line aux 0
!
! Only allow Telnet to this router if the source address is in access list 70.
line vty 0 4
 access-class 70 in
 password 7 1511021F0725
 transport input telnet
!
! Configure NTP so that all the routers have the same time in the network.
ntp clock-period 17179770
ntp server 172.26.71.2
end
```

Example 11-25 *ISP NAS Configuration*

```
Hostname isp-nas
!
aaa new-model
aaa authentication login default enable
aaa authentication login console none
aaa authentication enable default enable
aaa authentication ppp default tacacs+ local
aaa authorization exec default none
aaa accounting exec default start-stop tacacs+
!
enable secret 5 $1$2Ezj$2ygSyGTzphmQadmU854aL1
enable password escape
!
ip domain-name isp1.net
!
! Enable VPDN on the NAS and make the source of tunnels to be the loopback.
vpdn enable
vpdn source-ip 201.1.1.1
!
! VPDN group 1, connection to the home gateway Denver-gw, use LT2P,
! and the ppp name isp1.
!
vpdn-group 1
 request dialin l2tp ip 207.1.1.1 domain mkos.com
 local name isp1
!
crypto isakmp policy 10
 authentication rsa-encr
 group 2
 lifetime 240
!
! Define the IPsec transform policy set; because an L2TP is used, run IPsec in
! transport rather than tunnel mode.
crypto ipsec transform-set auth-mkos-dial esp-3des esp-sha-hmac
  mode transport
!
```

continues

Example 11-25 *ISP NAS Configuration*

```
crypto ca identity vpnnetwork
 enrollment url http://mkosca
 crl optional
cryto ca certificate chain vpnnetwork
  certificate 44FC6C531FC3446927E4EE307A806B20
! Certificate is multiple lines of hex digits
quit
  certificate ca 3051DF7169BEE31B821DFE4B3A338E5F
! Certificate is multiple lines of hex digits
 quit
!
! Crypto map to encrypt traffic destined to Denver home gateway for mkos.com:
!
crypto map VPDN_MKOS local-address Loopback0
 crypto map VPDN_MKOS 1000 ipsec-isakmp
 set peer 207.1.1.1
 set transform-set auth-mkos-dial
 match address VPDN_mkos_tunnel
!
! All L2TP traffic is sourced off the loopback, apply the crytpo map for IPsec.
!
interface Loopback0
 ip address 201.1.1.1 255.255.255.255
 no ip directed-broadcast
crypto map VPDN_MKOS
!
interface Ethernet1/2
 ip address 207.7.31.1 255.255.255.252
 no ip directed-broadcast
 no ip mroute-cache
 crypto map VPDN_MKOS
!
! ACL to determine what traffic IPsec should be applied to.
ip access-list extended VPDN_mkos_tunnel
 permit ip host 201.1.1.1 host 207.1.1.1
 !
```

Summary

This chapter described the implementation considerations for providing secure remote dial-in and virtual dial-in access. This includes establishing proper authentication and authorization for any telecommuters, mobile hosts, and remote branch offices attempting to gain access to resources in the main corporate network.

It is often necessary to restrict access to certain areas of the corporate network depending on who the remote user is and from where he or she is trying to obtain the connection. Also important is keeping track of connection details (such as who connected where and the duration of the connection) to keep accurate accounting statistics for an audit trail or billing purposes.

Finally, virtual dial-in environments require some special considerations because the data is traveling over shared public networks. Usually, you will want to ensure authenticated and private (confidential) delivery of the data packets over these public networks. It is usually a good idea to incorporate firewall functionality into the dial-in access perimeters and to implement some kind of auditing and intrusion detection system to keep accurate connection and traffic statistics.

Review Questions

The following questions provide you with an opportunity to test your knowledge of the topics covered in this chapter. You can find the answers to these questions in Appendix E, "Answers to Review Questions."

1 What are five security concerns for remote dial-in environments?

2 What are the two levels of authentication that can be performed for dial-in connectivity?

3 Which of the following is *not* a true statement?

   A CHAP and PAP are two mechanisms used for PPP authentication.

   B RADIUS and TACACS+ used in conjunction with EAP is a flexible and scalable dial-in authentication mechanism.

   C PPP CHAP and PPP PAP cannot be used with either RADIUS or TACACS+.

   D None of the above

4 When configuring RADIUS or TACACS+ authentication in Cisco IOS Software devices, what is meant by a method list?

5 True or false: A defined method list overrides the default method list.

6 Why is authorization a useful step after a user has successfully authenticated?

7 Which of the following is *not* a valid field in the first six fields of a AAA accounting record?

   A Time stamp

   B Password

   C NAS name

   D Username

8 For a user to gain access to a host through a router with lock and key configured, what must the user first do?

9 Why is IPsec the better choice over the Cisco Encryption Technology for providing security services for IP-based networks?

10 What is required in an IPsec environment if there is a requirement to encrypt an IP routing protocol that uses multicast packets to distribute its routing information?

## CHAPTER 12

Securing VPN, Wireless, and VoIP Networks

A multitude of security technologies have been discussed in this book, and many features specific to Cisco equipment were highlighted. This chapter pulls all of the information together and provides comprehensive design considerations and examples for securing VPN, wireless, and Voice over IP (VoIP) networks when using Cisco-based equipment for your network infrastructures. Specific configurations are not shown because the products to implement the designs vary greatly and have different syntax depending on the products and software versions used. However, references for relevant commands and detailed configuration examples are provided to simplify searching through the Cisco website. Security technologies and features for both wireless networks and VoIP networks are still under development, and the considerations for securing these types of networks in a Cisco-based environment are detailed as much as possible given the information available at the time of this writing.

Virtual Private Networks

The security technologies used to create virtual private networks (VPNs) were discussed in Chapter 3, "Applying Security Technologies to Real Networks." VPNs are used to establish secure, end-to-end private network connections over a public network infrastructure. VPNs are not by nature secure. Take, for example, Multiprotocol Label Switching (MPLS) VPNs, which are gaining deployment momentum. MPLS VPN-based services are starting to replace some of the more traditional Layer 2 VPNs, such as ATM or Frame Relay networks. Although security is mainly touted through the use of address and routing separation and the hiding of core infrastructure and network topology, MPLS VPNs and other Layer 2 VPN scenarios should not be thought of as secure. MPLS itself does not provide encryption, integrity, or authentication services. If these features are required, IPsec should be used over the MPLS infrastructure, firewalls should be deployed between different VPNs, and neighbor authentication should be deployed between peer routers. A detailed description of MPLS is beyond the scope of this book. However, for readers who want to deploy MPLS VPNs and are looking for more detailed information regarding MPLS networks, refer *MPLS and VPN Architectures, Volume II* (Cisco Press, 2003). For detailed security considerations specific to MPLS networks, refer to the white paper titled "Security of the MPLS Architecture" at http://www.cisco.com/warp/public/cc/pd/iosw/prodlit/mxinf_ds.htm.

For any VPN, only after the appropriate security controls have been put into place can you state that you have a secured VPN. Chapter 11, "Securing Remote Dial-In Access," covers securing remote dial-in environments, which the savvy reader has recognized as being part of an access VPN. Access VPNs can impose security over the analog, dial, ISDN, digital subscriber line (DSL), mobile IP, and cable technologies that connect mobile users, telecommuters, and branch offices. In this section, some more complex scenarios are shown, including the use of Network Address Translation (NAT) and IPsec with legacy user authentication mechanisms.

The design methodology for creating secure VPNs is in large parts constrained by the security policy. Before any network can be designed or configured, you need to understand what you are trying to protect and from what. Let's start by looking at a typical corporate VPN requirement that consists of three parts: a remote-access VPN for telecommuters and traveling corporate personnel, an intranet VPN to interconnect the branch office and corporate headquarters, and an extranet VPN to connect any third-party manufacturer or corporate partner to the corporate network.

The questions that first need to be asked are similar to the ones that someone would ask regarding a basic security policy because the VPN policy is close to, if not the same as, the corporate security policy. The corporate security policy should be reviewed to determine whether there any special considerations and modifications are needed for VPN users. The answers to the following questions need to be determined:

- What do I want to authenticate, devices or users or both?

- Will specific application access be authenticated? (Which ones?)

- Will there be restrictions on what a specific authenticated entity will have access to?

- How will access control be provided?

- What communication should be kept confidential?

- What are the origin and destination points for confidentiality? (That is, will the communication be kept confidential from sender to recipient or will there be intermediary encryption/decryption points?)

- How will confidentiality be provided?

- How many different users will need to be supported?

- Will there be any requirement to use private addresses and therefore NAT?

- Are there any routing considerations?

- How critical is it for the VPN to be available all the time? (That is, are short downtimes acceptable?)

- Where are potential points of infrastructure attacks?

After the answers to these questions are ascertained, the next set of questions can be tackled:

- What technology do I use to authenticate the devices, users, applications?
- What technologies are under potential consideration for other security services?
- How difficult is the configuration of a particular technology?
- What are the maintenance and management issues?
- Are there multiple mechanisms that may accomplish similar security services?
- What are the security versus usability and implementation trade-offs?

You want to make sure that the mechanisms you put in place are effective from an administrative point of view versus the trade-off in security that they provide.

Let's look at the potential answers and how they will affect the VPN design.

Identity

Identity in this book has coupled together the functions of authentication and access control. The following sections consider them individually because not all authentication is always coupled with access control—the situations in which this may be the case are pointed out.

Authentication

The decisions on how to implement authentication mechanisms depend first on what you want to authenticate followed by how the authentication will be provided—that is, which technology will be used.

What Do You Authenticate

For most VPN networks, there needs to be a combination of entities that need to be authenticated. These include devices and individual users:

- **Device authentication**—Devices will always be authenticated because all VPN-related security protocols were designed with the inherent belief that devices need to be authenticated.

- **User authentication for network access**—In earlier VPN deployments, it was common to only authenticate devices, mostly because in many situations there weren't any capabilities in products to support an additional user authentication mechanism. If user authentication was supported, the functionality was hard to maintain and control. This has drastically changed in recent years as more and more VPNs are being deployed for remote user access, where authentication of the user is a critical component before any network access is granted.

- **User authentication for application access**—Some companies have specialized applications that are restricted and require user authentication. The most common application that requires user authentication is the World Wide Web.

NOTE   In the remaining sections of this chapter, any reference to the term *user authentication* refers to user authentication for network access, and any reference to the term *application authentication* refers to user authentication for application access.

Most VPNs, whether access, intranet, or extranet use some mechanism of device authentication because the functionality is an inherent part of all security-related protocols such as Layer 2 Tunnel Protocol (L2TP), IPsec, or Transport Layer Security (TLS). Access VPNs, where a remote user is trying to gain access to corporate resources, should always require that both the device and the individual user be authenticated. By standardizing on this policy, it will make it easier to do access control. For intranet VPNs, where the network is a logical extension of the corporate environment, user authentication is not always required.

If all users first need to authenticate before gaining access to any corporate resource, it may not be necessary to authenticate users again when they access particular applications. The biggest problem in requiring a user to authenticate twice is the issue of a user having to enter his or her credentials multiple times, which isn't usually an acceptable procedure. This problem of double authentication has been recognized as being a hindrance for deploying effective VPNs in environments where there is a critical need to also authenticate critical application access. Many products now support automated mechanisms such that the user only has to enter his or her credentials once. Therefore, if you have specific restricted applications that also require authentication, you should have a policy that requires both user and application authentication.

A matrix of what to authenticate and recommendations as to where the authentication will prove useful is shown in Table 12-1.

Table 12-1   *Recommended Use of Device, User, and Application Authentication*

Type of Authentication	VPN Scenarios to Use It
Device	Between all VPN devices in the network infrastructure
Device and user	For remote access
Device and application	When restricted application access is necessary
Device, user, and application	For extremely secure access

How Do You Authenticate

There exist numerous technologies for authentication. Chapter 2, "Security Technologies," discussed the technical details of many mechanisms, and this chapter attempts to give some reasonable consideration options. The choice will depend on administration tasks versus the security the technologies provide.

Device Authentication Methods

For underlying communication protocols that require devices to authenticate each other, the features usually have a variety of mechanisms that can be used. Devices typically use their IP address or host name in conjunction with a credential to authenticate to each other. The following list identifies the typical credential forms:

- **Statically configured password**—A statically configured password is easy to configure but hard to maintain in a scalable manner. Even if AAA mechanisms can be used, there is the added task of modifying this password on a regular basis and redistributing it to all necessary devices. It is also not very secure if a statically configured password is sent in the clear and any mechanism that sends its password in the clear should be avoided (such as Password Authentication Protocol [PAP] authentication). Many protocols that use a statically configured password for its credential will use some sort of encryption technology to protect the password in transit, usually MD5 or SHA-1. If multiple devices require the same password to be configured, it is essentially a shared group key, which causes security risks if the key is compromised. A unique shared password (key) should be configured between each communication device, and they should be changed on a regular basis.

- **Public key cryptography**—This requires the use of public key encryption where a public/private key pair is generated and the private key is used to encrypt a credential known to both devices. For IPsec, this is the encrypted nonce device authentication. New public/private keys can be generated automatically in a user configurable timeframe. This automates the task of providing new secure credentials but also takes up device CPU cycles. The longer the key used, because many times the key length is also a consideration, the more CPU resources are taken. This method is more secure than a statically configured password, and even if short keys are used, this is a good middle ground.

- **Digital signatures**—This mechanism also uses public key encryption and requires the use of a public key infrastructure to exchange digital certificates. The digital certificates are used to securely exchange the public keys. Public Key Infrastructure (PKI) is not yet widely deployed due to the complexity of setting up the infrastructure and some technology hurdles that are still in the process of getting resolved. The main issue is how to bootstrap the system and initially enroll the public keys into a secure certificate authority (CA). Some vendors have proprietary mechanisms to make this process easier. Digital certificates provide the most scalable mechanism for device authentication, and larger corporations should look to deploy this method.

- **Kerberos authentication**—This requires the use of a Kerberos infrastructure where clients are members of a single trusted domain or mutually trusted domains. If an existing Kerberos infrastructure exists, this method of authentication can be easily incorporated as part of a VPN device authentication method. For corporations that do not have an existing Kerberos infrastructure, deploying a PKI infrastructure rather than Kerberos proves more useful because more vendors are supporting digital certificate-based authentication.

The L2TP protocol by itself only has simplistic device authentication via a Challenge Handshake Authentication Protocol (CHAP)-like protocol that requires a preconfigured shared password between the L2TP endpoints. When used with IPsec, however, the devices use more extensive authentication mechanisms, which usually include preshared keys, public key technology, or digital signatures. A few vendors also use Kerberos-based device authentication for IPsec, but it is not required in the standard and may cause interoperability problems in multivendor situations.

Many deployments use a preshared key because it is easy to configure and has in the past been the most interoperable IPsec device authentication method. It is an acceptable method for small corporations but does not necessarily provide strong device authentication. A preshared secret is problematic in larger environments if a shared group key is used and many entities share the same key. This causes severe security ramifications if the key is compromised. Using an encrypted nonce with public key cryptography is a more secure solution and is the one that Cisco IPsec implementations use as a default (using RSA signatures).

Digital signature-based authentication is the most scalable device authentication mechanism and should be seriously considered in large VPN deployments. What is large can be quite subjective, but I consider more than 30 devices a good candidate for digital, signature-based device authentication. Digital certificates are tied to unique, signed information on the device that is validated by the enterprise's CA. If a device is compromised, the certificate can be revoked and is added to a certificate revocation list (CRL). When using digital, signature-based authentication, CRL checking should always be used. On Cisco devices, it is a configurable parameter and not turned on by default. Cisco has a certificate enrollment protocol (the Simple Certificate Enrollment Protocol [SCEP]) that simplifies the certificate enrollment and renewal process. In addition, many CA vendors support web-based PKI enrollment services.

You can access a number of useful documents on the Cisco website that describe VPN device authentication features and configuration details:

- Step-by-step instructions on how to configure the Cisco VPN 3000 series concentrators to authenticate using digital certificates can be found at http://www.cisco.com/en/US/products/hw/vpndevc/ps2284/ products_configuration_example09186a00800946f1.shtml.

- A document that describes how to configure Cisco IOS CA interoperability, which is provided in support of the IP Security (IPsec) protocol, can be found at http://www.cisco.com/en/US/products/sw/iosswrel/ps1835 products_configuration_guide_chapter09186a00800ca7b2.html.

- The manual certificate enrollment (TFTP and Cut-and-Paste) feature enables users to generate a certificate request and accept CA certificates as well as the router's certificates; these tasks are accomplished via a TFTP server or manual cut-and-paste operations. You can find this feature description at http://www.cisco.com/en/US/products/sw/iosswrel/ps1839/products_feature_guide09186a0080110bd1.html.

- The certificate auto-enrollment feature enables you to configure your router to automatically request a certificate from the CA that is using the parameters in the configuration. Before the certificate auto-enrollment feature, certificate enrollment required complicated, interactive commands that had to be executed on every router. This feature enables you to preload all the necessary information into the configuration and cause each router to obtain certificates automatically when it is booted. You can find this feature description at http://www.cisco.com/en/US/products/sw/iosswrel/ps1839/products_feature_guide09186a0080087cc2.html.

- A document that demonstrates the use of enhanced certificate auto-enrollment commands can be found at http://www.cisco.com/en/US/tech/tk583/tk372/technologies_configuration_example09186a00801405ac.shtml. These commands provide new options for certificate requests and enable users to specify fields in the configuration instead of having to go through prompts. However, the prompting behavior remains the default if this feature is not enabled. Users can preload all necessary information into the configuration, allowing each router to obtain its certificate automatically when it is booted.

- The trusted root certification authority feature allows a router to be configured with multiple root CAs that it trusts. Therefore, the router can use a configured root CA (a trusted root) to verify certificates offered by a peer that were not issued by the same CA defined in the identity of the router. When a trusted root is configured in a router, the router does not have to enroll with the CA that issued the certificate to the peer. You can find more information on this feature at http://www.cisco.com/en/US/products/sw/iosswrel/ps1834/products_feature_guide09186a008007fecf.html.

- The exporting and importing RSA keys feature enables you to transfer security credentials between devices by exporting and importing RSA keys. The key pair that is shared between two devices will allow one device to immediately and transparently take over the functionality of the other router. The feature is described in greater detail at http://www.cisco.com/en/US/products/sw/iosswrel/ps1839/products_feature_guide09186a00801541cf.html.

- A document that describes how to configure CA interoperability for a PIX firewall can be found at http://www.cisco.com/en/US/products/sw/secursw/ps2120/products_user_guide_chapter09186a00801aed7a.html.

- A document that describes configuring Kerberos can be found at http://www.cisco.com/en/US/products/sw/iosswrel/ps1835/products_configuration_guide_chapter09186a00800ca7ad.html.

Addressing Issues

Two important issues that need to be considered are dynamic addressing through the use of Dynamic Host Configuration Protocol (DHCP) and private addresses using NAT. Because most device authentication is done using an IP address, if the IP addresses change, this can be problematic and additional considerations need to be taken into account.

For environments with DHCP addressing, a specific pool of addresses should be allocated for VPN devices. This will greatly simplify access control issues and authentication issues for devices that use IP addresses for identification. In addition, more recent IPsec implementations incorporate the extensions that allow an IP address to be assigned to a remote client and use two addresses; the one from the VPN gateway is the source address for packets it inserts into the IPsec tunnel, and the one from the ISP is the source for the tunnel itself. Cisco devices use the *mode configuration* extension, which was discussed in Chapter 2.

In NAT environments, whether IPsec is used before or after NAT is important. The IPsec NAT Traversal extension provides a solution for IKE and Encapsulating Security Payload (ESP) UDP encapsulation for passing IPsec ESP transport or tunneled traffic across NATs that exist between the IPsec peers. It is not a solution when using NAT for traffic from a remote private address after IPsec encapsulation. Generally, one should do NAT followed by IPsec on outbound traffic and reverse the process on the receiving end. When using NAT before IPsec, the addresses should be mapped into a unique address range that will not interfere with IPsec tunnel establishment. In addition, application protocol-aware devices should be used to perform the NAT translation to ensure that the address translation is also carried out in the data portion of the packet for protocols that embed IP addresses in the data portion.

Cisco IOS Software features that prove useful in NAT VPN environments include the following:

- The IPsec NAT Transparency feature, which introduces support for IPsec traffic to travel through NAT or Port Address Translation (PAT) points in the network. The feature was introduced in 12.2(13)T. You can find the command reference here:

    http://cisco.com/en/US/products/sw/iosswrel/ps1839/products_feature_guide 09186a0080110bca.html

- The NAT Support for IPsec ESP—Phase II feature allows multiple concurrent IPsec ESP tunnels or connections through a Cisco IOS NAT device configured in PAT mode. This feature can be used only if both VPN endpoints are Cisco devices running Cisco IOS Software Release 12.2(15)T or later. You can find the command reference here:

    http://cisco.com/en/US/products/sw/iosswrel/ps1839/products_feature_guide 09186a00801541de.html

User Authentication Methods

User authentication refers to what individual users will use to identify themselves and what credentials they will supply. The credential typically associated with the authenticator's identity can be a static password, one-time password, Kerberos token, or public key. Static passwords should be avoided because they are the most insecure method of providing a user credential. A one-time password mechanism is the minimum form in which user authentication should be performed for any VPN environment. L2TP/IPsec VPNs can authenticate both machine and user independently. First an IPsec tunnel is established (Microsoft uses a machine certificate if it exists and negotiates Internet Key Exchange (IKE) tunnels with machine certificates) followed by the L2TP control channel setup. User authentication is done using PPP authentication methods during establishment of the L2TP control channel. All other L2TP traffic is protected using the IPsec security association (SA). The L2TP user authentication support for legacy authentication is flexible enough to support many existing authentication methods via EAP, which preserves any existing authentication infrastructures. The following document provides a sample configuration for L2TP authentication with RADIUS:

> http://www.cisco.com/en/US/products/sw/secursw/ps4911/
> products_configuration_example09186a00801175d1.shtml

For VPNs that don't require L2TP but use IPsec, the issue to look out for with user authentication is interoperability, because not all vendors support the same user authentication mechanisms. However, the IPsec Xauth extension is widely supported by many vendors even though the draft document itself expired and never reached standard status. The following references show varying configuration examples for user authentication based on Xauth:

- A document that describes how to configure a host-to-router easy VPN solution based on the Cisco VPN client and Cisco IOS remote-access server. Xauth is used to identify the user who requests the IPsec connection. http://www.cisco.com/en/US/netsol/ns110/ns170/ns171/ns27/networking_solutions_white_paper09186a00801890e4.shtml

- A document that describes how to configure a router-to-router easy VPN solution based on the Cisco IOS easy VPN client and Cisco IOS remote-access server features. The Cisco easy VPN negotiates tunnel parameters and establishes IPsec tunnels. Xauth adds another level of authentication that identifies the user who requests the IPsec connection. http://www.cisco.com/en/US/netsol/ns110/ns170/ns171/ns27/networking_solutions_white_paper09186a0080189111.shtml

- Examples that show how to configure interoperability between a PIX firewall and PIX firewall-supported VPN clients. http://www.cisco.com/en/US/products/sw/secursw/ps2120/products_user_guide_chapter09186a0080106f8b.html

- A document that shows sample configurations for TACACS+ and RADIUS used with Xauth. http://www.cisco.com/en/US/products/sw/secursw/ps2308/products_configuration_example09186a0080094848.shtml

Note that the 802.1x wireless community has added user password-based authentication inside a VPN server-authenticated TLS session (EAP-TLS). User authentication is done using user ID/password via CHAP, PAP, MSCHAP, MSCHAPv2, and so on, and using EAP-TLS (RFC 2716), which provides certificate user authentication, either using smart cards or certificates in the user's account on a disk. The following three references describe how to configure IEEE 802.1x port-based authentication on the Catalyst 2940 switch, Catalyst 4000 series switches, and Catalyst 6500 series switches, respectively:

- http://www.cisco.com/en/US/products/hw/switches/ps5213/
  products_configuration_guide_chapter09186a0080192697.html

- http://www.cisco.com/en/US/products/hw/switches/ps663/
  products_configuration_guide_chapter09186a00800ddb0d.html

- http://www.cisco.com/en/US/products/hw/switches/ps708/
  products_configuration_guide_chapter09186a00801a5b0f.html

Application Authentication Methods

Application authentication mechanisms can vary greatly, but in many networking environments they are based on username and password. The following features that provide application authentication should be considered when using Cisco-based equipment:

- The Cisco IOS **ip auth-proxy** command is used to enable a named authentication proxy rule at the Cisco IOS firewall interface. Traffic passing through the interface from hosts with an IP address matching the standard access list and protocol type (HTTP) is intercepted for authentication if no corresponding authentication cache entry exists. If no access list is defined, the authentication proxy intercepts traffic from all hosts whose connection initiating packets are received at the configured interface. The command reference can be found at http://www.cisco.com/en/US/products/sw/iosswrel/ps5187/products_command_reference_chapter09186a008017cf1a.html#1069569.

- The **ip auth-proxy** command was enhanced in Cisco IOS Software Release 12.3(1) to include a firewall authentication proxy for FTP and Telnet access. Authentication proxy for FTP and Telnet sessions functions like authentication proxy for HTTP; that is, FTP and Telnet are independent components in the Cisco IOS Software and can be enabled or disabled on the interface of an unauthenticated host. A comprehensive document that describes the feature and configuration steps can be found at http://www.cisco.com/en/US/products/sw/iosswrel/ps5187/products_feature_guide09186a00801b0683.html.

- The Cisco IOS **ip trigger-authentication** command is used to enable automated double authentication for a device. The command reference can be found at http://www.cisco.com/en/US/products/sw/iosswrel/ps5187/products_command_reference_chapter09186a008017cf1b.html#1069489. A comprehensive document for configuring automated double authentication can be found at http://www.cisco.com/en/US/products/sw/iosswrel/ps1826/products_feature_guide 09186a00800d9df4.html.

- The PIX firewall provides the **virtual http** command that redirects the browser's initial connection to another IP address, authenticates the user, and then redirects the browser back to the URL that the user originally requested. The **virtual telnet** command allows the Virtual Telnet server to provide a way to pre-authenticate users who require connections through the PIX firewall using services or protocols that do not support authentication. The command reference for these commands can be found at http://www.cisco.com/en/US/products/sw/secursw/ps2120/ products_command_reference_chapter09186a0080104256.html#1037665.

Additional Authentication Considerations

Authentication is by far one of the most critical aspects of a secure network infrastructure. As such, it is important to understand all the subtle nuances when using a particular authentication mechanism.

When considering using L2TP with IPsec as a VPN tunneling solution, you need to carefully consider what is being authenticated. Although PPP provides initial authentication, it does not provide per-packet authentication. With IPsec, when the asserted identity in IKE is authenticated, the resulting derived keys are used to provide per-packet authentication and as a result the identity verified in the IKE conversation is subsequently verified on receipt of each packet.

If PPP uses user identity but IKE uses machine identity, only the machine identity is verified on a packet-by-packet basis and there is no way to verify that only the user authenticated within PPP is using the tunnel. Any user on a multi-user machine will be able to send traffic down the tunnel. If IPsec also uses user authentication, the problem goes away and provides segregation of traffic between users.

Certificate credentials, when used, must be adequately managed. Both machine certificate enrollment and user certificate enrollment should be strictly controlled. For user certificates, if a username/password is used by individuals to obtain a certificate, the security is as valuable as the password. Therefore, it is also useful to limit the user certificate enrollment time. This will prevent an attacker obtaining the password of an unused account and obtaining a user certificate after the enrollment process has expired.

Table 12-2 summarizes the authentication methods available for the VPN protocols that are to be considered.

Table 12-2 *Authentication Methods for Various VPN Protocols*

Authentication Method	L2TP	PPTP	IPsec	L2TP/IPsec	TLS
Device Authentication					
Shared password	Yes	Yes	Yes	Yes	N/A
Kerberos	N/A	Yes	Yes (not Cisco)	Yes (not Cisco)	N/A
Public key encryption	N/A	N/A	Yes	Yes	N/A
Digital certificate	N/A	N/A	Yes	Yes	Yes
User Authentication					
User ID/password	CHAP, PAP, MS-CHAP, MS-CHAPv2, EAP	CHAP, PAP, MS-CHAP, MS-CHAPv2, EAP	Xauth	CHAP, PAP, MS-CHAP, MS-CHAPv2, EAP	N/A
One-time-password	EAP	EAP	Xauth	EAP	N/A
Kerberos token	EAP	EAP	Xauth	EAP	N/A
Digital certificate	EAP	EAP	Xauth	EAP	Yes

Access Control

After an entity has been authenticated, restrictions may apply as to which parts of the network or which applications the entity may access.

Where Do You Provide Access Control

Access control is necessary to protect the resources that are critical, and the decision needs to be made to determine what resources are open for whom. VPNs that are a logical extension to the corporate network may sufficiently trust the authenticated entity such that all corporate resources are available to them. A major consideration is how likely is it that the authenticated entity is an imposter. If very secure authentication mechanisms are used, the likelihood is lessened. However, impersonation is always a possibility, and a risk assessment is crucial in the event that imposters were successfully authenticated. What potential damage could they cause to the network? In many situations, it is best to restrict access from any VPN to specific network subnets to which the necessary network resources that need to be accessed are connected to. Perimeter network points should always be the point where access control is applied. This is the demarcation point between a trusted and an untrusted network. In addition, internal security instances are continuing to be a large issue and access control mechanisms are needed inside the trusted network. This can require a secondary authentication mechanism once inside the trusted network.

Allowing any VPN traffic through a corporate perimeter network firewall is a serious consideration. Chapter 10, "Securing Internet Access," discussed a number of firewall scenarios, the most effective being a combination of a screening router and stateful firewall. If VPN traffic is defined to be end-to-end between devices, firewalls will need to allow the tunneled traffic through without performing any stateful inspection. This could be reasonable if the VPN is an extension of the corporate network and there is greater trust in the participants of the VPN. In many extranet and remote-access VPN scenarios, however, a design where a VPN concentrator is deployed between a perimeter screening router and a stateful firewall should be considered. This will allow the VPN concentrator to decrypt any incoming traffic, which will then traverse the stateful firewall to ensure that any corporate firewall policy is not bypassed.

How Do You Provide Access Control

Access control can be provided by using filters at perimeter devices that can include any of the following parameters: MAC source address, MAC destination address, IP source address, IP destination address, protocol type, protocol source port number, and protocol destination port number.

When filtering, the following are some guidelines to adhere to:

- Allow only users on specific subnets to specified corporate subnets.
- Use port number filtering to allow specific VPN tunnel traffic.

Table 12-3 lists the more common protocols and port numbers that should be allowed through a network perimeter firewall device.

Table 12-3   *Common VPN Protocols and Port Numbers*

Type of Traffic	Protocol	Destination Port Number
L2TP	UDP	1701
PPTP	TCP	1723
GRE	Type 47	N/A
IPsec IKE	UDP	500
IPsec AH	TCP or UDP	51
IPsec ESP	TCP or UDP	50
IPsec NAT Traversal	UDP	4500

IPsec traffic selectors are defined by access lists. The granularity of these access lists will depend largely on what traffic is protected by the VPN. In some cases, the VPN protects specific subnets; in others, it may protect certain hosts and specific applications. This is very much site dependent.

NOTE It is important to understand how addresses and port numbers are used in your VPN. IP addresses and port numbers may change during L2TP tunnel negotiation to accommodate load balancing and quality of service (QoS). In addition, IPsec tunnel mode may cause IP addresses to change. Be careful when constructing your filters to make sure you use the appropriate IP addresses and port numbers.

Access control can also be applied using the authorization function of a AAA server, as discussed in Chapter 11, "Securing Remote Access." This proves a useful function in environments where it is a requirement to restrict access to network devices or applications per individually authenticated users.

In very small corporations, it may be easy to manage passwords and access control by individually configuring every device. As the VPN gets beyond 5 devices and 20 users, however, it can be difficult to effectively manage these functions. AAA functionality provides a scalable mechanism to keep track of passwords and authorization attempts.

More recent developments have added access control via the use of digital certificates. Under the IPsec protocol, CA interoperability permits Cisco IOS devices and a CA to communicate so that the Cisco IOS device can obtain and use digital certificates from the CA. Certificates contain several fields that are used to determine whether a device or user is authorized to perform a specified action. For Cisco IOS devices, the certificate security attribute-based access control feature adds fields to the certificate that allow specifying an access control list, to create a certificate-based access control list. You can find a description of this feature at http://www.cisco.com/en/US/products/sw/iosswrel/ps1839/products_feature_guide09186a00801541ce.html.

Integrity

Integrity in this context pertains to having traffic be verified that it hasn't been modified in transit and is origin authenticated. IPsec inherently provides this capability. The problem is that environments with NAT will cause a problem if IP addresses are included in the integrity check and usually mechanisms are used where the IP addresses are not part of the integrity check computation. In IPsec, for instance, Authentication Header (AH) is hardly ever used for the integrity check. Instead, ESP is used with MD5 or SHA1, which provides an integrity check on the packet and most of the original header but not the outer IP header when tunnel mode is used.

If an IP address is spoofed for VPN-type traffic, typically the traffic can cause only a limited denial-of-service (DoS) attack and take up limited resources. In many cases, the IP address is assumed to be trusted and other mechanisms are used to protect against potential DoS attacks.

Confidentiality

Secure VPNs almost always require that some of the data be encrypted. You need to be selective as to the traffic to be encrypted only if there is a severe constraint in processing power. It is common to either encrypt all traffic going to a specific destination or to encrypt only certain application traffic. IPsec ESP is generally used to encrypt traffic. L2TP can use PPP encryption, but it is a weak form of encryption, and L2TP is therefore most often used in conjunction with IPsec when confidentiality services are required.

NOTE	In some cases, it may be required to modify the maximum transmission unit (MTU) on the PC/host side to avoid receiving devices perceiving the packets as oversized. If this is necessary, adjust the total maximum size that the packet can take so that it does not exceed the normal size of a nonencrypted Ethernet packet (1400 bytes). VPN applications typically provides the option of customizing the MTU size.

The devices that you must configure for IPsec or L2TP/IPsec in a VPN network infrastructure include the Cisco IOS routers, PIX firewall, VPN concentrators, and IPsec clients. The following web pages show numerous configuration examples for a variety of IPsec and L2TP/IPsec scenarios using user-based authentication, digital certificate authentication, and multiple combinations of devices:

> http://www.cisco.com/pcgi-bin/Support/browse/psp_view.pl?p=Internetworking: IPSec&s=Implementation_and_Configuration

> http://www.cisco.com/en/US/tech/tk583/tk372/tech_configuration_examples_list.html

Availability

VPNs have the same requirement as any other network, which is minimal downtime. Availability refers to having redundancy in place as well as having the capability to forward packets in the event of an attack. How much redundancy is in place depends on the decisions made when a risk assessment was done—remember that it is sometimes not necessary to overly protect network devices or information when the cost of protecting it far exceeds the cost of what the information is worth. Smaller corporations will probably not have the monetary resources to buy redundant devices, but larger corporations should definitely deploy redundancy in all critical VPN infrastructures. For any redundant configurations, the features should be enabled that provide for automated failover scenarios in the event of a link or device failure.

Audit

An auditing function is necessary to determine that the VPN has been appropriately configured. If encrypted traffic is being used, don't just rely on a device counter to show that traffic is being encrypted. Put an actual traffic analyzer on the network to verify that the traffic is indeed confidential and that anyone inadvertently sniffing the network can't see the traffic. A network intrusion detection system should be used at the network perimeter points to detect a potential attack to the corporate network at the earliest possible moment.

Intrusion detection was discussed extensively in Chapter 10, and you should refer to that chapter for specific configuration details. In addition, Cisco IOS Software has an IPsec VPN accounting feature, introduced in Release 12.2(15)T, which allows for a session to be accounted for by indicating when the session starts and when it stops. A VPN session is defined as an IKE SA and the one or more SA pairs that are created by the IKE SA. The session starts when the first IPsec SA pair is created and stops when all IPsec SAs are deleted. Session-identifying information and session-usage information is passed to the Remote Authentication Dial-In User Service (RADIUS) server via standard RADIUS attributes and vendor-specific attributes (VSAs). You can find more specific information about this feature at the following website:

> http://cisco.com/en/US/products/sw/iosswrel/ps1839/
> products_feature_guide09186a00801541ba.html

It can also prove useful to audit your VPN networks using freely or commercially available software to emulate some common attacks and to verify that your VPN infrastructure is indeed secure from at least the more commonly known exploits.

VPN Design Examples

This section shows two common designs. The first scenario is shown in Figure 12-1 and is for a small corporate VPN that has a remote branch office as well as a number of telecommuters and traveling personnel who will access the corporate network. Therefore, the VPN is a mixture of an access VPN and intranet VPN. Device authentication is performed using preshared keys for Ipsec, and remote users are individually authenticated using the IPsec Xauth extension and one-time passwords. A Cisco IOS router is used as the VPN firewall, which is also an IPsec peer. The router is also used as a network intrusion system to audit any incoming traffic and provide first-level defense against any potential network attacks.

Figure 12-1   *Small Corporate VPN Scenario*

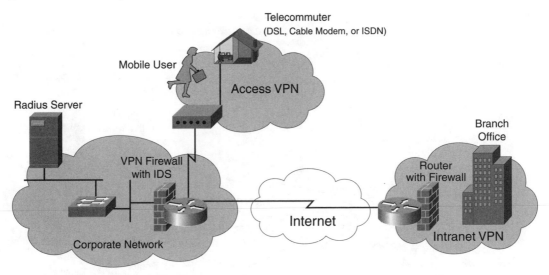

The second example is for a larger corporation that has a number of remote offices and telecommuters as well as corporate personnel who travel and need access back to the corporate resources. In addition. a number of third-party places need access back to the corporate network. Figure 12-2 shows this scenario. Device authentication in this scenario is via digital certificates, and remote user authentication is performed using one-time passwords and the IPsec Xauth extension. At the perimeter, a screening router is used to perform access list checks. The VPN termination point is at the VPN concentrator, which acts as an IPsec peer. All traffic is subsequently passed to the stateful firewall before being allowed to pass to the corporate network. An important point here is that access lists configured on the screening router may potentially check different IP addresses than the filters on the stateful firewall because the screening router may be using tunnel mode. A network-based intrusion system is also used to audit any incoming traffic and to provide first-level defense against any potential network attacks.

Figure 12-2 *Large Corporate VPN Scenario*

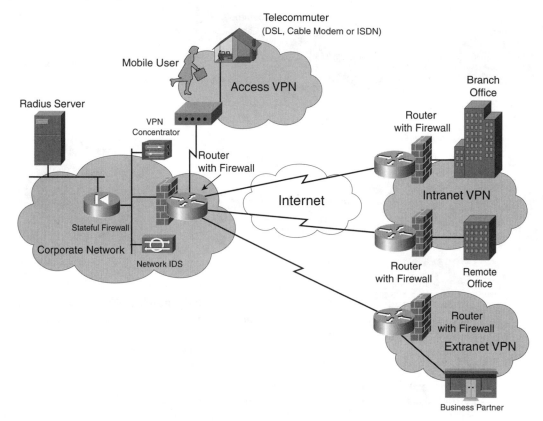

Wireless Networks

To deploy secure wireless networks, you need to apply the same kind of design methodology as for VPN networks. In many cases, the wireless networks are actually part of a
remote-access VPN. The following sections do not repeat any of the previous discussion
relating to VPNs, and only the features and configuration examples relevant to wireless
network access are referenced. Therefore, use this section as an extension of the previous
VPN discussion.

Identity

Identity considerations for wireless LANs also encompass both authentication and access
control functionality. The 802.1x standard, which uses EAP for authentication, is gaining
wide acceptance and should be considered in conjunction with AAA to provide identity
protection.

Authentication

Authentication for wireless networks can be device-based through the use of a shared WEP key. It can also be user-based through the use EAP. As discussed in Chapter 3, "Applying Security Technologies to Real Networks," wireless EAP authentication can be used in many ways (EAP-TLS, EAP-TTLS, LEAP, and PEAP). Because not all vendors are using all these mechanisms, the decision as to which to use depends mostly on interoperability constraints. Both device and user authentication should be deployed in wireless networks to most effectively secure them. User authentication should be carried out through a secure tunnel so that the authentication exchange is encrypted. Therefore, for all environments, I recommend the use of EAP-TTLS or PEAP.

You can find information about setting up PEAP on the Aironet 1200 series at the following website:

> http://www.cisco.com/en/US/products/hw/wireless/ps430/
> prod_technical_reference09186a008014626b.html

You can find information about setting up PEAP on the Aironet 350 series at the following website:

> http://www.cisco.com/en/US/products/hw/wireless/ps458/
> prod_technical_reference09186a008014626b.html

Access Control

Restricting access to who is allowed to connect to the wireless network is primarily carried out through the use of a AAA server, such as the Cisco Secure Access Control Server (ACS). The Cisco Secure ACS version 3.2 has features that include EAP enhancements to support Protected EAP (PEAP) for Microsoft Windows clients. PEAP retains the security benefits of Cisco EAP wireless (LEAP) while providing more extensibility and support for one-time token authentication. Cisco Secure ACS version 3.2 also supports machine authentication (using EAP-TLS or PEAP) on secure 802.1x ports. This capability is crucial for device control access in an 802.1x secure environment where port access is blocked until a user has successfully been identified behind an 802.1x-provisioned port. You can find configuration examples showing the setup EAP-TLS and EAP-PEAP with Cisco Secure ACS at the following website:

> http://www.cisco.com/en/US/products/sw/secursw/ps5338/
> products_user_guide_chapter09186a0080193add.html

In addition, MAC address filtering can be used in environments that want to impose stricter controls, although it is important to keep in mind that MAC addresses can be spoofed and additional access controls should be used as well.

To make access control at perimeter firewalls easier for wireless networks, wireless clients can be allocated a DHCP address from a specified pool of addresses. Traffic from the wireless subnet can then have specific filtering rules applied that apply only to wireless VPN traffic. These rules are site-specific depending on the defined security policy. In most instances, it is prudent to follow the rule of "deny all and permit only what is needed."

Integrity

Wireless networks provide packet origin integrity through the use of Wired Equivalent Privacy (WEP) or Temporal Key Integrity Protocol (TKIP). Because WEP has limited capabilities, deployment of wireless networks should look to have updated software on the wireless APs and clients to use TKIP.

Confidentiality

WEP provides confidentiality but uses a weak algorithm that can easily be exploited. Again, through the use of TKIP, which provides for an enhanced encryption scheme, better confidentiality of traffic can be ensured. In addition, some deployments may consider using IPsec ESP to provide a secure VPN tunnel. A wireless client would need to have IPsec enabled, and an IPsec transport mode tunnel would be created between the client and a VPN concentrator:

- You can find information about how to configure WEP, Message Integrity Check (MIC), and TKIP on the Aironet 1400 series at the following website:

  http://www.cisco.com/en/US/products/hw/wireless/ps5279/
  products_configuration_guide_chapter09186a0080184b01.html

- You can find information about how to configure WEP and WEP features on the Cisco Aironet 1100 series at the following website:

  http://www.cisco.com/en/US/products/hw/wireless/ps4570/
  products_installation_and_configuration_guide_chapter09186a008017285f.html

- For examples on how to configure IPsec, refer to the references under the "Confidentiality" section in the previous discussion about VPN networks.

Availability

Wireless networks have the same requirement as any other network, which is minimal downtime. Whether due to a DoS attack or equipment failure, critical pieces of a wireless infrastructure need to be made available for wireless client access. The amount of effort and money spent on providing this availability depends on how important it is to keep the wireless network access up and running. In some environments, such as airport lounge or coffee shop wireless access, the event of limited downtime may just be an inconvenience to clients. However, some corporations are starting to rely on wireless access for more critical business operations and need to provide greater resiliency to avoid network downtime.

In addition to any redundancy and failover features discussed in previous chapters, such as load balancing and hot standby, wireless networks have additional availability considerations that largely relate to issues surrounding loss of signal strength and losing connectivity with an associated access point (AP). Having the capability to quickly and securely re-associate with another AP can greatly increase availability by reducing lost sessions.

The Cisco Aironet products support fast secure roaming, which allows authenticated client devices to roam securely from one AP to another without any perceptible delay during re-association. For more information about how to configure a Cisco AP for fast re-association of roaming client devices, access the following website:

> http://www.cisco.com/en/US/products/hw/wireless/ps4570/
> products_configuration_guide_chapter09186a0080184acc.html

Availability issues can also arise from having the authentication server be unavailable when a client is trying to associate to a given AP. Sometimes this is due to congested links that can prevent the authentication exchange, such as RADIUS packet exchanges, from taking place. This issue can be overcome by giving the RADIUS packets priority on transmissions both from the AP to the RADIUS server and from the RADIUS server to the AP. When priority is given to the RADIUS packets, the WAN routers service them before lower-priority traffic. The end result is that LEAP clients can authenticate successfully during times of WAN link congestion. The Cisco document, "802.1x and EAP-Based Authentication Across Congested WAN Links," shows how to configure RADIUS packets to have higher priority. You can find this document at the following website:

> http://www.cisco.com/en/US/netsol/ns110/ns175/ns176/ns178/
> networking_solutions_white_paper09186a00800a9e8e.shtml

In addition, the Aironet series devices support an IEEE 802.1x local authentication service that allows the wireless AP to act as a local RADIUS server to authenticate wireless clients when the AAA server is not available. This provides remote site survivability and backup authentication services during a WAN link or server failure, allowing users in remote site deployments with nonredundant WAN links access to local resources such as file servers or printers. How to configure the AP as a local authenticator to serve as a standalone authenticator for a small wireless LAN or to provide backup authentication service is shown at the website:

> http://www.cisco.com/en/US/products/hw/wireless/ps4570/
> products_configuration_guide_chapter09186a0080184a9b.html

Audit

An auditing function is necessary to determine that the wireless network has been appropriately configured. If encrypted traffic is being used, don't just rely on a device counter to show that traffic is being encrypted. As with VPN networks, place an actual traffic analyzer on the network to verify that the traffic is indeed confidential and that anyone inadvertently sniffing the network can't see the traffic.

To address auditing needs, network administrators need a centralized method of configuring, gathering, storing, and retrieving information about all the APs and bridges on their network. They must be able to configure many APs and bridges, monitor the performance and availability of the wireless LAN (WLAN) infrastructure, and generate reports for capacity planning and client tracking. The ability to upgrade or downgrade software on many APs at one time is also essential. The CiscoWorks network management applications offer solutions for managing the Cisco WLAN infrastructure. CiscoWorks Wireless LAN Solution Engine (WLSE) is a specialized appliance for managing the Cisco WLAN infrastructure and, in conjunction with the CiscoWorks Resource Manager Essentials (RME), can greatly simplify many auditing tasks. The WLSE provides centralized template-based configuration, security misconfiguration detection, fault/performance monitoring, AP/bridge reports, and wireless client reports. CiscoWorks WLSE and CiscoWorks RME are complementary products that together offer a complete management solution for the Cisco WLAN. A document that describes how network administrators can use CiscoWorks WLSE and RME to help manage Cisco Aironet APs and bridges and describes configuration can be found at the following website:

> http://www.cisco.com/en/US/tech/tk722/tk809/technologies_white_paper
> 09186a00800c9617.shtml

Wireless Network Design Examples

Figure 12-3 shows an example of a typical secured wireless network scenario. The wireless network is essentially an extension of a remote-access VPN, in which IP addresses are assigned from a specific network access block obtained from the RADIUS server after the client has been successfully authenticated. The wireless clients and AP have 802.1x and EAP software to provide for device and user authentication prior to connecting to the switch and obtaining access to the corporate network. In addition, if confidentiality were desired, IPsec would be used between the wireless clients and a VPN concentrator. Smaller networks may opt to just use WEP encryption between the AP and the wireless client, but IPsec would give a more robust solution. The CiscoWorks WLSE/RMS solutions are used to manage the WLAN. Also, as with any network perimeter, an intrusion detection device can be used to help audit network traffic and detect a potential attack to the corporate network.

Figure 12-3 *Secure Wireless Network Scenario*

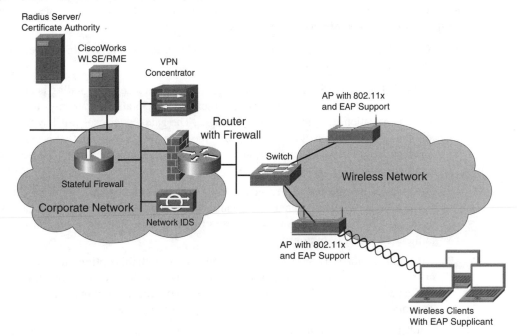

Voice over IP Networks

Voice over IP networks also have similar design methodology as VPN networks and the same questions need to be considered as were discussed for VPN networks. Security features in VoIP networks are still under development, and this section focuses on features that are currently available and that should be considered. However, you should follow the latest developments from Cisco in this area.

Identity

Identity considerations for VoIP networks also encompass both authentication and access control functionality.

Authentication

Most IP phones currently only provide device authentication, although user authentication will be available in ongoing developments. The Cisco H.323 gateways support the use of a crypto token for authentication that uses the "password-with-hashing" security scheme as described in Chapter 3, "Applying Security Technologies to Real Networks." A crypto token can be included in any RAS message between the VoIP gateway and a gatekeeper and is used to authenticate the sender of the message. It is possible to use a separate database for user ID and password verification.

As of Cisco IOS Software Release 12.2, Cisco H.323 gateways support three levels of authentication:

- **Endpoint**—The RAS channel used for gateway-to-gatekeeper signaling is not a secure channel. To ensure secure communication, H.235 allows gateways to include an authentication key in their RAS messages. The gatekeeper uses this key to authenticate the source of the messages. At the endpoint level, validation is performed on all messages from the gateway. The crypto tokens are validated using the password configured for the gateway.

- **Per call**—When the gateway receives a call over the telephony leg, it prompts the user for an account number and personal identification number (PIN). These two numbers are included in certain RAS messages sent from the endpoint and are used to authenticate the originator of the call.

- **All**—This option is a combination of the other two. With this option, the validation of crypto tokens in call initiation messages is based on an the account number and PIN of the user making a call, and the validation of crypto tokens sent in all the other RAS messages is based on the password configured for the gateway.

Crypto tokens for registration request (RRQ), unregistration request (URQ), disengage request (DRQ), and the terminating side of admission request (ARQ) messages contain information about the gateway that generated the token, including the gateway ID (which is the H.323 ID configured on the gateway) and the gateway password. Crypto tokens for the originating-side ARQ messages contain information about the user who is placing the call, including the user ID and PIN. This feature provides sender validation by using an authentication key in the gateway's RAS messages. The gatekeeper uses this key to authenticate the source of the messages and ensure secure communication.

Use the following Cisco IOS Software features for H.323 authentication/authorization:

- The interdomain gatekeeper security enhancement feature, introduced in Cisco IOS Software Release 12.2(2)XA and Cisco IOS Software Release 12.2(4)T, provides a means of authenticating and authorizing H.323 calls between the administrative domains of Internet telephone service providers (ITSPs). An Interzone ClearToken (IZCT) is generated in the originating gatekeeper when a location request (LRQ) is initiated or an admission confirmation (ACF) is about to be sent for an intrazone call within an ITSP's administrative domain. As the IZCT traverses through the routing path, each gatekeeper stamps the IZCT's destination gatekeeper ID with its own ID. This identifies when the IZCT is being passed over to another ITSP's domain. The IZCT is then sent back to the originating gateway in the location confirmation (LCF) message. The originating gateway passes the IZCT to the terminating gateway in the setup message. The terminating gatekeeper forwards the IZCT in the ARQ answerCall field to the terminating gatekeeper, which then validates it. You can find more detailed information about this feature at the following website:

http://cisco.com/en/US/products/sw/iosswrel/ps1839/
products_feature_guide09186a00800879e4.html

- The gatekeeper-to-gatekeeper authentication feature provides additional security for H.323 networks by introducing the capability to validate intradomain and interdomain gatekeeper-to-gatekeeper LRQ messages on a per-hop basis. This feature provides a Cisco access token (CAT) to carry authentication within zones. The CAT is used by adjacent gatekeepers to authenticate each other and is configured on a per-zone basis. In addition, service providers can specify inbound passwords to authenticate LRQ messages that come from foreign domains and outbound passwords to be included in LRQ messages to foreign domains. You can find more information about this feature at the following website:

http://cisco.com/en/US/products/sw/iosswrel/ps1839/
products_feature_guide09186a00800b5d6e.html

SIP authentication in Cisco devices uses the following:

- Authentication and authorization via Hypertext Transfer Protocol (HTTP) Digest and MySQL or via CHAP password and RADIUS
- Accounting via RADIUS

Access Control

Because dynamic Real-Time Transport Protocol / RTP Control Protocol (RTP/RTCP) ports are used by the endpoints for voice calls, firewalls can be problematic unless they have some capability to recognize voice traffic and dynamically allow traffic. You can use the **fixup protocol** command on Cisco devices to give them the capability to look into the Layer 4 through Layer 7 information within the IP payload and make the necessary changes to the embedded IP address and ports used. If encryption is involved, such as TLS or IPsec, this feature will not work.

On a PIX firewall, the commands for stateful firewall VoIP intelligence are as follows:

```
fixup protocol h323 {h225 ¦ ras} port [-port]
fixup protocol sip [5060]
fixup protocol skinny [2000]
fixup protocol skinny port [-port]
```

The defaults are as follows:

```
fixup protocol h323 h225 1720
fixup protocol h323 ras 1718-1719
fixup protocol sip 5060
fixup protocol skinny 2000
```

Table 12-4 shows a matrix of Cisco solutions for firewall and NAT when used with the VoIP **fixup protocol** feature.

Table 12-4 *VoIP* **fixup protocol** *Feature Support for Various Cisco Firewall Solutions*

VoIP Protocol	PIX Firewall	Cisco IOS Firewall	Cisco IOS NAT
H.323v2	5.2	12.1(5) T	12.1(5) T
H.323 RAS	5.2	No support	12.2 (2) T
H.323 w/NAT	5.2	No support	No support
H.323 w/PAT	6.2	No support	No support
SIP	6.0 / 6.1	No support	Near future
SIP w/NAT	6.0 / 6.1	No support	Near future
SIP w/PAT	6.2	No support	Near future
MGCP	No support	No support	No support
SCCP (Skinny)	6.0 / 6.1	No support	12.1(5) T

Table 12-5 lists the more common protocols and port numbers that should be allowed through a network perimeter firewall device in VoIP networks. It is recommended that the RTP audio stream ports listed here be constrained to a specified range of port numbers for media communication and then to specifically permit that range through the firewall as deemed necessary for proper VoIP communication.

Table 12-5 *Common VoIP Protocols and Port Numbers*

VoIP Protocol	Protocol and Port Number
H.323	
Unicast gatekeeper discovery	UDP port 1718
Multicast gatekeeper discovery	UDP port 1718 (to address 224.0.1.41)
RAS	UDP port 1719
H.225 call signaling for hosts	TCP 1720
TLS for H.225	TCP port 1300
H.245 capability exchange	negotiates TCP ports 11000 through 65535
RTP audio stream	UDP ports 16,384 through 32,767
SIP	
Signaling	UDP/TCP port 5060
RTP audio stream	UDP ports 16,384 through 32,767
User agent registration	Multicast address 224.0.1.175

Table 12-5   *Common VoIP Protocols and Port Numbers (Continued)*

VoIP Protocol	Protocol and Port Number
MGCP version 0.1	
Media gateway and call agent signaling	UDP port 2427
RTP audio stream	UDP ports 16,384 through 32,767
MGCP version 1.0	
Signaling to call agent	UDP port 2727
Signaling to media gateway	UDP port 2427
RTP audio stream	UDP ports 16,384 through 32,767

When using the Cisco secure PIX firewall with SIP, be aware of the following:

- If a firewall proxy is placed outside the firewall in the demilitarized zone (DMZ) network with Record-Route enabled, the list of allowed IP addresses from the outside SIP proxy server's IP address should be small and manageable, thus allowing for manageable security.

- Outside callers cannot make calls to inside the firewall unless they have been defined as an allowed device.

In addition, the following features in Cisco IOS Software can be useful to provide access control in VoIP networks.

Firewall for SIP

The Cisco IOS firewall extends the concept of static access control lists (ACLs) by introducing dynamic ACL entries that open on the basis of the necessary application ports on a specific application and close these ports at the end of the application session. The Cisco IOS firewall achieves this functionality by inspecting the application data, checking for conformance of the application protocol, extracting the relevant port information to create the dynamic ACL entries, and closing these ports at the end of the session as determined through a timeout value. This feature supports only the SIP UDP format for signaling; the TCP format is not supported. The feature is available in Cisco IOS Software Release 12.2(11)YU and 12.2(15)T.

The firewall for SIP support feature allows SIP signaling requests to traverse directly between gateways or through a series of proxies to the destination gateway or phone. After the initial request, if the Record-Route header field is not used, subsequent requests can traverse directly to the destination gateway address as specified in the Contact header field. Therefore, the Cisco IOS firewall is aware of all surrounding proxies and gateways and allows the following functionality:

- SIP signaling responses can travel the same path as SIP signaling requests.

- Subsequent signaling requests can travel directly to the endpoint (destination gateway).

- Media endpoints can exchange data between each other.

More information for the firewall for SIP feature is available at the following website:

> http://cisco.com/en/US/products/sw/iosswrel/ps5012/
> products_feature_guide09186a0080146557.html

Tokenless Call Authentication

The tokenless call authentication feature uses a statically configured ACL of authorized
H.323 endpoints for the Cisco IOS gatekeeper. The gatekeeper accepts calls from endpoints
on the list. This security feature is an alternative to Interzone ClearTokens (IZCTs) and
Cisco access tokens (CATs), and can be used with Cisco Call Manager (CCM). More
detailed information on the tokenless call authentication feature can be found at the
following website:

> http://cisco.com/en/US/products/sw/iosswrel/ps1839/
> products_feature_guide09186a00801541d1.html

Binding Specific Gateway Interfaces for MGCP

The current Media Gateway Control Protocol (MGCP) implementation does not allow the
assignment of particular IP addresses for sourcing MGCP commands and media packets,
which can cause firewall and security problems. This feature enables you to configure interfaces on which control and media packets can be exchanged. This new functionality enables
you to separate signaling from voice by binding control (MGCP signaling) and media (RTP
voice, fax, and modem) to specific gateway interfaces.

This feature includes a new command-line interface (CLI) that you can use to configure the
required interface for MGCP control and control of the required media packets. The feature
was introduced in 12.2(13)T and more specific information on it can be found at the
following website:

> http://cisco.com/en/US/products/sw/iosswrel/ps1839/
> products_feature_guide09186a0080110bd2.html

Binding Specific Gateway Interfaces for SIP

The **h323-gateway voip bind srcaddr** *x.x.x.x* command enables you to bind the source IP
address for the signaling and media traffic. This allows the downstream firewall to know
where the source signaling is coming from, which allows it to set up the trust associations
or policy for the VoIP traversal through the firewall. It forces the signaling and media traffic
source IP address to be defined specifically and doesn't allow the router to randomly choose
an IP address from one of its interfaces.

With Cisco IOS Software Release 12.2(2)XB, there is support for SIP bind addresses with
the **bind all source-interface** *x.x.x.x* command.

Integrity

VoIP networks provide packet origin integrity through the use of inherent protocol features. H.323 uses a crypto token, which in Cisco devices is currently based on a hashed password. The passwords should be configured on all gateways and gatekeepers that are part of the VoIP network.

Confidentiality

Confidentiality for VoIP traffic can be accomplished, but a number of pitfalls need to be taken into consideration. If NAT is being used and there are firewalls in the path, TLS and, or IPsec encryption is not an option for voice traffic. You should consider each leg of the VoIP network to ascertain where it is feasible to use encryption and then decide whether there is a large risk in someone eavesdropping on the signaling or voice traffic. It may prove useful to just encrypt some parts of the network. If you have an environment that could handle hop-by-hop encryption, IPsec should be configured. Consider this carefully, however, because at each hop the encryption/decryption can be problematic and cause too much latency.

The SIP extensions for caller identity and privacy feature provides support for privacy indication, network verification, and screening of a call participant name and number. This feature was introduced in 12.2(13)T.

Cisco implements this feature on SIP trunking gateways by supporting a new header, Remote-Party-ID, as defined in the IETF specification, draft-ietf-privacy-.02.txt, "SIP Extensions for Caller Identity and Privacy." The Remote-Party-ID header identifies the calling party and carries presentation and screening information. In previous SIP implementations, the From header was used to indicate calling party identity, and once defined in the initial invite request, could not be modified for that session. Implementing the Remote-Party-ID header, which can be modified, added, or removed as a call session is being established, overcomes previous limitations and enables call participant privacy indication, screening, and verification. The new feature uses the Remote-Party-ID header to support translation capability between Integrated Services Digital Networks (ISDN) messages and Remote-Party-ID SIP tags. The new SIP header also enables support for certain telephony services, and some regulatory and public safety requirements, by providing screening and presentation indicators. Detailed information on this feature can be found at the following website:

> http://cisco.com/en/US/products/sw/iosswrel/ps1839/
> products_feature_guide09186a0080110bfb.html

Availability

VoIP networks have the same requirement as any other network, which is minimal downtime and the capability to still make calls in the event of a DoS attack. There should never exist a single point of failure in the VoIP network infrastructure if the VoIP service becomes a critical mechanism of communication in a given network environment. Smaller corporations will probably not have the monetary resources to buy redundant devices, but larger corporations should definitely deploy redundancy for the networking infrastructure. For any redundant configurations, the features should be enabled that provide for automated failover scenarios in the event of a device failure.

Cisco provides for a specific telephony-based feature for redundancy. The Survivable Remote Site (SRS) telephony feature provides Cisco Call Manager (CCM) with fallback support for Cisco IP phones attached to a Cisco router on your local network. The SRS telephony feature enables routers to provide call-handling support for Cisco IP phones when they lose connection to remote primary, secondary, or tertiary CCM installations, or when the WAN connection is down.

CCM supports Cisco IP phones at remote sites attached to Cisco multiservice routers across the WAN. Prior to the SRS telephony feature, when the WAN connection between a router and CCM failed, or connectivity with CCM was lost for some reason, Cisco IP phones on the network became unusable for the duration of the failure. The SRS telephony feature overcomes this problem and ensures that the Cisco IP phones offer continuous (yet, minimal) service by providing call-handling support for Cisco IP phones directly from the SRS telephony router. The system automatically detects a failure and uses Simple Network Auto Provisioning (SNAP) technology to autoconfigure the branch office router to provide call processing for Cisco IP phones registered with the router. When the WAN link or connection to the primary CCM is restored, call handling reverts to the primary CCM.

When Cisco IP phones lose contact with primary, secondary, and tertiary CCMs, they must establish a connection to a local SRS telephony router to ensure call-processing capability necessary to place and receive calls. The Cisco IP phone retains the IP address of the local SRS telephony router as a default router in the Network Configuration area of the Settings menu. This list supports a maximum of five default router entries; however, CCM accommodates a maximum of three entries. When a secondary CCM is not available on the network, the local SRS telephony router's IP address is retained as the standby connection for CCM during normal operation.

When the WAN link between the router and the CCM fails, calls in progress are sustained for the duration of the call so long as the WAN link is not part of the call connection itself. Calls in transition and calls that have not yet connected are dropped and must be re-initiated after Cisco IP phones reestablish connection to their local SRS telephony router. Telephone service remains unavailable from the time connection to the remote CCM is lost until the Cisco IP phone establishes connection to the SRS telephony router.

You can find more information about the tasks and commands necessary to configure and maintain Cisco SRS telephony for systems with Cisco Call Manager v3.0.5 and higher at the following website:

> http://cisco.com/en/US/products/sw/iosswrel/ps1839/
> products_feature_guide_book09186a0080153d24.html

Audit

An auditing function is necessary to determine that the VoIP network has been appropriately configured and that the proper security services are being effectively deployed. Accounting is an important part of many voice networks to keep track of calls—who originated calls, what the call destinations were, and what were the call durations.

A specific feature to look at is gateway accounting for SIP, which is configured with the command **gw-accounting** {**voip** | **syslog** | **h323** [**syslog**]}. The **voip** keyword sends the call data record (CDR) to the RADIUS server. Use this keyword with the SIP feature. The **h323** keyword sends the call data record (CDR) to the RADIUS server. The **syslog** keyword uses the system logging facility to record the CDRs.

In addition, all the other auditing functions mentioned in earlier parts of this chapter, such as making sure that encrypted traffic is indeed encrypted through the use of traffic analyzers and traffic monitoring for potential network attacks through the use of intrusion detection systems, should be used.

VoIP Network Design References

Because practical security in VoIP networks is still largely evolving, two relevant papers written by Cisco that detail currently available security design solutions are referenced here. The first paper is titled "Security in SIP-Based Networks" and describes network security solutions based on Cisco SIP-enabled products. It is located at the following website:

> http://www.cisco.com/en/US/tech/tk652/tk701/
> technologies_white_paper09186a00800ae41c.shtml

The second paper is titled "Stealth VPN" and details a Cisco IOS Software site-to-site and small office / home office remote-access VPN solution. It encompasses myriad Cisco IOS technologies, including security and voice. This paper can be found at the following website:

> http://www.cisco.com/en/US/netsol/ns110/ns170/ns172/ns271/
> networking_solutions_white_paper09186a0080187b4e.shtml

Summary

This chapter focused on providing comprehensive design considerations and examples for securing VPN, wireless, and VoIP networks when using Cisco equipment. Useful features and references to configuration examples were given. Many of the security features for wireless and VoIP networks are still evolving, and newer software releases should be considered in these networks to deploy the latest security functionalities.

You can find a comprehensive Cisco IOS Software security Command Reference for Release 12.2 at the following website:

http://cisco.com/application/pdf/en/us/guest/products/ps4032/c1051/ ccmigration_09186a008011e003.pdf

Review Questions

The following questions provide you with an opportunity to test your knowledge of the topics covered in this chapter. You can find the answers to these questions in Appendix E, "Answers to Review Questions."

1 True or false: Any VPN is a secured VPN.

2 The design methodology for creating secure VPNs is constrained by what?

3 What kind of device authentication is used with L2TP/IPsec technology?

4 At what points of the VPN network should access control be applied?

5 How would you provide confidentiality services if you were using the L2TP protocol in a VPN?

6 True or false: Authentication for wireless networks can only be device-based.

7 Which of the following is a valid mechanism to restrict access to a wireless client?

   A Using the authorization function of a AAA server

   B Using MAC address filtering

   C Using special filtering rules for a specific pool of DHCP addresses only assigned to wireless clients.

   D All of the above

8 How would you go about verifying that confidentiality services are appropriately deployed in a wireless network?

9 What is the access control issue with RTP/RTCP port numbers in VoIP networks?

PART IV

Appendixes

Sources of Technical Information

Cryptography and Network Security Books

Denning, Dorothy E. *Information Warfare and Security*. Reading, MA: Addison-Wesley, 1999.

Kaufman, C., R. Perlman, and M. Speciner. *Network Security: Private Communication in a Public World*, Second Edition. Upper Saddle River, NJ: Prentice Hall PTR, 2002.

McCarthy, Linda. *Intranet Security: Stories from the Trenches.* Palo Alto, CA: Sun Microsystems Press, 1998.

Pfleeger, Charles, et al. *Security in Computing*, Third Edition. Upper Saddle River, NJ: Prentice Hall PTR, 2002.

Rescorla, Eric. *SSL and TLS: Designing and Building Secure Systems*. Reading, MA: Addison-Wesley Professional, 2000.

Schneier, Bruce. *Applied Cryptography*, Second Edition. New York, NY: John Wiley and Sons, 1996.

Stallings, William. *Cryptography and Network Security: Principles and Practice*, Third Edition. Upper Saddle River, NJ: Prentice Hall, 2002.

Firewall Books

Chapman, D. Brent and Elizabeth D. Zwicky. *Building Internet Firewalls*, Second Edition. Cambridge, MA: O'Reilly and Associates, 2000.

Chapman, Jr., David W. and Andy Fox. *Cisco Secure PIX Firewalls*. Indianapolis, IN: Cisco Press, 2001.

Cheswick, William and Steven Bellovin. *Firewalls and Internet Security*, Second Edition. Reading, MA: Addison-Wesley, 2002.

Intrusion Detection Books

Carter, Earl. *Cisco Secure Intrusion Detection System*. Indianapolis, IN: Cisco Press, 2001.

Northcutt, Stephen and Judy Novak. *Network Intrusion Detection: An Analyst's Handbook*, Third Edition. Indianapolis, IN: New Riders, 2002.

IETF Working Groups and Sites for Standards and Drafts on Security Technologies Developed Through the IETF

The working groups that define the Internet standards last only as long as until the work is completed, at which time the working group shuts down and the resulting documents are published. The main IETF site is the best start to search for relevant RFC standards:

http://www.ietf.org

You can find ongoing work in the security area here:

http://ietf.org/html.charters/wg-dir.html#Security%20Area

Documents on the Scope and Content of Network Security Policies

RFC 2196, *The Site Security Handbook*. A guide created by the Internet Engineering Task Force (IETF) to develop computer security policies and procedures for sites that have systems on the Internet:

ftp://ftp.rfc-editor.org/in-notes/rfc2196.txt

The Federal Agency Security Practices (FASP) website whose areas contain a slew of information that incorporates the Federal CIO Council's best current practices pertaining to security issues:

http://csrc.nist.gov/fasp/
Numerous documents on security policies can be found under the topic FASP Areas.

FIPS PUB 191. Created by NIST. Although it is written specifically for LANs, this publication is applicable to any computer network environment. The use of risk management is presented to help the reader determine LAN assets, to identify threats and vulnerabilities, to determine the risk of those threats to the LAN, and to determine the possible security services and mechanisms that may be used to help reduce the risk to the LAN:

http://www.itl.nist.gov/div897/pubs/fip191.htm

NOTE   Federal Information Processing Standards Publications (FIPS PUBs) are issued by the NIST after approval by the Secretary of Commerce pursuant to Section 111 of the Federal Property and Administrative Services Act of 1949, as amended by the Computer Security Act of 1987, Public Law 100-235.

Incident Response Teams

NIST Special Publication (SP) 800-3, *Establishing a Computer Security Incident Response Capability (CSIRC)*.

Computer Security Resource Center (CSRC):

http://csrc.nist.gov/publications/nistpubs/

Handbook for Computer Security Incident Response Teams (CSIRTs):

http://www.sei.cmu.edu/publications/documents/03.reports/03hb002.html

Other Useful Sites for Security-Related Information

The CERT Coordination Center provides comprehensive information that ranges from protecting systems against potential problems to reacting to current problems to predicting future problems:

http://www.cert.org/

Electronic Privacy Information Center (EPIC):

http://www.epic.org/

Comprehensive archive of security-related links:

http://www.cerias.purdue.edu/infosec/hotlist/

Cisco Security Product Information

At the following website, you can find general information on Cisco security offerings with links to detailed security products, services, and solutions:

http://www.cisco.com/security/

Cisco IOS 12.0 Network Security. Indianapolis, IN: Cisco Press, 1999. Provides information about Cisco IOS security features.

Reporting and Prevention Guidelines: Industrial Espionage and Network Intrusions

In today's high-technology environment, thefts of proprietary material and network intrusions are a major organizational threat. This appendix is designed to help organizations develop the ability to prevent such proprietary theft and network intrusion—and, when they do occur, to know how to respond to recover their property and stop further intrusions. I hope you can review this information quickly and easily, and that it will function as a check list as you review your organization's needs. If you have questions regarding this appendix, please call or e-mail me at:

John C. Smith
Prevention and Recovery Consulting
Trade Secret Theft and Network Intrusions
Mountain View, CA 94040
(650) 964-1956
e-mail: John@JCSmithInv.com
Web site: http://www.JCSmithInv.com
Copyright © 1997

The information in this appendix comes from my eight years of experience as the senior criminal investigator, High Technology Theft/Computer Crime Unit, Santa Clara County District Attorney's Office, working in high-technology crime in Silicon Valley. This appendix includes the insight I gained from investigating 50-plus trade secret/proprietary theft (industrial espionage) cases; recovering hundreds of millions of dollars' worth of stolen proprietary property; investigating more than 40 network intrusions; searching countless personal computers in various types of criminal cases; and interviewing many suspects, witnesses, victims, and other people involved in these crimes.

It has been my experience that, to determine the extent of your loss or the extent of a network intrusion, it is necessary to conduct an investigation and execute a search warrant on the suspect's workspace and/or personal computer system. We generally found more property than the victim thought had been taken. Such investigations allow investigators to search for the types of hacking tools and programs (such as backdoor logins) that may have been used on your systems.

For Immediate Problems

- *When a crime has been committed, do not confront or talk with the suspect.* If you do, you give the suspect the opportunity to hide or destroy evidence.

- *Know your options about talking with law enforcement.* Most agencies will not start an investigation unless the victim wants to do so. An official report must be filed before a search warrant can be issued.

- *Do not wait too long to call.* It is best to immediately consult with law enforcement to learn about your options. Evidence can be lost if you wait too long.

Reporting Options

- Call our office or your local law enforcement agency and make a police report. Request a search warrant to recover your property. You can use this information to file for an injunction.

- Make an official report to the federal authorities, probably the FBI.

- File a civil law suit and seek an injunction when appropriate.

- Take appropriate disciplinary action against any involved employees.

- Do nothing and hope that the problem stops before your organization suffers any substantial damage.

Conducting an Investigation

To conduct an investigation, think of Smith's Seven Step System, which consists of the following:

1 *SPEED.* The case should be handled quickly before evidence and property are destroyed.

2 *STEALTH.* The investigation must be done quietly or the suspect will learn of it.

3 *SYSTEM SECURITY.* No further damage should be allowed to your system.

4 *SECURE EVIDENCE.* Chain of possession to ensure it is admissible.

5 *SUSPICIOUS/SUSPECT EMPLOYEES.* Most thefts are done by employees.

6 *SHOW and TELL REPORTING.* Learn how to make a report understandable.

7 *SEARCH WARRANT.* Prepare and serve a warrant when necessary.

Workplace Philosophy

An organization is less likely to be victimized if it has the following characteristics:

- Has adopted security policies to protect its systems and data.
- Makes its security policies known to all who work in the organization.
- Has planned on how it will react to intrusions and losses.
- Encourages the reporting of suspicious incidents and has a method in place that makes reporting easy and confidential.
- Attempts to recover its stolen material.
- Makes it known that offenders will be criminally prosecuted.
- Has analyzed the major threats to the organization and has considered how to deal with them.
- Realizes that the major threat is probably a person authorized to be on the premises.

Organizations should continue to provide ongoing awareness training to remind everyone that the organization could be a target for the theft of proprietary data or a network intrusion.

Your plan and your working environment must be balanced. Your rules and operating instructions cannot be so severe that work and creativity are restricted, yet rules and accepted security practices should convey the message that thefts, acts of vandalism, and computer misuse will not be condoned.

Management should take security seriously and allocate the resources needed to implement and inspect the correct policies. Training should be provided. Business goals (such as deadlines) should not be allowed to take precedence over security.

Most importantly, your company should develop an attitude and mind set that it is not willing to be a victim and that it will *not* tolerate people who steal from or attack its site. Law enforcement has long known that thieves and predators pick on easy and willing victims. Realize that incidents *do happen* and *can happen* to your company. Your company management must also understand this fact.

Written Plan

Your written plan should be approved by corporate legal, corporate security, management, and the computer/network manager. The plan should be agreed on, be in writing, and be approved by the head of the organization.

Organizations should involve employees in developing a plan. Employees know organizational weaknesses and how to exploit them.

Identify the decision-maker who is authorized to call law enforcement. Identify who will be the day-to-day coordinator of an incident and who will work with law enforcement and attorneys. Provide for a response team that is trained to investigate network intrusions.

All managers, supervisors, and systems administrators should be very familiar with the plan and have a copy available. All employees should receive a copy of the plan or a briefing on the contents of the plan. Your plan should specify that any employee who learns of a theft or network intrusion *will not* discuss it with anyone except management, security, the legal department, or a designated person.

Remember that rumors fly at the speed of sound.

Law and the Legal Process

Know the appropriate state and federal laws. Include copies of state and federal laws with your plan. Determine your guidelines for prosecuting. Prosecution is necessary for a law enforcement investigation and if you want to use the search warrant process.

Know the appropriate local or federal law enforcement agency that has jurisdiction for any problems you might have. Establish the appropriate contacts. Keep names and phone numbers updated. Talk with law enforcement at least once a year. Offer tours or briefings. Know the capabilities of your law enforcement resources.

Know how long it will normally take local law enforcement and federal law enforcement to obtain a search warrant. Discuss what information or reports law enforcement will share with you. Know whether you will be able to obtain law enforcement reports for use in civil cases. Know whether you can you get reports from federal cases.

Plan for filing a civil injunction or temporary restraining order (TRO) as soon as law enforcement has completed the search warrant or covert investigation. Injunctions are frequently used by victims to prohibit suspects from using proprietary information that has been taken under questionable circumstances.

Computer and Network Systems

Make sure the audit or accounting functions are turned on.

Have servers in a physically secure location to prevent unauthorized access.

Control modem connections; use smart cards or a call-back system.

Make sure secure firewalls are set up and configured properly.

On a regular basis, run programs (for example, Crack, Tiger, COPS, and Satan) to check for system weaknesses.

Keep current on new programs designed to find system vulnerabilities.

Use a virus-checker program.

Have a password file in a hidden location (that is, a shadow password file).

Close holes in operating systems.

Do not allow the importation of software into the system.

Monitor the size of outgoing mail and notify the system administrator of large outgoing messages.

Track and audit company proprietary data when it is copied and printed.

Watch for the computer system behaving strangely or improperly.

Put names or hidden markers in source code—unusual code that would work only with something you have done or misspelled words.

Make timely system backups.

Keep one copy of backup tapes in a secure facility offsite.

Plan on how to handle various intrusions, such as broken accounts, system or root access, backdoor logins, sniffers, and Trojan horses.

Ensure that patches have been made to networks and that you apply the patch whenever a new one is made available. Watch CERT bulletins.

Employees

Several studies and my experience indicate that employees and other persons who are authorized to be on the company premises or who are in a trusted relationship commit most computer crimes.

Do complete background checks before hiring someone or allowing someone access to company resources.

In new employee indoctrination, stress the importance of proprietary data and that any compromise of proprietary data will result in discipline, termination, or prosecution.

Warn against bringing in other companies' proprietary data.

Conduct thorough exit interviews.

Advise departing employees that it is against the law to take proprietary material, and that you will prosecute anyone caught taking any type of proprietary information.

Determine whether the employee who is leaving has worked on important-enough material that a letter should be sent to him or her or to the new employer reiterating the non-disclosure and confidentiality documents signed by the former employee. Letters are frequently used by companies to warn other companies when an employee has changed jobs and the former employer is concerned that the employee may divulge proprietary information.

Set up an easy-to-use system that allows employees to covertly or anonymously report suspicious behavior.

Set up a reward system for preventing loss of data or helping to recover data.

Develop a method to combat the belief by many employees that anyone who has worked on something has a right to take a copy. This feeling of ownership occurs regardless of the signing of non-disclosure agreements and ownership/invention agreements. One of the most common criminal defenses used is that the ex-employee just wanted a sample of their work.

Control and approve any articles written about the company by employees.

Educate current employees on the cost and impact to the organization—and to them personally—of the loss of proprietary information.

Do not give prospective or new employees an email account or access to their new work environment before they have officially terminated from their last employer.

Methods of Safeguarding Proprietary Material

For your proprietary material to be considered secret, you must be able to show that you took adequate steps to protect it.

In both civil and criminal cases, you must explain what steps or methods your company used to protect its property.

The following are measures that can be used to protect proprietary information:

- Require non-disclosure agreements from employees, contractors, and anyone with access to the protected material.

- Require non-employees to sign a contract describing their access to protected material before the non-employee is given any type of proprietary material.

- Conduct thorough exit interviews.

- Collect all documentation of terminating employees.

- Maintain secure and locked facilities.

- Require employees to wear badges; require visitors to wear badges and be accompanied by escorts.

- Maintain document control.

- Ensure that all documents are marked and numbered.
- Keep logs of who is issued what documents.
- Use a need-to-know policy to determine who can access proprietary material.
- Restrict on a need-to-know basis access to networks where proprietary data is kept.
- Password-protect computers and networks where important data is kept.

Document Control

Properly mark proprietary and confidential documents. The confidential markings can be minimized if they are seen on routine documents. Mark only proprietary documents, not everything.

Do not have more than two security classifications.

Have an easy-to-use accounting system in place to track who checks out and returns proprietary documents. Require that the document-control system be used and inspect its use. Have the document-control processes audited by management on a random basis.

Track printouts from the computer accounting system. Have confidential and proprietary markings automatically put on every printed proprietary document.

Track and audit downloads of computer files.

Set up a disposal method for documents when they are no longer needed.

Limit access to source code; limit physical access to documents.

Foreign/Competitor Contacts

Train employees in how to protect proprietary data when they are traveling. Discuss hazards and how employees can protect themselves or detect methods such as these:

- Microphones in hotels, meeting rooms, and transportation
- Searches of rooms and briefcases by unknown persons

Train employees in what to do when they are approached by representatives of a competitor, a foreign company, or a foreign country.

Require that employees report when they are asked to be a guest or a speaker, to serve on a committee of a foreign country, or are put in a situation of working with a person who may be collecting information. Debrief employees when they return from overseas trips.

Determine how to handle visitors who take photographs and notes while touring your facilities.

Determine how to handle employees who are asked to lunch or other social functions by competitors.

Managers and Supervisors

Managers and supervisors should be trained to recognize and report employees who manifest behavior that may lead to acts against an organization. Such behavior may include the following:

- Employees who are angry at the company or a supervisor for being passed over for promotion, for not receiving a raise, for a perceived lack of respect, and so on.
- Employees with an unusually high fixation on making large sums of money, getting promoted in a company, acquiring a lot of stock from a start-up company, and so on.
- Employees acting strangely or being spotted with suspicious people.

Management should continually reinforce that first-line managers and supervisors will often be the first to learn of unusual employee behavior and that most problems are caused by insiders.

Reporting Process—Rewards

Create an environment in which employees will report suspicious behavior or actions. Have in place an anonymous reporting or call-in process and ensure that management takes this seriously. Offer rewards for saving data in the face of thefts or attempts at theft.

Train managers, supervisors, and all staff on how to make reports and explain why it is important to react *quickly and quietly*.

Intelligence-Gathering Methods

There are many ways for people to get at confidential information:

- Dumpster diving
- Obtaining your data from other companies
- Hiring your key employees
- Sniffing data on networks
- Going through trash inside the building

- Monitoring unsecured faxes and telephones (particularly true in other countries)
- Voice gathering by using sound-directional equipment
- Foreign or competing representatives who visit or tour your facilities
- Interns or students assigned to your facilities

Look for Weak Links

Often, the employees who make the least money have the most access in a company: security personnel, maintenance personnel, and janitors. The following are possible weak links:

- Is the company contracting for services, and are those employees bonded or backgrounded?
- Don't overlook trash being put in unlocked dumpsters.
- Social engineering of unsophisticated employees who talk about passwords in front of others.
- Employees with gambling or drinking problems, or employees who hang around card clubs.
- Allowing non-employees and employees of contractors too much access to sensitive areas or documents.
- Allowing too many employees without the necessary need-to-know access to sensitive areas or documents.
- Allowing work to be done that is not understood by a supervisor or management.
- Unlimited access to copy machines or downloading of documents.
- Allowing computer data to be sent out of the company without some type of check or monitoring.
- Allowing employees to write papers or to give presentations about the company or its products without the information going through a review process.
- Not enforcing company policy.
- Allowing engineers or other technical employees to use their own equipment, computers, or notebooks.
- Not protecting customer information, strategic forecasts, or business plans.
- Not running Crack or other tools that check for network vulnerabilities.
- Not closing computer accounts of employees who have left the company.
- Proprietary documents that are not marked or that are printed from a computer without adequate proprietary notice.
- Allowing a proprietary document to be moved, downloaded, or printed from a computer network without a warning that the material is proprietary.

California State Laws

The following are the California state laws that are used in a majority of high-technology cases. They can be downloaded from this site:

http://www.leginfo.ca.gov.calaw.html

- 499c PC—Trade Secret Theft

  Trade secret means any information—including formula, pattern, compilation, program, device, method, technique, or process—that derives independent economic value, actual or potential, from not being generally known to the public or to other persons who can obtain economic value from its disclosure or use. A felony. See the California Penal Code for complete wording.

- 502 PC—Computer (Network) Related Crimes, Illegal Intrusion

  Primarily a felony. See the California Penal Code for complete wording.

  1   Accesses, alters, damages, deletes, destroys, or uses data to defraud or obtain something of value.

  2   Knowingly accesses and without permission takes, copies, or makes use of any data from a computer system or a computer network.

  3   Knowingly and without permission uses or causes to be used computer services. (Misdemeanor)

  4   Knowingly accesses and alters, damages, deletes, or destroys any data on a computer or network.

  5   Knowingly and without permission causes the disruption of computer services or denies or causes the denial of computer services to a computer, computer system, or computer network.

  6   Knowingly and without permission accesses or causes to be accessed any computer, computer system, or computer network. (Misdemeanor)

  7   Knowingly introduces any computer contaminant into any computer, computer system, or computer network. (Misdemeanor)

  If the computer used by the suspect is located in Santa Clara County, we can prosecute even though the suspect broke into a system in another state.

- 641.3 PC—Commercial Bribery

  A felony. Any employee who solicits, accepts, or agrees to accept money or anything of value from a person other than his or her employer, other than in trust for the employer, corruptly and without the knowledge and consent of the employer, in return for using or agreeing to use his or her position for the benefit of that other person, and any person who offers or gives an employee money or anything of value under those circumstances is guilty of commercial bribery. The money or thing of value must exceed $100.

United States Code

Section 1832, Theft of Trade Secrets. Whoever, with intent to convert a trade secret that is related to or included in a product that is produced for or placed in interstate or foreign commerce, to the economic benefit of anyone other than the owner thereof, and intending or knowing that the offense will injure any owner of trade secret, knowingly (steals, copies, duplicates, sends, receives, buys, or possesses knowing it to be stolen).

Examples of Cases in Santa Clara County (Silicon Valley)

The following are some of the more serious cases of proprietary theft and network intrusions that the Santa Clara County District Attorney's Office has investigated:

- Kevin M. used the name of a victim company manager and obtained a modem account. He uploaded his own code and obtained superuser status on several systems. He then downloaded source code through cutouts and cellular phones.

- BV used cracking tools obtained on the Internet to gain system administration status at an Ivy League university. He then inserted a back-door login program into the operating system.

- RY, after leaving a company, gained access to the network through a security hole. On two occasions, he erased the manufacturing database and made hidden changes in the system. He almost stopped company operations for two days.

- MI, who wanted to make more money, gave notice and then compressed the victim company's source code. He emailed it to his account on a public provider and then to his home.

- CVD was the manager of the computer center. He used his employees to rewrite the company's source code and then sold it. He formed a company with the profit and was trying to sell the program overseas. The code was moved using modem and tape.

- Marc G. was caught trying to get on a flight back to France after working in a local software development company. He had taken enough papers to replicate that company's program. Five `tar` (`copy`) commands were found on the company's system.

- WBS, an angry employee in the defense industry, took a few papers at a time concerning a non-classified part of a proprietary project. By the time he was fired, he had an 18-inch-thick stack of papers. He also took a copy of the company's business plan. He was offering these to the victim company's competitors to get a job.

- INT wanted schematics and manufacturing/process information to help start up a new competing company. He hired a victim employee as a consultant who brought the information he needed to the new company. During a search warrant in a case over disputed source code, we found a proprietary document that would allow the replication of the victim's product. The engineer with the document said it had been given to him when he was a scientist in the Soviet Union, within six months of the publication date. He was able to retrieve it after the fall of the Iron Curtain.

- JW is an engineer who took processing data for a product and used it to obtain consulting fees and to get a job in another country. We arrested him two days before he was to leave for his new job in South America. This information may have been used as the basis of a partnership with a business in Europe.

- T & G took documents and source code. We found that T was, at the same time, also serving as the vice president of a company in Beijing. Further investigation revealed that T was sending documents to a company in Beijing.

- HT, while visiting a company with whom he had a business association, downloaded their customer database into his laptop computer and sent it to his company in Europe.

- F was employed as an engineer to develop computer instructions for manufacturing. He became angry and erased all the programs on the company computers. We recovered the programs at his home.

- AK acquired proprietary documents on his employer's new technology. He quit and obtained several jobs where it appeared he was using the documents to make himself look good and to advance in the new company.

- RC broke passwords on a network; using those accounts, he sent messages to the president of the institution trying to get the system administrators fired.

- A software engineer left the company where he developed the nucleus of a software program. In an extremely short time, he produced a similar competing product. Many lines of code are the same.

- A technician took prototype circuit boards out of new computers and sold them.

- Raj, an Indian electrical engineer, was working as a security guard in an R&D facility for one company while working in several other companies that had similar products. He had not listed his EE degree on his application for the security guard position. Raj was stopped trying to get back into the R&D facility six months after he had walked off that job.

- A local manufacturing company, trying to do business with a Pacific Rim company, entered into a working agreement. When the local company stopped visitors from the other company from taking notes and photos of their equipment, a representative of the foreign company tried bribery to get manufacturing details. The victim did not prosecute for fear of not being able to do business in that country. A second local company discovered that a company from the same Pacific Rim country hired away a manager. That manager put together a team of former employees from the victim company. The team developed a duplicate product to put on the competing market in an extremely short time.

Port Numbers

This appendix lists the assigned port numbers from the Internet Assigned Numbers Authority (IANA). For a more complete list, go to http://www.isi.edu/in-notes/iana/assignments/port-numbers.

The port numbers are divided into three ranges, which are described in Table C-1:

- The *well-known ports* are those in the range 0 through 1023.
- The *registered ports* are those in the range 1024 through 49151.
- The *dynamic* or *private ports* are those in the range 49152 through 65535.

Table C-1 *Port Assignments*

Keyword	Decimal	Description
ssh	22/tcp	SSH Remote Login Protocol
ssh	22/udp	SSH Remote Login Protocol
tacacs	49/tcp	Login Host Protocol (TACACS)
tacacs	49/udp	Login Host Protocol (TACACS)
domain	53/tcp	Domain Name Server
domain	53/udp	Domain Name Server
tacacs-ds	65/tcp	TACACS-Database Service
tacacs-ds	65/udp	TACACS-Database Service
kerberos	88/tcp	Kerberos
kerberos	88/udp	Kerberos
https	443/tcp	HTTP protocol over TLS/SSL
https	443/udp	HTTP protocol over TLS/SSL
smtps	465/tcp	SMTP protocol over TLS/SSL (was ssmtp)
smtps	465/udp	SMTP protocol over TLS/SSL (was ssmtp)
isakmp	500/tcp	ISAKMP protocol
isakmp	500/udp	ISAKMP protocol
nntps	563/tcp	NNTP protocol over TLS/SSL (was snntp)

continues

Table C-1   *Port Assignments (Continued)*

Keyword	Decimal	Description
nntps	563/udp	NNTP protocol over TLS/SSL (was snntp)
sshell	614/tcp	SSL shell
sshell	614/udp	SSL shell
kerberos-adm	749/tcp	Kerberos administration
kerberos-adm	749/udp	Kerberos administration
kerberos-iv	750/udp	Kerberos Version 4
ftps-data	989/tcp	FTP protocol, data, over TLS/SSL
ftps-data	989/udp	FTP protocol, data, over TLS/SSL
ftps	990/tcp	FTP protocol, control, over TLS/SSL
ftps	990/udp	FTP protocol, control, over TLS/SSL
telnets	992/tcp	Telnet protocol over TLS/SSL
telnets	992/udp	Telnet protocol over TLS/SSL
imaps	993/tcp	IMAP4 protocol over TLS/SSL
imaps	993/udp	IMAP4 protocol over TLS/SSL
ircs	994/tcp	IRC protocol over TLS/SSL
ircs	994/udp	IRC protocol over TLS/SSL
pop3s	995/tcp	POP3 protocol over TLS/SSL (was spop3)
pop3s	995/udp	POP3 protocol over TLS/SSL (was spop3)
socks	1080/tcp	SOCKS
socks	1080/udp	SOCKS
pptp	1723/tcp	PPTP
pptp	1723/udp	PPTP
radius	1812/tcp	RADIUS
radius	1812/udp	RADIUS
radius-acct	1813/tcp	RADIUS Accounting
radius-acct	1813/udp	RADIUS Accounting
http-alt	8080/tcp	HTTP Alternate (see port 80)
http-alt	8080/udp	HTTP Alternate (see port 80)

Mitigating Distributed Denial-of-Service Attacks

Distributed denial-of-service (DDoS) attacks are causing havoc in networks around the world, but in many instances there are steps that you can take to mitigate these types of attacks. This appendix attempts to detail some of the steps that you may take on network infrastructure routers to cause the least amount of harm in any network.

Understanding DoS/DDoS Attacks

Denial-of-service (DoS) attacks are common on the Internet. The first step in responding to such an attack is to find out exactly what sort of attack it is. Many of the commonly used DoS attacks are based on high-bandwidth packet floods, or on other repetitive streams of packets. Many of these attacks were described in Chapter 5, "Threats in an Enterprise Network." Attackers choose common exploits because they are particularly effective, particularly hard to trace, or because tools that enable execution of the attack are widely available. Many DoS attackers lack the skill or motivation to create their own tools and use programs found on the Internet; these tools tend to fall in and out of fashion.

A wide variety of DoS attacks are possible. Even ignoring attacks that use software bugs to shut down systems with relatively little traffic, the fact remains that any IP packet that can be sent across the network can be used to execute a flooding DoS attack. When you are under attack, you must always consider the possibility that what you're seeing is something that does not fall into the usual categories.

The Filtering and/or Rate-Limiting Issue

There are many schools of thought regarding filtering and rate limiting, especially on routers. Filters (or access lists) permit or deny traffic, whereas rate limiting constrains the amount of traffic being sent or received. The worst offenders of propagating DDoS attacks are people who refuse to apply any kind of filtering on their routers. It will not stop more sophisticated attacks, but even simple "no-brainer" filters will mitigate having obviously spoofed packets traverse corporate or Internet-connected networks.

The characteristics of the source IP address is typically a large factor in deciding whether to filter and/or rate limit traffic. The source IP addresses from DDoS attacks can have one of four characteristics:

- **Spoofed RFC 1918 and special-use addresses**—These are well-known addresses that should never be used or seen as part of the global Internet. Most can be found from an Internet draft by Bill Manning titled "Documenting Special-use IPv4 Address Blocks That Have Been Registered with IANA/RIR." This list includes the network addresses in Table D-1.

Table D-1   *Special-Use IPv4 Address Blocks Registered with IANA/RIR*

Description	Network
Default	0.0.0.0 /8
Loopback	127.0.0.0 /8
RFC 1918	10.0.0.0 /8
RFC 1918	172.16.0.0 /12
RFC 1918	192.168.0.0 /16
Net test	192.0.2.0 /24
Testing devices	192.18.0.0 /15
IPv6 to IPv4 relay	192.88.99.0 /24
RFC 1918 name servers	192.175.48.0 /24
End-node auto configuration	169.254.0.0 /16

- **Spoofed addresses that are not in the global Internet routing table**—Routable IP networks are allocated via delegations of authority from the Internet Assigned Numbers Authority (IANA). The list of IP addresses that have not been activated is easily accessible at http://www.iana.org/assignments/ipv4-address-space. This makes it easy for someone to create an attack with spoofed addresses based on this list. Because these addresses are not in the global Internet routing table, a simple check in the forwarding table can easily aid in their identification. Some tools, such as unicast reverse path forwarding (uRPF), make this check straightforward, making it harder for these attacks to be successful.

- **Valid address from a DDoS agent**—When a compromised host acts as a DDoS agent, it is possible that the source IP address will be that of the penetrated system. In this case, filtering must be applied with care, because dropping all packets from the penetrated machine will also drop any valid user traffic being sourced from that address. In some situations, it may make more sense to apply some rate-limiting tactics instead.

- **Spoofed address using a valid address from the Internet**—Sometimes the attacker's target is actually the spoofed addresses. Instead of trying to directly take down a large corporate network, the addresses from that network are spoofed so that other entities (typically upstream connected networks) will isolate the corporate network through the use of filtering. As in any valid address DDoS attack, this is a case where rate-limiting tactics may make sense depending on severity of the DDoS attack.

Steps to Take Before a DDoS Attack Happens

It is always a good idea to be proactive rather than reactive in mitigating any kind of network security attack. Chapter 8, "Incident Handling," discussed incident handling and the importance of having procedures in place to handle attacks, incorporating intrusion detection systems into your network architecture, and using tools to perform regularly scheduled host and network audits.

Specifically for DDoS attacks, there are additional ways to prevent your networks from becoming overloaded with unwanted traffic. These include the use of filtering and rate limiting and are discussed in this appendix. All examples are for Cisco IOS Software router configurations. For more detailed explanations of any filtering techniques listed here, refer to Chapter 10, "Securing Internet Access."

Network Ingress/Egress Filtering

All networks should implement some degree of network ingress/egress filtering to avoid spoofed attack traffic from being propagated across networks. Ingress filtering defines the traffic that is allowed to enter your network, whereas egress filtering defines the traffic that you send out to other networks. Filtering will not stop attacks that use valid source addresses, but all routers should incorporate filters that deny packets with spoofed RFC 1918 and special-use addresses from propagating through the Internet. In addition, all networks should consider following the recommendations in RFC 2827, "Network Ingress Filtering: Defeating Denial-of-Service Attacks Which Employ IP Source Address Spoofing," by P. Ferguson and D. Senie. It recommends ingress filtering on the ISP/customer edge of the network to ensure that a source address of a packet matches the IP address block allocated to a customer. This recommendation can be extended to corporate networks, many of which are large enough to follow security principles that apply to Internet service providers (ISPs). The corporate network should only accept traffic from outside connections with source addresses other than the corporate network block. In addition, it should only permit outbound traffic with valid corporate network addresses.

Although these may seem to be simple rules to follow, networks are complex beasts and how to apply these rules can vary. It is easy to get confused and go filter crazy or just not deploy them. A simple rule to follow is to at minimum, apply both ingress and egress filters at any router interface that connects to any remote connection, especially the Internet. In addition, for consistency, it is good practice to use the same fixed access list number for ingress and egress filters in your routers. It simplifies troubleshooting when, for example, you know that access list 103 is used for ingress filters and access list 104 is used for egress filters to remote connections. Of course, when routers have multiple remote connections, the consistency scheme may have to be modified. The following examples illustrate some common scenarios and offer recommended ways to apply these rules.

Example 1: Simple Filtering

The first example is that of a corporate network illustrated in Figure D-1. Here, the corporate network has been assigned the network address 144.254.0.0/16 and connects two remote offices with network addresses 171.71.32.0/27 and 192.150.42.0/27. The filtering policy and configuration examples follow.

Figure D-1 *Corporate Network with Simple Filtering Policy*

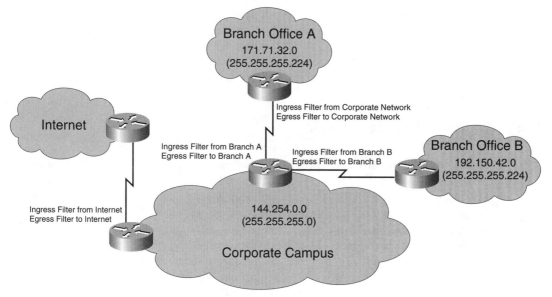

Branch Routers

The branch routers are assumed to have no other connection to the Internet, and filters are only applied on the interfaces that connect to the corporate network, in this case BRI 0.

The branch router ingress filtering policy is as follows:

- Deny all RFC 1918 and special-use addresses from entering the branch network. (The assumption is made that even if the corporate network is using some private address space, the traffic should stay within the corporate network.)
- Deny all traffic with an IP source address that matches the branch network address allocation.
- Permit all other traffic.

The branch router egress filtering policy is as follows:

- Permit only traffic with an IP source address that matches the branch network.
- Deny all other traffic.

The branch A router configuration is displayed in Example D-1.

Example D-1 *Branch A Router Configuration*

```
access-list 133 deny    ip host 0.0.0.0 any
access-list 133 deny    ip 127.0.0.0 0.255.255.255 any
access-list 133 deny    ip 10.0.0.0 0.255.255.255 any
access-list 133 deny    ip 172.16.0.0 0.15.255.255 any
access-list 133 deny    ip 192.168.0.0 0.0.255.255 any
access-list 133 deny    ip 192.0.2.0 0.0.0.255 any
access-list 133 deny    ip 169.254.0.0 0.0.255.255 any
access-list 133 deny    ip 240.0.0.0 15.255.255.255 any
access-list 133 deny    ip 171.71.32.0 0.0.0.31 any
access-list 133 permit ip any any

access-list 144 permit ip 171.71.32.0 0.0.0.31 any
access-list 144 deny ip any any

interface BRI0
description To Corporate Network
ip access-group 133 in
ip access-group 144 out
```

NAS Router

Filters are placed on only the interfaces that connect to the branch networks, which in this case is a PRI.

The NAS router ingress filtering policy is as follows:

- Permit only traffic with an IP source address of branch networks.
- Deny all other traffic.

The NAS router egress filtering policy is as follows:

- Deny all RFC 1918 and special-use addresses from propagating to branch networks.
- Deny all traffic with an IP source address that matches the branch network address allocation.
- Permit all other traffic.

The NAS router configuration is displayed in Example D-2.

Example D-2 *NAS Router Configuration*

```
access-list 133 permit ip 171.71.32.0 0.0.0.31 any
access-list 133 permit ip 192.150.42.0 0.0.0.31 any
access-list 133 deny ip any any

access-list 144 deny    ip host 0.0.0.0 any
access-list 144 deny    ip 127.0.0.0 0.255.255.255 any
access-list 144 deny    ip 10.0.0.0 0.255.255.255 any
access-list 144 deny    ip 172.16.0.0 0.15.255.255 any
```

continues

Example D-2 *NAS Router Configuration (Continued)*

```
access-list 144 deny    ip 192.168.0.0 0.0.255.255 any
access-list 144 deny    ip 192.0.2.0 0.0.0.255 any
access-list 144 deny    ip 169.254.0.0 0.0.255.255 any
access-list 144 deny    ip 240.0.0.0 15.255.255.255 any
access-list 144 deny    ip 171.71.32.0 0.0.0.31 any
access-list 144 deny    ip 192.150.42.0 0.0.0.31 any
access-list 133 permit ip any any

interface Serial 0:23
description To Branch Offices
ip access-group 133 in
ip access-group 144 out
```

Internet Router

Filters are placed only on the interface that connects to the Internet, which in this case is a T3 circuit.

The Internet router ingress filtering policy is as follows:

- Deny all RFC 1918 and special-use addresses from entering the corporate network.
- Deny all traffic with an IP source address of the corporate network or branch networks.
- Permit all other traffic.

The Internet router egress filtering policy is as follows:

- Permit only traffic with an IP source address of the corporate network and branch networks.
- Deny all other traffic.

The Internet router configuration is displayed in Example D-3.

Example D-3 *Internet Router Configuration*

```
access-list 133 deny    ip host 0.0.0.0 any
access-list 133 deny    ip 127.0.0.0 0.255.255.255 any
access-list 133 deny    ip 10.0.0.0 0.255.255.255 any
access-list 133 deny    ip 172.16.0.0 0.15.255.255 any
access-list 133 deny    ip 192.168.0.0 0.0.255.255 any
access-list 133 deny    ip 192.0.2.0 0.0.0.255 any
access-list 133 deny    ip 169.254.0.0 0.0.255.255 any
access-list 133 deny    ip 240.0.0.0 15.255.255.255 any
access-list 133 deny    ip 144.254.0.0 0.0.255.255 any
access-list 133 deny    ip 171.71.32.0 0.0.0.31 any
access-list 133 deny    ip 192.150.42.0 0.0.0.31 any
access-list 133 permit ip any any

access-list 144 permit ip 144.254.0.0 0.0.255.255 any
access-list 144 permit ip 171.71.32.0 0.0.0.31 any
access-list 144 permit ip 192.150.42.0 0.0.0.31 any
```

Example D-3 *Internet Router Configuration (Continued)*

```
access-list 144 deny ip any any

interface Serial 0/0
description To Internet
ip access-group 133 in
ip access-group 144 out
```

Example 2: Advanced Filtering

Now look at a more complex example that is illustrated in Figure D-2. Here some complexity is added; each of the branch routers has its own Internet connection, which can act as a redundant path for the corporate network to the Internet. Additionally, the corporate network and branch networks use some private RFC 1918 addressing, which needs to only be available from within the corporate or branch networks. In other words, no private address space traffic should traverse the links connecting the corporate and branch networks.

Figure D-2 *Advanced Filtering*

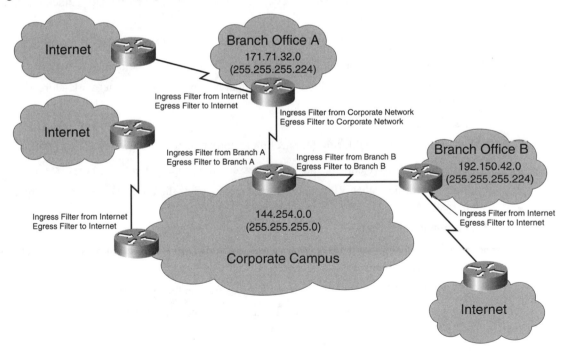

NOTE In some scenarios, corporations can coordinate the use of private address space between their corporate and branch sites and may want to allow propagation of these addresses between the corporate and branch networks only. Care must be taken that traffic from these private addresses are not leaked out to other networks, such as the Internet.

The filtering policy and configuration examples follow.

Branch Routers

The branch routers will now have to take into consideration that it's a backup connection for the corporate network and possibly the other branch network. Both ingress and egress filters are applied on the interfaces that connect to the corporate network—in this case BRI 0, which connects to the corporate network, and serial 1/0, which connects to the Internet. Because there is more likelihood that spoofed traffic may enter from the Internet connections, the filters should be stricter to ensure that the corporate network will not be affected by a DDoS attack from the Internet using spoofed addresses.

The branch router ingress filtering (connecting to corporate network) policy is as follows:

- Deny all RFC 1918 and special-use addresses from entering the branch network.
- Deny all traffic with an IP source address that matches the branch network address allocation.
- Permit all other traffic.

The branch router egress filtering (connecting to corporate network) policy is as follows:

- Deny all RFC 1918 and special-use addresses from propagating to the corporate network.
- Deny all traffic with an IP source address that matches the corporate network address allocation.
- Permit all other traffic.

The branch router ingress filtering (connecting to Internet) policy is as follows. (Note that this is the same as ingress filter above.)

- Deny all RFC 1918 and special-use addresses from entering the branch network.
- Deny all traffic with an IP source address that matches the branch network address allocation.
- Permit all other traffic.

The branch router egress filtering (connecting to Internet) policy is as follows:

- Permit only traffic with an IP source address that matches the corporate and branch network allocations.
- Deny all other traffic.

The branch A router configuration is displayed in Example D-4.

Example D-4   *Branch A Configuration (Advanced Filtering)*

```
access-list 133 deny    ip host 0.0.0.0 any
access-list 133 deny    ip 127.0.0.0 0.255.255.255 any
access-list 133 deny    ip 10.0.0.0 0.255.255.255 any
access-list 133 deny    ip 172.16.0.0 0.15.255.255 any
access-list 133 deny    ip 192.168.0.0 0.0.255.255 any
access-list 133 deny    ip 192.0.2.0 0.0.0.255 any
access-list 133 deny    ip 169.254.0.0 0.0.255.255 any
access-list 133 deny    ip 240.0.0.0 15.255.255.255 any
access-list 133 deny    ip 171.71.32.0 0.0.0.31 any
access-list 133 permit ip any any

access-list 144 deny    ip host 0.0.0.0 any
access-list 144 deny    ip 127.0.0.0 0.255.255.255 any
access-list 144 deny    ip 10.0.0.0 0.255.255.255 any
access-list 144 deny    ip 172.16.0.0 0.15.255.255 any
access-list 144 deny    ip 192.168.0.0 0.0.255.255 any
access-list 144 deny    ip 192.0.2.0 0.0.0.255 any
access-list 144 deny    ip 169.254.0.0 0.0.255.255 any
access-list 144 deny    ip 240.0.0.0 15.255.255.255 any
access-list 144 deny    ip 144.254.0.0 0.0.255.255 any
access-list 144 permit ip any any

access-list 166 permit ip 171.71.32.0 0.0.0.31 any
access-list 166 permit ip 144.254.0.0 0.0.255.255 any
access-list 166 deny ip any any

interface BRI0
description To Corporate Network
ip access-group 133 in
ip access-group 144 out

interface Serial 1/0
description To Internet
ip access-group 133 in
ip access-group 166 out
```

NAS Router

Filters are placed on only the interfaces that connect to the branch networks. Because you now must allow potential traffic other than that sourced by the branch network allocation itself to enter the corporate network, there is more likelihood that spoofed traffic may enter from the branch connections. Therefore, the filters should be stricter to ensure that the corporate network will not be affected by a DDoS attack propagating from the branch networks using spoofed addresses.

The NAS router ingress filtering policy is as follows:

- Deny all RFC 1918 and special-use addresses from entering the corporate networks.
- Deny all traffic with an IP source address that matches the corporate network address allocation.
- Permit all other traffic.

The NAS router egress filtering policy is as follows:

- Deny all RFC 1918 and special-use addresses from propagating to branch networks.
- Deny all traffic with an IP source address that matches the corporate network address allocation.
- Permit all other traffic.

The NAS router configuration is displayed in Example D-5.

Example D-5 *NAS Router Configuration (Advanced Filtering)*

```
access-list 133 deny    ip host 0.0.0.0 any
access-list 133 deny    ip 127.0.0.0 0.255.255.255 any
access-list 133 deny    ip 10.0.0.0 0.255.255.255 any
access-list 133 deny    ip 172.16.0.0 0.15.255.255 any
access-list 133 deny    ip 192.168.0.0 0.0.255.255 any
access-list 133 deny    ip 192.0.2.0 0.0.0.255 any
access-list 133 deny    ip 169.254.0.0 0.0.255.255 any
access-list 133 deny    ip 240.0.0.0 15.255.255.255 any
access-list 133 deny    ip 171.71.32.0 0.0.0.31 any
access-list 133 permit  ip any any

access-list 144 deny    ip host 0.0.0.0 any
access-list 144 deny    ip 127.0.0.0 0.255.255.255 any
access-list 144 deny    ip 10.0.0.0 0.255.255.255 any
access-list 144 deny    ip 172.16.0.0 0.15.255.255 any
access-list 144 deny    ip 192.168.0.0 0.0.255.255 any
access-list 144 deny    ip 192.0.2.0 0.0.0.255 any
access-list 144 deny    ip 169.254.0.0 0.0.255.255 any
access-list 144 deny    ip 240.0.0.0 15.255.255.255 any
access-list 144 deny    ip 144.254.0.0 0.0.255.255 any
access-list 144 permit  ip any any

interface Serial 0:23
description To Branch Offices
ip access-group 133 in
ip access-group 144 out
```

Internet Router

Filters are placed only on the interface that connects to the Internet. Note that the ingress filter differs from the first example in that it now must not deny traffic that may have IP source addresses from the branch networks. This is because the branch office-to-corporate network path via the Internet provides a level of redundancy in the event that the direct path fails.

The Internet router ingress filtering policy is as follows:

- Deny all RFC 1918 and special-use addresses from entering the corporate network.
- Deny all traffic with an IP source address of the corporate network.
- Permit all other traffic.

The Internet router egress filtering policy is as follows:

- Permit only traffic with an IP source address of the corporate network and branch networks.
- Deny all other traffic.

The Internet router configuration is displayed in Example D-6.

Example D-6 *Internet Router Configuration (Advanced Filtering)*

```
access-list 133 deny   ip host 0.0.0.0 any
access-list 133 deny   ip 127.0.0.0 0.255.255.255 any
access-list 133 deny   ip 10.0.0.0 0.255.255.255 any
access-list 133 deny   ip 172.16.0.0 0.15.255.255 any
access-list 133 deny   ip 192.168.0.0 0.0.255.255 any
access-list 133 deny   ip 192.0.2.0 0.0.0.255 any
access-list 133 deny   ip 169.254.0.0 0.0.255.255 any
access-list 133 deny   ip 240.0.0.0 15.255.255.255 any
access-list 133 deny   ip 144.254.0.0 0.0.255.255 any
access-list 133 permit ip any any

access-list 144 permit ip 144.254.0.0 0.0.255.255 any
access-list 144 permit ip 171.71.32.0 0.0.0.31 any
access-list 144 permit ip 192.150.42.0 0.0.0.31 any
access-list 144 deny ip any any

interface Serial 0/0
description To Internet
ip access-group 133 in
ip access-group 144 out
```

NOTE   Filtering is a fairly complex issue due to the variety of ways you can deploy filters. It is important to keep the maintenance of these filters as low as possible and to optimize the configurations for your environment. Ingress/egress filtering needs to be deployed because it facilitates the DoS originator to be easily traced to its true source, because the attacker would have to use a valid, and legitimately reachable, source address.

Rate Limit Some Network Traffic

A number of routers in the market today have features that enable you to limit the amount of bandwidth some type of traffic can consume. Sometimes this rate limiting is also referred to as "traffic shaping," and typically a vendor will allow you to enforce a bandwidth policy against network traffic that matches an access list.

You can use this proactively to create access list rules that match some of the network traffic used by the DDoS attack. If the attack is using Internet Control Message Protocol (ICMP) packets (as in Smurf attacks) or TCP SYN packets, for example, you could configure the system to specifically limit the bandwidth those types of packets are allowed to consume. This will allow some of these packets that may belong to legitimate network flows (such as datagrams being exchanged from established TCP microflows) to go through.

For Cisco routers, the committed access rate (CAR) functionality works with Cisco Express Forwarding (CEF), found in Cisco IOS Software Release 11.1CC and onward from 12.0. It allows network operators to rate limit certain types of traffic to specific sources or destinations. The main advantage of CAR is that it acts on packets as they arrive on a router's interface, dropping or rate limiting the DoS flow before any packet processing occurs.

The following two examples show how you can use CAR to rate limit ICMP packets and TCP SYN packets, two of the more commonly found DoS attacks.

Rate Limiting ICMP Packets

In this example, a corporation chooses to rate limit all ICMP echo and echo-reply packets received at its 2-Mbps connection from the Internet. The ICMP echo and echo-reply traffic is limited to 256 kbps, with a maximum burst size of 8000 bytes; all packets exceeding this rate are dropped. Multiple rate-limit commands can be added to an interface to control other kinds of traffic as well. Example D-7 shows the configuration commands for the previously described scenario.

Example D-7 *Configuration for ICMP Traffic Rate Limiting*

```
access-list 107 permit icmp any any echo
access-list 107 permit icmp any any echo-reply

interface Serial 1/1
rate-limit input access-group 107 256000 8000 8000 conform-action transmit
   exceed-action drop
```

Rate Limiting TCP SYN Packets

In this example, a corporation uses CAR to limit TCP SYN floods to specified servers. Typically these would be critical servers, and in this example they reside on the 144.254.2.0 network. The TCP SYN traffic is limited to 8 kbps, with a maximum burst size of 8000 bytes; all packets exceeding this rate are dropped. Multiple rate-limit commands can be added to an interface to control other kinds of traffic as well. Note that the first access list entry ensures that established TCP sessions are not limited. Example D-8 shows the configuration commands for the previously described scenario.

Example D-8 *Configuration for TCP SYN Traffic Rate Limiting*

```
access-list 108 deny tcp any 144.254.2.0 0.0.0.255 established
access-list 108 permit tcp any 144.254.2.0 0.0.0.255

interface Serial 1/1
rate-limit input access-group 108 8000 8000 8000 conform-action transmit
   exceed-action drop
```

NOTE   It is recommended that you first measure the number of SYN packets during normal state (before attacks occur) and use those values to set the burst size. If you set the burst size too low, many legitimate SYNs may be dropped. During an attack, use the **show interfaces rate-limit** command to display the conformed and exceeded rates for the interface.

IP Unicast Reverse Path Forwarding (uRPF)

A routing based filtering feature called IP unicast reverse-path forwarding (uRPF) can also be used to prevent most forms of IP address spoofing. This feature examines each packet received as input on that interface. If the source IP address does not have a route in the routing table that points back to the same interface on which the packet arrived, the router drops the packet.

To use uRPF, CEF switching needs to be turned on in the router (CEF distributed switching for an RSP+VIP-based router). CEF is an enhanced Layer 3 IP switching technology in Cisco routers that avoids the potential overhead of continuous cache churn by instead using a Forwarding Information Base (FIB) for the destination switching decision. The FIB mirrors the entire contents of the IP routing table—that is, there is a one-to-one correspondence between FIB table entries and routing table prefixes; therefore no need to maintain a route cache.

There is no need to configure the input interface for CEF switching. This is because uRPF has been implemented to search through the FIB using the source IP address. As long as CEF is running on the router, individual interfaces can be configured with other switching modes. RPF is an input-side function that is enabled on an interface or subinterface and operates on packets received by the router.

NOTE   It is important that CEF be turned on globally in the router. uRPF will not work without CEF.

Cisco IOS Software Release 12.1 and later includes an enhancement to uRPF that allows access lists to be applied to work in conjunction with uRPF. When a packet fails reverse path verification, the access list is applied. If the access list permits the packet, it is forwarded. If the access list denies the packet, it is dropped. In this manner, the access lists enable you to create exceptions to uRPF's usual functionality. In addition, it provides for a logging mechanism for packets that do not pass the uRPF check.

uRPF is not supported in any 11.2 or 11.3 images. uRPF is included in Cisco IOS Software 12.0 on all platforms that support CEF. CEF-supported platforms include the Cisco 7X00 series routers equipped with RSP7000, 7200 series, 7500 series, as well as the 12000 series, and AS5800.

Example D-9 illustrates a simple configuration that you can use on a router to use uRPF. It is useful to deploy this in scenarios such as leased-line aggregation routers or on dialup ports on access server gateways such as the AS5800 where maintenance of access lists could be a major headache.

Example D-9 *uRPF Configuration*

```
ip cef

Interface serial 1/1/0
  ip verify unicast reverse-path
```

NOTE   Do not use uRPF if you have an architecture that may result in asymmetrical routing—that is, a packet can be sent out from one interface to a given destination and legitimately be received from that destination on a different interface. In future releases, Cisco will fix this issue.

Steps to Take During a DDoS Attack

Even with the proactive measurements that corporate networks take to mitigate DDoS attacks, because new attacks are constantly creeping up you must be ready to provide countermeasures during a new DDoS attack. When a potential new DDoS attack occurs, you need to be able to have the assistance and cooperation from your direct uplink network providers. Talk to your uplink providers and get the appropriate contact information for people who can help you with implementing routing access control that limits the amount of bandwidth and different source addresses that are let through to your network. Also, it is important to start countermeasures as soon as possible. Begin the backtracking of packets as soon as possible, and contact your uplink providers, when traces indicate that the DoS attack traffic came over their networks. Don't rely on the source addresses, because they can be arbitrarily chosen. (Of course, if everyone implemented appropriate filtering techniques in their corporate networks, the spoofed-address DoS attacks from invalid network addresses would be greatly minimized.) The overall effort of being able to determine origins of spoofed DoS attacks depends on your quick action, because the router entries that allow traffic backtracking will expire a short time after the flood is halted.

Capturing Evidence and Contacting Law Enforcement

If possible, capture packet samples for analysis. The best place to capture packet samples is at the edges of your network where there is a demarcation from a trusted network to a less-trusted network. It is recommended that you use a SUN workstation or a Linux box on a fast Pentium machine to capture the packet sample. For capturing, use the TCP dump program (Linux or SUN) or snoop (SUN Solaris only). The command syntax is as follows:

```
tcpdump -i interface -s 1500 -w capture_file
snoop -d interface -o capture_file -s 1500
```

The maximum transmission unit (MTU) size in this example is 1500; change this parameter if the MTU is greater than 1500.

Preserve these logs as evidence for law enforcement.

If you want to involve law enforcement and you are within the United States, contact your local FBI field office. More information is available at the http://www.nipc.gov/ website. If you are located in Europe, no single point of contact exists. Contact your local law enforcement agency and ask for assistance.

Tracing

The packets in many DoS attack streams can be isolated by matching them against filtering (access list) entries. This is obviously valuable for filtering out attacks, but is also useful for characterizing unknown attacks, and for tracing "spoofed" packet streams back to their real sources, if valid source addresses are used. Access lists and access list logging are the most useful features for characterizing and tracing common attacks.

The source addresses of DoS packets are almost always set to values that have nothing to do with the attackers themselves, and are therefore of no use in identifying the attackers. The only reliable way to identify the source of an attack is to trace it back hop by hop through the network. This process involves reconfiguring routers and examining log information, and therefore requires cooperation by all network operators along the path from the attacker to the victim. Securing that cooperation usually requires the involvement of law enforcement agencies, which must also be involved if any action is to be taken against the attacker.

The tracing process for DoS floods is relatively simple. Starting at a router (call it "A") that's known to be carrying flood traffic, one identifies the router (call it "B") from which A is receiving the traffic. One then logs into B, and finds the router ("C") from which B is receiving the traffic. This continues until the ultimate source is found. Note that it is often the case that more than one upstream router propagates attack traffic, so multiple upstream sources may need to be identified.

There are several complications in this method:

- The "ultimate source" may in fact be a computer that has been compromised by the attacker, but which is actually owned and operated by another victim. In this case, tracing the DoS flood will only be the first step.

- Attackers know that they can be traced and will usually continue their attacks only for a limited time; there may not be enough time to actually trace the flood.

- Attacks may be coming from multiple sources, especially if the attacker is relatively sophisticated. It's important to try to identify as many sources as possible.

- Communication problems slow down the tracing process. Frequently one or more of the network operators involved will not have appropriately skilled staff available. It is therefore important to first identify all network ingress points associated with the attack, mitigate the attack there as seen appropriate, and then (or in parallel) contact concerned upstream service providers to begin tracing the attack further upstream.

- Legal and political concerns may make it difficult to act against attackers even if one is found.

The fact is that most efforts to trace DoS attacks fail. Because of this, many network operators will not even attempt to trace an attack unless placed under pressure. Many others trace only "severe" attacks, with differing definitions of what is "severe." Some assist with a trace only if law enforcement is involved.

Tracing with log-input

If you choose to trace an attack passing through a Cisco router, the most effective way of doing so is to construct an access list entry that matches the attack traffic, attach the **log-input** keyword to it, and apply the access list outbound on the interface through which the attack stream is being sent toward its ultimate target. The log entries produced by the access list will identify the router interface through which the traffic is arriving, and, if the interface is a multipoint connection, provide the Layer 2 address of the device from which it is being received. You can then use the Layer 2 address to identify the next router in the chain, using, for example, the **show ip arp** *mac-address* command.

SYN Flood

To trace a SYN flood, you might create an access list similar to the following:

```
access-list 169 permit tcp any any established
access-list 169 permit tcp any host victim-host log-input
access-list 169 permit ip any any
```

This access list will log all SYN packets destined for the target host, including legitimate SYNs. To identify the most likely actual path toward the attacker, examine the log entries in detail. In general, the source of the flood will likely be the source from which the largest number of matching packets are arriving. Remember that the source IP addresses themselves may mean nothing; you're looking for source interfaces and source MAC addresses. Sometimes it's possible to distinguish flood packets from legitimate packets because flood packets may have invalid source addresses; any packet whose source address is not valid is likely to be part of the flood.

Remember that the flood may be coming from multiple sources—distributed SYN floods are a major concern to many large corporations.

Smurf Attacks

To trace a Smurf attack stream, use an access list like this:

```
access-list 169 permit icmp any any echo log-input
access-list 169 permit ip any any
```

Note that the first entry doesn't restrict itself to packets destined for the reflector address. The reason for this is that most Smurf attacks use multiple reflector networks. If you're not in contact with the ultimate target, you may not know all the reflector addresses. As your trace gets closer to the source of the attack, you may begin to see echo requests going to more and more destinations; this is a good sign.

If you're dealing with a great deal of ICMP traffic, however, this may generate too much logging information for you to read easily. If this happens, you can restrict the destination address to be one of the reflectors that's known to be used. Another useful tactic is to use an entry that takes advantage of the fact that netmasks of 255.255.255.0 are very common in the Internet. And, because of the way that attackers find Smurf reflectors, the reflector addresses actually used for Smurf attacks are even more likely to match that mask. Host addresses ending in .0 or .255 are very uncommon in the Internet, so you can build a relatively specific recognizer for Smurf stimulus streams like this:

```
access-list 169 permit icmp any host known-reflector echo log-input
access-list 169 permit icmp any 0.0.0.255 255.255.255.0 echo log-input
access-list 169 permit icmp any 0.0.0.0 255.255.255.0 echo log-input
access-list 169 permit ip any any
```

With this list, you can eliminate many of the "noise" packets from your log, while still having a good chance of noticing additional stimulus streams as you get closer to the attacker.

Tracing Without log-input

The **log-input** keyword exists in Cisco IOS Software versions 11.2 and later, and in certain 11.1-based software created specifically for the service provider market. Older software does not support this keyword. If you're using a router with older software, you have three viable options:

- Create an access list without logging, but with entries that match the suspect traffic. Apply the list on the *input* side of each interface in turn and watch the counters. Look for interfaces with high match rates. This method has a very small performance overhead and is good for identifying source interfaces. Its biggest drawback is that it doesn't give link-layer source addresses and is therefore useful mostly for point-to-point lines.

- Create access list entries with the **log** keyword (as opposed to **log-input**). Once again, apply the list to the incoming side of each interface in turn. This method still doesn't give source MAC addresses, but can be useful for seeing IP data—for instance, to verify that a packet stream really is part of an attack. Performance impact can be moderate to high; newer software performs better than older software.

- Use **debug ip packet detail** to collect information about packets. This method gives MAC addresses, but can have serious performance impact. It's easy to make a mistake with this method and make a router unusable. If you use this method, make sure that the router is switching the attack traffic in fast, autonomous, or optimum mode. Use an access list to restrict debugging to only the information you really need. Log debugging information to the local log buffer, but turn off logging of debug information to Telnet sessions and to the console. If possible, arrange for someone to be physically near the router, or access the router via remote out-of-band console port access, so that it can be power cycled as necessary.

Remember that **debug ip packet** will not display information about fast-switched packets; you will need to do a **clear ip cache** to capture information. Each **clear** command will give you one or two packets of **debug** output. Also note that this option applies primarily to software-based platforms.

Issues to Look Out for with Access List Logging

Remember that the counter on an access list entry counts all matches against that entry. If you apply an access list to two interfaces, the counts you'll see will be aggregate counts.

Access list logging does not show every packet that matches an entry. Logging is rate limited to avoid CPU overload. What logging shows you is a reasonably representative sample, but not a complete packet trace. Remember that there are packets you are not seeing.

In some software versions, access list logging works only in certain switching modes. If an access list entry counts a lot of matches, but logging nothing, try to clear the route cache to force packets to be process switched. Be careful about doing this on heavily loaded routers with many interfaces; a lot of traffic can get dropped while the cache is rebuilt. Use CEF whenever possible.

Access lists and logging have a performance impact, but not a large one. Be careful on routers running at more than about 80-percent CPU load, or when applying access lists to very high-speed interfaces.

Monitoring DoS Attacks with the VIP Console and NetFlow v1.0

NOTE	The material in this section was written by Rob Thomas and is reprinted here with his permission. You can find this information and ongoing updates from Rob on the web at http://www.cymru.com/Documents/dos-and-vip.html. The document has been modified slightly here to conform to Cisco Press book presentation.

Introduction

DoS attacks have become almost ubiquitous. While these attacks are often easily and quickly mitigated through the use of filters on the border routers, these filters can prevent the proper analysis of the attack by obfuscating the attack and its data. For example, an ICMP attack against a given host, from a range of source IP addresses, can be quickly blocked by an ACL [access control list] that blocks all ICMP to the victim host. However, this leaves only ACL counters as an indicator of the duration and intensity of the attack. Further, the ACL (presuming it does not include the **log-input** keyword) does not reveal the source IP addresses of the attack. Have the source addresses changed? Are there additional hosts joining the attack? Which source is producing the bulk of the packets? These are valid questions, and the data provided by ACL counters will not provide the answers. Clearly there must be a better way. With a Cisco VIP card and NetFlow, it is possible to both block and monitor the attack.

The Cisco VIP (Versatile Interface Processor) is a "router on a card." It contains a CPU, memory, an IOS image, and all of the necessary structures to perform packet switching. Often used in the Cisco 7513 router, the VIP improves performance by removing the burden of packet processing, in many cases, from the RSP (Route Switch Processor). Because the VIP is a "router on a card" that runs an IOS image, it also has many of the same commands and data structures as the RSP.

NetFlow is a data collection method in Cisco routers that allows router support personnel to trace the flows that pass through the router. NetFlow is often used for performance and trend analysis as well as billing.

Through the use of the undocumented VIP console and NetFlow, a DoS attack may be closely monitored and analyzed. The VIP console can also be used to perform the more routine and mundane router performance checks, such as **show proc cpu**.

This method has been tested, in the lab and in production (during actual DoS attacks), on a Cisco 7513 router with the VIP2-50 line card.

Note that methods exist to secure a border router prior to an attack. DoS mitigation methods and NetFlow configuration can be reviewed in the Secure IOS Template (http://www.cymru.com/Documents/secure-ios-template.html). If BGP is used, there are additional defense methods available as documented in the Secure BGP Template (http://www.cymru.com/Documents/secure-bgp-template.html).

Caveat

The **if-con** command used to access the VIP console is *undocumented* and *unsupported* by Cisco. Cisco will not assist anyone with the use (or misuse) of this command. While this methodology has been fully "battle tested" on both lab and production equipment, and has been successfully utilized during several DoS attacks, your mileage may vary. The author is not responsible for any damage caused by the use of this command. The author also won't take undue credit for any benefit derived from the use of this command.

Credits

My thanks to the following for input, reviews, and suggestions.

- Angelito Basa
- David Bergum
- Ton Schoenmakers

The VIP Console

The syntax for the **if-con** command is **if-con** *slot*, where *slot* is the chassis slot location in which the VIP is inserted. The **if-con** command can only be run from enable mode, and there is no online help available for it. This command will prompt for the mode of access, either **console** or **debug**. Unless you have access to the IOS source code and a tolerance for sudden router reloads, you will likely not benefit from entering debug mode. Here is an example:

```
secure-router01>if-con 9
Console or Debug [C]: [PRESS ENTER HERE]
Entering CONSOLE for VIP2 R5K 9
Type "^C^C^C" or "if-quit" to end this session
[PRESS ENTER HERE]
VIP-Slot9>
```

Note the prompt: VIP-Slot9>. This indicates that the user is on the VIP console for the VIP in slot 9 of the chassis. This makes it quite clear that this is not the RSP console. To exit the VIP console, the syntax is simply **if-quit**:

```
VIP-Slot9>if-quit
Disconnecting from slot 9 CONSOLE after 00:02:12
secure-router01>
```

The prompt has returned to the expected RSP CLI prompt, and the amount of time spent in the VIP console mode is noted.

Once in the VIP console, many of the RSP CLI commands will work as expected. This, combined with NetFlow, is what makes DoS monitoring possible.

Monitoring a DoS Attack

To illustrate the benefit of the VIP console during a DoS attack, presume the following scenario: A single host, IP address 1.1.1.1, is the target of a DDoS attack. The attack consists of a high rate of small UDP packets to an unused port. The source IP addresses of the attack are far too numerous, dynamic, and disparate to block with black hole routes or selective ACLs. The target host is also suffering a performance degradation due to the rate of packets flowing to the host. It is decided to block all UDP to this host with a simple ACL:

```
access-list 105 remark
Temporary ACL to block the DDoS attack against 1.1.1.1 - 20 May 2001 robt
access-list 105 deny udp any host 1.1.1.1
access-list 105 permit ip any any
```

Due to the high rate of packets, it is decided not to log the ACL, as this might negatively impact the performance of the router and syslog server. This ACL is applied to the external interfaces of the router, which are located on the VIP in slot 9. The external interfaces are HSSI interfaces, HSSI9/0/0 and HSSI9/1/0. The victim host is saved. However, this makes tracing the attack difficult. What source IP addresses are used in the attack? Are new source addresses entering the fray? Which source addresses are the key contributors? While ACL counters can be utilized to determine if the attack is still raging, it can be quite difficult to determine the intensity of the attack, as well as the contribution to the attack of each participating host. Fortunately, the border router utilizes VIPs and NetFlow, thus the data on the attack is still available. We move to the VIP console to learn more:

```
secure-router01>if-con 9
Console or Debug [C]: [PRESS ENTER HERE]
Entering CONSOLE for VIP2 R5K 9
Type "^C^C^C" or "if-quit" to end this session
[PRESS ENTER HERE]
VIP-Slot9>
```

While ACL 105 has been applied to the two interfaces located on this VIP, the VIP actually routes any denied packets to the Null interface. NetFlow caches these flows for a short time, allowing a user to monitor them and extract copious details about them. Note that these flows are routed to the VIP Null interface, and are not sent to the RSP. Thus, the NetFlow cache on the RSP does not contain any of these flows and cannot access this data.

The **show proc cpu** command can be used to determine if the VIP is still heavily utilized by the attacking packets. To wit:

```
VIP-Slot9>sh proc cpu
CPU utilization for five seconds: 80%/80%; one minute: 80%; five minutes: 70%
[ Output truncated. ]
```

Based on the CPU utilization statistics, it is clear that the VIP is spending most of its time switching packets. The first number in the 80%/80% entry indicates the CPU utilization. The second number indicates what percentage of CPU utilization is due to network interrupts—in other words, packet processing. Next, NetFlow is queried to see what sort of traffic is hitting this VIP. This is done with the **show ip cache flow** command, with referenced points shaded:

```
secure-router01#if-con 9
Console or Debug [C]:
Entering CONSOLE for VIP2 R5K 9
Type "^C^C^C" or "if-quit" to end this session

VIP-Slot9>show ip cache flow
IP packet size distribution (489639251 total packets):
   1-32   64   96  128  160  192  224  256  288  320  352  384  416  448  480
   .000 .992 .000 .003 .000 .000 .000 .000 .000 .000 .000 .000 .000 .000 .000
    512  544  576 1024 1536 2048 2560 3072 3584 4096 4608
   .000 .000 .000 .000 .003 .000 .000 .000 .000 .000 .000
IP Flow Switching Cache, 8913408 bytes
  5088 active, 125984 inactive, 1843766371 added
  805412120 ager polls, 0 flow alloc failures
  Active flows timeout in 30 minutes
  Inactive flows timeout in 15 seconds
  last clearing of statistics never
```

Protocol	Total Flows	Flows /Sec	Packets /Flow	Bytes /Pkt	Packets /Sec	Active(Sec) /Flow	Idle(Sec) /Flow
TCP-Telnet	28084	0.0	1	45	0.0	0.1	11.7
TCP-FTP	172835	0.0	1	47	0.0	2.4	13.7
TCP-FTPD	2818	0.0	1	40	0.0	0.2	11.3
TCP-WWW	5551226	1.2	1	53	1.3	0.1	5.0
TCP-SMTP	4179	0.0	1	42	0.0	1.0	12.2
TCP-X	2594	0.0	1	40	0.0	0.6	11.2
TCP-BGP	2546	0.0	1	40	0.0	0.2	11.5
TCP-NNTP	2554	0.0	1	40	0.0	0.1	11.2
TCP-Frag	177	0.0	2	269	0.0	1.7	16.8
TCP-other	528636	0.1	1	40	65.5	0.6	35.5
UDP-DNS	11596	0.0	1	54	0.0	0.8	17.2
UDP-NTP	723	0.0	2	40	0.0	9.0	16.8
UDP-TFTP	763	0.0	3	37	0.0	10.2	16.9
UDP-Frag	25	0.0	1	40	0.0	251.4	15.0
UDP-other	169720402	39.5	1	40	46.2	0.6	11.3
ICMP	275131	0.0	10	759	0.6	7.7	14.2
IGMP	36	0.0	1789	1246	0.0	15.2	16.9
IP-other	7	0.0	19	64	0.0	18.9	17.5
Total:	176304332	41.0	2	44	113.9	0.6	11.2

```
SrcIf          SrcIPaddress    DstIf      DstIPaddress    Pr SrcP DstP   Pkts
Hs9/1/0        192.168.2.51    Null       1.1.1.1         11 04A9 0017   614K
Hs9/1/0        192.168.47.72   Null       1.1.1.1         11 05F9 0017   281K
Hs9/1/0        192.168.49.52   Null       1.1.1.1         11 08EA 0017    65K
Hs9/1/0        192.168.32.18   Null       1.1.1.1         11 08EC 0017  1463K
Hs9/1/0        192.168.208.208 Null       1.1.1.1         11 0411 0017  8351K
Hs9/1/0        192.168.77.66   Null       1.1.1.1         11 126F 0017  1763K
Hs9/1/0        192.168.184.159 Null       1.1.1.1         11 0609 0017   191K
Hs9/1/0        192.168.22.48   Null       1.1.1.1         11 0885 0017  1520K
Hs9/1/0        192.168.22.48   Null       1.1.1.1         11 0883 0017    66K
Hs9/1/0        192.168.7.44    Null       1.1.1.1         11 0F07 0017    97K
Hs9/1/0        192.168.7.44    Null       1.1.1.1         11 0F09 0017  2084K
Hs9/1/0        192.168.54.208  Null       1.1.1.1         11 040C 0017  3018K
Hs9/1/0        192.168.248.90  Null       1.1.1.1         11 0521 0017   201K
Hs9/1/0        192.168.201.177 Null       1.1.1.1         11 060C 0017   171K
Hs9/1/0        192.168.201.177 Null       1.1.1.1         11 054C 0017   107K
[ Output truncated. ]
VIP-Slot9>if-quit
Disconnecting from slot 9 CONSOLE after 00:03:25
secure-router01#
```

The host 1.1.1.1 is a web server, so web traffic (TCP-WWW) is expected. However, this site does not send or receive any UDP-based data, so the UDP-other entry is quite troublesome. We see very few entries for UDP fragments, so this does not appear to be a fragment attack. As noted in the 64 column of the IP packet size distribution stanza, 99.2% (.992) of the packets are 64 bytes in size. The Bytes/Pkt column of the UDP-other entry reveals that the packets are all 40 bytes in size (not counting IP header information). Thus, this is an attack of many small packets. This is the first indicator of woe, and requires further analysis.

The individual flows provide the granular detail necessary for proper analysis. Note that the listed IP addresses are directing a high rate of packets to the host 1.1.1.1. The entries indicate that the flows are entering the site through the HSSI 9/1/0 interface (SrcIf). None of the flows are entering through the HSSI9/0/0 interface. Due to ACL 105, the flows are sent to the Null interface (DstIf). The destination address is the target host, 1.1.1.1 (DstIPaddress).

The next three columns are all in hexadecimal. The protocol (Pr) is 11, which equates to decimal 17 – UDP. The source ports (SrcP) are varied. The destination port (DstP) is a consistent 17, which equates to decimal 23. UDP port 23 is an unused port on this (and most) system. Finally, we know the number of packets (Pkts) each host has generated in the poll interval. These are quite high.

So what have we learned? We know that this attack is UDP-based. We know that the packets are not fragments, nor do they claim to be fragments. We know that the majority of the packets are 64 bytes in length. We know of several source addresses used in the attack, and these are likely spoofed based on the address type (RFC 1918). These can be used in an effort to trace the source (see the "Tracking Spoofed IP Addresses" article [http://www.cymru.com/Documents/tracking-spoofed.html]). We know the source interface (HSSI9/1/0), which can be traced to an upstream router or provider. This greatly narrows the field when attempting to uncover the source of the attack. Since the attacks are all coming from the same interface, it is thus possible that the sources aren't so very disparate after all. Perhaps they are even in the same netblock or company! We know the intensity of the attack based on the packet counts. We can now monitor the duration and intensity of the attack.

In short, we have collected enough data to pursue the sources of the attack, involve the upstream ISPs in the pursuit, and possibly modify our ACL to accommodate the specific target ports.

Conclusion

While no tracking method is perfect, the VIP console combined with NetFlow adds another analysis tool to the network administrator's toolkit. This method provides both monitoring as well as data collection—data that can be used to track the sources of the attack and take appropriate action.

Tracking Spoofed IP Addresses Version 2.0

NOTE   The material in this section was written by Rob Thomas and is reprinted here with his permission. You can find this information and continual updates from Rob on the web at http://www.cymru.com/Documents/tracking-spoofed.html. The document has been modified slightly here to conform to Cisco Press book presentation.

Introduction

Tracking spoofed IP addresses back to the source can be quite a difficult task. For myriad reasons, such as limited router access, attacks of a short duration, and the manual nature of spoofed address tracking, finding the actual generator of the spoofed packets can be very difficult. For this reason, attackers often use the bogon address ranges, where a bogon address range is any unassigned and likely unrouted (by BGP4 in the Internet) netblock. This includes the RFC 1918 addresses as well as a collection of other address spaces, such as 1/8, 169.254/16, and the like.

However, with a certain combination of features enabled on a Cisco router, it is possible to determine the source of the spoofed packets. Further, this can be done without the laborious and CPU-intensive task of adding ACLs to filter the spoofed packets. The key features are CEF and NetFlow.

NOTE   Please be aware that router resources are never infinite. Both CEF and NetFlow require resources from the router, and therefore are not entirely immune to issues. NetFlow exports, in particular, may heavily load both the router and the export interface. Please take the time to test your configuration prior to deploying it in production.

While this document details a method for tracking the source of a DDoS attack that utilizes spoofed IP addresses, there are several other documents that detail methods of mitigating DDoS attacks. You can view my Secure IOS Template (http://www.cymru.com/Documents/secure-ios-template.html) and my Secure BGP Template (http://www.cymru.com/Documents/secure-bgp-template.html) to enhance your router and peering security. There are also several efforts currently underway to block DDoS attacks. Here are a few informative links. (Thanks to John Kristoff for passing these along.)

Pushback:

- http://www.research.att.com/~smb/talks/pushback-dodcert.pdf
- http://www.aciri.org/floyd/talks/pushback-Nov00.pdf

Traceback:

- http://www.cs.washington.edu/homes/savage/traceback.html
- http://www.research.att.com/lists/ietf-itrace/

CenterTrack:

- http://www.nanog.org/mtg-9910/ppt/robert/index.htm

Router Configuration

Most high-end Cisco routers on the Internet run either CEF or dCEF. This is because of the large performance gains to be realized with CEF, which stands for Cisco Express Forwarding. CEF has many benefits over fast switching, including a more reliable and sturdy method for building the forwarding table. CEF also offers some security benefits, such as RPF (reverse path forwarding). RPF provides a means of blocking packets that claim to originate from within your network, but present themselves on an external interface. Keep in mind that CEF can be a bit tricky to configure in an environment that has asymmetric data flows. You may wish to review the Cisco CEF white paper (http://www.cisco.com/warp/public/cc/pd/iosw/iore/tech/cef_wp.htm). CEF is, therefore, a wise choice for reasons of performance and security. CEF is enabled on a global basis with the command **ip cef**. To enable dCEF (Distributed CEF), the global command is **ip cef distributed**.

NetFlow provides a means of mapping traffic flows through a router. This can be of great use for capacity planning, statistical analysis of traffic patterns, and security reviews. Here is a sample of the output from NetFlow:

```
router1#sh ip cache flow
IP packet size distribution (11319 total packets):
   1-32   64   96  128  160  192  224  256  288  320  352  384  416  448  480
   .000 .016 .002 .002 .000 .000 .000 .000 .000 .000 .000 .000 .000 .000 .000
    512  544  576 1024 1536 2048 2560 3072 3584 4096 4608
   .000 .000 .000 .000 .976 .000 .000 .000 .000 .000 .000
IP Flow Switching Cache, 278544 bytes
  1 active, 4095 inactive, 19 added
  1909 ager polls, 0 flow alloc failures
  last clearing of statistics never
Protocol         Total    Flows   Packets Bytes  Packets Active(Sec) Idle(Sec)
--------         Flows    /Sec    /Flow   /Pkt   /Sec    /Flow       /Flow
TCP-Telnet           1    0.0       204     47   0.0      71.5         1.3
UDP-other            7    0.0         3    627   0.0       8.4        15.3
ICMP                10    0.0         5     91   0.0       4.1        15.4
Total:              18    0.0        15    103   0.0       9.5        14.6
SrcIf        SrcIPaddress    DstIf         DstIPaddress    Pr SrcP DstP  Pkts
Se1          192.168.88.5    Et0           192.168.77.2    11 0013 0007    31
```

From NetFlow, we can determine our packet distribution, protocol distribution, and current flows. Clearly this is valuable data. Enabling NetFlow is done on a per-interface basis with the command **ip route-cache flow**.

Once both CEF (or dCEF) and NetFlow are enabled on the router, we are ready to begin hunting the source of a spoofed IP address attack. It is recommended that the routers run Cisco IOS 12.0 or better.

Test Topology

In the example scenario, a malicious user on the host sweatpants, IP address 192.168.97.2/24, wishes to flood the host spanky, IP address 192.168.77.2/24, with copious amounts of bogus UDP traffic. To avoid being caught, the miscreant on sweatpants has decided to spoof his address to be 96.170.4.8. The miscreant knows that the entire 96/8 netblock is unassigned, and therefore any packets destined for this network will not arrive at an actual site. The spoofed packets are all destined for UDP port 7, the echo port. The source port is UDP port 19, the chargen port.

The network topology is displayed in Figure D-3.

Figure D-3 *Spoofed Traffic Attack Network Topology*

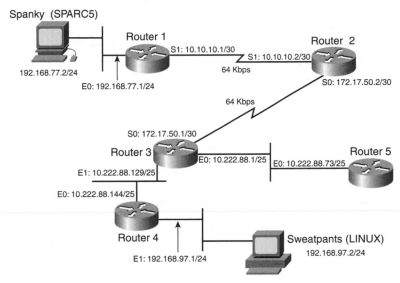

The routing is configured thusly:

```
Spanky
    Default route, gateway 192.168.77.1 (router1)
Router 1
    Default route, gateway 10.10.10.2 (router2)
Router 2
    Static route 192.168.77.0/24, gateway 10.10.10.1 (router1)
    Static route 192.168.97.0/24, gateway 172.17.50.1 (router3)
Router 3
    Default route, gateway 172.17.50.2 (router2)
    Static route 192.168.97.0/24, gateway 10.222.88.144 (router4)
Router 4
    Default route, gateway 10.222.88.129 (router3)
Router 5
    Default route, gateway 10.222.88.1 (router3)
Sweatpants
    Default route, gateway 192.168.97.1 (router4)
```

While static routing was used for this experiment, the experiment is not fundamentally changed by the use of a dynamic routing protocol, such as OSPF [Open Shortest Path First] or EIGRP [Enhanced Interior Gateway Routing Protocol]. While the responses to the spoofed address from spanky might be dropped sooner in the path, the result is the same—the spoofed packets never make it back to sweatpants, the source of the malevolent data stream. It is not uncommon to find the use of default routes for networks that are singly attached to the Internet.

The Game Begins

Using a packet generator, the attack is launched from sweatpants against spanky. A steady
stream of spoofed packets now present themselves on the network interface of Spanky. Due to
the interrupt saturation and higher than normal CPU load, the attack is detected by the system
administrator. The use of the snoop tool (Solaris-specific packet sniffer) determines the source
IP of the attack, 96.170.4.8. The network and security teams are alerted. After the source IP
address (96.170.4.8) and source port (UDP 19) are noted from the output of snoop, the first step
is to log in to the border router, router1, and take a look.

In this topology, it may seem quite obvious that the source of the spoofed packets, from the
perspective of router1, must be the serial interface leading to router2. However, it is wise to
validate this assumption to ensure that the source of the spoofed attack is not a host within the
same subnet as Spanky. First, the NetFlow cache is queried thusly:

```
router1#sh ip cache flow | include 96.170
Se1             96.170.4.8       Et0              192.168.77.2    11 0013 0007    159
```

Here we see that the source interface of the flow, which is listed in column one, is Serial1. So
it has been determined that the source is somewhere beyond the border router. Next, CEF is
queried. CEF inserts all active sources, on a per-interface basis, in its tables:

```
router1#sh ip cef se1
Prefix              Next Hop            Interface
0.0.0.0/0           10.10.10.2          Serial1
10.10.10.0/30       attached            Serial1
```

Here it is seen that the only next hop, according to the CEF cache, is 10.10.10.2. Consulting the
topology above, it is noted that the next-hop IP address is router2. The search moves one hop
further, to router2.

The process is repeated on router2. First, a check of the NetFlow cache:

```
router2#sh ip cache flow | include 96.170
Se0             96.170.4.8       Se1              192.168.77.2    11 0013 0007    299
```

The source interface of the flow is Serial0. Now for a check of the CEF tables:

```
router2#sh ip cef se0
Prefix              Next Hop            Interface
172.17.50.0/30      attached            Serial0
192.168.97.0/24     172.17.50.1         Serial0
```

Once again, the topology is consulted and it is determined that the next hop listed in the CEF
tables, 172.17.50.1, is router3.

On router3, the NetFlow tables are examined:

```
router3#sh ip cache flow | include 96.170
Et1             96.170.4.8       Se0              192.168.77.2    11 0013 0007    3235
```

Ah, perhaps the end is near! The source interface for the flow is Ethernet1. Is the source station directly attached to this router? A check of the CEF tables reveals:

```
router3#sh ip cef et1
Prefix              Next Hop            Interface
10.222.88.128/25    attached            Ethernet1
10.222.88.144/32    10.222.88.144       Ethernet1
192.168.97.0/24     10.222.88.144       Ethernet1
10.222.88.73/32     10.222.88.73        Ethernet1
```

This presents a bit of a conundrum; there are two possible sources. It may be necessary to check both IP addresses. First, a check of router5, 10.222.88.73:

```
router5#sh ip cache flow | include 96.170
router5#
```

This command returns nothing. After verifying that the attack is still underway, it is obvious that the attacker's data flow does not pass through this router. Moving on to router4 reveals:

```
router4#sh ip cache flow | include 96.170
Et1         96.170.4.8      Et0         192.168.77.2    11 0013 0007  6673
```

Ah, this looks promising. A quick check of the CEF tables finds:

```
router4#sh ip cef et1
Prefix              Next Hop            Interface
192.168.97.0/24     attached            Ethernet1
192.168.97.2/32     192.168.97.2        Ethernet1
```

So the only active IP address is 192.168.97.2. Since a quick check of either the MAC address (with **sh arp**) or other means reveals that this is not a Cisco router, this IP address begins to look more suspect. At this point, network sniffing can be performed to verify that the source IP of the attack, 96.170.4.8, is tied to the MAC address of 192.168.97.2. The source of the spoofed IP addresses has been found.

Limitations

While this method is fast and presents very little impact on the routers, it is not without certain limitations.

First, NetFlow must be running on the interfaces. NetFlow can be configured, in real time, during an attack. The NetFlow data is the key to this method.

Second, router access must be available. This can be a hurdle both technically (no access to the routers) and politically (the routers are owned by another entity). However, this can be a coordinated effort, with multiple teams handing off the tracing as each autonomous system boundary is crossed. If the trace is done completely within a single AS (autonomous system), however, many of the political and technical issues may not exist.

Third, the attack must be of a duration that allows for a trace. Short, bursty attacks may not allow for a full trace. While a partial trace may help to narrow the scope of the search, it will not find the culprit.

Fourth, this method is obviously limited to the Cisco IOS platform. Other platforms, such as a Check Point FireWall-1 firewall, will provide similar tracing capabilities through the rule base or tools such as tcpdump, snoop, and iptrace. However, some platforms may provide no trace method at all.

Conclusion

Uncovering the source of a spoofed IP attack can assure that the attacking host is removed as a threat to all networks. With a few relatively simple and quick steps, the source of such an attack can be revealed.

Additional DOS Information

Many companies are starting to create tools to help network operators handle DoS attacks. A rather clueful company is Arbor Networks, which provides tools to immediately identify, characterize, and trace back attacks to the network ingress. Additionally, incident data is automatically recorded for later analysis or law enforcement correspondence. You can find more information at http://www.arbor.net.

For more detailed information about DoS attacks themselves, refer to the following DoS attack resource pages:

- http://www.denialinfo.com/
- http://www.pentics.net/

Answers to Review Questions

Chapter 1

1 Cryptography is the basic building block that enables which of the following?

A Authentication

B Integrity

C Confidentiality

D All of the above

A, B, and C. Cryptography is the basic building block that enables authentication, integrity, and confidentiality. Most current authentication, integrity, and confidentiality technologies are derived from the following three cryptographic functions: symmetric encryption, asymmetric encryption, and one-way hash functions.

2 True or false: The best security algorithms are designed in secret.

False. Most good security algorithms undergo years of scrutiny by the world's best cryptographers, who validate the strength of the algorithm.

3 What is a brute-force attack?

In a brute-force attack, you apply all combinations of a key to the algorithm until you succeed in deciphering the message.

4 Name three fundamental cryptographic functions.

The three fundamental cryptographic functions are as follows:

— Symmetric key encryption

— Asymmetric key encryption

— Hash functions

5 What is the inherent weakness in the ECB chaining mechanism?

The ECB chaining mechanism encodes each 64-bit block independently—but uses the same key. An avid snooper interested only in changes in information and not the exact content can easily exploit this weakness.

6 Which of the following algorithms is specified as the symmetric key encryption AES standard?

A 3DES

B RC4

C Rijndael

D IDEA

C. The Rijndael algorithm became the symmetric key encryption AES standard.

7 What are three challenges with secret key encryption?

The three challenges with secret key encryption are as follows:

— Changing the secret keys frequently to avoid the risk of compromising the keys

— Securely generating the secret keys

— Securely distributing the secret keys

8 What is another term for asymmetric encryption?

Public-key encryption is another term for asymmetric encryption.

9 Name three common uses of asymmetric encryption algorithms.

The following are common uses of asymmetric encryption algorithms:

— Data integrity

— Data confidentiality

— Sender nonrepudiation

— Sender authentication

10 True or false: The crucial aspect of asymmetric encryption is that the public key needs to be kept confidential.

False. For asymmetric encryption algorithms, it is crucial that the private key be kept private.

11 Which of the following properties is *not* suitable for a hash function?

A It must be random—or give the appearance of randomness.

B It must be unique.

C It must be reversible.

D It must be consistent.

C. It must be one way (irreversible); that is, if you are given the output, it must be extremely difficult, if not impossible, to ascertain the input message.

12   What is a digital signature?

A digital signature is an encrypted message digest that is appended to a document.

13   How do keyed hash functions and digital signatures differ?

A keyed hash function uses a shared secret key and a message as input to the hash function and produces a message digest. A digital signature is an encrypted message digest.

14   A centralized key distribution model relies on what entity to issue keys?

A centralized key distribution model relies on a trusted third party, sometimes referred to as a KDC (key distribution center), to issue keys.

15   Which algorithm is commonly used to create secret session keys in a distributed manner?

Diffie-Hellman is the algorithm commonly used to create secret session keys in a distributed manner.

16   Name 5 elements commonly found in an X.509 certificate.

The following are elements commonly found in an X.509 certificate:

— Version number

— Serial number of certificate

— Issuer algorithm information

— Issuer of certificate

— Valid to/from date

— Public key algorithm information of the subject of the certificate

— Digital signature of the issuing authority

Chapter 2

1   What three concepts are encompassed in the term *identity*? Give a brief definition of each.

The three concepts encompassed in the term identity are authentication, authorization, and access control. Authentication is the process of validating the claimed identity of an end user or a device (such as clients, servers, switches, routers, firewalls, and so on). Authorization is the process of granting access rights to a user, groups of users, or specified system. Access control is limiting the flow of information from the resources of a system to only the authorized persons or systems in the network.

2 True or false: Passwords can never be compromised if they are easy to guess, if they are not changed often enough, and if they are transmitted in cleartext across a network.

False. Passwords can easily be compromised if they are easy to guess, if they are not changed often enough, and if they are transmitted in cleartext across a network.

3 Token password authentication schemes are based on the following:

A PAP authentication

B Publicly available encrypted hash function

C Challenge-response and time-synchronous authentication

D All of the above

C. Token password authentication schemes are based on one of two alternative schemes: challenge-response and time-synchronous authentication.

4 True or false: The PPP protocol requires that authentication be used to authenticate PPP peers before proceeding to the network layer protocol phase.

False. After the link has been established, PPP provides for an optional authentication phase before proceeding to the network layer protocol phase.

5 What is EAP?

EAP is a general protocol for PPP authentication that supports multiple authentication mechanisms. It provides its own support for duplicate elimination and retransmission.

6 Which of the following is *not* true?

A TACACS+ uses TCP port 49 for its transport.

B TACACS+ uses fixed-length and fixed-content authentication exchanges.

C In TACACS+, authorization does not merely provide yes or no answers—it may also customize the service for the particular user.

D Transactions between the TACACS+ client and TACACS+ server are authenticated through the use of a shared secret, which is never sent over the network.

B. TACACS+ allows for arbitrary length and content authentication exchanges.

7 Which transport protocol is used by RADIUS?

RADIUS uses UDP as its transport. Although some early implementations of RADIUS used port 1645, the official UDP port to use is 1812.

8 True or false: Using RADIUS, communication between the client and server is in the clear except for the user passwords, which are encrypted.

True. Using RADIUS communication between the client and server is in the clear except for the user passwords, which are encrypted.

9 Fill in the blank. Kerberos is based on the concept of a trusted third party that performs secure verification of users and services. In the Kerberos protocol, this trusted third party is called the _____, sometimes also called the authentication server.

Kerberos is based on the concept of a trusted third party that performs secure verification of users and services. In the Kerberos protocol, this trusted third party is called the Key Distribution Center (KDC), sometimes also called the authentication server.

10 What are the three main entities defined in the IEEE 802.1x standard?

The three main entities defined in the 802.1x standard are the supplicant, authenitcator, and authentication server. Supplicant refers to a device that needs access to a LAN (for example, a laptop or workstation). Authenticator refers to a device that is responsible for initiating the authentication process and subsequently acts as a relay between the actual authentication server and the supplicant. Authentication server refers to a device that is responsible for performing the actual authentication and authorization on behalf of the authenticator. It contains profile information for all the users on the network and can use that information to authenticate and authorize users to connect to the ports on the authenticator.

11 What are four characteristics of S/MIME that make it a very flexible security solution for a variety of messaging applications?

Any four of the following:

— **Multiple signers**—Because CMS supports multiple signatures on a single message, S/MIME supports having a message signed by multiple senders.

— **Multiple recipients**—It is possible to send the same message securely to multiple recipients by encrypting the message with a single CEK and then encrypting the CEK individually for each recipient.

— **Receipt**—The capability to provide a receipt allows a sender to be sure that the recipient received a message and that it wasn't altered in transit. However, the recipient is not required to generate a receipt and, therefore, lack of a receipt does not indicate that the recipient did not receive the message.

— **Forwarding**—Messages can be forwarded from one recipient to another while leaving the message signature intact and verifiable. This is possible because S/MIME uses a digital signature that signs the whole message.

— **Transport independence**—S/MIME provides end-to-end security at the application layer and is independent of any underlying transport. Therefore, in IP networks it can run over either TCP or UDP.

12   Which of the following is *not* part of the SSL/TLS specification?

   A   Handshake protocol

   B   Hello protocol

   C   Alert protocol

   D   Record protocol

B. Hello protocol. The SSL protocol consisting of five protocols: the record protocol, which provides the envelope and security services for the four content layer protocols (handshake, alert, change cipher spec, and application).

13   What transport protocol is commonly used for SSL? Why?

SSL assumes that the underlying packet delivery mechanism is reliable and, although in theory there are a number of transport protocols that could provide this service, SSL nearly always uses TCP as its transport.

14   What is the mechanism in IPsec ESP whereby authentication but not confidentiality services is provided?

ESP NULL encryption is used for providing only authentication services and not confidentiality.

15   What are five things included as part of an IPsec security association (SA)?

An IPsec security association includes the following:

   — The ESP encryption algorithm and key(s)

   — The AH authentication algorithm and key

   — A shared session key

   — Mode, tunnel, or transport

   — SA source address

   — SA lifetime

16   In IPsec AH transport mode, which fields in the IP header are not protected?

In the case of AH in transport mode, all upper-layer information is protected, and all fields in the IPv4 header excluding the fields that are typically modified in transit. The fields of the IPv4 header that are *not* included are, therefore, ToS, TTL, Header Checksum, Offset, and Flags.

17 Which of the following statements is *not* true?

   A All ISAKMP messages are carried in a UDP packet with destination port number 500.

   B Through the use of main mode or aggressive mode, an IKE SA is created.

   C Either peer can initiate the IKE phase 2 exchange.

   D IKE supports only the preshared key authentication mechanism to perform the authenticated DH exchange.

   D. IKE supports multiple mechanisms to perform the authenticated DH exchange: preshared keys, public key cryptography, and digital signature.

18 Which of the following IKE extensions allows an IP address to be assigned to a remote client?

   A Mode configuration and DHCP configuration

   B xauth and mode configuration

   C PIC and xauth

   D DHCP configuration and PIC

   a. Mode configuration (mode config) and DHCP configuration are IKE extensions that allow an IP address to be assigned to a remote client.

19 True or false: For L2TP, the control connection is the initial connection that must be established between a LAC and LNS before sessions can be brought up.

   True. For L2TP, the control connection is the initial connection that must be established between a LAC and LNS before sessions can be brought up.

20 A PKI comprises of which five types of components?

   A PKI of the following five types of components:

   — Certification authorities (CAs) that issue and revoke certificates

   — Organizational registration authorities (ORAs) that vouch for the binding between public keys, certificate holder identities, and other attributes

   — Certificate holders that are issued certificates and that can sign digital documents

   — Clients that validate digital signatures and their certification paths from a known public key of a trusted CA

   — Repositories that store and make available certificates and certificate revocation lists (CRLs)

21 What are the three main fields in an X.509v3 certificate? Give a brief description of each field.

The three main fields in an X.509v3 certificate are the body, the signature algorithm, and the signature. The body of the certificate contains the version number, the serial number, the names of the issuer and subject, a public key associated with the subject, and an expiration date (not before and not after a specified time/date); some certificate bodies contain extensions, which are optional unique identifier fields that associate additional attributes with users or public keys. The signature algorithm is the algorithm used by the CA to sign the certificate. The signature is created by applying the certificate body as input to a one-way hash function. The output value is encrypted with the CA's private key to form the signature value.

Chapter 3

1 What is the primary reason for classifying VPNs into access VPNs, intranet VPNs, and extranet VPNs?

The primary reason for the three distinct classifications is due to security policy variations. A good security policy will detail corporate infrastructure and information authentication mechanisms and access privileges, and in many instances these will vary depending on how the corporate resources are accessed.

2 Which of the following is *not* a link-layer or network layer VPN tunneling solution?

A IPsec

B L2TP

C SSL/TLS

D PPTP

C. SSL/TLS is an application layer protocol that secures communications end to end for specific applications and is sometimes used in conjunction with L2TP, PPTP, or IPsec tunneling protocols.

3 What is NAT and why is it used?

Network Address Translation (NAT) is often used in environments that have private IP address space as opposed to a globally unique IP address. NAT will translate the unregistered IP addresses into legal IP addresses that are routable in the outside public network.

4 When creating an L2TP/IPsec VPN, what is the problem if user authentication is used for PPP but device authentication is used for IPsec?

In an L2TP/IPsec VPN, if PPP uses user authentication, but IPsec uses device authentication, only the device is authenticated on a per-packet basis and there is no way to enforce traffic segregation. When an L2TP/IPsec tunnel is established, any

user on a multi-user machine will be able to send traffic down the tunnel. However, if the IPsec negotiation also includes user authentication, the keys that are derived to protect the subsequent L2TP/IPsec traffic will ensure that users are implicitly authenticated on a per-packet basis.

5 In a wireless LAN, what mechanism is used to solve the hidden-node problem?

In a wireless LAN, the hidden-node problem is solved by the use of the optional RTS/CTS (Request To Send / Clear To Send) protocol, which allows an access point to control use of the medium. For example, if client A is using RTS/CTS, it first sends an RTS frame to the access point before sending a data packet. The access point will then respond with a CTS frame indicating that client A can transmit its packet. The CTS frame is heard by both client B and C and contains a duration field for which these clients will hold off transmitting their respective packets. This avoids collisions between hidden nodes.

6 True of false: When configuring a wireless access point (AP) with a unique SSID, it provides a good security measure even if the SSID is broadcast out to the rest of the wireless LAN.

False. A unique SSID provides only minimal security functionality for accessing an AP; the security is compromised if the AP is configured to "broadcast" its SSID. When this broadcast feature is enabled, any client computer that is not configured with a specific SSID is allowed to receive the SSID and access the AP. In addition, because users typically configure their own client systems with the appropriate SSIDs, they are widely known and easily shared.

7 Why should SSIDs and MAC address filtering be configured in wireless devices even though they offer limited security functionality?

Many small networks, especially home-office networks, should configure MAC address filtering and SSIDs. Even though it offers only limited security, it will mitigate a casual rogue wireless client from accessing your wireless network.

8 Which of the following is not a true statement regarding the original WEP encryption specification?

A WEP uses the RC4 encryption algorithm.

B WEP use different keys to encrypt and decrypt data

C WEP uses a 24-bit initialization vector (IV), which is concatenated with the symmetric key before generating the stream ciphertext.

D WEP can use variable-length keys.

B. Because WEP uses RC4, which is a symmetric keystream cipher, the same key is used to encrypt and decrypt the data.

9 What protocol is being standardized as a replacement for WEP?

The Temporal Key Integrity Protocol (TKIP), being standardized in 802.11i, provides a replacement technology for WEP security and improves upon some of the current WEP problems. TKIP will allow existing hardware to operate with only a firmware upgrade and should be backward compatible with hardware that still uses WEP. TKIP requires dynamic keying using a key management protocol. It has three components: per-packet key mixing, extended IV and sequencing rules, and a message integrity check (MIC).

10 In the context of an 802.11 wireless network, which protocol requires a wireless client to authenticate before gaining access to the wireless network through an associated AP?

In the context of an 802.11 wireless network, 802.1X/EAP requires that a wireless client that associates with an access point cannot gain access to the network until the user is appropriately authenticated. After association, the client and a RADIUS server exchange EAP messages to perform mutual authentication, with the client verifying the RADIUS server credentials and vice versa. An EAP supplicant is used on the client machine to obtain the user credentials, which can be in the form of a username/password or digital certificate. Upon successful client and server mutual authentication, the RADIUS server and client derive a client-specific WEP key to be used by the client for the current logon session. User passwords and session keys are never transmitted in the clear, over the wireless link.

11 Using the protected EAP (PEAP) protocol, how are clients and servers authenticated?

When using protected EAP (PEAP), server-side authentication is accomplished by using digital certificates, although client-side authentication can support varying EAP-encapsulated methods and is accomplished within a protected TLS tunnel.

12 Which ITU-T standard specifies the security services for H.323 networks?

The ITU-T recommendation H.235 defines security and encryption for H.232 and H.245 multimedia terminals. It includes the capability to negotiate services and functionality in a generic manner, and to be selective concerning cryptographic techniques and capabilities used. There are no specifically mandated algorithms; however, it is strongly suggested that endpoints support as many of the applicable algorithms as possible to achieve interoperability.

13 True or false: H.225 allows for the negotiation of security algorithms and keys to secure the H.225 call setup channel.

False. Because the H.225 messages are the first exchanged when establishing H.323 communications, there can be no security negotiations "in band" for H.225, and both parties must know a priori that they are using a particular security mode. For H.225 call setup, the TCP port 1300 is used for TLS secured communications.

14 What are the three subscription-based authentication mechanisms defined in ITU-T recommendation H.235?

The ITU-T recommendation H.235 defines three mechanisms for subscription-based authentication: password-based with symmetric encryption, password-based with hashing, and certificate-based with signatures.

15 Which of the following is *not* a true statement regarding SIP authentication using HTTP digest authentication?

A The HTTP digest authentication technique requires shared secrets between the client and the server.

B The HTTP digest authentication is based on a cryptographic hash that includes the username, password, and a challenge provided by the server.

C The HTTP digest authentication can be used to authenticated SIP user agents to a SIP proxy server as well as the SIP proxy server to the SIP user agent.

D RADIUS cannot be used with HTTP digest authentication.

D. Some extensions to RADIUS have been made to support the HTTP digest authentication so that it can be used with SIP. The user agents authenticate themselves with the proxy by using the HTTP digest authorization header. The proxy, acting as a RADIUS client, sends the username, nonce, and other information required to compute the digest authentication hash value, except the password, along with the hash to the RADIUS server. The server retrieves the password from its database and computes the hash from the password and other values it received. If the computed hash matches the received hash, the client can be authorized.

16 Why is it problematic to encrypt SIP request and response messages end-to-end?

SIP requests and responses cannot be naively encrypted end-to-end in their entirety because some message fields need to be visible to proxies in most network architectures so that SIP requests are routed correctly. Note that proxy servers need to modify some features of messages as well for SIP to function. Proxy servers must therefore be trusted, to some degree, by SIP UAs. To this purpose, transport and/or network layer security mechanisms for SIP are recommended, which encrypt the entire SIP requests or responses on the wire on a hop-by-hop basis, and that allow endpoints to verify the identity of proxy servers to whom they send requests.

Chapter 4

1   What are the four primary mechanisms routers use to create and modify their routing tables?

The four primary mechanisms routers use to create and modify their routing tables are:

- — Direct connections
- — Static routing
- — Dynamic routing
- — Default routes

2   How do you define an interior gateway protocol?

An interior gateway protocol is the routing protocol used within an autonomous system, i.e. within a single administrative control.

3   Name four commonly used interior gateway protocols.

The four commonly used interior gateway protocols are RIP, EIGRP, OSPF, and IS-IS.

4   What are the two basic approaches for protecting routing table integrity?

The two basic approaches for protecting routing table integrity are to use static routes or neighbor authentication.

5   Describe the general steps used for plaintext neighbor authentication.

For plaintext neighbor authentication, the following steps are carried out:

1. A router sends a routing update with a key and the corresponding key number to the neighbor router. For protocols that can have only one key, the key number is always 0.

2. The receiving (neighbor) router checks the received key against the same key stored in its own memory.

3. If the two keys match, the receiving router accepts the routing update and incorporates the route information into its routing tables.If the two keys do not match, the routing update is rejected.

6   True or false: For keyed MD5 neighbor authentication, a digital signature is appended to the routing updates.

False. The message digest (or hash) is appended to the routing update. A digital signature is an encrypted hash, which is not used in keyed MD5 neighbor authentication algorithms at this time.

7 What field in the RIPv2 packet indicates the use of authentication?

The Address Family Identifier is set to 0xFFFF.

8 How many authentication schemes does EIGRP support?

EIGRP supports only the keyed MD5 authentication algorithm.

9 What authentication mechanisms are supported in the OSPFv2 protocol?

OSPFv2 specifies three types of authentication: null authentication, simple password authentication, and cryptographic authentication.

10 True or false: All OSPFv3 packets must be authenticated using either AH or ESP in tunnel mode.

False. The OSPFv3 packets require AH or ESP in transport mode.

11 Why is simple password authentication not very secure?

Simple password authentication is vulnerable to passive attacks where anyone with physical access to the network can learn the password and compromise the security of the routing domain.

12 True or false: In the IS-IS protocol, the use of authentication is mandatory.

False. Use of the Authentication field is optional. Routers are not required to be able to interpret authentication information.

13 What is used as input to the BGP-4 MD5 authentication algorithm?

The following are used as input to the BGP-4 MD5 authentication algorithm:

— The TCP pseudo-header (in the order source IP address, destination IP address, zero-padded protocol number, and segment length)

— The TCP header, excluding options, and assuming a checksum of zero

— The TCP segment data (if any)

— An independently specified key or password, known to both BGP speakers and presumably connection specific

14 Why are there no confidentiality mechanisms for routing security?

At the time of this writing, privacy has not been a major concern in routing infrastructures. It is more important to receive routing updates from valid neighbors than to ensure that the valid neighbor has sent the correct routes. The latter is a problem that is still being investigated.

Chapter 5

1 What are three basic categories of threats?

Three basic categories of threats are unauthorized access, impersonation, and denial-of-service attacks.

2 True or false: Network reconnaissance attempts can be completely avoided with appropriate security measures in place.

False. Network reconnaissance cannot be prevented entirely. If ICMP echo and echo-reply is turned off on edge routers, for example, ping sweeps can be stopped, but at the expense of network diagnostic data. However, port scans can easily be run without full ping sweeps; they just take longer because they need to scan IP addresses that might not be live. Intrusion detection systems at the network and host levels can usually notify an administrator when a reconnaissance attack is underway. This enables the administrator to better prepare for the coming attack or to notify the ISP that is hosting the system that is launching the reconnaissance probe.

3 What technique is commonly used to gain unauthorized access to networks that use modems?

War dialing is a technique that involves the exploitation of an organization's telephone, dial, and PBX systems to penetrate internal network and computing resources. All the attacker has to do is find a user within the organization with an open connection through a modem unknown to the IT staff or a modem that has minimal or, at worst, no security services enabled.

4 True or false: For wireless networks, it doesn't make sense to enable WEP because it is inherently insecure.

False. It still makes sense to enable WEP and to ensure that all defaults have been changed so that some reasonable authentication and confidentiality services are being used.

5 What is a man-in-the-middle attack?

A man-in-the-middle attacks is where an intruder is able to intercept traffic and can as a result hijack an existing session, alter the transmitted data, or inject bogus traffic into the network.

6 Which of the following are well-known denial-of-service attacks?

A Smurf, TCP SYN, and Stacheldraht

B Land.c, Ping of Death, and wizard.c

C Both A and B

D Neither A nor B

A. Some well-known DoS attacks include TCP SYN, Ping of Death, Land.c, teardrop.c, Smurf, and Fraggle. In addition, the more common DDoS attacks include Stacheldraht, Trinoo, and TFN. There is no known attack called wizard.c.

7 What are four common motivations for a computer network attack?

Common motivations for a computer network attack are as follows:

— **Greed**—The intruder is hired by someone to break into a corporate network to steal or alter information for the exchange of large sums of money.

— **Prank**—The intruder is bored and computer savvy and tries to gain access to any interesting sites.

— **Notoriety**—The intruder is very computer savvy and tries to break into known hard-to-penetrate areas to prove his competence. Success in an attack can then gain the intruder the respect and acceptance of his peers.

— **Revenge**—The intruder has been laid off, fired, demoted, or in some way treated unfairly. The more common of these kinds of attacks result in damaging valuable information or causing disruption of services.

— **Ignorance**—The intruder is learning about computers and networking and stumbles on some weakness, possibly causing harm by destroying data or performing an illegal act.

8 What is a TCP SYN attack?

The TCP SYN attack exploits the three-way handshake design for a TCP connection establishment by having an attacking source host generate TCP SYN packets with random source addresses toward a victim host. The victim destination host sends a SYN/ACK back to the random source address and adds an entry to the connection queue. Because the SYN/ACK is destined for an incorrect or nonexistent host, the last part of the three-way handshake is never completed, and the entry remains in the connection queue until a timer expires—typically in about 1 minute. By generating phony TCP SYN packets from random IP addresses at a rapid rate, an intruder can fill up the connection queue and deny TCP services (such as e-mail, file transfer, or WWW service) to legitimate users.

9 What are two common DoS attacks that exploit fragmentation vulnerabilities?

Ping of Death and teardrop.c are two common DoS attacks that exploit fragmentation vulnerabilities.

10 True or false: To effectively stop invalid DNS zone transfers but still allow valid DNS traffic, it is best to block traffic to destination port 53 only and allow traffic to source port 53 that already has an established connection.

True. In addition, newer releases of BIND have configurable parameters that should be used to enable an administrator to specify IP numbers or subnets authorized to do zone transfers.

11 What enhancement does passive mode FTP offer over the original FTP?

With passive mode FTP, the client initiates both the control connection and the data connection so that a packet-filtering firewall can provide some protection and not block data transfers.

12 Why is MAC address filtering in wireless LANs not an effective security control?

All MAC addresses are sent in the clear, and there exist programs such as Network Stumbler that a malicious user can use to eavesdrop on a wireless network and to obtain valid MAC addresses. The eavesdropper could then use a wireless LAN card that can be loaded with firmware to define its MAC address. Using this spoofed MAC address, the malicious user can attempt to inject network traffic or spoof legitimate users.

13 True or false: In WEP, the initialization vector is encrypted, so anyone eavesdropping on a wireless LAN cannot see what it is.

False. In WEP, the IV is transmitted as plaintext and placed in the 802.11 header; anyone eavesdropping on a wireless LAN can see it.

14 What is the main issue today that makes Voice over IP networks insecure?

The main issue with voice networks today is that they are generally wide open and require little or no authentication to gain access.

Chapter 6

1 What are three characteristics of a good security policy?

The following are characteristics of a good security policy:

— It must be capable of being implemented technically.

— It must be capable of being implemented organizationally.

— It must be enforceable with security tools where appropriate and with sanctions where prevention is not technically feasible.

— It must clearly define the areas of responsibility for the users, administrators, and management.

— It must be flexible and adaptable to changing environments.

2 What is the purpose of an anonymous user survey?

The purpose of an anonymous user survey is to gather information about a corporate security policy.

3 Which of the following form part of a risk assessment?

A Critical asset identification

B Asset valuation

C Asset vulnerability assessment

D All of the above

D. All of the above. A risk assessment should include identifying critical assets, providing a value to the assets, and determining the possible threats to the assets and the likelihood that the asset is vulnerable to a given threat.

4 What are the two ways of evaluating risk?

The two ways of evaluating risk are quantitative and qualitative. Quantitative risk evaluation uses empirical data and known probabilities and statistics. Qualitative risk analysis uses an intuitive assessment.

5 What are the five elements of a security architecture?

The five elements of a security architecture are identity, integrity, confidentiality, availability, and audit.

6 Can a weak algorithm and short key stop attackers from gaining access to valued information?

Yes, although a stronger algorithm and a longer key would take more sophisticated machines and more time to break any encryption scheme.

7 Why must identity mechanisms be carefully deployed?

Identity mechanisms must be carefully deployed because even the most careful of security policies can be circumvented if the implementations are hard to use.

8 Define confidentiality.

Confidentiality is the element of the security architecture that ensures that data communication is kept private between the sender and receiver of information.

9 When logging networking events, should you log everything?

No. If you log too much data, some problems or potential intrusions can be overlooked. It is best to carefully select the events to be logged.

Chapter 7

1   Why do you want physical security controls?

Physical security controls are needed to ensure that no intruder is able to eavesdrop on the data traversing the network and that all critical systems have a high degree of availability.

2   What are two factors to consider for physical device security?

Identifying the location of the device, limiting physical access, and having appropriate environmental safeguards in place are factors to consider for physical device security.

3   Is traffic filtering an adequate security control?

No. Traffic filtering provides some measure of security, but it is easy to spoof IP addresses and other filtering parameters. Filtering should be used in conjunction with other security measures.

4   What are 5 characteristics of choosing a good password?

Answers can include any of the following:

- — Do not use your logon name in any form (as-is, reversed, capitalized, doubled, and so on).
- — Do not use your first, middle, or last (current or former) name in any form.
- — Do not use any of your immediate family's names (spouse, offspring, parents, pets, and so on).
- — Do not use other information easily obtained about you, including license plate numbers, telephone numbers, social security numbers, the brand of automobile you drive, the name of the street you live on, and so on.
- — Do not use a password of all digits or of all the same letter. These types of passwords significantly decrease the search time for a cracker.
- — Do not use a word contained in any English or foreign language dictionaries, spelling lists, or other lists of words.
- — Do not use a password with fewer than six characters.
- — Use a password with mixed-case alphabetics, if possible. (Some systems use passwords that are case sensitive.)
- — Use a password that includes some nonalphabetic characters, such as digits or punctuation marks.
- — Use a password that is easy to remember, because you don't want to write it down.
- — Use a password you can type quickly without having to look at the keyboard.

5 Why should security mechanisms not be overly complex?

If security mechanisms are overly complex, users will find a way to circumvent the security practices, thereby creating more vulnerabilities. The most common problem is too many complex passwords, which users will write down to remember. Any password that is written down is no longer secure.

6 What is a common way to ensure infrastructure integrity?

A common way to ensure infrastructure integrity is with firewalls.

7 Name and describe the three common classifications of firewalls.

The three common classifications of firewalls are as follows:

— **Packet filtering**—These firewalls rely solely on the TCP, UDP, ICMP, and IP headers of individual packets to permit or deny traffic. The packet filter looks at a combination of traffic direction (inbound or outbound), IP source and destination address, and TCP or UDP source and destination port numbers.

— **Circuit filtering**—These firewalls control access by keeping state information and reconstructing the flow of data associated with the traffic. A circuit filter won't pass a packet from one side to the other unless it is part of an established connection.

— **Application gateway**—These firewalls process messages specific to particular IP applications. These gateways are tailored to specific protocols and cannot easily protect traffic using newer protocols.

8 What needs to be combined with checksums to protect against replay attacks?

When checksums are combined with a sequence number or other unique identifier, they protect against replay attacks.

9 Name three attacks that can be made more difficult with firewall-type products.

Any of the following attacks can be made more difficult with firewall-type products:

— Attacks against any random host behind a firewall

— Attacks against exposed services

— Attacks against internal client hosts

— Spoofing attacks

10 Why is Network Address Translation (NAT) not a security feature?

The only way NAT serves as a security feature is if no one knows the internal corporate network address being translated into a valid legal address. If the corporate office were the target for an attack, some forms of attacks would be harder to carry out because the corporate network address is unknown. However, in most cases, the network addresses are well known, even if they are illegal.

11   Why should cleartext passwords not be recorded in audit trails?

Recording cleartext passwords in audit trails creates an enormous potential security breach if the audit records should be improperly accessed.

12   Who should receive security awareness training?

Security awareness training should be provided to all personnel who design, implement, or maintain network systems.

Chapter 8

1   What are three causes of a security breach?

Any of the following can cause a security breach:

— External intruder attack

— Unintentional damage

— Inadvertent exploit of a software vulnerability

— Disgruntled employee causing intentional damage

2   What was the first major publicized security incident?

The Internet Worm in 1988 was the first major publicized security incident.

3   What are four possible signs of a security breach?

The following are signs of a security breach:

— Accounting discrepancies

— Data modification and deletion

— Users complaining of poor system performance

— Atypical traffic patters

— Atypical time of system use

— Large numbers of failed login attempts

4   Many intrusion detection systems are based on what two methods?

The statistical analysis method and the rule-based analysis method are the two methods on which many intrusion detection systems are based.

5   Name three methods to overcome limitations when using a NIDS in a switched environment.

Embedding the IDS functionality into the switch, using monitor/span/mirror ports, and passive cable taps are three methods to overcome limitations when using a NIDS in a switched environment.

6   What is the fundamental objective of handling a security breach?

One of the most fundamental objectives of handling a security breach is to restore control of the affected systems and to limit the impact of the damage.

7   What are three considerations when prioritizing actions to be taken during incident handling?

The following are considerations when prioritizing actions to be taken during incident handling:

- — Protecting human life and people's safety
- — Protecting sensitive or classified data
- — Protecting data that is costly in terms of resurces
- — Preventing damage to systems
- — Minimizing the disruption of computing resources

8   True or false: When a security incident occurs, anyone who inquires about the incident should be informed in full detail as to what happened.

False. Although a security incident should be reported to all affected parties, it is prudent to limit the scope and details depending on the incident. Widespread panic and embarrassing leaks should be avoided.

9   What are some things to be included in a post-mortem analysis?

A post-mortem analysis of the security breach should include information on what happened, how it happened, and what steps should be taken to prevent a similar incident from occurring again.

Chapter 9

1   True or false: If network infrastructure devices have strict security features and functionality configured, physical access does not have to be taken into consideration.

False. It is critical to control physical access to any infrastructure device. All network infrastructure equipment should be in areas accessible only by authorized personnel. Without physical access control, the rest of the control measures are useless.

2   What is the difference between the Cisco IOS enable password and enable secret?

The enable password uses a type of encryption that is reversible. The enable secret uses MD5 encryption and is much more secure.

3   Which Cisco IOS command encrypts passwords with type 7 encryption?

The command service password-encryption encrypts all passwords that support the type 7 password algorithm. It should be enabled on all routers to ensure that none of these passwords are stored in readable text form in configuration files.

4   Which four forms of authentication modes are possible to access enable mode in Cisco
Catalyst switches?

**The Cisco Catalyst switches can be authenticated for enable mode by using a
TACACS+ server, a RADIUS server, Kerberos, or a locally configured password.**

5   What are three important points to keep in mind when crating a device login banner?

**Any of the following four points are important to keep in mind when creating a
device login banner:**

— Do *not* include any wording that even remotely can be construed as an invitation
to access the device (such as using the word "welcome").

— Do *not* include any information that can divulge which operating system is
being used, what the hardware is, or what logical interface has been accessed.

— Include statements that advertise that unauthorized access is prohibited and
violators will be prosecuted under the full extent of the law.

— Include statements that advertize that access to the device will be logged and
monitored.

6   What is required for Telnet to be used on a PIX outside interface?

**For Telnet access to work from the outside interface, an IPsec client needs to be set
up to initiate a VPN connection to the PIX using IPsec.**

7   What are the trade-offs in using SSH versus Telnet access?

**SSH is encrypted so that communication is not in the clear. Telnet communication is
in cleartext. Telnet communication can be protected by IPsec to provide security.**

8   What are four good password management rules?

Good password rules include the following:

— Privileged-level passwords should be unique from any other password.

— Username/password privileges should be configured on a per-user basis and
group shared keys should be avoided.

— Create passwords that avoid dictionary words, dates, phone numbers, and names.

— Always change any default passwords.

— Change passwords on a regular basis.

9   What security functionality differences are there between SNMPv1, SNMPv2, and
SNMPv3?

**SNMPv1 has no security mechanisms, whereas SNMPv2 added authentication for
communication between the SNMP server and client using the MD5 algorithm.
SNMPv3 added authentication through the use of the HMAC-MD5 or HMAC-SHA
algorithms as well as confidentiality through the use of 56-bit DES encryption.**

10 Why is RADIUS the recommended mechanism for a Catalyst switch 802.1x port authentication?

In Catalyst switches, TACACS+, RADIUS, or Kerberos can be used as the authentication protocol, although RADIUS is generally recommended because it has built-in extensions that support EAP frames.

11 What kind of traffic should be encrypted and kept confidential for network infrastructure devices? Name three specific examples.

Network infrastructure devices should encrypt any traffic that can potentially cause a device compromise, including the following:

— Telnet sessions to devices

— TFTP configuration downloads

— SNMP transactions to and from network devices

— HTTP access to device information

12 Why is the audit element necessary when implementing a secure network infrastructure?

The audit element is necessary to verify that the security policy is being adhered to. This includes making sure that the network infrastructure is configured as expected and that networking activity is effectively monitored to detect any unusual behavior and possible intrusions.

13 True or false: Syslog messages are typically 1500 bytes to enable as much information as possible to be sent in a single packet.

False. Syslog messages are based on the User Datagram Protocol (UDP) and are received on UDP port 514. The message text is kept under 512 bytes to ensure that the UDP packet is smaller than 576 bytes—the smallest packet that must be accepted by a host without packet fragmentation.

14 Which of the following statements is *not* true when gathering data from network devices that are under a suspected security breach?

A Access the device through the console port.

B Immediately reboot the device.

C Gather all volatile information via **show** commands.

D Initiate a port scan or SNMP scan if you cannot access the device due to password compromise.

B. You should never reboot a device when gathering forensics data because you may lose valuable information.

Chapter 10

1 In a firewall strategy that includes an external screening router, what is the role of this router?

The exterior screening router acts as a first-level filter to permit or deny traffic coming in from the Internet to the internal campus. It validates most incoming traffic before passing it on to the firewall.

2 Which of the following is a good strategy to adhere to for providing services such as DNS, HTTP, and e-mail to outside users?

A Distribute all services to different subnets.

B Place all services on a single subnet.

C Do not offer any services to outside users.

D Interview all users before allowing access.

B. Restricting the services offered to Internet users to a single subnet, if possible, is a good strategy to use to simplify the administration of access control filter lists.

3 Why can it be more important to create filter lists based on destination UDP/TCP ports rather than source UDP/TCP ports?

When dealing with TCP or UDP port numbers, commonly known port numbers are always used as the *destination* port number. The *source* port number is more or less arbitrarily picked by the originating host from the range of numbers 0 to 65,535.

4 What are three characteristics of Cisco IOS standard and extended access lists?

The Cisco IOS standard and extended access lists have the following characteristics:

— By default, the end of the access list contains an implicit deny statement for everything if it does not find a match before reaching the end.

— After the access list is created on the router, any subsequent additions are placed at the end of the list.

— The order of access lists is important. The entries are searched in sequential order; the first match is the one acted on.

5 What is one of the important characteristics of Cisco IOS named access lists?

The advantage of using Cisco IOS named access lists is that you can selectively remove entries. However, you still cannot selectively add access list command lines to a specific access list—subsequent additions are still placed at the end of the list.

6 True of false: A robust firewall must have the capability to do packet-by-packet inspection and filtering on specific packet session information.

True. A robust firewall must have the capability to do packet-by-packet inspection and filtering on specific packet session information. The firewall should inspect traffic that travels through it to discover and manage state information for TCP and UDP sessions. For many corporate environments, FTP, Telnet, HTTP traffic, Java applets, e-mail, DNS, and some popular voice and video applications must be supported.

7 Why can encrypted confidential traffic pose a problem for firewalls?

When encrypted confidential traffic reaches a firewall, the only filtering that can be done is on IP addresses and the destination protocol that is being used (IPsec IKE, IPsec ESP, SSL, and so on). This is usually not sufficient for more sophisticated stateful firewalls that also need information from the application data portion of the packet. If that application data is encrypted, the firewall does not have enough information to properly inspect the packet and apply the specified security policy.

8 True or false: The use of NAT provides a security feature because private addresses are kept private.

False. The use of NAT does not provide a security feature because, more often than not, the private address will be known.

9 Identify the Class A, Class B, and Class C networks that have been reserved by IANA for private address space use (that is, NAT)?

The Internet Assigned Numbers Authority (IANA) has reserved the following three blocks of IP address space for private networks:

— 10.0.0.0 through 10.255.255.255

— 172.16.0.0 through 172.31.255.255

— 192.168.0.0 through 192.168.255.255

10 Which of the following is *not* true?

A CBAC examines the application layer protocol information to learn about the state of a TCP or UDP session.

B CBAC does not provide intelligent filtering for all protocols; it works only for the protocols you specify.

C CBAC has mechanisms that can protect against DoS attacks.

D None of the above; they are all true statements.

D. All of the statements are true. CBAC examines the application layer protocol information to learn about the state of a TCP or UDP session; CBAC does not provide intelligent filtering for all protocols—it works only for the protocols you specify; CBAC has mechanisms that can protect against DoS attacks.

11 True or false: The default behavior on a PIX firewall for traffic coming in from an interface with a lower security level and going to a destination interface with a higher security level is to allow all IP-based traffic unless specifically restricted by access control lists.

False. The default behavior on a PIX firewall for traffic coming in from an interface with a lower security level and going to a destination interface with a higher security level is to drop all traffic unless specifically allowed.

12 What is the one significant difference between how Cisco IOS IP addresses are defined and how they are defined on a PIX firewall?

The IP address netmask is defined in the opposite way. For Cisco IOS access lists, the netmask is represented by using 0s to represent the network number and 1s to represent the host number. For PIX firewall access lists, the netmask is represented by what's referred to as the natural mask, where 1s are used to represent the network number and 0s are used to represent the host number. The following example shows the difference when defining the network mask:

```
Cisco IOS: access-list becareful permit tcp any 144.254.0.0 0.0.255.255
PIX Firewall: access-list becareful permit tcp any 144.254.0.0 255.255.0.
```

Chapter 11

1 What are 5 security concerns for remote dial-in environments?

Security concerns for remote dial-in environments include the following:

— Identifying the caller

— Identifying the location of the caller

— Identifying the destination of the call

— Keeping track of accessed applications and data

— Keeping track of the duration of a connection

— Ensuring authenticated communication

— Ensuring private communication

2 What are the two levels of authentication that can be performed for dial-in connectivity?

A key element in allowing dial-in connectivity is to know who is accessing your corporate network by establishing an initial authentication mechanism. Authentication can be performed at the device level or at the user level.

3 Which of the following is *not* a true statement?

A CHAP and PAP are two mechanisms used for PPP authentication.

B RADIUS and TACACS+ used in conjunction with EAP is a flexible and scalable dial-in authentication mechanism.

C PPP CHAP and PPP PAP cannot be used with either RADIUS or TACACS+.

D None of the above

C. Although CHAP and PAP can be used with RADIUS and TACACS+, a more flexible PPP authentication method would be to use EAP.

4 When configuring RADIUS or TACACS+ authentication in Cisco IOS Software devices, what is meant by a method list?

A method list is just a list describing the authentication methods to be queried, in sequence, to authenticate a user.

5 True or false: A defined method list overrides the default method list.

True. Although any name can be used to define a method list, there is a reserved name known as default. The authentication methods defined within default are applied to any interface or line that does not have any other list linked to it. However, any named list overrides the default method list.

6 Why is authorization a useful step after a user has successfully authenticated?

Authorization is the process by which you can control what users can and cannot do. Often it is not enough to just establish a link connection on authentication. After the device or user has been authenticated, a subsequent authorization step may be required to permit access to a specified area of the network. Many corporate environments restrict access to some company branches or limit certain users to only particular areas of the network or particular applications.

7 Which of the following is *not* a valid field in the first six fields of a AAA accounting record?

A Time stamp

B Password

C NAS name

D Username

B. Accounting records are text lines containing tab-separated fields. The first six fields are always the same and contain the following:

— Time stamp

— NAS name

— Username

— Port

— Address

— Record type

8 For a user to gain access to a host through a router with lock and key configured, what must the user first do?

For a user to gain access to a host through a router with lock and key configured, the user must first Telenet to the router. When a user initiates a standard Telnet session to the router, lock and key automatically attempts to authenticate the user. If the user is authenticated, the user gains temporary access through the router and can reach the destination host.

9 Why is IPsec the better choice over the Cisco Encryption Technology (CET) for providing security services for IP-based networks?

The Cisco Encryption Technology is a Cisco proprietary protocol. IPsec is the preferred method for providing security services for IP-based networks because it is standards-based and can operate in multivendor environments.

10 What is required in an IPsec environment if there is a requirement to encrypt an IP routing protocol that uses multicast packets to distribute its routing information?

GRE tunneling is required in an IPsec environment if there is a requirement to encrypt an IP routing protocol that uses multicast packets to distribute its routing information (for example, OSPF or EIGRP). In its current form, the IPsec standard supports only unicast IP packets. For small environments, static routes should suffice, and GRE tunnels are not necessary.

Chapter 12

1 True or false: Any VPN is a secured VPN.

False. For any VPN, only after the appropriate security controls have been put into place can you state that you have a secured VPN.

2 The design methodology for creating secure VPNs is constrained by what?

The design methodology for creating secure VPNs is in large parts constrained by the security policy. Before any network can be designed or configured, you need to understand what you are trying to protect and from what.

3 What kind of device authentication is used with L2TP/IPsec technology?

The L2TP protocol by itself only has simplistic device authentication via a CHAP-like protocol that requires a preconfigured shared password between the L2TP endpoints. When used with IPsec, however, the devices use more extensive authentication mechanisms, which usually include preshared keys, public key technology, or digital signatures.

4 At what points of the VPN network should access control be applied?

Perimeter network points should always be the point where access control is applied. This is the demarcation point between a trusted and an untrusted network. In addition, internal security instances are continuing to be a large issue, and access control mechanisms are needed inside the trusted network. This can require a secondary authentication mechanism once inside the trusted network.

5 How would you provide confidentiality services if you were using the L2TP protocol in a VPN?

L2TP can use PPP encryption, but it is a weak form of encryption; therefore, L2TP is most often used in conjunction with IPsec when confidentiality services are required.

6 True or false: Authentication for wireless networks can only be device based.

False. Authentication for wireless networks can be device-based through the use of a shared WEP key. It can also be user-based through the use EAP.

7 Which of the following is a valid mechanism to restrict access to a wireless client?

A Using the authorization function of a AAA server

B Using MAC address filtering

C Using special filtering rules for a specific pool of DHCP addresses only assigned to wireless clients.

D All of the above

D. Restricting access to who is allowed to connect to the wireless network is primarily carried out through the use of a AAA server. A successfully authenticated client would subsequently be provided authorized access to specified network services. In addition, MAC address filtering can be used in environments that want to impose stricter controls, although it is important to keep in mind that MAC addresses can be spoofed and additional access controls should be used as well. Finally, wireless clients can be allocated a DHCP address from a specified pool of addresses. This range of addresses can then have specific filtering rules applied at network infrastructure firewalls, which apply only to wireless VPN traffic.

8 How would you go about verifying that confidentiality services are appropriately deployed in a wireless network?

If confidentiality services are being used in a wireless network, don't just rely on a device counter to show that traffic is being encrypted. Place an actual traffic analyzer on the network to verify that the traffic is indeed confidential and that anyone inadvertently sniffing the wireless network can't decipher the traffic.

9 What is the access control issue with RTP/RTCP port numbers in VoIP networks?

Because RTP/RTCP ports are dynamically assigned when used by the endpoints for voice calls, firewalls can be problematic unless they have some capability to recognize voice traffic and dynamically allow traffic. It is recommended that the RTP audio stream ports that can be used be constrained to a specified range of port numbers for media communication and then to specifically permit that range through the firewall as deemed necessary for proper VoIP communication.

GLOSSARY

A

802.1x: A standard developed by the IEEE that enables authentication and key management for IEEE 802 local area networks.

access control: Limiting the flow of information from the resources of a system only to authorized persons, programs, processes, or other systems in a network.

access point (AP): In the context of wireless networking, it is a device that coordinates the wireless clients' use of wired resources.

accountability: Holding people responsible for their actions.

accounting: The methods by which one can establish who or what performed a certain action, such as tracking a user's data connection and logging system users.

Advanced Encryption Standard (AES): A NIST–endorsed encryption standard in replacement of DES. It uses the Rijndael symmetric block cipher algorithm and can process data blocks of 128 bits, using three different key lengths: 128, 192, and 256 bits.

amplifier: A device used in wireless networks that increases the strength of received and transmitted transmissions.

antenna: A device that radiates or receives a modulated signal through the air so that wireless clients can receive it.

asymmetric algorithm: A cryptographic algorithm that uses different keys for encryption and decryption; also called a *public key algorithm.*

attack: The act of trying to bypass security controls on a system. An attack can be active, resulting in the alteration of data, or passive, resulting in the release of data.

audit trail: A chronological record of system activities that is sufficient to enable the reconstruction and examination of a given sequence of events.

authentication: The process of validating the claimed identity of an end user or a device such as a host, server, switch, router, and so on.

authentication, authorization, accounting (AAA): The security elements usually used to provide secure access to resources.

Authentication Header (AH): The IPsec header used to verify that the contents of a packet haven't been modified in transit.

authorization: The act of granting access rights to a user, groups of users, system, or program.

availability: A state in computing systems and networks in which the system is operable and can run the services it is supposed to offer.

B

biometrics: The process of using hard-to-forge physical characteristics of individuals, such as fingerprints and retinal patterns, to authenticate users.

block cipher: An encryption method in which data is encrypted and decrypted in fixed-size blocks.

brute-force attack: A way of trying to break an encryption algorithm in which every possible key is applied to the encrypted text to determine whether the resulting plaintext is meaningful.

C

callback: A security mechanism for dial-in connections to a network in which a user calls in, requests a connection, and then hangs up. The destination system calls the initiator back at a known number and therefore reliably confirms the identity of the caller.

call-processing manager: A server that provides call control and configuration management for IP telephony devices.

certificate: A message, digitally signed with the private key of a trusted third party (*See* certificate authority), stating that a specific public key belongs to someone or something with a specified name and set of attributes.

certificate authority (CA): An entity trusted to sign digital certificates and, therefore, vouch for the identity of others.

certificate revocation list (CRL): A digitally signed list of all certificates created by a given certificate authority that have not yet expired but are no longer valid.

Challenge Handshake Protocol (CHAP): An authentication protocol used to authenticate peers in a PPP connection.

cipher: A procedure that transforms data between readable text and ciphertext.

Cipher Block Chaining (CBC): A method of using a block cipher to encrypt an arbitrarily sized message in which the encryption of each block depends on the previous blocks. This links the blocks into one logical "chain."

ciphertext: Encrypted plaintext that must first be decrypted to produce readable text.

cleartext: A message that is not encrypted (synonymous with *plaintext*).

compromise: In the context of security, to invade something by getting around its security procedures.

computer emergency response team (CERT): A formal organization of system administrators whose members provide services pertaining to issues relating to computer and network security.

confidentiality: Assurance that data is not read or accessed by unauthorized persons.

cryptographic key: A digital code that can be used to encrypt, decrypt, and sign information.

Cryptographic Message Syntax (CMS): A protocol for cryptographically securing messages; it provides encryption and signatures for arbitrary content.

cryptography: The science of writing or reading coded messages.

D

data confidentiality: The process of ensuring that only authorized entities that are allowed to see the data can see it in a usable format.

Data Encryption Standard (DES): A secret key cryptographic scheme standardized by NIST; it has been deprecated by NIST in favor of the AES algorithm.

data integrity: The process of ensuring that data has not been altered or destroyed during transit.

decipher, decryption: A method of unscrambling encrypted information to make it legible.

denial-of-service (DoS) attack: Any action that prevents any part of a network or host system from functioning in accordance with its intended purpose.

Diffie-Hellman key exchange: An algorithm that provides a way for two parties to establish a shared secret key that only they know, even though they are communicating over an insecure channel.

digital signature: A string of bits appended to a message (an encrypted hash) that provides authentication and data integrity; typically this term applies only to signatures generated using public key encryption.

Digital Signature Standard (DSS): A digital signature algorithm developed by the NSA.

Distributed Computing Environment (DCE): A set of distributed computing technologies that provide security services to protect and control access to data.

distributed denial-of-service (DDoS) attack: When multiple machines in separate locations are used to launch a denial-of-service attack.

documentary evidence: Where computer-produced evidence for a court of law takes the form of a printout.

Domain Name System (DNS): A protocol used to map host names to IP addresses and vice versa.

E

Encapsulating Security Payload (ESP): The IPsec protocol that provides the security services of confidentiality, traffic-flow confidentiality, connectionless integrity, data origin authentication, and an antireplay service.

encryption: A method of scrambling information in such a way that it is not readable by anyone except the intended recipient, who must decrypt it to read it.

Extensible Authentication Protocol (EAP): A general protocol for PPP authentication that supports multiple authentication mechanisms.

F

Federal Information Processing Standard (FIPS): Standards published by NIST with which all U.S. government computer systems should comply.

firewall: A system, based on either hardware or software, that applies rules to control the type of networking traffic between two networks.

FORTEZZA card: A cryptographic peripheral (a PCMCIA card) that provides encryption/ decryption and digital signature functions.

H

H.323: A standard created by the International Telecommunications Union (ITU) that provides specifications for real-time, interactive videoconferencing, data sharing, and audio applications such as IP telephony.

H.323 gatekeeper: A device used in IP voice networks that provides central management and control services that are needed to ensure reliable, commercially feasible communications.

H.323 gateway: A device used in IP voice networks that provides data format translation, control signaling translation, audio and video codec translation, and call setup and termination functionality on both sides of the network.

H.323 multipoint control unit (MCU): A device used in H.323 networks that enables conferencing between three or more endpoints.

H.323 terminal: An endpoint where H.323 data streams and signaling originate and terminate.

hash: The resulting string of bits from a hash function.

hash function: A mathematical computation that results in a fixed-length string of bits (digital code) from an arbitrary size input; a one-way hash function is not reversible to produce the original input.

I

impersonation: The ability to present credentials as if you are something or someone you are not.

integrity: Assurance that the data has not been altered except by people who are explicitly intended to modify it.

International Data Encryption Algorithm (IDEA): A cryptographic algorithm taking a 128-bit key, which is more efficient to implement in software than is DES.

International Traffic in Arms Regulation (ITAR): The collection of laws in the United States that regulates the export of dangerous technologies; until recently, ITAR had jurisdiction over all software with data encryption capability.

Internet Address and Numbering Authority (IANA): An administrative organization that assigns standard IP-related constants, such as IP addresses and IP protocol numbers.

Internet Engineering Task Force (IETF): A standards body whose focus is to design protocols for use in the Internet. Its publications are called Requests For Comments (RFCs).

Internet Key Exchange (IKE): The protocol that specifically defines the negotiation and keying exchange for IPsec.

Internet Security Association and Key Management Protocol (ISAKMP): A framework for a key management protocol for IPsec that is a required part of the complete IPsec implementation.

IP Phone: Any device that supports placing and receiving calls in an IP telephony network.

IP Security Protocol (IPSec): A set of network layer protocols that collectively can be used to secure IP traffic.

K

Kerberos: A secret-key network authentication protocol, developed at Massachusetts Institute of Technology (MIT), which uses the DES cryptographic algorithm for encryption and a centralized key database for authentication.

key escrow: The practice of storing cryptographic keys with one or more third parties.

key fingerprint: A human-readable code that is unique to a public key; it can be used to verify ownership of the public key.

M

man-in-the-middle attack: When an intruder is able to intercept traffic and can as a result hijack an existing session, alter the transmitted data, or inject bogus traffic into the network.

Media Gateway Control Protocol (MGCP): A VoIP protocol standard.

Message Authentication Code (MAC): A fixed-length quantity generated cryptographically and associated with a message to reassure the recipient that the message is genuine. The term is most often used in connection with secret-key cryptography. (A public key MAC is usually called a *digital signature*.)

message digest: The value returned by a hash function (same as a *hash*).

Message Digest 5 (MD5): A one-way hash algorithm that generates a 128-bit output.

Message Integrity Check (MIC): Another term used in place of MAC (*see* MAC).

N

National Institute of Standards and Technology (NIST): An agency of the U.S. government that establishes national technical standards.

National Security Agency (NSA): An agency of the U.S. government responsible for listening in on and decoding all foreign communications of interest to the security of the United States.

Network Address Translation (NAT): The process of converting one IP address to another IP address; often used to connect networks with a private address space to the Internet.

NAT-Traversal (NAT-T): A specification for use with IPsec that determines how to detect the use of NAT and how to handle addressing in those environments.

nonrepudiation: A property of a cryptographic system that prevents a sender from denying later that he or she sent a message or performed a certain action.

P

password: A protected, private character string used to authenticate an identity.

Password Authentication Protocol (PAP): A simple authentication method used with PPP.

Point-to-Point Protocol (PPP): A standardized Internet encapsulation of IP over point-to-point links.

PPP over Ethernet (PPPoE): An IETF standard that specifies the means to encapsulate PPP packets over the Ethernet link layer.

port scanning: A technique used by potential network intruders to discover which application services are available for exploitation.

private key: A digital code used to decrypt information and provide digital signatures. This key should be kept secret by its owner; it has a corresponding public key.

proxy server: In the context of SIP, it is an intermediate device that handles the routing of SIP messages.

public key: A digital code used to encrypt information and verify digital signatures. This key can be made widely available; it has a corresponding private key.

Public Key Infrastructure (PKI): A trusted and effective key and certificate management system.

R

redirect server: In the context of SIP networks, it provides the client with information about the next hop or hops that a message should take so that the client can directly contact the next-hop server or user agent.

registrar server: In the context of SIP networks, it is a device that processes requests from user agents for registration of their current location.

registration, admission, status (RAS): Messages used in an H.323 network to define communications between endpoints and a gatekeeper.

Remote Authentication Dial-In User Service (RADIUS): A protocol developed by Livingston Enterprises, Inc., as an access server authentication and accounting protocol.

Request For Comments (RFCs): Documents that specify Internet standards; some documents contain informational overviews and introductory topics.

risk: The possibility that a particular vulnerability will be exploited.

risk analysis: The process of identifying security risks, determining their impact, and identifying areas requiring protection.

Rivest Cipher 2 (RC-2): A variable-key-size block cipher designed by Ron Rivest for RSA Data Security, Inc.

Rivest Cipher 4 (RC-4): A variable-key-size stream cipher designed by Ron Rivest for RSA Data Security, Inc.

Rivest, Shamir, Adelman (RSA): A public key cryptographic algorithm that can encrypt or decrypt data and can apply or verify a digital signature.

router: An internetworking device that directs traffic between networks.

routing: The method by which a host or gateway decides where to send a datagram.

S

S/Key: An authentication program that relies on a one-way function for its security.

secret key: A digital code that is shared by two parties; it is used to encrypt and decrypt data.

Secure Hash Algorithm 1 (SHA1): A one-way hash algorithm designed by NIST that has a 160-bit digest.

Secure Multipurpose Internet Mail Extensions (S/MIME): An IETF specification that builds security on top of the industry standard MIME protocol.

Secure Shell (SSH): A protocol for secure remote login and other secure network services over an insecure network.

Secure Sockets Layer (SSL): A cryptographic protocol, designed by Netscape, which provides data security at the socket level; widely used to protect World Wide Web traffic.

security perimeter: The boundary at which security controls are placed to protect network assets.

security policy: The set of rules and practices that regulate how an organization manages, protects, and distributes sensitive information.

Session Initiation Protocol (SIP): The principal IETF standard for multimedia conferencing over IP.

Smart Card: A credit card-sized device with an embedded computer chip, also called a *token*, which can store digital certificates that can establish one's identity.

social engineering: The process of using human fallibilities to bypass security systems.

Socket security (SOCKS): A transport layer-based secure networking proxy protocol.

spoofing: An attempt to gain access to a networked device by posing as an authorized user, device, or program.

stream cipher: An encryption method that encrypts and decrypts arbitrarily sized messages one character at a time.

symmetric algorithm: A cryptographic algorithm that uses the same key for encryption and decryption; also called a *secret key algorithm*.

T

Terminal Access Controller Access Control System Plus (TACACS+): A AAA protocol largely used for dialup connection management.

threat: Any circumstance or event with the potential to cause harm to a networked system. A threat can take the form of malicious demands, such as network intruders, and nonmalicious dangers, such as lightning strikes.

transport layer security (TLS): An IETF standard that provides transport layer security over connection-oriented protocols.

triple DES (3DES): An algorithm that uses DES and one, two, or three keys to encrypt/decrypt/encrypt the data.

trust: The firm belief or confidence in the honesty, integrity, reliability, justice, and so on of another person or thing.

tunnel: A vehicle for encapsulating packets inside a protocol that is understood at the entry and exit points of a given network; also, a secure virtual connection through the Internet or an intranet.

U

unauthorized access: The capability of reaching a certain area, either a physical location or a logical computer network, without permission.

Uniform Resource Locator (URL): The path descriptor to a specific network resource and the protocol used to accesses it (for example, http://www.cisco.com/).

user agent (UA): In the context of SIP-based networks, it is the combined functionality of a user client agent and a user client server.

user agent client (UAC): In the context of SIP-based networks, it is the client application that initiates SIP requests.

user agent server (UAS): In the context of SIP-based networks, it is the server application that responds to a SIP request on behalf of the user.

user ID: A unique character string or numeric value used by a system to identify a specific user.

V

voice-mail system: In the context of VoIP networks, it provides IP-based voice-mail storage and an auto-attendant (an automated attendant providing voice services) for services such as user directory lookup and call forwarding.

voice gateway: A general term used to refer to any gateway that provides voice services including such features as Public Switched Telephone Network (PSTN) access, IP packet routing, backup call processing, and voice services.

vulnerability: A weakness in security procedures, network design, or implementation that can be exploited to violate a corporate security policy.

W

war dialing: A technique that involves the exploitation of an organization's telephone, dial, and private branch exchange (PBX) systems to penetrate internal network and computing resources.

Wireless Equivalent Privacy (WEP): The protocol used in 802.11 networks to provide link-level encrypted communication between the client and an access point.

E

F

P

O

S

W

X–Z

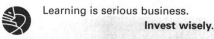

□ **YES!** I'm requesting a **free** subscription to *Packet*™ magazine.

□ No. I'm not interested at this time.

□ Mr.
□ Ms.

First Name (Please Print)   Last Name

Title/Position (Required)

Company (Required)

Address

City   State/Province

Zip/Postal Code   Country

Telephone (Include country and area codes)   Fax

E-mail

Signature (Required)   Date

□ I would like to receive additional information on Cisco's services and products by e-mail.

1. Do you or your company:
- A □ Use Cisco products
- B □ Resell Cisco products
- C □ Both
- D □ Neither

2. Your organization's relationship to Cisco Systems:
- A □ Customer/End User
- B □ Prospective Customer
- C □ Cisco Reseller
- D □ Cisco Distributor
- E □ Integrator
- F □ Non-Authorized Reseller
- G □ Cisco Training Partner
- I □ Cisco OEM
- J □ Consultant
- K □ Other (specify): _____

3. How many people does your entire company employ?
- A □ More than 10,000
- B □ 5,000 to 9,999
- c □ 1,000 to 4,999
- D □ 500 to 999
- E □ 250 to 499
- f □ 100 to 249
- G □ Fewer than 100

4. Is your company a Service Provider?
- A □ Yes
- B □ No

5. Your involvement in network equipment purchases:
- A □ Recommend
- B □ Approve
- C □ Neither

6. Your personal involvement in networking:
- A □ Entire enterprise at all sites
- B □ Departments or network segments at more than one site
- C □ Single department or network segment
- F □ Public network
- D □ No involvement
- E □ Other (specify): _____

7. Your Industry:
- A □ Aerospace
- B □ Agriculture/Mining/Construction
- C □ Banking/Finance
- D □ Chemical/Pharmaceutical
- E □ Consultant
- F □ Computer/Systems/Electronics
- G □ Education (K–12)
- U □ Education (College/Univ.)
- H □ Government—Federal
- I □ Government—State
- J □ Government—Local
- K □ Health Care
- L □ Telecommunications
- M □ Utilities/Transportation
- N □ Other (specify): _____

CPRESS

PACKET

Packet magazine serves as the premier publication linking customers to Cisco Systems, Inc. Delivering complete coverage of cutting-edge networking trends and innovations, *Packet* is a magazine for technical, hands-on users. It delivers industry-specific information for enterprise, service provider, and small and midsized business market segments. A toolchest for planners and decision makers, *Packet* contains a vast array of practical information, boasting sample configurations, real-life customer examples, and tips on getting the most from your Cisco Systems' investments. Simply put, *Packet* magazine is straight talk straight from the worldwide leader in networking for the Internet, Cisco Systems, Inc.

We hope you'll take advantage of this useful resource. I look forward to hearing from you!

Cecelia Glover
Packet Circulation Manager
packet@external.cisco.com
www.cisco.com/go/packet

PACKET